The Century

The

Century

*Peter Jennings
and Todd Brewster*

Photographs Edited by Katherine Bourbeau

DOUBLEDAY

NEW YORK   LONDON   TORONTO   SYDNEY   AUCKLAND

The Century

Staff for This Book

Writers
Todd Brewster
Peter Jennings

Editor
Todd Brewster

Picture Editor
Katherine Bourbeau

Associate Editors
Amy Faust
Tim Frew
Elisabeth King

Assistant Picture Editor
Audrey Landreth

Designed by
Elton Robinson

PUBLISHED BY DOUBLEDAY
a division of Bantam Doubleday Dell Publishing Group, Inc.
1540 Broadway, New York, New York 10036

DOUBLEDAY and the portrayal of an anchor with a dolphin are
trademarks of Doubleday, a division of
Bantam Doubleday Dell Publishing Group, Inc.

Library of Congress Cataloging-in-Publication Data
Jennings, Peter, 1938-
     The century / Peter Jennings & Todd Brewster. —1st ed.
p. cm.
     Includes bibliographical references (p.   ) and index.
     1. History, Modern—20th century.
     I. Brewster, Todd.
     II. Title.

     D422.J46 1998   98-13774
     909.82'1—dc21   CIP

ISBN 0-385-48327-9

Printed in the United States of America

November 1998

First Edition
10 9 8 7 6 5 4 3 2 1

WELCOME 1901

20TH CENTURY

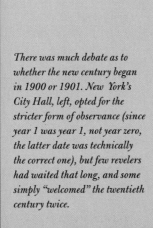

Contents

There was much debate as to whether the new century began in 1900 or 1901. New York's City Hall, left, opted for the stricter form of observance (since year 1 was year 1, not year zero, the latter date was technically the correct one), but few revelers had waited that long, and some simply "welcomed" the twentieth century twice.

Introduction

This work is an examination of life in the one-hundred-year period known as the twentieth century, a time of grand success and equally grand failure, of ideas both great and evil, and of the great and evil men and women who sought to carry them out. It is a story of progress and regress, of hubris and humility, of man majestically asserting control over his destiny and, just as often, shrinking from despair and confusion in the shadow of forces beyond him.

Boys bathing at Shelter Island,
New York, 1904.

When did the twentieth century begin? One may argue, and many will, that the "twentieth century" of history began not in 1901, but in 1870, when the Age of Invention started establishing the technological foundation for the society we live in today. Or, as others may assert, in 1914, when the First World War erupted, dismantling the nineteenth century's class and political structures and introducing the experience of mass death and destruction that would, in the end, be one of the century's greatest (and saddest) legacies. Or in 1917, when the Russian Revolution established the ideological competition that would define a bipolar world for seventy-two years. Or even in the 1920s, when our fast-paced urban society began to take shape. And years from now, when historians have come to grips with the forces that shaped our own time, no doubt there will be just as many theories on when the "twentieth century" truly ended. But this book, above all, is a chronicle of how ordinary people experience history; and in popular experience and imagination, the twentieth century began in 1901 and will end on December 31, 1999.

A time frame, however, does not by itself make a history. For that we needed a concept, a framework, a methodology, a point of view, and we arrived at ours through examination of a major theme of this time. The history of the world is but the "essence of innumerable biographies," wrote Thomas Carlyle, but the rigid hierarchical world to which both Carlyle and this "great man" theory of history belonged departed with the business of the nineteenth century. And while our history of the world is filled with the stories of both great men *and* women — scientists and inventors, statesmen and artists, adventurers and entrepreneurs, revolutionaries and politicians, even a couple of ballplayers — we have chosen to include them only as their lives intersect with what became, in this period, an even more powerful force: the humble masses, who by their numbers and the utter restlessness with which they greeted a dynamic time, created the story of the twentieth century.

How else to explain that the two most vital and competing ideologies of this time — communism and democracy — both preached the virtues of centering power with the multitudes and away from a privileged elite? Or that the century's greatest force of evil, the Nazi regime of Adolf Hitler, relied in large part on a manipulation of the force of popular will? Or that the most dynamic development of the last decades of the century has been the global reach of the new communications technologies, linking the lives of billions? Or that the most distinctive art of this time is not painting or sculpture or literature (though the century is amply, and impressively, represented in each), but a new kind of art, a popular art, distinguished not so much by its appeal to the minds of critics as by its appeal to large audiences of ticket buyers? If there is a twentieth-century *Pietà,* it is as likely to be made of celluloid as of stone.

Immigrant workers learning English in a Ford Motor Company classroom, late 1910s.

Listening to the voices of the "masses," to people who have lived through this century, has been our assignment for several years as this book and the ABC and History Channel television series to which it serves as a companion were created. And in so doing, we have asked our subjects to commit themselves to a deceptively simple act: to remember. History is an elusive target. Even when we ourselves have lived through a time, we tend to describe it, at first stab, the way we have been *told* it was. Thus, it sometimes seems that all women in the twenties were "flappers"; every family in the fifties lived in the suburbs; and the whole world was naked in the rain at Woodstock. We think you'll find that the subjects we chose resist such temptations; they look upon "remember" as an active verb, helping us to fulfill one determined goal of this project: to not just recite the events of the past, but help readers (and viewers) experience (or *re*-experience) them. For while it may be comforting, from our vantage point, to look back smugly at the mistakes of history and see them for what they are, it is much more challenging to feel the conflict of emotions present then — in the moment. The best histories don't soothe; they stir. And what more stirring experience than to truly feel oneself inside the catapulting forces that shaped, say, Germany in 1933, Birmingham in 1963, or Chicago in 1968, and ask, "How might I have behaved?"

The voices of our witnesses appear here in "boxes," edited narratives derived from the interviews done for *The Century* television series. But even in the primary text, we have sought to distinguish our story from other histories by holding each chapter up to a litmus test: Have we looked at this time from the perspective of someone who lived through it? And in so doing, have we captured a sense not only of the events of a particular era, but of the mood, the prevailing attitudes, what Germans call the *Zeitgeist*? Ironically, we have found that process to be a humbling experience all by itself. For while a study of history's greatest people might lend insight into the extremes of the human example, a study of the mass experience focuses by definition on the very extraordinary nature of the commonplace, which is to say, life itself in all its glory and mystery.

Thus, we hear from a woman who gave birth by the light of the 1940 London blitz and from a German soldier who, while invading the Soviet Union, fell in love with a Russian girl. We listen to the disappointment of a child arriving home during the Depression to discover that her father, in a

Black sharecroppers on the way to town, Hinds County, Mississippi, 1939.

moment of desperation, has removed the money from her piggy bank, and to the thrill of a young boy who, in 1920, twisting the dial of his crystal radio set, suddenly comes upon a miracle: the sound of music arriving out of the thin air. We listen to the story of a young seminary student who participates in the 1967 march on the Pentagon, protesting American policy in Vietnam, aware that his father is inside, helping to execute that very policy. We are witness to the anguish of a young gay man who handles the phones at an AIDS hotline in the 1980s, contemplating the fears of thousands who are certain that they have contracted the deadliest plague of our time. And along the way, we chart the ever-changing popular attitude, from the heady progressivism of the century's first decade to the fear and hopelessness of the mid-century, to the social strife of the sixties and seventies, and the more cautious technological excitement of our own time. Imagine an Everyman who comes of age in 1900 and lives to 1999. That is our story.

Our history spans the world, but only in the way that Americans' own experience of this time has. For, in determining what to include and what to exclude from the international scene, we asked ourselves other questions: Was this an event that affected American life, either directly or indirectly? Did it force an evolution of Western thought or experience? Are Americans different because it happened? Did Americans care? And the simple fact is that Americans in the twentieth century cared deeply about events in other parts of the world — sometimes in the interest of keeping themselves apart (the persistence of isolationism), other times to manipulate events to serve their national interests (the persistence of interventionism), and often when the sheer power of theater made something irresistible. The story of the United States in the twentieth century was, to borrow from the title of a Stephen Ambrose book, "the rise to globalism"; and to make that journey, as you will in reading this book, is to become acquainted with a path that brought a sometimes stubborn America into relationship with the rest of the world.

While traditionally organized — that is, in a chronological sequence — our history is meant to be read not as an exhaustive study, as one might find, say, in an encyclopedia, or even a dutifully thorough one, as could be discovered, perhaps, in a textbook, but rather, as a selective look at the past hundred years, a series of story-filled essays that together, we feel, offer a coherent picture of a remarkable time. There are many important stories we do not cover in detail (the massacre of more than a million Armenians in 1915, the genocidal crimes of the Khmer Rouge in Cambodia in the 1970s and '80s, and the occupation of Wounded Knee, South Dakota, by Native American activists in

Car enthusiasts at the Motorama auto show, New York City, 1953.

1973, to mention only three). But we ask you not to look upon this book as a reference, to be pulled from the shelf to answer the nagging trivia question; instead, read it like a novel, peruse its pictures as if you were walking through a well-curated gallery show, and glance at the first-person testimonies as if you were culling the diary of a beloved ancestor. The century is there.

The book leans heavily on the scholarship of others (and we firmly suggest that you take time to study both the chapter notes and the recommended reading list at the back of this book). But while, with the exception of the hundreds of interviews conducted for this series, we didn't work from primary source materials, we did occasionally call upon original experience. As working journalists, we have covered many of the events in the latter chapters of this book. Peter, for instance, was on the plane with Ayatollah Khomeini when he left his exile in France and flew to the open arms of a revolution in Iran. And he was in the White House, waiting to lunch with Ronald Reagan, when a presidential aide burst in with news of the *Challenger* disaster. In the middle of the 1989 rebellion in Czechoslovakia, Todd walked with Vaclav Havel down the streets of Prague to the chant of "Havel Na Hrad," or "Havel to the Castle," the presidential residence. While he was at the time but a long-jailed playwright, Havel soon took his seat as both the head of the new Czech state and the conscience of a new postcommunist Eastern Europe. And Peter was in Berlin to watch the erecting of the Berlin Wall in 1961, a memory that served him well twenty-eight years later when he stood in the same place watching the hammers chipping away at its once impenetrable concrete.

Still, a journalist's perspective, while closer than the average reader's, is not necessarily different; and in many ways, one of the most exciting parts about creating this history is that it was ours in the same way it was yours.

The fact that our unusual and lucky assignment has been to tell the story of a period in which we both have lived has alone made this a different kind of challenge than that faced, say, by a historian writing a biography of someone he never knew, or a survey of a time he never witnessed.

Even the events of *The Century* that lie beyond the life experience of its authors are never further away than the memories of a grandparent. As an enthusiastic enlistee in the First World War, Peter's own grandfather was among the first casualties in the gassings that surprised the Canadian soldiers on the Western Front in 1915, and the fact that he refused to speak of his experience filled his grandson with a sense of awe (even today, pictures of that grandfather, in uniform, sit to the side of Peter's desk). Todd's uncle, barely two years old, was a fatal victim of the 1918 flu epidemic, the worst in history; and Todd's maternal grandparents were traveling performers in the vaudeville circuit of the 1910s whose careers were soon displaced by the popular preference for that newest of entertainments, the movies.

Peter's father, Charles Jennings, was among the pioneers of radio news in Canada, and Peter still remembers the challenge he brought to a budding television newsman, unsure of the power of words. "Describe the sky," he said to his son, and after Peter complied, he sent him out to observe one more time. "Now, go out and slice it into pieces and describe each piece as different from the next." And Todd grew up hearing his own father's stories of a Great Depression childhood, when Ralph Brewster would watch a lonely drifter chalk the sidewalk outside the family home in Clifton, New Jersey, as a sign to the next hungry traveler that a knock on the door there would bring a sympathetic smile and a bowl of soup. The reader, we trust, has memories no less compelling, and no less formative, than these.

Antiwar activists locking arms in protest, New York City, 1964.

We all have many reasons to thank those previous generations — for the twin victories over fascism and communism; for the enormous strides toward conquering disease; for the moral awakening that cast light across the racist sins of a society too long proud of its highly dubious claims to equality; perhaps for our own gargantuan nineties prosperity, a standard of living many in the desperate thirties, and again in the despairing seventies, never dreamed we would achieve.

We can even thank them for our modern historical consciousness, for one of the by-products of the inventive genius of the twentieth century is that we possess a more dynamic archive of life in this time (sound, picture, *moving* picture, video, and, of course, artifact) than can be assembled for any time previous — and not just a public archive, but a private archive, too, as anyone with a camcorder and an attic filled with eight-millimeter films of birthdays and graduations and baby's first steps can attest. It may not always seem so ("Americans," complained the historical novelist Gore Vidal, "are not concerned with anything that happened before yesterday"), but thanks to all of these, we are the most historically aware population in the history of the world.

In recent years, a popular historical exercise has been to ask a simple question: What if? It is a natural query for an age when computer programs allow "readers" to make plot choices in novels *as they read,* and when — thanks to the Internet — virtual realities abound. But as *you* read through *this* book, you, too, may be tempted to wonder what your world would be like had some of its critical turns been reversed. What if the soldiers of Operation Overlord had not met success on the beaches of Normandy in 1944? What if the Manhattan Project's diligent physicists, many of them racked by guilt over their mission, had failed to beat the Germans to the atomic secret that would end the war in the image of a mushroom cloud in 1945? What if the Polish dockworkers in Gdansk had paused in fear instead of uniting behind the courage of Lech Walesa in 1980? Would the collapse of communism have come as swiftly? At all? The list is truly endless.

And yet, when considering the twentieth century, "What if?" is a question that brings as much lament as gratitude. For it is just as valid to ask, What if those foolish men who set the globe on its course toward the misery of World War I had chosen a more prudent and peaceful method for working out their differences? Might the Russians have never responded to the pleas of a long-exiled revolutionary whose dream of a workers' state hung like a dark cloud over the Urals for a lifetime? Might the German state have evolved more quickly into a respectable democracy instead of the fragile Weimar Republic, whose failure encouraged Berliners to listen seriously to the delusional rantings of a madman? And absent the awful scenes of mass carnage from that first "great" war, might we all have avoided the heavy blanket of cynicism that has disturbed our sleep for decades, and find ourselves still adhering faithfully to the optimistic liturgy of progress that informed life in the century's first innocent years?

Alas, unlike a computer novel, history does not reveal its alternatives. For better and worse, the story of the twentieth century, *our* story and *your* story, is what you hold here, a noisy human carnival throbbing with scenes both spectacular and outrageous, tawdry and radiant, reckless and heroic.

...UNTIL JUSTICE ROLLS DOWN LIKE WATERS AND RIGHTEOUSNESS LIKE A MIGHTY STREAM

MARTIN LUTHER KING JR

Learning from history at the Civil Rights Memorial, Montgomery, Alabama, 1995.

TheCentury

Seeds of Change
1901–1914

Seeds of Change 1901–1914

Previous spread: More than any other, this was the century of the city. And more than any other city, New York would become the emblem, the steel and concrete center, of the modern era. It was at the turn of the century that the New York we know today began to be built. Here, a worker helps to top off the new Woolworth Building, c. 1912, one of the first of many skyscrapers which by the twenties would make Olde New York into new New York.

Left: In 1900, when Oliver Lippincott's two-cylinder "Locomobile" became the first horseless carriage to edge out onto the top of Yosemite Park's Glacier Point, one of the hottest friction points of the century — technology versus nature — was dramatically illustrated. Lippincott declared that his "unassuming little machine" would never "detract from the sublimity of the great valley or lessen the majesty of the eternal hills." Then again, his was an optimistic age.

Frederick Jackson Turner was a young and not yet particularly distinguished American historian from the University of Wisconsin when, in 1893, he was invited to join a list of speakers scheduled to address a gathering at the World's Colombian Exposition in Chicago. The fair, which was held (one year late) in acknowledgment of the four hundredth anniversary of Christopher Columbus's journey, was an odd setting for a conference of the American Historical Association, and the thought that they would be reading their latest papers over the din of what was really an oversize carnival prompted many of the nation's best scholars to defer from appearing there. For Turner, it was a career breakthrough and an opportunity to expound upon his pet theory, developed over years of study: An avid fisherman, hiker, and proponent of the American West, he had determined that American life and character owed much to the pursuit of the frontier. And now that the 1890 census had declared that frontier closed — all of the land explored, claimed, and settled — the professor saw the nation as facing a turn-of-the-century crisis.

On July 12 Turner skipped Buffalo Bill's Wild West Show and the docking of a replica of a Norwegian Viking ship on the banks of Lake Michigan — just two of hundreds of events that attracted more than 28 million spectators to the Chicago fair — and chose instead to touch up his thesis before its appointed delivery at the Art Institute that night. Then, after waiting through discussions of "Early Lead Mining in Illinois and Wisconsin" and "English Popular Uprisings in the Middle Ages," he stepped forward and pronounced what was to become the single most significant historical statement of its time (and, as regards American history, of any other). Turner's "closing of the frontier" thesis was so rich and compelling it would eventually deliver him to the highest ranks of his profession and establish him as a friend of Teddy Roosevelt and Woodrow Wilson.

Turner's idea was elementary and attractive. He declared that Americans were not simply transplanted Europeans but a people unto themselves and that they were shaped not so much by their history or their institutions as by their

Frederick Jackson Turner,
1861–1932

"The wilderness masters the colonist . . . It takes him from the railroad car and puts him in the birch canoe. It strips off the garments of civilization and arrays him in the hunting shirt and the moccasin . . . Little by little he transforms the wilderness, but the outcome is not the old Europe . . . here is a new product that is American . . ."

Frederick Jackson Turner,
Significance of the Frontier
in American History

environment. To Turner, the root impulse of the American character was the pull westward, toward the adventure and possibility offered by the frontier. If the original Americans had come west from Europe to settle on the shores of the Atlantic, escaping from advanced civilization and its injustices, so, too, some of these same people continued to be pulled even farther westward as the East Coast began to exhibit some of the characteristics of the Old World from which they had fled.

Turner saw the quintessential American as constantly in motion, always in the act of remaking himself, and in that process the frontier was his church: the source that cleansed him of the sinful world and reintroduced him to life's most basic virtues. The historian detected in wilderness life the genesis of many of the American man's most distinctive qualities: the ready availability of free land made him generous and optimistic; frontier hardship made him self-reliant and individualistic; and frontier challenges made him willing to adapt, innovate, and even cooperate democratically with others. In the frontier, men lived with their "bark on" (painter Frederic Remington's phrase); were judged by their accomplishments in their own day, not those of their ancestors; and got by with a minimum of government, for what government was needed in a tiny backwoods outpost? Of course, as greater numbers of people arrived, the settlements began to exhibit more of the complications of civilization — government grew and the social structure became more rigid — until the move even farther westward was broached by the most adventurous. Yet gradually, as the settlers traveled from east to west, the societies they left behind were increasingly more "American," less encumbered by archaic tradition, and so a national character was forged. "American democracy was born of no theorist's dream," Turner declared. "It came out of the American forest and it gained new strength each time it touched a new frontier."

As long as there was free land to be found, the process Turner described could go on unimpeded, but now that the explorer had met his horizon, the nation faced perhaps its greatest challenge: whither? Turner saw in the closing of the frontier an end to the first great era of American history, but the author also tentatively saw a beginning. Since "American energy," he wrote, would "continually demand a wider field for its exercise," another frontier — or, more appropriately, its moral or spiritual equivalent — could and would be found. Indeed, Turner predicted that Americans would acquire a social conscience when they could no longer evade the problems of society by merely moving on. Others were not so sure. To them, Turner's thesis seemed to describe a future of inexorable decline, the first signs that America was entering a lethargic middle age. For with the frontier gone, what was there to ensure that the United States would not ossify like Europe? And even if it did not, what was there to guarantee that the urge to expand would be translated into the promotion of social welfare and not into, say, an aggressive foreign policy dedicated to acquiring new lands and markets abroad?

Turner himself underwent a reverse migration, the success of his paper leading in 1910 to a post at Harvard, where he reigned for a generation as America's preeminent historian. There, encamped in the refined world of Cambridge, he declared himself "a Western man in all but my residence," occasionally reinforcing the point on himself by dragging a tent out onto the porch of his Brattle Street home and sleeping in the "wilds" of urban Massachusetts. Turner's profes-

A pioneering British aviator demonstrates his "aeroplane" just feet from the White House, 1910. "Flight was generally looked upon as an impossibility," recalled Orville Wright, "and scarcely anyone believed in it until he actually saw it with his own eyes."

sional life also became somewhat compromised. While his thesis was enormously well regarded (in part because it reinforced an image of ruggedness that fit many Americans' sense of themselves) and the myth of the frontier would become central to twentieth-century popular culture (encouraging, among other examples, Zane Grey novels, John Wayne movies, and the fifties fad for Davy Crockett), the great book that many thought Turner would deliver to scholarship remained unwritten, and in the years after his death many historians eventually derided his idea as unprovable or nostalgic.

Still, there is no denying that Turner was a man of his time and that his thesis spoke to the fears and dreams of a people at the brink of extraordinary social, political, and spiritual tumult. The winds of transition were blowing across America at the turn of the century and for many the only way to hold steady was to dig their feet deeply into their long-fertile soil.

For most of the two thousand years since the birth of Christ (or the date established as such) Western civilization greeted the close of one century and the opening of the next as insignificant. In what was essentially an agrarian world, the cycles of nature — God's clock — were deemed to govern life, the passing of one day into darkness and the arrival of the light of the next thought to be nothing more than the continuation of a divine process, no matter how it coordinated

The cover of this song sheet paid tribute to the era's fascination with technology.

with the calendar. But with the end of the 1500s and the beginning of the modern age, and especially with the establishment of a mercantile economy (in which time began to be viewed as a commodity) and its attendant devotion to the concept of uninterrupted progress, respect for the calendar grew. And with that, a feeling of nervous tension began to be associated with the ends of centuries, the sense that with the turning of that penultimate year would come an almost magical transaction, in which the certainties of the past would be exchanged for a mysterious future, holding both the thrill of possibility and the terror of the unknown. This attitude became most powerful in the 1890s when the term *fin de siècle*, the French words meaning simply "century's end," came to stand for the feeling at once of impending ruin and revelation that caused havoc not only in the lives of Parisians but throughout much of the Western world.

The end of the nineteenth century carried so much more tension and foreboding because it coincided with the end of the absolutes that had governed life for so long. Charles Darwin's theories of evolution and natural selection, introduced in 1859 and refined in 1872, had shaken man's understanding of his origins *and* his purpose, challenging religion to evolve from a comfortable fundamentalism and convincing many to see life not as the unfolding of a plan designed by a benevolent creator, but as a morally neutral, competitive process rewarding the most aggressive participants. At the same time, socialism and democracy began to dominate world political thought, agreeing at least on one tenet, growing undeniable in these times: that the social order needed to be amended to take power from the elites and provide it to the masses. Finally, the growth of science and industrialism in the last days of the 1800s and the first of the new century had begun to prepare people for a new relationship with their natural environment, technology promising conquest of the darkness (the lightbulb), the sky (the airplane), the horizon (the automobile), and many of the burdens of work, even as it introduced new avenues to entertainment (the phonograph, the movies) and communication (the telephone, the wireless).

The machine, it appeared, was poised to become everyman's slave, devoted and reliable, an inexhaustible ox, and a testament to man's ability to master his surroundings. Increasingly, people were even leaving the farm to live in a machine-made world, the city, knowing that it was there that the new life would emerge. Some of the biggest of these fast-growing metropolises — Paris, St. Louis, Buffalo, Atlanta, and, of course, Chicago — held turn-of-the-century fairs displaying the enormous promise of the industrial future — and this to people for whom the paved road was still a novelty.

The census takers had been right, and not only about the American West. Everywhere one looked, there was the sense of being at the end of one kind of history and the start of another. By 1911 the edges of the earth had been reached — the American explorer Robert Peary tackling the North Pole, the Norwegian Roald Amundsen landing on the South — forming, in a way, the most direct analogy to Turner's observations. But the sense of an exhausted past was not limited to geography. In the years that straddle 1900, art abandoned all pretensions to reproducing the realistic image, first shattering it into "little cubes" (as Henri Matisse announced, giving the name to one of painting's newest and most violent ideologies) and going onward from there to spend the rest of the century exploring the fecund frontier of abstraction; music rejected traditional harmony for the

With the Wright Brothers at Huffman Prairie:
"Dad said, 'Our boys are going to try a flight today . . . if it's successful . . . it'll make history'"

When I was growing up, we didn't have electricity. We used a lot of candles for light and of course we had gas fixtures. And then outside in the streets, we had street lamps. Every evening at sundown the lamp boys would come around with their pole slung over their shoulders and they would light the lamps one by one. All the little kids would rejoice when the lamp boys would come, because it meant we could still play outside, even though it was dark. We even had a few parades some nights after it got dark. We would build these lanterns out of old shoe boxes and candles. All the kids on my block would line up and parade down the street with these makeshift lanterns while the parents and grandparents sat on the front porches and watched.

My father, who was an architect with an office in downtown Dayton, Ohio, was designing and building a new house for us in the country, and it was to be fully equipped with electricity, which was pretty modern back then. There was just so much change going on in those early years of the century. I remember when we got our first telephone. You would have to stand at the wall and talk into this contraption, and we shared the line with four or five different neighbors who would all come on the line at the same time. Sometimes you didn't know who was talking to who. Still, it was all very exciting. Life was changing so much and so quickly that it made some people anxious. But not my father, he was extremely interested and excited by what was going on.

One day he came home from work early and said, "Get your things ready. Our boys are going to try a flight today, and it may be the first one!" My father always referred to the Wright brothers as "our boys." He said, "We'll go out and if it's successful we'll be there to see it. It'll make history." Then he hitched our horse, Old Nip, up to the surrey and we headed out to Huffman Prairie where the flight was to take place. We were good friends with the Wright family. Orville and Wilbur's niece, Ivonette, was my best friend as a child, and their bicycle shop was down the street from our home. Orville and Wilbur had always been interested in flying. I remember playing with Ivonette on the Wrights' front porch while Orville and Wilbur sat at the other end watching the birds fly. And when they started working on their flying machine in the bicycle shop, the word spread pretty quickly around town. Some of the neighbors were pretty skeptical about what they were trying to do. They were always saying, "They're back in that bicycle shop again. I don't know what they think they're going to do. They will never make a machine that can fly." Now, being as close with the Wright family as we were, that kind of talk hurt us terribly. It was like our own family was being ridiculed. My father would always defend them. He

would say, "You just let those boys go, those boys know what they're doing." They weren't secretive about what they were doing. Their bicycle shop was open to anyone who wanted to come in and visit. The Wright brothers were so sold on building a flying machine that none of the negative talk bothered them at all. They just kept working.

Our father had driven us out to Huffman Prairie a number of times. That's the place that Orville and Wilbur used as a testing ground. All the other times we were out there, there was no flying going on. They would just be testing their machine: working on the propeller, or motorizing something, or making it move here or there. But this time my father had heard that they were actually going to make it fly. Now, the Wright brothers had already had a successful flight down in Kitty Hawk, North Carolina, but none of the newspapers really reported on it, and most people didn't believe it actually happened. So as far as we were concerned, they were attempting the impossible that day.

Dad knew of a place at Huffman Prairie that was on an incline, and it offered us a pretty good view of what was going on. Nip knew exactly where the place was too, because he had been there so many times before with my father. Nip pulled the surrey right up on that hill where we sat like statues waiting for things to happen. There was much activity going on down in that field, and we had the bird's-eye view of it. Dad was so excited, he turned to us, shaking his fist, and said, "Are you all paying attention to this? Now listen to me, you're going to remember this to your last day." The horse kept getting agitated and my father would have to get out of the surrey and rub Nip's nose and pat his head. He had to keep a tight hold on the horse's lines because the noise from the flying machine's motor was so terribly

loud. The outer part of the field was crowded with people. We felt we had just about the best seat where we were. We may not have been as close as some people, but we could sit in the surrey and look right down at everything that was happening. People applauded as they tested the motors, but for the most part, everyone was speechless. Every time either Orville or Wilbur did something the crowd would inch a little closer to try and see what was going on. They were constantly trying to keep people from getting too close. I think everybody was a nervous wreck.

When that plane took off the ground, I just can't describe how I felt. I think I held my breath the entire time, and I'm sure an awful lot of people said a prayer. It was spectacular — just unbelievable. That's all I can say. The plane lifted sort of level at first and then started to rise up. I don't know just how far they went. The whole flight couldn't have lasted longer than a minute, but it proved that it could be done. When the plane landed, the whole field just exploded with applause. And then it got strangely quiet. Nobody could believe what they had just seen. People stood around kind of dumbstruck. Everyone I looked at as we drove away had this blank, incredulous look on their faces. They were on their horses and in their carriages, and they were just shaking their heads. It was such a surprise. Not many people were even talking about it. I couldn't help but think about all of those mouthy people who said it would never happen. I was just exhausted when it was all over. It was like witnessing a miracle. I sat in the surrey and reasoned with my father, "I know you can fly a kite that way, but how did they get that machine up like that?" And Dad said, "That I don't know. You'll just have to ask Orville and Wilbur."

—*Mabel Griep was born in 1896 in Dayton, Ohio, just a few doors down from the Wright Brothers' bicycle shop. She married, raised a family, and lived in the Dayton area her entire life.*

Above: Griep (right) and her sister Lorine Hyer, c. 1905.
Left: The 1904 Wright Flyer during a test flight at Huffman Prairie.

otherworldly sounds of what composer Arnold Schoenberg called "pantonality"; literature played with the narrative; and physics, with the discovery of the electron, turned from the study of the macrocosmic forces of matter and energy that had dominated the field in the nineteenth century to the microcosmic world of subatomic particles that would lead eventually to Hiroshima. Finally, there was the 1901 funeral of Queen Victoria, all by itself an impressive piece of timing, the monarch whose name had been synonymous with the passing era now herself passing along with it.

In Europe, art and culture guided the march into *le moderne,* but in America, technology loudly announced the promise of the future, bringing the enthusiasm of discovery and the confidence that the new age would be a better age. It was American inventors whose genius thrilled the world with possibility (Edison, the Wrights) and, perhaps even more important, American industrialists (Rockefeller, Carnegie) and systems-builders (Ford, Taylor, Insull) who understood how to deliver the new technology into the lives of the masses. And who could not see the excitement in this? Design by design, piece by piece, object by object, America's crusading capitalists were replacing the natural world with a new man-made world, promising to establish a new life not just for the privileged few but for *mankind,* a world set in defiance of natural limits, a world shaped to fit man's needs, giving him comfort and pleasure and most of all freedom. And yet precisely because it *was* a defiance of nature and because it was a life with so little precedence, because it offered none of the comforts associated with tradition, the thrill of the new was received by nervous hands.

For now it was mostly anticipation. A few more years and a horrific war would pass into history before the world would finally cast off the yoke of the 1800s and enter into what some were calling nothing less than a second creation. Yet even in the years leading up to World War I, Americans found themselves anxiously making adjustments to prepare for life as they imagined it would soon be, and in the process, tentatively approaching some of the challenges that would inform their lives onward throughout the 1900s. How, for instance, to put an *American* imprint on the exciting yet foreign age that they now faced? How to fit a society conceived as a decentralized agrarian republic into a century of urban and industrial might? How to adjust a mostly white, Anglo-Saxon nation to the arrival of new immigrants from backgrounds alien to American traditions? How to reconcile competing notions of environmental and biological determinism with the American ideal of racial equality? How to execute the divine mission so many Americans believed to have been given to them as "trustees of the world's progress, guardians of its righteous peace"? Indeed, how to be an American in the alternately terrifying and exhilarating epoch unfolding before them as the twentieth century?

If the future had a shape, a logo, it was undoubtedly the skyscraper. The architectural wonder of the late nineteenth century had risen, literally, from the ashes of Chicago. The city had burned into history in 1871, then reconstructed itself not in wood or brick or iron, but in the very modern materials of steel and glass and steel-reinforced concrete laid out in a grid, so that the load was not borne by the walls, as had been previous practice, but dispensed throughout the structure, allowing it to rise toward the clouds, an urban silo. The skyscraper was

The excitement that attended the building of the new urban infrastructure was palpable. Here, engineers, politicians, and financiers gather underground to celebrate the completion of a river tunnel, c. 1907, in New York City. The men had already witnessed enormous technological change, and some — those old enough to have served in the Civil War — had been alive for the entirety of the Industrial Revolution.

"With me, architecture is not an art, but a religion and that religion is but part of Democracy."

*Chicago architect
Louis H. Sullivan*

The Woolworth tower — shown here in 1912, just prior to its completion — held the honor of being the world's tallest building for seventeen years.

almost too obvious a response to the closing of the frontier (vertical space replacing horizontal), and it became so commanding an image of the time that it inspired a Connecticut manufacturer to create one of the most durable and popular of twentieth-century toys, the Erector set. But even more important, as the new buildings began to reflect not the simple squared-off roofs that were common to the work of the great Chicago architect Louis H. Sullivan, but the striking, piercing verticality of church spires, they spoke to the aspirations of a new age dedicated to new values. By 1913, when New York City's Woolworth Building was opened, reaching for the heavens at sixty stories and 792 feet, the structure was boldly declared to be "the Cathedral of Commerce."

New York took to verticality like few other cities, the island of Manhattan being truly fixed space, and as the primary port of entry to the United States its newest buildings presented an image of upward motion to the throng of immigrants that in the century's first years pushed toward American shores. On his way to the administration center at Ellis Island, the immigrant first looked up as he passed the Statue of Liberty — an initial gesture of optimism demanded of him by his new homeland — but in fact he needed little encouragement to feel enthusiasm for the world he would now enter. For the millions making their way across the Atlantic, a new breed of immigrant from central and southern Europe fleeing pogroms and poverty, America was truly the land of opportunity.

From 1890 to 1910 nearly 13 million immigrants came to the United States, swelling the population and dramatically changing the nation from a mostly homogeneous citizenry descended from English, German, Scotch, and Irish ancestry to a population of dramatic ethnic diversity. If nineteenth-century America was white, Anglo-Saxon, and Protestant, then twentieth-century America would be white *and* black (the freed slave moving to stake his claim to a better life) *and* yellow. And it would include not only Protestants but Eastern Orthodox peoples from Russia and Greece, Latin peoples from the Catholic Mediterranean states, and Jews from Russia and Poland. The incorporation of immigrants from such vastly different backgrounds, holding vastly different beliefs and following vastly different customs, would pose one of the century's greatest challenges to American ideals.

The fresh arrivals were mostly rural peoples, but they came to the New World in search of jobs in industries that were centered in American cities and towns. And whereas they had sweated under the sun to till the earth in southern Italy, Russia, and the eastern European Slavic states, here they would work to the demands of a backbreaking foreman listening for the sound of the whistle that would announce the end of their workday. In the early years of the century, millions of new immigrants were packed into midsize American factory towns (in 1900 someone calculated that twenty-five languages were being spoken in the textile mills of Lawrence, Massachusetts) while millions more undertook a quintessentially modern mission: the building of the big city. Weeks after he left the soil of Sardinia, a young Italian worker could find himself digging subway tunnels, laying trolley track, paving roads, constructing bridges or sewers or electrical lines, even sitting atop a steel girder erecting one of the vaunted new skyscrapers. And thanks largely to the help of such eager new Americans, the city of San Francisco, felled by a tremendous earthquake in 1906 that left 200,000 people homeless, was able to rebuild itself in less than three years, the precarious

An immigrant's story: **Fleeing pogroms for the land "where there is gold in the streets"**

I was born in a small Russian town of about ten thousand people. We were a poor family. My father made the horse-drawn carriages that the bourgeoisie used on Sundays to promenade down the street. It would take him about six months to build each carriage because he couldn't afford any tools and he had to build each one with his own ten fingers. He even ground the colors and boiled down the oil for the paint he used on the carriages. I'll never forget the smell of the paint shop and the sight of my father meticulously mixing paint. It helped to cultivate in me an early love of painting. During the six months it took my father to finish a carriage, the family starved. We had no money, and the rich people wouldn't pay my father until he finished his carriage. It was a very hard life. My mother helped out by selling cigarettes and candy at the marketplace once a week, but we still barely had enough money to survive.

My family was part of a population of about two thousand Jews in our city. We were subjected to all sorts of slurs. People yelled out "Bad Jew" and "Christ Killer," and they said that we shouldn't be allowed to live. There was a pogrom in 1905 where the Russians looted every store that was either owned or operated by a Jew. I remember my mother pulling me into a hiding place for fear that I would be hurt. It was this abuse against the Jews that made my two brothers decide to go to the United States. In Russia, everyone thought that America was such a rich country that you could literally find gold in the streets. At home there were no jobs for Jews, but in America surely my brothers would find work. They went to New York, worked hard as house painters, and accumulated enough money to buy passage for the rest of the family.

I had never seen an ocean before we got on the boat for America. I looked out onto the sea and saw these huge waves crashing up against the rocks. It was a frightening experience. But then I saw the openness of the ocean, and that great body of water opened my mind to a world that I never knew existed. As we approached New York Harbor, I saw the Statue of Liberty and I was overwhelmed with a feeling of hope for a beautiful life in a new nation. Then we headed toward Ellis Island and I could see the big buildings of New York. It was an amazing site. The city I came from only had little shacks made of wood and stone. Here, everything was big and new. At Ellis Island they looked in my eyes to see if I was healthy and they checked my hair for lice. When they determined that my family and I were not sick, they put us on another boat and we were finally admitted to the United States.

When I saw the Woolworth tower I just couldn't believe how a building could pierce the sky like that. These great buildings gave me hope that I would grow up as a man sustaining his own life in a legitimate, honest, creative way. But looking at all of these powerful buildings also made me feel completely lost. New York was so much bigger than my city in Russia — like a splash of paint compared to a dot on a piece of paper. I walked into the Woolworth Building on lower Broadway and the elevator shot me up to the top floor. I never conceived that anything like that could be possible.

At first, I was afraid to go in the subway. I didn't want to climb down into that dark hole. In Russia, the only means of transportation that I knew about were horses and bicycles. One day I talked to a man who ran the newsstand near the subway entrance at 110th Street and Lenox Avenue. He explained to me that it was a nice railroad and that there was nothing to be afraid of. He gave me the courage to finally go down into that dark hole. And when I did go in, I discovered a whole new world. There were advertisements that told me what to buy and what not to buy. And I saw people — blacks, yellows, all sorts of different facial looks and ethnic groups — people like I had never seen before. Most of all I was amazed that I could go anywhere for five cents. I was able to go all the way down to Battery Park, and then, if I chose, I could transfer and turn around and go all the way up to Yonkers for the same nickel!

My first school was on 103rd Street near Third Avenue, but when I discovered that there were too many foreign boys in the same class, I left it, because I wasn't learning the American language fast enough. I wanted to learn the American language because I wanted to understand the American people, the American mind, and the

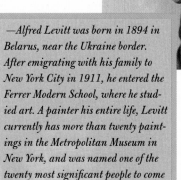

Levitt in 1914.

—*Alfred Levitt was born in 1894 in Belarus, near the Ukraine border. After emigrating with his family to New York City in 1911, he entered the Ferrer Modern School, where he studied art. A painter his entire life, Levitt currently has more than twenty paintings in the Metropolitan Museum in New York, and was named one of the twenty most significant people to come through Ellis Island.*

American culture. I wanted to be completely American, and that couldn't happen in a school full of foreign boys. Mostly I wanted to get a good job somewhere, and I knew if I didn't speak English, I couldn't get a good job. So I walked down to another high school in Harlem on 116th Street and asked the supervisor to give me an audience. I told him I wanted to learn the American language, and I wasn't getting it on 103rd Street. He said, "I will give you two questions, if you pass them, you are admitted." He asked me to spell "accident" for him, and did right away, with two *c*'s. Then he asked me what two-thirds of fifteen was, and I said "Ten," so he admitted me to high school. In Russia, only a small percentage of Jewish children could go to school, and then it had to be a special Jewish school. Once that school was filled, no more children could go. In America, I could go to school with everyone else.

After living in New York for a little while, my mother told me to get a job. At the time women used to wear coats with cloth buttons and each button had a metal ring around it. Since I loved painting and wanted to be an artist, I got a job for six dollars a week painting rings around buttons. Around that time I heard about a school on 107th Street called the Ferrer School that had an art program. I decided to go see if I could get in. When I knocked on the door a woman came out and asked me what I wanted. I asked her if there was an art school in there. She said, "Yes, but it is not open today. We have no money to pay for a model." I said, "Don't worry," and I stripped out of my pants and I got on the stage. I said, "Here you are, you have got a model." For that they allowed me to come to their school.

At the Ferrer School I heard about the Armory Show, which was a great exposition of modern art and painting. I went there and saw Marcel Duchamp's *Nude Descending a Staircase*. I was amazed at the painting; I couldn't understand how the artist could have even conceived it. And I saw many other things at that show that were very, very good. The Armory Show helped me make up my mind that I was going to dig into the unknown myself, and that I was going to become a good artist. It showed me that you could do a lot of things with paint that were not merely copying. It showed me that you could copy what's inside your mind.

America opened my eyes to a wider horizon of life. I began to understand that the Russian people were not the only people on this globe: there were French, there were Germans, there were English, there were Spanish, and there were Americans. There were all sorts of people that I never dreamt of, let alone understood. America was a place for all of these people to come, as I did, to seek their fortunes, to seek a hopeful place to spend their lives.

Although they enjoyed greater freedom and opportunity in the United States, many immigrants were dismayed by the squalid living conditions in the overcrowded urban ghettos such as New York's Lower East Side, left. "Was this the America we had sought?" remarked a Jewish immigrant. "Or was it only, after all, a circle that we had traveled, with a Jewish Ghetto at its beginning and its end?"

wooden structures erected during the city's days as a gold rush boomtown now wisely replaced by the kind of sturdy steel foundations that had a better chance of withstanding another tremor.

For the old-stock Americans, the ones whose parents and grandparents had arrived in previous centuries, the new immigrants and the new age came at once, and it was easy to confuse them. Many Americans were greeting the problems of big-city life for the first time, confronting the grime, corruption, disease, and overcrowding that came with such rapid, unrestricted growth, and they tended to see it not so much as a product of urban congestion as the work of foreign peoples defiling the American system. Indeed, in the century's first years, New York City had become Europe-on-the-Hudson, an amazing conglomeration of ethnicities — each group clinging to its heritage in tenement neighborhoods where there could be ten people packed in a room, more than two thousand in a city block. And the suddenness with which the character of that city and others was changing roused the voices of those who claimed the new immigrants were less in search of a new life centered around American ideals than in carrying the decadence of the Old World to American shores ("these bringing . . . unknown gods and rites . . . those, tiger passions here to stretch their claws").

The argument was, in fact, an old one. Americans had been grappling with the nativist urge throughout the nineteenth century, with some of their most distinguished political leaders lending credibility and eloquence to feelings that were at root nothing more than the coarsest form of bigotry. But the restrictionist fears at this moment were perhaps that much more vigorous for the stakes many people believed were at hand: for if the nation was remaking itself, Americans wanted to ensure that the new image retained some of the familiarity of the old.

America in 1900 was a provincial society of just 76 million citizens, a place of such innocence that it is hard for people at the end of the twentieth century to contemplate its quiet life: a nation of dirt roads and horse-drawn carriages, of tight corsets and Victorian pretensions, of kerosene lamps and outhouses, top hats and bowlers, McGuffey Readers and the *Ladies' Home Journal*. Cities were crowded with smoke-filled men's clubs and ornate wood-paneled bars like McSorley's Old Ale House in Manhattan (which prided itself on providing "good ale, raw onions and no ladies"), while country towns, which were still home to 60 percent of the nation's population, remained ensconced in Turner's frontier ethic, villages of stark simplicity and virtue. The average American adult had but five years of schooling (and only recently had the nation made dramatic strides at reducing a substantial rate of illiteracy). Yet, even in such absence of worldly sophistication and learning, many people felt confident of two critical judgments: that America was earth's Eden, its people God's chosen.

The 1904 St. Louis fair, which commemorated the hundredth anniversary of the Louisiana Purchase (also a year late), was striking for the arrogance with which it viewed the place of Americans in the parade of humanity. Along with the ice cream cone, the hamburger, and iced tea — all introduced here — the fair featured an anthropology exhibition (inspired by Darwin) that attempted to explain human progress according to the principles of "cephalization," or the gradual increase of the size of the human cranium across different races. Anthropologist W. J. McGee, who designed the display, admitted that traditional forms of proof

Turn-of-the-Century Arrivals, Ellis Island

- *Emmanuel Goldenberg (Edward G. Robinson), 1903*
- *Israel Baline (Irving Berlin), 1893*
- *Lily Chouchoin (Claudette Colbert), 1912*
- *Angelo Siciliano (Charles Atlas), 1903*
- *Schmuel Gelbfisz (Samuel Goldwyn), 1896*
- *Leslie Townes Hope (Bob Hope), 1908*
- *Knut Rokne (Knute Rockne), 1893*
- *Julius Stein (Jule Styne), 1912*
- *Rodolfo Guglielmi di Valentina d'Antonguolla (Rudolph Valentino), 1913*
- *Israel Straasberg (Lee Strasberg), 1909*

"Not yet Americanized. Still eating Italian food."

Early-twentieth-century social work report

The early years of the century repre-sented the waning days of the more formal, Victorian life. Here, a New England family dines, c. 1906, beneath the embroidery declaring a familiar nineteenth-century vow: "In God We Trust."

"God has marked the American people as His chosen nation to finally lead in the regeneration of the world. This is the divine mission of America, and it holds for us all the profit, all the glory, all the happiness possible to man."

Albert J. Beveridge,
Indiana senator

were unavailable, yet the evidence of his assertions, he claimed, was "within con-stant sight of all whose eyes are open," and to that end he presented groups of Pygmies from Africa, Ainu aborigines from Japan, Patagonian giants from Argentina, Negrito peoples from the Philippines, and Native Americans in live ethnological settings — what was, effectively, a zoo for *human* animals — demon-strating to the millions who came to St. Louis how "perfected man" (that is, the Caucasian and, specifically, the American Anglo-Saxon Caucasian) represented the peak of the upward movement of human development, from "savagery" to "barbarism" to "civilization" and, finally, through the miracle of industrial expan-sion, "enlightenment." The implicit message of the exhibit was that the distinc-tive American alchemy had transformed people to a higher state of being. And going beyond even his fundamental racist premise, the designer suggested that while the new immigrants speeding to American shores were, for the most part, white, they were merely whites of the "civilized" rank awaiting the "enlighten-ment" that the Yankee atmosphere would provide them.

No doubt many of those attending the St. Louis fair found comfort in such declarations of racial superiority (a theme addressed in various ways by nearly every celebrated turn-of-the-century festival), and yet, at the same time,

they were just as fascinated with the way in which the exhibit put them face-to-face with their caged primitive "selves." For if, indeed, man had evolved from apes, as was the popular understanding of Darwin's work, just how far *had* he come from his animal instincts? And if the advanced industrial society of the American Anglo-Saxon represented the peak of civilization, just what had he lost in getting there?

Throughout the late nineteenth and early twentieth centuries, scientists and pseudoscientists around the world had been consumed by a furious competition to discover evolution's "missing link," the one that would show how the ape made the transition to the human form, and in so doing claim progress's lead position for their own race. All, of course, turned out to be bogus. Americans had been excited by the 1868 discovery in Albany, New York, of the Cardiff Giant, which turned out to be a gypsum statue aged with an acid bath, a hoax worthy of P. T. Barnum (and indeed Barnum constructed his own "Cardiff Giant," which he passed off at his circus as the "real" one, a hoax of a hoax). Germans, on whose soil the remnants of Neanderthal Man had been found, later detected in the ridges of ancient bone the signs of a decidedly German braincase. In perhaps the most celebrated of discoveries, Britain's Piltdown Man, which was "unearthed" in 1912, establishing Old England as the cradle of civilization, would set the course of evolutionary studies for forty years before it, too, was declared phony, a mixture of orangutan bones assembled by an amateur paleontologist eager for fame.

So fascinated were people of this time with the relationship between civilization and the wilderness, between primitive and modern man, that a New Englander named Joe Knowles proposed in 1913 to spend sixty days in complete isolation, sensationally stripping to his nakedness at the edge of the Maine woods before going off to live off the soil. And live he did. Writing birch-bark letters with a stick of charcoal and leaving them under a stump where they could be retrieved by newspaper reporters, Knowles kept readers up on his success at catching fish and killing deer, even taking time to philosophize along the way, extolling the virtues of the natural life and scolding readers for being too "civilized."

Knowles's expedition may have been a hoax itself, as one Boston newspaper claimed, but it touched something deep in contemporary sensitivities. This was, after all, a time when Jack London's *Call of the Wild* — the story of a pet dog who escapes from his owner to return to the wilderness and revert to life as a wolf — was by far the most popular novel, and when the Boy Scouts of America was established, in part to ensure that children did not lose touch with the skills necessary for survival in the forest. After emerging from the Maine woods, Knowles made his way to a ceremony at the Boston Commons clad only in a bearskin, and was greeted by no fewer than 20,000 people. More than 300,000 purchased Knowles's book, *Alone in the Wilderness*, and, after his return, the *Boston Post* published full-page color reproductions of his "paintings" of wild animals, ready, the paper claimed, to be framed and hung "in your den." Even as they marched eagerly into the exciting, industrial future, proud of their accomplishments, people simply could not resist looking back.

"Progress" was a word that carried a multitude of meanings at the turn of the century, and both the positive one embraced by the organizers of the St.

Left: Dubbed the "overlord of the savage world," anthropologist W. J. McGee, shown here (center) in the Maricopa Indians exhibit, supervised the display and study of two thousand "primitive peoples" at the 1904 St. Louis World's Fair. "Human culture is becoming unified," wrote McGee, "not only through diffusion, but through the extinction of the lower grades." Above: A pamphlet for McGee's "Philippine Exposition," which featured over a thousand Filipino natives.

In 1913 newspapers throughout the East and as far west as Kansas City followed the wilderness adventures of the "modern primitive," Joe Knowles (in loincloth, above). "The way the world is living at present is entirely wrong," preached Knowles to reporters. "Civilization has carried us along to a point where . . . we are not living, but merely existing."

Louis fair and the negative one Joe Knowles preached from his perch atop the birch trees of Maine contrasted sharply with the creed of those who actually called themselves progressives. Concerned about the harsher edges of the modern workplace, these reformers directed their attention less toward the perfectibility of man than toward the perfectibility of industrial capitalism, the trimming and pruning of the economic frontier that had been heretofore governed only by the "natural" laws of the free market.

The conditions that inspired the progressives to act were, to say the least, appalling. At the turn of the century, the average industrial laborer's workweek involved fifty-nine hours on the job (in the steel industry, that could stretch to eighty-four hours). Pay was scant and many industries worked seasonally, shutting down for months at a time and leaving people without a paycheck until the factory opened again. Textile workers faced a particularly brutal situation, crammed into tiny urban garrets where many were paid not by the hour, but by the piece, an arrangement that forced them to work at a pace so frantic it would inspire a new word, "sweatshop." And coal workers — delivered by the company doctor, taught in the company school, housed in the company house, and buried in the company graveyard — lived lives but a step from the misery of indentured servitude.

Journalists like Jacob Riis exposed the workers' plight to the broader public, shocking Americans who had always prided themselves on living in the land of opportunity. When it was reported in 1904 that 10 million of their citizens and, later, more than double that amount could be classified as poor (lacking, read one study, even the "standard that a man would demand for his horse or his slaves"), the sense that something had to be done became pervasive.

Riis was joined by other reform-minded writers (sometimes derided as "muckrakers"), among them Lincoln Steffens, who exposed municipal corruption, and Ida Tarbell, who became famous for her reports on corporate greed in the oil and meatpacking industries. But the key to change in the early years of the new century was the constituency that now embraced it. In the past, progressive reforms had appeared radical and un-American, smacking of socialism (and socialists would indeed gain a footing in the electorate that would peak in the presidential contest of 1912), but, in part because the nation was enjoying the kind of prosperity and stability that historically nurtures a quest for betterment, reform seemed now to excite even the middle class, inspiring millions toward compassion for those caught in the sweatshops and the mills. As Kansas newspaperman William Allen White later described it, the image of the disenchanted American had changed. He had "shaved his whiskers, washed his shirt, [and] put on a derby."

America's urban nightmare: "Coal dust so black you couldn't see the sun at noontime"

Rohleder in 1908.

—*Charles Rohleder, born in 1905, supported himself by running a newspaper stand on the north side of Pittsburgh while attending the University of Pittsburgh and Duquesne University Law School. During the 1920s he wrote numerous articles for the* Northside Chronicle *and began a career at Dravo Corporation, which lasted for thirty-eight years. After he retired, Rohleder continued to work at his newsstand, as he did throughout his career at Dravo, until he was seventy-nine years old. He died in April 1995.*

When I was growing up at the beginning of the century, times were very hard for the poor. Very tough. There was no welfare to help you out. If you were hungry, the only places you could go to were the missions. There was one little mission behind the library that my mother went one day to beg for a load of coal. A load of coal was worth about three dollars back then, and it seemed as though it took my family forever to pay that mission back.

My mother rolled tobacco into cigars at home to try and raise a little extra money. Actually we all pitched in and helped — my father, my grandfather, me — everybody who was in the house. Back then, very few cigars were actually made in a factory; most were made in people's homes. We would spread out these big leaves of tobacco on the kitchen table and just roll and roll and talk and talk. And then my mother would take them in and sell them to a cigar company, which paid her according to how many she rolled. Of course, she didn't get very much money for them. Cigars at the store only cost about three or four for a dime, so you can imagine what the cigar company paid my mother for them. One time when I was a little boy I got into a box of tobacco clippings and just started chewing. I had seen all of these other people chewing on tobacco, and I thought, "Oh boy, I'd like to try that!" I couldn't even go to school that afternoon. I was sicker than two dogs.

At that time, there were a lot of foreigners moving to Pittsburgh — a lot of immigrants. There were also a lot of blacks moving up from the South. People came from all over because they could get a job right away. People used to say that if you couldn't get a job anywhere else, you could get one in Pittsburgh. There was a Greek family that moved in next door to us, and we used to laugh at them and make fun of them because they were immigrants and they spoke a language that we didn't understand. And even though they were really hard workers and were making a go of it, we used to look down on them. I guess it was just ignorance on our part. But back then we just thought that all immigrants were no better than the dirt under our feet. There were a lot of Poles, Greeks, and Germans in town. Pittsburgh even had two German newspapers. Most of the immigrants came to Pittsburgh to work in the factories, especially the canning factory and the steel mills. And despite what we thought about them, they worked very hard to try and get ahead — twelve-hour days, six days a week.

I guess you could have considered us German, at least of German ancestry — my mother was Pennsylvania Dutch — but I always considered myself an American. Both my mother and my grandmother would speak in German when they didn't want us kids to know what they were talking about. I knew a few words, but not enough so that I could carry on a conversation. As far as the real immigrants were concerned, I didn't want to have anything to do with them. I just didn't concern myself with them, I was too busy trying to make a living to fuss with them. I started working when I was six years old, selling newspapers out on the street.

Pittsburgh was very dirty back then. Everyone burned coal for heat, and it was soft coal, which emits a lot of sulfur and black fumes. Even in the summer, the factories were burning coal for steam to drive the machines. It got so bad that on some days you couldn't see the sun at noontime because of the thick smoke from the factories. There were steamboats on the river, and they had had these big smokestacks. When the boats went under low bridges, the smoke would come right up and cover the whole bridge. There were times when I walked across a bridge and went in clean on one side, but by the time I reached the other side, I needed a new shirt.

And the rivers themselves were even worse. They put these big sewers in, so that everybody could have flush toilets. The sewers must have been about ten feet in circumference and they just dumped right into the river. I used to see just awful stuff coming out of there. There was a hospital nearby, and if they had an operation and they chopped off a few pieces of that person — cancer or anything else — they just threw it right in the sewer. Before you knew it, it would come out in the river. One time I even saw a little baby floating down there. And of course, there was the sewage from all the toilets. Big long ugly things, paper and everything else would float right out of there. The worst of it was that kids used to fish right where that sewer came out because that's where the catfish were. I tried it a few times, but luckily I never caught anything.

There were also all of these factories and slaughterhouses and steel mills along the river. And they would just dump their refuse right in the water. You could always tell when the canning factory was processing tomatoes or making chili sauce, because the river would run red with tomato skins. And you would see chunks of fat floating down from the slaughterhouses. At night, the sky above the river would look like it was on fire from the open hearths at the steel mills. It was lit just like it was daytime. What a beautiful sight that was; it looked as if the whole city had burst into flames.

Occasionally I would go down to watch them make steel. There was this big beehive-looking thing that they made coke in. There would be a terrific hot fire going with a big ball of steel in there. And this man would stick this long bar into the fire to turn the steel. He wore heavy red flannel underwear to make him sweat, because the perspiration would keep him from getting burns. Of course the open hearths also blew a lot of soot in the air which would just cover the roofs and porches of all the houses in Pittsburgh. People would have to sweep a couple of times a day just to keep up.

Now, although the streets were really dirty and we all worked very hard — children started working in the factories around twelve, thirteen years old — we seldom complained about any of it. The immigrants, the blacks, everybody came to Pittsburgh to start a new life and earn a little money. But even though we were working towards our future, we never forgot about our past either. Every Memorial Day, we would have a special program where all the schoolchildren would march in this long parade up to the cemetery, all carrying potted flowers. We would plant those flowers by the Civil War graves. And then Civil War vets would come and talk to us about their escapades. They would tell us about how they shot people from the South and how they made the enemy soldiers turn tail and run from the battle. Of course, we all thought it was great fun and we laughed and laughed as they told their stories. Even so, there was something tragic in it all. That war must have been horrible for them, but it was because of that war that a place like Pittsburgh, with all its different groups of people, could start to thrive.

Progressives became increasingly concerned with the appalling conditions that many workers faced in mines and factories across the United States. Of particular worry was the fate of the nearly 2 million child laborers. "Breaker boys," such as these at a Pennsylvania coal mine, often suffered debilitating injuries as they worked ten-hour shifts in the dangerous mines.

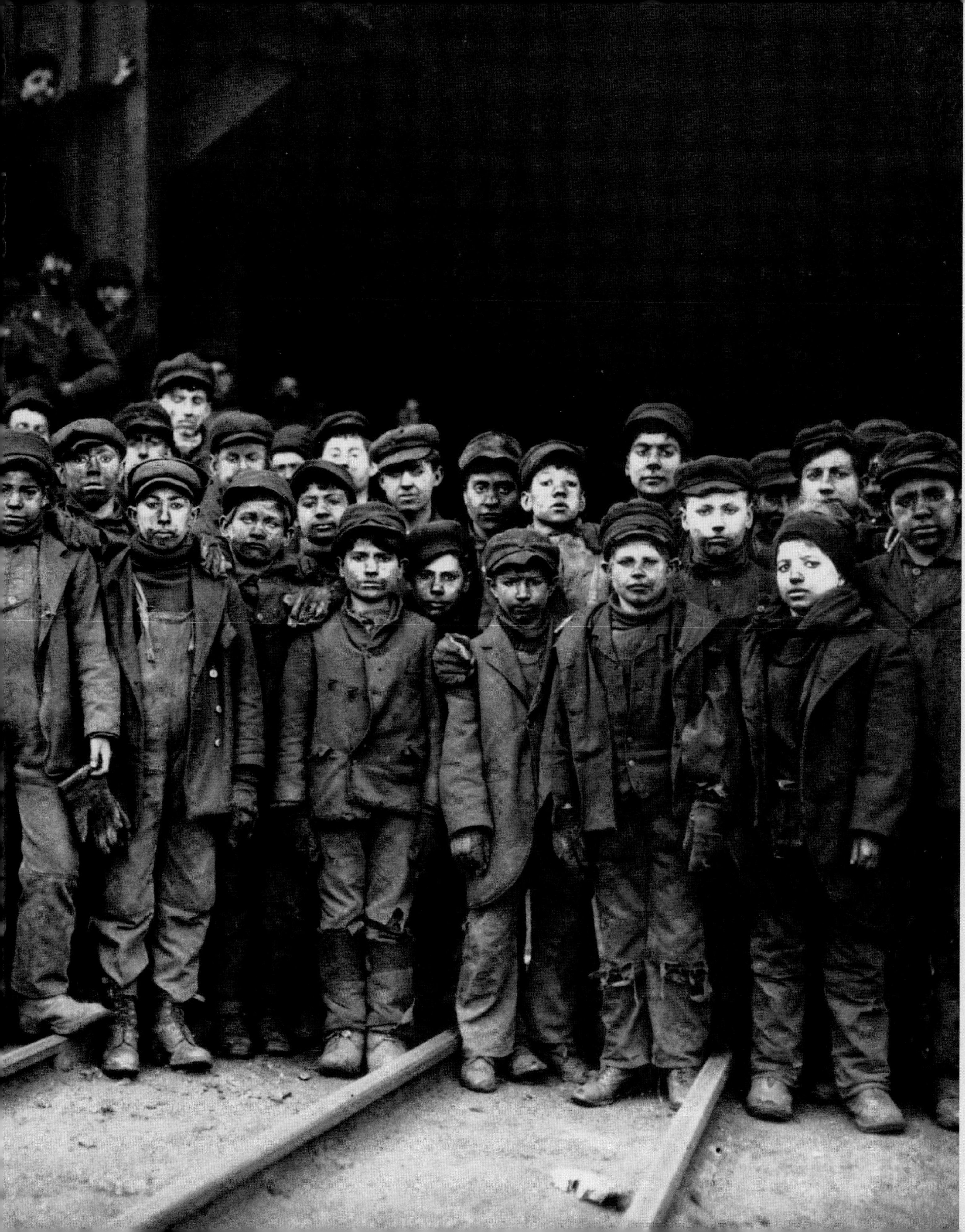

Thomas Edison, shown here, at right, and the "insomnia squad" at his West Orange, New Jersey, research laboratory, where they worked virtually around the clock perfecting the incandescent light-bulb, the durable storage battery, and the motion picture camera. "I never did any-thing worth doing by accident," Edison once proclaimed, "nor did any of my inventions come by accident; they came by work."

"If you should tell me that you could make babies by machinery, I shouldn't doubt it . . ."

Journalist Daniel Craig, writing to Thomas Edison

At least some of the public's willingness to address reform at this time could also be laid to its newfound faith in science as the unchallengeable Truth, the explicator of all human activity. The great age of invention (usually defined as across the years 1870–1920) fostered the heroic image of the genius-inventor, of which Thomas Edison was only the best known, the confident, self-made man who combined elements of American frontier mythology with the promise of the future (Edison, the uneducated, battling the wilderness of technology), a com-forting grandfatherly guide to a strange world. But a large part of the romantic aura surrounding science also went beyond machines to systems and the growing sense that science in this form could render benefit upon *any* problem or task: improve the speed of work and the competitiveness of business, the raising of children and the management of the house, the eradication of the slum and the successful maintenance of the urban society. Social work was the most obvious outgrowth of this mind-set, as evidenced by the growing number of "settlement houses" dotting the urban landscape, each of them dedicated to the progressive belief that the immigrant's plight was a by-product of his circumstances, *not* his racial or ethnic limitations.

But if efficiency was the new goal and experts were the new heroes, the ideas of Frederick Winslow Taylor surely made him the greatest scientific thinker of the day. Determined to stop what he referred to as "soldiering" (the more common term would be "goldbricking"), Taylor had stood with a stopwatch and timed workers tasked with shoveling coal, iron, and coke at the Bethlehem Steel plant in Pennsylva-nia. Convinced that there had to be "one best way" to execute any job, he calculated that the shoveler's work could be done most efficiently if he filled his tool with pre-cisely twenty-one and a half pounds of material in each lift. To help the company increase productivity, Taylor (who had once created a spoon-shaped tennis racket to improve upon his favorite game) then aided in the design of shovels that would lift exactly that amount, no matter the material to be lifted — a flat shovel for ore; a gigantic scoop-shaped shovel for the relatively lightweight rice coal — while at the same time establishing rules for a perfect shoveling "technique," even con-vincing Bethlehem to hire "shoveling coaches" to ensure that workers maintained the proper form. At first, Bethlehem's management thought him insane, but soon, 140 shovelers were doing the work that had been done by 500, and with that the Taylor legend began to grow.

Gradually, "Taylorism" became the doctrine of "scientific management," the system by which work is disassembled into its component parts and the tasks divided among laborers to provide for the kind of maximum efficiency Henry Ford hoped to achieve, for instance, with his automobile assembly line. And Tay-

To realize his dream of building "a car for the great multitude," Henry Ford developed the assembly line around Frederick Winslow Taylor's ideas of "scientific management." By 1914 Ford's plants were producing up to one thousand cars a day.

Below: An advertisement for a Taylor–inspired shovel that lifted the requisite twenty-one pounds.

lor, and others, imagined that it would bring only benefit, not only to profit-seeking capitalists but to the hardworking laborers, too, for high wages were part of his prescription for a well-run industry ("Men will not do an extraordinary day's work for an ordinary day's pay," he pronounced), even if the routinization of labor and the separation of the mind from the hand made many workers feel as if they had themselves become nothing more than a part in a gigantic well-oiled machine. To progressives like Taylor, conflict was regressive, for the very essence of the movement was that the various competing factions (management, labor, capital, government) function in harmony (or, to put it bluntly, *also* like a well-oiled machine).

Taylor himself was only interested in industrial management, yet before long his ideas were being applied to everything from church worship to housekeeping. And ironically, given how the ideas of scientific management would come to be viewed as antagonistic to labor, Lenin would study them carefully as a model for industry in the Soviet Union, Mussolini as a prototype for fascist Italy. Perhaps most important, Taylor's ideas became the basis for a kind of thinking that dominated life in the twentieth century, the belief that, as author Neil Postman has written, "society is best served when human beings are put at the disposal of their techniques and technology, that human beings are worth less, in a sense, than their machinery."

Progressives were split on the issue of women's rights. On one side were the suffragists, who insisted that all good things would flow from the extension of voting privileges to women. Not only did these activists claim the vote as a demo-

WOMEN
VOTE

WE DEMAND AN
AMENDMENT TO THE
CONSTITUTION OF THE
UNITED STATES
ENFRANCHISING THE
WOMEN OF THIS COUNTRY

Suffragists chose dramatic forms of demonstration and faced fierce opposition. At parades such as this one in Washington, D.C., 1914, they were often "spat upon, slapped in the face, tripped up, pelted with burning cigar stubs, and insulted by jeers and obscene language," reported one government official.

cratic principle, they also argued that it would improve society, predicting that when women could use the vote to affect social policy, society would become more receptive to reform, leading to a lessening of crime and vice, even the elimination of war.

On the other side of the issue, however, were progressives who saw suffrage as dangerous for women in the way in which the vote might work to *overvalue* equality and make it harder to push, for instance, for special legislation protecting women and children in the workplace. "Social feminists," as historian William O'Neill calls them, had made great strides for women, albeit in areas that were extensions of the woman's traditional role: the "helping" professions of social work, education, and health ("May we not say," offered activist Jane Addams, "that city housekeeping has failed partly because women, the traditional housekeepers, have not been consulted as to its multiform activities?"). And yet they were resented by more radical feminists who believed that by settling for achievements in the traditionally female occupations, the social feminists had delayed the march toward true equality.

Suffragists were also attacked by both women and men who saw the vote as undermining the family or, more precisely, the understanding that the division of

family life into spheres of responsibility — women maintaining the home, men providing financial and physical support — was an essential aspect of civilization, supported not only by tradition but also by biology. "What sort of next generation would evolve," asked these "Antis," as they were sometimes called, "if all women considered their first duty to be themselves, and overlooked the fact that their strongest power and highest possibility is that of unselfish — and often unnoticed — service?"

Suffragists had some strange allies: nativists, for instance, who felt it unfair that women of Anglo-Saxon stock be denied rights afforded to men from the "ignorant immigrant" classes, and southern racists, who saw in suffrage an opportunity to instantly double white voting power in the face of the threat of the freed slave. In the nineteenth century, suffragists had allied themselves with the abolitionists; in the twentieth century, however, they often pursued their cause at the expense of the African-American. "American women who know the history of their country," wrote feminist Carrie Chapman Catt, "will always resent the fact that American men chose to enfranchise Negroes fresh from slavery before enhancing their wives and mothers." In fact, the southern white man was already working hard to undo the vote that had been given to the black man, but on this, as historian Ann Douglas has pointed out, he now received the encouragement of activists like Catt, who insisted that when women were enfranchised, "rule by illiteracy" would end, and another suffragist suggested that once women received the vote, "immediate and durable white supremacy, honestly attained" would follow on.

By the early years of the century's second decade, suffragists had decided to put all their attention on a constitutional amendment, resorting to displays of civil disobedience to force the national leadership to comply. And indeed, with women being enfranchised in other parts of the world, an air of the inevitable entered the suffrage issue that needed only the force of the coming war and its demands upon women as laborers to become a reality.

The era's most famous progressive sported a prominent set of whiskers, a distinctively toothy grimace, pince-nez eyeglasses, and a jaw as solid as rock. Theodore Roosevelt was the kind of president that Frederick Jackson Turner could appreciate, a New York aristocrat who by dint of his enthusiasm for the rugged life had every right to claim that he, too, was a "Western man in all but my residence." Except that TR, as he was affectionately known by the nation he led for seven years, was really most at home in a seat of power, and at that, preferably the one in the White House.

Roosevelt became president when a young anarchist named Leon Czolgosz — the son of a Polish immigrant, he had been a disgruntled laborer at a Cleveland wire mill — sidled up to President William McKinley at the 1901 Pan-American Exhibition in Buffalo (which sported ethnological exhibits anticipating the St. Louis display) and with a pistol concealed under a handkerchief proceeded to enter his name as the first on the list of twentieth-century assassins who changed history. The vice president was, typically, at the apex of a climbing expedition in the Adirondacks when he heard that McKinley was about to succumb, and his trip down the slope to the train that would take him to the president's bedside and his own swearing in — Roosevelt rode through the night on a buckboard,

Peter, Peter, pumpkin eater,
Had a wife and tried to beat her;
But his wife was a suffragette,
And Peter's in the hospital yet.

Progressive era jingle

Marching with the suffragettes: "Mom said I was too young, but I insisted"

I came from a long line of New Englanders. One of my ancestors was on *The Mayflower,* and others fought in the Revolutionary War. My more recent ancestors had been abolitionists in the Civil War, and my parents and grandparents were all very active in town meetings and other political events. So I grew up with this tradition of public interest and public service. When I was still a young girl, my family moved to Washington, D.C. For me, Washington was an incredibly exciting place. There was the Washington Monument, the Tidal Basin, the cherry trees, and, of course, the Capitol and the White House. From the time we moved there, I just loved Washington. Occasionally my mother would take me out of school to go see Congress in session. We would sit up in the gallery and watch all of these men giving speeches and debating issues. I just loved the importance of it all and the ceremonial aspects of it. It was very exciting for a little girl.

On Sunday afternoons my parents would invite their friends over to our house in Georgetown for potluck dinners. These were people who worked for Congress or who worked in government offices, or sometimes they were just enlightened people who were interested in the progressive issues of the day. Needless to say, there was always a lot of political conversation on those Sunday afternoons. My brothers weren't at all interested, but I would always hang around and listen to everything that was discussed. This was where I first heard talk about woman's suffrage — about women's rights and about women getting the vote. It wasn't just that women didn't have the right to vote, they didn't really have the right to own property, they didn't have the right to custody of their children, there were just all kinds of ways in which they didn't have rights. Even at my school, girls weren't noticed as much as boys were. If a teacher asked a question, and the hands went up, it was always a boy that was called on to answer. I was on the debating team and even there the boys were always picked over the girls. It was little things like that. Men and boys enjoyed all the privileges and all the rights. The campaign to win women's suffrage was just a start, but it was a big step.

I hardly ever heard the suffrage issue discussed outside my home. In school I think only a few of my girl-friends even knew what the word meant, and even they knew very little about the issue. Washington was a very conservative city in those days, and a very southern city, and my intimacy with other girls was more about parties and walks and going downtown for lunch on Saturdays and things like that. It was at home that I really learned about suffrage. You see, my mother was very involved in the issue. And being the only girl in my family, it was just natural for me to listen to her, and to do things with her.

I admired my mother very much.

The suffragettes had a big headquarters in downtown Washington, almost across from the Supreme Court Building. My mother would take me up there on Saturdays when she volunteered to help out with mailings. I remember helping out by folding letters, licking envelopes, doing all sorts of things. The backbone of the suffrage movement was composed of well-to-do, middle-class women, both Republicans and Democrats. There weren't many working-class women in the movement. Most of them were too busy working to get involved. The suffragettes organized pickets and marches and rallies. It wasn't anything comparable to the violence that the British women were going through in their fight for suffrage. Those women were being arrested and beaten and jailed. Nothing like that happened here, but there was a lot of agitation.

I was only ten years old the first time I went to a march with my mother. She told me, "Oh, you're too young, you can't go." But I said, "I *am* going, because you're going to win the right to vote and I'm going to vote when I'm grown up." So she let me march. It wasn't a particularly large parade. We had permission for a group of about fifty women to march from the Capitol to the White House. There was a marching band — made up of men — playing music right behind us as we marched. Everyone there was much older and bigger than me, and they took longer steps than I did. So I had to really hustle to keep up with my mother, but I managed to do it. Just like all the other suffragettes, I wore a white blouse and skirt, and a purple and gold sash that came across my front. Purple and gold were the colors of the women's suffrage movement. We walked right up to the White House gates. They were locked, of course, so we couldn't get in. We ultimately moved across the street to Lafayette Park, where we demonstrated and we

Haessler, as a teenager. Right: Haessler's parents, Celia and Charles Whitaker.

—Lucy Haessler, born in 1904, was a volunteer activist with numerous labor, civil rights, peace, and community organizations. During World War II, she helped with Russian war relief and served with the Women's Auxiliary of the Michigan State CIO. In the 1960s she worked with the Women's International League for Peace and Freedom, the Women's Strike for Peace, and Students for a Democratic Society.

picketed. I was so excited because I just felt that something was going to be done. The more marches that were held, the more you could feel the movement just building and building. But the sad thing for my mother and for me and for all the suffragettes was that it took too long for any changes to happen. Even so, in my heart, I knew that this movement was going to go somewhere, and it was going to help with the struggles of women, and the difficulties of women.

A few years later in 1917, Jeannette Rankin became the first woman elected to Congress. When she got to Washington, everyone in the women's suffrage movement was just overwhelmed. She got a hero's welcome. You see, the suffrage fight was still on. Most women across the country still didn't have the right to vote. There were a few western states that allowed women to vote in federal elections before the federal government allowed it. And that's how Jeannette Rankin had been elected. She could sit in Congress, but in most states she still wasn't allowed to vote. My mother took me out of school so that I could go down to the Capitol to see her sworn in. There were people and press everywhere. I could barely control myself. I started to talk fast and loud, but then my mother said, "Shh, they'll put us out of here. You'd better keep quiet." Jeannette Rankin was a really heroic and outstanding woman; not only was she the first woman to be elected to Congress, and the first woman to speak out on issues of world peace. Later, when Congress was voting on whether or not to enter the First World War, she stood up and said something that took a lot of courage; she said, "I love my country, but I cannot vote for war." For someone like me, who had been brought up with the beliefs of women's rights and peace, hearing her say those words was one of the greatest moments of my childhood.

dodging trees and soaking up the forest mist — surely qualifies as among the oddest of inaugural parades.

Legend has it that TR's driver, concerned that his speed might endanger the man who was poised to lead the nation, shouted back "Too fast?," to which Roosevelt retorted, "Go ahead . . . go on . . . go on," but even if that is not true, it would fit the image that surrounded the twenty-sixth president, a man with a personality so commanding it would render him the most popular leader since Abraham Lincoln (to whom he constantly compared himself) and as one of a handful of twentieth-century chief executives who imprinted themselves upon the public mood.

TR stood just five feet nine inches, and at forty two, he was the youngest president in history — even younger than John F. Kennedy — yet he possessed an unquenchable thirst for activity, a boundless source of energy, and a zest for the "strenuous life" which made up for his lack of years. As Kennedy would more than half a century later, Roosevelt served as an inspiration to the nation's youth, a role he assumed enthusiastically, and so proud was TR of his physical strength that little boys visiting the White House were invited to take a swinging punch at his muscled stomach.

Fittingly for an era so enamored of the machine, Roosevelt's contemporaries consistently described him in technological terms: "a steam engine in trousers," said one senator; "a wonderful little machine," wrote novelist Henry James, "destined to be overstrained, perhaps, but not as yet, truly betraying the least creak." And the goal of all Roosevelt's energy, the proposed product of the "machine's" working parts, was nothing less than the preparation of his nation for the twentieth century.

Roosevelt was so much a man of his time, he embodied so many of its popular preoccupations (even some of those that seemed to be in conflict), it is hard not to think of him except as a caricature of the age. Who could better represent America's fresh sense of geographical definition than TR, who as biographer Edmund Morris points out was born of a southern mother and a northern father, yet was himself an easterner whose fascination was with the West? Who could better stand for the sometimes racially questionable declaration of a new American "breed" than this passionate follower of social Darwinism who had come to national attention with his charge up Cuba's San Juan Hill in the Spanish-American War of 1898, a triumph that helped claim, he said, the place of Americans among "the great fighting races" of the world? Who could better display America's emerging social conscience than a chief executive who believed not only in the natural right of the strong to prevail over the weak but also that the strong should, by moral purpose, work in *defense* of the weak, a president who wrote his senior essay at Harvard on "The Practicability of Equalizing Men and Women Before the Law" and who saw the government as responsible for curbing the abuses of the wealthy and standing up for the interests of both labor and the consumer? And who could better represent the modern quest for efficiency than this dynamo who by the age of forty-three had authored dozens of books and served as New York State assemblyman, United States civil service commissioner, police commissioner of New York City, assistant secretary of the navy, governor of New York , vice president, and, finally, president?

Roosevelt's brand of progressivism put him foursquare in the middle of the national mood: for while people wanted change, they did not want radical change, and while Roosevelt's reforms were progressive, they were a *conservative* sort of progressivism that policed more by threat than by action (it was TR who declared the presidency as a "bully pulpit"), more by regulation than by prosecution, and used power more symbolically and rhetorically than in fact. In a very public confrontation, Roosevelt did prosecute John D. Rockefeller and J. P. Morgan, two of the most celebrated titans of American business, for their railroad monopoly in the Northwest; he righteously took the side of labor and the consumer in the great coal strike of 1902; and by 1906, two years after he had been elected in his own right, TR increased the pace of reform by creating standards for food and drugs, tackling the corruption in the meat industry (in response to novelist Upton Sinclair's best-selling *The Jungle*), and, in the cause that he perhaps held dearest, aggressively limiting development of public lands (he would double the number of national parks and establish fifty-one wild bird refuges). Like Turner, Roosevelt believed that the experience with the natural world was a renewing one and if the country was to foster the kind of citizenship it needed to prosper morally, intellectually, and physically, that experience needed to be available to all.

Yet even as Roosevelt was initiating the nation's first tentative steps toward the social conscience that Turner had envisioned as America's next great adventure, he was also prodding the nation's attention toward what he saw as the preeminent civilization's responsibilities abroad. And while much of that was rhetoric, too, the debate that it prompted would, like most conflicts of this time, foreshadow a discussion that would run throughout the century. Consistent with his belief in the superiority of Anglo-Saxon society, Roosevelt saw American foreign policy much as he saw his progressive domestic policy, as a policing mechanism meant to maintain stability and protect American interests, the "civilized" nations of the world lording over the uncivilized both as right and as duty. Roosevelt felt Americans were naive about foreign policy, that they relied too much on the natural protection offered by the two oceans, and that developments in transportation and communications had created a more interdependent world, making it necessary to extend the Monroe Doctrine (which insisted that Europe stay out of affairs on this side of the Atlantic) into a natural right for American intervention in the Caribbean and the Pacific Basin. "Chronic wrongdoing," he declared self-righteously, "or an impotence which results in the loosening of ties of civilized society . . . may force the United States, however reluctantly . . . to the exercise of an international police power."

Still, the president's interest in the world of international politics was more personal than political. Like most of the chief executives who would follow him in this century, TR's ego sought the exposure that only the grander stage of world politics could provide him. In 1905 he personally forged an end to the Russo-Japanese War (earning himself a Nobel Peace Prize), and his parade of the United States Navy fleet around the world in 1908 (done in defiance of Congress) was a muscle-flexing gesture more demonstrative of the scrappy boyhood boxer's instincts that remained with Roosevelt his entire life than a popular mood. Most Americans simply did not yet want the role in international affairs that TR was ready to thrust upon them.

Teddy Roosevelt had been out of office for nearly two years when he appeared at Grant's Tomb Decoration Day, above, in 1910. TR's strong will and ebullient spirit kept him in the public arena. "He brought in a stream of fresh, pure, bracing air from the mountains," noted literary critic Harry Thurston Peck, "to clear the fetid atmosphere of the national capital."

My father was born in Oslo, Norway, and as a young man he went to sea and traveled around the world several times. On one of his trips, he ended up in California, and he liked it so much that he decided to stay. While he was in California, the Spanish fleet sunk *The Maine* in Havana Harbor and the United States entered the Spanish-American War. My father was so incensed that the Spanish would attack a ship from his adopted country that he volunteered for duty and went to war for the United States Navy. He was always very proud of his service in the war, and he was particularly enthralled by the story of a lieutenant colonel named Theodore Roosevelt who led the "Rough Riders" up San Juan Hill.

As much as my father loved America, he decided to go back to Norway after the war. Supposedly it was to see his family, but really I think he just wanted to get back with my mother, who was living in Oslo at the time. They were married soon after, and then I was born in 1901. Now, my mother wanted to stay in Oslo to be near her family, but my father was determined to return to America. He was convinced that we would all have a better future in the United States, so despite my mother's protestations, he set sail for New York, just a few months after I was born. Once he got a job and found us a home, he sent for my mother and me. I was barely a year old when I moved to America.

I grew up in Borough Park, Brooklyn, which back then was the outskirts of the city. A lot of Brooklyn was still like the country. Part of Borough Park was settled with nice homes and things, but we lived on what you might say was the other side of the street. Our part of the neighborhood was still pretty undeveloped; there just weren't very many houses. In front of our house was a great big field that I used to play in with some of the other kids. The neighborhood was made up mostly of immigrants who were just trying to get ahead. The shopping area consisted of about two blocks, and it seemed as though each store was owned by somebody of a different nationality. There was a butcher, who was a German; a grocer, who was Jewish; a shoe maker, who was Italian. It was just a huge mix of people from very different places. But they all gathered together in our neighborhood to try and become Americans. Everybody tried to help each other out, because we were all in the same boat. Everyone knew they had to work for a living. The ones that didn't start their own businesses were either carpenters or electricians or factory workers. The idea was to be part of the country, and to support yourself.

My father got a job in the Brooklyn Navy Yard as a mechanic in the Ordnance Department. He was in charge of mounting guns onto warships, so it was a natural extension to his navy experience. He was an extremely patriotic man. He just loved America. I was practically brought up with an American flag in my hand. Memorial Day was one of our favorite holidays. I loved seeing my father dressed in his navy uniform march down the street in the parade. And then we would meet in the park with other veteran families and have a big picnic. Although I was born in Norway, I felt American through and through. We were a real navy family.

I feel like I've heard about Teddy Roosevelt practically from the time I was born. My father was such an admirer of the man that it felt as though he was just part of my life. Teddy Roosevelt represented just about everything that my father admired. He had fought valiantly in the war; he had been an assistant secretary of the navy; he was gregarious and forthright. And although he had come from a very rich family, he fought hard for the common man. Teddy Roosevelt had this sense of adventure and spontaneity that my father respected. My father could find no wrong in TR.

I remember him laughing and telling me about how TR was such an independent and headstrong man that people had a hard time keeping track of him, even when he was in the White House. He would get up early in the morning and just take off and leave the White

Left: Freeman in 1903. Below: Her father, Carl Pederson, in his navy uniform.

—*Anne Freeman was born in 1901 in Oslo, Norway. In 1918 she joined the U.S. Navy and was among the first women to serve during World War I. After the war, she married and had two daughters. In October 1997 she took part in the dedication ceremony for the Women in Military Service Memorial in Washington, D.C.*

House, unbeknownst to anyone. They didn't have the Secret Service or things like that to keep an eye on him, so he would just take off and go for a walk around Washington before coming back to go to work. You'd think he would have been a little more careful seeing as he originally got into office when President McKinley was shot.

One day when my father was working at the Brooklyn Navy Yard, there was this strange man walking around and looking at things. He must have come in as part of a tour group or something, because they had gates and fences to keep people from just walking in. But here was this short man with thick glasses and a mustache walking around as if he owned the place. And then all of a sudden he pulled out a camera and started taking pictures. Well, this one guard immediately went up to the man and told him that he was not allowed to take pictures in the Navy Yard.

"Oh, I can take a couple of pictures," the man replied. "It's okay. I'm not a spy."

"Oh no," the guard said, "you are not allowed to do that. And if you do, I'm going to have to take you in."

After a gentlemanly argument, the man agreed not to take any more pictures. Well, what this guard didn't know was that the man with the camera was actually Teddy Roosevelt. Somehow he had gotten into the Navy Yard and decided he wanted to take some pictures. Even when the guard approached him, he didn't say, "I'm Teddy Roosevelt." He just acted like he was a normal citizen. I think he was trying to test the guard. It wasn't really that odd that the guard didn't recognize TR. You see back then, before television, the president wasn't as recognizable as he is today. You might see his picture in the paper, or a cartoon drawing of him, but you just didn't see his face all that often. And you certainly wouldn't expect to see him by himself, with a camera, walking through Brooklyn!

Nobody found out that day that it had been Teddy Roosevelt snooping around. But a little while after the episode, the guard received a letter saying that he had been accepted to the Naval Academy — and he hadn't even applied. I guess Teddy was so impressed by the young man's persistence that he pulled some strings to see to it that he got ahead.

To my father, America was a young country full of promise. And Teddy Roosevelt was a president who typified that. He, too, was young, and he wanted America to be noticed and to be a leader around the world. Teddy Roosevelt had an incredible strength of will that really appealed to new Americans who were trying to make their way. Once he set his mind upon something, he felt he could accomplish it. And that's the way my father approached his life as well.

Roosevelt considered the fourteen-month 1907 tour of the "Great White Fleet" to be "the most important service I rendered to peace." Here, in Japan, the sailors are greeted enthusiastically.

The Statue of Liberty hung her head;
Columbia dropped in a swoon,
The American eagle drooped and died,
When Teddy dined with the coon.

*Popular children's verse,
after Roosevelt invited Booker T. Washington
to the White House, 1901*

In an atmosphere so damp with racial chest-thumping, where immigrant cultures were being looked upon with suspicion and the undeveloped world examined as ripe for Western exploitation, it would only seem to follow that America's own caste system, the one that continued to separate black from white, would receive fresh examination. And indeed it did, for the worse. Just as it is hard at the end of the twentieth century to contemplate America's early-century innocence, so, too, is it hard to contemplate the nation's unashamedly high level of bigotry, a time when popular magazines regularly described blacks as "niggers" or "coons," "darkies" or "pickaninnies"; when adult black men were called "boy" and the caricatures of the time — Uncle Ben and Aunt Jemima — demonstrated the depth of understanding with which white America viewed the black personality. This was a day when the term "race riot" referred most likely to white people bringing violence down on blacks (not the opposite, as it came to mean in the latter half of the century), when a visit to the White House by black leader Booker T. Washington in 1901 was greeted with public censure ("Roosevelt Dines with a Nigger," read the headline of one paper), and when, in some places in the South, it was deemed so entertaining to see a black man suffer that theaters were reserved for lynchings.

While it had appeared, for a short time after the Civil War, that a more generous social structure might evolve in the South, one in which blacks and whites would share authority, the latter years of the nineteenth century were characterized instead by a vigorous white campaign to reclaim power over their dominion through the disfranchisement of the black voter (using, most notably, the poll tax and the literacy test) and the institution of a system of segregation that became known as Jim Crow. Like most folk terms, its origin is in doubt (some say it was intended as a simile, as in "black as a crow"; others, that it was derived from an early-nineteenth-century minstrel song, meant, like most minstrel songs, to portray the black man's life as a farce), but whatever its beginnings, by the 1890s Jim Crow had become synonymous with an order that prescribed a clear definition between the lives of southern blacks and those of southern whites. Remarkably, so long as they were serving as slaves and therefore offering no threat to white political or economic supremacy, black Americans had been allowed to live in relative intimacy with their masters — domestics on the plantation, for instance, worked and lived in close proximity to whites — but now that the African-American had been emancipated, he was seen as posing an intolerable danger, both sanitary and sexual, that could only be controlled through humiliation and degradation, or, as in the view of the most violent of white racists, death.

Jim Crow meant separate schools, trolley cars, buses, restaurants, inns, rest rooms, swimming pools. In some places, the services of prostitutes were separated; in some courts, black defendants were sworn in with a separate

The Suwanee, Georgia, train depot with separate accommodations for "Colored" and "White" passengers, c. 1915.

One day I was walking down the road outside Frankfort, Kentucky, on my way to a white person's house where I was doing some work, when I saw this dance pavilion over across a field. It looked really nice, and even though I was in a white part of town, I got off the road and cut through this field just to get a better look at this pretty pavilion. But then when I turned around to head back, there was a white man standing there with his rifle pointed right straight at my head. Now, I was scared, but I didn't show it. I just walked right up to him and as I passed him I told him that all I did was stop to look at the pavilion on my way to work. I showed no fear whatsoever, and he just let me pass.

I was born at a time when they still did things the old slave-time way. They felt that you had to lynch a black man every so often to keep him in his place. And that was the general idea. When I was very young they lynched a black man right here in Frankfort. He was accused of robbing someone and they strung him up right out in the open. My dad took me down there to see that dead man. He even lifted me up so I could get a good look at him. When I turned around and looked at my dad, there were tears rolling down his face. And he said to me, "George, when you grow up, I want you to do something about the way these white people are treating us black people." I promised my dad that I would, and I'm still trying to do something about it.

There was a lot of trouble going on between the whites and the blacks back then — a lot of mistrust. We had separate schools, separate parts of town, racial separation in everything. Even as a young boy, I knew a lot of very fine white people and we usually got along. Some of the finest people I knew were white southerners. Even so, most whites wanted blacks to stay in their place. They wanted to keep the slave system. When I was little, someone hired a couple of black fellows to do some advertising in the streets. One would tap a drum, the other would have a sign with some sort of message on it,

and they would dance around and cut up like a bunch of monkeys. And they were very popular. As long as you acted like a monkey, you'd get recognized. But as soon as you started to be intelligent, well, that was a different story.

My grandparents constantly told me, "Listen, don't get in no trouble and you'll be all right." And my great-grandmother, who had been a slave, said to me, "Boy, if you make waves, you're gonna be in prison before you're twenty years old." Now, I knew that I would have to make waves in order just to get ahead. But the most important thing that they taught me was just to get along with people, no matter what. Booker T. Washington said that the trouble with the black people was that they wanted everything to happen in one generation. He knew we weren't going to make it happen all in one generation. Progress is going to be made gradually, he believed, generation after generation. Now, that made a lot of sense to me. And the more that I could do to make things better now, the better things will be for future generations.

When I was a bit older, I got this job working at an ice plant. Then one day they were short on labor on the ice wagons, so they pulled me out of the plant, and put me on one of the wagons a couple of nights a week. Now, this was still pretty unusual. Everybody else who worked on the ice wagons was white. I was the only black man. And because of that, a lot of people on the streets — especially the kids — would yell at me when they saw me up there on that wagon. "Look, they got a nigger on the ice wagon. Who would have ever thought they'd put a nigger on the ice wagon?" They would run after us and yell, "See the nigger, see the nigger, see the nigger?" Well, the white fellow that I was working with hated those kids. But not because they were calling me names. He hated them because they would jump up on the wagon and steal little bits of ice. And he'd throw his thongs at them and try to shoo them away. That made

me think of a way to try and get those kids to see me as a person. As much as it hurt and humiliated me, I didn't get angered at all the bad words that were said about me. I didn't get angry at them at all. If I had done that, I would have gotten in trouble. Instead, I tried to win them over through kindness. So, as soon as my white coworker would go into a house to make a delivery, I would chop up some ice and put it on the sidewalk for the kids. Before too long, they stopped calling me nigger and they started to look at me for who I was and not for the color of my skin. I knew I had to endure a lot. I had to just stand up and take it. And if I were going to change things, the first thing I had to do was to get people to see me as a human being. I knew that this was just a small step, and there was a long way to go. I knew that it was going to take blood. *We* were going to have to bleed. If we wanted our rights in America, we were going to have to bleed for them.

—George Kimbley, born in 1896, served overseas during World War I. After working in a Gary, Indiana, tin mill for seventeen years, Kimbley became staff representative for the United Steel Workers Union, District 31, where he served for twenty-two years. From 1976 to 1979 he was the chairman of the Older Americans Congress in Gary, Indiana. Kimbley died on July 2, 1996.

Even though my grandparents had been slaves, I was born long enough after slavery that the slave element didn't really exist in my world, or even in my thinking. The beginning of the century was a time when we dreamed that things were going to get better for blacks: better housing and neighborhoods, better schools, better jobs. As a little girl my dream was to grow up, get married, and have a big house on a large farm with horses and cattle and people working for me. As a people, we had high hopes. But we also knew that to get there we would need an education.

My father was an itinerant teacher. He traveled from one village to another, and would hold classes for children — or adults, for that matter — that had never been to school but still wanted to learn. He and people like Booker T. Washington would go from village to village after harvesting time or planting time — the times when children didn't have to be in the fields working — and they would hold classes either in a church or at the village hall or even in a clearing out in the woods, anyplace where people could gather. Parents wanted their children to have an education. They wanted them to learn to read, write, and do arithmetic, so that they would have the opportunities to make a good living and have a better life.

other people"

We were coming out of a time where people actually belonged to other people. And while we no longer belonged to the white man, the white man was still saying, "I don't want my white child seated beside a black boy or a black girl. I want my child to go to a school where there are whites only. I don't want them with black children, Negro children, colored children, Indian children." It was that kind of prejudice that separated the races and brought about discrimination. Of course, black people worked with white people all the time. Black people cooked for white people; black people took care of white children; they took care of the white people's houses. Even so, people at that time thought that there must be a separation of the races in order to get along. In the South, we had "Jim Crow" laws. There were separate facilities for whites, and separate facilities for blacks. Out in public, we were always separated from the white people. When people traveled, I mean when *white* people traveled, they didn't want to sit in the same coach or car with black people. So the black people had to sit in a designated Jim Crow car, which was either up in the front of the train, right in back of where they shoveled coal into the furnace of the engine, and cinders would fly all over you, or in the caboose, the last little car on the end of the train.

Despite these laws that separated us and humiliated us, black people were starting to develop a sense of unity and pride. When Jack Johnson won the heavyweight title, we all felt so proud that a black man had done something like that. He was really respected in the community. Here was a man who had come out of hard times and tribulations, and who had done well in a white world. But when he married a white woman, a lot of black people were down on him. After all the trouble that black people had had with white people, to think that a man who had made a name for himself and who had made some money would just jump up there and marry a white woman. It was as if he was saying, "There's no black woman good enough for me, now I gotta go get a white woman." You figured that as many black women as there were — I mean, there were black schoolteachers and lawyers and doctors and all — with all of these women you would have thought that he could have found somebody equally as important as this white woman that he married. A lot of people felt that when he up and married a white woman, that he disgraced us as a race.

— Marjorie Stewart Joyner, born in 1896, was known as the Grande Dame of Black Beauty Culture. In 1926 she became the first black woman to receive a patent, for her permanent hair-waving machine. She died on December 27, 1994.

Roosevelt had calculatedly issued the press release announcing his 1901 dinner with Booker T. Washington (depicted in the drawing at right) in time to make the morning papers and, as historian Edmund Morris described it, cause "white supremacists all over the South to gag on their grits."

"Negro Bible." Oklahoma required separate telephone booths (to the extent that there were *any* telephone booths); Florida, separate textbooks. What was worse, the Supreme Court, in a landmark 1896 case known as *Plessy v. Ferguson,* had provided the judicial justification for segregation, declaring separate but equal facilities consistent with the Constitution and depriving opponents of Jim Crow of at least one avenue of challenge.

Segregation posed black Americans with an appropriately contemporary dilemma: whither? They had, in some ways, merely traded in one set of chains for another, their lives now circumscribed by fiercely defended borderlines that allowed white America to keep them from mixing too closely, even as they continued to look upon them with curiosity, the St. Louis fair's ethnographics played out across the lines of the Old Confederacy. And yet at the same time, in the short run, segregation protected them, at least in the minds of a small number of white southerners, from some of the more violent racist elements freely wandering the South. Indeed, this had been the professed goal of those white southerners who described themselves as more "paternalistic": the belief that while black Americans had no right to think of themselves as equal to whites, they didn't deserve to be murdered; rather, they could be protected from the more bloodthirsty southern bigots and still "kept in their place" by being allowed to live among their own and thrive in the limited way offered to them by their "inferior" biology.

For blacks living under such conditions, life became defined by a kind of repeated duality: they were both black *and* American, free *and* enslaved, equal *and* "inferior." Writing in his landmark 1903 book, *The Souls of Black Folk,* W. E. B. Du Bois declared that the African-American's life was defined by this "two-ness—an American, a Negro, two souls, two thoughts, two unreconciled strivings, two warring ideals in one dark body, whose dogged strength alone keeps it from being torn asunder." And yet Du Bois himself, along with Booker T. Washington, defined still another "two-ness," in the way that each chose to advocate for a separate path to black progress: Du Bois, the voice of protest pushing the white power structure to grant greater freedom and ensure equality; Washington, the spokesman for self-improvement, whose philosophy had been so eloquently uttered in his speech at the 1895 Atlanta Exposition (yet *another* signifi-

Such subservience attended the southern black experience in the early years of the century that it is hard to believe that the forces of slavery had been defeated a generation before. Jim Crow so penetrated life that signs delineating black areas from white were barely needed; people just understood. Here a Florida tobacco farmer and his farm-hands stand for a portrait, c. 1910.

cant fair), an address in which he became the first black leader to advise the African-American to acquiesce in both disfranchisement and some manner of Jim Crow and to "cast down your bucket where you are" and build a life apart from mainstream white society.

> *"In all things that are purely social, we can be as separate as the five fingers, yet one as the hand in all things essential to mutual progress."*
>
> Booker T. Washington

Much of the white population liked Washington, both for his message to black Americans that they cooperate with the white ruling class and because Washington, while an enthusiastic advocate for education (he wanted schooling to become "as common as grass, and as free for all as sunshine and rain"), saw black Americans as benefiting most from *vocational* training, not the kind of mind-opening liberal arts schooling that southerners feared would put "ideas" into the black man's head. Washington urged blacks to remain on the farms (he, too, believed in a form of the frontier ethic, insisting that a relationship with the soil was essential to a moral life) and not, like so much of the rural population, move to the city; to train as farmers and mechanics and domestic servants, jobs that many whites saw as appropriate for blacks, since, scattered across the countryside, they would find it harder to organize and create "trouble," and because their "inferior makeup" made them ill suited for the more complex industrial future being created by the "advanced" races anyway. That Washington did not push for civil rights pleased many whites, too, yet on this issue, they may have been reading him wrong. For many historians believe that Washington's strategy was one of "gradualism" and that (while he never publicly declared so) he did not see black Americans as occupying a subservient position to whites permanently; rather, only that they *postpone* the campaign for full equality until later. In a time when some white southerners were hell-bent on nothing less than the complete destruction of the black race, Washington, it appears, was most concerned with survival.

Booker T. Washington, 1856–1915

Registered Negro Voters, State of Louisiana

1896 130,334
1904 1,342

Had black Americans chosen to follow Washington, the history of race relations in the twentieth century might have been very different, but Du Bois, while in agreement with Washington on some matters, eventually offered an alternative philosophy, and in the end, it was his that won the day. Anyone looking for the roots of the American civil rights movement of the latter twentieth century should start with the decision to follow Du Bois: a walking-cane and white-glove mulatto elitist who had been born into freedom in the North, was educated at Harvard, and believed that "the Negro race" could be saved by "its exceptional men."

Where Washington was practical, Du Bois was intent upon ideals; where Washington claimed that black America should lift itself up, Du Bois declared that the oppressive white class must first lift the barriers to black advancement. Where Washington believed in the slow evolution to a color-blind society, dependent upon blacks working their way to acceptance in what he saw to be the more advanced white civilization, Du Bois preached that black civilization did not need to aspire to white achievement, was no less dynamic than that of whites, and that it had simply suffered from white oppression. Only on the complete rejection of the white notion of biological supremacy did the two agree: the lower standing of blacks was not due to their makeup, each man declared separately, but (and here's where their emphasis critically diverged) either to black under-development (Washington) or white racism (Du Bois).

In 1905, after the two men and their followers had grown even further apart, Du Bois and his partners formed the Niagara Movement at a meeting in Canada near Niagara Falls (the name alluded to the conference site as well as to the "mighty current" of protest they hoped to inspire), dedicating their efforts to "secure just legislation for the colored people" and to "complain loudly and insistently" about white oppression, which they did. But the campaign needed an event to inspire the masses to protest, and in 1908, at Springfield, Illinois, the onetime hometown of Abraham Lincoln, it got one.

After the wife of a Springfield streetcar conductor asserted (falsely) that she had been raped by a black handyman, a white mob entered the city's substantial black district destroying homes and carrying out all manner of violence. "Lincoln freed you," was their chant, "we'll show you your place." As the riot raged, eight blacks were killed, and two thousand others, fearing for their lives, fled the city. Flaunting two turn-of-the-century stereotypes at once, Springfield's white leadership first blamed the riot on the black population's tendency to vice and, while embarrassed by at least some of the violence, then insisted that if there was any unlawful or inappropriate behavior, it had to have been the work of the city's grow-ing "immigrant" population. But with Springfield, a line had been crossed. Nation-wide, the reaction to this and other stories of anti-black violence was growing. And in 1909, invoking the memory of Abraham Lincoln, a group gathered in New York City to establish the single most impor-tant civil rights organization in American history, the National Association for the Advancement of Colored People (NAACP), and make Du Bois the editor of its influential magazine, *Crisis*. Now, for the first time, there was an organization to speak for black America (even if most of its leadership in these early years was white), and speak it did, urging blacks forward to a new era of activism that would lead the way to the great civil rights advancements of the mid-century.

W. E. B. Du Bois,
1868–1963

> *"We claim for ourselves every single right that belongs to a free American, political, civil and social and until we get these rights we will never cease to protest and assail the ears of America."*
> *W. E. B. Du Bois*

On July 4, 1910, the sleepy little frontier town of Reno, Nevada, became the setting for a dramatic sporting event that riveted the nation ("Reno Now Cen-ter of the Universe" read the headline in the *Chicago Tribune*) when thirty-two-year-old John Arthur "Jack" Johnson, the heavyweight champion of the world, lifted his gloves against James Jeffries, a former champion who had come out of retirement for one last celebrated clash. So popular was this fight that odds-makers were predicting that nearly $3 million would be bet on it, particularly after Johnson, a celebrated black boxer thought to be so fast a friend once claimed that "he could block a punch and hit you with the same hand," confi-dently telegrammed "Bet Your Last Copper on Me" to hometown fans in Chi-cago. Yet the thrill owed little to sport and everything to race; with the enmity between blacks and whites in America growing, Reno would be the symbolic

I grew up on a farm in the country, outside of Danville, Kentucky. Of course we didn't have running water out there, nor electricity. They had them in town, but out on our farm it was just gas or kerosene lights, a well with a pump, and an outhouse. And we had to cook on a coal and wood stove. My mother used to take my sister and me to school every morning in a horse and buggy — four miles each way. It got awfully cold in the winter in Kentucky, so we rode in what was known as a cozy cab. That was a buggy that had an enclosed top on it with glass windows all around. And there was a little slot for the reigns to come through. It was supposed to be much warmer than the buggy with just curtains buckled on, but it could still get pretty cold. Sometimes we'd put hot bricks in the bottom of the cab to try and keep our feet warm.

We had to go into town for everything that we didn't already have on the farm. My father even had to ride into the little village store to pick up the mail. That's where the post office was, in the back of the village store. We were pretty cut off from things out there. When I was seven years old, my mother became gravely ill. There wasn't a hospital in Danville back then; the closest one was in Louisville, about seventy miles away. My mother was so sick that she couldn't be moved, so our family doctor came in from town and operated on her right in our house. My father stood right there and held the lamp so the doctor could see what he was doing. My mother never recovered. Living out in the country most definitely had its hardships.

I remember coming home from school one day to find that my father had had a phone put in. I mean, there were phones in town at that time, but out in the country, it was still quite unusual. I was so excited, I just couldn't wait to call a friend of mine who lived in Danville. That was the first time I ever talked on a telephone. Of course it was a party line, so if one of our neighbors was already on it, we had to wait till they got off. Even so, just having a phone made it feel as though things were really changing.

We had a cook named Fanny. Her husband, George, worked on the farm, tending to the milking and working the garden. Fanny was a large colored woman who used to joke around with my sister and me quite a bit. When she made us waffles, or berry cakes, or something that we liked a lot, why, we'd jump down from the table and run to the kitchen and say, "Oh, Fanny, I ate three. I ate three." And she'd look down at us with this stern face and say, "Well, you two go on back in there and eat three more!" She was a good jolly person. And we loved her. She loved to play cards. She had this old

Cash (center) with her sisters Eoline (left) and Katherine in 1904.

—*Minor Cash was born in 1901 in Richmond, Kentucky. After attending Colorado State University, Kentucky Wesleyan, and Berea College, she taught high school English and social studies in Stanford, Kentucky, until she retired in 1962.*

beat-up deck and she could play for hours. But my sister and I were never allowed to play with her. So when my father wasn't looking, we'd slip out to the cabin where she lived and play with those crazy old dirty cards that Fanny had.

My father was always kind of prejudiced against black people. A lot of that was passed down to him from his family. They lived near Fredericksburg, Virginia, during the Civil War, and the Union Army was just tearing things up around there. At one point things got really bad and they had to move. My father's oldest brother, who was just a boy, was sent out with one of the Negro servants to hide the horses. But instead of taking the horses and my father's brother away from danger, the servant took him right toward the Union Army. They met the army right at a bridge, and the soldiers threatened to throw the boy in the creek. Somehow he got away, but it scared him to death. Of course, my father's family believed that that servant led that boy to

the Union Army on purpose. They eventually made their way to Georgia, but got there just about the time that Sherman marched through and destroyed everything. My father said that he was brought up to think that the Devil was the worst person on earth, and Abraham Lincoln was number two.

But when I was growing up in Kentucky I never noticed anything like racial tension. I never heard of anybody not getting along. Of course in Kentucky we had separate facilities for blacks and for whites. There were Jim Crow laws. The philosophy was that it was all right to be friendly, but the blacks must stay in their place. And they had a definite place. They didn't go to our churches. They didn't go to our schools. And they had a certain area that they lived in – the Negro section. Jim Crow didn't apply everywhere; it was a state law. Ohio, just to the north, didn't have Jim Crow. I remember being in Cincinnati once and thinking that it was strange to see Negroes getting on the train along with whites. You just didn't see that in Kentucky. From the time I was born, the blacks and whites were kept separate. I didn't know any different.

I didn't feel as though I had any prejudices. There was no need for them, you see. It was all right for me to play with black children. I could associate that way. Fanny had a little girl, named Annie, and we used to run together all the time. We were buddies. We used to go out and play a game called Annie Over. That's where we would get on opposite sides of a building and then try and throw a ball over the roof to the other person. And we'd yell "Annie Over!" as we threw. You couldn't see the ball coming till it got over the peak, and then you had to try and catch it. One day I got stung by a bumblebee and I cried and screamed and carried on. And my mother came out and doctored me, but I kept on crying. She asked, "Why are you still carrying on like that?" And I said, "I'm crying 'cause the bee didn't sting Annie, too." I thought that if I got stung, then Annie should get stung, too.

Annie and Fanny and George were like part of the family. I just loved them. But then my father sold the farm and we moved to a county in Kentucky where there were very few colored people. Fanny and her family came along with us, but they felt really out of place there. They stayed for a little while, but eventually packed up and left and moved to a place where they felt more at home. I was very sad to see my friends go. From then on we always had white help.

confrontation between the "Bad Nigger," as white racists saw Johnson, and "the Great White Hope."

The stage for the bout had been set two years before when Johnson, a six-foot-three-inch, two-hundred-pound free-swinging African-American, beat white fighter Tommy Burns in Sydney, Australia, prompting calls to Jeffries to avenge the indignity suffered by the white race. Since then, Johnson had further alienated whites with his flamboyant manner, strutting confidence, free spending, and, in what was surely to whites the most distasteful of his habits, a preference for white women (and lots of them). Writer Jack London, author of *The Call of the Wild*, voiced the popular opinion that the Sydney fight had been a fluke, in which "a playful Ethiopian" had bested "a small and futile white man." And it was London, writing in the *New York Herald,* who urged Jeffries to "emerge from his alfalfa farm and remove the golden smile from Jack Johnson's face," following on with what became a rallying cry of the time: "Jeff," wrote London, "it's up to you!"

A promotional poster for the 1910 heavyweight bout between Jim Jeffries and Jack Johnson betrays none of the racial hostility that accompanied the fight. "If Johnson wins," wrote one frightened white journalist, "the Negroes in the Southern states . . . may be encouraged to acts which formerly they would not dare to commit."

Twenty thousand people crowded into the Reno arena for the fight, nearly all of them Jeffries's supporters. The house band declared Jeffries its favorite, too, taunting Johnson in a prefight overture with choruses of "America," "Dixie," and a popular racist melody, "All Coons Look Alike to Me." Still, there was little chance that the white man would win. Having recently lost a third of the three hundred pounds he had grown to since his glory days in the ring, Jeffries was enervated and showed it. Johnson, on the other hand, was in peak form. The black boxer had been preparing for this bout for most of his career, having begun his fighting toward the end of the last century by participating in a humiliatingly racist entertainment, reminiscent of a cockfight, in which eight or more blindfolded black boxers were set against each other at once, the winner rewarded with loose change from the white crowd.

On fight day, Jeffries made a grand entrance wearing a gray business suit over his boxing shorts, an aide shielding him from the blinding sun with a five-foot round paper shade. But it was Johnson, reported the *New York Times,* who earned a gasp from the crowd when he stripped to fight attire, the audience emitting "a sigh of involuntary admiration as his [nearly] naked body stood in the white sunlight." The reporter for a press syndicate described him in equal terms of awe: "a rounded symmetry more in line with the ideals of the great Greek artists," his head resembling the size and smoothness of "an ostrich egg," from "crown to sole . . . a living life-size bronze chiseled by the cunning hands of a master."

Jeffries emerged from the corner in his patented "crouch," his erect left arm projected toward his opponent in a gesture of intensity, but Johnson simply

ridiculed him and pummeled the white man mercilessly until the fifteenth round, delaying his knockout punch until then, some said, simply to ensure that Jeffries suffered long and hard. Now Johnson was the undisputed heavyweight champion, yet so passionate were the feelings attached to the fight, and so determined had white Americans been that this duel would correct the suggestion that a black man might best a white man in anything, even a contest of fists, that riots broke out across the country, leaving eleven dead and hundreds wounded. Having brought an undeniable challenge to white America's sense of itself, Johnson was soon pursued by law enforcement officials on a trumped-up morals charge that secured him a year's sentence in jail. After serving his time, he lived out the rest of his life fighting in small-time matches, hustling jobs as a trainer, and appearing as a curiosity in vaudeville shows.

Nineteen thirteen was a year of cultural turmoil in America and abroad. In Paris, Igor Stravinsky's ballet *The Rite of Spring,* with choreography by Vaslav Nijinsky, created a near riot at its premier performance. For the score, the Russian composer had relied upon pulsating, percussive sounds that critics found savage; and in Nijinsky's movements, they detected a pagan feel. If this was "spring," it was a different kind of spring than composers had evoked before, for there was nothing luscious and dewy to what Stravinsky wrote; instead, he had presented nature as Darwin might have heard it: violent, aggressive, unsentimental.

In New York that same year, an exhibition of paintings by Europe's and America's newest artists created a similar reaction. The Armory Show of 1913 (the display was erected at the 69th Regiment on New York City's 25th Street) had been conceived with a chauvinistic flair in keeping with the times. Hoping to demonstrate that Americans could be just as "modern" as Europeans, the exhibition's organizers announced, in a tone reminiscent of the circus barker, that they intended to put on the "greatest show on earth," and to underscore the American sponsorship of their endeavor, they decorated the armory's cavernous space with potted pines, a reference, they explained, to the American Revolution, where the pine had appeared on the Massachusetts flag, a symbol of liberty. But if it was only attention they were after, the curators could have simply let the art speak for itself. More than seventy thousand people walked the length of the armory to witness the visions of Picasso, Léger, Brancusi, Braque, Matisse, and Duchamp, masters of modernism each. And judging by press reports from the time, not a single person left without voicing an opinion, and most likely a negative one. Who, they asked, could ever call such rubbish art?

The show was grandly titled "The International Exhibition of Modern Art," but the dynamite, as the *New Yorker* later commented, was in the word "modern." And while the new painting and sculpture declared itself with the confidence that comes with a revolution, there were many in the New York crowd and in even larger gatherings that greeted the show when it moved on to Boston and Chicago (where art students burned Matisse and Brancusi in effigy) who would have nothing of it. One of America's more distinguished artists, Kenyon Cox, a longtime holdout against the trends that seemed to be undermining the traditional image, saw in the show nothing less than the "total destruction of the art of painting," and on this he could find only one bit of good news: that the Americans represented here seemed to him to have resisted the "depth of badness [attained] by the French and the Germans." Indeed, many of those attending the show looked upon the works before them as the perverse fantasies of the foreigner, *Ellis Island* art they called it. And no less a chauvinist than Teddy Roosevelt himself, fresh from his unsuccessful 1912 attempt to reenter the White House with the backing of a third party (Roosevelt and his handpicked Republican successor, William Howard Taft, had had a falling-out), was said to have stomped about the opening, waving his arms and declaring in a loud voice his disapproval of all but the American entries, even as he gave praise to the show's general spirit, in particular in the way that it tolerated no "simpering, self-satisfied conventionality."

The star image of the exhibition was most certainly Duchamp's *Nude Descending a Staircase* (or, as TR called it, "a naked man going downstairs"), a painting so abstract it defied its own title, which, of course, was the point. As critic Robert Hughes has pointed out, the nude had a long and distinguished history with painting, where she (and, more rarely, he) was usually portrayed in a blissful state of recline; by contrast, Duchamp's nude, to the degree that it looked at all like what it was supposed to be, was a nude on the move (indeed, the painting had the quality of a photographic motion study), a metaphor for the change that it heralded. Still, most people saw something else entirely — "an explosion in a shingle factory," "an earthquake on the subway," "a *staircase* descending a *nude*" — jokes all, uttered even as the jokesters themselves stood in long lines, necks craning, to see the object of their ridicule. The modern era might be abhorrent, absurd, unnatural, but oh to get a glimpse of it!

TR said Duchamp's *Nude* reminded him of a Navaho rug he stood upon while shaving each morning in his bathroom. And indeed, to the degree that Roosevelt, Cox, and others saw *any* merit to modern abstractions like

---

"You will see stranger things than you ever dreamed were on land or sea — and you'll hear a battle cry of freedom without any soft pedal on it."

Photographer Alfred Stieglitz, on the 1913 Armory Show of modern art

Marcel Duchamp's Nude Descending a Staircase, No. 2, *1912*

Duchamp's, it was as decoration, fancy wallpaper. But the fact that these artists attached meaning to their creations, that they saw themselves as articulating an ideology, an "ism" of the new, and one that quite blatantly intended to disassemble the world as men and women had known it, was simply too bold and raw for mainstream temperaments. This *modern* art was, as its name suggested, something different — art as *cause* — and the condemnation brought upon it by Roosevelt and others was a denunciation of the new work's politics. After all, when before had reasonable men discovered in painting, as they did here, "the chatter of anarchistic monkeys" or "the harbinger of universal anarchy"?

Anticipating a reluctant audience, the organizers of the Armory Show had included an editorial in the exhibition catalog urging viewers to greet the new art with an open mind. "Art," it read, "is a sign of life. There can be no life without change, as there can be no development without change. To be afraid of what is different is to be afraid of life . . ." Then, perhaps with Roosevelt's legendary machismo in mind, they added a challenge to contemporary pretensions to the rugged life, concluding with the statement that their exhibition was a proclamation "against cowardice."

At roughly the same time that New Yorkers were scoffing at modern painting, a project more uniformly pleasing to contemporary sensibilities was nearing completion 2,300 miles south of Manhattan. The dream of uniting the Atlantic Ocean with the Pacific, of a canal bisecting the thin strip of land connecting North America to South America, had dated back to the time of Spanish exploration in the sixteenth century. Ever since gold was discovered in California in 1848, prompting the building of a Panama railroad connecting steamships on either side to rush prospectors to their dreamland and back home again, Americans had been especially frustrated by their desire to have a connecting waterway all their own, a way to move freight and passengers from coast to coast with ease.

Still, as the century turned, a canal seemed unlikely, a French company having failed, miserably, in their attempt to dig across Colombia's Isthmus of Panama in the 1880s and no other immediate prospects at hand. Malaria and yellow fever had crippled the French plan, felling twenty thousand laborers and destroying the reputation of Ferdinand de Lesseps, the builder of the Suez Canal, who had expected to claim a similar success for French civilization in Panama, and instead became known as the Great Undertaker, his bankrupt project as "de Lesseps' graveyard."

The equatorial rains were another problem, diaries of workers reporting half-submerged trees black with tarantulas, as was de Lesseps' insistence on a sea-level canal which forced upon his team the removal of extraordinary amounts of terrain at a time when the equipment and know-how to do so did not exist. Upon hearing reports of the French workers' unhappy experience, people began to sense an air of the forbidden to any canal plan. After all, no one had ever attempted such an intrusion upon nature's domain before (the site required the excavation of three times the amount of dirt removed to create the Suez), an unprecedented fifty-mile reconfiguration of the earth itself.

But no president loved a challenge more than Teddy Roosevelt, and, just as John Kennedy would set his sights on the moon more than a half century later, TR set out to claim for America the rights to the world's greatest technological

4070

Thousands of tourists traveled by special train to the Panama Canal Zone to witness the excavation of the tremendous Culebra Cut (above), which became known as the "special wonder of the canal." "He who did not see the Culebra Cut during the mighty work of excavation," proclaimed one writer, "missed one of the great spectacles of the ages . . ."

feat. America itself would dig the "Big Ditch," as it became popularly known. And by the time the canal opened in August 1914, a good six months ahead of schedule, TR, though long out of the White House, would remain the personality most associated with it. For it was TR who bullied the Colombians for the rights to dig at Panama and, frustrated by them, gave tacit approval to the revolt that led to Panama's independence, even sending American warships to the isthmus to prevent Colombian troops from defending against the rebellion (within days the new Panamanian state gave Roosevelt the rights he wanted for the price he wanted). And it was TR who, in a light linen suit bestride the seat of a ninety-five-ton Bucyrus steam shovel, dominated one of the most famous photographs of the canal under construction, a picture in which you could almost hear the former president eagerly pronounce, "Now here, *here* is a new frontier."

Like Roosevelt himself, the canal was a bridge between two eras. The idea belonged to the 1800s — its grandeur, its hubris, its brazen display of the colonial mentality — but its execution would have been impossible without the tools of the modern period. There was, for instance, the new century's miracle science at work in army doctor William Gorgas's solution to the tropical disease dilemma, a problem that so worried John F. Wallace, the first American engineer assigned to run the project, he arrived for work on the isthmus carrying two expensive coffins, one for himself, another for his wife. Gorgas had long suspected that the spread of malaria was the work of mosquitoes and not the "noxious jungle vapors" or the Frenchman's lack of "morals" that had been originally suspected; at his direction, protective netting reduced the incidence of disease dramatically.

After Wallace made a poor start (aware of the boredom of the workers and the general incompetence of the operation, people at home had begun to refer to Panama as "the Great Sinkhole") he was replaced by John Stevens, a character worthy of Roosevelt (TR described him as "a backwoods boy"), a man of so many cigars his staff nicknamed him "Big Smoke." Stevens understood that the challenge of Panama was not the digging; it was the transportation of all the dirt once it had been dug. And as if he were reading from a page of Taylor's *Principles of Scientific Management,* he simply applied modern ideas on work efficiency to his task, immediately doubling the capability of his team. Donning work boots and overalls to join the men in the mud, Stevens also addressed workers' morale. "There are three diseases on the Isthmus," he declared, winning many fans back home, "yellow fever, malaria, and cold feet and the worst of these is cold feet."

Stevens concluded that de Lesseps' biggest mistake had been the sea-level plan. The American engineer's decision to build the canal with an elaborate system of locks instead was probably the crucial blow for his success. The great locks with their thousands of moving parts became an element of fascination both on-site and back home — each measuring one thousand feet long and eighty-one feet high, they were like skyscrapers turned on their sides, enormous concrete monuments. And yet, as author David McCullough has pointed out, they were "much more than monumental, [for] they did not, like a bridge or cathedral, simply stand there; they *worked.*" Like Duchamp's nude, this was a monument on the go.

But perhaps the canal's most commanding statement of the modern age came in the way in which it would be used. TR was said to have come to push for American sponsorship after a reading of Alfred Thayer Mahan's *The Influence of Sea Power upon History* convinced him to perceive his nation's chance for world leadership as intertwined with a firm presence on the seas. And Roosevelt saw such leadership as more than just a worthy national goal; to him, it was America's destiny to use the two oceans to safely convey the civilized world into the new century.

To that end, the canal would correct the embarrassment felt by American officials when the *Oregon,* desperately needed in Cuba during the Spanish-American War of 1898, had been forced to sail sixty-seven days around the Horn. And to demonstrate their new naval power with a flare, officials planned an

In November 1906 Theodore Roosevelt became the first American president to travel outside the country when he visited Panama to inspect the construction of the canal and sit atop one of the project's gigantic steam shovels, above.

elaborate opening day ceremony for Panama. At the behest of Portland's school-children, President Woodrow Wilson agreed to let the *Oregon* itself lead a grand armada through the locks, with plans to land at San Francisco in time to initiate the proceedings of yet another fair, the Panama-Pacific International Exposition. The ship's retired admiral was to command her; the president by his side. But it was not to be. A simple cement boat would be the first vessel to make its way through the gap that now chopped the continent in two, and in the end, Panama's "grand opening" would go on with little fanfare. For at almost the precise moment that America's great engineering feat became a reality, declaring in the minds of many the arrival of an age of unambiguous technological achievement, popular attention turned elsewhere, toward Europe and the event that would soon consume the world in darkness.

The Gatun Locks alone made the Panama Canal an engineering wonder. "The impression," wrote historian David McCullough, "was of looking down a broad, level street nearly five blocks long with a solid wall of six-story buildings on either side; only here there were no windows or doorways, nothing to give human scale."

2

Shell Shock
1914-1919

Shell Shock 1914–1919

Previous spread: The 10th Scottish Rifles Raiding Party of the British army huddles in a trench near Arras, France, waiting for the signal to advance. When the soldiers charged forward moments later, one of their own artillery shells fell short, killing seven. British and Canadian forces were able to push the Germans back four miles during the six-day battle of Arras, at a cost of over 36,000 men.

Left: In a scene that repeated itself across the western front, British and German soldiers at Ploegsteert, Belgium, greet each other in no-man's-land on Christmas Day, 1914. This would be the last impromptu truce of the war. The following year, the British infantry was ordered to "maintain a slow gun fire on the enemy's trenches" throughout the festive season.

On Christmas Eve, 1914, four months and twenty-two days into the bloodiest conflict the world had yet known, a handful of German infantrymen of the 133rd Saxon Regiment began assembling holiday candles along the parapets of their muddy trenches. Members of the Queen's Westminster Rifles, watching them from their own dugouts across no-man's-land a hundred or so yards away, were shocked by what they saw ("like the Thames on Henley Regatta night," said a startled British lieutenant) and sensed a ruse until they heard one of the Germans call out "Englishmen, Englishmen, don't shoot" and follow on with a full-throated version of "God Save the King."

With that, the frightened Brits quietly struck up their own rendition of an Austrian hymn, watching all the while for the signs of an ambush in the making, but there would be none. Before long, a few daredevils from each side had ventured out of their pits and onto the pockmarked battlefield, where, among corpses frozen stiff, they shook hands, agreed on an impromptu Christmas truce, and celebrated the moment with an exchange of cake and biscuits.

All over the western front that 1914 holiday season, men who were enemies met as friends. They took snapshots of each other and traded supplies, a tin of British jam for a piece of German chocolate. They sang carols, swapped stories, and analyzed each other's chances for victory as if they were handicapping a sporting event. They played spontaneous games of football, a spiked German helmet serving as one goal, a British or French cap the other. Then, just as quickly as it had all begun, the excitement ended. "I know this statement will take a bit of believing but it is absolutely correct," wrote gunner Herbert Smith in his diary. "Fancy a German shaking your flapper as though he were trying to smash your fingers, and then a few days later trying to plug you."

The latter half of the century's second decade was dominated by a war so brutal and so unnecessary it would give new meaning to the word "absurd." Nearly 10 million people died and 20 million more were wounded — many of them maimed for life — on battlefields across three continents. Not only were

French, British, Germans, Canadians, Russians, and Americans its victims, so were Serbians, Italians, Japanese, Turks, Bulgarians, Belgians, Chinese, Australians, Indians, South Africans, and members of dozens of other nationalities. For most of it, soldiers stood across from each other in a ridiculous stalemate, like two bullies in a playground. And during its biggest and most tragic battles, the same pieces of meaningless landscape were traded back and forth a dozen times, every mound of earth around them turned over by powerful explosives and joined with the flesh of the innocent.

Much more than human life was lost. At places with names like Passchendaele and Verdun, Argonne and Somme, Belleau Wood and Gallipoli, our European and American ancestors relinquished the jubilant sense of promise that modernity appeared to offer, and replaced it with a cynicism we have yet to shake. The excitement born of the machine in the century's first decade was now challenged by different, more sinister machines in its second. Stuck in endless battle, men even wondered if their plight was a by-product of the machine age: you may enjoy the good machines only if you agree to kill each other with the bad.

World War I changed art and science, language and politics. It divided families and sent new Americans back to the old country to raise their rifles against men from the same neighborhoods they had only recently departed. It left countless widows and orphans to fend for themselves in devastated postwar economies and robbed Europe of a generation whose talents were never allowed to flourish. Was there a scientist among the dead who would have led us to a cure for cancer? Did we lose a diplomat who would have prevented the onset of one of the century's other crippling wars? Did England bury another Wordsworth? France, a successor to Manet? The answers lie interred in the soil of the western front.

In many ways, the war was a wild, convulsive birth pang and death rattle rolled into one, signaling the departure of the old order and the entrance of the new. When it began, political life in Europe was governed by a small circle of men drawn from the upper middle class and aristocracy. Five empires — the Austro-Hungarian, the Russian, the German, the French, and the British — dominated the map, each of them, with the exception of France, led by a monarch. In Vienna, the eighty-four-year-old Franz Josef presided with weary grandeur over the decline of his bickering, multinational realm — a bizarre amalgamation of 50 million Czechs, Austrians, Magyars, Slovaks, Croats, Serbs, Turks, Transylvanians, Slovenes, Gypsies, Jews, and Poles. In Germany, Kaiser Wilhelm II sat on the throne of an ambitious and energetic new country possessing the most powerful army in the world and building a navy to match it. In Great Britain, King George V held sway over that island and a dominion that stretched across more than one-quarter of the earth's surface, while in Russia, Tsar Nicholas II sat weakly in wait for the popular rebellion that would fell his family's three-hundred-year dynasty.

Democracy, as we know it today, had only begun to make inroads in Europe. Of the major European powers, only the parliaments of Britain and France had the power to dismiss the prime minister. There, and especially else-

How the Civilian May Help in This Crisis

Be cheerful.

Write encouragingly to friends at the front.

Don't repeat foolish gossip.

Don't listen to idle rumors.

Don't think you know better than [British Commander] Haig.

Advice for the British public
as delivered in a World War I newspaper

"You can be sure of the thanks of the Fatherland."

German government slogan

Kaiser Wilhelm II, 1859–1941

"I am a South Slav nationalist. My aim is the union of all Yugoslavs, under whatever political regime, and their liberation from Austria by terrorism."

Gavrilo Princip, speaking at his trial for the murder of Archduke Franz Ferdinand

Princip (above right, with two of his coconspirators) would not see the war's end. He died of tuberculosis in a prison hospital in Austria, 1918.

where, politicians and civil servants of Europe were almost invariably members of the privileged classes, as ignorant of the plight of their countrymen as they were determined to preserve their authority over them. Three of the four empires were governed by men who were in fact related (George, Wilhelm, and Nicholas were all descendants of Queen Victoria), making World War I, in one sense, nothing more than an enormous family squabble, a fratricidal bloodbath.

But tiny cracks had appeared in the prewar imperial facade. Europe's population had grown enormously — in 1800, there had been only 50 million people; by 1914, there were 300 million — and the Industrial Revolution had helped to propel its growth, creating a gigantic working class. Though there had been much progressive social legislation, most Europeans still led hard lives, toiling in factories, mines, and sweatshops, what poet Siegfried Sassoon described as an existence of "unending struggle against unfair odds, culminating in a cheap funeral." Unhappy with their conditions, they had begun to listen to the champions of socialism.

A second, and somewhat contradictory, force also preoccupied the peoples of prewar Europe: nationalism. While the aristocracy remained cosmopolitan, a fervent belief in nationhood had taken hold among the middle and lower classes, another by-product of the Industrial Revolution and the sense of community it encouraged. In the great and powerful states, this nationalism motivated campaigns against the minority populations; while among the minority populations, it fomented independence movements toward new, ethnically determined "nations," undermining the stability of the great and powerful states. Age-old boundaries were about to burst, even if it would take a war to wrest them free.

Gavrilo Princip was a nineteen-year-old student at the beginning of 1914, immersed in the study of ethics, literature, and politics. Born to a *kmet* (the Serbian version of a serf) family in a rural part of Austrian-controlled Bosnia, Princip had grown up in extreme poverty. His father struggled to till wheat over four acres in the Bosnian hills, and while the crop was barely enough to feed his own family, he was nonetheless required to give the cash equivalent of one-third of it to his landlord each year. Six of the family's nine children died in infancy — a fate they expected for the sickly Gavrilo — and though Gavrilo survived, he was a scrawny and distant child who was described as suffering from feelings of inferiority.

As a teenager, Princip buried himself in books and dreamed of becoming a professor. But the urgencies of political rebellion proved too distracting. Like many other young Serbs, he had grown frustrated with the conditions endured by his people under the control of the Austro-Hungarian empire and dreamed of liberating them to join the Serbian kingdom next door. His was a popular opinion in the southern Slavic regions of Europe in those days. Most Serbs believed that the "purest" members of their race lived in Bosnia and Herzegovina. With nationalism rising and the empire of Franz Josef teetering, they felt that the moment to free their "weeping brethren in chains" had finally arrived.

Princip chose Sunday, June 28, 1914, to stake his claim on history. While Archduke Franz Ferdinand — the heir apparent to the Austro-Hungarian throne — and his wife, Sophie, prepared to visit Sarajevo on that day, Princip and six other members of the Black Hand — a Serbian nationalist terror group — plotted his assassination. Their scheme was anything but professional. The group consisted of a printer, a carpenter, a teacher, and four students. Five of them were under twenty; the eldest was twenty-seven. None had ever handled a weapon before they conceived their deadly plan. And they knew little about their target except that he was in line to succeed Franz Josef. (Had they been aware of Ferdinand's attempts to achieve a limited autonomy for the Slavic members of the empire, they might even have reconsidered.) Weeks before the planned visit, the terrorists secured six makeshift grenades, four aged Browning pistols, and seven vials of cyanide (to induce their suicides after the plot had been carried out) and set off for Sarajevo.

On the morning of June 28, as Franz Ferdinand and Sophie climbed into the back of a black convertible sedan, ready to tour the Bosnian capital, the seven plotters took their positions along the parade route. The first two assassins to encounter the archduke lost their nerve. A third lobbed a grenade toward the car and missed, striking the vehicle behind Ferdinand's (and then, bungling even his suicide, swallowed only enough cyanide to vomit). But fate had decided to give the Serbian murderers another chance.

An hour later, when Ferdinand resumed the parade, his driver took a wrong turn landing their car outside a delicatessen where Princip himself stood, barely five feet away. The Serb hesitated, then, turning his head away, fired two shots. "Es ist nichts" (It is nothing), muttered Ferdinand as he and Sophie both collapsed. He could not have been more wrong.

War meant something different to the generation that came of age in 1914. Partly because so few of them had ever fought in one and partly because most of the wars those few had fought in were quick, tame affairs carried out on colonial soil (the last major European conflict was the Franco-Prussian War of 1870), many men of the time saw in battle little more than a test of manly virtue and national fidelity. War was cleansing. War was adventure. War was honorable. War was renewing. War was sport. War was glamorous. War was a rite of passage. War was a way to sacrifice for one's country and experience the comradeship of other men. War was, in short, good.

When the archduke's murder triggered a feud between Austria-Hungary and Serbia that prompted Russia to come to the aid of the Serbs, and Germany to the aid of the Austrians, and when France then came to the aid of Russia, and England to the aid of Belgium (which had been overrun by German troops on their way to invade France), it was not hard to rally the masses of any nation to the cause. The politicians justified their actions by pointing to carefully negotiated alliances conceived to protect both property and business interests and to

As German citizens sent their smiling, confident soldiers off to battle, few people could have realized the devastation the war would wreak. By the end of 1914 alone, 400,000 of Germany's finest soldiers lay dead on the western front.

"Crowds of people everywhere and soldiers marching out of the city, showered with blossoms as they went. Every face looks happy: we've got war! Bands in the cafés and restaurants play 'Hail to You in the Battle for Victory' and 'The Watch on the Rhine' non-stop, and everybody has to listen to them standing-up. One's food gets cold, one's beer gets warm: no matter, we've got war!"

German actress Till Durieux, August 1914 diary entry

Germany's prewar pride: "Deutschland ist ein Kaiserreich!"

Before the war, I was just a young boy, but nevertheless I had a certain feeling about Germany's role in the world. I felt it was a true empire. There was an emperor, after all, who wore a uniform and had shiny boots, and that kind of thing was very impressive to a young boy. But I also had the feeling that Germany was really better than all other states. The president of the French republic was, of course, a civilian. And I always felt that at international conferences or gatherings of heads of state, the emperor would shine brightly next to the civilian president of France.

Of course we didn't call him the emperor; we called him the kaiser and the empire he ruled was called the Kaiserreich. *"Deutschland ist ein Kaiserreich,"* they used to say. And that was something which lifted you up, the very thought of it. We revered the kaiser. In my diaries, I referred to him as "His Majesty, the kaiser." He was the summit, the pinnacle of the political structure of Germany and we thought of him as a sort of half man, half god. I saw the kaiser three times during that period and I count those moments as among the greatest experiences of my life.

Similarly, I thought of Germany as a great power among nations, equal to other great powers like England. There was a certain competition between Germany and England then. Indeed, England had many colonies and Germany had only a few, and the emperor was building a big navy in order to get more colonies and be equal to his cousins overseas. A popular movement was created in order to support the kaiser in this endeavor. And private people — even children — were expected to contribute money to the cause. Children were expected to take, say, fifty pfennigs from their allowance and give it to the general collection for the support of the navy. When you did this you would get a little flag which you could wear in your lapel. We wore it proudly, happy to be a part of this tremendous popular movement in order to support the building of the German navy. The imperial navy. The kaiser's navy.

A feeling of international tension penetrated deeply throughout Europe then. I remember we went on vacation to the Belgian coast at a little resort called Middelkerke. And it was customary that people playing on the beach would build fortresses out of sand and hoist the flag of their nation. When my brothers and sisters and I hoisted the German flag, we felt a lot of hostility. People from other countries resented the Germans openly. As for us, no one needed to insist that we be patriotic; we just were. We believed the words of the German *Lied*, "Deutschland über Alles," which means "Germany above all." Not that it should be above all other nations, but above all else in our hearts, above all other things.

Above: Von Elbe at the age of ten. Below: Photographs from the scrapbook he kept documenting the soldiers' stay at his house.

—*Joachim von Elbe, who was born in 1902, went on to become a lawyer and public servant in Weimar Germany. Dismissed from his position during the Hitler regime because he had a "non-Aryan" grandmother, he emigrated to the United States in 1934 and became a citizen in 1941. After serving in World War II with the U.S. Army, he joined the foreign service, where he was involved in the treaty negotiations that admitted West Germany into the postwar NATO alliance. He is the author of* Witness to History: A Refugee from the Third Reich Remembers.

The first thing that shook all of this up, of course, was the assassination of Archduke Ferdinand. It was such a shattering event at that time, that a person of such great importance would be killed. Everybody, even we young people, felt the importance of the event. Early on, we hoped that diplomacy would pull us through. The kaiser went on his regular trip to Norway and it seemed that maybe nothing very serious would happen after all. Then suddenly my father appeared in the garden and read to us from the paper: there was a proclamation by the kaiser stating that there was an imminent danger of war. Constitutional rights would have to be restricted, such as the right of public assembly. Even the sanctity of the home was no longer assured. The awful conflict was about to begin.

One day, a soldier came to our house with a sheet of paper announcing that a platoon of nine soldiers would be billeted at our house. They arrived a few days later in full dress with their spiked helmets and rifles, ready for war. That was the first time I had the feeling that our house was no longer our own, that it could be taken over whenever the authorities pleased, and that it was not our place to object. There were planes roaring overhead and soldiers marching to the train station to report for duty.

There was of course great enthusiasm about the war then and everybody thought these poor soldiers must be hungry and thirsty. Baskets full of sandwiches were carried to the station by eager townspeople, so many that most of them ended up spoiled. The soldiers just couldn't eat them all. As they boarded the trains the men gleefully sang a song: *"Auf, auf zum Kampf, zum Kampf sind wir geboren. Auf, auf zum Kampf, zum Vaterland. Dem Kaiser Wilhelm reichen wir die Hand"* (On, on to fight, we are born. On, on, to fight for the fatherland. To Kaiser Wilhelm we give our hand).

In school, they told us it would be a very short war and that it would end with the total defeat of France and England, much as France had been defeated in the Franco-Prussian War of 1870. We had been educated to think of France as the hereditary enemy of Germany. France and Germany were rivals for the leadership of Europe. To us it went no further than that. Only the politicians cared about acquiring new territory. But to defeat the hereditary enemy, and claim the leadership of Europe, now that was a worthy goal.

long-established military defense plans that relied upon their taking swift and decisive action. But in fact the elite classes of the belligerent states saw the incident at Sarajevo as less a tragedy than an opportunity, a chance to both compete for a larger say in world affairs and, through the call to arms, squelch the popular movements that threatened their rule at home. There were, at first, some superficial attempts at diplomacy, but at 10:00 A.M. on August 2, 1914, when eight German cavalrymen marched forthrightly up to a French sentry post in the border town of Belfort and began firing, a tragic war, fought over little of consequence, had begun.

THERE IS STILL
A PLACE IN THE LINE
FOR
YOU

THIS
SPACE
IS
RESERVED
FOR
A
FIT
MAN

Will you
fill it?

Left: When, in 1914, more than one million of Britain's youth volunteered for war at recruiting stations like this one in Southwark, the army found them in desperate need of basic training. By the following year, recruitment posters, above, stressed physical fitness as a prerequisite for service.

The clash of old and new was almost too pitiful to watch. In their first battles with Germany, the French arrived on horseback, wearing bright red pantaloons and plumes in their hats. They then proceeded to march into combat in the only way they knew how — bayonets fixed, sabers skyward — and were brought down, row after row, by rapid machine-gun fire. "The sense of the tragic futility of it will never quite fade from the minds of those who saw these brave men, dashing across the open to the sound of drums and bugles," said a despondent French general. "They thought it chic to die in white gloves."

With losses mounting to fifteen thousand men a day, Paris seamstresses began sewing gray uniforms to replace the red and white ones, infantrymen were equipped with shovels with which to dig their cover, and the expectation that it all would be over by Christmas — a view once shared on both sides — faded. Even the most die-hard old liner had to admit that war was a new enterprise.

The change was from offense to defense. For centuries, men had deemed war a competition of the spirit won by the side with the most grit and determination. Offense won wars and it won them quickly. But what good was grit in an age of sophisticated war machinery? Modern weapons had put an end to hand-to-hand combat. The machine gun and heavy artillery made the assault on enemy lines little more than a suicide run. All a soldier could do was dig in and wait the other side out. The long stalemate had begun.

It is hard to imagine the shock and disappointment of a soldier arriving on the western front in late 1914. Urged on to enlist by a torrent of publicity describing the Great War as both a religious battle of good and evil and a street scrap (a good time proving oneself with the lads), he landed instead in the mud and stench of the trenches, sometimes a mile from the nearest enemy soldier.

With rats and corpses at every turn, the trenches of the First World War served as the perfect metaphor for war itself: a grave for the living. Across Belgium and France, there were thousands of miles of trenches, zigzagging this way and that. There were frontline trenches and support trenches, reserve trenches and communication trenches all tied together to form huge underground cities. Men even labeled them with the names of hometown streets.

Inside, soldiers lived the lives of rodents. Enlisted men slept in holes scraped in the trench walls, while officers lived in slightly bigger bunkers buried deep below them. Like moles, engineers even burrowed out from the trenches into the territory beneath no-man's-land to plant mines under enemy dugouts, sometimes encountering hostile tunnelers with the same designs going the other way.

The combination of boredom and sudden danger was overwhelming. During the years that the enemies stood ground against each other, the trenches were regularly shelled and were always under the threat of sniper fire. Still, as historian and critic Paul Fussell has noted, soldiers spent most of the time lying in wait. The day began with a "stand-to" (dawn being the preferred time for attack), which ended by breakfast. Thereafter, men cleaned their weapons, repaired their trenches, and wrote letters. (Many say that it was the ennui of trench life that turned this into history's most literary war, inspiring novels from Ernest Hemingway and Erich Maria Remarque, poetry from Siegfried Sassoon and Wilfred Owen, and lesser verse from the pens of literally thousands of long-forgotten

Life in the trenches: "And to think we wanted to come here"

Francis (seated) at age eighteen, with his brother Harry, twenty, in late 1914, just before going to France.

—*Edward "Ted" Francis, who was born in 1896, was a private in the British army throughout World War I, refusing promotion because he believed it would place him in more danger. He fought in most of the major battles of the war, including the Somme, Ypres, and Passchendaele. Afterward, he became a banana salesman, working his way up to chief of sales over a forty-one-year career. In 1994, he was celebrated at ceremonies honoring the eightieth anniversary of the Birmingham City Battalions as the unit's sole surviving member. He died in 1996.*

I had been a Boy Scout and I used to love marching up and down with the tin drum in front of me. So when young men started enlisting for the war, I thought, "Well, perhaps it would be a good holiday." I stood in a queue at the Birmingham Town Hall and joined up and when I got home my mother said to me, "Have you enlisted as a soldier?" I said, "Yes." She said, "You little fool. Only thieves and vagabonds join the army." And she said, "You go back and tell them you've changed your mind." But of course I couldn't.

The mood among all of us young men was that we couldn't get to be a soldier quick enough. In Birmingham, where I enlisted, they expected to make one battalion, which would be made up of about 1,000 men. But within the first few days of war they had 4,500. We had a wonderful time training. I was in a section of about fourteen men, all from the same area, all speaking the same language with the same twang, more or less. We were like one big family. And then came the great day for us young ones when they issued us a rifle — the newest Lee Enfield rifle. You should have seen some of the lads looking at it, those who had never held a gun in their life. We went through eight months of training until we were so itchy to get to France we couldn't stand it. All we were thinking was, "We must get to France before the war's over."

The men training us were old soldiers of the South African war who were old enough to be my father. None of them had experienced a war where you're in trenches facing each other, with shells coming at you every minute. So we had no idea what it would be like when we got there. We crossed over to France after we finished our training, and we walked fifteen miles to our base camp. When it was our turn to go up into the trenches, the regiment coming out had been there almost since the start, and they looked at us as if to say, "Heh, you're smiling now but you won't be later." We passed seven days and nights in there and, after a rest of six or seven days, we went back in again. Then came the day when someone said to us excitedly, "Jack Smith!" I said, "What about him?" I knew Jack Smith. "He's dead. He's been shot." The first one of the battalion to be shot. I said, "What?" And the man replied, "Yes, he's dead. Been shot. He put his head too far over and a sniper got him." And that caused a bit of a sensation amongst the lads. They thought, "Well, this is not exactly what we came for." And from that day onwards when we went to the trenches, it was three killed, four killed, five killed, twenty killed, a hundred killed. By then, we were veterans.

We learned all about the trenches and their risks and what we had to do to fight the Germans. And of course the morning came when we had to "go over the top"— which meant you'd leap over the trench and cover three, four, five hundred yards toward the enemy lines. So when the officers blew their whistle, we were to dash out of the trenches and make our way toward the German trenches. And it was then that we looked at each other and wondered if we'd ever get through it. Some were visibly shaking. Some were crying. Some were almost shell-shocked before they started. But of course when the whistle went, we had to scramble over. There was always an officer a few yards behind you with a loaded revolver in his hand. And anyone who was a bit slow to go would receive a shot in the foot just to remind him that he was there.

We would only learn later what happened. If we took the trench we went over to capture, then we'd have time to rest and talk. And one would say to the other, "Where's Bill So-and-so?" And someone else would say, "Oh, he's got it. He's killed." And then you see that friends of yours or people you know are missing — some are wounded, some are killed. And you could be talking to a man in the trench, and while you're talking he accidentally looks over the top of it, and in that few seconds he might get it in the head. The German snipers, who were the best in the world, they had the finest rifles with telescopic sights, so just to show your forehead for a few seconds might mean you were dead.

We spent a lot of time walking from one trench to the next, and when the weather changed to rain and mud, well, it's almost impossible to describe what that

British soldiers rest in a reserve trench during the battle of the Somme, 1916.

was like. If you've seen pictures of the surface of the moon, it was something like that, only worse — all dug up and wet through with mud. Impossible to walk. To get two miles would take seven or eight hours. Sometimes you were in water up to your waist, and had to walk in it for a week to get to the firing line. And under those conditions, they couldn't bring food or water up to us — all the people bringing it were shot down or shelled. So we were hungry and thirsty most of the time. When we'd been there about six or eight months, covered in mud, wet through practically all day, absolutely chewed up by lice — we used to say, "and to think, we wanted to come to this hole."

In our first month there, we could smell the dead bodies. But after a while we took no notice of it. For a

person just arriving there, it would stink. But, to us, who were used to it every day, we didn't think a lot of it. The noise was always on. And, when you'd been as long in the trenches as I was, you could almost say for sure if a shell was going to drop by you by the sound it made. If you thought it was going to get you, you'd flatten yourself in the mud, however deep it was.

Everywhere you looked for miles were great holes full of water and mud. This was dangerous for those who got a small wound, because if they were near a big shell hole they couldn't get up and they would feel themselves slipping into the hole. Once the water — which was poisoned with gas and God knows what — got into the wounds, it was certain death. All the shouting in the world did no good because we couldn't even give them a hand. That would seem the usual thing to do when a man you'd joined up with as a friend and a comrade was shrieking for help, but we had orders not to help a wounded man. Once on the way out from the front lines we were walking out in the pitch dark and I heard a chap crying for help in a big shell hole. His hands were scraping the edge, and he was crying to everybody passing for help. Well, I couldn't stand that. So I got my rifle, and we pulled and pulled and pulled, and he was saved from drowning. But this was forbidden.

Practically everyone had shell shock, but there were two kinds: one for the privates, and one for the officers. With an officer, at the slightest trembling of the lips, they would be sent to the hospital for a week, and then to England to recover. But privates would get a dose of medicine and be sent back onto the line. That was the difference. You could easily see when a man had shell shock. He was crying, shaking, his face was absolutely a different color. It was all we could do in the trenches to hold him back. Sometimes we'd even sit on him. Because, once he got out of the trenches, he was a dead man. Some couldn't stand it and walked out. And inevitably they got shot for deserting.

In the later years of the war, we got used to the dead bodies and treated them as nothing, like pieces of wood. Everything had a use. We'd even put the bodies in the bottom of the trench and stand on them to keep dry. Of course, these bodies were recovered later, but if they were left too long, they became skeletons, because the rats chewed them. To see a body with no face but a skeleton would shock most men. We also searched the dead bodies in the hopes of finding some food on them, or perhaps a flask of water. Some of them had food which had been sent by relatives from England, and that was a godsend, because other than that we could not have stood up to the conditions we were forced to fight in.

"He loved no-man's-land and constantly crawled out there at night. On one occasion a star-shell revealed his tall figure, not lying down but standing erect in the open. Whereupon, instead of throwing himself flat, he flung out his arms. 'Tell me if I look like a tree,' he shouted back to the British trenches."

British infantryman, describing his colleague, a former schoolmaster

No other war had ever utilized so much artillery. At a notoriously brutal British training camp in Etaples, France, shells explode the night sky into daylight, preparing newly arrived soldiers for the surreal experience of the battlefield.

poet-soldiers in Germany, France, and England.) Finally, with nightfall, the real work began as men emerged to retrieve casualties and repair the barbed wire protecting them from assault. Borrowed from the American West, where it was used to prevent the passage of farm animals, barbed wire became a symbol of the First World War, a confused and tangled mess of metal that was nearly impossible to penetrate on foot.

The trench conditions were so miserable and so unanticipated that they gave rise to an array of strange psychological maladies grouped loosely under the heading of "shell shock." Constantly handling dead flesh, listening for the faintest sound of danger while unable to show fear, always prepared to defend but almost never on the attack, shooting at an enemy that appeared to them as nothing more than an abstract gray blob darting behind sandbags a distance across the mud, many men effectively shut down. In 1915, when the first great wave of conscripts began to appear at the front, 9 percent of the battle casualties were reported as "without physical cause." Some went "blind," others were "deaf" or "dumb." Soldiers suddenly shook uncontrollably, lost their memory, or experienced paralysis.

Watching them, doctors were baffled and imagined that the men must have suffered some bodily injury too small for medical equipment to record; equally confused, superior officers suspected the odd behavior to be nothing more than an elaborate charade masking cowardice and ordered the men court-martialed for desertion. When it became clear a few years into the war that the men were suffering from a trauma of the mind, they were sent to new kinds of clinics called, simply, NYDN hospitals (for "not yet diagnosed, nervous").

Just as odd was the way that some men embraced the horrors of the front. It had not been the war experience they had imagined when they left from London, Paris, or Berlin, but it had been a war experience nonetheless, and its peculiar horror, its indescribable grotesqueness, made men feel a profound bond both with each other (many felt that only someone who had seen what they had seen could understand them anymore) and with the trenches themselves. "We welcomed an occasional ten days leave," wrote poet Robert Graves, "but, if slightly wounded, soon grew bored with hospital and depot and schemed to get back again, our wounds half-healed. The trenches made us feel larger than life: only there was death a joke, rather than a threat."

The fighting went on for what seemed to all an eternity, each side caught up in the same mad idea that the enemy could be brought down by force of attrition. Week after week, month after month, desperate generals prayed that tomorrow's raid would bring the knockout punch. It never did. From 1914 to the spring of 1918, the line on the western front moved less than ten miles in either direction.

The home fronts were at war, too. World War I involved massive armies commandeered across enormous battlefields for years at a time, and doing so required a total mobilization of the population. The professional fighting units — primed only for a short war — were spent quickly, and after a few months, the battle was being fought in large part by amateurs on both sides. Nearly every man between the ages of eighteen and forty, including drunkards, criminals, and the mentally ill, was called to service. Getting them into uniform, showing them how to use a rifle, delivering them to the front, and then feeding and clothing them

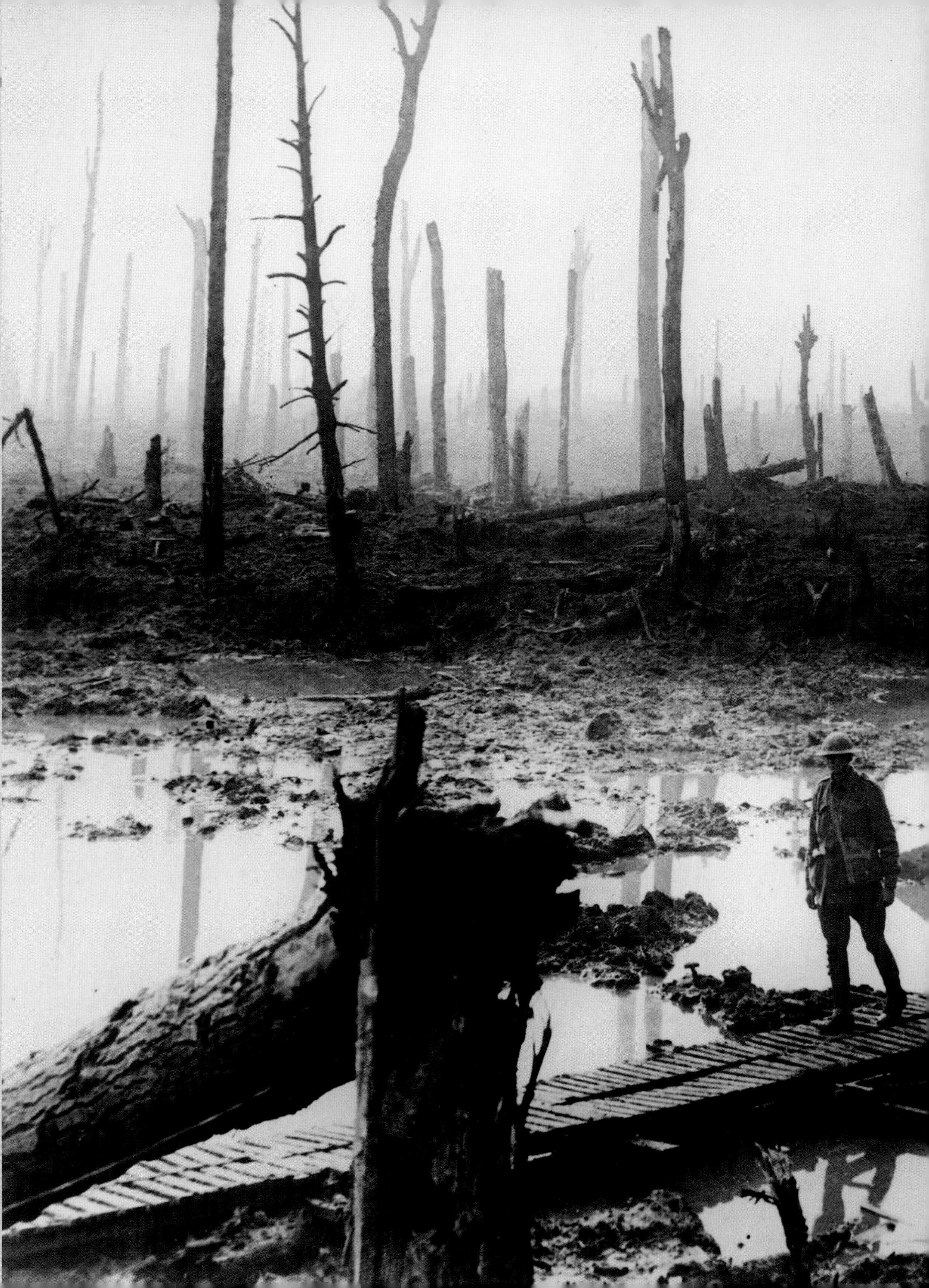

Morning revealed the extent of destruction brought by dawn raids. Here, Australian soldiers negotiate the smoldering wasteland that was once a verdant forest.

"Munitionettes" assemble shells in a factory in France. In order to fill wartime demand, many women moved into areas of skilled and industrial labor traditionally held by men, presenting a challenge to established sex roles.

while they were there took a Herculean effort from all parts of society.

People eagerly complied. Much of the class warfare and social unrest that had preceded the war was erased for a time by the push to victory. Within a few days of the onset of hostilities, 5 million Germans, 4 million Frenchmen, and 1 million British had enthusiastically left civilian life for the battlefields. Socialists who had presumed that people would choose class struggle over nationality were wrong; even some of the most radical laborites saw their duty as including an embrace of country in a moment of need. Likewise, industry, hiring women and children to replace the departing men, had begun to direct all of its energies toward producing war essentials.

Life in the belligerent states was completely transformed. In England, parks and golf courses became temporary drill grounds. In the war's early months, men who had been dentists, cobblers, and factory workers could be seen there marching in tattered civilian clothes, looking more like children playing soldier than real infantrymen just a few weeks shy of the killing in Belgium. Country estates became makeshift medical wards, and servant girls used to tidying aristocratic homes were packing shells in munitions factories. At schools, young boys were taught to march and young girls, the art of bandaging, for who knew how long the war was to go on and how deep into the nation's youth the order to serve would be heard? The situation in Paris was more dire. With the city at times only fifty miles from the fighting, large sections had to be evacuated. Rationing was severe and unemployment reached 44 percent. The city was under siege not so much by any enemy as by war itself, the eerie stillness of the once-busy streets broken only by the sounds of soldiers marching off to battle. The clientele of the famous cafés and nightclubs now consisted almost exclusively of nurses, war-industry workers, and the occasional soldier on leave. With most men at the front, Paris became a city of women, many of them young widows. Shops that had carried the world's most sophisticated fashions now displayed mourning clothes and "mourning brooches." Even the taxis and buses had largely disappeared, employed to carry enlisted men back and forth from the front.

Both the Allied and German press became unofficial (and in some cases official) agents of the government. Reporters were not allowed to accompany the armies into battle and had to submit their dispatches to military censors for approval. As a result, good news was exaggerated, bad news ignored. The distortions, as Paul Fussell also observed, turned the war into a fantasy: to anyone reading the papers in those days, the fighting on the front was easy work, victory was always within reach, and the enemy was a complete and total beast.

Propaganda was delivered at a fever pitch. Posters, poetry, theater, and song were all dedicated to the fighting cause. In Britain, which until 1916 relied on assembling its troops purely from volunteers, the message was most often directed at recruitment. Popular songs included ditties like "We Don't Want to Lose You, but We Think You Ought to Go," and a poster showed a young girl sitting in her father's lap asking, "Daddy, what did YOU do in the Great War?" (Ensuring that those without children would also experience a healthy bit of guilt, there were others that showed a mother scolding her son: "Go, it's your duty, lad!")

In Germany, the refrain of "The Watch on the Rhine" became the anthem of war hysteria. Soldiers would sing it as they marched to the railway stations and

German immigrants carrying both German and American flags march down New York's Broadway during a pro-kaiser parade in August 1914. That same month, President Wilson declared U.S. neutrality.

"What have the Russians, Poles, Bulgarians, and Serbs ever done for civilization? They have never made an invention, they have developed no political system, nor given us any ideas. All that this race possesses has been adopted from others . . . This is the ignorant, half-civilized, barbarous and sinister race which has declared war against the civilized races of the European order."

1914 editorial in a Chicago German-language newspaper

recruit passersby — Pied Piper style — along the way, arriving at their destination with a full-city chorus rushing alongside. The phrase *"Gott strafe England!"* (God punish England!) was rubber-stamped on letters and postcards and engraved on everything from cuff links to wedding rings. People even saluted to the phrase in much the same way that they would salute to "Heil Hitler!" a generation later.

The effect of all this was profound, and tragically ironic. For even as a steady stream of the dead and wounded began to flow back from the front, many young men continued to enlist with fervor. Urged on by the propaganda campaigns and left unaware of the battlefront's harsh realities by an impotent press, they jumped to get in, fearing only that the Great War might end before they had their chance to be a part of it.

Almost from the moment that the conflict in Europe began, America started a debate of its own, with many of the country's German-Americans defending the kaiser. In Chicago, where two-thirds of the people were recent Central and Eastern European immigrants, German-Americans held the edge on public opinion. Joined by Irish-Americans (who were not so much pro-German as anti-British) and Russian-American Jews (who were decidedly against their former tormentor the Russian tsar), they made a vocal display of their feelings. Pro-kaiser rallies were held at the Chicago Auditorium and parades marched through the Loop. The city was even the site of some Central Powers mobilization: German reservists stranded in Illinois at the outset of the war took over the campus of Chicago's Elmhurst College and used its grounds for military exercises.

The scene in Chicago and other American cities with large German populations contrasted with the rest of the country, where supporters of the Allies far outnumbered those of the Germans, particularly after one of the kaiser's submarines sank the British liner *Lusitania* on May 7, 1915, killing more than a thousand, among them 128 American vacationers on their way to Liverpool. But just as significant was the strong American feeling against any kind of war at all. To the growing number of American socialists, for instance, the war in Europe represented nothing more than a clash over capitalist greed — millions of young men sacrificed to a battle between Britain and Germany for commercial supremacy. Like many feminists, who had also come out vocally against the war, they worried that if America entered the conflict, it would slow their efforts for reform at home.

Many more Americans saw the war in starkly moral terms: as a deviant episode in modern history, a reversion to the barbarism of medieval times. It confirmed their image of the Old World as corrupt and stagnant. If Europe wants to commit suicide, they argued, why should we help her? With the debate raging throughout the country, President Woodrow Wilson declared American

"Once lead this people into war, and they'll forget there was ever such a thing as tolerance . . . and the spirit of ruthless brutality will enter into the very fiber of our national life."

President Woodrow Wilson

When it was sunk by a German submarine, the luxury liner Lusitania, *shown here on a period souvenir postcard, carried over twelve hundred vacationers and a cargo that included ammunition and small arms.*

neutrality in August 1914 and in 1916 ran for reelection with the slogan "He Kept Us Out of War."

But even without the presence of U.S. soldiers, the conflict was having a dramatic effect on American society. American businesses took advantage of the sudden European need for food, raw materials, and munitions, and as they did, the increased business activity boosted America into a period of prosperity. Labor, in turn, took advantage of the improved bargaining position they were in as business, deprived of the regular flow of immigrants from Europe, fell short of workers. At the outset of the war, immigrants traveled across the ocean at the rate of 1 million a year and American unemployment stood at 15 percent; by 1918, barely 31,000 made the same trip and the jobless rate had dropped to just 2 percent.

Confident that they held the upper hand, labor unions enjoyed a period of new militancy. In 1916 alone, the country witnessed 2,093 strikes and lockouts, and employee earnings rose by 26 percent. Still, the working conditions at many factories remained uncivilized: one-third to one-half of the working people in the United States were still required to work twelve-hour days, often seven days a week, and many workers and their families had no choice other than to live in factory-town shanties where they remained under the eyes of their foremen.

Wartime labor shortages also helped the cause of women. Even though the war had forced a split between those who argued for America's entry and those who argued against it, the opening of nontraditional jobs to women (which started with the war and then accelerated enormously once America got into it) helped further their common cause. Over the four years from 1914 to 1918, the number of female railroad workers increased threefold. Women were hired for metalworking and munitions jobs and as streetcar conductors. The resulting change in social attitudes made people more receptive toward granting the feminists their primary goal: the right to vote.

But perhaps the most enduring effect of the war on American domestic life occurred in the African-American community. In 1910, four out of every five African-Americans lived in the rural South, where most were migrant workers. As America's wartime economy took hold, thousands of these men and women made their way to the big cities in the industrial North in search of jobs in the steel, auto, and mining industries. The enormous demographic shift, which was part of an overall trend away from rural life in America, was called the Great Migration, and it happened to the accompaniment of sloganeering straight out of the book of Exodus. Chicago, in particular, was the dream destination of the movement. There, black southerners, urged on by visions of freedom and jobs, imagined they would find nothing less than the promised land.

White southerners, aware that they were losing their labor force, reacted angrily with a rash of violence. And at least some black northerners, fearful that the southern blacks would embarrass them with their lack of urban sophistication, resented the newcomers. But the movement, which predated the war and continued long after it, had the feel of the inevitable to it. And by the time it began to slow in the 1930s, the black populations of cities like New York and Chicago had already increased several times over, forever changing American urban life.

The excitement of the great migration: "We're going to Chicago!"

When I was growing up in Vicksburg, Mississippi, the South seemed like a happy place to me. My mother had gone to Chicago, so I lived with my grandmother, who was born a slave. I never went hungry, never missed a meal, and my mother would send me nice, decent suits to wear to church on Sunday. I didn't know what the word "segregation" meant. I knew that black people were the inferior people and they had to do all the dirty work and weren't allowed to go into certain places. Nobody ever had to explain all of this to me; I just knew it. But by the time I was eight years old, I had seen my first lynching. I was on my way home from school, and I saw a black man who'd been hung up on a tree. A bunch of white men were standing around him — they had poured gasoline on him and set him on fire, and now they were shooting at his body. I didn't really understand what was happening. The tradition in Mississippi was that if you lynched a "nigger," you would cut the tree down and paint the stump red. And on my way to school the next day, there was this red paint dripping on the bottom of the tree.

I knew people were leaving Mississippi and going North. The church we went to in Vicksburg was ministered by a man named Dr. Edward Perry Jones. And in his services on Sunday he would tell his audience to try to get their young people out of there because there was no future for them in Mississippi. Of course, the white "powers that be" heard this and they didn't like it, so they ran him out of town. My mother had been a pianist and an organist at this church, and that's when she decided to go to Chicago and leave me in Mississippi with my grandmother.

It was no problem for a black woman to leave town, but a black man couldn't go to the railroad station and buy a ticket out of Mississippi because the white people didn't want to lose all of that cheap, unskilled labor. In 1910, the year I was born, my uncle was working at a white barbershop in Vicksburg. His friends who had gone up North would write back and tell him what a wonderful place Chicago was. There was a lot of work there because it was more or less the center of the United States in that era. To take a train across the country back then you had to stop in Chicago and change lines, so a lot of businessmen would have their meetings there. All of the big hotels in the United States at that time were in Chicago — the Palmer House, the Blackstone, the Congress — and they all needed porters. So black people from all over the South were coming up to try to get decent jobs.

My uncle wanted to get up there, so he faked a letter from somebody in Memphis, and told his boss that he had an aunt who was dying and wanted to see her nephew. His boss read the letter, took him down to the railroad station, and used my uncle's money to buy him a round-trip ticket. He said, "Now, you go up to Memphis and you come on back here, you hear?" My uncle said, "Yes, sir." But of course when he got to Memphis he sold the other half of that ticket and kept on going to Chicago. My mother joined him after I was born, and that was the beginning of the exodus of my family from Mississippi. From 1910 to 1917, my uncle and my mother worked and saved up enough money to rent an apartment and bring the old folks and the children up to Chicago.

I was eight years old when we left, and all it was to me was a wonderful train ride. It was all happiness to me, you know, "I'm going to Chicago to see my momma!" And my grandmother really felt good because she had made great progress from where she had started out, being born a slave and all. Here she was with all of

—Milt Hinton, who was born in 1910, left Northwestern University in 1930 to pursue a career as a jazz bassist in Chicago. In more than sixty-five years of performing, he has played with such greats as Louis Armstrong, Cab Calloway, and John Coltrane, earning him the title of "dean" of jazz bassists. On his eightieth birthday, one hundred bassists serenaded him at New York's Lincoln Center.

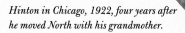

Hinton in Chicago, 1922, four years after he moved North with his grandmother.

her children migrated up North, and earning enough to send for her. I'm sure my grandmother was thinking only of the future, of our future. Her children would have better opportunities, and her grandson would have a better chance in life. And she was very delighted with that.

We didn't make the morning train, because by this time my grandmother was a pretty old lady, slow getting around. It poured down rain as we waited for the evening train, and the nice little cap my mother had

bought me got all wrinkled up. We boarded the train, and the coach we were allowed to sit in was right next to the coal engine, so the smoke and soot were horrible. My grandmother had made hard-boiled eggs and fried chicken, and we sat back there brushing the coal soot off the chicken and eating it and enjoying every morsel of it. My mother used to love to tell the story of when they met us at the railroad station in Chicago, because we looked so very bad! Totally disheveled. They threw coats around us and took us home to clean us up so we would look presentable.

Having lived all of her life in the South, my grandmother was very disturbed by Chicago — it was completely different. And I can remember it all so vividly because I loved her so much — she was like a saint to me. She would be fixing dinner and she'd say, "These chickens don't taste like the chickens in Mississippi."

"These mustard greens don't taste like the ones in Mississippi." Everything "wasn't like Mississippi." But to me as a child, things seemed pretty much the same. You could even join a club called the Vicksburg Club and hang around with people from your home town if you wanted. The people in Chicago didn't strike me as being different because they were all from the South like we were. And they'd gone through all the same pressures that we had gone through, and had made the same escape.

By the end of the Great Migration, Harlem was the cultural, artistic, and intellectual hub of the African-American community. Here, residents dance at a block party in 1915.

*Torrential rains in October 1916 turned the war-scarred Somme Valley
into a muddy quagmire and mercifully brought the offensive to an end.
During the five-month battle, the Allied advance never exceeded seven miles.*

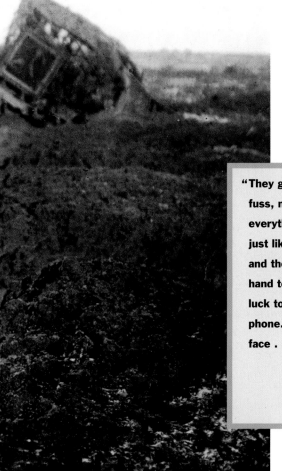

Two of the most disastrous battles in the history of warfare occurred in 1916, and neither was able to break the awful deadlock. On February 21, Germany attacked France 137 miles east of Paris, at the fortress-ringed town of Verdun. The old village served no strategic importance: winning it would not have helped Germany achieve a foothold against the Allies; losing it would not have been a tragedy for the French. Yet, the battle there became a symbol, a line in the mud, so to speak, and the more the attacking army seemed to want it, the more the resisting army felt compelled to protect it. France sent 259 of its 330 infantry regiments to defend Gallic pride at Verdun, the line of transport vehicles (some of them Parisian taxis, others the vegetable trucks of local farmers) stretching for miles along La Voie Sacrée (the Sacred Way), as the lone road in and out came to be called. When the battle finally ended, 700,000 from both sides lay dead.

Only a few months later, Britain began a battle just as bloody in the valley of the river Somme. In their own attempt to break the stalemate, they struck at the German trenches with an enormous barrage of artillery fire (so enormous the guns were heard at Hampstead Heath, north of London) and then followed up with an infantry assault. The strategy was a colossal failure. British cannons were unable to silence the German machine guns, meaning that row upon row of infantry marched point-blank into the line of fire, arriving "at a steady, easy pace," said a German officer later, "as if expecting to find nothing alive in our trenches."

> "They got going without delay, no fuss, no shouting, no running, everything solid and thorough — just like men themselves. Here and there a boy would wave his hand to me as I shouted good luck to them through my megaphone. And all had a cheery face . . ."
>
> *Officer of Ulster battalion, describing the infantry on their way to assault the German trenches at the Somme*

More than 22,000 were sacrificed in the first day alone — one of the deadliest single days at war for any army — and by the end of the battle five months later, more than half a million German, French, and British soldiers had perished. Even England's newest weapon proved to be a dud: forty-seven tanks were brought to the battlefield at the Somme, and while they frightened the German infantrymen, each and every one of the newfangled "landships" collapsed from technical difficulties by the end of its first day.

As miserable as the war had been to that point, the Somme and Verdun took it several steps further into the abyss. French soldiers receiving the brunt of the German artillery barrage at Verdun were so outgunned at first that one of them said it felt like the enemy "had one cannon for each of us." If they did, they also had more than that: poison gas was used with a vengeance there and in nearly every successive battle of the war.

First deployed in 1915 by German troops assaulting the Allied forces at Ypres (where it disabled nearly half of the Canadian troops), chlorine gas had been rendered ineffective by the development of the gas mask later that year. Upon seeing the clouds of poison coming their way, soldiers would simply don their protective contraptions and continue to fight. But phosgene gas, introduced at Verdun, and mustard gas, which arrived in 1917, were invisible and thus came without warning; the effects, in turn, were devastating. One whiff of mustard gas was enough to create sneezing, aching gums, a burning throat, and, occasionally, a loss of reason. More important, it sent men into a stupor, an irresistible lassitude that stunted their ability to fight back. Those unlucky enough to have breathed in great quantities of phosgene were sent gasping and retching to their deaths, the end coming slowly, while the victim's lungs filled up with fluid.

The chaos in and around Verdun was overwhelming. High explosives turned over the battlefield repeatedly until it no longer even resembled a negotiable plane; men trying to move across it found themselves frustrated by avalanches of earth, each new shock to the surface throwing them like seeds across a planting field. Unable to see through the clouds of dust and smoke, men advanced by compass bearing alone, blindly stepping over bodies and parts of bodies that had been churned over almost as much as the soil.

Men watched other men dismembered in an instant by artillery fire and obliterated by explosives, leaving barely a trace. In some sectors, the stench of decaying flesh was so powerful the soldiers wished for a gas attack if only to change the aroma. In one of Verdun's cruelest ironies, water was alternately too plentiful and too scarce, the former condition adding to the quicksandlike mud, the latter forcing men to lick the slime off walls and drink their own urine. Men treated their circumstances with black humor — shaking hands with corpses and then robbing them — but the joke, it seemed, was always on the living.

If there were two acts to the First World War, the second one began with the response to Verdun, the Somme, and other wholesale slaughters that year at Passchendaele and Chemin des Dames. Nationalism and an archaic war ethic had fueled the unexamined loyalty brought to the front by soldiers in the conflict's early years. But by the beginning of 1917, it was evident that the horrendous failure of both sides had seeded doubts among enlisted men and civilians. Over the next few months, thousands of French soldiers were arrested for various acts of mutiny, mostly their simple refusal to return to the front lines. Authorities looked to blame the influence of revolutionaries, but in fact it was war, much more than politics, that the men were fed up with, and the frustration was spreading.

The confusion on the battlefront was matched by a confusion at home. Men returning from the front wondered what war they had been fighting, the one they remembered or the one they read about. The ever-lengthening casualty lists (in the first four weeks of the battle of the Somme, the *Times* of London published sixty-eight columns of names) helped put the lie to government propaganda and the fiction-filled reporters' accounts. A will to question authority took hold: Just who were these people in control of this horrible tragedy? And why should we fight to the death to see that they stay in power?

Not only did trust in the government and the press suffer, so did trust in the church and traditional religions. Overcome by grief brought on by battles in which communities lost not just one or two men, but nearly every male between the ages of eighteen and forty, people sought comfort wherever they could find it. A vogue for spiritualism set in, with wives and mothers using fortune-tellers and crystal gazers to "get in touch with" their dead husbands and sons.

A collective mentality emerged that crossed battle lines. Many people began to see with more clarity the yawning gap between the privileged and the deprived, the powerful and the powerless, the satisfied and the hungry, the few

> **"It's time this bloodthirsty war was over . . . The women have become thin, worn out by this distressing anxiety, the constant expectation of disaster."**
>
> *French writer Louise Deletang, 1916*

Aristocratic and Russian: **Life inside "the class that had to be destroyed"**

I was only ten years old when the war began, but I do remember that there was a tremendous sense of heroism connected to those first few months. We were staying in the country that summer when the rumors began to circulate that a war was coming. I asked my aunt, "Will it be a real war?" And she answered very sadly, "Yes, I think it's going to be a very real war."

My eldest brother had just graduated from college, the Imperial Alexander Lyceum, and he was doing his military service. He wrote us a letter in which he said, "Sonia and Iuri [Sonia was my name then], I'm leaving for war, and if anything happens, remember, it is for Russia." And we both ran out of the room all excited that my own brother was going to be a part of this tremendous adventure. We had a very primitive telephone in our house then and at ten o'clock one night the phone rang and it was the old man from the post office who read us a telegram saying that my brother had been lightly wounded and that he had received the Saint George's Cross for heroism. The old man then added in a trembling voice: "Please accept my congratulations."

That feeling of the heroic adventure changed later as Russia began to face its own problems. Ours was an upper-class family. We had a house in St. Petersburg and a country estate and we had a team of about twelve or fourteen servants so we were rather well taken care of. And my father was very much involved in politics. He was a type of statesman and there were many like him in pre-revolutionary Russia: liberal in their opinions, wanting reforms, probably wanting a constitutional monarchy but certainly not socialist. He was a member of the Duma, the Russian parliament. And around 1916 there was the feeling that things were not going right with the tsar's regime. We heard stories about various cabinet ministers being changed, about wrong people being appointed, about Rasputin's influence. And we didn't know what to believe. There was with us children a tendency to glamorize the imperial family, especially the young Alexis, who was exactly my age. Then came the two revolutions.

First, it was the February Revolution. My father was sick and was staying at home, and there was suddenly a phone call from the Duma, telling him that he had to come, whether he was ill or not. He had difficulty getting to the building because of the crowds and he didn't return home for seven days. He stayed at the Duma with all the other parliament members, hoping to hold off the rioters, but the politicians were helpless. The revolution was happening. There were huge, frightening crowds in the street. They were not the friendly

Left: Koulomzin at age thirteen and, below, at eleven, in front of Volchi, her family's country house.

—Sophie Koulomzin, who was born in 1903, left Russia in 1920. After living in Estonia, Berlin, and France, she settled in New York State in 1948. In 1970, she returned to Leningrad and visited her old family home; seventeen families were living there.

people you talked to and dealt with, but impersonal. I have experienced crowds later in life, and I have always kept that feeling that a crowd of people is less than human. You can't reason with a crowd.

The result of this first revolution was the installation of a provisional government under Alexander Kerensky. We very reverently took down our picture of the tsar and his wife and little Alexis and put up a photograph of Kerensky. At this point, we were hoping that something good might finally come out of the revolution. Later on, when Kerensky also proved unable to lead, we took down his picture, too. We had lost our feeling for any leader at all.

We spent a happy summer at our country house that year, but we knew it was the last one. One evening that summer, I was running down the lawn towards the kitchen garden to call my mother to tell her that supper was ready. And I suddenly stopped and looked around

me and took in all the beauty — the roses, the trees, the park, the lawns — and I realized that this was all about to disappear. It was scary. I went back up to the house, carefully wrapped up my favorite doll, and put it in a chest of drawers in my nursery, thinking that maybe when everything is destroyed some child will find it and play with it.

Then, in the fall we came to Moscow, where my father and mother had found an apartment. The mood had gotten worse. Kerensky's government was about to collapse. The Bolsheviks seized the Winter Palace in Petrograd without a fight, but in Moscow the October Revolution was bloody. Sitting in our little apartment, my sister and I listened to the shooting going on. We saw the fires in the night. And then, after five or six days the shooting ended. We knew it was over and that the Bolsheviks had won.

After the revolution, it was a very difficult time. Everything was being nationalized. By the winter of 1919, things started to unravel. There was no electric light, no water supply, no heat. We burned the shelves of our bookcases and a partition separating parts of one room, just to keep warm. And because it was a Moscow winter, all the plumbing burst. The food shortage was also very bad. There was a tiny piece of very bad bread which was given twice a week and we could get turnips. But it was difficult to find potatoes. And there was no meat or milk. Our St. Petersburg house and our country estate were taken away. A committee came and took out all the furniture and everything. Then the money that we had in the bank was seized. So we had no more money and just the apartment in Moscow.

Our lives had certainly changed. My mother and I would go to the open market in Moscow to sell our clothing just so we could have food to eat. I tried to unravel some old sweaters, and make baby's socks, and sell them. I was uncomfortable, shy. But I got used to it, gradually. What troubled me was that we had no choice: we belonged to a class that had to be destroyed and that was a little painful.

In the first months after the October Revolution in Moscow they would put up lists of "enemies of the people" to be executed. And I remember that on the first list was the headmaster and the headmistress of a private school where my brother was registered. Each day we'd look at the list to see if it included someone else we knew. My father thought he'd try to find me a job of some kind and he went to an agency they called the work exchange. He approached the clerk and gave his name and she looked up and said: "You are alive? You are not executed?" We did everything we could after that to escape.

With shouts of "Down with hunger! Bread for the workers!" female textile workers turned the 1917 International Women's Day march in Petrograd into an insurrection that brought down tsarist Russia and paved the way for Lenin and his Bolsheviks to seize power.

and the many; and as they did, the enemy in uniform no longer appeared to be as responsible for their suffering as did the "enemy" sitting on their own country's throne.

The fomenting class struggle, held in abeyance during the war's early years, now returned with fresh vitality. Workers in Paris, Berlin, Turin, and other cities went on strike. In Germany, the rebellion was particularly fierce. Deprived of many goods by an Allied naval blockade (which was respected by "neutral" America), the German leaders had elected to use what little they had to supply their soldiers first, infuriating the civilian population. The resulting "turnip winter" of 1916–17 in which people existed on "turnip bread," "turnip soup," and whatever else their imaginations could create from the tired old vegetable, sapped home front morale. When the material deprivation forced upon them became worse the following year, more than a million Germans participated in the largest protest since the war began.

The situation was even more desperate in the East. Russian soldiers had begun the war with the same enthusiasm as their counterparts in France and England and the same expectations for a quick end (tsarist officers, leaving for battle in 1914, were tempted to bring their dress whites, so convinced were they that a victory parade through Berlin was in their immediate future). But, of course, they fared no better. Led by an aged war minister who thought the machine gun and other modern weaponry to be cowardly, Russia suffered 4 million casualties in the first year alone. By 1916, with Tsar Nicholas himself ineptly commanding the army and rumors of shortages of ammunition, the troops were rapidly losing the will to fight.

Both the war and a particularly harsh winter had forced enormous sacrifices back home. Short of fuel, many factories closed. Bread lines wrapped around the block, and refugees, driven east from Poland by the fighting, crowded the streets of Moscow and Petrograd (the new name for St. Petersburg, chosen in the nationalistic fervor of 1914, because it sounded more Slavic). Busy with the war, Nicholas had entrusted his country's fragile domestic life to the rule of his wife, Alexandra. And she, in turn, had come under the influence of a maniacal faith healer, Gregory Rasputin, who wreaked havoc throughout the government. Amid the chaos, the pleas of the nation's disgruntled peasants, who had long been demanding their own land, now merged with the larger population's demands for peace. Russia was ripe for revolution.

The revolt began over the scarcity of bread. On February 23, 1917, a parade of female textile workers, marching to celebrate International Women's Day, erupted in protest; the next day, some 200,000 workers went on strike, protesting the food shortages. Over the next few days, as their demonstrations escalated, the entire city of Petrograd shut down. Army units were assigned to put down the rebellion, but after some sporadic fighting, the troopers — a motley force composed mostly of men in their thirties and forties, drafted when the sup-

> **"Colorless, expressionless, endless regiments marching through dead cold . . . They were not individual Russians anymore; they were not men who were going to die for their country, they were just men who were going to die."**
>
> *Russian soldier, describing the scene on the eastern front, 1916*

Revolutionary troops occupy the Winter Palace soon after the February uprising. More than seventeen thousand soldiers from the Petrograd garrison joined the crowds in the streets rather than defend the tsar.

ply of younger recruits went dry — sided with the rioters. Trams were overturned
and bakeries were looted, all while the soldiers watched. Prisons were seized and
the inmates freed. Artillery depots were commandeered, their supply of rifles and
ammunition distributed among the rioters who then went marauding through the
streets.

Out of touch, Alexandra thought the disturbance to be little more than children at play. But Nicholas, heeding the advice of those on the scene, rushed back
from the front by train, only to be stopped a hundred miles short of the capital by
revolutionaries. He signed the abdication papers in pencil, he later said, "as others do when they make a list of dirty laundry," the collapse of the three-century-
old Romanov dynasty having taken but a few days.

News of the February Revolution was greeted warmly by many in the
West, for it was hoped that the establishment of a liberal parliamentary government might shore up the Russian position and keep them in the war. The provisional regime of Prime Minister Alexander Kerensky, which soon succeeded the
tsar's rule, instituted universal suffrage, equal rights for women, and basic civil
liberties while keeping Russian soldiers at the front. But the revolution also
inspired Vladimir Ilyich Ulyanov to leave his exile in Switzerland and return to
his native land, and with him came a very different agenda.

Ulyanov, who was better known by his revolutionary name Lenin, was the
leader of the Bolsheviks, a minor workers' party whose call for the revolt of the
industrial proletariat had fallen flat in Russia, a backward agricultural economy
with no industrial proletariat to rebel. Lenin had always imagined that the workers' revolution would begin somewhere else in Europe and spread to his homeland, but the collapse of the tsar prompted him to seize one of history's most
romantic moments and return to Russia now to realize his dream. He returned
his library books and settled up with his Swiss landlady before boarding a train
out of Zurich and beginning the journey that would result in the establishment of
one of the twentieth century's most potent and powerful societies.

Lenin's safe passage through Europe was guaranteed by the German gov-

Witness to the revolution: "Lenin arrived in a third-class train car, a bourgeois bowler hat in his hand"

When Lenin arrived in Petrograd on April 16, 1917, I was at the Finland Station to welcome him. I had been a revolutionary from the time I was a child, because growing up in poverty under the tsar's regime had taught me very early about exploitation. My father worked as a tailor, and I had a very hard childhood — sometimes we were starving. I went to work at a very young age and then educated myself, with some help from my friends. In 1905, I learned about Lenin, how he wanted to change life so that everyone would be equal, so that

Bryansky (with beard and hat, second row right) stands behind Lenin (front row, right).

—*Alexander "Sasha" Bryansky, who was born in 1882, was targeted for execution by the anti-Bolshevik White Guards in 1918 but managed to escape. He also avoided execution or imprisonment during the Stalin-era purges despite his connection to the early years of Soviet communism. An artist and poet, he published works throughout the century until his death in 1995 at the age of 113.*

there would be no poverty and exploitation. This affected me greatly; I learned to hate the regime and I started writing revolutionary poetry.

In 1914, I was sent off to fight in World War I. I was awarded the St. George's Cross, and then ended up in the Petrograd Reserve Regiment after some time in the hospital. That's how I happened to be in Petrograd in 1917 when the February Revolution happened. Of course I wanted to take an active part in it, so I pinned my St. George's Cross to my coat to look more presentable and headed out into the people. I joined a crowd of workers moving toward Nevsky Avenue. The Cossacks [peasant soldiers loyal to the tsar] were deployed at Znamenskii Square. There was a police officer in charge of the Cossacks, and he shouted into the

crowd, "Move back, or I'll shoot!" A woman ran up to him and got his horse by the bridle. She wanted to take him aside. He shot her dead right away. Then the crowd shouted, "Cossacks! Why do you keep silent? A police bastard just killed a Russian woman! Cossacks, go home!" And all the Cossacks rode away.

Then the demonstration moved on along Nevsky Avenue. People shouted, "Down with the war! Down with autocracy!" Machine guns rattled from the roofs where policemen were stationed, and several people were wounded. The crowd hesitated. Then a student, a small man with both hands amputated, cried out: "Soldiers, come on! Defend the revolution! Take them down!" A bunch of people broke into the building, went up to the roof and took the machine gunners down. Soon all the policemen disappeared from the streets to avoid being beaten.

After the February Revolution we saw that nothing had really changed. The new leaders were not going to put a stop to the war. At home, capitalism remained, and life for the poor did not change. There were rallies when Bolsheviks were beaten up by crowds of thugs. But

worst of all, there was no bread! Bakeries and shops were stormed to provide the people with food. The starvation was universal.

One morning in April I was at the Kshesinskaia Palace, and we were visited by Lenin's sister, who said that he would be arriving that day. Podvoiskii [commander of the Bolshevik Military Organization] started dancing, and then he said, "We must welcome him properly." Because it was the second day of Easter, all soldiers were on leave, and all workers had the day off, so we called them all to a rally at the station. Lenin's train was late and Podvoiskii kept sending me to find out when it was expected. He kept getting angry at me, as if I was to blame for the train being late. But finally the train was coming. And then we saw Lenin, standing in a third-class car, a bourgeois bowler hat in one hand. He was wearing a black coat with a velvet collar. When he came off the train he gave a small speech saying, "Long live the social revolution!"

I met him a few days later, and my impression was that he was just an ordinary man. He had a huge bald head covered on the sides with curly reddish hair; he was of an average height and had a common Russian face, maybe with some Mongolian blood. His eyes were lively and he was a very cheerful man. He always spoke with no preliminary notes, and with a lot of gestures. His hands would thrust forward calling to advance, then be stuck into his waistcoat armholes. Then he would lean back, laughing out loud, all shaking with laughter. I have never seen a man laugh like Lenin did. Evil people do not laugh like this. Lenin was a kind person. He seemed to me just like one of the comrades. I thought, such a man could not be bloodthirsty, and he wasn't; he made sure the October Revolution was bloodless.

When that moment arrived, Podvoiskii arranged for the employees of the Winter Palace to give servants' uniforms to one hundred sailors. They crept into the palace through a back door and convinced some of the White Guards to give up fighting against the Bolsheviks. I was outside the palace waiting, and when the sailors opened the gates, I ran up the carpeted stairway. In the very first room I saw cadets standing with their rifles ready. I shouted, "Put down your weapons or you'll get it!" When they saw a big crowd of soldiers behind me, they dropped their rifles and raised their hands. One of them said: "We were told that you are going to shoot us." I said, "No one will shoot you. We will let you go free, if you promise not to raise arms against the Soviet power." Then all the soldiers left, and only the government members remained. They were all arrested without any violence and released, even the worst enemies of the people. So in this way, Lenin was able to accomplish a revolution that turned the whole world upside down.

Pacifism versus preparedness: "No member of my family," insisted Grandma, "will fight a war in Europe!"

I was at a boys' camp in 1914 when war was declared. It was sensational news — the newspapers had huge headlines: "Germany declares war." "Germany marches into Belgium." "German atrocities reported in Belgium." "Russia comes in." These headlines stretched all the way across the front page, they were the biggest ones I had seen in my lifetime. It was a shock to a very peaceful world, but nobody took it too seriously and nobody believed it would last very long. Certainly nobody dreamed that the United States would someday be in the war. From the point of view of a schoolboy, it was just something to read in the papers and be excited about.

I come from a family of pacifists. My mother and father were active in the movement, and my grandmother was a suffragette who was also bitterly against war in any form. Once war was declared in Europe she took part in all kinds of meetings, conventions, parades and demonstrations against the war. She even went on a peace mission to Stockholm with Henry Ford, who was a leading pacifist at that time. He assembled as many peace-minded people as he could lay his hands on and sailed to Europe on a steamer, and my grandmother was one of the first people to sign up as a passenger.

I remember seeing them off on their mission to ensure that the war was over before Christmas, and I suppose they thought that after that the world would calm down and then war would be banished in the Wilsonian way. Of course, a mission like that accomplished nothing — they went over there and they came back, and there were no results whatsoever. The war went on and on.

The people who were against the war were not too well organized. The theme song of the pacifists was "I Didn't Raise My Boy to Be a Soldier." Their demonstrations were on a much smaller scale than the preparedness demonstrations, because preparedness was gradually becoming the great theme of the day. There wasn't exactly an outright militaristic attitude that we've got to fight, it was more that we ought to be prepared for national safety. By 1916, my cousin and I — being red-blooded schoolboys — were all for preparedness. We were swept up in the excitement of it all, and we thoroughly believed that America should be militarily prepared. We went to meetings where little buttons were distributed and flags were passed out, and feelings of patriotism ran very high.

As time went on, the patriotic fever increased and there was terrific indignation about the atrocities being committed by the Germans. In the papers and the magazines, Germans were portrayed as the most despicable members of the human race, ferocious-looking in their spiked helmets with blood dripping from their mouths.

Above: Villard, in uniform. Top: Antiwar demonstrators in New York, February 1917.

—Henry Villard, who was born in New York City in 1900, was the youngest Red Cross ambulance driver in Italy during World War I. In 1918, he came down with jaundice and malaria and was hospitalized with fellow ambulance driver Ernest Hemingway. He went on to become a diplomat, serving as U.S. ambassador to Libya and Senegal. Villard wrote about his experience meeting Hemingway in his book Hemingway in Love and War. He died in 1996.

I remember the story of the Belgian children having their hands cut off, which was a favorite propaganda story at that time. There was terrific indignation about the kaiser, and the slogan "Hang the kaiser" was common everywhere. All of this was emotionally designed to stir up the blood, and the cumulative effect was that Americans were very satisfied when we entered the war in 1917.

There were posters everywhere: "I Want You," "Join the Air Force," "Join the Marines," "Join the Army." And there was an irresistible feeling that one should do something. Most of us students were susceptible to a Wilsonian doctrine that promoted the idea of making the world safe for democracy. We shared in Wilson's idealism, and we believed him when he said that this would be "the war to end all wars," the last great war. This had a strong appeal, and it certainly influenced me a great deal. I said to myself, "If there's never going to be another war, this is the only opportunity to see it." I was at an age where it seemed that going to a romantic foreign country where I would be saving human lives — not fighting, but saving lives — was a noble thing to do. Everybody talked about what we should do for the war effort. Perhaps it's hard to imagine that with today's view of war.

I was studying at Harvard when the Red Cross sent a recruiting officer there seeking thirty men to go to Italy as ambulance drivers. There was a regular stampede to join, and I couldn't just stand by and watch all of my friends depart. I wanted to join them. The selection process was rigorous. You had to have a physical exam, you had to prove you could drive a car, but the most difficult part for me was that you had to have the written consent of your parents. At first my father was inclined to think that my patriotism should be recognized. But my grandmother exerted her influence and said this would be the last thing in the world she would tolerate, to see a member of her family go to war in Europe. So, in order to gain the consent of my family I persuaded them to come up to Cambridge and listen to my arguments.

My parents took the midnight train up from New York to Boston, and we had it out. My main argument was that this was a humanitarian mission. It was not a mission to stick a bayonet into somebody and kill them, but to save people's lives. And that was the argument that finally won them over. The next thing was to convince my grandmother. "No member of my family will fight a war in Europe," she said. But she ended up approving and giving her blessing to my going. In retrospect, this was probably one of the most important decisions I made in my life.

The first person that I put into my ambulance was a man who had just had a grenade explode in his hands. Both his legs had broken off, so he was a legless creature. I put him in the ambulance, as he moaned and groaned, and I took him from the front lines to the hospital. He kept calling out to me to drive slower, and by the time I reached the hospital, he was dead. Well this was a kind of cold water treatment for me, to realize all of the sudden what war was like. There wasn't time to try to think about it and adjust. I eventually became immune to it because as an ambulance driver, I saw everything. And it changed me — I grew up very quickly. This was no longer freshman studies. It was the real world.

Vladimir Ilyich Lenin, 1870–1924

ernment, which hoped that his presence might work to further destabilize the Russians and force them out of the war. Yet he traveled in a sealed boxcar ("a plague bacillus," Winston Churchill would later write, directed across Europe into the veins of the Russian nation), and the members of his party were not allowed to speak to even a single German, lest they draw too much attention to the deal that had a Russian revolutionary traveling at the aid of the kaiser.

Delivered to Sweden, the exile and his colleagues hopped sleighs to cross into Finland, then boarded trains for the final leg to Petrograd, where he was greeted by a crowd of admirers and a band playing the "Marseillaise." Most in the audience were surprised at the radical nature of reform advocated by Lenin and his closest advisers. But they cheered when he declared himself in favor of an end to Russian participation in the war, in the reestablishment of food supplies, and in land for the peasants. The people lifted him onto their shoulders and carried him to an armored car reserved for the occasion, and as they did, the other cars dimmed their lights to bring out the brightness of their new savior's. He had been an obscure intellectual haunting Swiss cafés only days before, but Vladimir Ilyich Lenin, it turned out, knew how to turn a revolutionary situation into a revolution.

By summer, Lenin's message had dramatically increased membership in the Bolshevik Party (25,000 in February; 240,000 in July) and further eroded morale on the war front. The rank and file, made up almost exclusively of land-hungry peasants, responded to his pledge to parcel out the earth to those who worked it. More than a million men abandoned their stations and returned home rather than lose out to their neighbors. When it arrived, the October Revolution that installed Lenin to power was an anticlimax (so much so that the story had to be fictionalized by succeeding generations), a forty-eight-hour coup accomplished with a bare minimum of bloodshed.

Whatever it would eventually become, the revolution in its early years was infused with an idealism that inspired the downtrodden. Emboldened by Lenin, socialists in France, Germany, and England began to assert their opposition to the war, dreaming of the day when the conflict would end and the workers' revolution would spread across the continent; and the socialists, in turn, inspired radicals. In France, strikes at munitions plants were now accompanied by sabotage. Even pacifists and anarchists, silenced by the patriotic orgy of the war's early years, found the will to speak up, and their literature began arriving on the front, where it was avidly read by the disheartened troops.

Germany's own desperate scarcities soon forced its generals to consider a drastic military move on the high seas. Hoping to break the blockade of their ships and disturb the flow of goods to the Allies, they began to target American merchant vessels in the early months of 1917. Germany knew that it risked drawing the United States into the conflict by its actions, but decided that it was worth the gamble. It wasn't. After enduring several months of submarine attacks, and news of a telegram from the German foreign secretary in which he suggested a secret alliance with Mexico against America, the United States declared war on Germany.

The decision remained controversial. Since President Wilson asserted the country's neutrality three years before, Americans had continued to show little

The savage image on this U.S. Army recruitment poster would come back to haunt Americans. This same picture was used by Nazi propagandists to encourage anti-American sentiment during World War II.

In order to boost the ranks of a decidedly meager force, the United States instituted conscription on May 18, 1917. A mere eighteen months later, the army would be more than 4 million strong.

enthusiasm for going "over there." (One of the most popular songs of 1915 was "I Didn't Raise My Boy to Be a Soldier.") Wilson himself had long argued that America play a diplomatic, not a military role, that it act as a catalyst for a "negotiated peace," a "peace without victory" that would end the bloodshed without gain to either side. But neither Germany nor the Allies took up his offer. Instead, the killing went on and on, with the war sucking in nations and peoples from all parts of the globe. Almost immediately after the first shots rang out in 1914, Turkey had joined the side of the Central Powers, battling the British throughout the Ottoman Empire. That same year, Japan had seized German colonies in the Pacific (though it joined the war in only a limited capacity). By 1915, Bulgaria had signed on with Germany; Italy, which had earlier been neutral, switched to the Allies. In 1916, Romania became an Allied state; in 1917, Greece. Because the war involved many imperial powers, colonials had been enlisted in large numbers: the Senegalese fighting on the western front in French uniforms, the Indians on behalf of the British in Belgium. In battles that underscored the irrational nature of both war and imperialism, French and British colonials even pursued German colonials in wild chases throughout the deserts of Africa, surrogate against surrogate.

Still, there was no convincing the citizenry of the United States to join up without settling on some legitimate war aims, and President Wilson, who began referring to the war in religious terms as a war of redemption, even a crusade, came up with a compelling one: the future of democracy. People began to rally to a concept of a war to protect liberalism, to reject militarism, to champion national self-determination. If the battle across the Atlantic represented the outgrowth of a corrupt and barbarous civilization, the new credo now read, then America must fight to rescue the Continent from corruption and barbarism. Even some pacifists had to admit that a "war to end all wars" was, curiously, a goal they could appreciate even if the means to it remained abhorrent.

Despite their previous ambivalence, most Americans embraced the Allied cause. As an aid to financing the war effort, the government sold "Liberty bonds"

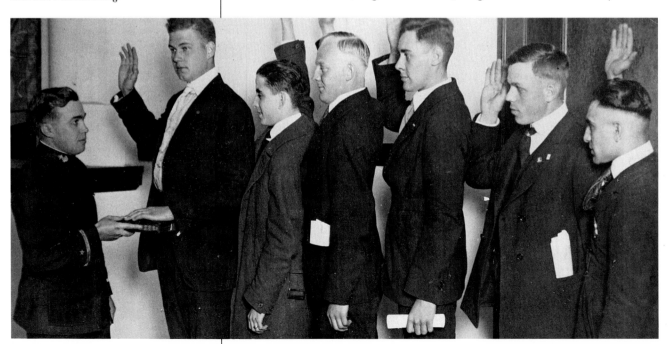

Doing one's bit on the home front: Victory gardens, Liberty bonds, and hatred for the dreaded Germans

When America entered the war, I was nine years old and completely caught up in the super-patriotism of the times. I even tried to read Wilson's declaration of war, which was hard reading, and though I couldn't finish it I was persuaded that he was absolutely right. It seemed to me that the United States had been patient and neutral for a long time, but that they had to get involved because the Germans were cruelly killing people and sinking our ships with their torpedoes. I felt that our soldiers going over were tremendously brave, but I didn't understand the awful things that happened to people until long after the war was over. To me it all seemed like a kind of glorious episode.

In Chicago, there were sharp divisions in people's beliefs about the war. Even in my own family there was a division, because my mother's side of the family was German. One of my uncles was very bitter toward Wilson and very pro-German, while my other uncles were for the Allies. When we used to gather at my aunt's and grandmother's on Sunday evening there would be frightful arguments. It was always the men who argued, not the women, and by the time we sat down for supper the men would be exhausted — totally spent from arguing.

This was a time of great bitterness towards the Germans. There was no feeling that the war was the result of long economic rivalries or anything of that sort. It was purely an evil thing, perpetrated solely by the kaiser. Since part of my family was German, we had been accustomed to speaking German around the house, but once the war began we stopped speaking it. We turned our backs on anything German — literature, music, history. In school I had been taking German-language classes but I went to the principal and asked him if I could be excused from attending them. I thought that that was the patriotic thing to do. He was very supportive and told me to go to the library during the hour of German class. I went to the library for a while, but after five or six weeks I was bored, so I returned, rather shamefaced.

A German name was a great liability during World War I. The Bismarck Hotel changed its name to the Randolph. The Kaiserhof Hotel became the Atlantic. Families changed their names. There was a boy in my class whose last name was Kirshberger, and his family changed it to Churchill. It seemed downright unpatriotic to keep a German name and very patriotic to change your name. People were fleeing anything Teutonic. In fact, anyone who was known to talk positively about Germany was thought to be a spy. We went to a resort one summer that consisted of just three cottages and an old frame hotel. There was an assistant Austrian counsel who was there, and I remember my mother saying there

Left: Despres holding a day's catch in Pentwater, Michigan, 1918, and right, with his sister Claire, 1917. Above: A group of boys from Cooperstown, New York, knitting warm clothes for American doughboys.

—Leon Despres, born in 1908, has remained in Chicago, where he worked as an attorney and served as an alderman. He was very active in the civil rights movement during the 1960s, joining Martin Luther King, Jr.'s 1963 March on Washington.

was no doubt that he was a German spy. Here was this poor civil servant, with his family in a place where he couldn't spy on anything but an ice house, but yet we felt he was very dangerous. It was a genuine spy scare, and of course to me as a child it seemed very exciting.

I was totally caught up in the righteousness of the war and I wanted to "do my bit," to use the phraseology of the time. I wanted to do everything I could, and it wasn't entirely unselfish because the only way you got any glory or recognition was doing your bit. I wrote letters to the soldiers, and I learned to knit scarves for them, though I never really caught on to it so I don't think my scarves amounted to anything. Liberty bond drives absorbed a great deal of my energy. I got bond subscriptions from friends of my parents, from anyone I could get hold of. I had a victory garden, and that was very exciting, though I don't think I ever grew anything more than radishes. We collected salvage for the Red

Cross; I was very conscientious in collecting and tying up newspapers, collecting as much metal as I could. They would give you coupons, which you would paste on a card, and when you filled the card, then you could put the card in your window. It was an exciting time, and everything we did — knitting, gardening, selling Liberty bonds, rolling bandages, walking in parades — we felt was part of winning the war.

It was a wonderful time to be a young boy. I remember going to see the war games on the lakefront in Chicago. It was a dark night, and there were no lights on, so all you could see were these soldiers advancing on both sides and tanks moving along. They had rifles and terribly loud explosions and flashes, and I thought it was glorious. That was my idea of war. It was totally sanitized but it made me feel that everything we were doing for that war was worthwhile. You know, it didn't occur to me that people were getting their faces blown off, that they were losing limbs, that they were being wounded forever, that young men were being killed. I was aware that young men died in the war, but to me it was kind of a beautiful sacrifice, sad but very beautiful.

Comfort for the dying: **Memories of a World War I nurse**

The day that the war was declared, my boyfriend went to enlist and the line was so long they couldn't receive everyone who showed up. I was just finishing nursing school in 1917, and our whole class enlisted with the Red Cross as soon as we graduated. We were sent down to New York where we marched in a parade wearing our nurse uniforms. Everyone waved their flags and applauded as we went by; there was so much enthusiasm for the war. I don't think we knew what we were getting ourselves into. We hadn't seen a war in so long that we had forgotten how terrible they can be. We had heard all kinds of stories but you don't believe everything you hear, especially the silly stuff about Germans cutting children's arms off. I wasn't scared at all. I didn't know enough to be scared.

We sailed across the Atlantic, which was a little scary because you never knew whether a submarine might attack, but we still had fun on board the ship. All those nurses, with all those wonderful soldiers on board and a live band for dancing, you can imagine what a good time we had! Some of the soldiers seemed very young, though, because they lied about their age to enlist, whereas we had to be twenty-five to be nurses. Crossing the English Channel was much scarier. We sailed at night so the submarines wouldn't see us. Some people were so afraid that they stayed up all night, fully dressed, but I had no trouble sleeping.

I got my first dose of the real war when they put me on duty in the amputation ward of a hospital in Paris. I had to help a doctor amputate a young man's leg. When the doctor cleaned off the leg, the flesh just quivered, I think because the boy was in such pain. It was very difficult to look at. That's when I learned what I was going to be up against. I think they put us there just to prepare us for what we would be doing on the front. And what made me so sad was that the boys in the ward were all so full of fun — happy and joking. I just cried all day. I told myself I was going to forget everything, and I deliberately closed my mind to a lot of things that even now I can't remember. I can still recall the sound of a leg being sawed off, though, and that's the one thing I wanted to forget.

They sent us out to our evacuation hospital, which was a group of tents about twenty miles from the front lines. Each tent held twenty cots, and the boys were sent down from the front in ambulances. We cleaned them up, dressed their wounds and let them sleep, but there wasn't too much we could do for them. They came in so dirty, with fleas and all, that some of them had to be deloused. Red Cross gave us wonderful flannel pajamas to dress them in, and they were just glad to be clean and out of those trenches. Sometimes they came in so many at a time that we had them lying on the ground outside

Above: Smith (right) with fellow nurse Marian Jones, Paris, 1918. Right: Smith's nurse corps with American soldiers at Dunkirk, shortly before returning home, 1919.

our tent because there wasn't room for them. Once, over a two- or three-week period, we passed four thousand patients through our evacuation hospital.

The horrible thing about dressing the wounds was this technique that we used, which I think was started in the Spanish-American War. When the soldiers lay wounded out in the battlefield, the flies would lay their eggs and leave behind these worms in the wound. Someone figured out that these worms worked around in the wound and cleaned it. This was a terrible thing to look at, but that was what they did to keep the wounds clean — certainly not something you would do today. I saw some other terrible things which I try to forget, like one man who had been shot in the face. He could still talk, and he could use his eyes, but his face and his mouth and his nose were hardly recognizable. One day he asked me, "Do I look bad?" And what can you say? I said, "Oh, no. The surgeon can fix you up when you get home." Later on, one of my nurse friends married a man whose face had a terrible scar on it, and I often wondered if he was the same one.

We tried not to attach ourselves to anyone, but my friend and I became so fond of one of the boys that was injured. He had a hole right in his forehead and he couldn't speak except for one word, which was "glass." One day, one of the nurses sang "Over There" to him, and he sang and sang, every word. For whatever reason, the music triggered something in his brain that allowed him, at that moment, to sing. My friend and I wanted to get him to talk again, so we kept him for two or three days, which was something we'd never done with any of the other patients. But we never got him to talk. He was so young, and he smiled all the time and didn't seem to be in any pain, but it was so sad to think that it was his

—Laura Smith, who was born in 1893, continued to work as a nurse in civilian hospitals in Massachusetts and Washington until she retired to marry and raise children in 1925. During World War II, she reentered the field of nursing, training Red Cross volunteers. She lives in Los Gatos, California.

brain that was affected in that way.

I didn't see many shellshock cases because they were handled by the main hospitals. But the man I was in love with then had it. I heard that his division was coming in on the train that day for R and R. So I arranged to meet him and when I got to the train, I saw him, but he didn't recognize me. There was certainly something wrong with him, and he had come down to rest because of it, but that was it — I never saw him again.

I was in Belgium in the countryside when the armistice was signed. When you're working near the front you hear the sound of the shells, night and day, just like thunder. So when November 11 came, it was completely quiet. It was so still you couldn't get used to the silence. No cows mooing, no birds singing — there were no cows left to moo anyway. A group of French musicians came and they played for us, which was nice, and it was the only celebrating we did because we still had a lot of patients and a lot of work to do. But it was strange to hear the silence after the guns had stopped.

I came home, and my father met me. But nobody else paid any attention. They didn't realize what we'd been through, I guess. I was never so lonesome in my life — I missed all the good friends I had made among the nurses. It took me a long while to get over it. I didn't want to see or take care of men anymore. I took baby cases and did maternity work. I married and had children, but my husband and I never talked about the war all through our married life and we never mentioned it to our children.

and raised nearly $17 billion. A wild, anti-German mood spread across the country. School districts banned the teaching of German, and teachers set out to instruct students in the differences between the tyranny of the German government and the justice of American democracy (conveniently leaving out any descriptions of the similarly undemocratic governments with which the United States had now associated itself). In an attempt to exorcise all German attachments, sauerkraut became "Liberty cabbage," dachshunds "Liberty pups," hamburger "Liberty steak."

Excesses were tolerated, even encouraged. A spy mania descended across the country focusing on anyone with a German last name. "German agents are everywhere," read one poster created by the federal government's new propaganda office. "Do not wait until you catch someone putting a bomb under a factory. Report the man who spreads pessimistic stories, divulges — or seeks — confidential military information, cries for peace, or belittles our efforts to win the war." The agency hired 75,000 "four-minute men" to deliver brief speeches of patriotism to theatergoers and encourage them to look for spies.

At a time when more than one-third of the American people had either been born abroad or had one parent born abroad, suspicion spread to anyone who held on to ethnic identity. Teddy Roosevelt led a campaign urging people to remove the "hyphens" from their names and become "100 percent American." Henry Ford instituted compulsory English-language courses for his foreign-born employees, even forcing them to "graduate" by participating in a pageant where they would dress in their national costume and march into a melting pot, then emerge in identical suits, happily waving American flags.

Repression was severe. A film producer was jailed for three years for depicting the American Revolution as including violence by British soldiers against Americans. Socialist leader Eugene Debs was sent to prison for speaking out against the war and against conscription (and ran for president from his cell in 1920, winning 1 million votes). The Post Office even refused to mail magazines and newspapers that didn't subscribe to the pro-war point of view.

Rested, well-fed, and confident, American troops march through London in August 1917, injecting new energy and enthusiasm into the war-weary Allied forces.

The United States was ill prepared for a major military conflict in 1917. The army had a grand total of 208,034 men (most of them national guardsmen); the "air force" was made up of about fifty-five dilapidated planes; and they had enough heavy guns and ammunition for only about a nine-hour bombardment. The draft soon brought many more men into the service, but most of them spent the better part of the year in training, marching with broomsticks over their shoulders instead of rifles.

Still, the specter of American participation in the war was almost more powerful a weapon than the reality. The fresh-faced, confident Yanks who started arriving in Paris toward the middle of 1917 were a

Mirroring scenes all over Europe at the beginning of the war, three years earlier, American civilians proudly bid their soldiers good-bye at a parade down New York's Fifth Avenue, 1917.

A black soldier goes to war for Wilson: **Fighting for "what we carry nearest our heart"**

Davis, in 1919, just after leaving the service.

When I was in my last year of high school down in Mississippi, I read this great speech coming from Woodrow Wilson, who was president at the time. I was so excited by it that I clipped it out of the newspaper and sat down and remembered it by heart. He said, "Gentlemen of Congress, I have called the Congress into extraordinary session, because there are very serious choices of policy to be made, and it is neither right, nor constitutionally permissible, that I should assume the responsibility of making them . . . It is a fearful thing for me to try to lead a great peaceful people into war. It could be one of the most terrible and disastrous of all wars. Because civilization itself could hang in the balance." But here is the thing I appreciated and got excited over. He then said, "Right is more precious than peace. We will fight for the things that we carry nearest our heart. For a universal dominion of rights, by a concert of free people, that is going to bring peace and happiness to all of this world."

That's what he said, "We will fight for the things that we carry nearest our heart." And I read that stuff, and went crazy over it. Don't you think that an African-American boy listening to that sort of speech would get excited? Wouldn't you, if you couldn't drink out of the same water fountain that white people drank out of? It excited me really, that's the truth. Oh, yeah, I said, that's the thing, a universal dominion of rights, where everybody is going to have the same rights. "A concert of free people." If you read that speech, you will find those words in there. And I thought I ought to get in there and help to bring about this universal dominion of rights, this concert of free people, because it sure wasn't free down where I was.

So that was one of the reasons I wanted to go off to war, but I also wanted to make some money so I could go to college. I thought maybe I could enlist and get a job with good pay, and then if I was lucky enough to survive, when the war was over I could support myself in school. So I went down and joined. But the question being debated at that time was whether or not they should really train black officers for the war that President Wilson had declared. There was quite a controversy about whether or not blacks should really go over there and whether they would be, I guess, accepted by the French. They only had about ten thousand African-Americans in the armies back in those days, but the number went up to about fifty thousand by the end of the war.

—Corneal Davis, who was born in 1900 in Vicksburg, Mississippi, was briefly a machine gunner and then served as a medic in the crucial battle of the Meuse Argonne offensive. After the armistice, he went home to Chicago (where his family had relocated), arriving on the day of the race riots of 1919. He served in the Illinois House of Representatives for thirty-six years and died in 1995.

I went over to France in a convoy that came out of Newport News, Virginia. It was a whole convoy of black soldiers, led by a black colonel who was highly educated and had all the military knowledge that we needed. We picked up more ships in New York City, an infantry outfit they called the Buffalo Soldiers. They had one of the great bands that became famous, even after the war was over. There were also a lot of Creoles out of New Orleans who could speak French. When our convoy landed in France, General Pershing was just landing there as well. From far away I could hear him hollering, "Lafayette, Lafayette, we are here!" I didn't know who Lafayette was! "Lafayette, Lafayette!" Now, I said, "What is he talking about Lafayette?" And someone said, "Lafayette, he came over in the Revolutionary War and helped us to retain our freedom." But because my history said five thousand or more black soldiers were with George Washington, I said to him, "Some other soldiers helped to get that freedom too."

I think we made a great hit with the French. I guess back home they thought the French were going to object to us, but we rounded up two or three French generals, and they gave us ammunition, and everything else they had. There were plenty of American marines who didn't want us to go into certain places in Paris — there was no "universal dominion of rights," so far as the marines were concerned, I can tell you. They used to say the nastiest things about us, telling the French women that we weren't even human. But the French people didn't feel that way. I don't know of anyplace where a black person couldn't go in France; if there was such a place I didn't know of it. And when the Buffalo Soldiers' band played in Paris, the French fought to hear them. They had a great song they used to sing, and the French women would go wild over it. It went something like:

Sweet little buttercup, fly little buttercup.
Dry your eyes of blue.
We will come back to you,
when this war is through.

Sing in your silver bells, or from the shouting shells,
Let your love light shine.
For God will guide you, watch beside you,
Sweet little buttercup of mine.

striking contrast to the war-weary people of France. They brought an enthusiasm to their task that the front hadn't seen since the war began. Parisians saw them as their last hope; they also saw them as attractively modern. For not only did Americans come from the New World, they arrived with the very radical intention of fighting for a set of ideas, and they were the same ideas that had recently come to be very appealing to the average European fighting man and his family: self-government, democracy, freedom.

Unfortunately, the war on the front remained brutal no matter what you were fighting for. American soldiers dove into the same trenches that had plagued the British and the French and suffered the same abuses. But at least the stalemate seemed ready to break. Lenin and his Bolsheviks remained true to their word. After murdering the commander in chief of the tsar's army — the last vestige of the Romanov era — they approached the Germans to negotiate an end to the war on the eastern front. The conversations were held at Brest-Litovsk, a Russian fortress about one hundred miles east of Warsaw (where, for appearances, the Russian entourage included a worker, a peasant, and a soldier), and when the deal was finished, Lenin had agreed to a humiliating peace, ceding control of Latvia, Lithuania, Poland, Finland, and the Ukraine.

Now it was a one-front war. But even with the Russians out of the way, Germany needed to move fast. Dwindling resources, unrest at home, and the vision of millions more American soldiers arriving on the front had put the kaiser in a desperate situation: he had to push for victory now or concede defeat. In March 1918, the Germans put on a last big offensive that brought them within fifty miles of Paris. It would not, it turned out, be big enough. In July, the Allies' renewed strength came through in the second battle of the Marne and sent the kaiser's army reeling into a final retreat.

American soldiers, derided by the Germans as a mongrelized army, had become an impressive fighting force in just a few months, and their eagerness for battle had proved infectious, inspiring the tired British and French armies to find new sources of energy. Once the technical problems they had exhibited earlier in the war were worked out, tanks proved to be a valuable Allied weapon, too, rolling over barbed wire, climbing parapets, and crossing ditches with an ease that made attacks on German entrenched forces now possible. That the Germans had elected not to pursue a motorized land force of their own was a major blunder. For at its end, World War I was a very modern war, fought across earth, sea, and sky, each with its own new machine: the tank, the submarine, and the airplane.

As they retreated, the German army continued to blaze a path of destruction, flooding French coal mines and cutting down telegraph and telephone poles. With all of the Central Powers teetering, there was a sense of chaos throughout Europe. Bulgaria fell first to the Allies; then Turkey. Polish and Czech soldiers broke off from the Austrian army to form rebel fighting units within the Allied forces. In October, the renegade Czechs declared their territory an independent state; eight days later, the Yugoslavs did the same thing. When Austrian and Hungarian units seceded from their own empire, the Hapsburgs found themselves leaders of little more than the hallways of their own castle.

Germany was next. They had rejected peace offerings from the Allies in January 1918, including Woodrow Wilson's declaration of the Fourteen Points,

Starving Berliners cut up a dead horse for food. By the middle of 1917, a demoralized German civilian population was beginning to break under the strains of war.

which, in addition to demanding that Germany cede occupied territory, underscored American democratic ideals. But now that they were losing the war, the German attitude had changed dramatically. After several diplomatic exchanges with the Allies, the Central Powers' high command visited Kaiser Wilhelm to recommend his abdication. Wilhelm refused. He was told that the number of German deserters was overwhelming and that the army simply couldn't carry on. He still refused. "What of their oath to the colors, to me as warlord?" the kaiser asked his generals. "Today," he was told, "oaths of loyalty have no substance." Even as he was convinced to sign the necessary documents and board a train to neutral Holland, the old monarch had not quite comprehended that his time had passed.

When the fighting stopped, the landscape, littered with so much death and wanton destruction, looked more like the victim of a natural disaster. And as with an earthquake, the seismic aftershocks continued long after the big event had ended. Some episodes, like the flood of refugees running rampant throughout Eastern Europe and the rash of revolutionary violence that engulfed the streets of Berlin, were directly related to the war; others, like the flu epidemic that struck in 1918 and over a few months killed more than twice the number that had died in all the fighting (including 550,000 in the United States and more than 6 million in India) felt more like God carrying out his punishment for the sins of the western front, or worse, like God joining in. When, in 1919, British astronomers proved Albert Einstein's theory of general relativity, making the German Jewish scientist world-famous overnight, the fate of the Almighty himself seemed in jeopardy, the notion of a singular order and grand design supplanted by an equation that, in the mind of one Boston bishop, "was cloaked in the ghastly apparition of atheism."

Though the celebrations of Armistice Day were as ebullient in New York as they were in Paris, Americans hadn't quite gotten the fighting spirit out of their blood yet. They searched for a new victim upon which to vent their rage and found one in communism. Labor organizers and socialists who dreamed that once the fighting ended people would return to the spirit of reform were disappointed. Instead, management sought to roll back some of the few advantages that labor had achieved in the wartime economy.

Fear of a worldwide workers' revolution following upon the success of Lenin's forces in Russia joined with the lingering wartime campaigns against foreigners to produce the century's first Red Scare. A handful of prominent labor organizers were rounded up and deported to Russia. Led by Attorney General A. Mitchell Palmer, federal agents arrested six thousand alleged communists, coercing confessions out of some of them in a manner so offensive it would eventually turn public opinion against the government.

The attempts to repress labor only seemed to increase its militancy. Strikes by workers in Seattle, New York, and Pittsburgh and by the police in Boston dominated the 1919 headlines. Some of labor's behavior seemed to confirm the fears of right-wing extremists, as when longshoremen boldly refused to send arms to groups fighting the Bolsheviks in Russia (among them five thousand U.S. sailors, soldiers, and railway engineers who had arrived in 1918 as part of a vain Allied attempt to hold off the Reds and keep Russia in the war) or when a few

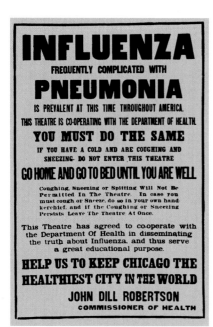

The "Spanish flu" (so dubbed after 8 million Spaniards fell ill in May and June of 1918) brought fear and death worldwide. The sign above appeared in a Chicago theater, 1919.

The 1919 Red Scare: **When every labor activist was labeled a Bolshevik**

When I was growing up my father worked at the U.S. Steel Mill in Gary, Indiana. You had to work 10- and 14-hour days of dirty, hard, manual labor at that mill. Wages were very poor, but if you asked for more pay the superintendent would say, "If you're not satisfied, you know where the gate is." There was no scheduling system of any kind, so you had no guarantee of work. You had to show up seven days a week just to get two or three days at a job. They used what they called the "bullpen" to line up people who had shown up to work. The coke plant was full of chemical fumes, and around the open hearths they had a lot of flue dust. They didn't have the sanitary conditions that you have now. My father worked on the train cars that would dump the cinder from the mill into Lake Michigan, which would light up the whole sky at night.

Gary was a company town, with company housing and a local government that was in the vest pocket of U.S. Steel. They elected the mayor, they appointed the chief of police, and they had full control of the police force. If you wanted a job in a mill, you would say you were a Republican, but then you'd better vote that way, for if you didn't you'd get in trouble. They had a way of checking up on all the voters. The mayor of Gary was a staunch Republican, very anti-labor, anti-union, and if you talked about being a union man, you were branded immediately. They didn't call you a Commie in those days; you were a Bolshevik, and you were given a hard time.

Gary was a town composed of a lot of ethnic groups. There were people from Poland, Greece, Czechoslovakia, Hungary, Italy, Germany, Sweden, and Romania. Most of them were not citizens in those days, and there was no pressure to become one either. The company was happier if you were not a citizen, because then you didn't participate in elections. But a lot of these immigrants were people who were oppressed in Europe. They left the old country and came here, chiefly on their own, with no one to fall back on. They were tough people, and they were determined to build a union. I sense that the company knew this and knew that they had to take pretty drastic action to keep them down.

In 1919, the workers got organized enough to strike for better working conditions and wages. The town was 100 percent union by this time, so the company actually had to import people from Mexico and blacks from the South to help to break the strike. They were recruited chiefly to keep the furnaces stoked with tires so that black smoke would come out of the stacks and it would look like they were producing steel in

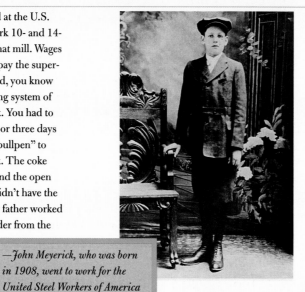

—*John Meyerick, who was born in 1908, went to work for the United Steel Workers of America in 1936, negotiating contracts for workers. During World War II, he performed a similar service for the War Labor Board. He has lived in Gary, Indiana, almost all of his life.*

Meyerick, when he was eleven, in 1919, the year the U.S. Steel Mill workers went on strike in Gary, Indiana.

there. But they weren't. These strikers were a tough breed, and the company knew that they had to get tough with them and scare the daylights out of them. And I have to give the company credit; they did. They were rough. The company men came out and started calling everyone on the picket line a Bolshevik. And that's when the strikers started getting pretty hot. Tempers started flaring because a lot of those people were very religious people and they didn't like being smeared like that. The police started getting rougher and rougher, and the company started recruiting more security guards to roam the town. That brought on a little violence in town, and that's when they started picking up the strikers and locking them up in jail.

The jail filled up, and the army came in and built a stockade made of chicken wire to lock up the strikers and make spectacles of them. If you tried to get near the factory gates, they threw you in the stockade. If you stood around on Main Street talking with a few other men you were thrown in there, too, because that was considered meeting or plotting. The army kept the strikers in there day and night, a couple of hundred at a time. I used to go look at them, but I had to be careful because if they caught you hanging around the stockade they'd throw you in there. I didn't like what I saw, behind that chicken wire — it's a scene I'll remember my whole life. Some of the strikers were beat up, and some of them were crying, heartbroken because they thought they'd be

deported. That stockade really scared some of them.

They were calling the people in there Bolsheviks, too. The company stooges would call out, "Look at those Bolsheviks in there." "Look at that one," and so on. They never said Commie, but "Bolshevik, Bolshevik, Bolshevik." That seemed to be the key word that they used to break the strike, because it made people feel like they were going to be deported or that their citizenship would be denied. I was a child then so I didn't really understand why this was having such an effect on people. But it did, and a lot of them started going back to work.

At first the local businesses were helping out the strikers — donating food and other goods to the soup kitchen that the organizers had set up as kind of a headquarters for the strike. But pretty soon the weather got colder and all the local businesspeople couldn't keep on giving credit, so they started urging people to go back to work. The churches even got involved, telling people they risked getting deported, and that scared the daylights out of the strikers. They had to feed their families so a lot of them had to give up. That's when the strikers started to riot. They would stop the streetcar at the railroad crossing and start harassing the people on their way to work. Even some of us kids got involved, throwing rocks at the streetcars, but we got in trouble with the organizers for that. "You're going to get killed," they told us, so we stopped doing that. But the violence got worse day by day. The strikers kept stopping the streetcars, but the militia was so powerful, the strikers couldn't compete. They were getting roughed up pretty badly.

My father was just as scared as the rest of them. He was on the picket lines and helping out in whatever way he could, but he was starting to worry, too. What was going to happen? He had come over from Europe — would he be deported? Would we have to move again, to look for a new job? It took a lot of courage back then to go on strike. There were no laws to back you up. As a kid, I didn't really appreciate the risks he was taking, not until I got older and started thinking about what those strikers went through to get a union. You have to give a lot of credit to those people in 1919.

The strike was broken, eventually, and everyone had to go back to work. And the union was broken as well — totally defeated. No meetings, no activity, nothing. And the Red-baiting continued for a long, long time. Even when we started forming a union twelve years later it was still going on. That strike really divided our town for many years. Some were mad at each other, telling people they gave up too quick. Others turned against the union. And pretty soon they started calling each other Bolsheviks too, which was exactly what the company wanted all along.

*Flowers poured from the windows and band music filled
the air as Parisians jammed the streets to greet President
Woodrow Wilson when he arrived in France to attend the
international peace conference.*

extremists of the American Socialist Party split with the group and went underground to begin the work of revolution.

Labor riots were only part of America's new domestic unrest. Twenty-eight episodes of racial violence erupted in 1919, including riots in Washington, D.C., and Omaha, Nebraska. In the worst uprising of the year, a group of white swimmers stoned a black swimmer to death for drifting into their section of a Chicago beach, sending blacks and immigrant whites to the streets for a brawl that lasted five days and left thirty-eight people dead. The incident had kindled rising tensions over housing and employment in that city, with many whites disturbed by the continuing migration of blacks from the South, and blacks outraged at being let go from jobs they had occupied while white workers were fighting abroad.

The fact that Chicago's rioters, black and white, were led by many veterans who had recently returned from the war in Europe served to emphasize a primary theme of the time: people who had fought for democracy and justice abroad were angry to have to come back to the United States and scramble for the same rights at home. They had, after all, fought not for the safety of their own land — as the French farmers did — but for a set of abstract principles like world democracy and the right of small nations to self-determination. Coming home, they discovered that such notions, noble though they might be, had little to do with better pay, more security, lower taxes, or fair treatment before the law.

When most of Wilson's Fourteen Points were whittled down in the peace treaty negotiations at Versailles (not even the victorious Allied nations would agree to the American president's demands for "freedom of the seas," an end to all trade barriers, and the self-determination of colonial states), many Americans felt they had been had. Wilson was a popular hero on the streets of Paris, but back home, the nation that had been so reluctant to go to war now blamed him for the disappointing peace that followed it. In an accurate demonstration of the national mood, the U.S. Senate refused to endorse the treaty, dooming to failure the one provision the president held most dear, the establishment of a League of Nations dedicated to resolving international conflicts peacefully. Americans had tried the life of the international policeman and found that they preferred to leave such work to others. By the 1930s, a poll would show that more than 70 percent concurred that it was "a mistake for the United States to enter the last war."

Exactly five years — to the day — after Gavrilo Princip shot the archduke, the treaty ending the First World War was signed. For the Germans, it was an oddly humiliating defeat. They were not, for instance, even allowed to participate in the formulation of the terms of surrender. And when they were finally handed the 230-page document detailing the conditions providing for the war's end, they discovered it to be unrelentingly punishing. Most noteworthy were the demands that Germany accept all guilt for the war and that it compensate the Allies for all costs incurred over the course of battle, from damage to farmland to war pensions due to be paid to veteran servicemen. Far from representing the end of hostilities, the treaty seemed to be continuing them, only by other means.

The French attitude was perhaps the harshest, since more than a million and a half Frenchmen had perished in battles fought mostly within their borders. But a punitive disposition was dominant among the Allies, in part because their populations at home would settle for nothing less. By contrast, the German pop-

*Germany's soldiers had the look
of a defeated army, which they were.
During the five years of the war,
1.8 million German men died on
the battlefields — nearly one out of
every six who served.*

> *"The King and Queen deeply
> regret the loss you and the
> army have sustained by the
> death of [your son] in the
> service of his country. Their
> majesties truly sympathise
> with you in your sorrow."*
>
> *Telegram sent to families
> of the British war dead*

ulation was stunned. Since the armistice had been signed before there had been an Allied invasion of Germany's borders, the people did not consider their army to have been defeated; instead, they insisted angrily that their leaders had only caved in to pressure. Upon hearing the terms offered to them by the Allies, the people formed mass protests in the streets. There was even talk of starting the war again.

The four-man German delegation at Versailles submitted a 443-page retort (nearly twice the size of the agreement itself) but won little sympathy from their enemies. Then, with slightly more than an hour remaining before their time limit expired, they gave in and signed. The bitterness would linger. And what should have been the closing chapter of a terrible saga would, in the end, become the beginning of another, as the German people sought ways to avenge their fate over the next two decades and, sadly, found them. Historians in search of the roots of the century's next big conflagration discover that all paths return here.

Still, there was, incredibly, some good that arose from the carnage of Europe. The war toppled cruel dynasties in Austria, Germany, and Russia; and it encouraged the downfall of the Ottoman Empire. In place of these tyrannies came at least a few legitimate republics. Many of the new states adopted democratic constitutions on the American model, complete with bills of rights.

The war helped to democratize society as well. The days of the aristocracy were over. A new egalitarian spirit spread across the Continent. Women were given new rights, and in Britain and the United States, these included the right to vote. Social distinctions lessened and the privileges of the elite were taken away. But, ironically, at the same time that individuals took more of a part in determining their own destinies, they also took less. In its unending death toll, the war had also introduced the notion of mass experience to modern culture, leaving more and more people with the feeling that they were not individuals at all, but tiny parts of a big, multiheaded organism. Never before had so many been affected so profoundly by the same event at the same time. Even contemporary sensibilities accustomed to the electronic byplay of the global village are challenged to contemplate the degree to which savagery, grief, and despair became universal during World War I.

Try, for instance, to imagine the torrent of sorrow that descended upon the wives, mothers, and children of British villages in late 1916 as telegrams arrived announcing the death of thousands of their young men in the Somme valley; now envision the scene in German towns at the same moment. And in the Bombay homes of British colonials who fought at the Somme. Add to that the grief of French families who lost soldiers at Verdun (since it was being fought at the same time), the kin of the Germans who were fighting them, and of the Moroccans marching side by side with the French. To anyone who was touched by the slaughters of 1916, it must have felt like the entire population of the world was grieving. And in a way it was.

The collective experience of the home front only mirrored the new collective nature of war itself. Deprived of close combat, soldiers no longer aimed at individual soldiers when they fired their weapons; they fired instead at "them," a vague sort of enemy that was much easier to dismiss because it *was* so vague, so devoid of human shape. The "camaraderie" of war now took a new, macabre twist: because machine guns and explosives killed huge numbers at once, thousands regularly shared not just the experience of battle, but the exact moment of death as well.

Despite its fascination with the ideals of self-determination and class consciousness, postwar Europe was a cynical place. How could it not be? Men returning from the front coped with missing limbs, chronic infection, and haunting images of the horrors they had witnessed, even as many of them, like deranged addicts, privately lusted for one more chance at battle. Women mounted framed pictures of their dearly departed husbands and sons, repeating an almost biblical phrase to themselves — "He died so we might be free" — partly to keep the memories of their men alive, partly to convince themselves that there was still reason left in the world. Stonemasons started carving the names of thousands into memorials for the dead, lists so long they were not yet completed when the century's next big war erupted twenty years later. The historians moved in to do their work; so did the accountants. The Carnegie Endowment for International Peace announced in 1920 that the war had cost a total of $337,980,579,560, a figure they arrived at by, among other things, calculating the value of each life lost according to his productive capacity. The robust American economy made a Yankee worth $4,720; a Russian brought barely half that.

Europe was done, at least for a while. American business produced more than all the European economies combined, and it would be a long time before the factories of the German and English working classes could afford to retool and compete. *Old* Europe — the continent of kings and queens and of the almighty birthright — was done forever, the excitement now residing with two systems, democracy and socialism, both of which preached the virtues of centering power away from a privileged elite. The world war had been just that: a war that destroyed a *world*. The challenge to the survivors was to construct something better in its place.

**"This is not Peace.
This is an Armistice for twenty years."**

Marshal Foch, reacting to Versailles

A Canadian transport struggles through the rubble of the French countryside, August 1918. After years of incessant artillery barrages and senseless killing, Europe lay in ruins.

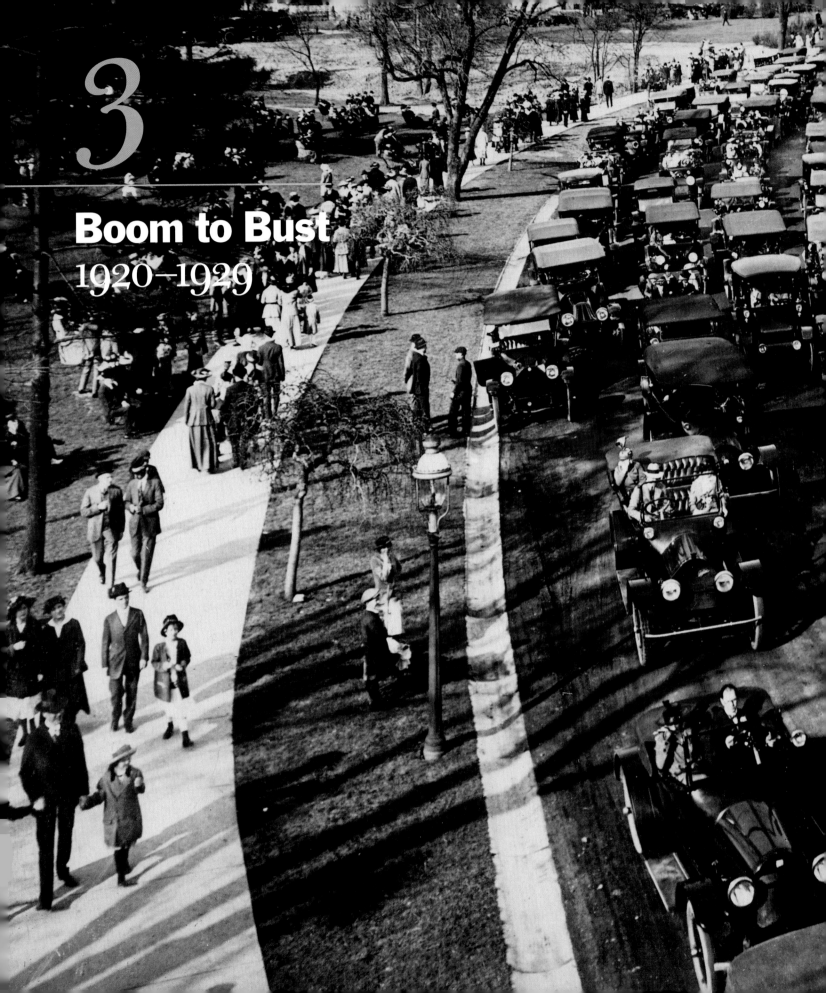

3

Boom to Bust
1920–1929

Boom to Bust 1920–1929

The crowd that assembled at the First Congregational Church in Washington, D.C., shortly before midnight on January 16, 1920, was filled with anticipation of a new era. Summoned by the imminent arrival of Prohibition, at the stroke of twelve, thousands of people had gathered there, and at other churches and town halls around America, to usher out the sinful past and greet the arrival of "a new nation." One by one, various speakers made their way to the pulpit, decrying the awful demon rum which, with God's help, had been "put to rest." And as they did, the wide-eyed audience dreamed of the world that would now emerge, a place where prisons would be turned into factories and slums would be nothing more than a memory. "Men will walk upright now," preacher Billy Sunday declared before a similar congregation in Virginia. "Women will smile and children will laugh. Hell will be forever for rent."

In the Washington audience that cold January night was the beaming Senator Morris Sheppard of Texas, author of the constitutional amendment establishing America as a "dry" nation. Sheppard listened with the rest of them as Navy Secretary Josephus Daniels described their purpose as the greatest reform movement in the history of the world, and he cheered when William Jennings Bryan, the evening's featured speaker, rose at midnight to pronounce that "they are dead which sought the young child's life." But a new morality, as the senator soon discovered, was easier to declare than to maintain. Only a few months later, a moonshine still, operated by renegade Texans and churning out more than 130 gallons of alcohol a day to thirsty constituents, was discovered buried in a thicket on the outer reaches of Sheppard's Austin ranch.

The 1920s were an era of painful contradictions. Still reeling from the Great War and the worldwide wave of disillusionment that it inspired; both dazzled and bewildered by their sudden access to such technological wonders as radio, movies, the automobile, and the airplane; torn between the traditional life of simple rural virtue and the exciting jazz age that beckoned to them from the streets of cities (a lure of sexual experimentation and freedom from responsibility), people attempted to make sense of their lives.

> *"Of all the nostalgic longing for the past that man had experienced since theology first taught him to look back toward Eden, hardly any was greater than the homesickness with which much of the world in 1920 looked back toward the world of 1914 . . . of all the speeches [Warren Harding] made in his [1920 presidential campaign] the one phrase for which he was most applauded was 'back to normalcy.' "*
>
> *Mark Sullivan*, Our Times

It was as if they had returned from the war to discover themselves living on a different planet, one made more by the hand of man than the hand of God, a world of neon and skyscrapers, of new mass-produced products hawked through new mass-audience media, and of new mores challenging Victorian notions of the proper and the civilized. The twenties were the decade when modern society was established, when the vast and complicated urban culture that reigned throughout the rest of the century had its beginnings. And those who lived through this time of transformation watched more things change more rapidly than have changed in all the years since.

No institution was spared turmoil. The church — and attitudes toward religion — changed. Whose faith, after all, could survive knowledge of the senseless deaths of ten million in Europe? Business changed, employing the techniques of modern advertising more effectively and encouraging a rush to the altar of materialism. Entertainment changed, led by the arrival of the first talkies, the first modern celebrities (among them, Babe Ruth and Rudolph Valentino), and the first tabloid newspapers, filled with gossipy tidbits to further inflate celebrity legends. Sex roles changed, with many women, newly enfranchised, displaying a new zestful spirit of independence. Even courtship changed, with cheap Ford cars now available to spirit young couples free from the disapproving eyes of chaperons. In the eagerness to keep up, people started buying household goods on credit and stocks on margin and at times seemed to care more about owning a car, and the license that it provided to the new age, than about feeding their families.

Europe, too, underwent a metamorphosis, entering into a period of social and political turmoil that would not be resolved until the 1930s, and then frighteningly so. But the spirit of this decade belonged decidedly to people of America — America and its pop culture, America and its production-crazy businesses, America and its thirst for the "new." For many people, there was an uneasy giddiness to it all, exemplified by the fast-rhythm jazz music blaring out of every city café and nightclub, a "pinch me, I must be dreaming" mood, and a sense that even if they couldn't understand their emerging world, even if they weren't sure they believed in it, they weren't going to be kept from partaking of its pleasures. For these people, the perfect metaphor for the 1920s was Prohibition and the tolerance for flagrant lawbreaking that it roused. In the twenties, all laws (*and* principles, *and* conventions, *and* traditions) seemed to be up for grabs.

But for others, especially the white citizens of small-town America, the developments of this turbulent time were a call to arms. Convinced that the world had lost its moral compass, they insisted upon righting the course. Many of them had been shut out of the era's prosperity (farming, for instance, slipped into a deep recession in the early twenties that lasted throughout the decade and well into the next), but, more important, they didn't share the era's values. Their vision of the future didn't include materialism, new technologies, or the overt expression of personal freedoms. Instead, they dreamed of a world built on a reestablishment of old-fashioned bedrock values, a fundamentalist creed, and a homogeneous culture. The clash between the forces of old and new, country and city, puritan and hedonist, would animate life for the better part of a dynamic decade.

Henry Ford, 1863–1947

**"I am careful and I am thrifty.
At least I was until I became a motorist."**

William Ashdown,
Confessions of an Automobilist *(1925)*

The construction of new roads could not keep pace with the popularity of the automobile. Few rural roads were paved, making intercity travel difficult at best. Here, a motorist in Adams County, Ohio, ponders his predicament.

Automobiles had been around a long time. Henry Ford had built his first one in 1893, and his first Model T was completed in 1908. In 1920, there were already 8 million horseless carriages sputtering and rattling around the poorly charted "roads" of the American countryside, most of them Tin Lizzies purchased for the unbelievably low price of $300. But it was in the succeeding years of this decade that the mass rush to the automobile began to have its impact. By 1929, more than one-half of all American families had a car; by 1930, there were more cars on the streets of New York City than there were on the continent of Europe.

The change was sudden and dramatic, and how could it not be? The automobile was, after all, the first significant improvement in self-guided transportation since the bicycle (which, after its introduction in Scotland in 1839, had a similarly dramatic effect upon the nineteenth century). And by the time it became widely available to anyone with a few hundred dollars, the car had already begun to redefine nearly every facet of life.

The burgeoning automobile age established a new sense of freedom and individuality: people no longer had to make their plans according to train schedules, and they traveled not with hundreds of strangers, but by themselves or with family and friends. At the same time, it also established a new, wider sense of community: small towns and villages that existed miles away from anyplace else were now connected to each other by roads, granting people who had long lived in isolation the opportunity to enjoy up-to-date medical care, higher-quality education, and whatever else lay "down the road."

Thanks to the car, thousands of new suburban communities flourished, providing people with the luxury of homes surrounded by green grass even if they now had to commute to their jobs in the big cities. And the car allowed Americans to make their first major forays into tourism, forcing a country of "regions" to meld together and break down differences that once sharply divided not just North from South or East from West but one town from the next as well.

The very landscape of the industrialized world took on a new shape to accommodate the car. Spurred on by demanding automobile owners, road building became one of the prime activities of government (in America, the second highest public expenditure after education). And with each new mile of road, it seemed, came something else new: the first "mo-tel" (San Luis Obispo, California, 1925), the first set of traffic lights (New York City, 1922), the first shopping center (Kansas City, 1924), the first national road atlas (Rand McNally, 1924), and the first public parking garage (Detroit, 1929).

With the gradual improvements in the nation's highway network, "auto camping" became a rage during the 1920s. Here, two families enjoy an afternoon picnicking on the banks of the Stewart River in Minnesota, 1922.

A 1920s joy ride: **Tourist courts, gravel roads, and (plenty of) breakdowns**

In the days before the car and the radio, we found ways to amuse ourselves. I always loved to read and that was a very important source of entertainment, particularly in the winter. In the summer the Chautauqua lecture programs were an important part of our life. That was our entertainment. When I was a young child, we would often walk to the Chautauqua programs. And I can remember many, many times I'd fall asleep during the entertainment and my grandmother would carry me back home, which was almost a mile.

Then, when I was quite young, my aunt bought her first car. And that was a big event. It was a Studebaker. No, a Dodge. Her first car was a two-toned brown Dodge. The salesman gave her the driving lessons. And I got to ride along in the back seat, which was a big thrill for me because I learned as much as she did. I watched all the things he told her to do. And that was how I learned to drive. At that time we didn't have to have a driver's license so I really did quite a bit of driving by the time I was thirteen. And got along fine.

Then in the summer we were able to get out and really have some good trips. My cousin was living in Huntington, Indiana, which was forty miles from us in Gary, so it wasn't too much of a problem to get over there. We could drive to Fort Wayne. And then very soon after she got the car we started really taking some fine trips. We saw all of the Indiana state parks, for instance, in the first year or two. It was such fun driving!

My aunt liked to stop before it was dark. So by four o'clock or so we'd start watching for a tourist court or a tourist home. No bed and breakfasts in that day, but many people would rent rooms in their homes to tourists. And they'd have a sign in the yard advertising tourist rooms. Usually about a dollar a night. There were many tourists courts available, too. They featured separate little cabins. Sometimes they'd be fancy and shaped like an octagon and other times they might be like an Indian tepee with anywhere from eight to twenty separate units spread out around it. And they would rent for maybe two or three dollars a night.

The roads were sometimes surprisingly good. From Warsaw to Fort Wayne we'd drive on Highway 30, which was a cement road. Of course, it was narrower than it is now and just two lanes. If you had a breakdown — and there were plenty of breakdowns — you'd hope you'd find a gas station soon. But even if you couldn't, there were always plenty of people glad to help you. When I started teaching in Ohio, I had a little Studebaker coupe that I'd bought for two hundred and eighty five dollars, and I think every truck driver between Warsaw and Ohio knew to watch out for me. You didn't hesitate to ask for help. If I had a breakdown

—Betty Broyles, who was born in 1919, attended Ball State University and then taught home economics to high school students. She retired from teaching in 1983 and remains in Gary, Indiana.

Broyles in 1928, prior to her car trip to New York.

I'd pull off the road and wait for the next truck driver to come by and know that I'd receive help. There was no concern as far as being robbed or mugged. You felt very safe.

In the late twenties, my father was stationed at Charleston, South Carolina, in the Navy. So we decided that the three of us, my aunt and grandmother and I, would go down and visit him. That involved, of course, going from Indiana to South Carolina. And we took several days to do it. I can remember driving into the area of the Smoky Mountains, on a gravel road from Gatlinburg into the Smokies. A gravel road! But we made it fine to Charleston. He was quite upset because we hadn't telephoned him along the way. "Where were you?" he said. "I was so worried about you." But we were fine. And on that same trip, after we left Charleston, we drove to Washington, D.C. And at that time I remember my aunt became ill as we were approaching Washington, D.C. So I took over the wheel. Why, I wouldn't attempt that now for anything. But we got where we

were going and drove on to New York City.

New York was frightening. I think my father was very worried about this, what three women were doing driving to New York City. But if there was the slightest doubt about the road we would stop and ask and get directions. I remember going through the Holland tunnel. I never had been in such a large tunnel before. And to go under a river, it just seemed incredible. And the lights impressed me so. I can remember being so thrilled by those. We had a wonderful time in New York City. We stayed with a relative who was a house mother for a musical sorority. And their headquarters was right at Central Park West. She knew places to go in New York City. We went to Central Park and she took us down to watch the sailing of a ship, the *Europa*. We got to go on board the ship and see all the tourists getting ready to leave for Europe that night. We enjoyed New York, stayed a few days, and then drove home, stopping at our little tourist courts along the way.

People who drove cars to work in the 1920s often spent their days working on some type of business related to cars. The automobile industry dominated the American economy, with one out of every eight workers employed in automobile-related jobs (including the petroleum, rubber, and steel industries). It was also one of the prime forces driving the stock market to record heights, and it revolutionized work conditions (both for better and for worse). The automobile business led the way to the five-day, forty-hour workweek and other forms of what became known as welfare capitalism, even as it institutionalized a demoralizing form of routinized assembly work.

But the joy of the automobile wasn't the job or the motel or the parking garage. It was the car itself, and the places that it could take you. Whether you were going from a small town to a bigger one or from a big town to a city, cars were, literally and figuratively, vehicles of escape. Farm people who had never been farther than the village general store could now go to a nickelodeon up the road and peek in on the glamorous world of the movies. The city dweller could opt for a reverse commute and spend a sleepy Sunday afternoon communing with nature. If you owned a car in the 1920s, the world seemed, quite abruptly, limitless.

The car was so attractive it even altered how people thought about money. For years, while people still thought of the automobile as a utilitarian vehicle, the inexpensive Model T commanded a clear lead in automobile sales. But as leisure and comfort became an increasingly popular preoccupation for the consumers of the mid-1920s, people saw more of what they wanted in the glamorous and expensive cars being produced by Alfred P. Sloan's General Motors.

The change marked a shift in consumer thinking. The Ford car had represented its creator's dream: a simple, durable machine that country people could use to get around and, more important, that they could afford (the Model T engine had been designed so that the owner could use it to run farm equipment when it wasn't propelling a car).

GM, in contrast, was interested in a different kind of consumer, a very modern consumer, one inspired not by practicality, but by speed, comfort, and styling. The company produced cars in different colors (the "T" had always been an unalterable black) and challenged customers to keep up with the times by changing models each year. While Ford stood steadfastly by his Model T, GM added new features to its cars: hydraulic brakes, chromium plating, six cylinders, and a lacquer finish. And the company convinced people to pay GM's higher prices by offering something that Ford considered immoral: the opportunity to purchase cars on installment.

A crowd gathers at the opening of a Gulf station in Louisville, Kentucky, 1925. Each oil company developed its own distinctive gas station architecture and company logo. The Texaco star and the Mobil flying horse are two of the more enduring emblems of the 1920s; Gulf stations were distinguished by a setback, towered entrance.

Tinkering with the wireless: **"Can anyone hear me west of Steubenville?"**

—Albert Sindlinger was born in 1907 in Tuscuras, Ohio. He graduated from Ohio University in 1928 with a degree in electrical engineering. During his long career in communications, he has managed movie theaters, distributed newsreels, conducted Gallup research polls, and invented a device to measure audience ratings which was widely used in the 1940s. He runs his own research company, which was founded in 1946 in Wallingford, Pennsylvania.

Above: Sindlinger (right) with his brother, Walter, and dog, Tippy, outside their house in Ohio. Right: Announcers at KDKA in Pittsburgh report the results of the Harding-Cox presidential election in the first official radio broadcast on November 2, 1920.

When I was about seven years old, in 1913, my uncle gave me a couple of books for Christmas. One was *The Boy's Life of Edison,* which I read three times on that day alone, and the other was a book by Marconi on how to build a wireless. To this day, I have both in my library. I was fascinated by Edison's life; inspired by it. And the Marconi book prompted me to build my first radio, which utilized a Ford motor. At that time, the Model T was the Ford car. And if you took the spark system out of an old Model T, you could build a wireless spark transmitter. I had a cousin about five miles away and we used to talk to each other by the spark radio.

A few years later, I read about the invention of the vacuum tube and discovered someone in Marion, Ohio, who had one he wanted to sell. I think the price was fifty-three dollars, which was a lot of money. But I had a newspaper route and had saved up. And so in the summer of 1920, my uncle drove me to Marion. I think it took us five hours to make the forty miles because there weren't any paved roads then. It happened that Warren Harding, the presidential candidate, was passing through Marion (his hometown) that day in a train

heading for New York. So I got to meet him and Herbert Hoover, who was fascinated by my vacuum tube. The next day we drove back home. We had to wait overnight because car lights weren't powerful enough for true darkness then.

About four or five days after I had gotten the vacuum tube hooked up, I started to hear music coming across the wires. Music! And then, between the music, I could hear somebody talking. It took me five or six evenings to put together what was being said, but I finally determined that it was "I am Dr. Conrad. I am experimenting with radio station 8XK. If anybody can hear me beyond Steubenville, Ohio, to the west please call me long-distance." And he gave his telephone number.

Now, there were only three telephones in our system. My father, as school superintendent, had one, the mayor had another, and the minister had the third. But none of us had ever called long-distance. So I ran across the street and knocked on the door of our local telephone operator and told her that I wanted to make a call to Pittsburgh, which was about a hundred miles away. It took her about forty-five minutes to go through the

manual and figure out how to make the long-distance call. But when we finally got through, I don't know who was more excited, Conrad or me. His signal was getting out a hundred miles! For the next three weeks, he would go on the air, and I would go on the telephone, and tell him whether the signal was better or worse.

Soon I got a letter from him, and he said that on the night of the presidential election of 1920, he was going to broadcast the election returns in what would be the first official radio broadcast and he wanted me to come celebrate the moment with him at the station. He did not have a call letter at that time, but this was the station that would soon be known as KDKA, the first radio station in the country. My family went to Pittsburgh with me and when he met my father, Conrad thought he was the guy he had been speaking to these many months, not some thirteen-year-old kid!

The transmitting station was at the top of a tall building and I went in and took an elevator to the top. It was my first elevator ride and I was impressed that there were so many elevators in the building. Then I found out that this was known as the K Building of the Westinghouse Company, where they tested elevators. So it was a building of elevators. And on the top floor, they had built this little shack, which was about twelve feet by sixteen feet. There were two men in there doing the transmitting and I was fascinated by their equipment. They had two microphones. One was held with rubber bands in front of a Quaker Oats box that had been propped in front of the speaker of a Victrola. This was the mike they used to transmit music. And then the other microphone was used for voice.

That night, one of the gentlemen in the shack was on the phone. And he was being read election returns from the *Pittsburgh Post Gazette* which he would then broadcast over the airwaves to the hundred or so people who had the equipment to hear us. But this was Prohibition time and so the man doing the talking was also busy sipping out of a flask he had in his pocket. Before long, he was too drunk to continue and decided to go out and get some fresh air. As he did, he handed the mike to me and for the next forty-five minutes, I read the 1920 presidential election returns to the nation.

Now by January of 1921, I had decided to build my own broadcast station. I built a hundred-watter and then applied for an experimental broadcast license. In March I got a letter saying: "One of my first official duties as Secretary of Commerce is to award you this license. Aren't you that young fellow I met back on the railroad platform in Marion, Ohio, with that vacuum tube? What's a fourteen-year-old kid going to do with a broadcast station? Signed, Herbert Hoover."

The poor had long been buying all manner of material goods on credit, but installment buying was a foreign and somewhat shameful concept to the great middle class. Houses were bought with borrowed money, but since real estate was considered to be a solid investment, few people thought of a home loan as true indebtedness.

An automobile loan, on the other hand, was real debt. From the moment that a car was purchased, it began to depreciate, and financing plans put many people in the position of mortgaging their futures for an automobile ride today. Still, the ebullient mood of the 1920s didn't allow for much patience. There were so many new things to experience, and the mantra running through the minds of many consumers was to "enjoy it now." Dazzled by steel and tires, people marched lockstep into an era of buy now, pay later. In 1927, more than three-quarters of American automobiles were purchased on time; a year later, even Ford had succumbed to the pressure, begrudgingly offering loan arrangements on the new, slightly less utilitarian Model A.

Once the threshold had been passed with cars, people felt free to purchase just about anything else on credit, too. By the end of the 1920s, more than 60 percent of all sewing machines, washing machines, vacuum cleaners, refrigerators, and furniture sales were made on purchase plans. And a full one-third of all money spent on furniture went to purchase the decade's other major plaything: radios.

Amateurs had been fooling around with makeshift radio sets since the early years of the century. In dusty attics, cow barns, and toolsheds, tinkerers (mostly young) sat with headphones strapped on, and tapped into the miracle of

the airwaves (or the "ether," as they commonly called it, a term that only added to the sense of magic). Wires were wrapped around baseball bats and Quaker Oats boxes to form receivers; transmitters were made from tinfoil, glass, and wire; and "speakers" were fashioned from newspapers rolled into cone shapes — all for the considerable excitement of picking up signals from far-off places, an event so special that it was sometimes reported in the local paper.

As early as 1911 instructions for building a radio receiver were listed in the manual of the Boy Scouts of America, underscoring the quality of boyhood adventure attached to radio experimentation, particularly when it involved tapping into signals from navy stations. During World War I, all nonmilitary radio broadcasters were ordered to suspend their use of the airwaves to allow for clearer communications. But even when civilian radio operation resumed in 1919, most people still thought of broadcasting (actually a farming term, meaning "the act or process of scattering seeds") as little more than an eccentric hobby.

*Reflecting a more genteel tradition of perfor-
mance, announcers and musicians, such as
these at the Nicollet Hotel Studio of WCCO,
Minneapolis, dressed formally, often wearing
tuxedos, even though they could not be seen by
radio audiences.*

With the licensing of the first stations in the early 1920s (Pittsburgh's KDKA officially began in November 1920), that all changed. Now there was something besides "Hello, out there!" to hear between the static, even if families still had to build their own receivers and listen, often, by tilting their ears toward a communal headset placed between them in something like an empty cereal bowl.

Suddenly, it seemed, every business, school, and public utility went on the air. In New Lebanon, Ohio, the Nushawg Poultry Farm had its own station; in Clarksburg, West Virginia, Roberts Hardware Store had one; the Detroit police ran their news over the appropriately titled KOP. "Programming" was primitive: a station announcement, a weather report, and a few strands of usually live music, but it *was* programming nonetheless, prompting at least a few people to dream of what the new medium might mean to the future of the country.

Commerce Secretary Herbert Hoover, himself an engineer, a profession held in high regard in this techno-crazy decade, saw radio as "an instrument of beauty and learning"; a Schenectady station manager mused that "the power to say something loud enough to be heard by thousands" would "give rise to the

desire to say something worthwhile." And *Scientific American* saw an age when we would raise children with radio mothers, "crooning songs and telling bedtime stories." But for now, it was the mere novelty that most excited people, the sheer thrill that came with watching a few wires and tubes light up and pluck a voice out of the open sky. Radio was to the air as the automobile was to the earth, an agent of transport to a world as wide open as the imagination.

In 1922, the medium really took off. At the outset of the year, there were 28 stations; at the end, 570, and hundreds of companies manufacturing stylish new sets with names like the Grebe, the Aeriola, and the Radiola. With all stations operating on just two frequencies, an on-air chaos ensued, and the traffic jam prevented listeners from enjoying a

As the popularity of the medium grew, radio design progressed from simple knobs and switches mounted on a breadboard to fancy mahogany sets that functioned as the centerpiece of the family living room. By 1926, one out every six American homes had a radio.

favorite pastime: hearing broadcasts from far away. After a public outcry, many stations began a practice of observing a weekly "Silent Night," in which they would go off the air, allowing, as one broadcaster described it, a man in San Francisco to say, "Last night, on my crystal set, I listened to the hoot owls up in Portland."

By mid-decade, the number of frequencies had expanded to allow clearer broadcasting, and two networks, NBC and CBS, had emerged to provide desperately needed programming (*The Maxwell House Hour, The General Motors Family Party, The Ipana* [toothpaste] *Troubadours*). But the issue of regulation hovered over radio like an evil stepparent. Some people argued for government control of the airwaves, as was imposed in Britain. Radio, they contended, was potentially too important to be left to the whims of business. But others eventually prevailed with their view that regulation would be a gross and unwarranted departure from American traditions of free speech and free enterprise.

An even more vigorous debate was pursued over the topic of commercial advertising. Hoover claimed that it would kill radio by diverting it from loftier goals, and how many listeners, after all, would stay by their sets to learn the advantages of one soap over another? Arguing that the industry should adopt a self-policing policy regarding advertising, he pronounced his worry that a presidential speech could be used "as the meat in a sandwich of patent medicine advertisements." But the broadcasters were too busy salivating over the possibilities advertising afforded for new revenues to worry about appropriateness. In 1926, an NBC variety show was interrupted for regular promotional announcements from Dodge cars and encountered little audience objection. From then on, advertiser-supported programming became the norm.

Early sponsors worried that people would be offended by their sales pitches and chose tasteful and discreet language (Announcer: "This morning, Mr. William Johns of Swift and Company has some practical suggestions for reducing your meat bill . . ."). But that quickly changed once they discovered that the consumer-crazy citizens of the 1920s were eager to embrace advertising on radio, just as they were embracing it every place else.

Up until the 1920s, most advertisements had appeared in newspapers and read more like announcements, providing the simplest information about a product ("P&G Naphtha Soap: The White Naphtha Soap in the Blue Wrapper"). But as people entered the new age, a new form of advertising urged them on. Whether it appeared on air, in one of the many flashy new national magazines now crowding the newsstand, or on billboards being propped up on country roads, the commercial message of the day operated as a kind of gospel proclaiming the new rules of modernity. With dramatic flair, it told people what new things they needed and what new habits they must now undertake (among them, daily teeth brushing, the use of an underarm deodorant and a mouthwash), lest they risk living only half a life or, worse, deny themselves admission to the "future."

The new ads featured drawings of people, rather than the products themselves, and they often appealed to the underlying emotional character of the consumer instead of attempting to persuade him or her to buy a product through cold hard facts. Sex was a selling tool; so was fear (it was more than mere coinci-

"A man in Pittsburgh said it was snowing there . . . Somebody sang in New York . . . a banjo plunked in Chicago . . . it was sleeting in Atlanta."

Sportscaster Red Barber, describing the first time he heard radio, 1924

dence that one of the decade's leading advertising men, Edward L. Bernays, learned his techniques at the knee of his more famous uncle, Sigmund Freud). Palmolive soap was sold as a way of achieving "that schoolgirl complexion"; Jordan automobiles were the route to a ride that crossed "the wild and the tame"; and Listerine took direct aim at the consumer's inferiority complex by portraying, in what may well be the most famous advertisement of the time, an old woman reminiscing about the love of her life who had run out on her years ago because she suffered from "halitosis." Listerine's slogan was "Suspect yourself first!"

Far from being insulted by these ads or any others, people actually *wanted* to hear their messages, if only to keep up with the latest technologies, the hippest fads, and the most modern ideas on behavior. The abuses were enormous. If you believed the advertising copy of the 1920s, you would have concluded that bathing in Linit laundry starch would make you beautiful; that eating candy could make you thin; that opting for the "tasteless bargain bread" over the fluffier Wonder brand might cause a husband to stray; and that constipation could be "cured" by twisting the body back and forth in a spectacular writhing motion.

Still, it is not hard to see why people of the time swallowed at least some of the more preposterous claims, particularly when an advertiser was clever enough to match his message with the image of a scientist in a white jacket, fresh from the laboratory. After all, people had just been dazzled by science in ways that would have seemed impossible only a generation before, and the news they heard had put them into a mood of perpetual awe that made a newspaper column like Robert Ripley's "Believe It or Not!" — celebrating the amazing and the bizarre — a mainstay in the popular press.

Not only advertising but advertising men gained prominence throughout the 1920s, often promoting themselves as heroic figures: swift, youthful, optimistic, and with rare powers of vision allowing them clearer sight of "what is to come." They saw themselves not as manipulators, but as facilitators, easing the transition to the new; as the most benevolent of revolutionaries, helping to show the great masses how the advancements of science could be integrated into their lives.

To help people adjust, advertisements in the 1920s regularly combined the excitement of the future with the certainty of the past. Factory-produced goods were glorified for their traditional craftsmanship; canned foods were "as good as homemade." In a book called *The Man Nobody Knows*, advertising man Bruce Barton claimed that the "founder of modern business" was none other than Jesus of Nazareth, and he referred to the stars as "the first and greatest electric sign," allying the glow of the heavens with the neon of New York City's newly buzzing Great White Way. Silly though such ideas may seem today, it was all in the interest of helping people to see the new as familiar, as not abandoning the past, but building upon it.

Of course, advertisers were also doing much more than that. They were helping to establish a whole new way of living: urban and feverish, driven by technology and dependent upon credit, encouraging the expression of personal freedoms and adhering to a belief in the infallibility of the machine.

Not only the car and the radio but dozens of other new machines came into

"Reason why" selling strategies, which gave readers specific (often bogus) incentives to use a product, helped change the face of advertising in the 1920s. This ad appeared in the Saturday Evening Post, *June 30, 1928.*

Bruce Barton, 1886–1967

Bromodosis *(odor caused by foot perspiration)*

Homotosis *(lack of nice furniture)*

Acidosis *(upset stomach)*

Sneaker Smell

Accelerator Toe

Office Hips

Vacation Knees

Ashtray Breath

Coalitosis *(use of coal, instead of oil, heat)*

Underarm Offense

*New "diseases" brought to you
by 1920s advertising*

*A salesman demonstrates the wonders of
a Hoover vacuum in the showroom of
Louisville Gas and Electric. Along with
modern appliances and machines, the
1920s gave birth to the "supersalesman,"
men who, as writer Sinclair Lewis sarcastically observed, were dedicated to "the
cosmic purpose of Selling — not of selling
anything in particular, for or to anybody
in particular, but pure Selling."*

common use in the 1920s, and some machines, particularly the new household machines, dramatically changed the lives of American women. Electric irons began appearing shortly after the war, and by the end of the decade, the old-fashioned flat iron was hardly in use. Electric washing machines did away with washing by hand; refrigerators began to put the iceman out of business; gas stoves replaced stoves heated by coal or wood. Central heating was now the norm; so, too, were indoor bathrooms (leading, in part, to the 1920s preoccupation with hygiene).

The house was a new environment, one less susceptible to the whims of nature, and the housewife's life was, just as suddenly, a less burdensome one: no more building fires and hauling water, no more slaving over a wood stove or washboard. The housewife as laborer gave way to the housewife as domesticator, beautifier, feminizer. And since so much of what she now did required her to enter into the marketplace and buy products — *many* products — advertisers seized the opportunity to help redefine her role for her. Washing the clothes was not a chore, but an act of love — why would a devoted wife let her husband go to work with graying shirts? A well-scrubbed bathroom wasn't just convenient; it was the way to protect the family from disease. Well-prepared food was a way of ensuring that the family felt close, and who doesn't want that? Even if their lives now involved less muscle work, many women, pressed onward by guilt, spent as many hours cleaning house and doing baby care as they had before.

For some — particularly the more affluent — the new domesticity included a fresh understanding of marriage. The nineteenth-century model that had hus-

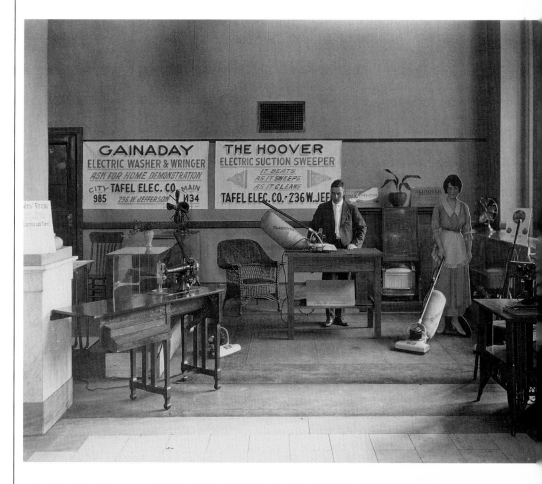

Twenties women: **New jobs, new fashions, new morals**

Since money was scarce in my family, it was very important for me to start working as soon as I could. And I was very fortunate to get a job with a publishing company, which I liked a great deal. After about one week in the business world I was absolutely in love with the corporate structure. But it was hard for women to get ahead, and we weren't encouraged to do very much. After two years with the company I was promoted and became a correspondent in the distribution department. But I was told, "When you correspond, be sure you don't sign your letters 'Lillian Hall.' You must write 'L. M. Hall,' because we do not want the news dealers to know that they are dealing with a woman." This didn't really bother me, because I was so thrilled that they were letting me do it; I was the only woman doing something at that level. Of course there were two men doing my same job, and they were making $35 a week to my $22.50 a week. But after that promotion, I was so excited, I thought, "Oh boy, I can just see myself becoming circulation director here." So I asked my boss what I should do. And he said, "Why, Miss Hall, you can't be a circulation director, you're a woman. The best thing for you to do is to train yourself so that you can be a good secretary." I was terribly disappointed.

> *—Lillian Hall Gerdau was born in 1913 in Brooklyn. She married in 1941 and continued to do secretarial work until she retired at the age of eighty.*

I remember one day my mother and I went to the barber. And I sat on the chair in the corner while she had things done to her. When she was finished, she was totally unrecognizable. Instead of wispy hair in a bun, she had short hair that swung out when she walked. This is a woman who was born in the old country where from the time they're born they have long hair. I always thought of her as a miserable old lady and suddenly she wasn't anymore — she was a young woman with swinging hair. And the smile that lit up her face! Suddenly she saw herself as a girl. I couldn't have been more than six years old at the time but even I sensed this. And that evening when my father came home and saw what she had done, he was speechless with rage and shock. "You????" he said. "It's all right for those other women, but you???". . . He got used to it. And my mother never let her hair grow long again.

> *—Clara Hancox was born in 1918 in the Bronx. Her parents came to America from the Ukraine during World War I.*

Policewomen confront four female bathers for disobeying an edict banning abbreviated attire at Balboa Beach, California, 1922.

After the First World War, things loosened up a bit between women and men. Most of us still went on proper dates, and all of that, but a lot of people went beyond that. I remember once when we were in England we got a long-distance call from some friends who wanted to tell us they were getting married. Now, it was very difficult to get a call through from America to England in those days, but they were just so excited to tell us. We pretended to be thrilled, but since they had been living together for two years, we just thought all of that excitement was kind of unnecessary. I remember a cartoon in the *New Yorker* around that time — it was a picture of a man and girl in bed, and she was shaking him and saying, "Wake up, you fool, we're getting married today." That wouldn't be funny now, but it certainly was then. I remember the first time my mother ever voted. It was when Al Smith was running against Herbert Hoover. As it turned out, my father voted for one of them and my mother voted for the other. My father said to her, "Don't you realize that you are simply canceling out my vote?" Mother knew it, of course, but that didn't stop her.

> *—Emily Hahn, born in 1905, was the first woman to graduate from the University of Wisconsin with a degree in engineering. She has been a correspondent for the* New Yorker *magazine since 1926.*

My mother was not very contemporary. She was very rigid and so my older sister and I were brought up according to very strict lines of deportment. We were not to flirt with anyone or wear too much makeup. We were to dress modestly, and we were never to be seen anywhere that ladies did not belong, which was just about everywhere. Having babies was never mentioned. I would just hear that someone was, well, *that way*. "She's *that way*, you know." And of course birth control was never mentioned. But my sister defied all of that. She was a flapper. She worked at the phone company, and she wore beautiful short dresses, fur coats, coach-style hats that covered up her head like a turban, and — of course — the galoshes, always unbuckled. That's where the term "flapper" came from because these things flapped, flapped, flapped. The day my sister came home with bobbed hair, my mother took one look at her and retired to the couch with her "aromatics" — her smelling salts that kept her from fainting. When my sister decided she wanted her own apartment, you can imagine how my mother reacted. She refused to let her move out until she was married, so my sister lived at home until she was forty-one years old!

—*Florence Arnold, born in 1918, grew up in Chicago. After marrying and raising three children, she went back to school and received a degree from Ball State University in 1973.*

When I was growing up, my family was very supportive and I felt like I could have any career I wanted. But in reality for women during that time, there weren't a lot of choices. You could go to nursing school, secretarial school, or teachers college and that was about it. My grandmother was a teacher, and so were my mother and my two aunts, and that's what I ended up doing as well. In those days, jobs were so scarce that it was frowned upon for a wife to work if her husband had a job. One breadwinner per family — that was it. I almost couldn't get work in the school system because of my aunts. And if I was married and my husband had a job, the school system would never have hired me. The husband was supposed to support the wife, and that was that.

—*Betty Broyles, born in 1919, retired from teaching in 1983 and lives in Gary, Indiana.*

band and wife existing in separate spheres, linked primarily by economic dependence, was now in a slow fade. In its place came the 1920s "companionate marriage," which put a higher value on maintaining the relationship between man and woman. Love — not children, not work — would be the glue uniting the family. Husbands and wives would socialize together, play sports together, and engage in conversation.

As with so much else in this era, the new marriage took its lead from the opinion of "experts." Colleges started including courses on "modern marriage" as a separate and different practice from that of the past, one informed now by sociological research. And "self-help" books began to appear, where, more often than not, women were advised that the success of the marital union was dependent upon their "rewinning" their husbands through charm and physical attractiveness. The air of uncertainty that had gathered around marriage — both modern *and* traditional — was borne out in one of the decade's more unfortunate statistics. By the late twenties, there was one divorce for every six marriages (up from one in seventeen in 1890), and two-thirds of those were initiated by the wife.

Encouraged by the growing tolerance for experimentation, some women in the twenties — particularly young women — felt free to venture beyond the home and enjoy forbidden pleasures. Many teenage girls drank, smoked cigarettes, dressed in suggestive clothing, engaged in premarital sex, and affected an air of sophistication. With their short, closely cropped hair and flattened breasts, these "flappers" (the name referred to the sound made by the unbuckled galoshes they wore) projected an androgynous look that insulted traditional notions of femininity. By spending too much of their time flirting, they also outraged feminists. But the thing that offended — and intrigued — people most about these new women was the carefree attitude they attached to sex.

Perhaps it was the open, free feeling of a ride in an automobile or the sense of despair that consumed so many people after the war; the desire to make a break with the Victorianism of the past or the growing anonymity of life as it became more centered in cities and away from the small towns; but sex, it seemed, was on everyone's mind in the 1920s. Not only advertising but books, movies, and plays were filled with sex (even as theaters were sometimes closed for showing indecent fare and the Post Office Department maintained a list of five hundred forbidden titles). So, too, was conversation. Though his seminal work had been completed long before the twenties (and in Vienna), Sigmund Freud and his theories of sexuality were a twenties rage. "Freudian" — the word — had only recently been added to Webster's dictionary, and the language of psychoanalysis — terms like "id," "superego," and "Oedipus complex" — was now entering into common use. If most Americans had oversimplified his groundbreaking studies to suggest that sexual repression was the root of neurosis (and they did), it was only a further demonstration of the decade's search for a license for hedonism.

The twenties even invented a new term, "sex appeal," describing what every woman hoped to achieve by going to the neighborhood beauty parlor. In 1922, New York City had 750 such shops, catering mostly to the very rich; by 1927, there were 3,500, offering permanents and manicures to eager salesgirls on

Women share a cigarette in the recently inaugurated woman's smoking compartment of a Pennsylvania passenger train. The men's smoker featured leather upholstery; the women's version was appointed with wicker furniture and a vanity mirror.

the way to Saturday night dates. Calorie counting became a national obsession; daily weigh-ins on the bathroom scale (yet another twenties discovery), a necessity. Only the twenties could have produced Margaret Gorman, crowned the first Miss America in 1921 from a field of eight, when the title was awarded without benefit of a "talent" competition. Within a few years, the pageant had become an American institution.

But sex in this time was more than posing and flirting. Thanks in part to the proliferation of birth control, middle-class people seem to have actually engaged in more of it — marital or otherwise — and become adjusted, though sometimes hesitantly, to the thought that sex could be enjoyed as sex, separate

> *"[The institution of marriage] is drafty, it's leaky, the roof sags, the timbers shake, there's no modern plumbing, no hard wood floors, no steam heat. We don't feel comfortable in it. We've outgrown the edifice . . ."*
>
> 1920s novelist Fannie Hurst

from any procreative aspect. When, in 1916, Margaret Sanger was arrested for disseminating information on birth control (it was she who coined the term) at her clinic in Brooklyn, New York, she was in the midst of a campaign to convince Progressives that contraception was a way of helping to free poor women from the burdens of large families. By the mid-twenties, the focus had shifted. Condoms were available at barbershops, pharmacies, and gas station rest rooms, and Sanger was the author of *Happiness in Marriage,* a manual for achieving sexual satisfaction.

If there was one persistent attitude to match the excitement for the new in the 1920s, it was nostalgia for the old, for a time when truth seemed absolute and one's worldview was shared by one's neighbor. In America, this took the form of a yearning for the simple, agrarian image that had come to be identified with the country in the nineteenth century, for a time when the United States was a nation of farmers, largely white, largely Anglo-Saxon, and largely Protestant.

Like most nostalgia, it tended to idealize, to remember a perfect past that never was, but with so much changing so rapidly around them, traditionalists could afford to define their cause in terms of their opposition and they did so, vigorously. If the new world was go-go-go, the old was slow and steadfast; if the new had sprung forth from science, the old would claim religion. If the new was cosmopolitan, the old was homogeneous. Most citizens of the time were possessed of some sort of duality: they liked much of what the new world was bringing them, but they also missed having some things the way they had been. For others, it was nothing short of war.

At the beginning of the decade, most people thought of the Ku Klux Klan as an embarrassing footnote to nineteenth-century American history. Yet, in fact, a new Klan had been founded in the years preceding World War I, and by 1921, it claimed more than a million members (4 million by 1924), spread out across both the North and the South. The new Klan was dedicated not only to harassing African-Americans but to a whole host of other causes as well.

The rural South and Midwest remained largely untouched by the economic boom enjoyed by urban America. For these potato planters in Princeton, Minnesota, the twenties had little to do with jazz, flappers, mah-jongg, and the speakeasy.

Although increasingly rare, lynchings, such as this one at the courthouse square in Lawrenceville, Georgia, continued throughout the 1920s despite legislative efforts to end the barbaric practice.

Expanding upon nativist feelings that had already been aroused throughout the early years of the century, the Klan now encouraged the hatred of Asians in California, of Mexicans in Texas, of Jews in New York, of Catholics in the Deep South, and, in general, of any of the many Mediterranean peoples who had settled in American cities throughout the early part of the century. The Klan now spoke for many old-stock Protestants, who worried that the new immigrants might displace them in their jobs and their homes, for small shop owners, who feared that national chains would run them out of business, and for farmers, who had been left behind by the percolating industrial economy of the 1920s.

But most of all, the Klan was a way for many of those people who objected to the growing national culture to fight back. Frightened by the frenetic and godless life they felt to be moving center stage in the cities, they joined up not so much to wear white robes and participate in lynchings as to reestablish a shared moral community. And they looked to the Klan not only to drive out "foreigners" (whom they suspected had brought all this craziness here to begin with) but to restore an old-fashioned morality as well.

In small towns all over America, the Klan's moral police squad, known some places as the Horse Thief Detective Association, would come riding into town like a sheriff's posse, determined to drive out prostitution, gambling, and other "lawlessness." But in their quest to rid society of its ills, the Klan's police often resorted to punishments worse than the so-called crimes they were targeting. They patrolled the back roads looking for teenagers in amorous embrace and if they found any, threatened to flog them. In Texas, they beat at least one man because he had separated from his wife; another for annoying girls; and a third for speaking German.

Many people cheered them on and put Klan members in positions of greater power. By 1924, the organization had become so powerful it was a significant player in the state governments of at least a half dozen states (especially Indiana, which was known as "the sheeted Tammany"). The Klan was almost mainstream. Future Supreme Court justice Hugo Black became a member; future president Harry Truman nearly did: tempted by the political advantage it might provide him in conservative Missouri, Truman gave ten dollars dues to a Klan organizer until the Klansman then insisted that Truman (running for a position equivalent to county commissioner) would have to agree, if elected, to hire no Catholics. Truman took back his ten dollars.

One cause that united minister and Klansman was the Eighteenth Amendment. The movement to ban the sale and distribution of alcoholic beverages had once been led by Progressives, who cited growing studies showing the medical risks of heavy drinking and alcohol's destructive influence on marriage and the family. But by the time that Prohibition was enacted, its driving force was the puritan, who hoped it would beat back the forces loosening modern morals, and the nativist, who saw it as a way of rejecting the wine-drinking immigrants of southern Europe. Of course, it did neither.

If anything, Prohibition served to quicken the pace toward a freewheeling, lawless society. While it actually did curb drinking somewhat, it also encouraged crime on an unprecedented scale, and not just by promoting big-time bootleggers

BOOTLEGGERS, PIMPS, HANGERS-ON, GET RIGHT OR GET OUT

WIFE-BEATERS, FAMILY-DESERTERS, HOME-WRECKERS, WE HAVE NO ROOM FOR YOU

GO JOY RIDING WITH YOUR OWN WIFE

Signs at a Klan parade in Texarkana, Arkansas

"Them" against "us": **The revival of the Ku Klux Klan**

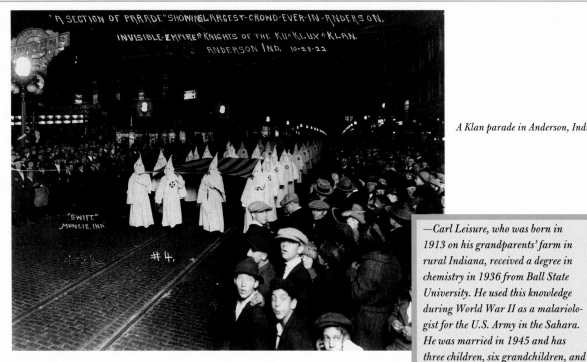

A Klan parade in Anderson, Indiana, 1922.

—*Carl Leisure, who was born in 1913 on his grandparents' farm in rural Indiana, received a degree in chemistry in 1936 from Ball State University. He used this knowledge during World War II as a malariologist for the U.S. Army in the Sahara. He was married in 1945 and has three children, six grandchildren, and one great-grandchild.*

A great many people think of the Klan as simply a hate organization and that it was. Hate is probably the easiest emotion to teach. It's very easy to be "us" against "them" and that, really, was a large part of what the Klan was about. My parents both belonged to the Klan and so did my sister and I. When I was old enough, I was made an officer in the Boys' Klan and the main thing I remember about that is that I had a beautiful blue satin cape to wear on top of my other uniform. That was what it meant to me.

But the Klan was also a natural outgrowth of the time, and movements like it were all over the world. We were changing from an agrarian society to a manufacturing society and the Klan was a reaction to it. People in Indiana had always been farming people. The land was there and that was your life. It was stable and renewable. But suddenly, in the twenties, the farming went sour and we changed over to a manufacturing existence. Unfortunately, the manufacturing plant wasn't as dependable as the earth. A factory would operate for twenty-four hours a day for three or four months at a time and then close, leaving everyone out of work. Jobs were precious. And while the Klan as I knew it was not a nice organization in many ways, a lot of the talk, when you were at home and with other Klan members, wasn't so much about hate as it was about how we had to stop the inroads of these outsiders into our jobs.

Anything that fought against the changing world was welcomed in these quarters and the Klan was certainly that even if it was trying to preserve a society that was no longer preservable. The Klan taught the sanctity of the home. They wanted prayer in school. They wanted you to follow the Bible as long as you didn't admit that any part of it was Jewish. The Klan was very patriotic. And you were never to have anything to do with drink or loose women, even though most Klansmen would wink at each other on these issues.

The parades and rallies were fun. Nothing is more gorgeous than a parade when you're a kid. My father had a truck at that time and I would stand on the hood of the truck, which was of course painted white. I'd be wearing my nice white uniform with the tall peaked hat and the mask thrown back. And I would sing up a storm. It was great fun singing hymns like "Onward Christian Soldiers."

They would have these lovely cross burnings, too, which were very much like big revival meetings where everyone shouts and gets religion. Everyone who was anyone showed up. Every businessman who was not Jewish belonged to the Klan, not necessarily because they believed in what the Klan said but because it was good business. Most ministers belonged to the Klan. Many teachers belonged to the Klan. In this state, we even had a governor who belonged to the Klan, who was later impeached.

The hatred was big. All new immigrants, regardless of where they came from, were bad. If they happened to be from England, that was pretty much acceptable. Some immigrants from Germany were acceptable. But Irish immigrants were more "them" than "us," because they tended to be Catholic and all Catholics, of course, were "them." Jews, of course, tried to control all the wealth. That was what the Klan claimed. Jews were international and anything international was suspect. And Negroes were unacceptable of course because it was a known fact that every black man's ideal was to rape a white woman. That was what the Klan taught. Even Chinese were a no-no, but we didn't have very many so we didn't hate them much. You can only hate what you have. We felt like we were just engulfed in a sea of people who were not us and had to fight back.

As a child, I was a "why" character. I was always asking questions. The Klan would wave the American flag, and tell you that you should hate people and I would always ask, "Why?" I knew a dozen black people, all of whom were fine, there was nothing wrong with them. I enjoyed them. You were supposed to hate Jews and our neighboring grocery man was a rabbi. I loved to go talk to him, because he was brilliant. You were bombarded constantly by misinformation. Listening to the Klan, I thought that if you looked carefully at an Italian of recent origin, you'd see a four-spiked tail and two horns.

Then it all collapsed. After some scandals, people lost the faith in it. When the power started to dissolve, the whole thing disintegrated. People became disillusioned, is all I can say. We suddenly realized that these people, whom we had built up to hero status, not only had feet of clay, they had legs of clay. And it was a good riddance.

and smugglers. Average citizens carried hip flasks, visited neighborhood speakeasies, and brewed their own booze by purchasing homemade stills for six dollars at the local hardware. For some, Prohibition had made alcohol even more enticing, by adding a flavor of criminality to even the most casual cocktail.

The amendment made lawmen into criminals and real criminals into folk heroes. Congressman Fiorello LaGuardia, New York City's future mayor, ridiculed the reformists by posing with a mug of near beer (a nonalcoholic beverage concocted by brewers throughout the dry era) mixed with an alcoholic malt tonic available at any drugstore. "Delicious," he declared. Chicago's mayor, William Hale "Big Bill the Builder" Thompson, announced with a smile that he was "as wet as the middle of the Atlantic Ocean." Meanwhile, many of the so-called enforcers were getting rich off bribes, and organized crime, in control of much of the illicit trade, was thriving.

Tales of the exploits of big-city mobsters like Al "Scarface" Capone, "Machine Gun" Jack McGurn, and George "Bugs" Moran filled the tabloids. Though his gang was credited with more than three hundred murders, Capone, and the other brutal mob figures, commanded more than a small measure of awe based not only on the power that they wielded but also on the image they projected of "getting away with it all." Capone's story seemed to suggest that you could bully, steal, and kill without ever having to pay for it. Indeed, in the automobile age, he drove around in what may have been the biggest prize —

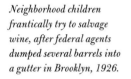

Neighborhood children frantically try to salvage wine, after federal agents dumped several barrels into a gutter in Brooklyn, 1926.

When a drink was a crime: "Some of the best customers we had were cops"

Patrons enjoying illegal brew at a local speakeasy.

My mother was Irish, from county Sligo, and for her making booze was a family tradition. In Ireland, everyone makes their own stuff. So when she got here to New York, she and my father bought some rooming houses, and when Prohibition hit, she just started making booze in the kitchen and selling it from the ground floor. She was a real businesswoman, my mother, and I guess I took after her. As a teenager, I was already driving around in a Nash convertible making deliveries and running four speakeasies.

The way it worked was we'd make some of our own stuff, and the rest we'd bring in from Scotland or Canada. Our speakeasies were just like a regular bar you'd see today except for the door with the peephole in it. We had to be careful who we let in and we knew our customers on a first-name basis — they were like family. If a stranger were to come in and he turned out to be a government agent and you sold him anything, you'd be finished. The minute you asked him for the money, he'd pull out the badge and pow! They would put a big lock on your door and close your joint down.

We had to watch out for cops, too, but we knew quite a few of them. Some of the best customers we had were cops. Sometimes they'd pay for their drinks but mostly we'd take care of them, you know, if they were working the beat. When we'd bring in barrels of beer we'd give the beat cop a dollar a barrel if he was watching. This kind of thing was going on across every level. If the Prohibition agents were going to raid us, we would usually get a call from the police captain at the desk telling us ahead of time. So we'd move everything next door and they'd come in and look around and there'd be nothing. Everyone was on the take back then, all the way up to the mayor, Jimmy Walker. In fact we used to make deliveries to his house every week.

We couldn't always know when they were coming though. Once, when I was about fifteen, the Prohibition agents came and broke down our door with an axe. I grabbed a broom and made like I was sweeping the joint. And when the guys came in they said, "Get the hell out of here. You're too young to be working at a place like this." Meanwhile I was running the joint! So they locked up the bartender and, boy, were they surprised when I was the one who came to bail him out. This kind of thing didn't happen to us too often, though, because we ran a respectable joint. As long as your joint was respectable, you were generally okay.

—John Morahan, born in 1915, attended Fordham University in the Bronx, and went on to own numerous music and entertainment clubs in Manhattan in the 1950s. He served in the U.S. Army in Japan during World War II and has been active in the American Legion since then. He left New York City in 1965 and now lives in New Jersey.

I grew up in New York City. For one month, that is, then I moved to Elizabeth, New Jersey, and finished my growing up over there. We had a sixty-acre cow pasture behind our house—that's how rural Elizabeth was at that time. Everybody was a bootlegger where I lived. Every corner of town had a saloon on it. Of course, you know, they were never raided by the cops, because the cops were a big part of that business, too. The guys that were selling the booze, they could hide it from everybody except the kids. Kids can get into places. If you hid the booze under a garage, kids would always get under there and find all these cases of booze. So we knew who was buying it, who was selling it, where it was going.

When I was a little kid I wrote this article that was supposedly about my school. But I was writing about the bootleggers — who was operating, where they were selling the stuff. Nobody paid any attention to this school kid saying all of this stuff — it was very primitive in writing form and all that, but I was exposing all the bootleggers in Elizabeth. Then they found out. I think I was on their hit list for a while.

I used to go down to Breezy Point, New York, and there was a boat down there called *Away in a Moment.* This was a beautiful boat that looked like a big speedboat. But it was a boat that brought in booze. I was sitting down by the water one night, and I saw the *Away in a Moment* coming in, and it had a little engine on it, going *chum, chum, chum.* Now, in fact, this boat had three great big Liberty engines on it, left over from World War I. Then across the way, I see this searchlight come and *Zroom!* the Coast Guard boat shoots out to intercept *Away in a Moment.* Now, they're not supposed to do that, because they're being paid off by these guys, but somebody must have forgotten to make the payoff that night. So here came this big Coast Guard boat, but all of a sudden the *Away in a Moment* stopped, and the *chum, chum, chum* noise stopped, too. Then, *Zroom! Zroom! Zroom!* The three big Liberty engines got going and wham, that boat took off, and they never caught it. Eventually the Coast Guard ran it down, and they made a Coast Guard chaser out of it. But by that time the bootleggers had replaced it with another boat that was even faster. It was all a great game.

—Mickey Spillane, born in 1918, is best known for his mystery-suspense novels, including I, the Jury, The Long Wait, *and* Kiss Me, Deadly. *In 1984, he created a television series,* Mike Hammer, *based on his well-known character of the same name.*

Al Capone, 1899–1947

jazzed

corked

potted

boiled as an owl

loaded to the muzzle

loaded for bear

tanked

burning with a blue flame

pie-eyed

slopped

lit

oiled

Prohibition terms describing
someone in a state of drunkenness

a $30,000 seven-ton, armor-plated Cadillac, sporting bulletproof glass and a special area behind the seat for a collection of firearms — leading millions to dream that one day they, too, could be like Al.

By the late 1920s, there were thirty-two thousand speakeasies in New York City alone (nearly double the number of bars in business before Prohibition), and at many places throughout the country, liquor was sold boldly and freely, within sight of the police. In 1926, *Time* printed a recipe for making gin. The Speaker of the House had a private still. The Eighteenth Amendment had changed the culture, all right, but not quite in the way that its authors intended.

In the 1920s, traditionalists also staked their claim in the church. Religious belief encountered some stiff competition in the years immediately after the war, especially from psychoanalysis, science, and a Sunday joyride in the sedan. It suffered, too, from its failure to give people adequate answers to the nagging questions of the war. Just how *did* one worship a God who tolerated suffering on such an enormous scale? Atheism gained favor, particularly among intellectuals. So did more than a few cultish ideas, including nudist colonies, yoga, Ouija boards, and an eccentric French self-help guru's notion that anything could be achieved if one began the morning by repeating, "Every day, in every way, I am getting better and better."

Still, more than one-quarter of the American population, mostly southerners, took this moment to seek comfort instead by embracing a literal interpretation of the Bible. Their idols were a collection of fire-and-brimstone preachers like Aimee Semple McPherson and Billy Sunday who rocked the churches of the time with colorful oratory filled with sensuous descriptions of Hell.

Like the Klan meeting, the evangelical gathering provided an outlet for many people who feared that their simple, rural way of life was in jeopardy. If the revival church was these people's social center, it was also their theater. McPherson, who spread the gospel both over the radio and in person, appeared in white satin robes and preached with the support of three bands, two orchestras, three choirs, and six quartets. Sunday, whose career had already spanned four decades by the 1920s, was a preacher known for his athletic style, in which he traveled back and forth across the platform, stomping, pounding, jumping, and sliding (he had, in fact, been a professional baseball player). Legend had it that Sunday covered more than a mile, back and forth, in a single sermon.

One topic of fixation for the fundamentalist crowd (even the word "fundamentalist" was a 1920s creation) was evolution. They worked hard to push bills through several state legislatures making the teaching of evolution a crime. In Tennessee, they succeeded, leading to a sensational 1925 trial pitting William Jennings Bryan, who argued for the state, against Clarence Darrow, who defended Dayton, Tennessee, high school biology teacher John Scopes.

Broadcast countrywide over radio (the first trial ever to be so aired), attended by a crowd so large that it spilled out onto the courthouse lawn (where people protected themselves from the heat with fans emblazoned with a toothpaste ad), and covered carefully by every tabloid in the nation, the Monkey Trial, as it became known, was a thoroughly modern event. The city of Dayton had even competed for the chance to host it, convinced that it would bring them a trove of tourist dollars (which it did).

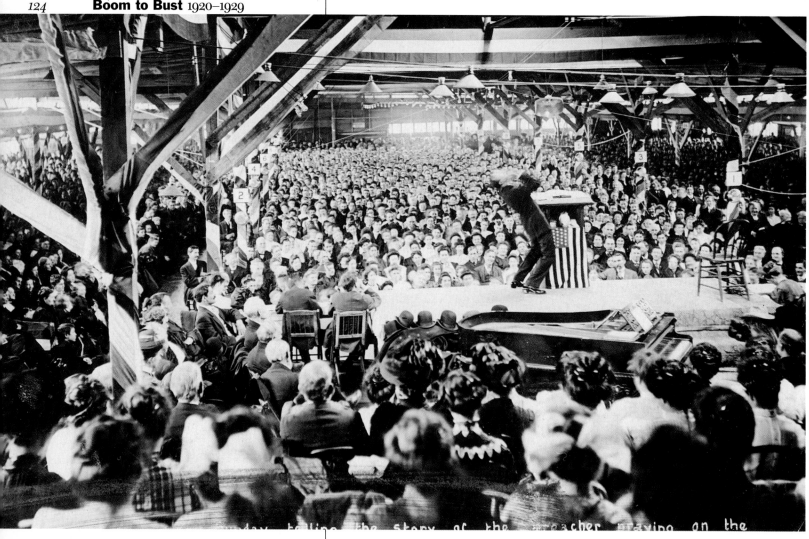

Evangelist Billy Sunday captivates the audience at one of his traveling revival meetings. Sunday held particular contempt for liberal theologists, whom he described as "hog-jowled, weasel-eyed, sponge-columned, jelly-spined, pussy-footing, four-flushing, charlotte-russed" Christians.

> **"Some folks work their hands off'n up'n to the elbows to give their young-uns education, and all they do is send their young-uns to Hell."**
>
> *Reverend Joe Leffew, preaching to the Holy Rollers of Dayton, Tennessee, at the time of the 1925 Scopes trial*

But people everywhere followed the trial not because they cared so much about evolution or Tennessee education, but because it brought the two conflicting forces of 1920s life into one courtroom, ready to fight it out. The aged and paunchy Bryan, who had once been known as "the prairie radical," argued for the traditionalists, claiming his belief in "everything in the Bible"; the sprier Darrow spoke for modernists, crowing that it was his purpose to prevent "bigots and ignoramuses from controlling the education of the United States."

Scopes was found guilty of teaching evolution (and was fined a mere $100), but the ridicule that Bryan endured at the hands of Darrow left a more lasting impression upon the national audience. In a time that worshiped the scientifically derived truth, the fundamentalist could only look old-fashioned. Bryan died five days after the trial closed, a victim of diabetes, but it was hard not to believe that he had been felled more by his humiliation than by his condition and that some part of the traditional world he represented was buried along with him.

For so many people, there was simply no resisting the modern age. Not when it had magical entertainment like the movies. Midway through the decade,

Creationism on trial: **"Defending God's word"**

Students being sworn in as witnesses during the Scopes trial in Dayton, Tennessee.

Early in 1925, a handful of men began to talk about the possibility of doing something that would create some interest to bringing people into Dayton. It seemed that we were just kind of drying up and we weren't getting any tourist trade, any travel coming through. And a group of men met at the Robinson's Drug Store around a Coke and they decided they would try the new Scopes law. At that time it wasn't known as Scopes, of course. So they went to look around and get a teacher that was willing to try this case. John T. Scopes, our coach at the high school, said, "Well, I wouldn't mind doing that. I will be the teacher, and I will let them say that I taught evolution against the law." And then they began to look around and see if they could find some lawyers that would be interested in coming. And one of them said, "Well, I'll write William Jennings Bryan, and see if he'll be interested in coming and testing the constitutionality of this law." So he got in touch with Bryan, he got in touch with Clarence Darrow, and both of them agreed to come and try the case.

As that shows, much of the impetus behind bringing the Scopes trial here was economics. But I also think that nearly every individual citizen in the Dayton area believed in the Bible's story of how man was created by God and not raised up from a lower form of animal. And of course it disturbed them to hear that there was a teacher that was going to teach their children that the Bible story was not true. I was about seventeen years old and my father was a deputy sheriff. And because we expected huge crowds for the trial and the weather then was almost a hundred degrees, we knew that our courtroom would be just a baking oven. So the judge agreed that one or two boys could bring Cokes in to the press people, to the jury, and to the lawyers, and I was one of those boys. They had three times the capacity of people in the courtroom for that trial and they were all rooting for Bryan because Bryan was defending God's word. At about the middle of the trial, the judge decided, "We

can't stand this baking oven of a courtroom with this size crowd. I'm going to permit the trial to go outside and we'll continue it under the shade trees out in the yard." And he took the jury, put the seats out there for them, and moved his platform out there so he could preside. When he did this, it happened to be a period when Bryan was witnessing and Darrow was digging in on him and being very rude in the kind of questions he was asking him. And the people were getting more and more irritated with Darrow. And of course, this disturbed the judge. And he finally said, "I have no control over this crowd out under the shade trees. We've got to go back in the courtroom." And in less than a couple hours they went back into the courtroom where he could announce, "I'll empty the courtroom if this fuss keeps going."

> *—Gilles Ryan, born in 1907, was seventeen years old during the trial and attending Ray Central High School, where John Scopes was a teacher.*

Most of the people in Dayton were fundamentalist Christians, but there were quite a few of us who felt otherwise, of course. My father was the county druggist during the time of Scopes. He went in business in 1898, and by 1925, he was chairman of the school board. He sided with Darrow and the evolutionists because he didn't believe that the state or federal government had a right to tell a local school board what they could or could not teach. Like most druggists, my dad was also a purveyor of textbooks, so he was as guilty as Scopes, I guess, in the sense that he had hired Scopes to teach school and was selling the textbook which was in question. Still, he really enjoyed the trial and all the hullabaloo and he saw it as an opportunity to promote the drugstore. From 1940 on, I don't think he ever filled a prescription. He just talked to people about the trial, people coming in and wanting to see the pictures and all

that. We lived less than a hundred yards from the courthouse and they had speakers out on the front lawn, bellowing the trial out to the crowds. The unit manager of the Underwood and Underwood photographic group and I would sit on the front porch in the swing and I would walk across with him when it looked like some excitement was brewing and we'd talk to his photographers. The trial really was a hullabaloo. Everywhere we had hucksters selling watch fobs and handmade dolls. When I die, I'll hopefully go to heaven, and I want to ask the Lord, what was it all about?

> *—Wallace "Sonny" Robinson, born in 1920, inherited his father's drugstore and managed it until his retirement in the mid-1980s.*

A lot of the newspaper people who came here for the trial looked upon the locals as rubes or hillbillies. The chief antagonist was H. L. Mencken, who really seemed to be making fun of our way of life. But we were proud of where we lived. My father's drugstore — where all these discussions about Scopes began — was the town gathering spot. In the morning, men would come to the store to chat. They'd each get a cigar at the counter and then chat. I remember one man would come in and take out a nickel and tap it on the counter and that meant that he wanted his cigar. The women did whatever their work was in the morning, and then after lunch, they'd get cleaned up and come to town to shop. And they'd come to the store for a Coca-Cola or a dish of ice cream. After school, children came in and they'd take the funny books off the rack, read them and then put them back. The papers were the same thing. People could come in and pick a paper up, look through it, put it back together, and put it back on the stand. Nobody minded having a secondhand paper. Bryan liked it here so much he stayed on after the trial for a few days. But he was a very different man from when he arrived. When Bryan came, he was smiling and seemed to be rested, and then, in the middle of the trial, it was just as if he had wilted. It just seemed that the starch had gone out of him, and Darrow did put him through a strenuous series of questions about how he believed the Bible. Darrow asked him something about "how is it that all this happened in one day?" And then Bryan made the mistake of saying that he felt the days then had more than twenty-four hours. And Darrow pounced on that, and made a big thing of it and you could just see that Bryan was more or less defeated.

> *—Frances Gabbert, born in 1916, was in third grade during the trial. In 1938 she began teaching biology at the same high school where John Scopes had taught.*

there were already twenty thousand theaters in small town and big city alike, showing silent films along with a live stage show, and all for a mere fifty cents. Every place that was anyplace had a theater and everybody who was anybody spent at least one night a week there.

More than the car or even the radio, the movie experience was the very epitome of escape, particularly in the big cities where theaters were built to rival the most garish palaces in the world. Their architecture looked like what you might get if you crossed the Taj Mahal with Versailles and added a movie screen: ornate, gilded places that were meant to release the imagination every bit as much as the movie itself (in fact, it was said that people showed up even when they knew the movie was bad, aware that the experience of the theater alone would be sufficient reward). Movie theaters had uniformed ushers and attendants in the rest rooms; pipe organs and orchestras to accompany the film action; and they were sometimes designed so that viewers had to take long, circuitous routes to get to the auditorium itself, giving them a chance to feel that they weren't waiting for a movie at all, but taking a stroll through some raja's palace, admiring the splendor of the rich decor.

Above: The Sheik *(1921) established Rudolph Valentino as the preeminent male sex symbol of the 1920s. H. L. Mencken once described Valentino as "catnip to women." Left: In the twenties, the theater itself was part of the show. Here, a New York movie house's "human billboard," featuring live showgirls on the marquee, attracts viewers to the premiere of* Hollywood Revue *(1929).*

Of course, when it was good, the film was still the primary attraction, and even before the first feature-length talkie appeared (*The Jazz Singer,* 1927), the decade's films were good. The movies of these years showcased at least one famous director in Cecil B. De Mille (whose work encouraged the decade's obsession with sex) and featured a handful of stars. Charlie Chaplin was the biggest. Ordinary people the world over identified with his lovable "tramp." But moviegoers also flocked to see Douglas Fairbanks, Clara Bow, Joan Crawford, and most of all, Rudolph Valentino, whose exotic Latin looks and sexy tango may alone explain why film audiences in the 1920s were 60 percent female.

Just as they had come to value advertising for its information on how to be jazzy in the jazz age, so people looked to the movies for guidance on how to dress, talk, smoke, and appear sexy. Girls mimicked vamps like Theda Bara and copied the sexual gestures of Clara Bow (the "It"girl). Joan Crawford encouraged the craze for flappers. After Valentino became a big hit with his performance in *The Sheik,* college-age men wore baggy-style Valentino pants, called themselves "sheiks" and their women, "shebas."

Not long before, people had identified themselves as part of a region that stretched little beyond where they could see out their farmhouse windows. But now a shared national culture was emerging. People in Maine were watching the same movies and listening to the same radio shows as people in California. Teenagers in Iowa were parting their hair just like teenagers in North Carolina. Everyone, it seemed, was playing mah-jongg and singing "Yes! We Have No Bananas." The obsession with American pop culture didn't stop at the borders,

The new divertissements: Movies, dancing, and "Come on, let's go see the Babe!"

When I was a kid in East Harlem, there were a lot of movie palaces with names like the Cosmo, the Beaumont, the Palace, and the Stadium. And then we had the Liberty theater, which was smaller and showed the older movies. We used to go to the Liberty because it was easy to sneak into. Sunday was the big day there. A lot of people would come and bring their food with them in a pail. They would sit in the theater, watch the movie and eat their Sunday afternoon dinner. And then Mrs. Columbo, the owner, would get up and make a speech. It was always the same thing: "Now, everybody get quiet and if you have to go to the toilet, get up and go into the goddamn toilet. Don't go on the floor." Everybody would clap and yell at that, but it didn't stop them. The place was always a mess. And you had to be careful where you sat because the guys in the balcony eating their dinner would set their pails on the railing and forget about them and then some macaroni would end up falling on your head. We kids would watch it happen and then laugh like hell. It was crazy but we had a great time.

Back then, many of the studios were in New York and we could go to them and watch movies being made. We got to see many of our favorite stars — Harold Lloyd, Douglas Fairbanks, Tom Mix. We got to see Harold Lloyd making a movie on 116th Street, hopping onto a bus and hanging out of the window. At the movie studios on 127th Street we would go to Mary Pickford Day. And then *The Jazz Singer* came out and it was all anyone talked about: "Did you see the talking picture? Did you see the talking picture?" It was a big topic, this new step in the movie industry because this was our main means of recreation, just going from one theater to the next and suddenly after years of watching the silents, we had sound!

—Pete Pascale was born in 1914 in East Harlem, where he has remained for most of his life. He has worked for LaGuardia House, a local community center, since 1931.

Sometime in the early twenties, it was discovered that if you built a movie palace, the grandeur of the place would attract as many people as the attraction on the screen. So there were these huge theaters in the cities. But I grew up in a small town, and the nearest movie palace was twenty miles away. So when I was about twelve or thirteen I had the idea to start showing movies in the local high school gymnasium. And since I had my own little radio station, I started advertising the films on the radio. This gave me a built-in audience, even though there were only about twelve people listening to my station at that time. Everyone found out about it one way or the other because every Wednesday and Saturday I

A crowd at the Astor Theatre, New York, 1929.

would pack that auditorium with four or five hundred people at twenty-five cents apiece. So here I was, making seventy-five dollars a month, more money than my father, who was the superintendent of schools! It took them a few years, but when the school finally figured out how much I was making they took it over themselves.

—Albert Sindlinger was born in 1907 in Tuscaras, Ohio. He ran a number of movie theaters in the Midwest during the 1930s.

I didn't go to the movies very much as a child because it cost money. And even when we had the dime for the Saturday movie my mother didn't want me to go. "You'd better be out in the sunshine and fresh air," she would say. But to go to the movies with my mother and father, that was different — that was a "family outing." I never will forget the first time that we actually heard voices on the screen. It was a Charlie Chaplin movie which was silent, but in one part of it he sang a song. And he was dancing. It was terribly exciting.

There was so much dancing at that time. When I was a kid I used to see adults doing the Charleston. And then there was something called the black bottom, which came out around the same time as the Charleston. It was quite a sexy-looking dance with lots of wiggling around. The name didn't come from what you might think. The name was actually taken from the type of stockings women wore. They were flesh colored, but at the heel they had a black bottom. What I realize now is that these were the first "jazzy" dances. And of course as a child I used to imitate that. But my

parents never did it. It required giving up your dignity to do that kind of dancing, and my parents had dignity so they danced waltzes and fox-trots instead.

—Clara Hancox was born in 1918 in the Bronx. Her parents came to America from the Ukraine during World War I.

We had so many heroes back then and we knew all about each one of them. We felt almost personally involved. We'd write and get their autograph or their picture. Even the local college football team! I think to this day I could still name the whole 1928 lineup because we were just so involved with them. I think we felt this way because they were coming to us through the radio. Sitting and listening to these games being broadcast we felt closer to the players than we do today. The sports heroes were different back then. We believed they had integrity and decency, but more importantly we thought of them just as regular human beings. I mean we were aware that Babe Ruth drank and all, but he was certainly no criminal. Most of them just led normal, private lives and weren't paid exorbitant amounts of money or anything. I used to think that maybe they went to church on Sunday just like I did, you know? And you can relate to people like that.

—Wallace "Sonny" Robinson was born in 1920 in Dayton, Tennessee. His father owned the drugstore that became a famous meeting place during the Scopes trial in 1925.

When we used to go to Yankee Stadium we never said, "We're going to go to Yankee Stadium." We'd say, "Come on, let's go and see the Babe." We all went up to see the Babe. And we all sat in the bleacher seats, because they were only fifty cents. And we'd sit as close as we could to the Babe, and shout, "Hey, Babe, how you doing out there?" Trying to talk to him, you know. And he would wave to us and things of that sort. But a true Yankee fan, he just went to see the Babe, and that was that. Of course, even if you didn't get to Yankee Stadium you could still keep up on what the Babe was doing. We used to go to the billiard room on Third Avenue between 117th and 116th. And they had this guy with earphones listening to the game on the radio and he drew a picture of the diamond that showed first, second, third, and home plate. Then if a guy got a base hit he would show the guy was on first base. And we didn't hear nothing. Because he had the earphones. But you could just look up from your billiard game and follow the Babe. If the Yankees were taking a big beating, then we used to go away. But if it was a close game, we'd stay right till the end.

—Pete Pascale

129

either. By mid-decade, most of the movies being watched in Britain and France, indeed three-quarters of the movies shown the world over, were made in the USA.

The biggest salesmen of this new national culture were the print journalists. With the literacy rate rising rapidly, newspaper and magazine reading became a favorite 1920s activity. Tabloids appeared in the big cities for the first time, combining a liberal use of photography with a breezy writing style and an eye for the lurid. People flocked to buy them and a host of new magazines, too: Henry Luce's weekly *Time,* which summarized the news in a lively format that could be purchased anywhere from coast to coast (in a way, America's first national newspaper), and DeWitt Wallace's *Reader's Digest,* which saved subscribers hours of unnecessary page-turning by summarizing interesting articles and tidbits from other publications into one easily readable volume. (The digest concept was a popular one in the twenties, if for no other reason than it made reading as fast an experience as everything else.)

> *"[From movies] we learned how tennis was played and golf, what a swimming pool was . . . and of course we learned about Love, a very foreign country like maybe China or Connecticut."*
>
> Writer Kate Simon, recalling the 1920s thrill of movie-watching

Movie stars and scandals took up more than their fair share of the decade's column inches. So did sports. Football player Red Grange became the first athlete to appear on the cover of *Time* (a distinction shared in the twenties by Sigmund Freud, Leon Trotsky, Albert Einstein, and Britain's Princess Elizabeth). By the end of the decade, he had been joined by pugilists Jack Dempsey and John Tunney. But the sports celebrity who commanded the greatest awe in the 1920s was almost certainly the man referred to simply as the Babe.

From the moment that he set foot on a baseball diamond, George Herman "Babe" Ruth changed the game, translating an old-fashioned sport played in cities but meant to suggest the joys of a lazy afternoon in the countryside into a faster-paced game more suited to its urban fans. Up until Ruth, baseball had been dominated by pitchers, a game of defense that was most satisfying when the score was low; after him, it was all offense, a hitter's game that was at its most thrilling when someone (usually Ruth) put ash to leather and delivered a souvenir to the fans sitting behind the outfield fence.

People who saw "the Sultan of Swat" hit a home run in the 1920s felt as special as people in later generations would feel having watched a rocket launch (and the image of a baseball freed from the tyranny of the arena, the way a missile is freed from the earth, was a potent one for the burgeoning freedoms of the time). There simply had never been a figure like Ruth before. An orphan from Baltimore, he had risen to become one of the world's biggest celebrities and, while dazzled by his new status, took to it with a naturalness that people found irresistible.

A hedonist of the first degree, Ruth had an appetite for life that simply would not quit. He overate and showed up at the ballpark drunk. Though married, he had dozens of girlfriends and appeared in public with them, one on each arm. One sportswriter called him "our national exaggeration." Like Capone, he

Bambino
Sultan of Swat
Mauling Mastadon
Behemoth of Bust
Mammoth of Maul
Colossus of Clout
Prince of Powders
Mauling Monarch
Blunderbuss
Rajah of Rap
Wazir of Wham

Nicknames for Babe Ruth,
as coined by the tabloids

Not even the ample twenties imagina-
tion was big enough to contain the
image of George Herman "Babe" Ruth.
His celebrity was so great that newspa-
pers ran columns entitled "What Babe
Ruth Did Today" and businessmen
turned him into the era's most sought-
after pitchman, endorsing everything
from cigars to underwear.

seemed to be living out a twenties dream — getting away with it all — but Ruth had another kind of appeal, too: he appeared to many people to be the kind of celebrity they might be if they ever received the chance — imperfect, uneducated, with anything but movie star looks; a little unsure of how he arrived here, but who's asking questions?

Jazz was the new culture's music. Begun in New Orleans during the last century, it had traveled north with the Great Migration of African-Americans and settled in Chicago. Once there, it took on a new sound. Gone were the complicated rhythms and overlapping melodic lines favored by the New Orleans ensembles; in their place was music that had "swing," a more lyrical, danceable sound that demonstrated the influence of white musical heritage as well. Jazz, simply put, had become America's music.

Throughout the decade, people moved to jazz's syncopated rhythms. Jazz inspired poetry and dances like the Charleston; it made stars of African-American bandleaders like Duke Ellington and Louis Armstrong; and it prompted George Gershwin — the son of Russian Jewish immigrants — to write dozens of songs and one symphonic masterpiece that epitomized the twenties sound, an *American* sound. When we think about this time, it is a recording of Gershwin that we are likely to play in our mind's ear, the soaring clarinet of "Rhapsody in Blue," the romantic lyrics of "The Man I Love."

Night after night, jazz lit up cafés and clubs, especially in the New York City enclave of Harlem. A white neighborhood until the turn of the century, Harlem typified the new black life. Out of the South for good now, many African-Americans had settled into ghettos — new, too, in the twenties — and become city people. From 1920 to 1929, New York City's black community grew six times over. By mid-decade, Harlem was almost entirely black, and an entertainment mecca.

For its many white patrons (and the bigger clubs opened their doors to whites only), the lure of Harlem was the lure of the "primitive." Eager to shed their Victorian ways, people went there to bathe in the sensuality of black culture and be entertained by a music that was unafraid to celebrate pleasure (the word "jazz" was said to be derived from a black slang term for sex). That jazz was much more, that it was an art form in the making, one capable of expressing the full range of human emotions, was lost for the moment in the urge to look in on what most clubgoers saw as a strange and exotic world. Even white bandleaders like

George Gershwin, 1898-1937

Paul Whiteman, whose "orchestral" jazz joined Western musical traditions with the rawer harmonies of the street, recorded compositions with titles like "Song of the Congo."

The rage for the "dark" went beyond music. In the 1920s, the tanned body became suddenly stylish (*Vogue* carried its first advertisements for sunlamps in 1923), and America's fascination with primitive cultures continued. American anthropologist Margaret Mead made the Pacific island of Samoa the subject of a best-selling book when she reported in 1928 that the people there practiced recreational sex without guilt. For a decade wild with curiosity for anything in the realm of the erotic, the news was positively riveting.

Followers of Marcus Garvey's Universal Negro Improvement Association gather for a "New Negro" parade in Harlem, 1920. The separatist leader attempted to establish a black shipping line dedicated in part to returning American blacks to their ancestral Africa, but the business quickly collapsed under mismanagement, and he was jailed in 1923 on what was probably a trumped-up mail fraud charge.

At the same time that white America was exchanging one stereotype of black life (the minstrel man) for another (the naturally rhythmic, sex-obsessed Harlem entertainer), black America began to focus even more on self-discovery. Marcus Garvey preached the spirit of pan-Africanism and described a new African-American identity, more African than American and impatient with the injustices endured at the hands of the white majority. A hundred thousand people joined Garvey's Universal Negro Improvement Association, which stood in direct contrast to the older and more established National Association for the Advancement of Colored People. And for each person with a membership in UNIA, there were hundreds more who joined Garvey in spirit.

Garvey opposed interracial marriage and looked upon light-skinned blacks as inferior. His newspaper, *The Negro World*, preached separatism and refused advertisements for skin lighteners and hair straighteners. Garvey declared that Christ was black, indeed that all civilization had sprung from the black peoples of North Africa, and his solution to America's race dilemma was the return of black Americans to Africa. Few Harlemites followed his message to the extreme, but with both the revival of the Klan and the race riots of 1919 very much in mind, the theme of black pride attracted them immensely.

The bulk of America's affluent and influential blacks, what W. E. B. Du Bois had referred to as the Talented Tenth, took this moment to promote awareness of Harlem's many poets, essayists, historians, playwrights, and high-culture musicians. Black Americans were still stymied at the ballot box, at the office, and in the labor unions, went their thinking, but with the fascination for Harlem entertainments running now at full speed, perhaps there was an audience in the wider culture for Negro arts and letters. And maybe there, in the books and drama readings, art galleries and concert halls, they could sculpt for the world the image of "a New Negro."

The movement, which became known as the Harlem Renaissance, helped to broaden understanding of the black American experience. Poets like Countee Cullen and Langston Hughes gave vivid expression to the pain of racism ("I, too, sing America," wrote Hughes. "I am the darker brother. / They send me to eat in the kitchen / When the company comes, / But I laugh, / And eat well, / And grow strong."). Historian Arthur Schomburg dispelled the myth of black passivity in the antislavery campaigns of the nineteenth century, and his collection of books and papers on Negro history became the focus of the 135th Street branch of the New York Public Library, Harlem's newest social center. And black spirituals were offered up in concert settings as formal and grand as would accompany a program of Schubert *lieder*.

If the focus on their heritage and identity helped black Americans assert their legitimacy in a white world, it also helped them cope with the ruptures caused by the Great Migration. For even as blacks emerged in a new urban setting offering greater freedom and more regular work, they longed for the sense of community that had been left behind in the South. Popular songs of the time often alluded to the sense of loneliness ("Alabama Bound," "Home Sweet Home Blues"), and movie houses in Harlem and Chicago regularly combined the latest from Hollywood with a live show of Delta blues just to make the cold, dark cities of the North feel a little closer to home.

One of the most powerful evocations of black history during this time was

Langston Hughes, 1902–1967

The Awakening: Harlem at the time of the "Renaissance"

As a young boy, growing up in Orange, New Jersey, I had the opportunity to meet Willie "The Lion" Smith and J. P. Johnson, two of the great piano players of the time, who also happened to be friends with my mother. They would commute from Harlem to Orange to record piano rolls at a local music studio. At the end of the day, they would get together with my mother and her sisters and cousins, and it would be party time in the community. Orange was sort of a fast town in those days. In fact, because of the Mafia, none of the saloons in Orange shut down during Prohibition; the booze flowed freely. It was exposure to musicians like these that led me to read about and appreciate what was being called the Harlem Renaissance, where artists, musicians, and writers were beginning to come forward.

The Renaissance sprang from the concept of the "New Negro," which was put forth by such people as Marcus Garvey, W. E. B. Du Bois and, later, Adam Clayton Powell. I heard a lot about Marcus Garvey from one of my father's best friends, whose nickname was "Ready Money." Ready Money owned a secondhand shop on Hickory Street in Orange, where he flew the red, black, and green flag of the Garvey movement. He was constantly espousing Garvey's ideas throughout the community and reading and handing out copies of *Negro World*, Garvey's newspaper. At the time, I didn't really understand everything he was talking about; he talked so much that some people thought he was crazy. But many other people listened, if not to Ready Money, then to Garvey himself. The whole point of the Garvey movement was to purge the community of the self-hatred that was created by white racism. In order to succeed, blacks needed a strong sense of pride in their own race. People like Ready Money may have sounded a little mad sometimes, but just the fact that he was flying that flag outside his little shop in Orange, New Jersey, showed that the movement was having an effect.

The time was ripe for a renaissance back then. After the defeat of the kaiser in Germany, a spirit of optimism and positive expectation swept across Harlem. The Allies won the war for democracy, so now it was time for something to happen in America to change the system of segregation and lynching that was going on in Europe, the black troops were welcomed as liberators; so when they came back to America, they were determined to create a situation that would approximate the slogans they had been fighting for.

They wanted democracy at home in the United States. And this general idea helped feed the concept of "The Renaissance."

Well, *my* first idea of renaissance was the Harlem basketball team, the Renaissance Big Five, with "Fats" Jenkins, "Pappy" Ricks, and "Tarzan" Cooper. They used to be known as the Spartan Five, when my father played with them, but they changed the name when the whole Renaissance concept swept Harlem. The black community used to turn up in droves whenever that team played. One of my greatest experiences as a child was when my father took me to a practice. We were standing around watching Fats Jenkins and Pappy Ricks shoot baskets, when my father said I could go out on the floor with them. One of them threw me the basketball and I threw it back. And from then on, I was a lover of basketball. Those players were world champions to us.

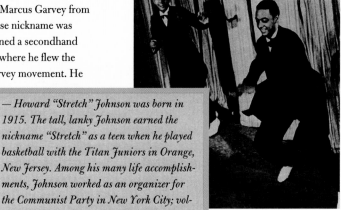

Johnson onstage at the Cotton Club.

— *Howard "Stretch" Johnson was born in 1915. The tall, lanky Johnson earned the nickname "Stretch" as a teen when he played basketball with the Titan Juniors in Orange, New Jersey. Among his many life accomplishments, Johnson worked as an organizer for the Communist Party in New York City; volunteered for combat with the Buffalo Soldiers in World War II; and founded and edited the Afro-Hawaii News,* the first African-American newspaper in Hawaii.

They played some of the big white professional teams and beat them handily. So as a kid, I never had any sense of inferiority about black athletes. But I was too young and not politically conscious enough to resent the fact that my father couldn't play on a white team.

A lot of people wonder how there could be joy and optimism in a community under the conditions of segregation and discrimination. But the black community had two very important forces that enabled it to survive and grow. One was the church, where you had the gospel and the spiritual, which were inspirational in their basic content. And the other was the entertainment world, where you had the music of the secular side, expressed in jazz.

The first time I was truly seized by jazz was in 1927 when I heard Duke Ellington broadcast from the Cotton Club. I think it was either Norman Brokenshire

or Ted Husing who said, "You're now listening to the jungle music of Duke Ellington played at the Cotton Club in Harlem where Broadway, Hollywood, and Paris rub elbows." When I heard that music, that sound that Ellington created, it just went through me. About a week later, I formed a band of my cronies, Irving Overby and Robby Benjamin. We played kazoos and used some whisk brooms for brushes, and we tried to imitate the Ellington sound. *Rah . . . Rah . . . Dah . . . Dom . . . Bah . . .* I still love that music today.

Of course at the time, I never thought I'd ever actually work at the Cotton Club; I was just a small-time kid from Orange. It was my sister Winnie who made that possible. She had been hired as a chorus girl when she was fourteen years old and had worked there for two years when I first went in to audition. My sister Winnie said, "Stretch, if you come down in the cellar with me, I'll teach you some steps and maybe you can pass the audition." So we went down in the cellar and woodshedded, as they say. I got a few steps down and my sister thought I was ready. She said, "Be sure to smile at the audition and make big movements." So I did, and they hired me. Since my sister was already a chorus girl, I never really felt that I beat the competition fair and square; I had a pretty good idea of what kind of a tap dancer I was, and it wasn't very good.

Now, the Cotton Club, with an all-black show, didn't admit black patrons. It wasn't a stated policy, but the black community just knew that they weren't expected to be there. They didn't put a sign up, "No Colored Wanted," but it was known in the community that it catered to a white tourist trade. At the Cotton Club, the whites from downtown could see a show right in the middle of Harlem with the cream of the black entertainment — Ethel Waters, Pops, Duke Ellington, Cab Calloway, Jimmie Lunceford, all the great black musicians — and not have to be bothered rubbing elbows with the people who actually lived in the community.

On Sunday the Cotton Club would have a celebrity night where top white performers, such as Sophie Tucker, Al Jolson, Maurice Chevalier, and George Raft, would come up and do a turn on the stage after the black show was finished. So on those wooden boards I had the opportunity to see the greatest entertainers in the world — black and white. I would say that the Cotton Club, in some respects, represented the epitome of what the literary and cultural mavens call the jazz age. You were not considered part of the hip crowd, or the cognoscenti, as the literary people would say, if you didn't conclude a night on the town with a trip to Harlem. There was *always* a visit to Harlem at the end of the night to get the real thing.

to be found not in Harlem or Chicago, but on Broadway in Jerome Kern and Oscar Hammerstein's 1927 Broadway musical *Show Boat*. Promoted, oddly, as "an All-American Musical Comedy" by its producer, Flo Ziegfeld, it is today regarded as a watershed event in theater history. Never before had whites and blacks been seen performing together in a hit Broadway play. Never before had a musical (despite its "comic" label) dealt with such serious themes as racial oppression and marital discord. Never before had white audiences seen a black character in such rich and human dimensions (even if, by today's standards, he would appear to be a stereotype).

> *"Niggers all work on de Mississippi,*
> *Niggers all work while de white folks play,*
> *Loadin' up boats wid de bales of cotton,*
> *Gittin' no rest till de Judgment Day."*
>
> Opening lines of the Broadway hit Show Boat, *1927*

Ziegfeld himself had thought that 1920s theatergoers wanted only frills and thrills in their entertainment and had gambled on *Show Boat* against his better judgment. He was wrong. *Show Boat* played to eager audiences for over two years, featuring a hit song, "Ol' Man River," that moved people to tears. The ballad, sung by a black riverboat worker, was popular for its evocation of the timeless quality of nature during a period when nothing seemed timeless or natural. But the fact that these words of wisdom were sung by a black man, and that they included references to the pain of oppression, was not lost on the crowds.

The vibrating national culture of the 1920s promoted one other magical machine, the airplane. Since the Wright brothers had flown their crude apparatus at Kitty Hawk in 1903, aviation had grown slowly. Planes had figured prominently in the First World War, but the dream of passenger flights had been just that, a dream, and most people had come to think of the sky as a place for birds, military hardware, and little else.

By the mid-1920s, the airplane seemed to have more potential as a circus act than it did as a vehicle for human transportation. Carnivals and country fairs featured daredevil riders performing stunts like wing-walking and parachute-jumping, and spectators bought rides at five dollars a thrill. Barnstorming pilots, evangelists for an aviation future, hopped from airfield to airfield, moving without maps, going as far as their gas supplies would take them, gathering curious crowds wherever they alit. But while people everywhere found the flying machines interesting, the general mood was one of "you'll never get me up in one of those things." Then came Lindy.

At 7:42 A.M., on May 20, 1927, Charles Augustus Lindbergh climbed into his single-engine *Spirit of St. Louis* and, clearing the telephone wires at the end of the runway by a mere twenty feet, took off from Roosevelt Field, Long Island, for a journey into history. Sixty-six people had already flown across the ocean. But Lindbergh aimed to go from New York to Paris (a flight measuring four hundred miles greater than had ever been accomplished before), and, most important, he intended to do it alone.

No one gave him much of a chance. Less than a month before, two French pilots attempting the same route had been killed in a crash short of their destination, but the twenty-five-year-old Lindbergh, a midwesterner through and through, was determined to succeed. He packed five sandwiches and some water,

Early airmen (and women): "Everyone thought of us as daredevils"

I was seven years old when I took my first ride in an airplane. It was just after World War I. There was a man out on Long Island who sold rides in a plane he had designed. He would sit there in the middle of this potato field with a big sign: "Rides for five and ten dollars." I was strapped in on my father's lap while my little brother sat on the pilot's lap. As we went up over Long Island, the clouds parted and we looked out over the fields. It was like a fairyland. The streaks of sun came down all around us and changed colors. And from that moment on, I knew I wanted to fly planes.

When people saw that little children like us were willing to go up in the plane, they felt it must be safe after all and they lined up for rides. We brought in so much business, the pilot began to give us free rides week after week. By the age of twelve I felt that I knew all there was to know about flying, but my father told me I'd have to be eighteen before he'd let me go up alone. I cried on my mother's shoulder and begged until finally, when I was fifteen, she let me take lessons. After two and a half flying hours my instructor told me it was time to do my solo. I was terrified, but I told myself, "You've always wanted to do this, and now you've got to do it." And once I got up there around one thousand feet, it was like I was home. That's the only way I can describe it.

At the age of fifteen I was flying and hanging around with some of the best pilots in the world. We were having so much fun flying around in those primitive planes. And they were primitive! If your engine didn't give out, that was considered a great flying day. We got to be experts at crash landings because you'd be flying along and suddenly have no engine. You'd look down, and find an open field and think, "Well, gee I can probably make it down there," and make a sudden landing. Of course, the farmers were not too happy about this. In fact they often got irate because it was said that the cows didn't like airplanes, and that they gave out less milk when we were flying around them.

We had no radar, and no way of communicating with the ground once we took off because radios were still too heavy. We navigated by using railroads or by just looking for landmarks. The scary times came when you were trapped above a cloud cover and couldn't see anything. Sometimes I had to just pick a spot in the clouds and fly back and forth until the heat off my tailpipe would make the clouds thin out. Other times, I'd have to land blind because I'd be stuck up in the clouds for so long that I'd run out of fuel. There were certainly some scary moments.

When I was seventeen I pulled my first major stunt — in order to prove myself to the male pilots. There was one who had just lost his license for crashing a plane while trying to fly under the Hell Gate Bridge on the

Smith at Roosevelt Field, Long Island, April 28, 1929, just before embarking on her attempt to break the world's endurance flight record for women.

—Elinor Smith Sullivan, who was born in 1911, won the Best Woman Aviator of the Year Award in 1930. During the Depression, she flew in air shows with Charles Lindbergh to raise money for the unemployed. She married and had four children, and after nearly twenty years of retirement was called by the U.S. Air Force in 1959 to help train pilots for combat. In 1960, she piloted her first jet, then retired permanently from flying.

East River. He was hanging around and griping about being grounded while "this little girl" was allowed to fly, and I decided to show him by trying the stunt myself. When I told my family, my father said, "Well, I don't like the idea of you doing it, but if you were to fly under all four East River bridges, they'd certainly never

forget that." So I did. Because of my age, it was supposed to be a secret, but a whole gang of newspaper reporters and newsreel photographers showed up. The Brooklyn Bridge turned out to be the only tricky part of the stunt — I had to fly through it sideways to avoid a big destroyer ship coming upstream. This was the shot they showed in theaters all over the country. The Department of Commerce sent me a letter reprimanding me, but enclosed in the envelope was a note from a secretary asking for my autograph!

Once I turned eighteen I was able to make a living doing air shows, flying passengers around and testing planes for designers. The designers needed us pilots because if we could break an international record in one of their planes, it was great publicity for their planes, like winning an Oscar or something. I was very popular for these runs because I was so much smaller than all the other pilots, so I broke a lot of records, especially for altitude. I also earned money flying photographers around. I took one guy out to get shots of the rumrunners — the men who brought boats into the city loaded with booze to sell to the nightclubs. We flew down so close to the deck of one ship that they shot at us.

Everyone thought of us as daredevils. We were the birdmen and birdwomen, and in the eyes of many we had achieved godlike status, though many people also thought we were all crazy. I still have letters from people who seemed to think we were from outer space or something. But after Charles Lindbergh's flight, we could do no wrong. It's hard to describe the impact Lindbergh had on people. Even the first walk on the moon doesn't come close. The twenties was such an innocent time, and people were still so religious — I think they felt like this man was sent by God to do this. That kind of public adulation is something that I doubt could ever happen again. And it changed aviation forever because all of the sudden the Wall Streeters were banging on doors looking for airplanes to invest in. We'd been standing on our heads trying to get them to notice us but after Lindbergh, suddenly everyone wanted to fly, and there weren't enough planes to carry them.

There weren't too many women fliers in the twenties, so I was kind of an oddity. But I was lucky in that no one ever gave me a hard time about it or harassed me. Strangely enough, though, when I would lecture to women's groups there would always be someone saying, "Well, she really belongs at home. A girl her age should be married. What right has she got to be out there wearing pants?"

"[The airplane was] no longer an unruly mechanical device, as it was during the takeoff . . . ; rather, it seems to form an extension of my own body, ready to follow my wish as the hand follows the mind's desire — instinctively, without commanding . . . [it] seem[s] more like a living partner in adventure than a machine of cloth and steel."

Charles Lindbergh

Charles Lindbergh and The Spirit of St. Louis *take off from Roosevelt Field, Long Island, en route to Paris, May 20, 1927. The plane, built to his specifications, was financed by Missouri businessmen and $2,000 of Lindbergh's own savings.*

*Skeptics had called him the Flying Fool, but when
Lindbergh returned to New York after his heroic
flight, he was welcomed with a Congressional
Medal of Honor and a parade up Broadway, which
attracted an estimated 4.5 million spectators.*

:

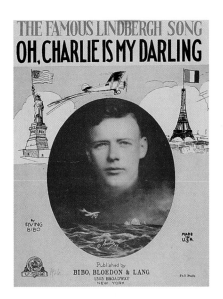

THE FAMOUS LINDBERGH SONG
OH, CHARLIE IS MY DARLING

by
IRVING
BIBO

MADE
U.S.A.

Published by
BIBO, BLOEDON & LANG
1505 BROADWAY
NEW YORK

Hundreds of songs were written in honor of Charles Lindbergh, but the man himself quickly grew tired of the excessive worship. After receiving an ecstatic reception in St. Louis, he confided to his publicist, "I was so filled up with this hero guff, I was ready to shout murder."

but no change of clothes. Flying initially at a speed of 102 mph, he encountered heavy rain and threatening turbulence, but, flying often as low as ten feet above sea level, he pushed on.

After Lindbergh had been in the air for fourteen hours, a crowd of forty thousand watching a prizefight at Yankee Stadium stood for a moment of silence. They had no news yet, but they feared the worst. After seventeen hours, the pilot found himself on the brink of exhaustion, unable to even prop his eyes open. Realizing that he had slipped into hallucinations, he slapped his face, opened the window for air, and somehow recovered his will. Then, twenty-six hours into flight, he saw a bird, the first sign of land and after it, a fishing boat. He called out to the anglers — "Which way to Ireland?" — and they looked back at him quizzically. Ireland followed, with eager villagers waving. Now it was only a matter of his fuel holding out; it did.

Thirty-five hundred miles into flight, Lindbergh ate his first sandwich and took a sip of water, anticipating the City of Light up ahead. Once there, he circled the Eiffel Tower before heading out to the airfield at Le Bourget. More than 100,000 French men and women greeted him as he landed, thirty-three and a half hours after departing New York. The hysteria that followed was frightening.

Before Lindbergh could remove himself from the plane, it was besieged by eager fans, who promptly began tearing parts of it off for souvenirs. The crowd was so unruly it carried Lindbergh aloft for more than half an hour, preventing the pilot from reaching the assembled greeting committee. Instead, he was whisked away by two French pilots who put him in their car and delivered him by back roads to the American Embassy. Lindbergh was wearing a pair of the ambassador's pajamas and sipping a glass of milk when the reception committee finally met up with him, hours later. By the time he went to bed, he had been up for sixty-three hours.

The earth seemed to glow in the aftermath of Lindbergh's accomplishment. Accolades came from all over. In Brussels, the mayor greeted the American pilot as a visitor of divine dimensions, sent to redeem a fallen people. "I salute you, dear Captain Lindbergh," he said, "a noble son of your great nation which at an hour when civilization was in danger came to its help and with us conquered."

In America, the praise was equally grand — and incessant. The *Washington Post* compared him to the Pilgrims; the *St. Louis Star* called him another George Washington. More than 1,750 tons of ticker tape were dropped on New York's Broadway during the parade after his return. More than 5,000 poems and 250 songs (including George M. Cohan's "When Lindbergh Came Home") were written in his honor. The Lindy Hop became a dance hall craze. And in the single month after he landed home, Lindbergh received 3.5 million letters (mostly from women interested in knowing if he was available).

Handsome, clean-cut, decent, Lindbergh was an easy hero to love. But his charm seemed to have a particular appeal in the cynical, tawdry twenties. Was there a better figure to straddle the decade's opposing forces? Lindbergh was a simple country boy who conquered the most modern and jazzy of machines. Was there a more effective antidote to the feeling that life was spinning out of control? Lindbergh had appointed himself a task and then accomplished it. Was there a firmer example for good in a society consumed with corruption and lawlessness?

Speculation fever: "You put up 10 percent and a broker covered the rest"

In the summer of 1929, I was a college student studying finance, so I was working at a brokerage firm in Baltimore, learning everything I could. My main responsibility was as a "board boy." When the stock prices came off the ticker tape, I had to run over and mark them on a big board that took up a whole wall of this huge room. I lost a lot of weight that summer, running back and forth marking those stocks up and down with each transaction.

People were making a lot of money in the stock market — you could sort of feel it when you visited customers or made deliveries. Everybody was really, really busy and they were feeling pretty good about themselves. It was around this time that the public got more interested in the market than they had been. Stock prices had been going up pretty steadily, and even though it was still mainly rich people investing, the average guy was starting to hear about friends making $20,000 or $30,000 dollars overnight. There was rampant speculation, and if you wanted to take part all you had to do was put up 10 percent of the money and a broker would cover the rest.

The market in those days was highly manipulated. You'd go out to lunch and you'd hear a rumor, and you'd rush out and call your broker, trying to get in on a good thing. The stock would run up, but what you didn't know was that a pool of investors had started that rumor, and that they were going to pull out as soon as the price got high enough for them. They'd make their money, but the price would fall back down and you'd be stuck with your shares. There were even people who would collapse whole markets just to make money. It was a very wild time because there was no regulation at all. There were some people who could see that this was all going to fall apart, but most people just kept on playing the game.

As people got rich, they felt like celebrating! I can remember these wonderful parties we went to up in New York. If you were a college fellow and you were on the right lists, you went to these debutante parties where the liquor would flow and maybe two big orchestras would play, and this would go on until five in the morning. The fathers of these young ladies were making so much money in the market that they didn't care how much these parties were costing them. It was a very exciting period, because all you needed was a tuxedo and tails and you could go out every night to one of these parties.

In that summer of 1929 there was a big boom. But in the fall, the bottom fell out. People didn't believe it could happen, but it did. A few years later I met Will Durant of General Motors, and he told me that in the fall of 1929 he had gone to President Hoover and

—*I. W. "Tubby" Burnham who was born in 1909, got his degree in 1931 from Wharton School of Economics, though the school dropped its brokerage courses after 1929. Graduating in the heart of the Depression, roughly 80 percent of his classmates were unable to find work. Burnham went to work on Wall Street in 1931, and he has remained there for over sixty-five years.*

Burnham in the garden of his home in Pikesville, Maryland, 1927.

warned him that the market was going to collapse. But Durant was so anxious to make more money himself, he stayed in the market. That really shows you something. Here was a man who knew enough to tell the president of the United States what was going to happen and then did nothing himself. And that was the case with lots of people. They stayed too long, they didn't sell, and they lost everything.

My father was one of those people. I first heard about the Crash when he called me at school and told me about it. He said he had lost money but not to worry, that we'd be fine, because he was a doctor and

there would always be work for him. Well, I was in college, and I didn't realize how serious it all was. I mean, at that time in my life the most important thing imaginable was buying a raccoon coat — everyone had one and it was all I could think about. So even after my father told me about the Crash, I begged and pestered him to buy me that coat. Finally he gave it to me and said, "Well, now you've got the coat, but we're broke. I got wiped out in the market." He had lost $200,000, which was everything we had. That's when I realized how bad it was.

Given the chance to capitalize on his feat (among the thousands of proposals was a million dollars offered by a movie company if he would marry before their cameras), Lindbergh refused all and instead joined the Guggenheim Foundation on a series of goodwill tours. For a moment, at least, people felt better about themselves and their times. They "set down their glasses in country clubs and speakeasies and thought of their old best dreams," wrote F. Scott Fitzgerald. "Maybe there was a way out by flying, maybe our restless blood could find frontiers in illimitable air."

Maybe, but not yet. As powerful as the story of Charles Lindbergh was, as great an effect as it had on the thoughts and dreams of the modern world, it would take something else to shake the decade out of its drunken stupor. After Lindbergh, people went back to the bar for one more round, and even when the stock market plunged to record depths in October 1929, few understood the rude awakening that lay ahead of them.

A solemn crowd gathers outside the New York Stock Exchange on October 24, 1929 — Black Thursday — the day the market crashed.

4

Stormy Weather
1929–1936

Previous spread: Desperate for jobs and searching for answers, unemployed men march on Boston City Hall, February 1934.

Left: In a scene that was all too prevalent during the Depression, a family finds itself in the street, evicted from a Brooklyn apartment. The homeless took shelter where they could find it: doorways, bridge abutments, packing crates, abandoned cars, or in crudely built shanties made of discarded wood and cardboard.

In early January 1931, a forty-six-year-old tenant farmer drew the nation's attention to a small event in rural Arkansas. Homer C. Coney harvested cotton and corn on land he rented at eight dollars an acre, but a tremendous drought the previous summer had meant that most of Arkansas's farmers had no crop and, hence, no money to make do through the winter. With unemployment at unprecedented levels, a good bit of the state's population was suffering. Coney offered his truck up for twenty-five dollars but found no takers. So the farmer and his family huddled in their one-room shack — newspapers plastered over the walls to keep out the draft, a Bible and a cheap print of *The Last Supper* propped up on the mantelpiece — and tried to exist on a Red Cross relief ration of twelve dollars a month.

All winter long, Coney, his wife, and their five boys fed on beans mixed with a bit of lard (to "give it flavor"), but as it turned out they were better off than some. Early in January, a young mother visited the farmer and frantically said that her children had not eaten anything in two days. The story motivated him to take action. "Lady, you wait here. I am a-goin' to get some food," said Coney, according to an account from the time which went to great pains to quote the farmer in his rural dialect. "Then I cranks up my truck you see settin' over yonder, and takes my wife and rolls over to Bell's place. Bell's the feller them Red Cross guys picks to run the relief, but he never give out nuthin'."

There, the farmer discovered a crowd of hungry people who were being denied their rations because the agency had run out of forms. "So I hollers out, 'All you that hain't yaller, climb on my truck.'" And, with nearly fifty men hanging off all sides of his vehicle, Coney drove off to the nearby town of England. The farmers confronted the mayor and the police chief, drawing a crowd of five hundred people who joined them in their plea. "We are not beggars," one of them shouted at the officials. "We are willing to work for fifty cents a day, but we're not going to let our families starve." Rumors spread that the farmers were carrying guns (they weren't), and desperate merchants feared that their stores would be

Land mismanagement and three years of drought destroyed agrarian communities throughout the Great Plains as the topsoil literally dried up and blew away. So many farmers from Oklahoma decided to move to California that the word "Okie" became synonymous with "migrant." Here a family takes to the road in Pittsburg County, Oklahoma.

looted. But before long, the Red Cross sent in a crew from the next town, providing immediate assistance. With the farmers forming a line to quietly wait their part of $1,500 worth of emergency rations, the tension was eased.

All over the country, people read about the brave souls who stormed an Arkansas town, demanding food. Some suggested that the episode had been instigated by communists (an idea that lost steam when it was pointed out that most of those in the uprising were unaware that *Russia* had experienced a revolution, much less contemplated one of their own). But as the details of the story emerged and a picture of Coney himself came into view, more people felt sympathy for the protesters than rancor, even seeing something of their own situations in the plight of the suffering. "You let this country get hungry and they are going to eat," wrote populist Will Rogers in his newspaper column, "no matter what happens to Budgets, Income Taxes or Wall Street values. Washington mustn't forget who rules when it comes to a showdown."

The Great Southern Drought of 1930 was a catastrophe, to be sure. But the scene of desperation that it encouraged was only a small part of a wider picture of want that greeted the world at the outset of the new decade. Rarely in history has the passage of one ten-year period to the next so neatly defined two distinct moments in time as it did when the panting, hysterical twenties gave over to the pathetic, hopeless years that followed immediately after them. It was as if one had walked from the light into the dark, from a freewheeling summer wind into an unforgiving January freeze. Everything was turned on its head. Choose a list of adjectives to describe the earlier decade — words like abundant, self-interested, confident, venturesome, prosperous — and you need only establish their opposites to depict the latter: needy, community-minded, fearful, protective, poor. If the twenties moved with a swagger, the thirties could barely muster up a crawl.

Only a small percentage of Americans was directly affected by the stock market crash in October 1929, when nearly $30 billion was lost in a matter of days. And those who were had reason to think the situation would quickly pass, especially when prices held steady throughout the rest of the year. But by the early months of 1930, more than stocks were in decline. Businesses were closing, jobs were scarce, and banks, holding the life savings of rich and poor alike, were shutting down. To this day, there is no agreement as to why the nation — indeed, the entire Western world — sank into what is known as the Great Depression and just what role, if any, the Crash had in precipitating it. But what people then knew, and what they passed on in colorful detail to the generations that succeeded them, is the pain and suffering of a time as tragic as any in modern history.

In 1930, 26,000 American businesses collapsed; in 1931, 28,000 more met the same fate. And by the beginning of 1932, nearly 3,500 banks, holding billions of dollars in uninsured deposits, had gone under. Twelve million people were unemployed (nearly 25 percent of the workforce), and the real earnings for those still lucky enough to have jobs fell by a third. In some cities, the toll was even heavier: 50 percent of Chicago was out of work; 80 percent of Toledo. Yet, striking though those statistics are, they don't do justice to the sense of ruin that pervaded the industrial world. To find that, one must contemplate the scenery of the time: soup lines stretching as far as the eye could see; respectable men knocking on the back doors of their neighbors (the front door would be too humiliating)

When "Father took my piggy bank": The Depression's darkest days

Hancox in 1923 with her parents, Solomon and Sarah.

My parents migrated to New York from the Ukraine in 1916, and when I was a young girl we lived in the slums of the Lower East Side. During the 1920s, we didn't know there was going to be a depression — we were just building ourselves up and struggling along. We lived in a poor place, but we were never desperate. My father started working in the flooring business, and as the building trade boomed, he really started making money. This allowed us to move uptown to the Bronx, which to us was like living out in the country. We had a four-room apartment, and my parents began to furnish it with hand-carved furniture and drapes for the windows with golden tassels. My father had this feeling of wanting things to look rich, to make up for the fact that we had lived through all those terrible years. There was nothing on the floor, until one day my father came home with this carpet, and as he unrolled it, it was like a cherry pie! It was a red, Oriental carpet, handwoven, and when you walked in and saw it, you just exploded with delight, it was so beautiful. My mother, ever the one who watched the pennies, said, "How much did you pay for this carpet?" My father said, "Two hundred and fifty dollars." My mother said, "Take it back." But he didn't.

My father was doing very well, and he got this marvelous order to do the floors in a building that could be called a skyscraper in those days. He went to the bank and borrowed a huge sum of money to buy the materials. And just as the work was about to begin, the market crashed. We weren't even paying attention to the stock market, so we didn't really know what was happening at the time. But almost overnight it was like a bomb had fallen. All of the sudden, faces were tragic, and people were walking around in the hallways of our building and in the streets, with inquiring eyes saying, "Has it happened to you?" It was awful. It was like a domino effect: everything that happened to one person gradually happened to other people who were connected with them until everything just shut down. The people who had given my father the contract lost all their money, and since my father had borrowed all of that money, he was wiped out. Psychologically, he never recovered.

People jumped off the George Washington Bridge, which had only recently been built. We heard about it. People we knew who were involved with Wall Street, people who had bought on margin — that funny word "margin" suddenly became a part of our vocabulary — couldn't meet their debts. They were so disgraced that they killed themselves in order to get their families the insurance money. It was incredible and horrible what happened in those years. Respectable businesspeople would walk around in the streets of downtown Manhattan with a tray of bright red apples, and they would ask you to buy an apple for five cents. And horrible as that was, it was even more horrible that we didn't even *have* five cents!

For about five years I had been saving money in a piggy bank — nickels, pennies, dimes. The only way you could get at that money was by breaking the bank or shaking it until the coins came out one by one. Even during those terrible days if I ever had a penny or two I would put it in the piggy bank, and I loved to shake it and feel the weight. But it turned out that I was the only one in the family that had any money. And one day I came home and grabbed hold of my piggy bank, just to give it a shake, and discovered that there was nothing in it. The bank was empty!

My mother was standing in the doorway of the room, looking at me, and she said, "Your father borrowed the money. He has to go out to look for work and he needed money to go downtown." So I said, "How much money was there?" She said, "About ten dollars." Ten dollars! My father took the whole thing. But she

— Clara Hancox was born in 1918 in the Bronx. She graduated from the University of Iowa in 1939, and upon returning to New York became a columnist for the Daily News Record, *a national menswear magazine. After fifty years with the magazine, she retired at the age of seventy-five to write a novel.*

said to me, "When your father comes home don't say anything. It's bad for him." And he came home and I didn't say anything but my face was swollen with tears. And my father took me in his arms and he said, "I'm sorry. I had to have money. But it's a loan. I'll pay it back to you." He never did. But it was so embarrassing for me and so painful, even then in my childish years, to have to see my father in this terrible state. That's what was bad. It wasn't the piggy bank, it was to see this happen to the man who in my eyes could do no wrong.

My father walked the streets every day and found something to do. My mother went to work, and I even worked, playing the piano for a dancing class on Saturday mornings for fifty cents an hour. My mother would find a few pennies and we would go to the greengrocer and wait until he threw out the stuff that was beginning to rot. We would pick out the best rotted potato and greens and carrots that were already soft. Then we would go to the butcher and beg a marrow bone. And then with the few pennies we would buy a box of barley, and we'd have soup to last us for three or four days. I remember she would say to me sometimes, "You go out and do it. I'm ashamed for the neighbors."

Then, one day, I came home from school and saw furniture on the sidewalk that looked familiar. We had been evicted. What hurt me most about it was the look of pain on my mother's and father's face. I couldn't bear to look at them. To see their disgrace. We found another place which was much smaller, but in later years I would say to my mother or father, What happened to that desk that we had? Where is the china closet? And they would say, oh, it got lost during the eviction, someone stole it. We kept having to move, and finally we ended up in another family's apartment; they lived in one of their rooms and we lived in their living room — my mother, father, and I. And in that room, with all of our furniture packed into it, that carpet was still on the floor, that wonderful Chinese carpet!

and asking if they might do odd jobs in return for a piece of bread; dozens of people fighting over a barrel of garbage behind a restaurant, lucky if they came up with an old bone bearing a rancid shred of meat; families with their furniture parked on the sidewalk moments after being evicted from their homes, their spirits broken by failure, their eyes looking downward in disgrace.

There was time, as there always is, for a little bit of moralizing. Convinced that the calamity represented the comeuppance of a culture that had been for too long hell-bent on greed, many Americans pointed their fingers at businessmen and politicians (and at Europe, whose war debt remained unpaid), blaming them for the troubles that now befell them. All over the country, shantytowns were christened "Hoovervilles," pinning the responsibility on the man in the White House, Herbert Hoover, whose first reaction to the crisis had been to wait it out, just as the country had waited out its many other economic dips. Even capitalism itself came under scrutiny, with many people questioning the viability of the free market system and looking at such "un-American" ideas as socialism and communism as realistic solutions. The odor of revolution was in the air.

Yet, few people could shake the persistent feeling that they themselves were to blame, too. One of the most admired figures of the twenties, after all, had been

Weary, dejected farmers in Spotsylvania, Virginia, look on as their land is sold at public auction. Crop prices plummeted, and farmers could not keep up the payments on their heavily mortgaged farms. In 1933, one-quarter of the farmland in Spotsylvania County went under the hammer, selling for as little as thirty cents an acre.

> *"Found starving under a rude canvas shelter in a patch of woods . . . where they had lived for five days on wild berries and apples, a woman and her 16 year old daughter were fed and clothed today by the police and placed in a city almshouse. The woman is Mrs. John Moll, 33, and her daughter, Helen, of White Plains, NY, who have been going from city to city looking for work since July, 1931, when Mrs. Moll's husband left her. When the police found them they were huddled beneath a strip of canvas stretched from a boulder to the ground . . ."*
>
> New York Times, *September 6, 1932*

the self-made man. And, for those who believed in him, it didn't take too much to conclude that if success could be self-generated, then failure could, too. Despite their anger at Hoover and the bankers, the debates over the merits of capitalism, and the flirtations with the Left, many people still saw the crisis as a very private one. Not only had the culture been greedy; they had been greedy, too.

They looked back longingly at the twenties, finding themselves more in agreement now with the traditionalists who championed the values of the past than with the evangelists of modernism who had been proved wrong by the Crash. Now it was the city that was suspect; the land, pure. The self-centered, materialist world that had reached its zenith in the twenties seemed cold and harsh; the small town, warm and welcoming.

Most of all, people at this time looked for a leader, someone to point the way out of their mess, and, if possible, a painless way; for Americans, that urge was to be satisfied by an energetic aristocrat fresh from the banks of the Hudson Valley. But for Europe, which coped, too, with economic disaster, the crisis would join with latent feelings of national pride and revenge to bring to the surface a demagogue whose demon eyes were fixed on visions of such grandiosity that he would ultimately challenge the very nature of civilization itself.

The Depression began at a time when most people in positions of power believed in laissez-faire economics, a philosophy that treated the marketplace as a self-regulating entity that should not be tampered with. Just as surely as this philosophy had brought prosperity to much of the industrial world in the twenties, they held that it must endure periods of hardship like the one they faced now. These people viewed the market much as one views the weather: when it is bad, there is not much to be done but to wait until it is good again. Yet the Great Depression wasn't just bad weather; it was a hurricane five hundred times over. And as it did its damage, it became increasingly clear that the old foundation under the economy would not stand and that the new one would have to be built soon — that is, if people were still expected to live above it.

The prevailing explanation for the economic crisis of the time is that a rise in industrial production throughout the 1920s was not met by a commensurate rise in wages; more goods were being produced more quickly than ever before (up 43 percent per factory man-hour in the United States), but because the big industrialists were pocketing so much of their profits, fewer and fewer people were in a position to purchase what the factories were making. For a time, the 1920s fascination with installment buying hid the economy's fatal flaw. People simply continued to buy more and more on time. But even with a bundle of credit, consumers still had to meet payments, and as things got tighter, one of the first things they did was to stop buying cars and toasters and radios and furniture. The markets, in turn, became glutted with product, and industry ground to a halt. When the layoffs then began (and they began before the Crash), the crisis became self-perpetuating: with no jobs to be found, even fewer consumers were in a position to buy.

The sense of betrayal was overwhelming. People had bought into the frenzied twenties with ardor, unconcerned that they would eventually have to pay the price for their spending spree. More important, they had expected that the system that was bringing them so much prosperity would not ever fail, or at least not fail like this. They had not become millionaires, but they had *dreamed* of becoming millionaires, the life of luxury seeming at times to be little more than a lucky break away. Now, while the truly wealthy were buffered from the crisis (or even profiting from it), the best off among the middle class were postponing marriage and education and childbearing; the worst off were scrambling to meet even a subsistence existence.

As leaders parroted each other with false claims that the crisis was over, a kind of perversity set into the system. Unemployed lumbermen turned into arsonists so they could earn a few dollars as firemen, putting out the same fires they started; even as millions went starving in the nation's cities, farmers — lacking a fair market for their crops — often let fruits and vegetables rot in their fields, there in full view of the hungry. And when the price for a head of cattle dropped to where it was lower than the price to ship it to market, some breeders began destroying their own livestock.

America had once been the land of possibility; now it was the land of despair. In the spring of 1931, the people of Cameroon, in West Africa, sent New Yorkers a check for $3.77, to aid the "starving"; and the nation's harbors were crowded with liners carrying immigrants not to America, but back home to Europe, where the passengers hoped things would be better (for how could they be worse?).

A period of mass migration began that in an eccentric way followed the logic of the free market. If, indeed, a capitalist economy was like the weather, people encountering its storms reasoned that they should simply move to the drier states. They crammed their belongings into rusting Fords and Chevrolets or hopped the freight trains and traveled across the countryside, rarely finding their destinations before a new set of hardships had done them in.

In many places, even the modest relief effort was corrupted. Fearing the creation of a national dole, Hoover insisted that the Red Cross — not the government — serve those suffering most. But while the organization had proved itself capable at handling an emergency (it was praised for its response to the Mississippi River flood of 1927), it was wholly unprepared for an ongoing crisis prompted by a systemic flaw. And local Red Cross chapters, like the one in Homer Coney's Arkansas town, were more often than not controlled by town fathers who were unsympathetic to the needy, who feared that providing for too many might encourage a kind of laziness that would survive the Depression and make workers less productive when the economy started up again.

Angry, people banded together and fought back. Farmers became particularly bold, often showing up at the auction when the bank had foreclosed on a neighbor's farm and hanging a noose around a tree to demonstrate what would happen to the auctioneer if the bidding on the property were to be seriously undertaken (at which times, of course, it rarely was). A similar militancy appeared in the cities, with tenant groups often carting the furniture of their evicted neighbors back to the apartment they had just lost, daring the landlord to come again. In the spring of 1932, three thousand factory workers marched on the employment office of Ford Motor Company's River Rouge plant in Dearborn, Michigan, engaging Ford's company police in a skirmish that left four marchers dead and

> **"Right here, in Mississippi, some people are about ready to lead a mob . . . In fact, I'm getting a little pink myself."**
>
> *Governor Theodore Bilbo*

"Cheered in '17, Jeered in '32"

*Slogan of World War I veterans,
marching on Washington*

*The Bonus Expeditionary
Force, popularly called the
Bonus Army, took up residence
in various shantytowns
around Washington, D.C.
Fearing violence from the disgruntled veterans, government officials ordered the
White House gates chained
and the building barricaded.*

sixty wounded. And later that same year, in one of the Depression's sorriest spectacles, twenty thousand armed forces veterans arrived at the Capital to demand
early payment of a bonus they were due for their service in World War I.

The bonus, which amounted to one dollar per day of duty, had been established in the mid-1920s and was to accumulate interest until 1945, when each
veteran's take would amount to, roughly, $1,000. But recently a Texas congress-
man, noting the intense need in his own district, had introduced a bill to provide
for immediate payment of the awards, a sum that would put the government back
around $4 billion but buy each of the recipients about five months of food and
shelter. Singing war songs and carrying signs, the enormous lobby of veterans
came to Washington to support their own cause — just as teams of lobbyists regularly came to support big business.

The Bonus Expeditionary Force, as the veterans called themselves, traveled
by truck, car, and on foot. And when they arrived, they set up camp along the
banks of the Anacostia River and in abandoned government buildings. Taking
sympathy upon them, Hoover secretly ordered the District police to see that they
were well treated and even provided tents and field
kitchens to make their stay bearable. Energized by
their solidarity, the bonus marchers felt optimistic
about their case, particularly after the legislation
passed in the House. But days later, it failed in the
Senate, whereupon thousands of the old soldiers
stood on the steps of the Capitol, singing a funereal
version of "America."

Afterward, most of them packed up their things
and went home. But nearly eight thousand of the
dejected men hung on in the Washington humidity,
one insisting that he would wait "until 1945" if he
had to, just to receive his money. Hoover set a date for
the veterans' complete departure (their presence was
becoming an embarrassment to him) and even autho-
rized $100,000 of government money to help ease
their going, though he impoliticly declared that the
dollars would eventually be subtracted from the
bonus pool. When his deadline passed and the
marchers were still encamped, the president decided
upon more drastic measures, ordering first the police
and then the army to dislodge the veterans from
Washington.

On the afternoon of July 28, 1932, General
Douglas MacArthur, side by side with Major Dwight Eisenhower, marched up
Pennsylvania Avenue with a parade of infantry, cavalry, and tanks. The troops
routed the squatters from the empty buildings and then chased the campers from
the marshes along the river, burning their shacks. Two veterans had already died
in the skirmishes with the police. Overcome by tear gas fumes, a baby now succumbed, too. Hoover had removed the straggling veterans, all right, but he would
pay a high price for his tactics.

A storm of protest followed. Americans who viewed the photographs and

In the event's ugly climax, a full-scale riot broke out as federal troops marched on the Bonus Army and, using tear gas, forced protesters back to their main encampment across Washington's Eleventh Street Bridge.

read the reports over the next few days found the actions of their government inexcusable. Any remaining faith they still had in Washington was now called into question, especially when Hoover and MacArthur attempted to justify their orders by saying that the marchers were criminals and communists. Far from a revolutionary crowd, the veterans seemed to most people to be little different than the rest of the nation: they had no work and they wanted to feed their families. Squeezed from all directions, the people needed an ally — desperately — and in the Democratic candidate for president in 1932, they finally found one.

It is hard, today, to imagine the level of expectation that greeted Franklin Delano Roosevelt when he ascended to take the reins from the much-maligned Hoover. The fifty-year-old aristocrat, distant cousin of the twenty-sixth president, had barely finished four years as governor of New York. His legs were so wasted by polio he had to strap on awkward braces merely to stand unaided. Yet the task ahead of him was, with the exception of Washington's and Lincoln's, the greatest challenge ever presented to an American leader. Within days of Roosevelt's inauguration, no fewer than half a million people had written letters to the White House, urging him on. "Yours is the first opportunity to carve a name in

Life "on the bum": Boxcars, jail time, and rumors of work

Bailey (right) and two friends, when he was working as a longshoreman.

—Bill Bailey, who was born in the 1910s, fought with the Abraham Lincoln Brigade during the Spanish civil war. When he returned to the United States, he became a labor organizer and longshoreman, retiring in 1975 to write, lecture, and appear in feature films. He died in 1995.

I had been a sailor. So, when things got really bad in New York City, a fellow seaman told me that I should head down to Florida because there was a shortage of sailors down there. "There's oil tankers just laying out in the bay out there," he says. "They haven't got no men, so they're just laying at anchor." Now, for an out-of-work seaman, that's a description of Utopia. So I stowed away on a ship headed for Florida, but when I got there the police came aboard and found me and took me off to jail. The next day I appeared before the judge and told him I came down there looking for work. The judge said, "You think we're gonna take a New Yorker over a kid from Florida? You're crazy!" So they put me in a chain gang for thirty days. And when I got out, I found out that there was no work in Florida anyway. That was just some wise guy trying to get me out of New York so he would have less competition up there.

I hit the road to look for work in other port cities, but as the Depression got deeper, things just got worse and worse. And while people may have wanted to help you, with a loaf of bread or a sandwich or something like that, they had to start getting selective: Should they give it to a thirty-five-year-old man, or to a woman with two kids? So bit by bit you began to see yourself getting less taken care of. There was this horrible law across the whole United States, called the vagrancy law. Any cop could come up to you and say, "Hey, you got a job?" "No." "Where do you live?" "Oh, I'm from another state." "You got any money with you?" "No." And then they'd have you for vagrancy. So I just minded my own

business and tried to avoid all that by moving on.

Soon I discovered that the best way to travel was by railroad boxcars. Of course, the railroad companies were opposed to the idea originally. But in towns where things were really bad, the people were going to the sheriff and saying, "You've got to do something about all of these people bumming on the streets." Then the sheriffs would call up the railroads and say, "We want your train to slow down in this little town every now and then to pick up all these hoboes." So because of the pressure from the sheriffs, these trains would slow down and we'd jump on and ride. It wasn't so bad. Some days if the weather was nice, you could sit up on the roof of the cars and sun yourself.

Heading westward into California, we joined masses of people, because everyone was under the illusion that there was work out there. Most of the people doing the traveling were just poor farmers or pickers trying to follow crop seasons around, but even with a crop in season there wasn't much out there. Who the hell needed a hundred guys picking oranges anymore when there was no market for the oranges? It was a very sad type of deal. But I will say this: as bad as things were, there was no violence. You'd never hear of a woman being attacked or beaten. And all the mothers on the road with families, they got the preference in the boxcars. When you were making a grab for a freight car and you were just getting ready to jump in, somebody might be there at the door and say "Sorry, fella, family car." That meant there was a whole family in there, and you

respected that and you stayed the hell out of it. That's just the way it was. As things got worse there were more and more families out there. Sad, but that's the way the country was.

Rumors were everywhere. You'd hear: "They're taking ten thousand men at Imperial Valley!" And everybody would head there, only to find nothing but masses of people there talking about some other rumor of work someplace else. So, you'd just have to learn to survive — somehow. I'd go to the shoe repair and say, "Anybody leave shoes here that are my size?" And maybe somebody did. I'd go to the undertaker and say, "Anybody leave a good coat here?" Because often they'd take the clothes off the dead people and bury them in their Sunday suits. And the undertakers were pretty good guys, so they'd say, "Well, why not? He don't need it anymore. Good luck." And if that stiff lying there was your size, then you were in luck.

Bumming was easy for me, because I was young and had a schoolboy face and I'd always say "Madam" or "Mister," and "I'm willing to work, if you will give me a meal." I think that sort of hit people more than, "Hey, any change in your pocket?" That type of stuff. Sometimes people would say "Okay, young man." Or "How long you been on the road?" Or "Where you from?" Or "What does your mother think of you doing this?" But it worked often enough. The main thing to remember was to try and keep clean, and always have a sandwich hidden someplace that you could chew on, because you might not always be able to bum a meal or get work every day. I've been in places where I was bumming at the front door and while I was trying to get their attention, I could hear a knock on the back door —someone else looking for a handout. Some people even put up signs saying, "Please do not knock. We have nothing for ourselves." And you always had to be careful that you weren't thrown in jail for asking for food.

One of the best ways to stay out of jail was to go to jail. Sometimes I'd get into a town, and if there was no work at the docks I'd go straight to the sheriff's office and say, "I want to know if you have a place I could stay in for the night." And he'd say, "Go down there to cell four, and flop in there." So you were safe, and he appreciated that, because it meant that he didn't have to go out and look for someone like you to throw in there. The next morning, he might come up with a pot of coffee, and you might get a chance to clean yourself up a little bit, and then you'd be on your way. So most of my time, I spent in these little sheriff's jails. And that proved to be a very smart idea, because if somebody got robbed and said, "It was one of them filthy hoboes coming through town that did it," they could never blame me because I was already locked up.

"He's honest, he's strong and he's steady, a chip off the block that gave us Teddy," read part of the chorus from this 1932 campaign song.

Results of the 1932 American Presidential Election

Roosevelt: 22.8 million votes
Hoover: 15.7 million votes

the halls of immortals beside Jesus," offered one. "People are looking to you almost as they look to God," said another.

Roosevelt would spend twelve years at the helm of the federal government, and when they were over, people would find it hard to remember a day when he was not their leader, when they could not expect, at a time of need, to hear his soothing voice. Aided by the intimacy of the radio, which he used to great effect, but mostly by a strong belief in using government to actively aid the lives of ordinary people, Roosevelt would become the most important president of the century, changing the office so completely that historians would measure all those who succeeded him against his extraordinary accomplishments.

When he campaigned for the office and even when he assumed it, Roosevelt had no grand plan to raise the masses out of their suffering (the term "New Deal" was a toss-off in his nomination acceptance speech and it surprised him when the phrase took hold). The Democratic platform of 1932 called for much the same approach that Hoover was following already: a balanced budget and a curb on government spending. But to the nearly 100,000 people who braved a blustery March morning to hear his inauguration address and the millions of others who gathered around their radios at the same moment, Roosevelt provided a sense of supreme confidence. He had no remedy, perhaps, but like Teddy Roosevelt, he did have energy — a buoyant, audacious spirit brimming with a captivating confidence — and he promised his constituents that he would use that energy to act swiftly in their behalf.

Striking at the most persistent emotion of the time, he borrowed from Henry David Thoreau ("Nothing is so much to be feared as fear") to pronounce that "the only thing we have to fear is fear itself." But Roosevelt received his biggest round of applause when he declared that he would seek from Congress a "broad Executive power to wage a war against the emergency, as great as the power that would be given to me if we were in fact invaded by a foreign foe."

Editorialists, writing in newspapers the next day, heard that line as the president's wish to assume the mantle of a dictatorship. And indeed, the power that Roosevelt wielded, fueled by the sense of awe that he inspired among his followers, prompted critics to accuse him of fostering an American tyranny (if Roosevelt was one of America's most loved presidents, he was also among its most hated). But the sense of urgency that gripped the nation had prompted many to put caution aside. No less a Republican than Governor Alfred Landon of Kansas pronounced that "even the iron hand of a national dictator is in preference to a paralytic stroke," while Senator David Reed of Pennsylvania went one step further. "If this country ever needed a Mussolini," he said, "it needs one now."

Roosevelt began work by declaring a bank "holiday." The euphemism was characteristic of the new president (pessimism being more or less banished in the Roosevelt White House), but the action was no less serious for it: bank reserves now measured $6 billion opposite liabilities of $41 billion, and anxious depositors, fearing default, were eager to retrieve their savings. Throughout the last week of the Hoover presidency alone, terrified investors had withdrawn $250 million of gold. No fewer than thirty-eight states had closed their banks in advance of the presidential edict. Now, with the rest of them forced to follow suit, the nation came grinding to a halt.

"The Greatest Man in the World"

"Benedict Arnold 2nd"

"My Friend"

"God's Gift to the USA"

"Chief Shooter at the Moon"

Names attached to mail addressed to President Roosevelt

Enthusiastic supporters welcome New York Governor and presidential candidate Franklin Roosevelt to Pittsburgh, 1932. Roosevelt's rapport with audiences was legendary, his charm a refreshing break from the stodginess of his opponent, incumbent Herbert Hoover.

Checks were not honored; payrolls not met. While housewives begged their grocers to give them food on credit and companies started bartering goods or issuing private scrip (Dow Chemical, for instance, paid their workers with something called Dowmetal), Roosevelt's financial advisers worked long hours to assemble a rescue bill that propped up the banks with federal loans. The following morning, when Congress opened in special session, the legislation was rushed first to the House, where (pushed along by cries of "Vote! Vote!") it was unanimously approved, then to the Senate, which provided an equally swift endorsement, before landing on Roosevelt's desk at precisely 8:36 P.M. If nothing else, the speed of the New Dealers had to impress America: the bill that the president signed that night was the government's only copy, and it still bore pencil marks from last-minute corrections.

With 60 million poised by their radios, Roosevelt then addressed the nation in the first of his "fireside chats." Beginning with "My friends," the president explained the government's newest moves, assuring people that it was safe to return their money to the banks that would open the next day ("You must have faith; you must not be stampeded by rumors . . ."). And when people did, in fact, redeposit their money — returning $600 million in hoarded currency by the end of the week, nearly $1 billion by the end of the month — it was clear that the presidential assurance much more than the legislation had turned things around. In a matter of days — hours, really — Roosevelt had personalized the office like no chief executive before him, and established the practice of substantial government participation in the nation's economy.

Over the course of FDR's legendary "first hundred days," the government established fifteen new legislative initiatives aiding farmers, providing for a federal relief program, developing the Tennessee Valley, mandating a minimum wage, regulating Wall Street, legalizing the manufacture and sale of beer, insuring bank deposits, and employing millions of jobless — without a doubt, the greatest period of reform in American history. The ambition of the smart and cocky New Dealers was matched only by their idealism, and they shook the old southern city of Washington to life. Intellectuals and social workers both, they were casting government anew, government as social engineer, executing Roosevelt's belief that the public sector not only had a mandate to dabble in the economy but was also charged with meeting people's social needs.

Roosevelt's NRA (National Recovery Administration) called upon industry to cooperate on pricing and wages; his AAA (Agricultural Adjustment Administration) monitored farm production, paying farmers to plow under crops in order to keep down surpluses; and his massive public works programs put people to work building roads, schools, parks, and dams. Before Roosevelt, when people spoke about "the government," they were usually referring to city hall; now when they used the term, they could only mean Washington, D.C.

Some of the new programs flew in the face of time-honored American traditions. Open markets are the essence of free enterprise, and here was Roosevelt replacing them with government management. The relief offered to the unemployed was welcome, yet the notion of government "charity" nagged at many people's pride. Following on the loss of real work, it felt like one more sign that they had failed. They accepted help only because their situations were so desperate they had no alternative, but they preferred those New Deal measures that pro-

Remembering FDR: Bold leadership and "that voice . . . that brilliant, ringing, uplifting voice!"

Roosevelt's chief of staff was probably the smartest chief of staff ever, because whenever Roosevelt would get into trouble, they'd arrange for a fireside chat. And from the mail and the phone calls they would get, they would gauge the public reaction and decide what to do or what not to do. And boy, was Roosevelt charming! Under my breath, I used to say, "Barnum is alive and well," because he was masterful. His strength was in his voice and his sincerity, and this would not have carried over into television, because what carried Roosevelt in my opinion was what you imagined in your head as he spoke. As a theater owner, I can tell you that if Roosevelt had a fireside chat you'd put in your newspaper ad that day that the speech would be broadcast in your theater as always. If you didn't interrupt your shows for his speeches, you didn't do any business. Roosevelt was magic.

> *—Albert Sindlinger, born in 1907, is an inventor and has worked for the Gallup Organization as an audience researcher.*

When Roosevelt came to power in 1933, there was an almost immediate change in attitude. By that time Herbert Hoover was the losing president, the beaten president, a depressed person. He rarely smiled. When Roosevelt came to power, that voice . . . that brilliant, ringing, uplifting voice which we all heard on the radio made an almost immediate philosophical difference. We felt better about things. We felt we could win, we could get ahead, we could come out of the Depression. This feeling was certainly reflected in the activities of the adults around me. And I even felt it as a kid. I liked Roosevelt. I liked his smile. Herbert Hoover was a dour individual, but Roosevelt, with that jaunty cigarette holder and that smile and that lift in his voice, he was a leader, a true leader. Perhaps the greatest leader we ever had.

> *—Marty Glickman, born in 1917, was a member of the 1936 U.S. Olympic track team.*

I think the only way to truly appreciate Mr. Roosevelt's speeches was to hear them the way I did. The government was worried about the mood of the country, and I was hired to travel around and find out what was going on. I was riding the rails and sleeping under bridges, living with hoboes and bumming food for dinner. One night, someone had a radio turned on, and we heard that magnificent resonance coming out, that voice saying, "We have nothing to fear but fear itself." The way he said "my friends," I can still see the hoboes looking at each other, and nodding, "Yes, he is a friend of mine. And I'm a friend of his, and he's a friend of ours." I only

Roosevelt, en route to a Democratic rally in Sea Girt, New Jersey, 1932, greets Jersey City Mayor Frank Hague.

wish he could have been there to see the response that he got. He had said it so many times, and it was true, they were his friends. They voted for their friend, not for a president of the United States. He was my friend when I voted for him.

> *—Melvin Belli, 1907–1996, achieved national notoriety as Jack Ruby's defense attorney in his trial for the murder of Lee Harvey Oswald.*

In traditional black culture, the church minister is the divinely appointed story teller. He gives meaning to existence. So for the black community in the 1930s, the use of the voice to affect us was nothing new. It was just that of all the voices that I heard and respected and loved, Roosevelt was the master. He could reach out and touch everybody and sort of bring us all together. He made us feel that all we needed to do to resolve our problems was to come together, work out a plan, and do it. And me, a little black boy down in Georgia, hearing that voice over the radio, I felt it. It wasn't that he told it to Daddy and then Daddy told me. He was talking to little Ossie sitting there listening to him. He engaged my support and my sympathy. It was very much one of the reasons why we Americans never gave in to despair. He was always there to spur the troops on. "Come on, fellas! One more time, and you're going to get it done! It's going to be wonderful." And you know, you felt better about yourself.

Franklin stayed at the White House and said these tremendous, marvelous things. But Eleanor went out and made them happen. Eleanor Roosevelt would do those little things that were louder than anything Roosevelt himself ever said. She went to Tuskegee, where they were training black pilots to fly planes, and of

course nobody believed that would work. "Black folks flying planes, oh, God! There are going to be crashes every time they go up!" Eleanor didn't make a speech. She just went to Tuskegee and got in one of the planes. The black pilot got in, and they took off. They went around, and they came back down. What could be more effective than that? No speech. No statement. Just did the little things that made the New Deal work. That was who she was. And we recognized her as a special friend of black people because of things that she did, and quietly said.

> *—Ossie Davis, who was born in 1917, is a stage and screen actor. During the Roosevelt years, he was a student at Howard University in Washington, D.C.*

I remember watching the radio, listening to the fireside chats, the dull glow of the dial, and feeling that Roosevelt was reaching out to us, and saying, "I'm in charge here, don't you worry, I will take care of you. Forget what the other people say, the ones who refer to me as 'that man in the White House,' because I will fight for you against the wealthy." He made you feel that you had a friend who had the clout to do something. It's nice to have an Uncle George or an Uncle Charlie who'll slip you a ten once in a while. But Uncle George or Uncle Charlie couldn't get you a job. Franklin Roosevelt would see that you got one. It was almost like you had a rich uncle, Uncle Franklin, who could make the factory hire you because it was his factory and it was his country. I never felt that he was demeaning the people. I always felt that he was a guy who really knew what was going on, even though he had never been through it himself.

The far right considered Roosevelt "that man in

the White House" who should be ousted as soon as possible before he ruins the country. The people on the far left said the man in the White House and his nice wife were doing the best they could but they should do more. The people in the center said, "Thank goodness we've got you here, Charlie." But as the election showed, there were more people that felt that he was doing well than those that felt he was doing poorly. He had the votes, he had the money and he had the charm. He was a picture-book type of leader. And it was pretty hard to feel nasty toward him. Oh, maybe in a cocktail party at the country club they'd be nasty. But come to think of it, they're still nasty at the country club.

—Bill Wilkinson was born in 1915 in San Francisco. He attended the University of California at Berkeley and worked in public relations for charitable organizations until his death in 1995.

My father felt that Franklin Roosevelt was the worst thing that had ever happened to the United States of America. He voted for him in 1932 but he said he regretted it ever after. At dinnertime, he would talk in very derogatory ways about the president and as a small boy sitting at that table I thought that was just terrible for my father to speak that way of the president of the United States. But on his left was my grandmother who thought that Roosevelt was the greatest man who ever lived, that the sun rose and set on Franklin Roosevelt. What made their debate so memorable was that each of them was quite hard of hearing, so the decibel level got very high. But neither of them changed their minds, to their dying day.

The people like my father who worried about Roosevelt felt that he had usurped too much power, that he was distorting our balanced system of government, that too much adulation and raw power was being taken on by the White House. Others thought he was a hypocrite, and Americans don't like hypocrites. His accent, his theatrical flourishes, the cape and the cigarette holder — those things didn't turn everyone on. But oh, boy. When he came on the radio, you listened whether you liked him or not.

—David McCullough was born in 1933 in Pittsburgh. He started his writing career at Sports Illustrated *in 1955, then turned to writing history books, including the award-winning* Truman *and* Mornings on Horseback, *a biography of Theodore Roosevelt.*

A Resettlement Administration (RA) client visits his loan officer in Smithfield, North Carolina, 1936. A precursor to the Farm Security Administration (FSA), the RA was an early New Deal attempt at curbing rural poverty.

vided them with jobs — no matter how menial or low-paying — to a life on the "dole." (Taking that sentiment to heart, one New Deal program hired people for such "essential" work as shooing starlings away from government buildings.)

Conservative politicians feared that so much government mingling in the affairs of people's lives would amount to creeping socialism. And once the government began providing direct aid to people, they predicted, it was only a matter of time before people would *expect* it to be provided, emergency or no emergency, creating an enormous federal bureaucracy structured around the needs of a dependent population. Their worries struck a chord with the rich, many of whom saw FDR as a traitor to his own class, but Roosevelt soon had a more pressing problem stirring among the masses: while his policies produced an almost immediate revival in national morale and a dent in the era's worst statistics, they did not put an end to the pain of the Depression. And by 1935, people were becoming impatient.

Two charismatic men — one a politician, the other a priest — became the spokesmen for a populist critique of Roosevelt. Huey Long was governor of Louisiana, then Louisiana senator, a tousled and sometimes vulgar figure who built his following around an appeal of Robin Hood simplicity: squeeze the rich to make "Every Man a King." Father Charles Coughlin was a Catholic cleric from Detroit whose sermons, delivered in a mellifluously seductive voice across CBS radio, blamed the Depression on the faceless forces of high finance and de-

The Huey Long legend outlasted the man himself. Here, the 1936 inaugural of Louisiana Governor Richard Leche, an ardent Long supporter, is dwarfed by an image of the Kingfish, who had been assassinated the year before.

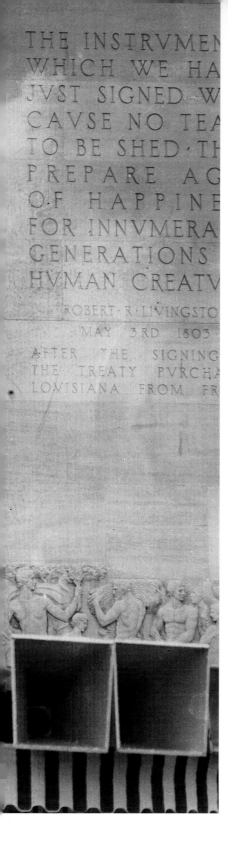

manded social justice for the little man.

Both men were outrageous. Coughlin was a masterful performer, calling upon sentimentality, anger, and patriotic fervor to rally the largest radio audience in the world (about 40 million) first in support of FDR (he called the New Deal "Christ's Deal") and then against the president as a "betrayer" and "liar," more a tool of the moneyed interests that created the Depression than an ally of the people. Long was contemptuous of Louisiana's democratic institutions, converting the state into his own private duchy. First elected governor in 1928, he shocked the South by single-handedly seizing control of the legislature, then installing a lackey in the governor's mansion after he left for the Senate. "All I care is what the boys at the fork of the creek think of me," he said defiantly. And because his firm control of the state allowed him to deliver on many of his promises — building bridges and roads; giving free textbooks to Louisiana university students — they loved him.

Long had his sights set on the White House, and when he arrived in Washington, he brought his ambition with him, soon taunting Roosevelt and his urban, well-bred New Deal reformers both on the Senate floor and during his own very popular radio appearances. (To assure his popularity, he employed no fewer than sixty clerks to send out pamphlets and leaflets proclaiming his triumphs.) There, and elsewhere, promoting his Share Our Wealth Club, the Kingfish, as he was called, proposed confiscating all estates over $1 million and redirecting the money to provide a home, car, and radio to everyone in America, as well as a guaranteed $2,500-a-year income.

Like Long, Coughlin reduced the mysteries of the Depression to easy answers, presented in an "us versus them" homily. Conspiracies, led by the "grinning devils" of Wall Street, were to blame, the same men who led America by deception and subterfuge into that "great contest for commercial supremacy" known as the First World War. Coughlin had his own group, the National Union for Social Justice, which, like Long's, denounced Roosevelt for doing both too much and too little: for creating an intrusive federal bureaucracy that meddled in the lives of honest Americans, while failing to establish a more equitable distribution of income.

Father Charles E. Coughlin, 1891–1979

Left: Lemoine as a student at LSU, 1932. Above: Long, c. 1930, addressing a committee meeting of the Louisiana state legislature.

— *Percy Lemoine, who was born on Christmas Day, 1909, served as a communications officer aboard the USS* Yorktown *in the Pacific during World War II. At the war's end, he returned to Louisiana and became state commander of the American Legion. Subsequently, Governor Edwin Edwards of Louisiana appointed him director of Veterans Affairs.*

Huey Long was a scoundrel in the eyes of most of the public. But to some, he was considered a savior and even the second coming of Christ. People would come in overalls, some were even barefoot, to hear him speak in public. He was so convincing. He could tell you in a few minutes what he had done and what he wanted to do, and you knew he was gonna do it. He would say, "I'm going to do this for you, right or wrong," and he would come through. The people would shout and clap and go back home and say, "I'm gonna vote for that man from now on." And when election time came, they voted for him and his slate of candidates all the way through. We didn't know any better. It was the height of the Depression, and Huey Long came along providing leadership and giving everybody an opportunity to do better. He wanted communities to be upgraded and roads to be built. He provided free schoolbooks. It had cost me forty dollars a year to buy books when I was in school, and, suddenly, I didn't have to pay that forty and that meant a lot.

I was in high school the first time I set my eyes on the Kingfish, as we called him. I went with some friends to the town of Marksville for a political rally in which Long was speaking for one candidate and the town mayor was speaking for the other. In those days, political involvement was sort of clannish. The Long supporters gathered at one end of the courthouse, and at the opposite end the anti-Long people, the mayor's supporters, stood together. It was the only time I ever saw Long speaking on the wrong side — for the opposition, that is. He was speaking without notes, and he just kept talking and talking with the help of a public address system to amplify his voice. Then, right smack in the middle of his speech, the mayor called out the fire trucks and had the sirens turned on, and they circled all around the square, drowning out Huey Long's voice. Long was furious. I never saw him so mad. He was blue in the face, and he shouted and waved his arms. He hollered something like, "I swear that this mayor will never serve as mayor again." And when the next election came, Long ran his own man for mayor and lo and behold his friend was elected.

My most direct experience happened a few years later when I was looking to get into Louisiana State Uni-

versity in Baton Rouge and decided to ask Governor Long himself for some help. I traveled to Baton Rouge with all of my belongings packed in my "please-don't-rain" suitcase (a flimsy cardboard box with a handle on it) and when I arrived at the governor's office, there was this tall guy standing guard outside. "What do you want?" he said and I said, "Somebody told me to come see the governor." And with that, they let me in. Mind you, I was just a country boy, and I was as nervous as could be. Governor Long was dressed as elegantly as always, in a suit with a clean, crisp shirt and tie. He had his feet cocked on his desk. I said, "Governor?" and he said, "Yes, what do you want, son?" I replied, "I want to go to LSU," and because I couldn't really stay in school unless I was working, I asked him if he could help me to get a job, too. Long didn't answer right then, he just wheeled around on his chair, grabbed the telephone, and put a call into somebody.

"I'm sending this young man to you," he said to the person on the other end, "see that he gets enrolled in LSU, and you can put him to work tonight if you want." With one call, I was enrolled and by the next morning I had my job, too, milking thirteen holstein cows by hand, three times a day, for twenty-five cents an hour. Sometimes I wonder why he was so quick to help someone he didn't know, but I think it was because Huey Long cared. I was just a poor farmer's boy after all, and he always catered to the downtrodden. Besides, he figured that if he helped me out, then down the line I'd help him out. And it was true, because after that Long kept up with me and always knew what I was doing, and from then on I supported him.

I felt very bad when Long was assassinated. The day of Huey Long's funeral, I had never seen so many people in one place. Everyone in Louisiana that had a way to get to Baton Rouge attended. Every politician of any consequence and men, women, and children from all walks of life — white and black — were there. Some of them were dressed up in suits and dresses, while others, farmers mostly who didn't have much of anything, came in their patched-up overalls. I remember several of them to this day. My family and I drove with friends about a hundred miles for the ceremony. The eulogy was given by Reverend Gerald L. K. Smith, who had been working with Huey Long on his Share Our Wealth Plan which was his program to redistribute money from the rich to the poor. It was really a political ceremony, but after the reverend spoke, people lined up at least four city blocks to walk by and pay their respects to Long and to bless his coffin. And everybody was crying and saying what a shame it was such a good man had been killed. He was buried right on the capitol grounds, and his grave is still there.

Long appeared ready to make a serious challenge at Roosevelt in the next year's election when in September 1935, in a corridor of the Louisiana capitol, he was gunned down by a prominent local doctor whose family he had wronged ("hit like a deer," said one witness). By then, FDR had already co-opted some of the populist fervor through the creation of the more liberal Second New Deal, featuring labor reform, a largely symbolic "Soak the Rich" tax bill, and, one of his most enduring legacies, Social Security. Coughlin tried to carry on, but the populist movement needed the Kingfish's bravura to thrive. The radio priest helped create a third political party which barely competed in the 1936 election; then, sadly, his rhetoric dissolved into a career of anti-Semitic sloganeering.

Using the radio to generate their message, Long and Coughlin established the appeal of demagogic politics in the burgeoning era of mass culture. But the constituency the two men brought into focus was motivated by more than the froth of overzealous orators. The Depression underscored the helplessness of people in the face of one of the twentieth century's most dramatic developments: the disappearance of individual autonomy in the face of the increasingly powerful industrial state. The salespeople, shopkeepers, barbers, farmers, and other middle-class people who followed Long and Coughlin were baffled by the continuing encroachment of the modern world. And like the traditionalists of the 1920s, they were willing to fight back.

The same winter that Roosevelt came to power in the United States, another leader assumed his country's highest office in Europe. The timing was ironic. For over the next twelve years, until their deaths just over two weeks apart in 1945, the lives of Franklin Delano Roosevelt and Adolf Hitler would grow increasingly intertwined, drawn together as archenemies in the conflict that stands as the century's grotesque climax.

Even sixty years later, the rise of Hitler baffles. His seduction of the German people was so sudden and complete, his assumption of power so total, his vision so ruinous and megalomaniacal, he defies comparison with the most evil of history's great conquerors. Because he lived, 40 million people would die, most of them in brutally agonizing circumstances, and because he provoked a war of unprecedented savagery, the geopolitical makeup of the world would stand throughout the last half of the century in a twisted distortion, a pretzel of suspicion and fear. He was, said one German philosopher, an "error" in history, as if the Fates had looked away from their plan in a moment of distraction, allowing a deadly mutant virus to take hold.

Like Roosevelt's, Adolf Hitler's journey to power was propelled by the world economic collapse. Along with America and most of Europe, Germany, too, had suffered a depression, with unemployment reaching as high as 25 percent. But if it had been hunger alone that motivated them, the people would have followed a very different leader. Hitler's enormous popularity, which extended well into the educated classes, was also a product of Germany's lingering desire for revenge.

Despite Germany's surrender in 1918 (an armistice arranged by the Reichstag, not the army), few Germans accepted that they had been defeated in World War I, least of all the former Austrian corporal who survived a poison gas attack on the western front to serve in the early 1920s as the chief propagandist of the

"The hand of Moscow backs Communist leaders in America . . . [and] aims to support FDR . . . I ask you to purge the man who claims to be a Democrat from the Democratic Party, and I mean Franklin Double-Crossing Roosevelt."

Father Charles Coughlin, 1936

A triumphant Hitler arrives at a youth rally in Berlin, 1934. "He had called from the depths of defeat the dark and savage furies latent in the most numerous, most serviceable, ruthless, contradictory and ill-starred race in Europe," wrote Winston Churchill.

Nazi Party. From Bavaria, which had become a haven for right-wing nationalists like himself, Hitler railed against the forces of Judaism and Bolshevism that were responsible, he said, for the collapse of the fatherland and mocked the fragile republican government established at Weimar as those "November criminals," a reference to the date of the World War I armistice.

At first, the movement was dominated by people like himself: outcasts and people from the fringes of society. Early meetings were attended, remembered one observer, by "men staring at the speaker with wide-open distorted mouths ... their weighty forms [filling] up whole rows, their heavy hands clasped around their beer kegs as though they were sacred relics." But after the complete breakdown of the economy in 1930, the message of resentment and revenge gained steam, spreading beyond the lower classes to recruit university students, professors, businessmen. Hitler's anti-Semitic message resonated with a deep-seated German suspicion of moneylenders, and his nationalistic ideas joined easily with the popular notion that Germany's present money crisis was rooted in the punishment handed them at Versailles. So energized, the campaign moved with the speed of a plague. As late as 1928, actors imitating Hitler's melodramatic gestures were reducing cabaret audiences to helpless laughter. Five years later, the mustachioed provocateur with the quivering forelock was the nation's undisputed chancellor.

The Nazi bible was *Mein Kampf*, a two-volume treatise begun by Hitler while he sat in prison serving time for his part in the 1923 Beer Hall Putsch, a bungled attempt by the party to seize control of the Bavarian government. In his book, he expanded upon his racist views, stressing the social Darwinist notion that man must fight or be doomed to extinction. Since the aggressive capacity of any race, he announced, was directly proportional to the purity of that race, its very existence was threatened by its tolerance of "foreign defilements." The Jews, being international and pacifist, were thus suspect, the "bacilli" that in the Weimar era were infecting every aspect of German culture and politics. Only the Bolsheviks were to be despised as much, for they stood in the way of Germany's natural right to expand its territory to the east.

German Nazi Party Membership
1926................17,000
1929.............120,000
1930.............210,000
1931..........1,000,000

As the movement gained in favor, *Mein Kampf* (My Struggle) sold briskly (becoming a popular wedding and graduation gift), and while few people actually took the time to read it, the fact that it existed gave Hitler a certain legitimacy. For many, it was proof that the excitable Austrian was worth more than an angry speech or two, that he actually had ideas, and it made Nazism seem like an ideology (or even worse, a religion, with Herr Hitler its god) rather than what it was: a movement motivated only by the lust for power, built around the rantings and ravings of a madman.

Still, it was Hitler's voice, much more than his pen, that struck close to the German heart, and it was the emotional appeal of the Nazi movement, much more than its political agenda, that brought it such a commanding following. In a moment of brilliant insight, Hitler had grasped that the pain of the German people at this time went beyond that of the rest of the Western world. They had been

Like an actor preparing for his big moment onstage, Hitler posed for this series of studio photographs in the 1920s. By analyzing them, he hoped to master a set of effective oratorical gestures.

"He thrust his chin forward. His voice, hammering the phrases with an obsessed energy, became husky and shrill . . . His whole face was covered with sweat; a greasy tress kept on falling on his forehead, however often he pushed it back. Speaking with a stern face, he crossed his arms over his breast . . . but a moment later a force bursting out of him flung them into the air, where they implored, threatened, accused, condemned, assisted by his hands and fists. Later, he . . . began to march to and fro along the platform, a lion behind the bars of his cage . . ."

victimized by the Depression, certainly, but that blow was only their latest. Having suffered through the war and then the humiliation of Versailles, a period of revolution and then an era of chronic inflation, they had enjoyed a few years of relative stability in the late 1920s only to be socked now with the collapse of the entire Western economy. In response, their spirit had devolved into a well-deserved mood of despair, a pit of fear, resentment, and shock. What they sought now from their leaders was not some rational argument for a set of policies that might cure the situation; instead, they needed something much more basic: a simple reassurance that they were a good people (indeed, a great people), that their suffering was unjust, that their lives would improve, and that those who were responsible for their pain would be punished.

Early in his career, Hitler had discovered that he had an extraordinary talent for the kind of oratory that would appeal directly to such feelings, and once the moment of public vulnerability arrived, he exploited it to the fullest. In speeches that often ran two hours or longer, he would hold a crowd of up to half a million spellbound, taking time first to warm up and sense the mood of his audience, then diving in to do his work. Sweating profusely, shaking with fury, he would build the attitude of his listeners into a frenzy, playing with an assortment of techniques that would make them first laugh, then cry, then explode in a fit of rage.

In the end it mattered not what he said, but how he said it. Few who came away from a Hitler rally were able to describe what policies he stood for, yet they had been dazzled by him nonetheless, thrilled by the pageantry and by the sense of historical inevitability that it seemed to provide. Germany would rise again, if only because Adolf Hitler said it would. And that, of course, was one of the hallmarks of his appeal: the movement could not be separated from the man.

No matter how spontaneous he may have seemed, no matter how impulsively the torrent of words appeared to come to him, Hitler masked a method of enormous calculation. For one of the many dubious contributions that the German leader made to the century was the concept of politics as high theater. He may have failed in his first choice of career (as an artist) and his second as well (architecture), yet when he finally landed upon politics, Hitler practiced it with a flair that utilized visual and dramatic techniques to enormous power.

Everything about the Nazi movement reeked of manipulation: the parades, the singing, the banners, the lights, the oratory. As early as the 1920s, Hitler was preparing his speeches in front of a mirror and studying photographs of his gestures and facial expressions so better to use them to his advantage. At the same time, he was assembling the collection of symbols that over the next twenty years would prove to capture the national imagination: the most enduring of them the *Hakenkreuz* (or hooked cross) set in a white circle on a red banner. "In red, we see the social idea of the movement," he explained, "in white, the nationalist idea, in the swastika, the mission of the struggle for the victory of the Aryan man." Nazis greeting each other with "Heil Hitler!" and the stiff-armed salute seemed silly in those beginning days, but by the early thirties, the pose was as much a part of German life as sauerbraten.

Hitler's love for stagecraft prompted him to make smart use of amplification and lighting. He studied acoustics (raising or lowering the timbre of his voice to

"I called him Onkel-dolph": **A childhood encounter with Hitler**

When I was a little boy, I loved when Hitler would come to visit my father. I called him Onkel-dolph, and I found him the most fascinating and imaginative companion. My favorite game was railroad. He would get on his hands and knees on the floor and pretend he was the tunnel, and then I would crawl under him and I was the engine, and behind me was an imaginary train and he would do all the sound effects. He would say, "You are now pulling out of the station," and he'd make the sounds of a steam engine. Then he would let his imagination go and describe the cattle cars, imitating the sounds of cows, sheep, chickens, and pigs. Finally we would pull into a station and then he would imitate the conversation of lots of people, and he was a very gifted actor, very good at doing sound effects.

I was simply delighted, and part of my fascination with him was a certain honesty he had, a certain candor on his part. Most grown-ups, when they come to visit your parents, they will see you there and pat your head and say, "My, how you've grown. And how are you doing in school?" And the way they say this, the kid knows perfectly well that they're just being polite, they want to get rid of you. Now, Hitler was quite different. He would come in, and he would greet me affably, most cordially. Sometimes he would say, "Sorry, fellow, today I've got no time for you at all," and this was an honest thing. But if and when he decided to devote himself to you, then he got down to your level, and he was there entirely for you. This is a fascination no kid can resist.

With adults Hitler was not prepared to engage in debate, but he was able to listen very patiently. I remember witnessing some of the conferences in my father's library, where they were planning the next election campaign, or something of that sort. Hitler would remain silent while his lieutenants would air their views, and make their suggestions. He would say nothing unless the debate among his lieutenants threatened to flag. Then he would either throw in a remark or ask a question to stir things up again. This would go on for a long time, and he listened to all the various suggestions, very carefully, quite quietly. He had the habit of sitting there, chewing his cuticles, while listening. And then, when he had made up his mind, he would slap his thigh, stand up, and tell Göring to do this and Goebbels to do that and Himmler to do this. And from that moment forward, there was no further discussion. He had made his decision. And everyone had to abide by that. He would broker no further objections. My father sometimes tried to object, but he was always shouted down. People were captivated by Hitler simply because of this immense assurance that he radiated. For people who are insecure and torn against themselves, it is a relief to have somebody come up and say, "That way. Let's go." That was

Hanfstaengl, in 1926, while on vacation in Poland.

—*Egon Hanfstaengl was born in 1921. His father was an early Nazi Party member and a confidant of Hitler. When that relationship became strained, Egon's father, believing his family to be in danger, fled with them to England and the United States in 1937. Egon served with the U.S. Army in the Pacific during World War II and eventually returned to Munich, where he is a retired schoolteacher.*

much of his secret.

I was never at the big Nuremberg rallies. But I was in a huge rally with many thousands of people outside Munich. I was on a big platform, hidden behind a tree looking out at the huge audience. Whenever Hitler spoke, people were always made to wait, so he could make a dramatic entrance. And then military music would start, and he would march down the center aisle, flanked by heaven knows how many gorgeously uniformed creatures. He had the ability to stand there, silently waiting, until the tension rose. It takes a lot of willpower to make a huge audience wait that long, but he could do it. And then he would begin, slowly revving up until he would finally reach a tremendous pitch. I looked out into the audience that day and recognized a teacher of my gymnasium sitting in one of the front rows next to two charwomen from the same school. There was this enormous class difference between the teacher and these charwomen, and they were obviously embarrassed to be sitting next to each other. But after Hitler

had got going in his speech, all three of them were yelling their heads off, and they had melded together, so to speak. It was quite an extraordinary thing to watch, and a specific illustration of what Hitler's oratory could achieve.

About 1934, my mother and I were guests at the Berchtesgaden. I was older then, and I no longer called Hitler Onkel-dolph. I called him Herr Hitler because my parents had said he didn't like that degree of intimacy from older people. He would take it from little children, but he was a bit squeamish about that kind of thing with adults. He had a terrace there — not the enormous showy terrace that was later built — and on a clear day, you could see Salzburg from there. We were out there one fine morning and he pointed out and said, "You see that there, boy? That's Salzburg, that is in my homeland of Austria. And one of these days, I'm going to see to it that it will join with Germany." And I thought that seemed perfectly correct.

Charwomen hang Nazi banners out to dry.
Once Hitler had gained power, the swastika
became ubiquitous, appearing on flags,
plaques, armbands, pins, and pennants, and
for a while at least, on such unofficial merchandise as hairbrushes, cigarette lighters,
toy horns, paper cups, and artificial flowers.
In 1933, the Ministry of Propaganda
instituted an antikitsch law, forbidding the
commercial use of Nazi symbols.

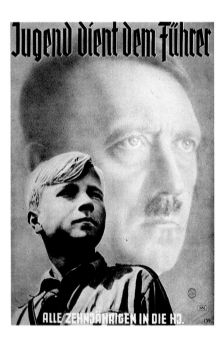

This 1935 poster reads,
"Youth serves the führer!
All ten-year-olds into the
Hitler Youth."

fit various halls) and carefully timed his entrance at rallies to build interest, arriving always late (but not late enough to "arouse hostility"). He even chose the style
of uniforms used by the Brownshirt storm troopers that served as the party's private militia. Once crowned the führer, he set upon schemes to raise his dramas to
an even grander scale, both in the bombastic state orgies that served as the yearly
Nazi Party rallies in Nuremberg and, ultimately, in plans (never executed) to
rebuild Berlin as the capital of the world and a monument to himself (including a
dome seven times the size of the dome of St. Peter's).

　　The effect of all this was to take politics into a new realm, the subconscious.
One of the questions that lie central to an understanding of the twentieth century
is why the German people followed Hitler, and to what degree they share responsibility for his crimes. Yet, without absolving them, it is fair to say that Hitler
practiced a deception of remarkable deviousness, not only in his use of drama but
in his uncanny ability to touch Germans at a level so primitive and profound they
seemed to respond more from instinct than determination.

　　The paradoxes are plentiful. People freely voted Hitler into office (though
they never actually gave him a majority, forcing the Nazis to join with other right-
wing parties in a coalition), knowing that once there, he would dismantle the
democratic republic in favor of a system built around himself. And helping to
assemble that system with him, they complied with a transformation of their society so total that they ceded all individual rights in favor of obedience to the new
order.

　　Mayors and other elected officials were replaced by party functionaries;
potential rivals to the führer were shot; "Heil Hitler!" supplanted "Praise be
Christ" in Catholic schools; and, in the new spirit of cooperation, laborers
accepted lower wages at factory jobs, happy not just to be working but to be
working *for the Reich,* as Hitler, in flagrant violation of Versailles, ordered the
armaments industry into full production in preparation for the war he knew he
must wage. The group that received the most punishing treatment was the Jews.
Within weeks of his assumption of power, Hitler had barred them from civil ser-

Hitler as "Savior": **"This man was not only admired but welcomed, longed for"**

I was born in the last year of the First World War, and from earliest infancy I was aware of Germany's hatred for the Treaty of Versailles. I remember very clearly my mother's grief over her fallen brothers and cousins, and my family's very strong antiwar feelings. The inflation that occurred after the war, which I remember even though I was only five, strengthened those feelings. Then we had a few calmer years, but the early 1930s was a catastrophic time for Germany. In Bremen, where I grew up, there were lines in front of the employment offices, lines in front of the food distribution centers, longer and longer lines every day. There were parades and demonstrations by the Communists and Social Democrats with their beating drums. And these demonstrations were not always peaceful: every night there was fighting, and we lived right next to the working-class district, so we often heard gunfire. There was a great sense of uneasiness everywhere. So when this odd Hitler came along with his slogans that captured the essence of what was in the hearts of the German nationalists, then it became clear, even to a child, that things would change very soon.

The mood of the country was explosive, and Hitler's slogans, which came more and more into the public sphere after 1931, resonated well among the people. At that time he never spoke of war. He promised us that unemployment would end, and that Germany would once again take its place in the world as a state worthy of respect. And I think that was probably the key thing, for the Treaty of Versailles had cut to the root of Germany's self-respect, and a people cannot survive for long without self-respect. So this man was not only admired but welcomed, longed for. When the change of power happened, and the streets were suddenly peaceful and clean, and there was no more fighting — then all of us, who hadn't really been for Hitler necessarily, were initially greatly relieved.

I must have been about fourteen years old the first time I saw him. The picture that was constantly shown in the newsreels and newspapers was very impressive, showing how Hitler and [President] Hindenburg greeted one another and how Hindenburg shook Hitler's hand as chancellor. As a young woman, I pinned all of my hopes on this new personality — the hope that now everything would be entirely different and better. I still remember January 30, 1933 [the day that Hitler became chancellor], very clearly. It wasn't a revolution in the real sense of the word, but rather a relatively peaceful transition. Now, suddenly, there were brown-shirted troops who marched around and made a very orderly and cheerful impression. The sidewalks were lined with people, there were nice marching bands, and there was a festival-like atmosphere every-

Fischer (second from left, wearing headband) at the moment when she met Hitler, 1936.

—*Margrit Fischer, born in 1918, became a kindergarten teacher, and in 1942 a Third Reich organization promoted her to a key teacher training position. Though she was pressured to join the Nazi Party, she never did. Since 1941, she has been married to Fritz Fischer, a historian who became a controversial figure due to his views that Germany was largely to blame for World War I.*

where. The people were astonished, curious, but also glad. There wasn't any jubilation yet, but there was expectation.

The jubilation came one or two years later, after unemployment had really been fought and the streets were clean. At that time there was still no mention of war, and no mention of persecuting Jews either, at least not publicly. The most important thing now was that the people really had a feeling of participation. It all happened so quickly in those first four years: first the creation of jobs, then the creation of all sorts of organizations. The previous private associations — the scouts, the religious groups, and so on — were gradually subsumed into the Hitler Youth. Not everyone had to join. I, for example, did not join the Hitler Youth at first, because I was raised to be very individualistic, and I was wary of big gatherings. But in high school, I had a wonderful teacher who completely embodied the ideals of National Socialism, and she was a role model for me.

It is very difficult to capture charisma in words. I was hiking, and I met up with a group of BdM girls [Bund deutscher Mädel, or League of German Girls] on the way up to where Hitler had his residence. I was wearing a *Dirndl* [the traditional German folk dress]. And merely waiting in this group created a feeling of suspense, which then relaxed when the door opened and the führer walked up to us very matter-of-factly and shook our hands and talked with us — not really like a father, but more like a comrade. He had a very deep understanding of young people, and had an ability to speak with youths. He joked around with us, and asked us where we were from and why we had come; it was a very natural half hour. But his entire personality, his bearing, touched a place in the heart that is quite seldom reached. At that moment there was a feeling of inner enthusiasm and approval that was not cerebral, not at all, but which carried us all away and bound us to one another — all of us who were standing there. Afterwards, when we hiked down the mountain, we felt like we were walking on air. We fell into each other's arms and exclaimed how we had been blessed to experience

such a half hour — that it was an experience we would never forget for as long as we lived.

We had no television then, only radio and newsreels, and of course everything we saw and heard was terribly slanted. Before every radio news announcement the government played a beautiful fanfare — Liszt, I think — that struck you to the very core. When you heard the fanfare, you went running to the radio thinking, "What has happened now?" It was very cleverly done, and very exciting. Whenever Hitler's voice came on the air, you felt a kind of inner attentiveness. His way of speaking was difficult for the ears to take for any length of time, but we got used to it, and somehow it was always something special to hear him speak. Of course we had to listen to Hitler speeches so often that ultimately we started to find them boring, but during those first years it was really remarkable what he was able to do with his voice.

We were never allowed to see anything that would tarnish Hitler or the image of his leadership. Of course we didn't see everything as positive. We were certainly not thrilled about the characters who worked with Hitler, for example. But we couldn't publicly rebel against the state. That was the price we paid, and we said to ourselves, "Well, we are really well off, and we have climbed so far." Basically people were satisfied. The fact that we had to keep our mouths shut, and to guard against being too critical, that we were not entirely free, that was the price that we paid for this positive feeling, this positive, upward movement of our nation.

During the Olympic Games in Berlin we had a friend from England visit us in Bremen. He thought Germany was incredible and he said to us, "This National Socialism has made Germany into an entirely different country and I only wish England could experience something like this." So by this time, the Germans could again look out on the world with heads held high, and we could again see ourselves as equals amidst the chorus of other countries. We received so much praise from the rest of the world — never was there so much praise for Hitler's *Reich* as in 1936.

*Toddlers carrying Nazi flags are paraded down
Berlin's Unter den Linden, 1934. Obsessed with
the future of the Aryan race, Hitler encouraged
ardent Nazi Party members to procreate and
recommended the preaching of the Nazi gospel to
children at a very young age.*

vice and, by the end of 1933, they had been excluded from universities and professional occupations.

Whenever it seemed that he might be going too far, that he might have to justify his actions to someone other than himself, Hitler resorted to an irrefutable argument: his stewardship of the mystical community of the German *Volk*. The term, which cannot be accurately translated into English, means, literally, "folk," but to German ears it is filled with overtones of race, tribe, blood, nation, family; and in the 1930s climate in which Hitler rose, a time when the German people felt themselves to be under siege from outside forces, the führer's misty-eyed use of it worked on the masses like a drug. Here, they thought — as they laid road for the mighty German autobahn, worked the assembly lines to build planes, tanks, and warships, and marched lockstep, carrying the materials to assemble the concentration camps — here we belong.

That the twentieth century had a Hitler would alone seem to be punishment enough on the human race. But the German leader was perhaps only the worst tyrant of the 1930s (and on that there is considerable argument). Italy's Benito Mussolini, who was a kind of mentor to Hitler, took this period to consolidate power over his dominion, building a national image around Il Duce (the leader) that was nearly as developed as the "führer myth" that absorbed the Germans (though not, thankfully, as vicious). And in the Soviet Union, the idealism of the Russian revolution evaporated under the murderous gaze of Joseph Stalin, who wielded an authority far more brutal than any tsar had ever dreamed.

Decades later, when the extent of his bloodthirstiness became known, historians would argue that Stalin was as evil as Hitler (and only in the century that invented mass culture could people engage in a debate to distinguish between two leaders, each the murderer of millions), but if there is a basic difference between their savageries, it is this: Hitler killed to create a racially pure state; Stalin, to effect a social and political transformation. And Stalin got to work first.

Joseph Djugashvili, son of a Georgian shoemaker, inherited his position at the helm of the Soviet Union from Lenin, peacefully, yet he presided over a second revolution of sorts, and a more significant one in many ways. After the bloody civil war that established the Bolsheviks in power (a war that ended the lives of 15 million) and a famine in 1921 that killed more Russians than died in the First World War, the Soviet Union's leaders were faced with a fundamental dilemma. Their struggle had been largely urban and industrial, yet more than 80 percent of the nation's people were rural peasants, a vast impenetrable mass that held itself apart from the cities as if it were from another culture (and, for that matter, another century).

The peasants had eagerly seized the farmland from the large estate owners during the 1917 revolution, but that was as far as their allegiance to the Communist Party went. While the nation's new flag held both a hammer and a sickle, few who used the latter bought into an ideology that demanded that they give the property they had just won from the landowners back to the state and work on a *kolkhoz*, or collective farm. In the mid-1920s, Lenin got around this quandary by adopting a policy of transition that allowed for a period of small-scale free enterprise until socialism could be achieved. The Soviet leader grudgingly admitted that it might take twenty years to bring his ideas successfully to the farms; by

Banners bearing the heroic images of Lenin
and Stalin adorn a square in Moscow, 1931.
Stalin linked his image with that of Lenin,
even going as far as doctoring photographs,
and rewriting history books so it would seem as
if Lenin had chosen him to be his successor,
which he had not.

Stalin poses with delegates at the 16th Party
Congress, Moscow, 1930. The two party officials standing to his right were eventually
killed in one of the Soviet leader's many purges.

allowing the farmers to work their own land for profit in the meantime, he could
generate the capital he needed to modernize Soviet industry. But by the time
Lenin's successor came to power and established his first Five-Year Plan in 1928,
the timetable for that "transition" had been sped up considerably. The days of
"creeping capitalism" were finished, and one of the most tragic periods of Russian history had begun.

Over the next few years, while the government forced the farmers to join
collectives or face deportation to work camps in Siberia, more than 14 million
people either died of starvation or were shot to death by the state. Whole villages
were leveled and millions of children were orphaned, set loose to wander the
countryside scavenging for food like lost animals. If the resistance was strong,
and it was — people slaughtered their own livestock and destroyed their farm
machinery rather than cede it to the Communists — the police were that much
stronger. At first, they targeted only the *kulaks,* those farmers who were more successful than the rest and who, in the eyes of Soviet propagandists, were the great
exploiting capitalists of the fields, a title slapped on peasants whose so-called
entrepreneurial activities often amounted to little more than owning a goat or hiring a relative to help out with the harvest. Then, in order to meet quotas established by the central authorities, they extended their campaigns to include random arrests of anyone, *kulak* or not.

The attack on the nation's peasantry was, in effect, a war fought by the government of the Soviet Union against its own people, by the ideological activists of the cities against the rural culture they saw as the source of Russia's "backwardness," and the battle was as profound as it was tragic, for like so many schisms of the time, it represented the clash between the future and the past, between this century and the last, between the new Russia and the old.

Since only one side was armed, it was clear who would win, but the peas-

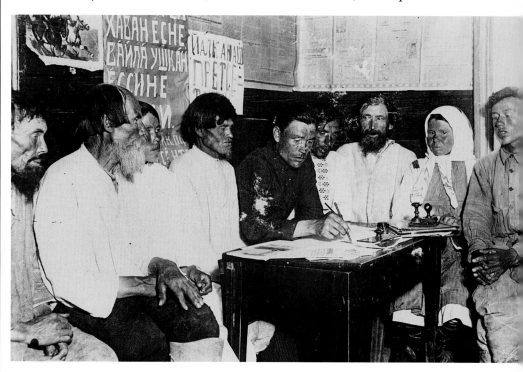

A party activist (in dark shirt) teaches Soviet agricultural "techniques" to peasant farmers in the Chuvash Republic. By converting private farms into collectives, Stalin hoped to transform the rural landscape into a series of "grain factories" and "socialist agrotowns."

"He who does not join the kolkhoz *is an enemy of Soviet power."*

Communist Party slogan, 1930

ants fought a cunning battle. In 1930 alone, they killed a quarter of the nation's cattle, sheep, and goats and a third of the pigs, feasting on them in a massive display of resistance that ensured that Soviet agriculture would lag behind past performance for years to come. And even after the state had broken them down and forced them to join the collectives, the farmers devised ingenious ways to sabotage the system, cultivating less of their land and slowing their work pace to spite their enslavers. Tied once again to "landlords," the peasants described the collectives as a "second serfdom," which is precisely what it was. The rural population was no more happy with this feudal world than it had been with their last.

In village after village, the churches were closed or destroyed, seen by the party as an obstacle to collectivization, as a relic of the Russian past, and as a power center that might try to compete with Moscow. Starry-eyed activists arrived in their place, preaching the new religion — Marxism — but achieving few converts. The bureaucrats had completed their two-week courses in crop management and were now ready to direct the new farms, searching their Marxist theory books in vain for directions on how to handle irrigation problems and crop spoilage. Unfortunately for them, the state had seen to it that they had no place to turn for advice: the best farmers were the ones who had thrived in the pre-collectivization days and now most of them were either wielding hammers in a distant gulag or lying in a mass grave with the other "enemies of the state,"

Peasants stand trial for hoarding grain in one of the Soviet Union's Central Asian republics, 1931. Party activists used false accusations, class hatred, and intimidation in an attempt to destroy the kulak *class.*

ready to fertilize next year's bungled planting.

The part of the Soviet Union where collectivization proved to be most diffi-cult and where the treatment of the peasants was harshest was the Ukraine, where the program awoke a fierce sense of nationalism that Stalin became determined to crush. Setting stiffer and stiffer procurement quotas, he pushed the Ukrainian peasant to the limit, insisting when they did not meet their targets that they must be hiding grain. In fact, the Ukrainians were truly starving, forced to harvest so much produce that they had none left over for themselves. Still, Stalin persisted. He sent thousands of party activists to the region to spy on the peasants (includ-ing the children of the Young Pioneers who stood on watchtowers and peered out over the fields looking for "thieves") and signed a decree ordering that any-one found hoarding grain was to be shot dead. Nearly sixty thousand people were convicted in less than six months, some for the high crime of "snipping," the lifting of an ear of corn or two while harvesting, which didn't carry the death penalty, just a mandatory ten years in prison.

"I heard the children . . . choking, coughing with screams. And I saw the looks of men: fright-ened, pleading, hateful . . . [One said,] 'Take it. Take everything away. There's still a pot of borscht on the stove. It's plain, got no meat. But still it's got beets, taters, and cabbage. And it's salted! Better take it, comrade citizens! Here, hang on. I'll take off my shoes. They're patched and repatched, but maybe they have some use for the proletariat, for our dear Soviet power!' . . ."

Communist activist, describing his work, overseeing the forced collectivization of the Russian farms, 1930

Death began on a gigantic scale in 1933, with 5 million peasants succumbing to starvation even as Stalin ratcheted up the quotas yet another notch. Corpses appeared everywhere, on the streets, in the fields, in the homes. Millions tried to flee, but they were refused entry at the train stations and arrested if they tried to make their way on foot. Because Stalin was obsessed with a fanatical fear of the nationalist impulses of people of the Ukraine, he had decided to tighten his grip on them, turning the nation into one massive six-hundred-mile-wide work camp in which his will was carried out by the cruelest forms of tor-ture.

People ate soup made from dandelions and ran to railroad tracks at the sounds of an oncoming train, begging that the travelers throw them crusts of bread from their windows. As the ordeal wore on, so many peasants developed the distended stomachs that are a signal of starvation and near death that those who still had "healthy" bodies became the targets of club-wielding activists. Surely these people must be hoarding food, the guards thought, or wouldn't they be dying like the rest?

Through it all, Stalin sat with a poker face, as if his program were coming off as planned, insisting that any information to the contrary was inherently sub-versive. Newspapers carried no mention of the mass death in the fields and noth-ing but stories of praise for the collectivization miracle, denials that were all part of the Soviet leader's devious method of operation. For where Hitler built his myth around the sense of drama he created in the Nuremberg Stadium, Stalin built his around the Great Lie and the threat of terror that he mounted toward anyone who dared to object to it.

Whatever idealism it had once had, Soviet communism had now evolved into an iron dictatorship, a society that — much like Hitler's Germany — began to revolve around the commanding presence of one man. The individual was

During the famine, when I was a student at the Soviet School of Mines, the government decided to send out some students to help the collective farmers with the harvest — those who remained alive, that is. So in 1933, I was sent with a group of other students out to the Ukraine. By this time, the famine had spread all over the territory of the black soil, which stretched from the Polish border across the Ukraine and into Russia. As we traveled into the area we noticed that there were no people left anywhere — they had all been deported or starved to death, all because of collectivization. Sometimes we would arrive at a place that our maps told us was supposed to be a village and there would be nothing there — just bricks and weeds.

When we arrived at Uman, the village where we would be working, we went to the family home in which we were supposed to stay and found only one girl there, of about thirteen years of age. Her wall was covered with photographs of nice-looking, healthy people. They were her grandparents, her parents, and her sisters; there were maybe twelve or fifteen of them altogether. We asked her, "Who are these people? Where are they?" She said, "They all died of starvation. I am the only one who's still alive, but I will die soon because I have already gone through the stage of being swollen." This meant that she was now in the dehydration stage and beyond medical help.

We were very depressed by that, and so we went on to another house where we met a widow with one daughter. She had taken in one other girl because this girl's mother had gone into a kind of famine rage — which was not uncommon — and was ready to cut her daughter's throat. But the girl escaped and this widow took her in. This woman baked us green pancakes which tasted and smelled very bad, almost like dung. She said, "These are made from beet leaves and the leaves of a cherry tree, which I dried and ground up and then put some water into it. This is what we're eating."

Living among the villagers I learned what was going on with collective farming. The peasants had to give all of their grain to the government, but the government thought they were holding out and hiding the grain. Some of them did try to hide it under a roof or a floor, or they would dig a hole three meters deep and bury canvas bags full of grain. But then the Communists would come with long, steel probes and wherever the ground was loose they would start digging. And when they took that grain away the family was left without anything. If a family had a cow or pigs they would slaughter them, too. In the villages, you would never see a dog, or a cat, or a goose, or a chicken. Everything was consumed.

In Uman there was a small pond for fishing. And

Workers dispose of the bodies of famine victims in the Ukraine, 1932.

one day, a group of men who were still strong enough were fishing there, and when they pulled in their nets they found a bundle of something. It was a human head, the head of a woman they knew, in fact, who had disappeared. When the authorities came to investigate they traced it back to the woman's neighbor. He had killed her and was living on her flesh. He was shot, of course. I also saw two people arrested in a railway station, near Kiev. They were a man and wife, peasants from some northern wooded area. When we asked the chief what was going on, he said, "They are cannibals. They are doomed to be executed by shooting." In fact, they were half insane, because when starvation starts, a person goes through various stages. The first one is a tremendous desire to eat something. Then the person gets almost insane. Then weakness appears. These people who were arrested were already in the stage of weakness. They were trembling, and not at all steady on their feet. Soon they would get swollen and desiccated, so they were doomed either way.

People are very able animals; they can survive all kinds of deprivations and adapt themselves. The collective farms continued to exist and somehow, people survived. Many years after the famine, I met someone from Uman and I found out what happened to the woman who had tried to kill her daughter. She stayed alive somehow, and the girl came back to live with her.

—Eugene Alexandrov, who was born in 1916, was deported to a German labor camp during World War II. In 1950, he emigrated to the United States and then earned his Ph.D. from Columbia University. He taught geology at Queens College of the City University of New York until retiring in 1987 as professor emeritus. He is a cofounder of the Congress of Russian Americans, Inc., an organization representing the interests of Russian immigrants.

subsumed now by the state, his survival dependent upon his ability to function usefully as part of a gigantic, pulley-driven national machine. And society now operated not according to the laws of nature, but according to the laws of Stalin: whatever he said was "true" if only because he had said it.

If there were problems with the harvest, Stalin declared, why then there was only one place to look for blame: the *kulaks* that must still be rooted from our midst; reports of the famine in the Ukraine were fiction, the kind that makes people laugh. The harvests were doing exceedingly well; so was steel production. There was no challenge too great for the Bolshevik society. Of course many people knew otherwise, yet they had to keep it to themselves, carrying around the image of a two-headed monster: on one side the rotting head of a corpse, on the other the smiling face with the wire-brush whiskers of the Great Genius Leader.

Even westerners were deceived. Hitler, Stalin, and Mussolini all came of age at a time when despotism did not have the dreadful reputation that it went on to acquire with the coming of the Second World War. Far from it, the bold leader with the simple solutions seemed, to many, like the perfect antidote to their festering wounds. Hitler rebuilt the German war machine and helped his nation escape the Depression, Mussolini made the trains run on time, and Stalin was in the process of converting a corrupt centuries-old society into a modern utopian state.

So long as the truth was denied, so long as people believed in the Great Lie, the "success" of the Five-Year Plan stood in stark contrast to the depression in the West (and while agriculture was a failure, Soviet industrialization did make significant strides). If Stalin encountered some resistance along the way and had

Two baseball teams made up entirely of American expatriates celebrate after a game in Moscow, 1932. While these men and scores of other Americans had voluntarily moved to the Soviet Union, Stalin quickly grew distrustful of their presence. By 1938, many of them had been arrested by the Soviet government, charged with espionage, and either killed or sent to Siberian work camps.

Dream destroyed: An American communist's harrowing journey through Stalin's terror state

You could almost say I was born into the revolutionary movement, because my father became a Communist in 1917, just one year after I was born. He had immigrated from Italy to America, but he soon became very attracted to the fine-sounding words of Karl Marx, and of course the propaganda he heard about the Soviet Union: no unemployment, no social classes, no racial prejudice and so on. When I was growing up, I was a member of a group called the Young Pioneers of America, which was for children of Communists. Our function was to support the party. We even had our own cheerleaders who would chant, "Two, four, six, eight, who do we hate? Capitalists, capitalists, rah rah rah!" I was told by my father never to salute the flag and never to say the Lord's Prayer, but I was too afraid my friends in school would make fun of me. So I used to salute the flag, but with my fingers crossed behind my back, always afraid that my father would somehow find out.

—Tom Sgovio, who was born in 1916, was not released from the gulag system until 1954. He returned to the United States in 1963 after spending several years in Italy, where he was married. He worked for General Motors in Buffalo, New York, and then retired to Arizona in 1982. For many years he has been campaigning for the State Department to acknowledge the plight of the hundreds of Americans who were imprisoned under Stalin.

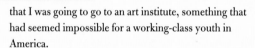

Left: Sgovio speaking at a Friends of the Soviet Union Workers rally, Buffalo, New York, 1933. Above: Sgovio's mug shot taken in Vladimir Prison after his second arrest.

We young Communists went to demonstrations wearing our Communist blouses, and our motto was "Always Ready." By the age of twelve I had already been arrested for handing out leaflets in front of a steel plant. When I was fifteen, I was at a protest where the police started arresting demonstrators and I jumped up on a platform and yelled, "Fellow workers! What you see here is capitalist justice, the lousy cops, the fascist police are arresting these innocent people!" After that, the police arrested me and I spent some time in a juvenile detention home. But my father was really proud.

When I was about seventeen, my father was arrested at a demonstration, sent to prison, and then held for deportation to Italy. With Mussolini in power, my father was sure to suffer as a Communist there, so the American Civil Liberties Union arranged for him to have voluntary asylum in the Soviet Union. Now at this time in America, William Randolph Hearst's papers were full of terrible things about the Soviet Union — stories about forced labor and terrible poverty. But I didn't really believe them because so many liberals from the West, like George Bernard Shaw, had traveled there, were given the red-carpet treatment, and came back trumpeting the beautiful things they saw. When my father moved to Moscow, he wrote me very nice letters, telling me all kinds of wonderful things, mainly that I could get a free education there, and that's what attracted me most. So when I found out that the family would be joining my father, I was very excited to think

that I was going to go to an art institute, something that had seemed impossible for a working-class youth in America.

My mother, my younger sister, and I arrived in Leningrad, in August 1935. Our trip had been paid for by the Communist Party, and all the arrangements were made by them as well. As I walked through the streets of Leningrad, I couldn't help noticing that most of the people did not look very happy — it wasn't at all as I had pictured it back in America. The guide who showed me around took me into a beer parlor, and my God, my heart sank! I had never seen such squalor, never seen so many drunks in my life! The guide ordered some food and it was so terrible I couldn't eat it. Then we went to Moscow, where my father was living under the status of "political immigrant," which meant that we had special treatment. Not really so special, but special in that we lived in a hotel. We had one room for four people, with four cots and a separate communal bath. But we all expected hardships in the beginning, so we didn't complain.

During my first two and a half years in the Soviet Union, we were really living like citizens of a state within a state, because of our political immigrant status. I found work as a commercial artist, and I studied in an art studio. We had our meals in a house for immigrants where there were communists from all over the world. In the beginning, my father was very enthusiastic. We even used to go around to different institutions and make speeches about how terrible things were in America, telling everyone how lucky they were to live under socialism. But things were starting to show themselves.

I usually found something to justify everything bad

I saw, but there were some things I couldn't help noticing that really bothered me. For instance, all this fanaticism about Stalin and Lenin. I was raised as an atheist, and so it disgusted me that the Soviets had basically created a new religion around these men. All you heard about day and night was Stalin. All the songs were about Stalin. It seemed to me that Lenin was like a god to the people and Stalin was a saint, but in fact they were beyond gods. They were deified in the newspapers, and their portraits were everywhere. I began to dislike Stalin, because I couldn't understand how he could stand in front of crowds and bask in applause for a full ten or fifteen minutes, just waiting while everybody applauded him.

I understood that this really was not the dictatorship of the proletariat. I realized that there were classes. They had done away with the old bourgeoisie, but there was another class, the *Soviet* bourgeoisie — in other words, the rich generals and their wives who went around in fur coats, who had beautiful apartments, and so on. Still, I didn't renounce communism in general, because I thought, maybe it was just Soviet-style communism. I thought if communism happened in America, it would be entirely different.

My first truly shocking experience was when I went with a Russian friend to a very run-down suburb of Moscow where there were many factories. We went to a restaurant, and the walls were lined with beggars: men, women, and children, with feet wrapped in rags because they had no shoes. They stood there, and as soon as anyone left, if there was any food on the plate, they would rush and jump on that food. I was so horrified, and I studied those faces, because we were always told by our guides that the beggars were just the leftover remnants of the Russian bourgeoisie. But those weren't the faces of nobility. They were the faces of peasants.

Then things began to change very quickly for us. The government told all of us foreigners that they could no longer support us — we would have to move out of our hotel and find our own place to stay. And every day on the radio, the propaganda machine cranked out stories about enemies of the people and saboteurs being arrested. The purge of millions of innocent people had begun, and suddenly foreigners were being arrested along with everyone else.

As the arrests got worse and worse, and more of my friends disappeared, I decided I'd had enough of the Soviet Union, and wanted to go back home to America. Then, one day, there was a tap on my shoulder, and a man asked to see my documents. He took me to a room full of people like myself and then they called my name and took me away to prison. I told myself, "Wait 'til the Communists at home hear about this. They'll write to Stalin and have me freed." One night they took about a thousand of us to a train station and told us we were sentenced to five or ten years in a gulag, which was a labor camp.

They put us in cattle cars and we waited for about two days without moving. We still clung to the belief that we would be released. But when the wheels of the train started to move, a strange thing happened: all the men who thought they'd be freed suddenly began to sob, and scream, and cry. The further east we traveled, the more I remembered William Randolph Hearst and all of the things he wrote. And I thought to myself that maybe everything he said was true after all. For twenty-eight days we rode in that train, until we arrived in a transit camp in Vladivostok and joined up with about eighty thousand other prisoners. Typhus and dysentery were raging, and we slept on the ground. One night I was sent out to dig a hole which they said was going to be a cesspool. But I think it was a mass grave, because while we worked, there was a constant procession of carts. They were taking the corpses out for burial.

Eventually I ended up in Kolyma in a labor camp. One man told me, "No matter how bad things are, if you look hard enough, you're always going to find some good. Look at it this way. You came to the Soviet Union for an education, right? So you're getting one. If you survive, you're going to graduate from the academy of the Gulag. You can learn more here than at Oxford or Cambridge." And it was true. I learned the utterly low depths that man can fall to. I learned that communism doesn't work. And I learned why it'll never work, because in order for it to work or succeed, you would have to change human nature.

to put it down, well, that was the price of a revolution. George Bernard Shaw visited the Soviet Union in 1932 and pronounced the reports of starvation and forced collectivization to be "nonsense." *New York Times* Moscow correspondent Walter Duranty, who later won a Pulitzer Prize for his reporting, wrote the same year that "there is no famine or actual starvation" in the Soviet Union. Fed up with the joblessness at home, hundreds of Americans went abroad to try the other life. And why not? If democracy was so great, why had it brought good people such misery of late? If Roosevelt was so perfect, why could his New Deal not erase unemployment?

After months of heated controversy, the Olympic Games opened in Berlin on August 1, 1936. The spectacle followed on the establishment of the Nuremberg Race Laws, a humiliating series of edicts depriving Jews of citizenship, banning Jewish-Gentile marriages, and forbidding Jews to employ Aryan housemaids. Over the next few years, the codes would be gradually extended until their goal was to erase the Jew from German society altogether. But even without the harsher laws, some German towns were extending the Nazi terror a step further: many drugstores refused to sell to Jews; hotels displayed signs declaring "Jews Not Admitted"; and food stores refused to allow them to handle, much less buy, their wares.

The world's outrage was vocal, but, in the end, ineffective. For by the time the Berlin Games began, Hitler had transformed the German capital into a $30-million public relations miracle. And how could he resist? The Olympics had been scheduled for Berlin once before, in 1916, but the war had canceled them altogether. As part of its punishment for that conflict, Germany had been banned from international sports competition until 1928. Now a new Berlin Olympics provided Hitler with the opportunity to show that Germany had risen again.

Hitler inspected the old stadium that had been built for the 1916 Games and pronounced it unfit, insisting instead that an arena be constructed that could hold 100,000 people. He then ordered the eight-mile-long route from the old royal palace to the new Olympic complex widened to accommodate the thousands of marching athletes, destroying, in the process, many of Berlin's prized lime trees. Enormous flagpoles displaying the Nazi banner trimmed the avenue. The anti-Semitic signs were painted over or removed; the doors of the concentration camps were swung open; and the repression of the Christian churches was eased. In this, the first Olympics to be broadcast on radio, Germany would show the world a "model" society bursting with pride. They even resurrected a simple bungalow from the 1932 Los Angeles Games and displayed it next to the grand accommodations offered at their Olympic village, a dart aimed directly at the American delegation.

At the center of the Games was the ten-foot-high, 16.5-ton steel Olympic Bell. Four years before, when the Weimar government was still intact, the bell had been conceived as Germany's Olympic emblem, and it included a ring of script just above the lip that read "Berlin 1936" followed by a grand but harmless phrase from the poet Friedrich von Schiller, *"Ich rufe die Jugend der Welt"* (I summon the youth of the world). But whatever the Weimar administrators had originally intended by it, the rise of Nazism had brought the phrase a new meaning. In all the advertising that accompanied the Olympics, an image of Hitler himself was superimposed over the bell, making it appear as though *he* was the "summoning" figure, and when the bell toured the nation in the months before the Games began, crowds of people came out to be in its presence, a symbol (yet *another* symbol) of the will of the new Germany.

Berlin attracted more than twice as many athletes as the Los Angeles Olympics four years before, and most of them (as well as most of the thousands of journalists, businessmen, diplomats, and tourists who were in attendance) fell under the spell of Nazi pageantry. Far from the terror state they had expected, Hitler's Germany looked like a happy, productive nation. Perhaps the stories of oppression, many thought, had been just that, stories. Maybe Hitler's brand of mass politics was to be praised, not condemned. Only the performance of an African-American sprinter would spoil the picture-perfect image of Aryan supremacy.

One of eleven children born to an Alabama sharecropper, James Cleveland "Jesse" Owens had traveled north to Ohio with his family during the Great Migration in the 1920s. There he had excelled as a track star (Jesse Owens didn't run, said one of his coaches; he "caressed" the ground), once arriving at a 1935 meet in Michigan with an aching back and proceeding to break three world records within forty-five minutes of competition. Remarkable though that feat was, it was just a prelude to Berlin. There, putting the lie to Hitler's racial theories, Owens dominated the track and field competition, winning four gold medals (in the long jump, the 100- and 200-meter dashes, and the 400-meter relay) and bringing the German audience to its feet.

The story that Hitler snubbed Owens and the other "black auxiliaries," as he derisively called the African-American athletes, at the winner's ceremony has been exaggerated by time; in fact, the führer, who had personally congratulated the first German victors, later stopped greeting any winners at the request of Olympic officials. But the American sprinter's performance was treated as a political triumph nonetheless, a symbol of a *different* kind that echoed over the sounds of the Hitler youth marching the streets of Berlin daily. "That's a grand feeling, standing up there," said Owens, of the awards ceremony, later confiding to friends that he was relieved not to have to confront Hitler directly and accept congratulations from one he so detested.

Owens's medals could not, certainly, divert the dark propaganda wave that was sweeping Germany (and the sad fact was that his own nation still confined African-Americans to the back of the bus). Yet, with an athlete's uncanny timing, his remarkable performance had seemed to stand up for democracy when the odds against it were quickly mounting, when the world seemed poised to choose organization over freedom, nationalism over internationalism, the highly regimented single-purpose state over the principle of individual liberty, and to be setting the agenda for another war even more horrible than the last.

The Berlin Games were the largest, most expensive, and most publicized Olympiad to date. This official Olympic poster was printed in nineteen languages and distributed in thirty-four countries.

*The stiff-armed salute of the host country's
devoted people was the Games' most
familiar sight, and a hint of the united
front that Nazi Germany would soon
present in its dreadful challenge to the world.*

5

Over the Edge
1936–1941

Over the Edge 1936–1941

Previous spread: Wary civilians respond to the sounds of planes overhead during the Spanish Civil War, May 1937. Hitler's prized Luftwaffe brought a reign of terror down on Spain's cities as it lent vital air support to fascist Francisco Franco's Nationalist Army.

The most popular show in America in the mid-1930s was NBC's *Chase and Sanborn Radio Hour*. A variety program, it featured the playful antics of ventriloquist Edgar Bergen and his dummy, Charlie McCarthy. More than fifty million people tuned in to hear McCarthy taunt Bergen each week (proving that there was at least one ventriloquist whose appeal had little to do with the thrill of *watching* him work) and by 1938, *Chase and Sanborn* had become so dominant in its Sunday evening time slot, CBS could not even find a sponsor willing to underwrite a show to go up against it.

Having already lost the low-brow audience, the network aimed instead for high culture and commissioned Orson Welles, a twenty-three-year-old director who had thrilled theater critics with his unusual staging of Shakespeare's *Macbeth* (set in Haiti with an all-black cast), to provide them each week with a one-hour, commercial-free drama aired directly opposite Bergen. On the night of October 30, Welles's *Mercury Theater* opted to present a radio play based on H. G. Wells's "The War of the Worlds."

Disappointed with the script they had assembled, the young director and his colleagues decided at the last minute to exploit the growing reputation of radio as the medium of truth and offer the play's events as realistically as possible. They would begin as if they were presenting an evening of music from a hotel ballroom and then interrupt the band with a sudden announcement that Martians had landed on the property of a farm near Grovers Mill, New Jersey. From there, the story would unfold much as a real crisis might, with radio reporters relaying dispatches from the scene.

"Ladies and gentlemen, this is the most terrifying thing I have ever witnessed . . ." sobbed Welles's "correspondent," as he encountered the invaders. "There, I can see the thing's body. It's large as a bear and it glistens like wet leather . . . The eyes are black and gleam like a serpent. The mouth is V-shaped with saliva dripping from its rimless lips . . ."

Welles had provided the proper disclaimer at the top of the hour, assuring

*The Hurricane of 1938 slammed into the coast of
Long Island and then ripped a path of destruction
north through New England and into Canada.
Downtown Providence, Rhode Island (above), was
completely flooded as six-foot waves crashed
through parts of the city.*

> *"[These years] were like
> the time you put in in a
> doctor's waiting room,
> years of fumbling with old
> magazines and uncon-
> firmed suspicions, the ante
> years, the time of the moist
> palm and the irresolution."*
>
> E. B. White

people that what they were about to hear was fiction and the *Mercury Theater*'s loyal listeners, few though they might be, no doubt took the show for what it was. What Welles had not anticipated was the large number of people who would join his drama after it had already begun, taking in the Chase and Sanborn show until it went to commercial, then spinning the dial around only to come upon a "news bulletin" describing an invasion from Mars.

In the course of a single hour, Welles's Martians landed on earth, constructed some deadly heat-ray machines, defeated the American Army, destroyed radio communications, and occupied large sections of the country. Remarkably, hundreds of thousands of Americans believed every word of it. Radio stations were inundated with calls from listeners who were gripped with fear; train stations became crowded with families demanding tickets "anywhere." In New York City, theaters were emptied in panic and in northern New Jersey — the site of the Martian "landing" — roads were jammed with people who had packed their cars with their most precious belongings and set out to flee extraterrestrial annihilation.

When Welles signed off at 9 P.M. he was greeted by a throng of New York City police, ready to arrest him for the hysteria his broadcast had set off, yet, in fact, he had broken no law. Instead, there was a mild reprimand from the Federal Communications Commission and for the next two days, CBS followed its regular network identification tag with a line saying "the entire story and all of its incidents were fictitious."

A nail-biting sense of apocalypse dominated the lives of people in the late 1930s. And why not? Everywhere they looked there was evidence that things were going more deeply awry. The American economy remained nearly as stagnant as it had been when Roosevelt took office in 1933. Reelected by a landslide in 1936, FDR found himself presiding over a country that remained, in his words, one-third "ill-housed, ill-clad," and "ill-nourished." Ten million people — nearly 15 percent of the American workforce — were still unemployed (though even these numbers, like many government figures of the time, may have been understated) and by the spring of 1938, five million who had found work since the Depression's darkest days were busy pounding the pavement once again. Perhaps we weren't on our way out of this thing, many thought; having taken one step forward, maybe we are about to be sent two steps back.

Nature, too, looked like an enemy. Only a month before "The War of the Worlds" broadcast, the East Coast of the United States endured a storm of such mammoth proportions, it felt like an invasion itself. The Hurricane of 1938 caused more damage than the Chicago fire and more deaths than the 1906 San Francisco earthquake. Seven hundred people were killed and the homes of more than sixty-three thousand were destroyed by the downpour, which arrived much to the surprise of the U.S. Weather Bureau. Forty-foot waves crashed against Long Island, with spray from them felt as far north as the state of Vermont.

Yet even as people struggled to keep food on the table and their houses on the ground, it was the rumblings of war around the globe that jangled nerves. At first, it was the news that Italy had seized Ethiopia in 1936; that same year, a group of army officers and their followers engaged the liberal government of Spain in a brutal civil struggle that eventually brought Generalissimo Francisco

Throughout Europe, people were growing increasingly concerned about the rise of fascism and the growing threat of war. This French poster reads, "If Hitler Attacked What Would the Pacifists Do?"

Franco to power. In 1937, two flights of Japanese fighter planes attacked an American gunboat in China, killing three Americans. And while the American government quickly shrugged off the incident, the Japanese continued their assault on the Chinese province of Nanking, torturing and killing 200,000 civilians and beginning a period of sustained war with China that would severely strain Japanese relations with the United States. Finally, the threat of a brutal international conflict reminiscent of the century's first seemed coldly genuine in September 1938, when Adolf Hitler, having already annexed the Rhineland and overtaken Austria, huddled with the aged, ailing British Prime Minister Neville Chamberlain in tense negotiations over the fate of Czechoslovakia.

In years past, Americans would have learned of events like these through

Radio's new immediacy: "In the morning people would say, 'Did you hear that last night?'"

In the middle of the 1930s, neither of the two big radio networks — NBC and CBS — had a news department. All we did was air a couple of five-minute news broadcasts a day which were supplied by the Press Radio Bureau. But toward the end of the decade, the country began to count on getting its news from us.

It was a standard evening ritual in houses: people would gather round these rather large radio sets when the news came on, and nobody would talk very much until it was over. They listened to H. V. Kaltenborn bringing them coverage of the Spanish Civil War with the crackle of the rifles in the distance, and certainly nobody had ever heard real gunfire on the air before. Radio was bringing things right into people's homes, and it was beginning to affect the way people felt about what was going on in the world. So when something important happened in Europe, the country was prepared to listen. Americans had always been somewhat interested in Europe's affairs, but they just didn't feel that they were intimately affected by them. Now they were fascinated.

When Hitler annexed Austria, we did a full half hour of reports from Europe, with correspondents in Paris, Berlin, Washington, and London, and me in New York, acting as what would now be called an anchorman. Then in 1939 came the Czech crisis, which was a major radio event, and the country was enthralled by it all. They listened as much as they possibly could. We just took over the radio, doing minute-by-minute coverage, monopolizing the attention of the country. It was a great novelty then to be able to hear somebody like Hitler speaking, or to hear Neville Chamberlain coming back from Munich and waving the paper and saying, "This means peace in our time." To hear his actual words was amazing.

It's no exaggeration to say that radio brought the

As part of their coverage of the London blitz of 1940, American, British, and Canadian radio commentators broadcast a joint program called Round London After Dark. *Edward R. Murrow is seated to the left of the lamp.*

whole country together, all at the same instant, everyone listening to the same things. And the country liked being tied together that way. In the morning people would say, "Did you hear that last night? Did you hear Hitler speaking again? What was he talking about? Did you hear them all cheering, '*sieg heil*'? What did you think?" It was on the tip of everybody's tongue. People didn't quite see, just yet, exactly how all these things overseas were ever going to intimately affect their daily lives. But it was the greatest show they'd ever been offered.

> —*Bob Trout, who was born in 1908, began his career in radio in 1931. Though he has worked in television during his more than sixty years in broadcasting, radio remains his medium of choice.*

Radio was of enormous importance in the 1930s. We listened to it morning, noon, and night. We only had one radio in the house — the big set in the living room, and we would gravitate to it in the evening, after school or work. This was not a formal, after-Sunday-dinner kind of family gathering, it was all very casual. But it made the nation seem to us rather like a national village, and I think it helped the country overall to achieve the melting pot effect.

Since I came from a funny family — my mother and father were professional comedy performers — it was inevitable that we would gravitate to the comedy programs. We listened to Jack Benny, Burns and Allen, Bob Hope, Fibber McGee, and all those popular shows of the day. The soap operas were never of any interest to me, but I was interested in news and sports.

The biggest sports events on the radio in the thirties were the prizefights. In Chicago, on the South Side, you could walk down the street in the summertime and not miss a minute of the fight, because the windows were open and every place you passed had that broadcast on the air. In order to imagine the fight you would superimpose your recollections of newspaper or magazine photos of Joe Louis or Max Schmeling, or whoever the fighters were. And then you could almost see the action.

As for "The War of the Worlds," I was sitting with my aunt and doing my homework when the first interruption came on, and I wasn't particularly interested because these interruptions were happening about fourteen times a day at that time. But here was this announcer who sounded like a typical radio newsman telling us the Martians had landed, and there was not the slightest reason to doubt what he said.

After a few more interruptions, my aunt and my mother went cuckoo, and they began to grab hats and

coats and things and we ran down the hall to the elevator, screaming like nuts. When we burst into the lobby, which I had expected to find in a state of general panic, there was nothing but peace and calm. And then I noticed that at the clerk's desk there was another program on the radio. And I thought if we were really being attacked, this would be on all the networks. So we figured out then that we'd been had, and we fell into hysterical laughter.

> —*Steve Allen, the comedian, was born in 1921. He became an entertainment pioneer, creating the original* Tonight Show *in 1953 and hosting it until 1957.*

The radio had an immediacy about it. You didn't have to wait to read the paper to find out what was going on. And it had an important quality that no other medium has: It made you use your imagination. And that was a fabulous thing. And the radio reached everyone, because almost everybody could afford one. People would gather around their radios, and they would get the word — from Washington, from their local station, and everywhere else. For the first time, you could find out what was happening in your community, in your state, in the world.

Around this time came the foreboding, black clouds of war developing in Europe. And we began to listen to the BBC, and we heard Churchill. You know, he was really talking to us, the Americans, when he did those famous broadcasts. Supposedly they went to the Commonwealth of Nations, but he was really speaking to us. We had the resources, we had the men, we had the facility, and the ability to do something about their situation. We were all concerned, because we were told that there could be dangerous times ahead. And to hear Edward R. Murrow, an American, covering what was happening in Europe, that really brought it home to us. He had a great voice, and he could describe a scene so beautifully — he really put you right over there. When London was on fire, you could hear British fire engines beeping, and then the crash of the walls, and the flames. And Murrow was there, describing it all so dramatically. This finally caused us to say to ourselves, "This is really war. How horrible that it's come to Europe." Because Murrow brought it right to us, at home, and made us feel very uneasy. And more and more, people were saying that someday we'd be caught up in this.

> —*Steve McCormick, who was born in 1914, was a radio correspondent at the White House during four administrations. He also served in World War II as a lieutenant colonel, receiving a bronze star for his performance on Saipan.*

dispassionate newspaper accounts, sometimes days after they had occurred. But world events in the late 1930s took on a new and frightening urgency in part because of the way that news was delivered. In the early thirties, radio programming was dominated by comedies and variety shows, but by the end of the decade it was also a prime news medium (trusted, reported a *Fortune* poll, even more than the papers) and the news bulletin — so artfully parodied by Orson Welles — had become a staple of modern life.

People no longer turned radios on only to hear specific shows; now they kept them on for long periods of the day in part to catch every news flash (radios were standard equipment now for cars and even for farm tractors). In 1938 alone, there were thousands of news flashes interrupting programming, an epidemic of sensationalism that spread jitters nationwide, and when the bulletin included a "live" report from the scene, the temperature of the moment was raised even higher.

British Prime Minister Neville Chamberlain and his wife, in window at top right, wave to an enthusiastic crowd after his return from Munich. Winston Churchill, who denounced the agreement, later wrote of Chamberlain, "His all-pervading hope was to go down in history as the Great Peacemaker . . ."

In the midst of the fighting in Spain, CBS radio correspondent H. V. Kaltenborn reported from an evacuated farmhouse along the Spanish border, the sound of bombs exploding behind his voice. In the spring of 1938, CBS brought live reports as German troops goose-stepped their way through the streets of Vienna. In September of that same year, Adolf Hitler, speaking to the awestruck throngs at the Nazi Party rally in Nuremberg, was heard live over NBC and CBS.

Throughout, whole families sat rapt by their Philcos and Zeniths, ears cocked to the strange sounds history was making across the great Atlantic. They listened, riveted, to the crisp diction of Edward R. Murrow and his team of international correspondents ("This is London . . .") as they described troops massing at borders throughout Europe, ready to invade. And they breathed a huge sigh of relief when the British prime minister returned from his diplomatic mission to Munich on September 30 waving an agreement ceding Czechoslovakia to Hitler, but assuring, he said, in a statement of astonishing naiveté, "peace for our time." For anyone alert enough to care about the news in the 1930s, it was a roller-coaster world.

Though they hung on every word coming from abroad and were frightened of the repercussions that a second European war would have for their own lives, few Americans were interested in seeing their country get involved just yet. The domestic struggles they faced were difficult enough and besides, there was a new earnest attitude emerging throughout the country focusing people more inward than outward. Dazzled by the documentary efforts of thirties' photogra-

Of her classic picture Migrant Mother, *above, photographer Dorothea Lange said, "I did not approach the tents and shelters of other stranded pea-pickers. It was not necessary; I knew I had recorded the essence of my assignment."*

In order to support and defend its aid programs, the Farm Security Administration (FSA) sent photographers, like Lange and Marion Post Wolcott (right), into rural America to document life in the 1930s.

phers, filmmakers, writers, and social scientists, people were gaining a whole new understanding of their country and its countrymen. Europe could wait.

Photography took on a new vitality. Like the radio news flash, it appealed by making the viewer feel like an eyewitness, absorbing the unfiltered experience of life firsthand. At the height of the Depression, when economic statistics were untrustworthy and even hyperbole seemed insufficient to the task, pictures provided the best description of American suffering (and the only one available to the illiterate). Commissioned by the New Deal, teams of cameramen roamed the country documenting the nation's woe, and when their work appeared in magazines and newspapers, it shocked viewers into an outpouring of sympathy (and, in turn, helped garner support for FDR's relief programs). One photograph in particular, showing a female migrant worker with her young children, so moved viewers it became the nationally recognized symbol of the era's misery.

Among the places the New Deal pictures appeared was a fresh new photo magazine called *Life*. Started in 1936 by Henry Luce, the founder of *Time*, *Life* was an instant success. The mere idea of a photo magazine was so exciting to thirties' readers, it inspired more than a quarter of a million of them to buy subscriptions even before the first issue had been published. And once *Life* hit the newsstands, its popularity rose so quickly, Luce nearly killed it when he couldn't raise advertising rates fast enough to pay for the magazine's skyrocketing circulation.

People liked *Life* because it showed them pictures not only of major news events but of everyday moments as well (an early issue featured a photo essay called "Birth of a Baby"). The magazine had the quality of a community journal; readers opened it up each week to find stories about people as ordinary as themselves. In its first year, *Life* did stories on a corset buyers' convention, a baby's first haircut, a night at the Savoy with "the boys and girls of Harlem." And even

Life founding publisher Henry Luce described the mission of the magazine as "To see life; to see the world; to eyewitness great events; to watch the faces of the poor and the gestures of the proud; to see strange things . . . to see man's work . . . to see and to take pleasure in seeing . . ."

**"From the mountains
To the prairies
To the oceans, white with foam . . .
God bless America"**

*Irving Berlin
1938*

when it did focus on the big stories of the time, it often looked at them from a vantage point that made people feel a common bond ("Today I may not be in the mood nor feel the need to read the finest article about the prime minister," wrote Luce, describing the mind-set of his readers, "but I will stop to watch him take off his shoe.").

Like much of the media, *Life* was obsessed with understanding America, and its essays and pictures were devoured by people who sought, through them, a clearer sense of national identity. The watchword of the day was "we," not "I," and the hero was the common man. Everywhere, people seemed eager to learn just what America *really* looked like and who Americans *really* were. Following the lead of photography, journalists on the road gathering facts about the country and novelists writing the new literature (like John Steinbeck's enormously popular 1939 novel *Grapes of Wrath*) tried to be as sharply observant and as quietly receptive as the lens of a camera.

Musical anthropologists roamed the nation recording folk songs; painters, working for the WPA, put abstraction aside to capture scenes of America in real-

Militant labor: "Do you think you can faint again, but this time on schedule?"

For me, the most exciting aspect of the mid-1930s was the growth of industrial unionism and the birth of the CIO [Congress of Industrial Organizations]. By "industrial unionism" I mean a concept of unionism that embraced the skilled, the semiskilled, and the unskilled as members of the same union. This was in great contrast to the old tradition of the A F of L [American Federation of Labor], which sought to unionize only the skilled elite. The way the AF of L saw it, unskilled factory workers didn't earn enough to pay dues, so why bother? By contrast, industrial unionists were committed to the well-being of the lowest paid, and also to the idea of bridging the racial gap. Black people worked beside whites in the coal fields, the steel mills, and auto and rubber factories.

The rise of the CIO was one of the most dramatic chapters in the history of labor —not only in the United States but in the world. And it came almost as a surprise to so-called labor historians, who as late as the twenties and the early thirties were talking about the great new partnership between labor and capital. This was, of course, a myth, because underneath it all was this terrible bitterness of the long Depression, which drained what little savings most workers had and degraded them. During that time a groundswell of discontent developed, and John L. Lewis and the other organizers of the CIO took full advantage of it. But what came as the real surprise to the historians — and I think to John L. Lewis himself — was how quickly the workers in

—Victor Reuther, born in 1912, has devoted his life to strengthening the voice of labor at home and abroad. Despite the loss of his right eye from the gunshot of an unknown assailant in 1949, he has had successful careers with both the CIO and the UAW, where he played a major role in the establishment of international bargaining councils for multinational automobile companies. He is the author of The Brothers Reuther *and the Story of the UAW.*

mining, steel, rubber, and auto responded to the idea of organizing. I know this came as a surprise to me and my brother, Walter Reuther, at the level we were organizing in Detroit.

I think I can best describe this rapid growth by telling the story of the factory in which I was working in the fall of 1936. I was running a punch press in a plant on the west side of Detroit which made wheels and brake drums for all the "Big Three," but especially for the Ford Motor Company. There were five thousand workers in these two plants on the west side of Detroit. And we had all of seventy-eight members signed up in the union. So how did we have the *chutzpah* to call a strike, with seventy-eight members and five thousand workers? Especially when we knew the fear that Harry Bennett and his thugs from the Ford Motor Company brought to bear on workers to prevent them from openly associating with union organizers or attending union meetings?

I was working in a department that had a higher percentage of union membership than any others — though still not great. And there was a Polish woman working at the punch press next to me who had two small children at home and I knew she worried about them. But the speed of the line and the pressure on all of the workers in there was so horrible in those days, that it caused her to faint one day. And visibly, she dramatized a problem that was common to every worker among the five thousand: the incredible pressure under which they were working. There was a look of awe and bewilderment on the face of every worker in that department as they looked at this woman. And they were angry. And I came home and I reported to my brother what had happened that day. And he said, I want to meet with this woman.

We went to see her at home, and Walter said to her, "It is time we do something dramatic to overcome

Reuther (seated at far left) at a strike meeting led by his brother Walter Reuther (standing).

the workers' fear of organizing. Do you think you can faint again, but this time on schedule?" She looked at him with bewilderment. Walter said, "Not Monday, but Tuesday. Give us a day to work on this. We'll get our second-shift people in a little early on Tuesday, and just before the end of the shift, I want you to faint again." She promised to do it. And on Monday we passed the word on to our trusted union members, hoping there was no stool pigeon among them to leak out the strategy. Tuesday came, and sure enough she went into a dead faint. I walked over and pulled the main switch, and gradually all these huge presses ground to a frightening silence. It was an awesome silence, because the workers had never been in the factory when it was quiet before. And suddenly, they realized the incredible power they had in their own hands. They could shut the damn place down, and they did. And the strike began.

The superintendent of the plant came pounding down into our department, shouting and cursing at us. And he found me standing on a box of parts, telling the workers they had to organize and build a union in order to change their own working conditions. He yelled at me, "You get the hell back to work, or you'll be fired." I said, "There's only one person that can get us back to work now." I had my brother's name typed out with a telephone number. I said, "This is the president of our local union. He's the only one who can get us back to work." So the superintendent called Walter, who was expecting the call. And Walter said, "Well, I'm sitting here in my little office and you're over there. Send a car." They sent a car for him. And when he came in, I introduced Walter. He made the same speech I had been making, and the superintendent grabbed his trouser leg and said, "Reuther, you're supposed to get them back to work." Walter said, "I will, but I've got to organize them first."

We had a ten-day strike. But as a result of that first stoppage that grew out of the woman fainting, we could not sign up workers fast enough. Fear was eliminated, wiped out in one dramatic move. Soon we had over three thousand workers signed up, and every effort on the part of the company to organize a phony company union and thwart our efforts failed miserably. We had the upper hand because we caught them off guard, by a clever strategy. When our company finally knuckled under and signed, it was because Ford Motor Company desperately needed the parts we were making. Ours was a short and quick strike, but we won, and we raised our wages in one simple move from twenty-two and thirty-three cents an hour to a minimum of seventy-five cents an hour for everyone — Blacks, women, it didn't matter. We were on our way.

istic splendor. And pollsters like George Gallup and Elmo Roper published extensive data, revealing American public opinion not only on presidential preference (most still liked FDR) but on venereal disease education (most were for it), the sterilization of hardened criminals (for it), the easing of divorce laws (against it), and dozens of other issues as well.

As people learned more about their neighbors, a kind of harmless chauvinism overtook much of the country, celebrating not so much America's system of government as the sturdiness of its people, the beauty of its countryside, and (in a phrase that originated with the period), the "American way of life." Flag sales soared for the first time since 1918. Songs like Irving Berlin's "God Bless America" took hold of the popular imagination. And a new enthusiasm for establishing an American cultural identity emerged in many places, built on the feeling that America was indeed a culture unto itself, its people sharing a common set of beliefs and customs.

A sense of "we" also energized workers. For most of the 1920s and early 1930s, organized labor had been impressively weak. At the outset of the new decade, there were only three and a half million union members, and as the Depression took hold, the numbers went down even from that. With so few jobs to be found, workers toiled at the mercy of management. But after Congress passed the Wagner Act in 1935, a landmark piece of pro-union legislation, the tide began to shift.

The jowly visage of United Mine Workers chief John L. Lewis, his steely blue eyes fixed in a stare of defiance, came to dominate the image of militant labor in the late 1930s. The son of a Welsh coal miner, Lewis changed union history by insisting on organizing his members by industry rather than by craft (combining skilled and unskilled workers). In a break with the American Federation of Labor (AFL), Lewis and his followers established a rival group known as the Congress of Industrial Organizations (CIO) and, almost instantly, union membership (and power) were dramatically increased nationwide.

Despite their newfound strength (or perhaps because of it) labor faced formidable opposition. Even with a Congress and president sympathetic to union rights, management was in no mood to budge. While maintaining assembly lines patrolled by club-wielding foremen and other working conditions as brutal as any in the civilized world (forced to work without the protection of the simplest safety devices, more than twenty thousand workers were maimed each year in accidents at the nation's steel mills), management resisted union efforts with a vengeance, sending out teams of strikebreakers brandishing machine guns and tear gas and using agents to infiltrate the unions and report on their activities.

To fight back, unions employed an unusually effective technique known as the "sit-down" strike. The strategy was used with abandon in the late 1930s, particularly after 140,000 workers sat down on the job at seventeen General Motors plants, bringing one of the country's largest industries to a standstill. Emboldened by their decision to join Lewis's CIO and by the overwhelming mandate given FDR in the 1936 election, the GM workers forced management to meet them at the bargaining table, and the success of the strike quickly swelled the UAW's ranks (only 30,000 auto workers had belonged in autumn 1936; a year later, there were more than 400,000).

Dubbed "the messiah of industrial unionism," John L. Lewis once declared, "A man's right to his job transcends the right of private property."

"We wanted peace. General Motors chose war. Give it to them!"

Union worker leading strike on GM, 1937

Shouting "CIO! Let's go!" striking workers and their families demonstrated in front of the Republic Steel plant in Chicago, only to be set upon by club-wielding police. Although the steelworkers lost the two-month strike, the Memorial Day Massacre of 1937 proved to be a moral victory for labor.

After staging several successful strikes against small automotive parts makers, the upstart United Auto Workers was ready to turn its sights against one of the "Big Three." Here, UAW members stage a sit-down at a General Motors plant in Flint, Michigan, 1937.

The CIO was on a roll. Having improved the lot of miners and auto workers both, Lewis now turned his attention to steel, where conditions were appalling. In addition to the dangers of the workplace, the average steelworker endured wages of less than $400 a year (and on this, he supported a family of six). His clothes caught fire once a week and if he did not die in the blaze (250 or so perished in the mills each year), he recovered to find yet another bill, this for replacing his charred shirt and pants.

As sinister as the steel industry could be, at least some of its executives recognized that it would be foolhardy to oppose labor at its moment of strength. The chairman of U.S. Steel (the largest company in the industry, indeed, the largest company in America) met privately with Lewis and yielded to most of his demands without a fight, agreeing to increased wages, paid vacations, and seniority. It would not be so easy with "Little Steel." The half dozen or so companies that made up the rest of the industry (and they were "little" only in comparison to U.S. Steel) resisted violently, forcing a protracted strike.

On Memorial Day, 1937, with seventeen thousand steelworkers on strike across the nation, a few thousand employees and their families gathered for a picnic and parade outside Republic Steel headquarters on the South Side of Chicago. More than five hundred city policemen awaited them. In the resulting clash, ten demonstrators were killed and one hundred more were wounded. Newspaper editorialists successfully portrayed the strikers as the aggressors, but the label was not to stick. The Memorial Day Massacre, as it came to be known, prompted Senate hearings (where, in the spirit of the day, the lawmakers looked at newsreel footage and photographs to determine culpability) and as it became clear that it was the police who had provoked the workers, public sympathy embraced the union's story. When labor's finest year concluded, they had won 7.7 million new members. The ranks of the United Auto Workers alone had swelled more than tenfold. And not only steel, but also rubber, textile, and electrical workers had successfully pushed their agendas upon management.

Of course Europe couldn't, and didn't, wait. Even as Americans embraced the spirit of the common man and endorsed his campaign for better treatment in the workplace, it was hard for them not to notice how poorly their brethren were being treated across the Atlantic, how quickly the Continent was being wrenched back and forth between the teeth of ambitious men, and how much it looked like the preamble to another, even more devastating, world war.

On April 26, 1937, a squadron of Heinkel 51 German aircraft buzzed over the tiny Spanish town of Guernica. It was market day and so the town's population had swelled to ten thousand, with peasants and others from surrounding villages milling about the square. Guernica had but a single munitions plant and one bridge that might have been deemed a strategic corridor for troop movements, hardly enough to make it an obvious target. Yet, starting at 4:40 P.M., the German fighter planes, ordered by Hitler to aid Franco's Nationalists, began a three-hour bombing assault on the town, slaughtering women carrying their babies, shopowners protecting their goods, and peasants running for cover in the fields. When the dust had settled, more than sixteen hundred people were dead and eight hundred others wounded. In fact, just about the only parts of Guernica not touched by destruction were the munitions factory and the bridge.

The awesome terror experienced by the people of Guernica frightened people worldwide. The Spanish Civil War had become an international cause of sorts, its liberal republic defended by tens of thousands of foreigners who volunteered to beat back Franco (among them, the "Abraham Lincoln Brigade," composed of 2,800 American devotees). And the story of the tiny town's gruesome slaughter at the hands of fascist barbarism, as preserved on canvas by Pablo Picasso in one of the century's greatest paintings, became a centerpiece of the 1937 Paris World Exhibition. But it was the new look of warfare, the wanton destruction of innocent lives and property for no purpose other than to terrorize the opposition, that seemed to shake people most. Was this, they wondered, how battles would be fought from now on, with bombs raining down on children?

They had little more than their fears to confirm such morbid suspicions as yet. But by the spring of 1938, when the *Anschluss* descended upon Austria, it became depressingly obvious that, at the very least, the new brand of politics

Picasso's 1937 Guernica, *below, may be modern art's greatest statement on the brutality of war. The painting hung for forty-three years in New York City's Museum of Modern Art, then moved to Spain in 1981, in compliance with the artist's wishes that it be returned to his homeland once democracy was restored there.*

After warning the Austrian chancellor, "I shall be suddenly overnight in Vienna, like a spring storm," Hitler sent troops into Austria to enact an Anschluss, or "union." In fact, the German army met little Austrian resistance. In some places, such as Vienna (above), cheering crowds lined the streets to welcome the soldiers.

being exported by the German führer aimed to threaten people as much as governments and armies, that he intended to make the rest of the world conform to the same insanity that he was instituting at home.

Hours after Hitler bullied the Austrian chancellor into capitulating to his demands, the nation was completely transformed into an extension of the Reich. As if on command, Viennese policemen took armbands emblazoned with swastikas out of their pockets and fitted them onto their sleeves; swastika flags were unfurled from windows of homes and businesses. Café patrons stood and sang chorus after chorus of "Deutschland über Alles." And almost immediately, a pro-Nazi majority emerged to begin a wholesale attack on anyone who had actively supported Austria's independence and, of course, anyone who was Jewish.

Shops owned by Jews were looted and synagogues were occupied by the SS. As crowds taunted them with insults, Jews were made to scrawl anti-Semitic slogans across their own storefronts and to get down on their hands and knees and scrub pro-Austrian resistance phrases from the streets. Policemen even forced them to clean the toilets in the SS quarters, using their precious prayer bands, or *tefillin*, in place of rags.

Austria was no longer Austria; now it was *German* Austria, closer to a province than a country, and anyone who had held a position of power in the pre-Nazi era was suddenly suspect. Not only those who had held influential govern-

Watching *the* Anschluss: "When the Nazis marched into Vienna, the world ended for me"

The winter before the *Anschluss* was a great time. We were happy, we danced the nights away, we made plans for the future. It never occurred to us that, as Jews, something bad could happen to us. Austria had always been an anti-Semitic country, but in a way it had never really touched us in Vienna. We thought that this was the place where we were born, that this was our country. There were really no restrictions at all. We could live in peace, and we lived a very good life. Every time we heard about what was going on with Hitler in Germany we said, "Oh, that can't stay that way. They'll get rid of that lunatic." And we believed it. That was our tragedy.

I led a very sheltered life, as my father was well off and could offer us everything we wanted. Our social life was mainly among Jewish people. I don't even think that my parents had friends who were not Jewish. But we went to great parties and balls at the opera or at the emperor's castle with sometimes as many as two thousand people attending. I went to college, and had a boyfriend, and I was looking forward to a very good future. I was a very happy person. So when suddenly on Friday the eleventh of March, 1938, the German troops marched into Austria, and were welcomed with open arms, the world ended for me.

A few weeks before the *Anschluss*, the chancellor of Austria had gone to see Hitler, and when he came back, he spoke on the radio and told us that there would be no changes, that Austria would always be Austria. We believed it, and we were lulled into thinking that everything was going to be just fine. So when we heard on the radio that German troops had crossed the border into Austria and were met by throngs of people welcoming them with flowers, we were very much surprised. There was no sign that our military had gone out to intercept Hitler's army. It was just open arms. They moved very fast from the border toward Vienna, and were greeted there on Sunday. It was said that 300,000 people congregated in the square in front of the former emperor's palace the next day to hear Hitler speak. There were Nazi signs everywhere. There were large groups of men in brown uniforms and the SS in their black uniforms, wearing their Nazi armbands. They unfurled enormous swastika banners on all of the official buildings.

We found out later that everything was prepared down to the very last detail. Many Austrians, it seems, had wanted to be part of Germany, especially those who had Nazi inclinations. They knew exactly what would happen, but they thought they would be much better off. The Germans came to Austria and trained people who wanted to be Nazis, though the Nazi Party was illegal at that time. We didn't know that this was going on,

Stept in Austria one year before the Anschluss.

—*Karla Stept, born in 1918, escaped from Vienna on August 7, 1938, with her parents and younger brother. After hiding in Italy for several months, she obtained a visa for Argentina where she lived for twenty years. In 1960, she moved to New York City and began a successful career in publishing that would bring her back to Latin America, as well as to Mexico and the Caribbean.*

that there were so many Nazis among us. There was a way to recognize Nazi sympathizers — they wore white kneesocks. But there were no Nazi uniforms on the streets, and no official hint of what was going on, absolutely nothing. All the preparation had to go on without anybody knowing, and I'm sure today that they trained tens of thousands of people. And not only that, they provided the uniforms, and all the outer trappings of the National Socialists. It was all just very well prepared.

So Austria converted to Nazism within an hour. It was unbelievable. Then the telephones began to hum. People who lived in sections of the city where they could see what was going on would call and say, "Don't go out. Stay in. You don't know what will happen to you." We were all on the phones to each other. "Is everything all right? What are you doing? What's going on? Look out the window. What's going on on the streets?" Because we weren't sure what was going on.

On Saturday morning, twenty-four hours after the German troops had crossed the border, the brown shirts and black shirts got to work against the Jewish

population of Vienna. They forced Jewish men and women to get down on their knees and scrub the sidewalks free of graffiti, all the while being kicked by the people standing around them. They put detergents and other things into the water, which would eat away at the skin, so these people had to scrub with bleeding hands. And seeing the faces of the bystanders, it was terrible. They were enjoying it. They really enjoyed what was happening to those poor people.

All of this was a complete shock to us, because we had never heard of things like this happening in Germany. And as we found out later on, they never did happen there. It was an Austrian specialty. What took the Nazis five years to accomplish in Germany took them only twenty-four hours in Austria. One should not forget that. For five years in Germany they had worked up to this by adding one thing to the next. In Austria, they did it in just one day. The Germans had to learn to be anti-Semitic. The Austrians always were. They must have harbored all that rage for hundreds of years. And now suddenly they were free to express it.

ment positions but also professors, newspaper editors, and theater directors had to resign. More than 79,000 "undesirables" were rounded up for arrest, and anyone who owned property was "asked" to declare his allegiance in time to greet the occupying troops due to arrive with Hitler. "During the coming week," read a declaration on March 12, 1938, "every house and every window in our city must testify to the unreserved support of the native Viennese for the National Socialist State."

When the führer returned in triumph to his native country days later (standing in the backseat of a gleaming new Mercedes, arm in erect salute) he was met by streets festooned with Nazi banners and cheering hordes shouting his name. The soldiers marching with him were presented with flowers, their horses fed apples and bread. Only twenty-five years before, Hitler had wandered this city's alleys as a struggling artist, living in cheap rooming houses and trying to make a living by illustrating postcards. Now, in a delicious irony, he returned a conqueror, without even having to fire a shot.

Across the ocean, people looked upon the situation in Europe with amazement, a mixture of fear and curiosity. It struck many of them as unreal, this German devotion to a lying tyrant. How could anyone fall for it? What they didn't understand was the führer's genius for manipulation, his ability to grab hold of the heartstrings of a nation and squeeze from it a fanatical loyalty. It may have seemed comical to the rest of the world — the voice growing from a low growl to a sputtering and spitting frenzy, the mass of lacquered hair responding with each angry phrase, the nervous eyes focused on some distorted vision of the future — but when Hitler spoke, he spoke the stuff of dreams to many of the German people; a Wagnerian opera played out in real time. And the better things got for them (while Americans continued to cope with the Depression, Germany's unemployment was shrinking rapidly, thanks, in part, to the Nazi policy

"Work for the Jews at last, work for the Jews! We thank our führer for finding work for the Jews!"

Crowd watching people forced
to wash the streets of pro-Austrian
slogans, March 1938

Vienna had long been a center for
anti-Semitism, but after the
Anschluss *life quickly worsened
for the city's Jews. Here, a group of
Jews is publicly humiliated in
what the Nazis sarcastically called
a "scrubbing party."*

*Herschel Grynszpan
1921–c.1942*

"It is not a crime to be a Jew. I am not a dog. I have a right to live. The Jewish people have a right to some part of the earth."

Herschel Grynszpan, seventeen, after murdering a German diplomat in Paris

of rearmament), the more they believed Hitler's oratory, the more they began to see him as their messiah.

The German leader had taken the first half of the decade to focus on domestic politics, on consolidating his power and reversing the country's economic slide. Now he moved to step up the campaign against the Jews and spread his influence deeper into Europe. While factories purred and wages rose, few people could see any reason to stand in his way.

Adding to the Nuremberg racial laws of 1935, Hitler declared that Jews would be forbidden to practice medicine and law. They would be barred from engaging in commerce. Certain stores were now to be off limits to them — groceries and pharmacies posted signs barring *Juden* — and Jews were to adopt "Sarah" or "Israel" as their middle names so that anyone looking at their papers would be forewarned of their racial identity.

Then in November 1938 the campaign took a violent turn. Distraught over the suffering of his family at the hands of the Nazis, a young Jew named Herschel Grynszpan walked into the German Embassy in Paris and asked to see the ambassador. He was just under five feet tall and so nervous, the guard who greeted him later remarked that he looked like nothing more than a frightened schoolboy. Since the ambassador was not in, Grynszpan was ushered instead into the office of the third secretary, Ernst Vom Rath, who was going through the morning's mail. When the diplomat turned to ask why he had come, the youth responded by removing a revolver from his pocket and firing five bullets at Vom Rath's head.

As word of the incident reached Germany, it inspired rage in the Nazi leadership. While Vom Rath had been anything but a faithful Nazi and had even been under investigation for opposing the government's torment of the Jews, his death was mourned by official calls for revenge that resulted in a night of unprecedented attacks on German Jewry. Ordered by Joseph Goebbels, Hitler's minister of propaganda, hundreds of SS men changed into civilian clothes and went out into the night to incite mobs to beat, burn, and loot. They didn't have to look far to find recruits.

Throughout Berlin, Stuttgart, Vienna, and other cities, crowds smashed Jewish store windows and broke into Jewish homes. They destroyed furniture and paintings and, in some cases, even raped Jewish women. One hundred and eleven Jews were killed and one thousand synagogues were destroyed in what came to be known as *Kristallnacht* ("the night of broken glass"). Thirty thousand people were hauled off to concentration camps, so many that officials at Buchenwald pleaded that it was filled to capacity. The people needed a little release from their tensions, said Hitler's aides, explaining the violence. And what better way for them to let off a little steam than to rough up a few Jews?

Kristallnacht spoiled a moment of international calm. Only a month before the murder of Vom Rath, tensions had risen over Hitler's claims on Czechoslovakia. After encouraging pro-Nazi sentiment among German-speaking people in the mountainous border territory of the Sudetenland, the führer had complained that Germans there were being denied the chance to join their ethnic compatriots as part of the Reich. In fact, Hitler was less interested in the Sudeten people than he was in the area's numerous industrial plants and in breaking the

The evil frenzy that was Kristallnacht: **"I thought it was great to bash some Jews!"**

After Herschel Grynszpan, the Jewish boy, shot the German diplomat Vom Rath in Paris, the newspapers carried banner headlines against the Jewish people: "The Jews have taken off their mask from their face. They have shown now what they want to do to us," and so on. It was dreadful. And this diplomat did not die instantly. He was seriously wounded, and they weren't sure whether he would die or not. So, the Jewish people, whenever we met we would say to one another, "If only this man does not die." But, of course, he died. And thus began the pogrom they called *Kristallnacht*. On that day, we did not leave the house. We only heard from friends who phoned to say what had happened. They had seen synagogues burned, and shops smashed. The next morning, my mother and my father and I went out to see what had happened. And when we saw the synagogues, some were still burning. People were going through the rubble to find silver and other precious things, plundering these places. The fire brigade was out, but they were not allowed to do anything except to see that the neighboring houses would not catch fire. And nobody stopped these people from plundering the remains of the synagogues. We saw the Jewish shops with windowpanes smashed — splinters of glass were everywhere and ashes were all around. It had been easy for the looters to make out the Jewish shops, because by that time, every one of them was required to indicate that the owners were Jewish. It was a terrible sight, and it made me furious, especially since I couldn't defend myself against any of it. I had learned that I had to fight injustice, and here I was, paralyzed. I could not do anything. I could not fight back. And that made it very difficult for me, because I had been brought up fighting.

Inge Deutschkron, born in 1922, is the author of the book, I Wore a Gold Star, *and a play titled,* From Now on Your Name Is Sarah.

Kristallnacht is a term that minimizes the event. It would be better to call it the "Night of the Imperial Pogrom." That night was a clear turning point, a great divide, the beginning of a new era, and not only for Jews. My family was not bothered on that night. But the next morning, on the way to school, there was a very strange, totally altered atmosphere. One could tell that the people were stirred up, that something had happened that was entirely new. And then I found out at school what had happened. There were some Nazis in my class, and they were happy, rubbing their hands together, saying, "Now the Jews will be dealt with, finally the time has come." And then after school, I went into the center of Hamburg, and I saw what damage had been done. It was so monstrous that you didn't want to believe it. It was like a terrible dream. Windows were

A synagogue in ruins after Kristallnacht, *Eberswalde, Germany.*

shattered, goods were scattered in the street. There was smoke and fire. Merchandise was thrown out onto the street. There were people who walked in the midst of it without any self-consciousness at all, who showed themselves to be completely indifferent, and who were quite clearly complicitous with what was going on. There were also other people who you could tell were troubled. They kept their heads down and were probably extremely disturbed by what they saw. And from that point in time, everything was clear. It was plain that the Nazi regime was capable of doing anything. Suddenly there was the feeling that we could meet with a violent death at any moment, not because we did anything against the system, against the regime, but because we existed in the world as Jews, because of our biological existence. This feeling was very tangible, very palpable from that moment on.

—Ralph Giordano, born in 1923, survived three brutal interrogations by the Nazis and spent the last year and a half of the war in hiding. He has written nine books, including The Bertinis, *an autobiography of his family.*

I heard about *Kristallnacht* the day after it happened, that Jews were being beaten up, killed, thrown into the river to drown. In the small town where I lived there was only one Jewish shop, and I went and saw that it had been smashed in and everything had been taken out. And I thought to myself, "Yes. That serves them right." Because with the Hitler Youth, I had done it myself. I had taken a bucket with whitewash and painted *Juden* on his window, and an arrow on the pavement. My father was very angry and sad about the

developments, and we had many bitter arguments about it. He said to me, "Can't you understand it? Can't you see it? The Nazis are bastards. You don't behave like that, in any sort of society, smashing windows and killing people." [Nazi Propaganda Minister Joseph] Goebbels claimed that it was "spontaneous," that the German people had gotten angry that one Jew had dared to kill a German. To this my father said, "Oh God, spontaneous? It happened in Berlin and Munich and Düsseldorf and every German city, all on the same night? It was organized!" Of course, everyone knew it was organized. And my father pointed out to me that all these SA people suddenly had expensive cameras and their wives had fur coats and he said to me, "You know where they got that from." But I thought all of it was great. It's shameful to sit here now and to admit it, but I thought it was great to bash some Jews up and smash their windows. "They have done so much harm to us and so they get some of it back." That was my view.

—Henry Metelmann, born in 1922, was a member of the Hitler Youth and served with the German army on the Eastern Front.

In the middle of the night after Vom Rath was assassinated by Grynszpan, my father was picked up by two or three Gestapo agents. They came and looked me over, too, but I was twelve years old, so I obviously wasn't fit to be arrested. My mother told me to go to school the next day but of course I didn't want to go. I already smelled that something was going on. She insisted, though, so I went. And when I got to school, the first thing I saw was one of my schoolmates telling another that his father had spent the night before out burning the synagogues, and what fun it had been for all the SA men to stand around and urinate into the burning synagogue. Well, at that point, I knew that my father's arrest was not just a happenstance. And after school, I immediately got on my bike and went down to the synagogue. And sure enough, it had burned to the ground. Police were there shooing people away. You couldn't get very close. That was it. I came home after that, and my mother said, "I know where your father is." He was up in the police station with a dozen others. So she made a big package of sandwiches and told me to take it to my father. Well, I did manage to get it to him. I dashed in the station when the guard was marching the other way, and I gave him the sandwiches. He said, "Now, get out of here, quick!" I did. The guards chased me but I got away, and I ran home through the streets, past all the shops with their broken glass.

—Hans J. Fabian was born in 1926 in East Prussia. He escaped from there in 1941 and went to New York via Berlin and Paris.

A synagogue burns in Graz, Austria, in the aftermath of Kristallnacht, November 1938. While violence against Jews was not new to Hitler's reign, this was the first pogrom organized and carried out by his government. In a crowning insult, German Jews were collectively fined one billion marks after the event for, as Nazi aide Hermann Göring put it, "their abominable crimes, et cetera."

> "If you have sacrificed my nation to save the peace of the world, I will be the first to applaud you. But if not, gentlemen, God help your souls."
>
> *Jan Masaryk*
> *Czech minister to Britain,*
> *reacting to the Munich*
> *agreement*

If you were a member of Congress, would you vote "yes" or "no" on a bill to open the doors of the United States to a larger number of European refugees than now admitted under our immigration quotas?

No:	**83.0 %**
Yes:	**8.7 %**
Don't Know:	**8.3 %**

From a 1938 Fortune *magazine poll*

resolve of a country that, through its various alliances with France, Great Britain, and Russia, could prove to be an obstacle to his wishes for further expansion.

The task of negotiating the Czech crisis fell to Prime Minister Chamberlain, who, like many who had lived through the calamity of the First World War, was acutely aware of the potential for international conflict and determined to do whatever he could to avoid it. Chamberlain shared a dim view of the Czech people ("not out of the top drawer, or even the middle," he said of them) and was hard-pressed to find a reason why British boys should die to protect the borders of a country rather hastily put together over a table at Versailles.

Late in September, while Londoners were being fitted for gas masks, subways were being fortified to serve as bomb shelters, and children were being sent to country homes for safety, the prime minister personally undertook a bold mission to Munich, confronting Hitler, and when he returned with an agreement that essentially abandoned the Czechs and gave the Germans everything that they wanted, he was nonetheless roundly cheered for keeping the world out of war. In Britain, streets were named in his honor; in Lisbon, a statue of him was erected by "grateful" Portuguese mothers; and there was talk that he would be a shoo-in for the Nobel Peace Prize.

Now, *Kristallnacht* had put a dent in Chamberlain's image ("Oh, what tedious people these Germans can be!" he remarked after hearing the news) and the euphoria of Munich was in a sharp fade. People everywhere were horrified by the news of the pogrom, both for the sheer ugliness of the event and for the outlaw picture it painted of the German leadership. Perhaps Chamberlain had been wrong, they now thought; despite the Munich agreement (or, worse, *because* of it), there would be another world war.

In the United States, there were calls for harsh sanctions against Germany and efforts in Congress to widen immigration quotas to allow for the safe harboring of German Jewish refugees. But the flip side of America's new fascination with itself was an even more cold and rigid attitude toward foreigners. Many people saw the acceptance of more European immigrants not as an act of compassion, but of weakness. In an attempt to keep Europe's problems in Europe (and America white, Protestant, and Anglo-Saxon), these people had worked successfully through the twenties and early thirties to make it harder for immigrants of any nationality to enter the country; the shortage of jobs brought about by the Great Depression had only made that policy seem more urgent.

Early in 1939, in response to *Kristallnacht*, New York Senator Robert Wagner introduced a bill calling for the admission of ten thousand German Jewish children in addition to the regular German quota. Despite the support of prominent Republicans and Democrats and the enthusiasm of thousands of American families who volunteered to adopt the children, the bill failed. "If we are going to keep this country as it is and not lose our liberty," said a lobbyist speaking against the legislation, "we have got to keep not only these children out of it, but the whole damned Europe."

News bulletins weren't the only thing on the radio keeping hearts beating rapidly in the late thirties. Every Sunday afternoon, Father Charles E. Coughlin, the Catholic priest who together with Huey Long had hectored Roosevelt in the early years of the decade, spent an hour ranting and raving about the Jewish conspiracy to take over the world. Coughlin's earlier prominence had focused on the sins of the New Deal, but his favorite targets were now more than likely "Jewish-sponsored" communism, and his biggest campaign was to keep America out of Europe.

No doubt some of Coughlin's forty million listeners tuned in so they could yell back at their radios in disgust at his narrow-minded diatribes, but there were just as many who found the priest's arguments persuasive. And while he tapped into a virulent strain of American anti-Semitism, the topic that appealed to most of Father Coughlin's supporters was isolationism.

The way these Americans saw it, they had gone over to bail the Continent out of trouble once before and gotten stuck with the bill (Britain alone owed the United States more than $5 billion, a sum which London showed no interest in ever paying back). Worse, the false prosperity brought on by the First World War had, in their eyes, helped to engineer the Depression, from which they now all suffered. Refugees from Europe might take the precious few jobs in America away from Americans or simply come over here and go on the dole. Given such feelings, why should they care if the sons of Europe's dead soldiers wished to repeat their fathers' mistakes and go to war again? Let them.

Meanwhile, the number of European refugees in search of safety was growing out of control. After *Kristallnacht*, thousands of German and Austrian Jews lined up outside the offices of foreign consulates, eager to apply for asylum. Most would be rudely rejected. For not only America but nearly all of the other Western democracies, too, balked at opening their doors any further.

Farcical ideas for a Jewish haven were tossed about. The French colony of Madagascar was one site repeatedly suggested (an idea advanced originally by Hitler himself), but France worried that German Jews might foment a revolution there. An American undersecretary came up with Portuguese Angola, but the Portuguese said no, presumably for the same reason. FDR offered the idea of Ethiopia and even sent his ambassador on a futile mission to get Mussolini's approval. A Bronx congressman insisted that the Jews could be sent to the underpopulated areas of Alaska. As the discussion raged, the Nazi leadership stood aside in bemused pleasure. See, they said, no one wants the Jews. Not even those who claim to be their defenders.

On May 13, 1939, a ship carrying 936 passengers departed from Hamburg, Germany on its way to Havana, Cuba. Most of the people on board the S.S. *St. Louis* were German Jews holding documents from the United States Immigration Service guaranteeing their eventual passage onward to the United States; they were going to Cuba only to get out of Germany and wait until their number came up on the American quota queue, which at this point was backed up for months.

The excitement on board ship was palpable. Many people had pooled their life savings in order to buy a ticket on the liner. For them, the hope of a future in America meant an end to the terror-ridden existence they had endured since the Nazis came to power. Unfortunately, it would not be that simple.

When the *St. Louis* arrived in Havana, friends and families gathered at the port to greet the travelers. But the authorities refused to let them disembark, arguing that their Cuban visas had been improperly processed. Over the next few

"November 10 opened the eyes of even the most devotedly home-loving Jews. Everyone who can possibly manage is trying to get out of the country."

Diary entry, 2/24/39
Ruth Andreas-Friedrich

The "America Firsters": Europe's troubles were "fundamentally not our concern"

Growing up in the thirties, I was educated by people who were seriously disillusioned about why we'd fought in World War I. So the general feeling of my generation was that we shouldn't do that again, especially during a time when we were just pulling ourselves out of a terribly tough Depression. When I was in college in 1937, I traveled all through Europe and saw everything that was going on there — the political turbulence in France, the militarism taking hold in Germany, the abdication of the throne in England — and I came back from that trip sort

A capacity crowd packs Madison Square Garden in New York for an "America First" rally, 1941.

of wondering if all of their problems were really our problems. I was young, and hardly thinking profoundly about anything, but my overall reaction to it all was just, "God, it's great to be an American."

The following year I married and moved to New Haven for law school, and I found myself in an environment with a lot of interesting people. The war clouds were gathering in Europe by this point, and as I talked about it among my good friends, we began to think about what we could do to keep America from getting trapped in another European war. They were in a hell of a mess over there — France seemed disorganized and the British didn't seem to have too much military capability either, but we felt that fundamentally it was not our concern as Americans. At that time our military was really very small. And we were just convinced, after the experience of "trying to make the world safe for democracy" in World War I, that we'd better take care of our hemisphere first and avoid entanglements.

In retrospect, it's clear that some of the events

going on in Europe, such as *Kristallnacht*, really didn't get the coverage that we now know they deserved. So our awareness level wasn't very high. Dorothy Thompson would write a column from time to time on the refugee situation, for example, but I don't think we were aware of how serious that was. I think we all would have been horrified if we'd really known and understood it. One must remember that we had been influenced by hearing the history of World War I, and learning about the propaganda stories put out by the Allies to encourage us to come over and fight. The horror stories of the Germans beheading babies and so forth, had proved to be just propaganda. So there was a built-in skepticism toward some of the stories that we heard.

In the spring of 1940, my friends and I started to worry about President Roosevelt, because it was clear to all of us that he was anxious to help Britain and France. We were very skeptical of his constant assurances — like in the

—Bob Stuart, who was born in 1916, disbanded America First and enlisted in the army after the invasion of Pearl Harbor. He served in the U.S. Army in Europe during World War II, and then attended Yale Law School. He was the CEO of Quaker Oats Company for fifteen years, ambassador to Norway from 1984–1989, and has served on the boards of numerous foundations, corporations, and charitable organizations.

1940 campaign when he said again and again, "I promise you, mothers of America, that your sons will not be involved in foreign wars." Everything he was doing seemed to lead toward more support and more involvement. We felt very strongly that there was still a lot to rebuild and do in the United States, and as we talked more about this, we decided to run a poll and check what the student body at Yale was thinking. We found that something like 85 percent of students were against our getting involved in the war in Europe. This got some publicity in the *Yale News*, and the group that was organized as a result of this would soon become known as America First. Interestingly, this original group included some people who would become very well known later, like Gerald Ford, Sergeant Shriver, and Peter Dominick, who later became a senator from Colorado.

Our plan was to get a whole group of people from all different universities involved in our organization. So we put out a letter and we got lots of responses. The

Republican convention was taking place in Philadelphia that summer, and we thought we should go down there and persuade the party to add to the Republican platform that their priority is defending our continent and rebuilding our own society. And so we testified before the platform committee, representing ourselves as "young college men for defense" or some such thing, since we hadn't really formalized a name yet.

And then we went down to Washington and talked with people, and the consensus was that we really ought to talk to General Robert E. Wood, who was the chairman of Sears Roebuck, because he agreed with us. Now we didn't have much clout, so I approached General Wood and told him, "We've got a group that is nonpartisan, that represents all shades of opinion, and if you'll be the leader, we'll have a shot at it." He agreed to act as our chairman, and that's when we changed from just being a university law school group to having some heavyweight members from across the whole spectrum — Republicans, Democrats, educators, novelists, and labor union leaders. We were not partisan, nor did we represent any particular ideology. We were together on this one issue that we all believed in, which was non-intervention.

The group we put together was not just a bunch of pacifists. We tried to avoid any of those "isms." We tried to run the ship very carefully, and avoid the kooky groups, like the Coughlinites and other anti-Semites. We insulated ourselves from that to some extent by involving a number of influential Jewish people, but we were still criticized quite a bit. They called us everything from pacifists to Nazis to tools of the fascist powers. The one member who really got the worst of the criticism, though, was Charles Lindbergh.

There was something about Charles Lindbergh, and at the rallies where he spoke people would hang on his every word. He was a legend, and to hear a legend who speaks articulately, looks young and vital and vigorous, it was very exciting. I think the crowds really felt his sincerity, too — he wasn't running for any office, he was doing this because he believed in it so strongly. He had nothing to gain by becoming involved with us, and he hated any press attention by this point, but he was willing to be a spokesman for our cause. And he took all kinds of slings and arrows in the process. I've really never forgiven FDR for the way he beat up on Lindbergh, implying that he was a tool of the Nazis.

Toward the end of 1940, our strength was growing in the Congress. And every poll taken at that time showed that something like 83 percent of Americans said they didn't want to get involved in the European war. The following year, all of that changed.

tortuous days, while the Cuban immigration authorities and a bevy of lawyers argued over what to do, the *St. Louis* became a kind of floating prison. Policemen patrolled the docks watching out for anyone who might attempt to jump ship and swim ashore. At night, searchlights panned up and down, looking for passengers moving to slip off in the cover of darkness. Families hired small boats and rowed out to greet the liner, shouting up to the people who stood, sobbing, at the ship's rail. A woman aboard ship propped her two babies up in a window in a vain attempt to show them to her husband, who paddled in a canoe below. Others tried, frustratingly, to communicate through sign language. But the situation was hopeless.

On shore, the Cuban government (and a host of corrupt rivals) couldn't agree on how much it should extort from families desperate to save their loved ones, so it ordered the *St. Louis* to sail back to Germany, prompting a near mutiny. Two people attempted suicide and dozens of others threatened to do the same, while authorities hurriedly contacted other countries, hoping to find someone who would accept them. Cables were sent to Roosevelt, pleading that he intervene on the Jews' behalf, but the American president's hands were tied by a public largely indifferent to the plight of the Jews and, in some cases, vocally anti-

In Havana Harbor, a fleet of small boats formed a suicide watch around the S.S. St. Louis *after the Cuban government announced that none of the Jewish refugees would be allowed off the ship.*

Semitic. The ship wandered throughout the Atlantic, homeless, a poignant symbol of the Jewish dilemma.

Finally, a month after it first left port, the *St. Louis* was allowed to land in Belgium and most of the passengers were given clearance to stay there or go on to England, France, and Holland. They were free, if only temporarily. Yet, throughout the ordeal, the country they had dreamed of joining, the nation of immigrants, had officially offered them little more than a bureaucratic back of the hand.

Spring 1939 was a season of triumph for Europe's new trio of dictators. Franco finished his work in Spain, at a cost of one million dead; Mussolini seized Albania; and Hitler marched unopposed into Prague, claiming, now, the *rest* of Czechoslovakia (and making Chamberlain and his Munich Pact a laughingstock). War fever was ratcheted up a notch or two by the news, but most of the world still tried, nervously, to look the other way. If the rational mind said there was danger ahead, then the irrational pretended not to notice. And, for the time being, the irrational won.

In the United States, people sought escape in entertainment, particularly in New York, where the flashy new World's Fair offered them a peek at "The World of Tomorrow." The pavilions of thirty-three states, fifty-eight foreign countries (minus Nazi Germany), and thirteen hundred businesses filled the imaginations of visitors by showing them such modern marvels as television, nylon stockings, robots, and man-made lightning.

The popular General Motors "Futurama" exhibit, which played to 28,000 people a day, featured their vision of life in 1960, when everyone would be fit and tan, take two-month vacations, live in collapsible houses, and drive cars (*General Motors* cars, that is) powered by "liquid air." Each visitor who went to the GM pavilion left with a button reading "I have seen the future" and tens of thousands of them, so pinned, wandered the fair's twelve hundred acres each day, wide-eyed, like a congregation at an evangelical tent meeting shortly after witnessing a miracle.

Still, there was something terribly strange and ironic about the fair, about nations standing eyeball to eyeball in real life joining together as part of one big friendly world in Flushing Meadow. The scene had the feeling of a family in the midst of a bitter divorce, when the parents are still trying to put on a happy face for the children, and the children, all too aware of what is going on, are too scared to do anything but pretend right along with them.

Even the architecture of the 1939 World's Fair — with its towers, arcs, fins, domes, and serpentine roofs — spoke to the hopes for an exciting future aided by advancements in science and technology. Shown here is the Perisphere, at the fair's Theme Center.

The 1939 World's Fair: Electric washers, television, and "a refrigerator that makes its own ice!"

Left: Snow's father, William (bottom row, fourth from right), with his co-workers in front of the yet-to-be-completed Perisphere. Right: Snow with her mother Lillian in a World's Fair souvenir photo.

New York World's Fair 1940

— Gilda Snow was born in 1929 in Queens, New York. After high school she went to work at Equitable Life Insurance, and then married in 1951. She left her job in 1953 to raise a family, and in 1964 she took her two children to the World's Fair held on the same fairgrounds as the one she attended as a child. Today she has five grandchildren and lives in Massapequa, New York.

My father was an electrician, and when I was about eight or nine he wanted to show me the kind of stuff he did. So he brought me to the place where he was working and it turned out to be the New York World's Fair! We went to the fairgrounds, which was really just a big marsh — a lot of unused land. My father took me around to all the buildings and exhibits that were starting to go up, and he said, "This is what I do, kid. This is it! And someday this place is all going to be lit up." He wanted me to see it firsthand and he wanted to show me that we were going to have a beautiful World's Fair, eventually.

When the fair opened up officially, it was quite an event, with lots of people there, of course. I had seen this place when it was going up, but all of a sudden it was alive. The crowds really gathered there because I think the American people were ready for a pick-me-up. Everyone had been down in the dumps for so long from the Depression, and this World's Fair was helping everybody come alive again. Being at the Fair was like having a bird's-eye view of the future, and people loved it, because isn't that what life is all about? I mean, we're always looking forward to the next day, the next hour, the next year. We all want to be there and see all the changes that have taken place. The fair was an opening into a new world, and I think we were ready for that.

The hub of the fairgrounds was the Trylon and Perisphere — a great big white ball and a three-sided tower set in a fountain. You couldn't miss them. And at night they'd light up the fountain with beautiful colored lights. It was quite a thing to behold. There were all kinds of exhibits — Wonder Bread, where they gave you a little loaf of bread; Heinz, where they gave you a little green pickle pin to wear; and the National Cash Register Company exhibit, which was a huge cash register that kept track of the number of people at the fair. Every time another person went through the turnstiles, a new number would pop up.

But the fair was called "The World of Tomorrow," and the most interesting exhibits were the ones that showed you what the future would be like. The highway exhibit had freeways that you could never imagine being used because there weren't that many cars around at that time. I also remember sitting in a dark room and watching a rotating stage that would display first the old and then the new. We would see all the old washing machines, refrigerators, cars, and so on, and then little by little the stage would move, and we would be in the future. There were televisions, electric washers, electric dryers — everything was electrified. It was almost like a fairy tale, like a whole different way of living. It was so easy. Take the refrigerator, for example. It made its own ice. You didn't have to do anything with it except open and close it! And, there was a light inside of it! There was a television demonstration where this man would film you. And to see your picture on the screen, well that was just unbelievable. How it worked, we did not know. I didn't even ask! I was just in awe of the whole thing. It was hard to believe that we would

ever see any of these things, because, let's face it, at that time we were just pulling ourselves out of a Depression. I was still a kid, and I couldn't believe it, but I don't even think any of the grown-ups could imagine these things happening either.

I can't vouch for everybody that was at the Fair, because everybody left with their own ideas. But I do believe that people who went to these futuristic exhibits took home a lot of what they saw. It had to do something to you inside. It had to say something to you like, "Hey, I could get involved in that." Maybe a young boy saw something and he said, "Gee, that's not a bad idea. Maybe I ought to get involved in something like that when I get older." It showed us so many openings in the future that we might someday fit ourselves into. It gave us hope that there would be a lot going on right after this World's Fair that everybody could get involved in.

But then I remember going to the Polish pavilion. We were going up this huge, beautiful walkway, with flowers all around us. But as soon as we got up to the building, the lights went out. My father, he figured they had an electrical short, because the rest of the fair was all lit up. And then we heard over a loudspeaker that Germany had just invaded Poland, and that they were closing down that pavilion. And that, of course, was the beginning of the war. I remember thinking, "War? Where?" I didn't even know where Poland was at that time. But there wasn't anything to see and we couldn't go into the pavilion, so we just walked away from it.

After the film's Atlanta premiere,
Gone With the Wind *author Margaret Mitchell said, "It was a great thing for Georgia to see the Confederates come back."*

In June, the King and Queen of England came to the United States (hoping to cultivate the assistance they would need if indeed a war did break out) and millions of people from the world's largest democracy strained to get a glimpse of the royal couple. Their parade in New York attracted more than three million people (making His Majesty second only to Lindbergh as a parade attraction); and in Washington, 600,000 lined the streets, including one starstruck Texas congressman who, melting under the royal spell, said that "if America can keep Queen Elizabeth, Congress will regard Britain's war debt as canceled."

Of course, fantasy was standard fare in the movie houses, where Walt Disney had introduced his first full-length cartoon, *Snow White and the Seven Dwarfs*, in 1937, and was hard at work on an animated paean to classical music, *Fantasia*. The nation's hottest box office attraction in 1939 was a freckle-faced teenager named Mickey Rooney, whose exploits as the innocent Andy Hardy made people long for the simple pleasures of small-town American life. And it was only a few short months before the most anticipated event in movie history, the premiere of *Gone With the Wind*, would bring the decade's favorite novel, an epic romance set in Civil War Georgia, to the big screen.

Awash in fairy tales and cartoons, science fiction and nostalgia, people had little patience for unpleasant news. As late as August, thousands were still entering a World's Fair contest in which they could win a trip abroad by writing one thousand words on "Why I Want to Visit Poland." While they sat with stubby pencils — visions of kielbasa and the sounds of sweet mazurkas swirling about their heads — nearly two thousand German panzer tanks were lining up on the Polish-German border ready to gut much of the nation and ignite the conflict that would soon bring civilization to the brink of extinction.

As it had all decade, the radio once again became the eyes and ears of the world. In late August, between the static, came reports of a surprise agreement penned by Germany and the Soviet Union. The cynical pact, which in essence split Poland into two spheres of influence, shocked faithful Communists worldwide who had always thought of Stalin as the last best hope for defeating Hitler's Germany. In fact, the two men held daggers intended for each other behind their backs as they shook hands, but for now each served the other's devilish purpose quite well: the Soviets buying time in which to improve their arsenal; the Germans removing the problematic prospect of a two-front war should they move soon to occupy the rest of Europe.

After staging yet another excuse for intervention ("persecuted" German nationals in *Poland*, now), the Germans began to institute trial blackouts in Berlin and move the tools of aggression into place. Then, at dawn on September 1, 1939, the killing began. First, Hitler's deputies faked a Polish "invasion" (by, among other things, commandeering a Polish radio station and screaming over the airwaves, in Polish, that the Polish raid on Germany was about to begin). They then unleashed one and a half million German soldiers in "response," backed up by the most powerful war machinery ever known to man.

For anyone old enough to remember 1914 and the mass slaughter that preceded the entrenchment of the western front, the moment had a familiar feel. But only Germany, it seemed, had learned from the last war. In the north, near Danzig, the Polish cavalry — their sabers poised, their horses moving at a gallop

German panzers head toward Warsaw after defeating a Polish battalion at the Brahe River. Once the front was broken, the Poles' only hope was for the British and French to attack Germany from the west. By the time the Allied forces were mobilized, however, Poland had already fallen.

"It is a wonderful feeling, now, to be a German... The row of tanks has no end. A quarter of an hour, tanks, tanks, tanks."

From the diary of a German soldier, describing the invasion of Poland

— advanced on the first signs of enemy troops only to be surprised by what lay behind the German infantry: panzers as far as the eye could see. They moved ahead anyway, futilely smashing their knives into hard metal, and dropping to the ground under intense fire. The frontier was lost in days.

In Warsaw, people greeted the news of the invasion with fear. The city's 400,000 Jews, one-third of the population, huddled in their synagogues, pleading for divine assistance. But not even God could move as fast as the Germans. Unusually dry and sunny weather allowed the tanks to advance rapidly toward the capital. By Sunday, September 3, the British and French had shaken the stupor of appeasement and declared war on Hitler, prompting crowds of Poles to rush to the French and British consulates, where they stood outside singing "La Marseillaise" and "God Save the King." But it was too late; the deluge was in full force and the inevitable was now in view.

By September 4, the Polish government was already moving from Warsaw to safer ground. Thousands of German soldiers, who had set off from Berlin in railway cars emblazoned with hook-nosed caricatures and the words "We're off to Poland, to Thrash the Jews!" now descended in tanks and troop carriers on the Polish capital. They were joined by row upon row of Stuka dive bombers,

which peeled down to blast road junctions and railroad lines. Chopin played on the radio (a signal to Polish citizenry that the nation had not given up) and snipers slowed the German advance, but the enemy air power was too much for them. The Stukas, which emitted a piercing noise that spread terror wherever they went, were backed up themselves by an even more powerful artillery: row upon row of Heinkel 111 heavy bombers, which proceeded to obliterate much of the city's prized medieval architecture.

Together, the tanks and bombers carried out the German *blitzkrieg*, a strategy that defied entrenchment by moving fast and furiously, hitting hard and heavily, from above and below, on both military and civilian targets. Hitler had studied such war plans for years, hoping to avoid a repeat of the stalemate of 1915. Now, over a few days, he saw his *blitzkrieg* at work, while the world, in turn, saw the awful promise of Guernica fulfilled: bombs, thousands of them, were indeed raining down on children.

By September 17, when the Russians invaded from the east to take their part of the spoils, Poland was finished. Chopin went off the air. "Deutschland über Alles" replaced it. An entire nation had been wiped from the map in a matter of a few weeks' time. A third of Warsaw was in flames. Food ran out. People stepped over stinking corpses to feed off dead horses, cutting away the flesh with penknives. All that remained now was for the SS to move in and do its work. Over the next few weeks, in an attempt to squash any chance of a political opposition, they went door to door, murdering two hundred people a day: teachers, intellectuals, doctors, clergymen, and, of course, the hated Jews.

Maps sold out across the United States in the fall of 1939. If Europe was going to go through another shakeup, people wanted to follow along. They mounted them on their walls, and, listening to their radios, marked the troop movements with colored pushpins. While arguments between interventionists and isolationists escalated, the war became, for some, an elaborate geography lesson.

In Europe, things first settled into an eerie silence, what the Germans christened the *Sitzkrieg* and others derisively called "The Phony War." But that was just a prelude to more stormy weather. By the spring of 1940, the Wehrmacht had taken Denmark with ease (the casualties of both sides came to only fifty-six). Norway put up more of a fight, aided by a poorly planned British campaign, but it, too, soon fell.

Next, Hitler looked toward France, where an elaborate defense strategy known as the Maginot Line had been built throughout the thirties. Based on the logic of trench warfare, the line was an eighty-seven-mile string of underground forts along the country's eastern border, protected by machine guns, barbed wire, and concrete walls ten feet thick. When it was erected, the French no doubt had the slaughter of Verdun in the backs of their minds; whenever it came, they thought, they would be ready for the next scrap with the Germans. But while the Maginot Line would have been a worthy sanctuary for the besieged soldiers of the Great War, it was useless in the age of the *blitzkrieg*. And with two-thirds of their border forces resting comfortably inside the embrace of an archaic defense, France was an easy target.

On its way west, the Wehrmacht first mowed over Holland, nearly destroy-

The SS began the immediate persecution of Poland's Jews. Here, after the shooting of a German police officer in the city of Olkusz, Jewish men between the ages of fourteen and fifty-five were systematically rounded up, forced to lie face down with their hands tied behind their backs, and mercilessly beaten for hours.

Remembering the invasion of Poland: "Huge planes with sinister-looking black crosses"

Just before the invasion of Poland, Hitler sent the third armored division through Berlin, and he was very disappointed by people's reactions. He thought they would be jubilant, as apparently the Germans had been in 1914 when World War I started. But the Berliners lined the streets and let the tanks go by, remaining totally silent. There was no movement, no reaction, nothing. I think this illustrates the general feeling among the people at that time, especially the young men in uniform like myself who would have to use their weapons sooner or later.

Not long after that, my company marched into Czechoslovakia and camped out on the Polish border. We were very scared because we didn't know what war was. We had only been told by our fathers that war was a horrible thing. And so we hoped and prayed that we would be spared. As a matter of fact, when Mussolini intervened with Hitler shortly before the war started, we were happy, thinking the war might never come. And then the order came to move into battle position. We were to march across the border at 4:45 A.M. on the first of September, 1939. For a young man, war means hearing the first shots, and suddenly having strange smells in your nose: Burning houses, burning cows, burning dogs, burning corpses. It means seeing the first people killed; in Poland it was civilians. And then seeing young men like yourself in foreign uniforms being killed or wounded.

I was in an armored tank division, and of course we rode on and on and just kept on rolling. We were the spearhead of the German army. The Poles were very tough to fight. They fought bitterly and desperately. But it was easy for a modern army like the German army to beat them, because here we were in tanks being attacked by Polish cavalry. Can you imagine? Soldiers on horses with lances moved against tanks. It was so easy to kill the horses. And by killing the horses, kill the men as well.

—Peter Pechel, born in Berlin in 1920, rose to the rank of captain during the war and later became a television correspondent.

In the summer of 1939, my father, who was the mayor of Warsaw, rented a house out in the Polish countryside because he knew the war was coming soon. One day I was playing in the woods with my friend; we were picking mushrooms, which was a favorite sport in Poland. And we heard this tremendous sound of motors, and watched the trees start bending. Huge planes with sinister-looking black crosses on them were flying over us, pretty much at the level of the treetops. They were headed north, toward Warsaw, and they must have been one of the first squadrons of the Luftwaffe. This

Left: Pechel in his Wehrmacht uniform, 1944.

Right: Kulski, standing, with his sister Wanda, 1934.

was when I realized that war had begun, and it was a terrifying experience.

The little medieval town near us was bombed a few days later. And since it was not defended, the Wehrmacht took it over immediately. I was near the market when I first saw them coming, and while I expected something like cavalry on horses, they came on motorcycles and trucks. They wore greatcoats covered with dust, goggles, and very scary gray helmets. Somehow I expected that the invader would come in looking very well dressed, but they looked pretty beaten up and bedraggled. The Polish army had given them a hard resistance on the border, so they had been fighting every day. They put up a field gun in the middle of the square near the cathedral. And they put up loudspeakers and announced that the town had been liberated, and that we wouldn't have to worry about anything because we were now going to be part of the great German Reich. They brought in a large military band and started playing "Deutschland über Alles" and other German marching songs.

At the same time, they started a fire in the synagogue and tied up the rabbi, letting the elders run into the temple to try to save him. I didn't know anything

about Dante's Inferno at the time, but my first impression was this was complete unreality. And absolute horror. With the music and the German flags — which were very beautiful red flags with swastikas — they turned the square into a theater. And they reassured us that nobody had to worry about anything. It was just absolute horror. I didn't stay in that town very long, but before we left, I remember that a nine-year-old peasant boy came over and touched the handle of a German motorcycle. And a soldier, who was inside the café, came out and shot him dead, right in front of my eyes. It was lucky that it wasn't me; I certainly felt like doing it. But after that I stayed away from Germans, period.

—Julian Kulski was born in 1929 in Warsaw, where his father was mayor during the Nazi occupation. As a teenager he was a member of the Polish underground, and participated in the Warsaw Uprising of 1944.

September 1, 1939, was my birthday, and it certainly wasn't a very beautiful birthday present to have the war begin. On that day, my life changed completely, just took a turn of one hundred and eighty degrees. In Warsaw, the war lasted several weeks. But finally we gave up and the city was conquered by the Germans. By the time the German army walked in I felt relieved. I was a young girl, and all it meant to me was that we wouldn't have the bombing anymore. In fact, I had been praying for the Germans to come in because it was just terrible to be bombed constantly from all sides — with the airplanes, the *blitzkrieg*, and so on, we hadn't slept in four weeks. The population was quite starved by that time, and the whole of Warsaw was on fire. When I walked down the street my hair would catch fire, because everything was burning.

Once the Germans came in, the people who had been hiding in basements for so long began to come out and line up for food and water. And that's when I got very disappointed with the Polish people, because as the German policemen walked by, the Poles would point at the Jews in line and say, "Look! *Jude! Jude!*" in order to get them thrown out of the line. They did this just so that they could move ahead more quickly in line — it was absolutely disgusting. Here the Germans had been our common enemy, and suddenly our own countrymen were singling us out as Jews the minute the Germans walked in. And pretty soon we were afraid even to leave our homes.

—Susan Bluman was born in Warsaw in 1922. In 1939 she and her family fled to Vilna, Lithuania, where they were granted an exit visa by the Japanese consulate.

ing the city of Rotterdam and unleashing a wave of civilian terror that forced thousands upon thousands to flee ahead of them, clogging roads. Belgium was next (as America's armchair strategists furiously moved their pushpins to keep up), and the Allied soldiers (primarily British) rose in force to meet the Germans there. Unfortunately, they fell into a deadly trap.

With the bulk of the French still at the Maginot and the bulk of the British in Belgium, Hitler calculated that he could send the mightiest regiment of his army through the Ardennes Forest that lay between them and enter France relatively unchallenged. He was right. General Erwin Rommel, commander of the 7th Panzer Division, helped crush the token French forces assigned to protect the Ardennes, and when he emerged on the other side, within striking distance of both Paris and the English Channel, he saw "civilians and French troops, their faces distorted with terror, [lying] huddled in ditches, alongside hedges and in every hollow beside the road . . . a chaos of guns, tanks, and military vehicles of all kinds inextricably entangled with horse-drawn refugee carts."

Convinced that Chamberlain's diplomatic mistakes had led them to the brink of extinction, the British had recently replaced him with Winston Churchill, a dramatic and surly leader who saw his role as nothing less than saving England. Churchill was an inveterate optimist, but he could find little to recommend in the Allied situation now, particularly after his French counterpart, Premier Paul Reynaud, telephoned and said, "We have been defeated. We are beaten. We have lost the battle." By sweeping "like a sharp scythe" (Churchill's phrase) through France and north to the coast, Germany had accomplished in eleven days what they had failed to do in four years of bitter fighting in the First World War.

The Allied forces that had engaged the Germans in Belgium were now nearly surrounded and the only strategy left to them was retreat. Reluctantly, Churchill ordered his troops to flee to Dunkirk, the sole remaining port, and he sent 165 ships of the Royal Navy to retrieve them there. But the waters proved to be too shallow for the Navy vessels, and London had to put out an emergency call for anything that could be used to float out and meet them. Some 850 crafts responded: yachts, coasters, fishing boats, steamers, fire-fighting boats.

While the Luftwaffe pelted the beaches with machine gun fire and bombed the waters, soldiers waded out until they were up to their necks, eager to reach the "safety" of a paddle-wheel steamer or a brightly painted ferry. The makeshift fleet brought 25,000 men to safety and then rushed back across the channel for more. Over nine miraculous days in late May and early June, the poor man's armada saved more than 200,000 British soldiers and another 140,000 French.

Many in France saw Dunkirk as a betrayal and Churchill himself, appearing before a shaken Parliament, announced "wars are not won by evacua-

After succeeding Neville Chamberlain as Britain's prime minister, Winston Churchill told the House of Commons, "I have nothing to offer but blood, toil, tears, and sweat," and he promised, "Victory. Victory at all costs. Victory in spite of all terror. Victory, however long and hard the road may be, for without victory there is no survival."

British Tommies gather on the beach during "Operation Dynamo," the evacuation of Dunkirk. In a decision that may have cost Germany the war, Hitler ordered his panzer commanders to halt their advance on the retreating French and British forces for fear of overextending his armies. The delay gave the Allied army the few precious days they needed to escape across the Channel.

On the beach at Dunkirk: "In between bombings, we looked for my father among the dead . . ."

Left: Rogalin in 1943. Above: British and French troops on the beach at Dunkirk.

—*Paule Rogalin, born in 1930, never found her father on the beach, for he had been captured by the Germans. Released after the war, he rejoined his family in Versailles. In 1946, Paule married an American soldier and moved to the United States. They had two sons and lived in Glen Rock, New Jersey, where she has taught English to recent immigrants for the past fifteen years.*

Just before the war began I was living in Dunkirk with my mother. My father had been drafted and was stationed nearby. Since so many of the French ships were coming through Dunkirk we saw soldiers all of the time, and we just knew something bad was going to happen soon. It was like living on dynamite. All of us children went to school each day with a gas mask on our back, a school bag, and a blanket, because there was no heat in the classrooms due to shortages. We were all given gas masks because they were expecting the Germans to use gas, as they had in the first war. I was given a real old-fashioned mask with a long tube and a canister, and it petrified me to put this thing on.

One night my mother and I went to see some friends who lived in a barge anchored in the port of Dunkirk. We started to hear these loud explosions, but the air raid signal had not sounded, so we didn't know what it was. And suddenly we were surrounded by fire. The big ships in the harbor were on fire, and men were jumping off them — some of the men were on fire as well. We were so shocked, but we ran off the barge, and jumped into a ditch shelter nearby. The bombs kept falling, and soon the shelter started collapsing. I was almost up to my nose in dirt. I was getting buried alive, and my mother was trying to get me out, but she couldn't move her arms. And these three young men, I don't know how they managed it, but they got my hands, and they pulled me out of the dirt.

We ran toward the town of Dunkirk, but bombs were just falling all over. It was terrible. It's something I cannot forget. Houses were collapsing, and we could

hear people down in the basement who were screaming because they were drowning in the water from pipes that had burst. And we just kept on running. My feet were not even touching the ground, because these two young men were kind of holding me on each side and dragging me so that we could run faster. It seemed like we ran almost all night.

In the morning the bombing stopped for a while, so we started walking back to our house. It was still standing up, but as we got nearer, we could see the drapes flying out of the windows, and we could see that a bomb had exploded inside the house. We stayed there for a few days, because there was nowhere else to go; the whole city of Dunkirk was just gone, all gone except for one statue, which still stands there today. We kept hearing that the German soldiers were marching toward our town, and the terrifying stories we heard were left over from World War I — that they would come in and rape the women, cut off children's arms, and all of that.

Though I can't remember the first German I saw, I do remember the sound of their boots and their voices speaking that very guttural-sounding language. That's what scared me the most. They came into our house, which was half gone, and they kept saying to my mother, "Where is the man of the house?" They thought we were hiding something. And she kept telling them he was in the French army. I guess they wanted to take him prisoner. I'm not a hateful person, but I felt hatred toward the Germans. I hated them with a passion. And I felt like we were not French anymore. We were invaded by these people, who had done so much

damage, and so much killing, and I'm sure a lot of them got killed too, but at that point, I didn't care.

After a few days we left the house, bringing with us a few things that we carried on our backs. When we got onto the main road we saw that many others were doing the same thing. We looked for our friends but we couldn't find them. As we walked along we saw a lot of dead people, old men with half of their heads blown off, children who were badly maimed; I remember seeing one man who had burned up inside his truck, and he was still at the wheel. Then the enemy started shooting at us from their airplanes, and even though we were mostly just women, children, and old people they would swoop down low and shoot at us. We had to scramble down the hill into the canal in order to avoid getting hit.

We saw French soldiers in trenches who had no idea what to do. They were lost just like we were, running in all directions with no general to tell them what to do, trying to get away from the Germans. Since I was just a little girl I was hoping that my father would be the hero and save us from all of these bad people. But when my father managed to find us he was just like those men. He had left the army because they had no guns, nothing to fight with. He was almost crying when he found us, saying, "We can't fight. We don't have anything."

We stayed on a barge in the canal for a few days with my father, trying to figure out what we should do, and we decided that my father should try to get to England. So he went back to the beach of Dunkirk, and we had no way of knowing what had happened to him. And then we heard that many soldiers had been killed there on the beach, so my mother wanted to go see for herself if my father had made it. And since she never went anywhere without me for fear that something would happen, she brought me with her to the beach of Dunkirk. It was utter confusion there with bombs going off everywhere and soldiers scrambling to get on ships. Some were drowning in the sea because the water was so rough and the waves were so high.

We took advantage of the breaks between bombings to look for my father among the dead men on the beach. It was a horrible sight, all of these men lying there, and when I would see a dead man with his eyes open I'd say to my mother, "He's awake. He's not dead. Maybe we can help him." My mother realized how awful it was for me, and luckily she didn't see my father there, so we left the beach. And I remember thinking, "When is this going to end?" And that was a question I used to ask my mother and it would drive her crazy. "When is it going to end, Mother? When? Tomorrow? Maybe tomorrow?" And she would say, "Yes, maybe tomorrow."

"I fly over the black road of interminable treacle that never stops running . . . Where are they going? They don't know. They are marching toward a ghost terminus which is already no longer an oasis."

French author Antoine de Saint-Exupéry, watching the flow of refugees from his plane

In what would become known as the "Exode," or Exodus, panicked civilians from northern and eastern France fled from the advancing German army. Entire towns and villages emptied as refugees headed south across the Loire and into cities such as Bordeaux, where the population tripled in a matter of weeks.

tions." Yet they had done a remarkable thing, he said, moving hundreds of thousands of men out of harm's way; the success of the maneuver would now allow England to regroup and strike back later. Then the prime minister, his considerable oratorical skills in full flower, followed with some of the most stirring language ever uttered by a world leader. "We shall not flag or fail," he said, his voice electric with purpose. "We shall go on to the end, we shall fight in France, we shall fight on the seas and oceans . . . we shall never surrender."

The tired old British politicians rose as one and cheered, their eyes alit with fresh vigor; they had found the man to lead them from their darkness and he would do so, in part, with every Englishman's favorite weapon: words. Throughout the war, Churchill's voice came thundering over radio speakers in the homes of workingmen and -women in Birmingham, of aristocrats in London, and vacationers in Blackpool, and as it did you could almost see the shine come back to England's faces, the renewed sense of nationhood, the rejuvenated attitude of resolve. Trains filled with haggard soldiers, their uniforms in shreds, were still arriving at Oxford Station. Day after day, as their railway cars passed through the countryside, people came out to greet them with cakes and biscuits and outstretched arms, just as they would victors.

Something like the same thing was happening in America. People had followed the story of Dunkirk; after all, it was the best drama on radio. And they had been moved by the plight of England, its soldiers and matériel nearly spent, as the lone force now against a Nazi juggernaut. Churchill's words had brought tears to the eyes of Americans, too. At the height of the Dunkirk crisis, a poll revealed that 47 percent of the nation was in favor of selling airplanes to England and France; after the prime minister's speech, 80 percent approved. The isolationist freeze was beginning a slow thaw.

In a few days, France fell, unleashing a new wave of refugees onto the streets of Europe. Now it seemed as if every nation on the Continent was a "Poland"; every man and woman one of "the hunted." More than two million people fled Paris alone (two-thirds of the city's population) in cars and on bicycles and on foot, pushing baby carriages; overall, ten million French were homeless. They wandered the countryside, aimlessly, moving they knew not where, abandoning whole towns to the Germans, searching, vainly, for someplace to hide.

A collaborationist government was established in Vichy, led by France's eighty-four-year-old World War I hero, Marshal Henri Philippe Pétain, and Hitler demanded that the armistice be signed in Compiègne, near Paris, in the same train car in which the Germans had forfeited World War I. The CBS correspondent, standing close by, reported that the führer was "afire with scorn, anger, hate, revenge, triumph." His whole posture was one of contempt for the French nation, "and all it has stood for" in the twenty-two years since it witnessed the humbling of the Kaiser's army.

The stone tablet marking the site and blaming World War I on "the criminal pride of the German empire" was blown up; the train car was shipped back to Berlin. Now France, too, was a German "province" and the number of non-German peoples squirming under Nazi rule had grown by forty million. But Hitler's aggression was far from sated. And as it became clear that Germany was in command of Europe, Mussolini's Italy joined him, sending troops from Libya into Egypt to challenge the British at the Suez Canal. Japan, still at war with China, was impressed by Berlin, too, and looked to Hitler with an eye on partnership. In a few weeks, Italy, Germany, and Japan would sign the Tripartite Agreement establishing the Axis alliance and only penniless Britain, which was hauling cannons out of museums to keep up with the artillery needs, was left to stand against them.

Churchill's phrase factory went into high gear. "Hitler knows that he will have to break us in this island or lose the war," he said. "If we can stand up to him, all Europe may be free and the life of the world may move forward into broad, sunlit uplands. But if we fail, then the whole world, including the United States, including all that we have known and cared for, will sink into the abyss of a new Dark Age, made more sinister, and perhaps more protracted, by the lights of a perverted science."

In July, nervous Britons looked up from their tea to see, in broad daylight, an amazing display of fireworks. The Luftwaffe had begun bombing strategic sites in England in preparation for a full-scale invasion. But, to the Germans' great surprise, the Royal Air Force had courageously fought back. Overhead, British Spitfires and Hurricanes engaged the German Messerschmitts in fiercely fought skirmishes over the cliffs of Dover, and, though grossly outnumbered, often bested them. The Battle of Britain was pure theater, like a series of medieval jousts carried off at 25,000 feet, and it made folk heroes of England's best airmen. Then the enemy's bombers gave the people an even closer look at war: they started striking at the heart of London.

The London blitz of 1940 began when an errant bomber, aiming for some aircraft factories on the outskirts, mistakenly hit the central city, destroying a church and killing people emerging from the pubs at closing time. Churchill responded by striking the core of Berlin, and in turn, Hitler unleashed wave upon wave of planes (he promised a hundred bombs for every one that struck the German capital) in an all-out assault on London's East End. No city had ever witnessed such a bombardment.

From September to November, nearly 250 German bombers attacked London each night, sending people into the blackness and packing the shelters with huddled masses. Entire blocks of row houses were leveled; factories were gutted, left for smoldering ash. Everywhere there were mounds of glass, deep bomb craters, and workmen busy cleaning up the debris so that life could go on, at least until the next night's bombs struck and the process started all over again. The sound of air raid signals became as familiar as police sirens, the smell of burning wood as common as kerosene.

The patterns of life changed. A trip to work was now an event: who knew,

Residents of Plymouth, England, search the casualty announcements the morning after an air raid. Reading the daily lists became a grim routine for civilians during the Battle of Britain.

*This downed German Messerschmitt
110 fighter/bomber was left in the
streets of London as a morale-boosting
exhibit and to provide concrete
evidence that the Royal Air Force was
holding its own during the blitz.*

The blitz: "London was ablaze and the docks were alight. That was the night I went into labor . . ."

When you're young and enjoying life, it's very difficult to take political happenings very seriously. Somehow you feel that the worst won't happen. In 1938 that was my attitude toward the thought of war. When Chamberlain came back from Munich, we were delighted with him. There were plenty of warnings: "The war will come. We must prepare." Particularly, of course, from Winston Churchill. But generally speaking, the people still hoped a miracle was going to happen and Chamberlain seemed to have provided it. Then, by the beginning of 1939, things had changed. People were sure there was going to be war. Companies moved their businesses, their factories, everything, out into the country, fearing that London would be a target. There was a feeling of unease.

Most of us learned that the war had begun when we heard it on the radio. There was a kind of silence before it and after it, or at least that's how it seems in my memory. It was a very short announcement: "We are now at war with Germany." But, of course, what *was* a war? Was it going to be the war of World War I when soldiers got shipped over and walked through trenches and tried to shoot the enemy, or what? We had no idea and we certainly didn't know then how much of the war would be in the air, right over our heads.

First, the men were called to join the military. Then there was the building of the air raid shelters. In our gardens we got "Anderson" shelters, which were tin huts buried under the earth. And in our homes we got what were called "Morrison" shelters, which were wrought-iron tables. We were to hide under these tables if there was a bomb. We also had to line all of our curtains with black fabric, to make sure our homes were absolutely light-tight. There was a group of men called the Home Guard who kept watch for bombs or other signs of invasion, and we were rather led to believe that at any moment a German might parachute himself into our midst. We were told to learn to recognize him in order to have him captured. It didn't happen, of course, but to us it seemed possible that these things might happen. So there was a national feeling that we had to be ready, and we were busy all the time, fussing about.

We were all issued gas masks, which were horrid things with eye-pieces, which you looked through, and long snouts, which you breathed through. They were bad enough as it was, but what was worse was the contraption they gave you for your baby. It was an enormous cabinet into which you fastened your child. And you had to pump fresh air into this for the baby to breathe. Ughhh! They were horrible things, and I think they made me feel more like we were in a war than almost anything else. The toddlers got what was called a Mickey Mouse gas mask, which was the same as the

Above: Black in 1939.
Right: Londoners stroll the streets the morning after an air raid.

—Sheila Black, who was born in 1920, was an actress until the outbreak of the war, when she went to work in an electrical engineering factory as part of the war effort. Since the mid-1950s, she has been a journalist, writing for such publications as the London Times *and* Punch.

adult model, but painted like Mickey Mouse. Extraordinary. This was totally unnecessary, though, because the children were fascinated with gas masks, as children are fascinated with anything. You know, they're not frightened, children.

During the Phony War [the period immediately after the declaration of war when, to nearly everyone's surprise, there were no overt hostilities], the initial feeling of panic that we felt when war was declared just died. It really did. People seemed to go about their business. Yes, it was different. You were preparing for war. But there was a kind of complacency, and also a tremendous camaraderie. Everybody was in the same boat. And everybody was doing strange things and strange jobs. And, then in 1940, the war picked up and finally came to our shores with the dogfights in the air over England. Now we really knew what we were in for because men were being killed.

I was married when the war actually started, and pregnant when the dogfights over Kent and London began. Then came the bombing. On the night of September 14, 1940, London was ablaze and the docks were alight. That was the night I went into labor. Our flat was at the end of a car park where antiaircraft guns were positioned. So the noise was absolutely deafening when the battle started. My midwife rode over on her bicycle at around midnight, and she stayed through the night because it wasn't safe for her to leave. My daughter was born at three o'clock that morning, and the midwife opened the curtains because we got more bright light from London burning than we got from the

electric light in the middle of the room. That was the Battle of Britain and that, for us, was truly the beginning of the war.

What else is there to say about the blitz? Yes, there was bombing, yes, we lived with it, yes, we woke up and some areas were devastated, but we got used to it. One day I was walking to the doctor's, pushing a pram, pregnant with my second child, and I passed through some trees. There had been some bombing there, the bodies hadn't yet been cleared, and there was one woman hanging in the fork of a tree. She was mutilated, but you could see her head, sort of hanging down, and she was blond with a dark parting. Two women were standing there looking, and one of them said, "My goodness, her roots needed doing, didn't they?" Now, that's probably going to sound terrible, but that was how much we were taking bombing for granted. The thing that these two women noticed was that her roots needed retouching, not that she was dead and that there were others dead around her. And that is an example of how we took it. Some people died, some didn't.

You lived for the day. And then at night, you would get under your Morrison shelter, into which you put your mattress. And you got into bed with the children. And others packed up their mattresses and blankets and went down into the tube stations. And when you came up in the morning, you saw dead people. You would think we would have all been terribly squeamish about it, but we got used to it. Human beings are extraordinarily resilient. They get used to anything. Or almost anything.

after all, if the office had survived last night's attack? So, too, was the trip home: many were blocked from their streets while police tried to defuse an unexploded bomb. More than 177,000 camped out in the London Underground stations each night. They cued up early, toting mattresses and rugs, then spread themselves out on the dank, cold concrete platforms or in one of the three-tiered bunks hurriedly assembled by the authorities. Privacy was nonexistent. People used pails of water for toilets; families ate and drank; and mothers nursed their babies in front of their neighbors. The British sculptor Henry Moore, working as England's Official War Artist, produced sketches of the shelter scenes and they later became his most popular work, looking at one moment like pictures of tangled humanity on a slave ship, another like the underground world of a pack of burrowing animals.

Awful though the shelters were, people found it a comfort to share disaster. Londoners played cards and joked and made dates to meet at the same curve in the tunnel wall, as if it were the corner pub. Even after the bombing stopped, many felt more comfortable sleeping below. There, they found camaraderie and

London's subways continued to operate throughout most of the blitz even though many of the tube stations were used as bomb shelters. At midnight, when the trains stopped, Londoners, seeking safety, bedded down on the tracks.

Tales of the Eastern Front:

"She gave me a quick kiss, and ran away . . . and I thought: 'second-rate human beings, *Untermenschen*' "

Metelmann during his service, 1942.

— Henry Metelmann, born in 1922, earned the "Crimean Shield" for his service as a driver in a German panzer unit. Captured by the Americans in the Rhine Valley in 1945, he was sent to work camps in America and England. After coming home to find his parents dead and his home destroyed, he decided to move to England permanently. He married a Swiss woman and they settled in Alton, England, where he worked as a railway signalman. His memoir, Through Hell for Hitler, *was published in 1990.*

When the war broke out I was too young to join the Wehrmacht. I was very disappointed because I was sure the war would be over before I could become a soldier and fight for my country. But soon I was eighteen and drafted and heading for Russia in the winter of 1941, ready to protect against the threat of Eastern barbarism and communism, the two great evils of the world. Barbarossa, the invasion of Russia, had taken place that summer, so the German forces had already moved quite a ways into Russia.

We traveled in troop trains that took us slowly through Poland. And as we came further east, we could see that the living standards were much lower. The villages looked very old, full of decrepit thatched cottages, and so on. We realized we were moving into a poorer part of the world, and that gave our arrogance a boost. We thought, "God, look at this here. They live like bloody pigs." In Germany, everything was better organized and tidier.

In Poland we stopped in a railway station, and saw another train with closed cattle cars. We could see people looking out through the windows and there was barbed wire around all the openings to prevent the people from putting their hands out. A woman looked at us and said, "Bread, bread," in German. We didn't want to be nasty. When an SS guard came along, we asked, "Would it be all right to give her some bread?" And he said, "No. They're bloody Jews and they were fed only a couple of days ago." We felt bad about it. To fight on a battlefield was great, to kill soldiers was great. But this had nothing to do with a battlefield, this was just a person.

As we moved into Russia, the poverty got worse, and now it was winter. It was cold, and the further east we got, the colder it became. Then one day we passed through a place where there were tanks lying all over the place, and they were rusting away. Some were turned over, and you could see that they were burned out. We had all the tanks for our division on the back of our train, and I remember looking out of the window and seeing an overturned German tank, exactly like mine, completely burned out. For the first time, it occurred to me: My God, how did the driver get out of there? Fear overcame me. It was great to talk about fighting, and heroism, and how we were the greatest soldiers, the Germans, and we beat the hell out of everyone. But when I saw that German tank I remembered my father saying, "Oh, it isn't as easy as that." When it comes down to it, you're young and you don't want to die.

When we got to the Crimea, we went into a very poor village of one-room cottages with earthen floors. We went into one of these cottages, and there was a young mother with three small children, living in very poor conditions. Our sergeant said to the woman, "Out!" She said, "This is our home — where can we go?" And the children started to cry. I thought to myself, here we had come a thousand miles, and now we were going to rob these people of what little they had. And the woman rolled up everything she had and dressed the children, and they went out. I stood in the house — it was nice and warm, they had a fire on — and looked out of the window. And I saw them standing there in the snow. The mother and the three small children, their bundles over their head. I thought, well, if that is war, I don't know.

It was very cold that first winter — the coldest temperature I remember is minus fifty-four degrees. It was so cold that you couldn't even touch metal with your bare skin because the skin would stick to the metal. When it's that cold, you reach a point where you don't care anymore whether you live or you die. And a lot of the German soldiers did freeze to death. Sometimes a man would fall down into the snow and we'd kick him and wake him up again, because if you lie for half an hour in minus fifty-four-degree weather, you're finished.

Napoleon went into Russia in 1812, with 670,000 troops, and arrived back in Paris, half a year later, with only a few thousand. Our defeat in 1941 was not as bad as that in numbers, but the retreat was Napoleonic. We lost, more or less, all of our cars and lorries. They were either shot to pieces, or their engines were frozen. We were forced to walk. I must admit to my shame, that it was only then, when my nose was rubbed into the dirt — or into the snow, really — that I lost my arrogance and started to think of other people and to question what I was doing there.

Very gradually during my time in Russia my attitude began to change. It started in the Crimea with the sad woman and her three children. And then when I was billeted in a house in another Crimean village, there was a girl called Anna, and somehow I fell in love with her. One day she took me down to the river nearby and she said, "Why did you have to come into our country like this? I love my country, and you have come here as an invader, as a German soldier. We can never be friends or anything more, because of who you are." She gave me a quick kiss, and ran away. And I walked after her, and the old thought was there: "second-rate human beings, *Untermenschen*." Anna was supposed to be a second-rate human being because she was Russian. But to me, Anna was not only beautiful, she was a valuable human being. And I was in love with her. What was going on? I was the superior human being, I had come to fight Anna's people, to fight Anna and rob her of her home. We were to destroy everything so that we could be their masters. I didn't understand it anymore. Unconsciously, that added to the growing realization that I was involved in something horrible.

But I didn't lose my arrogance yet. As long as we were going forward, I went with it. I still believed it was right. But there were human feelings, sometimes. I remember one of my first battle experiences attacking the Russians. I was driving a panzer and there was a river in front of us and a narrow bridge that they had not managed to blow up. And through my periscope, I could see Russian tanks and soldiers everywhere. We had to get over that bridge because it was one of the basics of being a tank soldier: in battle you must never stop — you must keep moving. But there were three Russian soldiers on that bridge, two of them carrying a wounded one. And when they saw me coming, the two of them dropped the injured man. I had to get over that bridge, and he was lying there, so I stopped. My commandant shouted out, "Don't stop! Go on!" And I said, "He's lying there! I can't go!" He said, "I give you the order to go on." So I went on, and I saw him looking at me, as if he couldn't believe it. And that is still with me now. Very heavily it lies on me, that I have done something like that. I know that if you lie down, an elephant doesn't tread on you. But yet I did that.

freedom from the harsh light of reality at street level. The subway was their cave, proving that Churchill was right when he said Hitler could drive things into a new Dark Age. In some ways, he already had.

I f the American public was warming to the idea of offering assistance to the Allies, it had not yet closed the debate. While London burned, interventionists and isolationists were at each other's throats: the president making the case for aid to Britain (though not even he at this point was suggesting soldiers) and a host of other voices (among them CIO chief John L. Lewis and America's aviation hero, Charles Lindbergh) trying earnestly to shout him down. The fall of France, shocking as it was, had given new impetus to the interventionist cause. Then, in December, after the election that brought him an unprecedented third term, FDR finally pushed ahead, introducing an ingenious idea by which to get Britain what it needed.

Saying he would take the dollar sign out of the argument, Roosevelt made an analogy that every American could understand: he said that he would lend war equipment to Britain much as one might lend a garden hose to a neighbor whose house was burning down. "I don't say to him . . . 'Neighbor, my garden hose cost me $15; you have got to pay me $15 for it.' I don't want $15 — I want my garden hose back after the fire is over." In fact, Roosevelt had no expectations that the equipment would ever be returned (calling him on it, Ohio Senator Robert Taft said, "Lending arms is like lending chewing gum . . . You don't want it back"); instead, he wanted to stress the humanitarian nature of the interventionists' argument. When the president later presented the idea to the nation in a fireside chat listened to by millions gathered around their radios in a national moment of homespun charm, it proved irresistible. FDR came across like a father speaking to his children, reducing a complex moral lesson down to terms they could appreciate. And as he finished, the letters and telegrams poured into the White House, supporting "Lend-Lease," one hundred to one.

Now, for all practical purposes, the Americans had joined the Allies. People added their own hard-earned dollars and cents to the cause; benefits like "Bingo for Britain" swept the nation, raising $50 million by the summer of 1941. But it would be some time before Lend-Lease would affect the conduct of the war. While the uniting of the United States with Britain had represented a tremendous moral victory for Churchill, the American arsenal was itself nearly empty. Factory workers put in overtime to meet the new demand, but America's own army was conducting drills with sticks instead of rifles and with trucks masquerading as tanks. Meanwhile, Hitler's aggression continued unabated.

In the spring of 1941, temporarily distracted from his unfinished work in Britain, Hitler marched his troops into the Soviet Union (Germany's sixteenth invasion in two years), putting the lie now to yet another agreement, the much ballyhooed 1939 nonaggression pact, and landing the Nazi troops face to face with Hitler's ultimate enemy, the nation he dreamed most of defeating. This time, the German forces added, incredibly, yet another level of ruthlessness to their tactics. They would not only slaughter civilians, they would starve whole cities. And because it was the capital of what he deemed a racially suspect people and the center of what he felt was a decadent ideology, Hitler had an even more dire plan for Moscow: he wanted to raze it and make it permanently uninhabitable.

"The three most important groups who have been pressing this country toward war are the British, the Jewish, and the Roosevelt Administration."

Colonel Charles Lindbergh, 1941

*Soviet troops attempt to repel the invading
German army. During the first months of
"Operation Barbarossa" — Hitler's code name
for the surprise attack on the Soviet Union —
more than a million Soviet soldiers were taken
prisoner, including Stalin's own son.*

In less than a month, the Germans advanced more than three hundred miles into Soviet territory. Then Hitler opted to delay his push and capture the agricultural regions of the Ukraine. In the end, it would be a fatal blunder. By October, when the Germans moved forward again, the season's first snow fell and the troops, ill-equipped for such weather, became crippled with frostbite. A hundred years before, the Russian winter had been Napoleon's undoing; now it would take out Hitler as well.

A Soviet general blamed the German dilemma on too much preparation: their boots actually fit, he said; any Russian knows that you need oversize footwear so you can stuff them with wool and straw to protect against the cold. But, whatever the reason, at the end of November, 162,000 German soldiers had perished, five times what they had lost in the entire Western campaign. Then, on December 6, a renewed Soviet army emerged to drive the Germans back fifty miles. That, and the news from another part of the world on the very next day, would shift the tide of the war forever.

Perhaps it was that most Americans came from European ancestry or that the personality of Hitler seemed to focus the mind at the expense of all else; the intense drama of the British and Soviet situations or simply the willingness to believe that the one and only place where they would eventually have to go to war was the place where they had gone to war a little more than twenty years before, but Japan was not in the forefront of the American mind in 1941. On the morning of Sunday, December 7, that all changed.

In the wee hours of that memorable day, a battalion of 189 Japanese bombers lifted off from a carrier deep in the Pacific and, like a flock of geese, moved gracefully through the skies on what would be a historic mission. On the East Coast of the United States, it was noon on a sleepy Sunday. President Roosevelt, wearing a looseknit pullover, sorted through his stamp collection and chatted with an aide. Celebrated newsman Ed Murrow, stateside for a benefit held in his honor, was getting ready for a round of golf, eagerly anticipating that night when he would be FDR's guest for dinner at the White House.

In New York, concertgoers dressed for Carnegie Hall's afternoon fare: a program featuring pianist Artur Rubinstein and the New York Philharmonic that would be broadcast live over CBS; elsewhere, people filed out of morning church, set the table for the day's big meal, or took a resigned look at a list of weekend chores. Many gathered at some of the nation's biggest arenas or, of course, in front of their radios, for a day of football. The Philadelphia Eagles were playing the Washington Redskins at D.C.'s Griffith Stadium; the Brooklyn Dodgers (the *football* Dodgers, that is) were facing off against the New York Giants at the Polo Grounds. And out deep in the Pacific, at Pearl Harbor, on the island of Oahu, a navy band on the deck of the U.S.S. *Nevada* prepared to play the "Star-Spangled Banner" for the morning's flag ceremonies.

As he neared Hawaii, Mitsuo Fuchida, pilot of the mission's lead bomber (a man who so admired Hitler, he had even grown a tiny "Hitler mustache"), strained to look through dense cloud cover for a view up ahead, but could see little. Finally, he, too, turned on his radio and, picking up some soothing music off KGMB in Honolulu, knew that he couldn't be too far from his target. When the clouds broke into a beautiful blue sky, the thirty-nine-year-old airman spotted

"This year, between twenty and thirty million persons will die of hunger in Russia . . . Perhaps it is well that it should be so, for certain nations must be decimated."

Hermann Göring, 1941

Pearl Harbor's Battleship Row. "What a majestic site," he said to himself, an executioner admiring the beauty of his victim. Then, dropping two flares (the first was unheeded), he signaled for the bombers to begin their attack.

If surprise had a sound it would have rocked the whole world at that moment, a primitive deafening roar of anguish and bewilderment. The sailors on the *Nevada* were standing at attention when the first bombs struck, listening to the last phrases of the national anthem. Seconds later, the scene was roiled in chaos. "A huge column of dark red smoke rose to 1,000 feet," Fuchida remembered years later in his next life as a Presbyterian missionary. "It was a hateful, mean-looking red flame . . . Terrible indeed." With Battleship Row an inferno, the bombers turned their attention elsewhere, crushing supply ships, destroyers, cruisers. Everywhere there were screams, the whining pitch of diving bombers, and more of that impenetrable crimson smoke.

Across the country, as word of the attack leaked out, spectators whispered to each other in the stands at Griffith Stadium; and in the middle of the Giants-Dodgers game, one of those familiar news flashes came across the radio, this the one listeners had always feared most. Everywhere people rushed outside and looked for a crowd to comfort them. In front of the White House a throng quietly sang "God Bless America," staring up at the north portico the way that mourners raise their heads at a funeral, as if to ask "What now?" Wandering the streets of the capital, CBS's Eric Sevareid saw in the faces of Americans the same frightened look he had seen in the faces on Paris's Quai d'Orsay a year before, while Murrow detected a fear he remembered from the worst days of the London blitz.

A bloodthirsty group gathered outside the Japanese Embassy in Washington, looking, said one bystander, like a lynch mob in Georgia; and on the West Coast people rushed to find cover, fearful that the Japanese strike was a preamble to invasion. They need not have worried just yet: a model of efficiency, Fuchida and his bombers did their damage in under two hours and then returned home, leaving the United States to cope with 2,433 dead, 1,178 wounded, 18 warships sunk, and 188 planes destroyed. It was the worst day in American naval history.

The isolationists hid. Now there was no doubt as to America's point of view. Armed with grim resolve, the country would go to war, in Europe and in Asia, sending soldiers as well as matériel. The recruiting stations were packed within hours of the nation's Pacific calamity, with many spurred on by a spirit of revenge. FDR himself, writing his speech to Congress the next morning, began with "Yesterday, December 7, 1941, a date which will live in world history . . ." and then replaced those last words to create the angry phrase every American alive then heard as a battle cry: "a date," he said, "which will live in *infamy*." Pearl Harbor was, after all, a distinctly American disgrace, the list of broken battleships reading like a roll call at a political convention — the *Arizona*, the *California*, the *Nevada*, the *Oklahoma*, the *West Virginia* — and even if it did not involve enemy troops landing ashore, the nation treated it like an invasion, a blow they must swiftly return.

"Hell, it's probably just a pigeon with a metal band around its leg."

Navy officer reading radar blips showing planes advancing on Pearl Harbor

With much of its Pacific fleet left in smoldering ruins, America was finally drawn into the fray. Four days after the attack on Pearl Harbor, above, Hitler, too, declared war on the United States.

6

Global Nightmare

1941–1945

Global Nightmare 1941–1945

Mordechai Chaim Rumkowski was a sixty-three-year-old widower when the Germans invaded Poland in 1939. A Jew and a Zionist, who managed an orphanage in the industrial city of Lodz, Rumkowski had served in the local *kehilla*, the Hebrew council charged with administering the Jewish communities in prewar Poland. Most of his fellow council members joined the exodus from Poland at the news of the Nazi invasion, knowing only too well the fate of their Jewish sisters and brothers in Germany and Austria. Rumkowski stayed. And when the Germans reached Lodz and burst in upon the *kehilla* headquarters, demanding to meet the leader of the Jewish community, it was he who stepped forward.

Rumkowski hardly fit the Nazi stereotype of a Jew — he was tall, blue-eyed, and had a dramatically coifed mane of silver hair — so it seemed perversely fitting, in some ways, that the Germans seized upon his forthrightness to make him head of the Lodz *Judenrat*, the Nazi term for the governing bodies of the Jewish ghettos they created throughout occupied Poland. Warsaw was the largest of these "Jewish Residential Quarters" (as the invaders preferred to call them), with 400,000 people housed seven to a room. Lodz (pronounced "Woodge") was next, with 200,000 in an area barely two miles square.

Most of the 48,100 rooms in the Lodz ghetto were without running water or sewer connections. Food was scarce and disease was rampant. ("It was recently discovered that the leaves of radishes and young carrots are edible if cooked," remarks a diarist in 1941. ". . . [Men's shirt collars] have become one or two sizes too large.") Barbed wire lined the perimeter of the area, which was patrolled by German police under orders to shoot without warning any Jew who might approach them. But, at Lodz, death by starvation, typhus, or suicide was more common.

Hoping to keep his community from further decline and stave off the fate of deportation he imagined they all faced, Rumkowski struck a deal with the Germans. He would cooperate with them, even assist them, with the hope that the

Lodz Jews would become an indispensable part of the German war effort. Rumkowski gave the Germans a list of fifteen thousand skilled workers and seventy different products that the ghetto's inhabitants could manufacture. Soon more than a hundred factories were in operation, turning out uniforms, helmets, and caps for the German army.

Many of the ghetto's inhabitants hated "King Chaim," as they derisively called him, for forcing them to work in concert with the Germans and for his strutting, dictatorial manner (he once attempted to issue ghetto postage stamps bearing his likeness, but the authorities disallowed it), but Rumkowski insisted that his designs would help to preserve their community. For a while, at least, the deal did help to save a semblance of civilization. Despite its scarcities, the Lodz ghetto continued to operate forty-five schools and provide weekly orchestral concerts. There were theaters, art exhibitions, and a lively political debate. Though all the synagogues had been destroyed, religious activities were openly carried out in the homes of worshipers. Then, in late 1941, the deportations began.

> "We arrived at the place after a long journey and at the front of the entrance is a sign BATHHOUSE. Outside, people receive soap and a towel. Who knows what they will do with us?"
>
> *An inmate arriving at one of the German concentration camps, unaware of his fate*

Told that twenty-thousand of the ghetto's inhabitants would have to be removed, Rumkowski again bargained with the Nazis, convincing them to reduce the number by half and letting him — not them — choose which people would go. Hoping to maintain his industrial production, Rumkowski provided them with what he referred to as "the scum" of the ghetto — thieves, wastrels, and their families. But less than two months later, the Germans were back for more. Rumkowski then extended his list to include anyone who could not work. By May 1942, nearly fifty thousand had been deported.

The deportees had no idea where they were going and neither did those who watched them leave. Rumors of death camps persisted, but they had to compete with the lies of the Germans, who had the deported sign preprinted postcards reading "I am well . . . and in good health" and send them back to their friends and families in the ghetto. Then, in September, the Germans demanded all those over the age of sixty-five and all children under the age of ten. Rumkowski complied. "Brothers and sisters," he said, "hand them over to me. Fathers and mothers, give me your children."

Rumkowski knew that the deportees were headed to their deaths, but he argued that he must "cut off the limb to save the body." In the end, neither survived. A quarter of the Lodz Jews died in the ghetto; nearly three-quarters in the gas chambers at Chelmo and Auschwitz. And among those ordered to join the last shipments east was Mordechai Rumkowski.

From 1941 to 1945, the world experienced the most terrible and exhilarating period of modern times, a moment when history's greatest conflagration accelerated beyond measure, bringing with it an unyielding sea of blood. The war that had dominated the lives of Europeans for more than two years became now a truly global conflict, with Americans fighting against the Japanese in the Pacific and joining the Allies to face off against the Germans in the Atlantic, in North Africa, and eventually, on the Continent itself. Meanwhile, fierce activity continued along the dreaded Eastern Front, where Hitler's rejuvenated forces tightened their grip on Leningrad — starving the historic city even as they rained

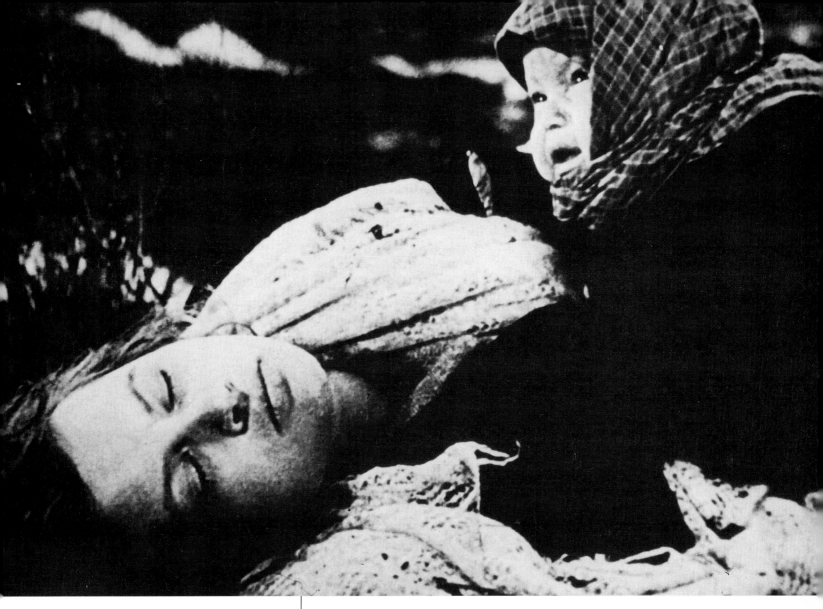

A Russian child weeps over her dead mother. In the Soviet Union alone, nearly seven million civilians succumbed to the war's violence.

bombs down upon it relentlessly — and pushed on to fierce hand-to-hand fighting in the homes and alleys and attics of Stalingrad.

The stakes had been raised. No longer did it seem that the war was being fought only to deter the intentions of an acquisitive nation. Now it was a fight to prevent the destruction of the world as people knew it, and the combat had no limits. The fear that civilians would become targets — so pronounced at the outset of hostilities — was realized to the point where it became commonplace, with millions of innocents perishing along with the cities and towns they had built over centuries of civilization. Amazingly, millions also fought back, determined to preserve not only their lives but their histories, too — particularly in Leningrad, where hundreds of thousands, nourished by little more than boiled leather wallets and the glue off their neighbor's walls, volunteered to build trenches and barricades, barbed-wire fences and pillboxes, all in a desperation driven not by their devotion to Stalin or communism but by the love of their glorious municipality, the home of all that Russians consider to be their essential culture.

When that city was then joined in horror by Hamburg, Stalingrad, Dresden, Tokyo, and finally Hiroshima, the archetypal symbol of this war became the image of a burning city, the pictures of the flaming carcasses of buildings as fa-

"...when those on earth

Die, there is not even a sound;

One is cool and enthralled in the cockpit,

Turned blue by the power of beauty,

...this detachment,

The honored aesthetic evil..."

From World War II veteran James Dickey's poem, "The Firebombing"

Posters like this one urged men to enlist, but the command to "remember December 7th" was hardly necessary: The shock of Pearl Harbor had been etched firmly upon the brain.

miliar as the mud-filled trench had been for World War I. With the flames came a burning cynicism bred from the sense of exasperation shared by the soldiers and the people on the home front alike, the feeling that there were no wars-to-end-all-wars, that war was instead a permanent state, the fighting interrupted by periods of relief, but never truly ending; and that the entire planet was giving up *its* children to the madness that was World War II.

It was hard — indeed, nearly impossible — to gain perspective. Caught in this dizzying battle for survival, people held on where they could, and, fired by adrenalin, enjoyed the one thrill that remained for them, the sense of camaraderie and purpose that came with fighting a war that even in its tragedy and confusion did seem to define a struggle between good and evil — and fighting it together. If World War I could be described as an epic of senseless violence committed toward no identifiable purpose, then the very least that could be said for its successor is that World War II was violence *with* purpose.

The entire populations of the belligerent countries were involved, from the women working in munitions factories to the men flying lonely combat missions, dodging enormous black carpets of flak. Still, the sense of "total war," as it is often used to describe World War II, was not only about the commitment of whole societies to the just cause (or the unjust one) in some regimented fashion. Total war also captured the sense of collective madness that this war produced, the kind of full-pitched insanity suggested by stories like that of the ghetto life of Lodz, where Rumkowski's attempts to save his people from Hitler turned him into a mini-führer himself, determining which citizens were "expendable" for the good of the whole; of All-American boys fresh off the farms of Kansas seeing the quaint sights of Old Europe for the first time from the seats of B-17s, and greeting each of their postcard views with five thousand pounds of destructive firepower; by the systematic slaughter of six million Jews in the gas chambers of Buchenwald and Auschwitz and Dachau and Treblinka, a fact reported in the American press as early as 1942 (where it generated reactions ranging from apathy to disbelief); by the second London blitz, the "little blitz" of 1944, in which the city was invaded by rockets and pilotless aircraft (confirming the sense that they weren't battling anything human after all, but demented science); and, finally, by the flash of primordial light that incinerated the Japanese city of Hiroshima and delivered into nervous hands the terrible knowledge of nuclear destruction. Even after the wild celebrations of May and then August 1945, when most of the world erupted in glee at the surrender of the Axis powers and an end to the killing, one had to wonder if the dark forces that Hitler represented had been partly the victor, if only because the conflict delivered mankind into a hell that defied defeat, that lingered in the cranium like a cancer.

After Pearl Harbor, there was no question: America would join the war. The isolationists stepped down from their platforms and joined arms with the interventionists. Casting the one "nay" vote against a war declaration on Japan, pacifist Congresswoman Jeanette Rankin broke down in tears. A few days later even she was unwilling to reject the plea against Germany, declaring herself "present" when the time came to vote so that her congressional colleagues could demonstrate unanimity against Hitler. Recruiting stations were soon jammed with eager young men; people rushed to buy defense bonds. By February 1942

America's armed forces were already on the way to combat readiness. In 1940, Congress had instituted the country's first peacetime draft. By the war's end, nearly 16 million Americans had served.

more than five million volunteers had emerged to help local community war efforts. And industry had moved into high gear, churning out so many tanks, planes, guns, and ships that their efforts jump-started the listless economy. At San Quentin, even the prisoners angled for a part in the war effort, winning contracts that required them to supply submarine nets and nightsticks for the National Guard.

The attack on Pearl Harbor was a singular moment in modern American history, a penetration of our borders by a hostile force, and it had the effect on the country that a burglary has on the family home: people never felt quite as safe again. The surprise had been largely an illusion (leaders on both sides had expected a war and it was assumed that an attack on Pearl was one of the scenarios the Japanese were considering). Still, for the public at large the news jangled the nerves and helped to create a sense of paranoia that prompted regular "sightings" of hostile aircraft, the cruel and unconstitutional incarceration of Japanese-Americans (one of the many persistent — and false — rumors was that the bombers had been guided to their destination by enormous arrows cut

"There were mock air raids, in which my father patrolled the darkened streets in a white helmet and the rest of us huddled on the stair landing, safe from hypothetical flying shards of glass . . . There were screaming black headlines every day and mountainous collections of tin cans and scrap metal on the school grounds, and little flags of blue stars appearing in our neighbors' front windows, signifying boys not much older than myself who had gone off to war."

Writer John Updike, describing the nervous weeks that followed Pearl Harbor

On Corregidor Island in the Philippines, thirteen thousand American troops were forced to surrender after withstanding a month-long artillery barrage; then, in a further humiliation, they were paraded before Japanese troops, above.

into the sugarcane fields by Hawaii's Japanese farm workers), and, in part, the witch hunt mentality that would survive into the Cold War. Americans simply did not want to be tricked again.

The paranoia, it seemed, was everywhere. The National Association of Broadcasters banned the playing of request songs on the radio on the grounds that it might allow the Japanese to send coded messages. Weather reports were discontinued, for fear that enemy fliers might take advantage of them to plan bombing raids on American cities. Man-on-the-street interviews were also ended, for what if someone inadvertently revealed a national secret? In the rush to identify the enemy, a 1941 issue of *Time* even taught its subscribers how to distinguish between our Chinese friends and the hated "Japs," who were, presumably, lurking around every corner: the Chinese, it declared, were less hairy, more kindly and open, while the Japanese were hesitant and nervous and "laugh loudly at the wrong time."

The enthusiasm for battle was one of revenge. And in the weeks after the invasion, there were plenty more reasons to wish for that. Wake Island, Guam, Borneo, Singapore, and the Philippines all fell, as the Japanese emperor — ruler, now, of one-seventh of the world — brought humiliation after humiliation upon the American forces in the Pacific. At Guam, U.S. Navy Captain George McMillin and his men were forced to undress to their underwear to watch the Japanese flag replace the Stars and Stripes over Government House. At Clark Air Force Base near Manila, the bombers arrived to find American warplanes sitting idly, fully exposed to enemy attack. "They squatted there like sitting ducks," recalled one Japanese pilot. Nearly half of the Pacific air force was destroyed. On the Philippines' Bataan Peninsula, more than 75,000 American and Filipino

Fleeing the Japanese onslaught: **One sailor's courageous tale**

I heard about Pearl Harbor when I was stationed in Iloilo in the Philippines on a flagship called the USS *Houston.* Just as we were heading out to sea, the Japanese began bombing the harbor we were in, too, and they reported to the world that they had sunk the USS *Houston,* President Roosevelt's favorite ship. Luckily they hadn't sunk us at all — we had been in the shadow of some mountains and they couldn't see us. But we were reported sunk so many times by the Japanese in those first few months that we were nicknamed the "galloping ghost of the Java coast." And that name stuck with us until the day we really did sink.

In February 1942, the USS *Houston* and thirteen other battleships were in an eight-hour sea battle with the Japanese in the Java Sea. Twelve of our ships were sunk, leaving only us and one other ship serviceable. Because we had been at our battle stations for weeks, we were at the end of our physical and psychological endurance. We were getting no hot meals and very little sleep, and we had been badly mauled in battle: the ship had been hit twice, so it was in a shambles. We were very confident, though, as we turned west and headed toward Australia, that there were no Japanese for at least 250 miles around us. And of course, being young American sailors, all we were thinking about was getting to Australia, to all the women and beer and dance halls, and so on — visions of sugar plums, basically. But this was not to be, because within a couple of hours, we ran into this huge Japanese armada of about sixty-five ships. There was nothing we could do but plunge right into the middle of them, train our guns port and starboard, and just fire away. There was no question about who the enemy was, because everybody was an enemy.

This battle evolved into almost a boxing match, really, because we were so close, almost like two people standing toe-to-toe fighting. We were close enough that the guys on our deck could see the Japanese on the deck

of their ship. My battle station was in the powder magazine, which means that I was in a little steel compartment as far down below the water as you could get. Our job was to send the bags of powder up a hoist and into the turret to be placed behind the shells and fired. So we were just busy as hell, and the ship was doing full speed, weaving and heeling, and it was very hard to keep our footing. Every time a shell would explode or a torpedo would hit us, everything would shudder and we would hear steel hitting the sides of the ship.

After being hit four times by torpedo fire, our ship ended up dead in the water, sinking and on fire. The engine rooms and fire rooms had been hit by torpedoes, the powder magazines were flooded, and we were out of ammunition. So we had to just lie there in the water while the Japanese formed a semicircle around us, turned their searchlights on, and started blasting us out of the water, piece by piece. When the word came to abandon ship, we had to get out of that powder magazine and try to make our way up. We decided to form a line, putting one hand on the shoulder of the guy in front, and the other hand over our mouths and nose, because there was so much fire and smoke. We had a long way to go to get out of there because we had to make our way up through three or four decks. At one point, there was a loud explosion and I was knocked unconscious. When I came to, I was the only one left — I never saw those other twelve guys after that. So, I started making my way up to where I was supposed to go, moving from one compartment to the next, not knowing what was in there, whether it was on fire, or full of smoke.

—*Otto Schwartz, born in 1923, was a seaman second class with the U.S. Navy. He spent four years in Japanese prisoner of war camps throughout Southeast Asia, working at one point on the infamous Burma-Siam death railway. When he was released in 1945, he weighed just over one hundred pounds. Retired and living in Union, New Jersey, he is the founder of the USS* Houston *Survivors' Association and publishes a newsletter that goes out to over five hundred survivors and family members of victims.*

When I finally got up onto the open deck, it was kind of mesmerizing to look out and see all these searchlights on us, and all these shells coming at us, but of course you couldn't stand around too long looking at it. The captain had been killed and the executive officer had issued a second abandon ship. Everyone was milling around trying to decide what to do. I looked over the bow of the ship, which was very high out of the water, and saw guys jumping off. As they hit the water they immediately disappeared, because the ship still had forward motion even though we had no engines. I decided that I wasn't jumping off that bow, so I went to get my life jacket but it had been hit by shells and was on fire. Luckily, I met some guy who had two life jackets, and he handed me one. I took it, and crawled over the side of the ship onto a boat boom, then I jumped off that and started swimming.

I estimate that I was in the water about fourteen hours. I swam all night, and I didn't run into any of the other crew members, or life rafts, or boats of any kind. At one point, I heard some screaming and machine gun fire in the distance, and I realized that the Japanese were machine gunning the men in the water. Pretty soon a Japanese torpedo boat approached me and there I was — an eighteen-year-old kid all alone in this big ocean. I didn't know what the heck to do. Our life jackets had very high collars, so I took the collar off my life jacket, and formed an air pocket that I could breathe in. I put my face in it, and just bobbed up and down in the water, pretending to be dead. They put a searchlight on me, and I could see the waves of light in the water. I kept waiting for the bullets to come — I *knew* they were going to come. I could hear people speaking Japanese on the deck of this ship, and then they poked me with some kind of a pole. But they turned the searchlight off, and left. I couldn't figure out why they didn't take a few rounds just to make sure that I was dead, but they didn't. So I kept swimming.

Sometime in the early morning, I came across another guy, and we swam together for a while. But I started getting a lot of leg cramps, so I had to keep stopping to work them out. This guy got annoyed at me and said, "You're going to get both of us killed if you can't keep moving." I told him it was a very big ocean, and he might just as well get lost. And he did. So I swam all day, and in the early afternoon I was approached by a Japanese landing barge that was bringing supplies to the troops that had landed on a nearby beach. They picked me up and threw me in the barge, took me onto the beach on the western end of the island of Java. I was now a prisoner of war — officially a guest of the Imperial Japanese, but at least I had survived, one of only 368 of a crew of 1,100.

Above: Schwartz while in boot camp, 1941. Right: The crew of the USS Houston *before setting sail for the Pacific.*

A boy's war: Keeping Detroit "safe" from enemy planes

In 1941 I was living in Detroit in an upstairs flat with my parents and my two younger brothers. I came home one Sunday afternoon from the Plaza Theater, having just watched another interminable string of westerns, to a household that was somber and quiet. The radio was on, and I was told that the Japanese had bombed Pearl Harbor. I spent the whole next day talking with other kids about this war and what it would mean, and the excitement level was high. I mean, I was eleven years old, and I just didn't understand that people died in wars and that war was a horrible thing. To us it was simply excitement. Airplanes from Suffrage Field air base were flying over the city and, God, we thought it was wonderful.

My parents understood what war was. My father was a veteran of the First World War; he was born in Ireland but he got his citizenship by fighting in France with the U.S. Army. He brought home all his stuff and we wore his helmet and leggings and we'd carry his canteen. My brothers and I were constantly asking him questions, but he didn't talk about it much. Once, after we saw a movie called *The Fighting 69th*, I asked my father on the way home, "Did we kill more Germans or did they kill more Americans?" And he didn't answer me for quite a while, but then he said something like, "It's hard to say because dead soldiers are all on the same side." I didn't know what he meant at the time.

To us kids, combat was sort of a lifestyle, what with cowboys and Indians, the good guys and the bad guys, World War I movies, and everything from King Arthur to the count of Monte Cristo. And suddenly, here was this exciting thing happening, with the good guys versus the bad guys and *we* were the good guys and *we* were going to win! We played war constantly. We made our own rifles out of wooden boards, machine guns out of fence posts, bayonets out of old poles. A boy named Richard, who lived down the street from us, had a father who was a disabled veteran of the First World War. He would get his father's helmet every now and then and wear it, and everyone would just be green with envy. If Richard felt like it, he would let you put it on for a while, and then you would have the kids beat you on the helmet with broomsticks, just to sort of test its protective nature. And, even though it did hurt, we pretended it didn't: "Can't feel a thing . . . can't feel a thing." We constantly roamed the empty fields near our house, attacking the abandoned buildings and hurling clumps of mortar at them. But nobody would be the Japanese, and nobody would be the Germans. We were all the good guys.

We watched the newsreels, the Hollywood version of World War II, with scenes from the battlefields where we were always winning. There was a lot of censorship,

Shine (back row center) at age twelve with his brothers and a neighborhood friend.

—Neal Shine, who was born in 1930, attended the University of Detroit and started working at the Detroit Free Press *as a copy boy in 1950. He remained at the* Free Press *for forty-six years and retired as publisher and president of the paper. Though he never fought in a war, he served in the Army Medical Corps in Salzburg, Austria, from 1953 to 1955. He is married and has six children.*

as we found out in later years, because nobody wanted anybody to know how bad it really was. If there were any dead bodies, they were Japanese bodies. But Hollywood's version of the war suited us kids just fine. We fought that war in the East End Theater, the Plaza Theater, and the Lakewood Theater. We were on Guadalcanal, we were in *Thirty Seconds Over Tokyo*, we were carried away to these places. I remember something called *The Boy from Stalingrad*, an absolutely hyped propaganda film about a kid who stopped the entire German army by himself. We identified with him because he was a kid and we were kids, and we damned well would do what he did if we had to. If the Germans ever ended up on the east side of Detroit, we would draw the line somewhere around Market Street and defend our territory, just like the boy from Stalingrad.

We would come out of the movies so fired up. In fact, we even got fired up in the movies. Once during a movie called *Bataan*, we were losing badly to the Japanese and Lefty Brosnan, one of the kids in the neighborhood, stood up and threw a golf ball at the screen to try to stem the Japanese onslaught. All he did was mess up the screen so that for the rest of the war it had a big patch in it that you could always see there. Eventually the newsreels became so popular that Detroit opened a newsreel theater downtown. It was all flamethrowers and bombs and shells, and we indulged ourselves in this chaos.

According to the propaganda, you *had* to hate the enemy. The Germans were despicable, and the Japanese were indefensibly horrible. I mean, they ripped people's tongues out and tortured people and killed innocent human beings. So we hated the Japanese, and we hated the villain in most of those Japanese movies, who was a Chinese actor named Benson Fong. Part of the propaganda was how to tell the Chinese from the Japanese, so we would keep our eye out for these specific racial identification points. You know, like "the first two toes are separated because of the sandals the Japanese wear"

and "the Chinese have smooth faces." We spent a lot of time staring at Asian faces in the restaurants and in the laundries to make sure that nobody was slipping in here, and that sure kept us busy.

We were always on the lookout for spies from the "fifth column," so to us, people with foreign accents were automatically suspect. Now, in an immigrant neighborhood, this is pretty ridiculous, right? I mean, my own father had a foreign accent. But we'd pick out people we thought were likely spies because they wore long overcoats and slouch hats. There was one old man who lived on Hart Avenue, and on the roof of his house he had what looked suspiciously to us like a short-wave antenna. How the hell did we know what a short-wave antenna looked like? But if we ever saw one, this might be one. So we followed him, back and forth, up to the corner, went over to the Hart Grill, where we would stand outside the window and watch him eat his bowl of soup. Then we found out that he was not a spy but a cook in a restaurant, and probably Greek. But he was swarthy and shifty, and fit the bill, so we took it upon ourselves to keep an eye on him.

We all felt Detroit was at risk, as much as anyplace else, that is. The word "enemy" was everywhere in capital letters, and we saw the enemy, leering at us from propaganda posters, with sharpened teeth and blood on his bayonet and we knew that unless we were vigilant, it could happen to us. We had to protect our shores from this "enemy." We learned the silhouettes of all the airplanes, and we spent countless hours lying on our backs at the playground, looking skyward, watching for Messerschmitts and Stukas and Mitsubishis and Zeros. But all we ever saw were the planes from the local air base. Every now and then we would think we spotted an intruder, but we never did. If they had ever tried to slip one airplane over Detroit airspace, without a doubt some kid in my neighborhood would have sounded the alarm.

My father was an air raid warden, but he could have been Eisenhower's aide-de-camp and I wouldn't have been any prouder. He had a white helmet with a symbol on it, an armband, a flashlight, and a whistle. And when Patrick Joseph Shine said "Lights out" in his rich Irish tenor voice, the damned lights went out all over the neighborhood. We were so absolutely proud of him as we watched him striding up and down the street, making people close those drapes and shut off those lights during the air raid drills. We also had air raid drills at school, where we would get under these tables in the basement. We always sang songs because there was this theory that if you sang loudly the bombs — which never came, thank God! — wouldn't crack your eardrums. So we sang nice, loud, good, rousing songs while we crouched under flimsy tables.

There was this thing called "the war effort" that took on a life of its own; you *had* to be doing something for it. We would demand that kids tell us what their fathers were doing for "the war effort." Mothers, too. One day, my mother got herself a pair of slacks, a cap that held her hair in the back, and a lunch bucket, and went to work in a factory. I think if you were to ask me to pick the most unlikely factory worker in North America, it would have been Mary Ellen Shine. I mean, my mother was this nice lady who baked and cooked and cleaned house and kept her kids in line, and suddenly she was running a machine at an aircraft supply factory. Every day for three years she marched off to Continental Motors and ran a machine, and I think she enjoyed it.

I remember being jealous that I didn't have an older brother; I was the oldest in my family. Other kids came to school with patches on their jackets that their brothers had sent them, souvenirs from overseas, stories that they had received in letters about dogfights with the Japanese, or about this or that invasion. I felt deprived because I didn't have an older brother who would send me a German helmet. But then there was a sort of ritual at my Catholic school when someone was killed, where someone would come into the classroom and get the siblings of whoever was the casualty, and then announce the name over the public address system, you know that "Jack Callahan had been killed in action," and we would all get up, put our coats on, go next door to church and pray, and then go home. There were only fifty students in my class, and two brothers of two of my classmates died. I found myself being thankful that I didn't have a brother who was at risk, so that I wouldn't have to sit with my mother while she wept in church, while they played "Taps" and folded the flag and gave it to her. So the realization that this was not so fun anymore finally came to me when the kids from the neighborhood started dying.

My friend Larry Keegan's brother Mike got drafted and went into the Air Force and became a pilot of a B-17. He did countless bombing runs over Germany, and when he came home we were all anxious to talk to him about the war, but he never talked about it. Never. No heroic tales, no stories about all the bombs they dropped and all the cities they leveled. I think the war changed people. It had to, when you saw all the destruction and found yourself doing things that you never thought you were capable of. I'm just glad I was never put to the test.

soldiers surrendered in the biggest defeat in United States military history and were then made to march sixty-five miles in the broiling heat. With the Japanese guards beating them with whips and rifle butts as they went, more than fifteen thousand prisoners died along the way.

Few Americans had heard of these distant island targets; even fewer knew of their strategic importance. Yet, people jumped at the news of their defeat as if the attack had been at the nation's heartland, convinced (as perhaps no Americans had been since the Civil War) that their lives were now vulnerable, that Japanese and German bombers would soon be striking at *American* cities the way the Germans had struck at London and Dover and Coventry, and that, far from being immune to the world's troubles, America, too, risked being subjected to the chokehold of tyranny.

This time, there were no nationalistic tunes beckoning men to the cause, no rallying cries like George M. Cohan's spirited "Over There," which had so many doughboys marching eagerly to Europe in 1918. The desire for revenge on the Japanese (and it was considerable) competed with the wisdom of experience: If they had to go to war again, these soldiers and their families had a keener sense of what that meant. Propaganda posters described their task more as work than duty, unpleasant but necessary. Popular songs stressed not the noble purpose of battle, but the sense of separation and loneliness that greeted the servicemen and their families, wrenched from quiet lives to join the noisome fighting. While federal officials pined for a militant march to urge the country on, the most popular song of 1942 — indeed, of the entire war — was Irving Berlin's "White Christmas," a sentimental ballad lifted from the lips of Bing Crosby to become the mantra of homesick soldiers and the loved ones who gazed from their windows, eager for their return.

The mood throughout much of the country was like that of an ad-hoc task force — inexperienced but ready to tackle the ugly job. In February, before addressing the nation in a memorable "fireside chat," FDR suggested that people buy an atlas to acquaint themselves with the geography of the war. In his address, the president, as the task force leader, then guided his millions of listeners through the maps, helping them to better understand how World War II was a different war from the last, how the security that the great oceans had long provided for America had been erased by the sophistication of modern weaponry.

The president would eventually define the American war goals much as Woodrow Wilson had defined them for the First World War twenty-three years before: this was a battle for democracy over totalitarianism; for freedom from want, freedom from fear, freedom of belief, and freedom of expression — the "Four Freedoms." And even as wartime America itself became less free (the draft had been reinstituted in 1940, government price controls were imposed in 1942, and rationing had already become a way of life even before war was declared),

"I'm Making Believe"

"I'll Get By"

"I'll Be Home for Christmas"

"Don't Sit Under the Apple Tree with Anyone Else but Me"

"I'll Walk Alone"

"I'll Be Seeing You"

"Good-bye, Mama, I'm Off to Yokohama"

"Ma, I Miss Your Apple Pie"

Wartime songs, appealing to the overwhelming sense of separation

"I want to talk to you about rubber, about rubber and the war, about rubber and the American people."

Roosevelt's "fireside chat," June 1942

"Today I am mailing you my old rubber girdle I have cut and torn into strips . . . I hope I may claim the privilege of being the first to donate personal wearing apparel for the good cause."

Mrs. Meta Kirkland
Santa Ana, California, responding to the
president's pitch

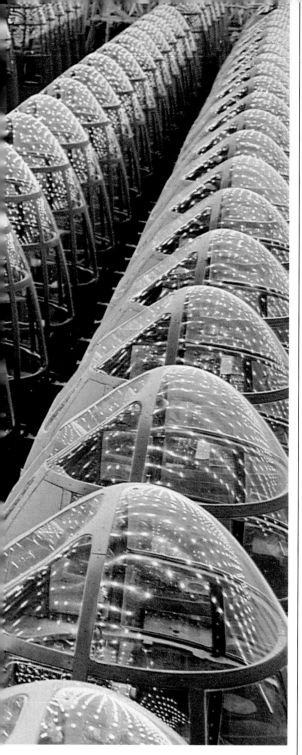

With much of the male population at war, women, like those at Douglas Aircraft's Long Beach, California, plant (above), became the backbone of the nation's war industry. At the peak of production, U.S. companies produced $6 billion of war materials each day. Even Russian Premier Joseph Stalin would later raise a toast "to American production, without which this war would have been lost."

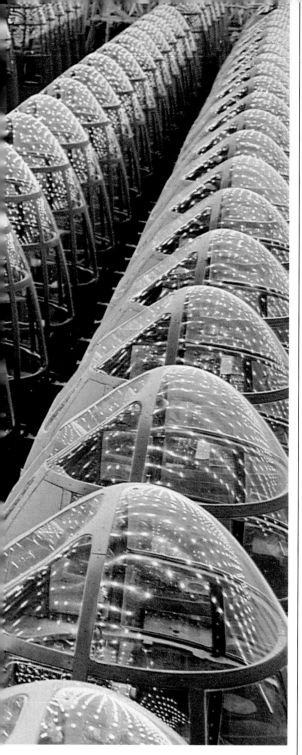

the government urged upon the nation a volunteer effort of extraordinary proportions.

This would be the people's war, fought by citizen soldiers, financed in part by citizen purchase of war bonds, directed by the citizens' freely elected representatives in Washington and their appointees. Student governments took on a more active role in community affairs, Hollywood director Frank Capra was commissioned to produce a series of films called *Why We Fight*, and the national anthem was reissued in A flat — a key, music educators declared, that put it "within reach of all" voices. Capitalizing on the interest in a self-conscious demonstration of democratic values, some advertisers described the war as little more than a threat to the ideal of consumer choice. "What this war is all about," claimed a pitch for Royal typewriters, is the right to "buy anything you want."

The call to patriotism was heeded by some, yet it did not speak directly to the national mood. For even as they threw themselves into the task, many Americans were in fact less interested in attaching meaning to the war — the attack on Pearl Harbor was enough to convince most people that we had to fight — than in moving beyond it to address their private crises at home. The war industries had catapulted the economy into prosperity, but most of those working in the busy factories and even more of those in uniform (many of whom, growing up in the thirties, had known no economy *but* the Depression economy) feared that the nation's struggle with hunger and joblessness was not over and that the suffering they had experienced before the war began would quickly return once the fighting had stopped.

If Britain was fighting the enemy with pluck and determination, Russia with sheer numbers and brutal conditions, then the success of the American war could only be described as the miracle of manufacturing. By the time the nation's factories were at their peak, cargo ships were being constructed in seventeen days (down from a prewar production pace of one year), and bombers in thirteen thousand man-hours (fifteen times faster than usual). A typewriter factory made machine guns, a corset company became a grenade belt manufacturer, and auto plants produced bombers, their employment ranks swelled by great numbers of women in blue overalls and hair bandannas, working in place of the young men who had been rushed off to hastily assembled military camps across the nation. Giant plants were built (Ford's at Willow Run, Michigan, employed 42,000) and whole towns were overtaken by industry.

The effort worked with amazing speed. Buttressed by an industry that was already producing more tanks, ships, planes, and other matériel than all the Axis nations combined, the Americans forced the Japanese into a corner by June 1942, first when Lieutenant Colonel James Doolittle led a surprise attack on Tokyo (so much a surprise that schoolchildren could be seen waving at the bombers as they passed overhead), avenging Pearl Harbor at least psychologically; later, when the American forces prevailed in their defense of the tiny islands of Midway. It would take three more long, hard years, but America's Pacific forces would never look back, proceeding on a string of victories lasting right up to the Japanese surrender.

In the eyes of almost everyone, the successful response of American industry had seemed to redeem capitalism. Incomes rose and liberals began to see a

more beneficent side to businessmen. But if capitalism was back in favor, it was at least an enlightened form of capitalism now, shaped and molded by government participation in the markets. The war seemed to be proving British economist John Maynard Keynes right: Massive government spending was the answer to the Depression, not austerity. By 1942, a third of the nation's economic activity was war-related; by 1943, federal spending alone had exceeded the total production of the entire 1933 economy and the American standard of living was on a rapid rise. The war had trumped the New Deal as the agent of recovery (just in time to save Roosevelt) and set the American system on a period of uninterrupted growth that would last more than thirty years.

The new economy put people in theaters, restaurants, and shops (and prompted some to secretly wish that the war would continue, at least until they had enough money to buy that new refrigerator). But at the same time, the social impact was devastating. In the three and one half years after Pearl Harbor, 12 million men left their homes to go to war and more than 15.3 million civilians moved, many of them in search of jobs at defense plants. Families that had only recently suffered a blow to parental authority in the failure of fathers to provide food and shelter during the dark days of the thirties, now had more money — but only at the price of separation and migration that forced many children to adapt to the prolonged absence of both their fathers *and* their working mothers.

Knowledge of the Great War may have tempered the Second World War soldier's enthusiasm for battle, but it did not remove it completely. War is funny that way. The horror fades, recast by memory into the adventurous anecdote or tidied up in the heroic narratives of literature (and, now, the action-packed Errol Flynn film). For too many of the men who had fought and survived the First War, battle was the one event that had given their Depression-filled lives meaning, and to their children, Dad's tragic tales, honed and shaped over the years, had begun to sound, if nothing else, like a life experienced more fully than their own, a vitality to aspire to. War was a horror, yes, but, oh, to have witnessed such horror!

Once in, a few of them even felt the adrenaline reward of the soldiers' life. The sophistication of World War II's war machinery allowed tank commanders and pilots, for instance, to utilize the soldierly skills that had seemingly been made obsolete on the western front. Unlike the poor infantry stuck in that war's trenches for years on end, the Spitfire pilots sparring with German Stukas in the Battle of Britain and the tank commanders in the African desert could both experience danger *and* respond to it in a way that helped determine their fate. Yet, for most of the fighting men of World War II — be they British, American, Russian, Canadian, German, Japanese, or any of the fifteen other nationalities that participated — the experience of combat in this war was, like the war itself, an extension of the misery and barbarity of the last. Bloodier, messier, and perhaps even more psychologically devastating. Consider only this fact: The two wars involved roughly the same number of combatants and the fighting occurred over roughly the same period of time, yet more than twice as many people died.

Perhaps the greatest difference, as far as the soldier's life was concerned, was this war's dependence upon the machine. Far more than its predecessor, World War II utilized the tank and the plane (in many ways, World War II was the bomber's war) and modern rifles that were capable of firing rounds more rapidly

Average American Family Income:

	1938	1942
Washington, DC	$2,227	$5,316
Hartford, CT	$2,207	$5,208
New York City	$2,760	$4,044

With a theme song entitled "Slap the Jap with the Scrap," the Office of Civilian Defense organized nationwide recycling drives to provide materials for the war effort and to boost the morale of the home front.

Even the best training could not have prepared America's GIs for the brutal fighting they faced in the Pacific. One soldier later wrote, "It was as though I was out there on the battle-field all by myself, utterly forlorn and helpless in a tempest of violent explosions." Above, a Marine at Peleliu.

(if less accurately) at the enemy. But in its twisted way, the newly advanced matériel, too, only represented the reverse progress of this war: more powerful armaments — and more of them — directed everywhere and nowhere at once. Skill might be called upon to fight air wars like the Battle of Britain, but it was of less importance when one's target was on the ground, approached in the frenzy of "assault fire" or obliterated in what became known, euphemistically, as "area bombing." With such disregard for precision, it is no wonder that friendly fire was more common than in any previous war and that the civilian became the accidental — as well as the intended — victim time and time again.

For the infantry (and even in the mechanized war of World War II, the infantry was still how most soldiers fought war), this war was as frustrating as the last and, despite its clearly defined moral objectives, almost certainly more dehumanizing. As critic and historian Paul Fussell has written, a solid meal was rare. The soldier lived on servings of Spam, powdered eggs, and dried vegetables. The food disturbed his stomach so that he often had to vomit, and when prompted by fear of combat, would frequently lose control of his bowels. The environment itself fought him, too, whether it be the scorching winds of the African desert, the coral atolls of the Pacific, or the freezing rains of northern Italy. And of course there was the mud — the same mud that had slowed the soldiers of the First World War.

Yet it was the machines, again, that took the infantryman's life to a new level of degradation. The bullet was the kindest sentence that a poor soldier could receive, for a lifeless body retains some shred of dignity; too many in this war perished, instead, under the wheels of tanks or in the vapor of powerful explosives. The living watched them, and recoiled at their fate, wondering when it would be their own; then stood at burials in which the dead — represented often

With the Marines at Tarawa: "I watched a young man die and broke into an uncontrollable laugh"

When the war broke out, I had graduated from college and was attending art school in New York. I went back to my hometown, Portland, Oregon, to enlist, and took physicals for the Navy, the Army, and the Marines. The Navy said that I might qualify for flight training, but since my teeth were crooked, I had to go to a dentist up in Seattle to find out. When I got up there, this young man took one look at me and he said, "Well, I passed one man like you today, and I don't think I should pass two." So that was the end of my flight career. And that's an example of how the most trivial thing can change your entire life.

I ended up in the Marines, in the Sixth Regiment of the Second Division. Boot camp was sort of brutal: they got us up early, they swore at us, threatened us, and intimidated us to eliminate our feelings and weed out the weaklings. One major effect of the training was to change your whole perspective on authority. It was the opposite of democratic; we were simply told what we were going to do and if we didn't do it, well, we'd end up in jail or punished.

As soldiers, we never saw a newspaper or heard any news. So the job had nothing to do with morals or politics or anything like that. When we were in training we heard rumors of Japanese cruelty and so on. In Guadalcanal we had a radio for a little while that we would tune in at night to San Francisco. The announcers would tell us what we had done during the day, "Well, the Marines advanced two miles and did this and that," and we'd say, "Oh, did we?" Maybe we had, maybe we hadn't. We didn't have any sense of what we were doing in a larger context.

Guadalcanal was our first real mission. We were sent there to secure the place and to mop up the remaining Japanese, who were half-starved by this point. By the time we arrived, there wasn't much left to do, but I saw a lot: degenerate corpses that were many months old, pieces of arms and legs everyplace. That was where I began to develop this very detached attitude toward what I saw. For a while I had a Japanese skull that I found near a big shell hole. To some people, that might seem gruesome, but to me, as an artist, it was just an object that I might sketch. One day, I was wandering through the corpses and bomb craters and somebody said, "Hey, who wants some gold teeth?" I went over and took my hunting knife out of its scabbard and I pried a bridge out of a dead Japanese soldier's mouth. I also kept the dog tags of this guy and at the time I thought that these were wonderful souvenirs.

Next, I was sent with my regiment to Tarawa in the Gilbert Islands. A battle was going on there on one square mile of sand. We arrived on the third day of the battle. It was scorching hot, and corpses were piled everywhere, bloated and blackened by the sun. I was the telephone man, which meant I had to string telephone wire from the command post to wherever the company was.

We advanced about two hundred yards and at nightfall we were attacked. At one point during the battle, I was left alone with the phone, and a voice came over it asking if we needed artillery support. I said yes, and some shells exploded. "Lower your fire," I shouted, because the Japanese seemed to be closer to me than the explosions. The next explosion was behind me, so I yelled, "Cease fire!" For the next few hours I ran back and forth through the battlefield and kept the phone working. I could hear our company captain begging for reinforcements because three-quarters of us were casualties, but command post refused to send any or to let us pull back.

Shells were exploding all around me. The first time you get shelled, it's a real rush. Especially when a piece of shrapnel bounces off your shoe or something like that. But the power of high explosives is very demoralizing, because it's this sudden force which has nothing to do with humanity; it's the force of an enormously powerful machine and there's nothing in the world you can do to resist that. After a while you start to feel like someone who's been in an automobile wreck; you get into a state of shock and you can't really comprehend everything that's happening around you. There really is no way in the world to prepare yourself for the reality of battle.

During my trips from the front to the rear of the battle, I was stopped every fifty feet or so by soldiers guarding their shell holes with rifles. The routine was that they would shout, "Who goes there?" and I would say, "Marine!" Then they'd say, "What is the password?" And I'd say, "Oregon." Then, "Repeat!" and I'd have to keep repeating states until they were sure I was not the enemy. I soon realized that all of these shell holes were full of Marines who were either wounded or too afraid to go out into battle. The war stories never seem to mention all of these guys who are literally paralyzed with fear, unable or unwilling to fight.

One shell landed so close to me that I was thrown to the ground. When I sat up, I had to pick the pieces of coral gravel out of my face. This was really the climax of my battle experience, and it put me over the thin, red line into shell shock. I went and told my captain that I needed a break, and I dug out a little area in a bomb crater and fell asleep. When I woke up a few hours later, a huge noise shook me, and I looked up to see an American fighter plane roaring straight toward me. I wasn't surprised or afraid at all. I was like a drunk watching television — nothing happening around me seemed to have any bearing on my life. When the plane opened fire I felt the muzzle blast of the machine gun on my face, but I wasn't hit. I scrambled out of my crater and saw that the battlefield had gone quiet. I soon figured out that the battle lines had moved, and that my sleeping place had become no-man's-land. But since the battle had just ended, I was safe.

A shouting voice kind of jolted me into reality; it was a corpsman looking for casualties. He had found a body, and he wanted me to help fix the guy up. I looked down at the man's face, and I realized I knew him. His eyes were open, rolling from side to side, the sightless eyes of a dying man. Then I noticed that his right leg was entirely missing. The absurdity of the whole situation suddenly hit me, and I broke into an uncontrolled laugh. All the fear and horror melted away, and I felt nothing but relief. Then suddenly, I was sober again. I was watching a man die, and the reality of the violence was back with me. All I could think was, "This is insane, this is too much. Nobody will ever get me to do this again." To live through a battle like Tarawa shakes your faith in humanity forever.

> *—Earle Curtis, Private First Class, who was born in 1918, was discharged from the Marines in 1944 due to shell shock and received a citation for bravery for his actions on Tarawa. He settled in San Francisco. Though he says he has "outlived" the effects of shell shock, Curtis rarely talks about his war experiences because his "insides still get knotted up."*

Above left: Earle Curtis at age twenty-five. Left: Marines advance after a destroyer bombardment on Tarawa, 1943.

Named after a "divine wind" that saved Japan from a Mongol invasion in the Middle Ages, Japanese kamikaze corps were made up of young pilots whose devotion to the emperor was so total, they were willing to perform suicide runs on enemy targets. Here, the men of one such unit pay a final respect before embarking on missions that will bring them certain death.

**"No part of the enemy's body
may be used as a souvenir . . ."**

*Order issued by the commander of
the American Pacific Fleet, 1942*

*Accounts of brutality by both sides in
the Pacific war helped to fuel an
intense hatred between the two
enemies. Here, American troops have
displayed the head of a Japanese
soldier on a captured enemy tank.*

by a collection of body fragments too gruesome and splintered to be called a corpse — were honored for their "service."

Not surprisingly, the fighting men of World War II suffered the same moral dissonance and mental decay that their fathers had experienced in Passchendaele, Verdun, and the Somme. Their supporters at home cheered them on with flags unfurled and even their field commanders were apt to spout a morale lecture or two, usually sprinkled with references to the rightness of the Allied cause, but a soldier's mind, so intent on survival, does not distinguish between a "good" war and a "bad" one; it is war itself that it finds so hard to process. The rate of psychological collapse for this war was so high, the count often exceeded the number of those with physical injury. The brutal fighting on the island of Okinawa in 1945, for instance, produced 8,000 American deaths, but 26,000 cases of what was kindly referred to as "the thousand-yard stare."

As in the First World War, the soldiers felt some camaraderie with their enemy counterparts, and even grudgingly admired each other's handiwork. But, strangely, one of the things that characterized this contest as separate from the last was the soldier's willingness to extend his aggression beyond killing to the perverse, to engage in torture and mutilation, and to target the innocent. The Pacific war was particularly brutal this way. In their raids on Hong Kong and Singapore, the Japanese bayoneted civilians and killed the wounded. They locked prisoners in packing crates for years on end and routinely finished off the enemy dead by cutting off their penises and sticking them in the corpses' mouths. Historians have never fully accounted for the level of Japanese barbarity (just as they have never fully accounted for German behavior in the Holocaust), though it does seem to relate to the same cultural factor that produced the *kamikaze*.

To the Japanese soldier, there was no higher calling than fighting for his emperor. Hirohito was tantamount to God, in Western terms, and even though the emperor himself was outraged by the atrocities committed in his name and said so, still it was taken as an article of faith among the Japanese fighting men that the greater the violence, the greater the demonstration of one's commitment to serve him.

Death was a sublime act, surrender an intolerable dishonor, not only unmanly in the sense of being unmasculine but also un*man*ly, as in rendering the soldier who did it as something less than human. (Three Allied soldiers died for every one who surrendered, whereas 120 Japanese died for every one of their surrendering men.) The corollary of this ethic could then be seen in the contempt with which the Japanese held the surrendering enemy: captives were objects to be scorned and defiled.

The Japanese behavior, which was also informed by a virulent racism, regarding all other peoples as inferior, shocked Americans and encouraged people to think of them as barely human, a nation of rabid animals. Yet, while they were hardly routine, barbaric acts were also committed by Americans. As early as 1942, Allied soldiers were opting to take home trophies from their kills, boiling the flesh off Japanese heads and carving out ears, hands, and even sexual organs as mementos, then swapping them among themselves like trading cards. Surveying their work after an assault, American soldiers sometimes urinated in the mouths of corpses. Pacific war memoirist Eugene Sledge recalls watching a fellow

Marine pry open the jaw of a wounded Japanese to extract the gold from his teeth. Frustrated by the man's thrashing about, the Marine finally cut his cheek from ear to ear, allowing him better access to his prize. Horrified, Sledge pleaded that the man be put out of his misery but his call went unheeded. Finally, another Marine ran up and put a bullet in the Japanese man's brain while the scavenger, unfazed, continued his work.

At least some of this behavior was inspired by the abstract way in which the Pacific war was fought. The Pacific battle differed from the European battle in many ways, but chief among them was the way the Pacific war was enacted apart from signs of civilization, on outcroppings of rock and coral that seemed almost like another planet. In Europe, the American soldier could see signs of the familiar; here, as historian Samuel Hynes has pointed out, he found in the cratered terrain and the strange languages, the inhuman fighting methods of his enemy (absent, even of the most basic of motives, self-preservation), only a "green and threatening mystery."

With their reservoirs in ruins, Leningrad residents tapped frozen canals, the Neva River, and streets that had turned to glaciers for drinking water. While many people became ill, the intense winter cold prevented full-scale epidemics from sweeping the city.

The suffering brought by the Second World War was enormous, and global, but when the total picture is considered, there is little to challenge the statement that the greatest pain was borne by the people who lived within the grasp of the century's two most vicious tyrants, Adolf Hitler and Joseph Stalin. While Americans were busily manning the factories that made them "the arsenal of democracy," and focusing much of their attention on the war with Japan, the people of Central Europe and western Russia were engaged, daily, in a life and death struggle fought out on the very streets of their cities.

Throughout the winter of 1941–1942 and onward for nine hundred days, the people of Leningrad suffered dramatically. Concerned that the German army might encounter enormous losses in an all-out assault, Hitler had ordered a blockade of the city instead, hoping to starve its three million people and destroy the Russian morale. Since Leningrad was closed off to the west by the Baltic Sea, to the east by the eighty-mile-wide Lake Ladoga, and to the north by the Finnish army (Finland was engaged in its own territorial war with the Soviet Union), the Wehrmacht needed only to seal the southern flank to divide the old imperial capital from the rest of the country. But even as the Germans closed ranks around them and began bombing warehouses and supply routes to erase their food supplies, Leningrad's hearty citizens

The first arduous journeys across the Lake Ladoga "ice road" were slow, and precious food shipments could not keep up with the needs of Leningrad's people. But through the winter, as the ice on the lake thickened, more than nineteen thousand people were put to work on the "road of life," increasing both the quantity and frequency of deliveries.

"Zehnya died 28 December . . .

Babushka died 25 January . . .

Leka died 17 March . . .

Dedya Vasya died 13 April . . .

Dedya Lesha, 10 May . . .

Mama, 13 May . . .

All died. Only Tanya remains"

Diary of eleven-year-old Tanya Savicheva, chronicling her family's suffering during the siege of Leningrad. By 1943, she, too, would die.

showed they would not be easily conquered. Volunteers built thousands of air raid shelters and pillboxes and felled trees in the enemy's path.

By late December 1941, Leningrad was down to two days' supply of flour. People were making "bread" by combining cellulose, sawdust, and the sweepings of flour from storage bins. Animal feed became human feed. Weeds were boiled to create soup. The starving died in the streets, falling beside the frozen trolley cars that stood silently in their tracks, and they died at home, whereupon the family quickly hid the corpse so they could continue to receive the dead person's 250-gram daily ration. Fifty-three thousand perished in December alone; by February 1942, another 200,000 had died. Somehow, the city held on.

Scientists studying the possibility of running a "road" over Lake Ladoga had declared that four inches of ice could support a horse; that a horse and a ton of freight would require seven inches; and that a truck would demand a minimum of eight. When the winter proved to be brutally cold, the Leningraders then cautiously began sending convoys across the "road of life." In the first seven days, forty trucks slipped through to the bottom of the lake, but dozens of others arrived on the western shore and, despite the strafing of Nazi bullets from overhead, soon returned carrying precious food.

A way out had been found. Women and children were evacuated and the city limped onward, in darkness and silence, for there was no fuel oil to light the

A mother's desperate journey out of Leningrad: **"People say things are forgotten with time, but that? Never!"**

On the twenty-first of June, 1941, I was so happy. I was six months pregnant, and my husband invited me to go to the park in the evening. Everything was so nice; the night was so still, all the trees were in blossom. The next morning we went to Nevsky Avenue to buy a paper, and when we entered the shop, we saw a crowd of people near a radio. They were very frightened, and when my husband asked what was the matter, people answered, "War." Germans had bombed Kiev and many other small cities just on the border of the Soviet Union. Everyone was shocked, because we had only heard that "Our country is so strong," and that "Hitler respects Russia." Hitler told us that he would never attack, never. But he deceived us.

People rushed to the shops to buy food, and I told my husband, "Let us buy food. If there's a war, we might starve." But he told me, "No, silly girl. There is enough food in Leningrad. And if our house is bombed, and we lose everything, we will just go to the shop and buy everything again." But all the food in Leningrad was in one place, and when bombs were thrown on that store-house, the city was left without food.

My husband told me I should leave the city and go somewhere, but how could I go, alone, pregnant? And I did not want to leave him. He packed all my things in suitcases, and that night, I threw all these things away and told him, "No. We shall live here together in Leningrad." When the bombing started, we had alarm signals every fifteen or twenty minutes, and it was very hard for me to go to the safe places because being pregnant, I could not run. Very often during the bombings I was in bed, and the bed would be jumping from place to place. So we moved out of our apartment and into the Polytechnical Institute, where my husband was a post-graduate. Under the laboratory there was a very big basement. We felt much safer down there because it was built by the tsar and the walls were one meter thick. We thought that the bombing would stop soon, that maybe the war would stop soon, because in all the newspapers, Russian people were told that we could finish with Hitler in two months. But soon, we heard on the radio that Germans were coming closer and closer to Leningrad. People rushed from small towns into Leningrad because they didn't want to live under German power. Leningrad became overcrowded, and a lot of people were evacuated to Siberia or other places. And then the Germans surrounded the city and there was no way to escape in any direction.

My baby was due on the first of October. All through September, Leningrad was bombed. We were living in the basement with nineteen other people, and I hoped that as soon as the war stopped, we could go back to our apartment with the baby. I was sent to a maternity home on the first of October, and since I had a very hard delivery I was there a long time. When I got out on the nineteenth of October, the winter had already started. It was very, very cold. When my husband came to take me from the maternity house, he told me, "Zina, I don't know what to do, because our house is without windowpanes."

We went back to the basement and lived there without light, without water, without heating. That winter was so severe, you cannot imagine. And I was the only woman in the basement who had such a small baby. When I gave birth to her, she was such a nice big girl. And my husband wanted to have a girl, so we were very happy. But he understood that this beautiful girl, she wouldn't survive, because I had no natural milk in my breast, nothing. All we had for her were the four small bottles that were provided for her in our food rations. And my husband was becoming so pale with hunger, almost blue; he could not even move anymore. Once a woman told me, "What are you doing? Your child will die, so give all the food to your husband, and save him. If he survives, he can give you a second baby." I gave the milk to him once, but then the baby started crying, and I decided that food belonging to the baby must be eaten by her. So I told my husband, "Keep to your bed. Take care of the baby, and I will do everything else myself."

In the morning, I would rush into the park, gather snow, and melt it for the baby to drink. From the ration cards they gave us, we received 125 grams of bread and one pound of meat for a month. Plus each day we were given one tablespoon of cereal, and one teaspoon of oil. How could people live on that? People were getting so weak, that sometimes if they fell down, they could not get up. I, too, was getting weaker and weaker. Once, on

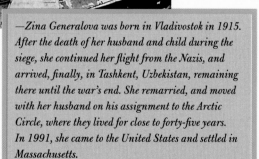

A grieving mother lays the body of her dead infant on top of a coffin, one of thousands who died of starvation every day during the siege.

—*Zina Generalova was born in Vladivostok in 1915. After the death of her husband and child during the siege, she continued her flight from the Nazis, and arrived, finally, in Tashkent, Uzbekistan, remaining there until the war's end. She remarried, and moved with her husband on his assignment to the Arctic Circle, where they lived for close to forty-five years. In 1991, she came to the United States and settled in Massachusetts.*

my way home I was in such despair that I decided to hide and sit somewhere to have a rest; I had no strength left to go. I was dying. And suddenly in my ears I heard the cry of my baby. Ooh! I jumped and rushed. Two minutes before, I did not think that I could have run so fast. And so my baby saved my life.

By the end of January, people began saying that soon there would be a way out of Leningrad. People would go across Lake Ladoga, which was frozen, and was the only place you could get through the blockade that surrounded the city. When my husband first told me about that, I told him that we would die. How could we go? It was forty-one degrees below zero, and we had no warm clothing. How could we do it with the baby? But he told me, "We shall die here of starvation." We took a train to Lake Ladoga that had a very nice passenger carriage. And it was so warm inside, ah! Everyone looked at me and said, "You have a baby! How did you save your girl?" When we got to the lake we had to wait until nighttime to cross it because the Germans were watching. Also, many trucks full of people were falling into the holes in the ice, because the Germans were bombing the lake. We waited the whole day on the bank. I don't know how we survived. But when night came, we were taken across, and we were safe.

My husband and my baby were with the driver, because my husband was already so blue, so sick. And the baby did not cry; she weighed less than when I gave birth to her. When we got to the other side of the lake, hot food was given to us — big loaves of brown bread. But that was very sad because people were so hungry they tried to eat the whole loaf, which is dangerous when you are starving. They were also giving chocolate to the children, but my baby was too young to eat it. Then we were put into train carriages which were very bad, like the kind used for cattle. When I entered that carriage, I understood that my baby would die. Well, she died on the fourth day. A few weeks or so later, I don't know, people knocked at the door and asked if there were dead people in this carriage. I covered the baby and gave it to them, and they told me, "Mommy, take the blanket off. Only bare bodied." I did as I was told and put the baby on the heap of dead people. People say such terrible things are forgotten with time. But that cannot be forgotten, never.

When we made it across, my husband told me, "Zina, send me to the hospital. I am dying." And so people came and took him to the hospital. Now why did I not jump off that terrible carriage, and rush after him? I was very, very weak. I was so weak and so tired, that I decided that I would go to our final destination, a small town called Pyatigorsk, and then come back when I was okay and pick him up. But I did not do that. He died at the hospital. And then I was alone.

"We have fought during fifteen days for a single house. The 'front' is a corridor between burned-out rooms; it is the thin ceiling between two floors . . . From story to story, faces black with sweat, we bombard each other with grenades in the middle of explosions, clouds of dust and smoke, heaps of mortar, floods of blood, fragments of furniture and human beings . . ."

A German officer describing the fighting at Stalingrad, 1942

lamps and not even a bird to sing. Every creature — living or dead — had been picked over by the hungry hordes, including many of the human creatures whose corpses lay collapsed in the gutters. Leningrad Radio, run from a generator of a ship frozen in a river, aired the sound of a metronome between programs to let its listeners, few though they were, know that the city was still alive. By the time the city was liberated in January 1944, nearly a million people had died, including more civilians than in any city in any war in history.

While the siege of Leningrad was settling in, and the Germans appeared in a freshly ascendant position, a ferocious battle was beginning over Stalingrad, a sprawling provincial city of half a million, outlining the western bank of the Volga River. If there was one battle that defined the struggle between fascism and Bolshevism — the essential confrontation that Hitler had so long dreamed of winning — it was this one. From a strategic vantage point, the modest industrial city was important because its conquest would allow Germany to cut off the supply route to the Russian army up north and open the way for the Wehrmacht to control the oil fields surrounding the Caucasus mountains.

But Hitler wanted Stalingrad for another reason as well: in an act of brazen self-congratulation, Stalin had named this, Russia's third largest city, after himself in 1925, honoring the battle he had led there during the Russian civil war; its capture would thus provide a symbolic as well as a strategic victory and a challenge to the Russian will. In the end, Stalingrad would prove to be so important to both Russians and Germans, they would together expend the lives of one million people in just five months.

The drama began with the German troops cutting their way through the residential areas on the city's northern edge. There they encountered sporadic shelling, oddly imprecise. Only after they caught up with the emplacements did they discover that the guns hadn't been operated by Russian soldiers at all, but by Russian civilians, many of them women in housedresses. The legendary Russian resistance was here, too.

That night an enormous roar deafened Stalingrad: the sound of six hundred German planes descending upon the city at once. The enemy fliers dropped bombs carrying incendiary devices, and when they ignited they left the city so bright with flames German soldiers forty miles to the rear said they could read a newspaper from the light. More than forty thousand civilians died in this initial blitz, but the worst was yet to come.

Fought in alleyways and in the shells of burned-out buildings, around street corners and inside homes, the Battle of Stalingrad became the Verdun of the Second World War — a fierce contest that grew well beyond its relative importance. Since the city was home to several of the Soviet Union's prized industrial armaments plants, tanks rolled off the assembly line and directly into battle. Yet it was hand-to-hand combat that came to dominate the Stalingrad fighting. Verdun had its no-man's-land, but here, soldiers fought face-to-face, barrel-to-barrel. Buildings changed hands several times a day; so did streets, so did rooftops. Piles of rubble became a conquest and, then, just as strangely, something to protect. Snipers worked from every garret, booby traps appeared at every turn. Grenades came flying at soldiers from above, behind, even below.

The insanity of the battle became obvious even to its impotent commanders (for how was an officer to lead an army that was dispersed into the city's streets?). Yet from their headquarters in Moscow and the occupied Ukraine (Hitler had moved his operations there and was directing one of the battles himself, by radio), the two dictators insisted that their armies fight on. In October, the Germans still held the upper hand: they had cornered the Russians on the banks of the Volga, holding them to just three factories and a bridgehead four thousand yards deep. But, ignoring the pleas of his advisers, Hitler had failed to protect his flanks. A month later, fresh Russian troops encircled the city, trapping the German army inside. Now it was the Wehrmacht that was under siege, starving and freezing while they waited for promised reinforcements that never arrived. By January 1943, the battle was over and more than eighty thousand German prisoners were marched off to Soviet camps where all but a few of them would eventually die.

Stalingrad marked a turning point in the European war. Soon the German nation was to revert to a defensive position, the guns of the world trained on her. Hitler had not planned for a long war and his factories, lacking sufficient quantities of oil and gas, were not up to the demands of the battlefront. There were other problems, too. The German public was no longer quite as enthralled by their führer. Dissent was beginning to emerge. And while they reacted to the news from the East — the public avidly followed the drama at Stalingrad, though the news they were receiving was heavily skewed to mask German defeat — Germany's citizens raced for cover from a barrage of Allied bombing.

The first raid came at Cologne and lasted a mere ninety minutes. But when it was over, the Allies' 1,080 bombers had dropped more than two thousand tons of explosives. It was, surely, the most successful air attack in the war thus far. Fewer than 500 people were killed, but 600 acres of the city were destroyed and 45,000 people were left homeless. Now it was *German* refugees who began to clog the roads in search of shelter.

The response of the high command was to introduce the nation to a more intense war effort. Air raid shelters were built. Rallies were held. All men, aged sixteen to sixty-five, and women, seventeen to fifty, were told to report for compulsory labor. But the impact of the bombings on home front morale was significant. Mindful of the turnip winter of 1916 and the desperate conditions that attended the home front in general throughout World War I, Hitler had always been careful to create as little disruption of German life as possible. Now that their own people were suffering (the way that Britain and Russia and Poland had suffered), the public's enthusiasm for battle predictably waned.

On January 13, 1943, a local Nazi Party leader spoke to students at the University of Munich, and, after recounting the disaster at Stalingrad, deposited blame for the German defeat squarely on the shoulders of the nation's youth. Those German boys who had avoided service in the Wehrmacht by studying at the university were behaving like malingerers, he said. If they could not serve in the army, they must reaffirm their devotion to the Nazi cause by signing up for work in one of the war industries. As for the women, he added, they should look to bear children, a son for each year they were attending university.

The reaction of the students was outrage. They stormed the lectern, expelling the official and his SS entourage from the hall, then ran out onto the streets, where they staged a demonstration against the Nazi regime. After Munich's riot police arrived on the scene, the uproar was put down (and, in time, the riot's leaders were beheaded). But smaller protests followed in the Ruhr, Frankfurt, and Stuttgart.

Nazi officials tried to boost the people's morale by increasing their rations (and Goebbels, bizarrely, instituted a campaign for civic "politeness," offering to reward the waiters, transit employees, clerks, and others who maintained the most courteous manner throughout their present ordeal). But, by midsummer 1943, the pace of the Allied bombing raids had increased and life on the German streets had become a fight for survival. More than 75 percent of the port city of Hamburg was destroyed, leaving 800,000 homeless. In time, Berlin would collapse, too; so would Dresden.

With lines of people gathering outside the shelters each day, the streets of Berlin began to look like the streets of London in 1940, when Germany was battering the British capital daily (only Germany never hit London as hard, or as frequently). And, as in London (and Coventry and Warsaw and Leningrad), the camaraderie generated by the bombing provided the glue that held the nation together. People scurried to move out of harm's way at night; then rebuilt their shattered homes during the day, all the while putting their hope in Germany's chances to repel the Allied land invasion, which they knew was imminent.

In the spring of 1944, the destruction was so enormous and proceeding at such a terrific speed, the Nazi propaganda ministry sent some of Germany's best photographers to take pictures of the art and architecture that were still standing and undamaged. After all, they might never be seen again. Sadly, it was one of the few acts of preservation undertaken by a regime intent, more than ever now, on razing the rest of civilization. Orders given to German troops retreating from the Eastern Front demanded that they destroy everything in their path, a dictate which included destroying things German, too. If he was going to lose, Hitler did not want the nation to survive him under enemy rule. Cattle, grain, farm equipment, and peasantry were to be moved westward with them; the rest of Eastern Europe was to be ground into a desert.

Germany's Eastern strategy was in shambles. But there was one part of it which had proceeded according to plan. In the earliest days after the invasion of Russia in 1941, the führer and his deputies had stumbled over how to deal with the enormous numbers of Jews living in the new German "territories." Before the war, they had pressured the Jews to emigrate from Germany and Austria. Those that remained were herded into ghettos and slave labor camps where they could do those tasks deemed too low for the Aryan population. But Germany's acquisition of Poland and Czechoslovakia had placed a large number of Jews under their control; with war raging, there was no easy way to expel them. When Russia and its large Jewish population then seemed ready to give way, too, Hitler and his deputies seized upon the chance to combine their strategic needs with their race-based ideology and execute the "final solution" to the Jewish "problem." They would simply exterminate the Jews.

In fact, the killing began long before fifteen top government officials met in the Wannsee suburb of Berlin on January 20, 1942, and declared it an official (if still secret) aim of government policy. As the fighting men of Operation

> " Without screaming or weeping these people undressed, stood around in family groups, kissed each other, [and] said farewells . . . An old woman with snow-white hair was holding a one-year-old child in her arms and singing to it and tickling it. The child was cooing with delight. The parents were looking on with tears in their eyes."
>
> *German engineer Herman Graebe, describing the scene at an execution pit in the Ukraine*

A member of the Einsatzgruppen *targets a mother and child at point-blank range. Women were often ordered to hold their children so that one bullet could do the work of two.*

"What really boggled my mind was that the only sounds made were by the tools and the stones. The people didn't speak. Their eyes seemed extinguished, and the overall impression was that these were not men but, rather, beings from another, fearful world — the world of the dead."

German businessman Hans Deichmann, describing a visit to Auschwitz, 1942

Barbarossa spread through the Soviet Union in late 1941, divisions of the SS followed after them, rounding up Jews for mass execution. The victims were marched to the countryside where they were forced to dig their own graves, then shot in front of them. And when that method of slaughter proved to be too much for even the hardened Nazi officers to bear, they began using mobile gas vans, herding the Jews into the vans under the pretext that they contained delousing chemicals, filling the chamber instead with carbon monoxide, then dumping their dead bodies out to make room for the next group.

The evil campaign, which killed over a million Russian Jews before the German army was driven back in 1944, was carried out with the help, in many cases, of the local Ukrainian and Lithuanian populations, whose own anti-Semitism meshed sinisterly with their will to please the occupying authorities. The activities of the *Einsatzgruppen*, as the German mobile killing squads were called, were kept remarkably quiet. To remove all physical evidence of the massacres, additional units would sometimes arrive after the SS work was completed and burn the bodies on oil-soaked grids, then grind any remaining bones in special machines. Yet things didn't always go according to plan. When the chief representative of an American Jewish relief committee returned from a visit to Eastern Europe in 1942, he reported hearing of a vast pit near Kiev, where seven thousand Jews — some dead, some still alive — had been buried under a layer of dirt so thin it looked to be "heaving like a living sea."

The second phase of the "final solution" was even more evil than the first. As the war dragged on, Hitler's deputies organized and carried out the deportation of millions of European Jews, from Berlin, Vienna, Prague, and the rest of the Reich. Telling them that they would be "resettled" in the East, they then stripped the Jews of their belongings and hauled them in crowded boxcars to any

Hiding from the horror: "'If there's anyone in the attic,' said the SS officer, 'you're kaput'"

The war between the Germans and the Russians broke out in June of 1941. Our town, Maciejow, had been in Poland until Russia occupied it at the start of the war, and a lot of the people in town were not happy with the Russians because so many businesses had closed down. When the Germans came, I think at first people thought that things couldn't be much worse — that they might even be better.

The first clue that things weren't going to be good was when the Germans saw the rabbi sitting at a table with some bread and salt, which is the traditional way to welcome people. One of the officers went directly to where the rabbi was sitting, turned the table over, and told him, "You there, Jew: Get out of here." I was nine years old and didn't fully understand what this meant for us.

After the Germans had secured the town, they gave an order that all Jewish men between sixteen and sixty should report to authorities to change their passports. I happened to be in the town square that morning, and saw the Jewish men lined up. The Germans marched those men to their headquarters, which was a mile outside of town. Later, I heard shots coming from that area, and I noticed local Ukrainian men walking in that direction with shovels. It turned out that some men who were trained in certain occupations were let go, but about four hundred of the Jews never came back.

Later on, the Germans spread the word that those men were taken to work camps, but of course that was a lie; they were all dead. The Germans even forced a young boy to write letters signed by all of those people that were killed. The letters said these people were someplace else but still alive, and the Germans delivered these letters to the families. Some of the wives, mothers, and sisters of these men chose to believe that these people really were away for work, and would be back. Nobody could imagine that you could take a man that did nothing wrong and shoot him, just like that.

When rumors started that something even worse was going to happen, a lot of people went into hiding. My mother, my brother, my sister, and I went to our grandparents' house, which was away from the Jewish community. The women of the family hid in an attic while my brother, my grandfather, and I stayed downstairs. We were young and my grandfather was old, and at that point they didn't bother very old or young people. One night, I heard German voices across the street, then suddenly they were shining a flashlight into the house, knocking on the door, and yelling, in German, "Open up!" When I opened the door and these two SS officers walked in, and asked me where my sisters were, I said, "I don't know where they are, you took them away already. Maybe *you* can tell *me* where they are."

Leon Ginsburg at age thirteen, after the war.

—Leon Ginsburg, who was born in 1932, was sent to the United States with a group of orphans when the war ended. He worked his way through college and became an inventor and manufacturer of high-tech dental equipment. He married another Holocaust survivor, who was also hidden as a child. They have three children and live in Rockland County, New York.

They started searching the house, and when they asked me if anybody was up in the attic I said no. One of them drew out his revolver, which to me looked like a cannon, and put it to my head and said, "Is anybody up there? If I find anybody up there, you're *kaput*." They went up and looked, but luckily my family was hiding in a narrow part of the attic and they weren't found. After they left, my teeth started chattering. I got into bed with my brother, and he held me to stop me from shaking.

The main population in our area was Ukrainian and many of them saw the Germans as liberators, because as soon as the Germans came in they let the Ukrainians take over the government. They also formed a militia-type of group that worked with the Germans, persecuting Jews and hunting them out. They even helped with a lot of the killing. The Ukrainians became very good at finding the places where people were hiding. And they had an incentive because if you captured a Jew, you were given five hundred German marks plus the clothes that person was wearing. For many of them, it was a hunt they carried out with glee.

For a while, they stopped the killings, and they told us that everything was back to normal. So those who were hiding came out, and people started working again. Then in May of 1942 we heard that they were killing all the Jews in Kovel, the next town. So we went back into hiding in a cellar. Almost every night, I could hear the soldiers approaching, usually two of them walking together. One night when I peeked out I saw them drag a young girl out of a room and shoot her right there on the sidewalk.

One night they stuck a rifle into the door where we were hiding and told everyone to come out. My mother saw an area that was boarded up inside the basement, and she ripped off a board and told me to get inside. She put back the board and I held it in position. Two Ukrainian policemen came down to the basement with rifles and bayonets, and my mother was hiding under some bedding. They searched the room and stabbed through the bedding until she screamed, "No! No! I'm coming out." They took her away. They came so close to where I was that I had to stop breathing because I was afraid they would hear me. But then they left, and I was all alone.

My brother ran away into the woods that night, but was captured and taken to a synagogue where they rounded up Jews. Once you were in that synagogue, you were on the way to your death. While in there he saw the names of all the people who had been captured, because people would write their names on the walls. My brother found my sister's name there. She had written, "My dear brothers, take revenge." Since she was basically a good-natured soul, she must have already seen some horrible brutality in order to make that statement. My brother was determined to escape, so he and another boy sneaked up the chimney of the wood stove in the synagogue. The Ukrainians spotted the other boy, and they killed him, but my brother managed to escape. He made his way out of town that night.

As for me, I really didn't know what to do when my family was taken away. I went from one hiding place to the next, always managing to survive. Eventually I made it to a farm owned by some Polish Christians who knew my uncle and agreed to take me in and so I lived with them and hid my Jewish identity. We were only about ten miles from Sobibor, the camp, and the trains headed there used to pass near the farm. I saw trains headed to the camp with the windows closed up and SS men sitting on top of the train with machine guns. Once, there was a window on the last car, and these two young faces were looking out — a boy and a girl, around fourteen or fifteen. They were looking right at me with this frightened look, but I couldn't show any emotions about it. I felt so embarrassed to be standing there, seeing my people being taken to be killed. I will never forget those two faces, because probably within a day or so they were dead.

Jews lived in constant fear of a knock on the door or a light shone through their window in the middle of the night. Here, in Wiesbaden, Germany, a deportation begins.

Prisoners line up at an unidentified concentration camp. "During roll call they would kill many of us," recalled one survivor. "Kill us for the simple reason that someone soiled their pants, soiled their uniform . . . Dysentery was something very common. After two weeks at Auschwitz your eyes would swell up . . . your legs would puff because of malnutrition and hygiene. And then you became a skeleton."

of several death camps. There, after an initial examination, those who were deemed fit to work were separated from those who were not. But since the labor was demanding and the conditions were atrocious, nearly everyone eventually faced the same fate: they were told to remove all clothing and jewelry and ordered into bathhouses armed with water jets holding Zyklon B, a poison gas used to kill rats. Once the screaming subsided, and the doors were opened, the inmates' bodies were still standing, so many of them had been crowded in at once. Then the corpses were hauled off to the ovens for burning.

The six most active camps were located throughout Poland (Hitler wanted them out of sight of the German people), but as the war neared its end, even the facilities at Dachau (near Munich) and Bergen-Belsen (near Hamburg) had been equipped with ovens. The camps took the industrialization of killing to a new level. Now there were not only weapons factories but actual killing factories, too, depositing the stench of their work into the surrounding communities, fertilizing the neighborhood flower beds, employing the local talent, and working hard to meet "productivity" quotas. The staff of Auschwitz, the most notorious of the Polish camps, proudly claimed to be able to "process" twelve thousand inmates a day.

Life (and death) at Auschwitz:
"In the morning we were shorn of hair, then . . . tattooed. That's when I got my number, 104995"

I was living in a work camp called Paderborn in northern Germany, cleaning the streets and sewers in the town. We were guarded by policemen, but at least we had something to eat and nobody got shot or killed. In February 1943, we were told to get ready because the entire camp was going to be evacuated toward the east. We walked at night, through the streets that we had been cleaning for a year, to the train station, where we were put on cattle cars. We spent five days and five nights in these cars with hardly any food or water, never knowing where we were going. There was no room to sleep or sit down. Several people couldn't take it and they died right in the car; we had to just put them in a corner. Then we came to a place, and somebody called out "Oswiecim!" That's the Polish word for Auschwitz.

There was a peculiar, sweet smell in the air. I couldn't figure out what it was. It was the smell of excrement, urine, death, hunger, dirt. It was the smell of the gas chambers, but we didn't know that, of course. We heard noises — dogs barking — and all of a sudden, it became very light. The doors of the car were opened up and we heard, "Everybody out. Leave your luggage." Everywhere there was screaming and yelling: "My son, my father, where are you?" We saw for the first time that we were in a line of thirty or forty cars, full of old people, young people, children.

We were forced into two columns, women on one side, men on the other side. I held on to two of my friends. The screaming and yelling continued as mothers looked for their children, and mothers tried to hold on to their babies. I would never have believed that anything like this could happen to human beings, but this was just the beginning. At the end of the line, there was an SS man in a beautiful leather coat, and as we walked by he asked us, "How old?" If you were between the ages of sixteen and thirty, the thumb went up and you went to one side. Over thirty, the thumb went down, and you went to the other side. Why were we being separated? The screaming, the whips, the dogs, that picture will be with me as long as I live. "How old?" he asked me. I said, "Nineteen." The thumb went up.

They piled us into trucks, and then a guard said something to me that I didn't understand. He said, "You're the lucky ones." I said, "What do you mean?" And he said, "The others are already up the chimney." That's when we started to realize what this place was. All the girls were gassed that same day. But they needed labor, so when the thumb went up, I was given a chance, together with my other friends, to live. We were taken to a place where they told us to undress. I don't know how long we stood there. I wasn't hungry anymore. I was scared for my life. "The others are already up the chimney." So that was the smell.

Left: Michel in 1939. Below: Michel's sister, Lotte (far right), and their parents in 1939. Lotte left for France the day after this photograph was taken. She survived the war and lives in Israel. Michel's parents died in Auschwitz.

—Ernest Michel, born in 1923, survived the Auschwitz "death march" in 1944. He settled in Allied Occupied Germany and was sent to cover the Nuremberg trials as a reporter for a German newspaper. He emigrated to the United States in 1946 and began a long career with the United Jewish Appeal of New York, eventually serving as executive vice president. In 1981, he realized his lifelong dream, organizing the World Gathering of Jewish Holocaust Survivors in Jerusalem. He is the author of Promises to Keep.

In the morning we were shorn of hair. Then, every one of us was tattooed. That's when I got my number, 104995. I was sent to the camp that was used as slave labor for I. G. Farben, a company that was trying to manufacture artificial rubber. We were slaves, but there was a difference between us and the slaves who were brought to America from Africa. They were treated poorly, but at least they were a commodity, so they were given some food. With us it was totally different, because the supply of Jews in Europe was unlimited; there were millions of us. The normal food rations in Auschwitz were such that you had approximately half a year until your body gave out — they had figured it out very scientifically. And after that, up the chimney. When you got down to eighty, ninety pounds you knew you were about to be taken out and gassed.

We didn't live, we existed. That's all it was. The camp was surrounded by two sets of electrically charged wire. The moment you touched it you were electrocuted. I saw inmates by the hundreds run into that barbed wired just to get it over with. But I never wanted to. My parents instilled in me a feeling of responsibility, even during very difficult times. So I told myself and the others around me, some of us have got to hang on in order to tell the story of what happened. So despite the horror, the hunger, the fear, and the death all around us, some of us kept up the hope that it had to end some-

time. I was convinced that what was happening to us was probably one of the worst things that ever happened to any people at any time.

To survive under those circumstances took fortitude and a desire to hang on, but it also took plain old dumb luck. Without a lucky break, something extra that helped you survive, you would never make it. And eventually, I got my lucky break. Now, I was getting very thin — probably eighty-five pounds or so, and my bones were starting to show. One day I got hit over the head, and I went to the prison hospital to get taken care of. I didn't want to stay there overnight because if I did, the next day I'd be put in the truck, and sent up the chimney. But by some fluke, a man came through the hospital and asked if anyone had good handwriting. Now, in 1939 my father had sent me to take calligraphy lessons. At the time I said, "What do I need this for?" And he said, "You never know when it could come in handy." That ended up saving my life. They sat me down with a logbook and told me what to write: "Weak of body." "Heart attack." The Germans kept immaculate records, and of course, nobody was ever gassed. Everybody died of weak body or heart attack. So because I could write neatly I became an official recorder.

One of my other duties was to work in the medical area, where Dr. Joseph Mengele did his experiments. We were asked to bring in blankets for the women who were being given electric shock in order to find out how much strain a person could take. After the experiments we would bring the women out and put them on the truck that would take them to Birkenau. None of them survived. We took out bodies, one after another. After a while, death was like breathing to us.

This hospital job allowed me to witness one of the most important events during my stay in Auschwitz. Three men — very popular guys whom I had known — attempted to escape and were caught. First, they were tortured, then they were brought to the roll call place. In front of ten thousand inmates, they were brought to the gallows. There was total silence, and we were surrounded by SS men with machine guns because they feared something might happen. Just before the men were hanged, one of them shouted out, "Don't forget us!" And then they were killed. Now being an aide in the hospital, it was my job, along with a friend of mine, to take the bodies down from the gallows and put them in the morgue. We laid them down, separate from all the others. At Auschwitz I must have carried more bodies than I can even count. But these were men that I had known, and when I saw that they were gone forever, it had a major impact on me. It made me want to live even more. I looked down at them lying there, and I said to them, "You will not be forgotten."

Jews weren't the only victims. Gypsies, Slavs, Catholics, homosexuals, and the mentally retarded were sent to their deaths, too. When information on the camps reached the West throughout 1942 and 1943, it prompted a few protest rallies and considerable discussion among Jewish leaders and members of the State Department as to an appropriate response (State was remarkably indifferent to the plight of the Jews and Roosevelt's failure to order the bombing of Auschwitz is viewed by some as the greatest failure of his presidency) but most people, reading articles that were usually buried in the inner pages of their newspapers, were inclined to discount the story as preposterous. In World War I, the Allies' propaganda had created numerous lies about the Germans, reports of soldiers raping nuns and cutting off the hands of babies. Surely this was yet another exaggeration.

On the night of June 5, 1944, Americans tuned their radios to hear FDR announce that the Italian fascists had been deposed under the force of Allied troops. The Italian and African campaigns had always been sideshows to the war in Europe and Russia, but the fall of Italy was symbolic, the first of the Axis nations to surrender. In the Roman square where *Il Duce* had once whipped crowds into a frenzy, the celebration was enormous.

Roosevelt was happy over the news ("One up and two to go!" he said), but he was understandably preoccupied. For even as the president spoke, 175,000 young Allied soldiers (many of them teenagers about to witness their first days in combat) were pushing off from the coast of England toward France in the largest amphibious operation in the history of war.

Operation Overlord, as it was called, was a massive logistical challenge. Along with the enormous fighting force (which was scheduled to grow to 2.5 million before the invasion was completed), it involved moving 50,000 motorcycles, tanks, and bulldozers across sixty miles of open water, employing 5,333 ships and 11,000 airplanes. All told, the operation of D-Day (the "D" stood for nothing more than a reinforcement of the word "Day") was roughly comparable, historian Stephen Ambrose has written, to transporting the cities of Green Bay, Racine, and Kenosha, Wisconsin, across Lake Michigan — every man, woman, child, car, and truck — and doing it all in one night.

But it was the strategy, much more than the logistics, that was the gamble. An amphibious invasion is an inherently dubious idea; historically, most have failed. The landing army arrives on a fortified coastline with its back already pushed to the sea and until it can sufficiently secure the beachhead to allow for trucks and artillery to come ashore, the attackers must move about on foot, a disadvantage that is rarely overcome. With Operation Overlord, there was all this against the Allies and more: the untested citizen-soldiers, tens of thousands of young men barely out of boot camp. On the morning of June 6, 1944, no one knew if they were up to the job.

Touring the bases under clearing skies (a torrential rain had forced the postponement of D-Day by twenty-four hours), General Dwight Eisenhower, the Supreme Commander of the Allied troops, went down to a Portsmouth pier to see off British units boarding a landing craft. He said farewell to twenty-three thousand Allied paratroopers at Newbury, aware of predictions that as many as 75 percent of them would be casualties. Holding lucky coins he had saved from

"Do you realize that by the time you wake up in the morning, twenty thousand men may have been killed?"

Winston Churchill, speaking to his wife, Clementine, shortly before retiring on the night before D-Day

"I've done all I can . . ." proclaimed General Eisenhower to the 101st Airborne Division (above) before the invasion of Normandy. "Now quit worrying, General," replied one soldier, "we'll take care of this thing for you."

Landing at Normandy:
"A buddy . . . started to scream, 'I can't go in, Clair, I can't.' . . . I said, 'You gotta go, you gotta'"

Just before they shipped my infantry unit, the 90th, over to Europe, we were given a ten-day furlough to visit our wives and children. I, being single, went back and spent those ten days with my mother and dad. For me, it wasn't a joyful occasion. I tried to put on a pretty good front for them, that things were going to be okay. I didn't tell them that I knew we'd be going into combat; I tried to spare them as much as I could. There's a song from that time that has always stuck with me, "Dear Mom, the weather today is cloudy and damp, your package arrived but was missing a stamp. The bugle just blew and tomorrow there's a big day with plenty to do. I like it here, Mom, but I'm kind of homesick for I love you, dear Mom." To me that song is sort of a prelude for when we headed for Normandy on D-Day.

We embarked from New York on a British luxury liner called the *Affluent Castle*. There were 4,500 of us, and we all had to go directly down below for security reasons. I'm sure the Germans must have had some people there watching to see what kind of movement there was toward England. We sailed for fourteen days, and for fourteen straight days I was seasick. Sometimes you figure you're better off not even living! Our living quarters were hammocks strung three deep, and I spent most of my time down below. Every day when we went up on the deck for calisthenics, I would look up and see those gigantic swells of the Atlantic Ocean and I'd just want to head straight for the railing.

When we got to England we were stationed in a huge tent city outside of Devonshire. We got there in March of 1944 and trained a bit. By May we still hadn't heard what we were doing there. Then on June 1, all letter writing was stopped, and that was our first clue that something was ready to happen. The following day we were told that D-Day was set for June 5.

On the third of June, all the troops were assembled and it was just a mass of humanity — people loading the ships, loading trucks and tanks onto ships. It was a pretty gratifying feeling, looking at this and saying, "Holy smokes, look at all this stuff. How could we lose the war?" When we got on our liberty ship we were told what our destination was, and there wasn't much we could do at that point but prepare ourselves. We were very well trained, physically, for what lay ahead. Mentally, though, each person is different. When you think you are going to face the enemy and you wonder, "How long have I got? Will I survive?" you want to be in the best shape spiritually to face your creator. I just said to myself, "Well, I'll put my trust in the Lord and take it from there."

There were three hundred of us on my ship, and for the next three days we sat in the harbor. We passed the time lying around on deck — some were playing

Left: Galdonik in Germany near the end of the war. Right: American soldiers in a landing craft off Omaha Beach.

—*Clair Galdonik, who was born in 1919, worked in Texas for several years after the war. In 1954, he came home to Minneapolis and took a job at an oil refinery, where he worked for thirty-two years. He was married in 1957 and has three sons. He is very active in veterans organizations and volunteers regularly at a nearby veterans hospital. In 1984 he attended the fortieth-anniversary commemoration of D-Day in Normandy.*

cards or shooting dice to keep their minds off what was to come. We watched as more ships came into view. It was gratifying to see that we were not alone. The weather was absolutely terrible — overcast and very windy. When we found out that our mission was postponed another day, some people were happy, but I was disappointed — just another twenty-four hours to lie in wonderment.

When we finally crossed the Channel on the morning of the sixth, we had to go from the ship onto those landing crafts that would take us to the shore. There were big scramble nets that led down into the landing crafts because they were probably about twenty-five or thirty feet below the level of the ship. Here we were with all of our gear — I don't know how we even got our legs over the side of the ship. We had a gas-resistant suit that was very cumbersome, we had our rifle belt, and we had to carry ninety-six rounds of ammunition, our canteens, our entrenching tool, our gas mask, our life jacket, our K-rations, and our rifles. I mean, we were *weighed down*. I had a strange, nightmarish feeling, sort of like, "Is this a dream or is this reality?" But then we lined up and they called my name and over the side I went. I don't know how we did it, but somehow we got down that net, even with the huge waves bobbing up. And I wasn't seasick at all.

Our battleships had already started firing on the beach by the time my unit got there and it was glorious to see the big belches of orange flame coming out of our guns. Then we saw the 82nd and 101st Airborne, and to see those darlings up there gave us a marvelous feeling. It was reassuring to think that we might have it relatively easy going in. But as we got closer to the beach we saw these big, black plumes of smoke, and we knew that the German artillery had opened up and was zeroing in on the beaches where we were headed.

Then the ramp on the landing craft went down. A good buddy of mine started to cry and scream, "I can't go in, Clair, I can't." The poor guy just broke up. I said, "You gotta go, you gotta," and I grabbed him with one arm and inflated our life jackets, and threw him in the water. I jumped in and tried to help him by myself, but he was hysterical. Another one of my buddies came along and got on the other side of this guy and I said, "We gotta go, we gotta go," because the longer we were out there the longer we were subjected to artillery fire, and we could get hit at any time. I don't know for how many yards we kept this guy with us, but then the artillery fire kept getting more intense, and he broke away from us. I told him, "You've got to go get on shore as fast as you can and get up that beach." Just then a round came in very close to us, but it was behind us, thank God. That guy got to the beach safely, but I don't know what happened to him after that.

We held our rifles over our heads and submerged ourselves in the water to protect us as much as we could. After the second salvo, total fear had left me. I was exhausted, weighed down, but then I got mad. I started cursing, and I told myself, "Nothing is going to stop me until I get on that beach." Fortunately, I got there, and I took off as best I could up the beach to some kind of wall, where we took cover until we could regroup.

It was a heck of a letdown for me seeing our first casualties. To see a dead GI, who just a few hours ago was full of life, full of hope, to see it end for him so suddenly, well, that sets you to thinking, "How much longer have I got?" At a time like that you don't hold out too much hope that you're going to survive this whole war. Some of us did, and some of us didn't. God rest their souls that lie over there in foreign soil.

"My decision to attack at this time and place was based upon the best information available. If any blame or fault attaches to the attempt it is mine alone."

Note carried in the wallet of Supreme Commander Dwight Eisenhower on the morning of D-Day, the invasion of Normandy

his successful invasions of North Africa and Sicily, he made small talk with the men of the 101st Airborne. Then, after saluting the planes as they took off for France, the stiff-lipped Kansan who would later occupy the White House turned aside in tears.

An American electrician's mate, who was in the first wave of American soldiers to land at Omaha Beach, later recalled, "We hit the sandbar, dropped the ramp, and then all hell poured loose on us."

For most Americans, D-Day was the climax of the war. It was *their* war, the trucks and tanks and armored vehicles carrying the Allied soldiers having recently slid off the assembly lines in Michigan and Illinois; the bombers and fighters ready for takeoff having emerged from assembly plants dotted throughout Ohio, Oregon, and California; the battleships, cruisers, and destroyers having been hammered together at shipyards on both coasts. People cheered the news of the invasion, which they had eagerly awaited. Churches rang their bells, factories sounded their whistles. Then, just as suddenly, everyone huddled in fear for the fate of their young boys, whose lives hung in the balance. On the night of June 6, Roosevelt, who had been too sick to go to London and participate in the planning of D-Day, came on radio to do the only thing that he, or for that matter, any American could do — pray. But the comfort that prayer provided at this moment was undermined by the knowledge that the God they depended upon now was the same one who had tolerated the carnage of Europe and the awful slaughters in the Pacific.

Off the English Channel, thousands of terrified infantrymen from twelve Allied nations, many having already vomited their breakfasts, floated in flat-bottomed landing craft toward shore beaches code-named Sword, Juno, Omaha, Gold, and Utah. As the coastline grew near, appearing to them through thick gray fog, the soldiers, carrying seventy pounds of wet battle gear apiece, jumped neck-deep into the waters and waded ashore. Now the battle was theirs to win or lose, all theirs. The first units, taking advantage of the element of surprise (the Germans had predicted that the Allies would invade at Pas-de-Calais, the channel's narrowest point, and were thus underfortified at Normandy), made their way quickly into the farmland at Gold, Juno, and Sword beaches. But the Americans pushing in at Omaha were not so lucky. There, in the center of the front, soldiers walked into a wall of German gunfire and paid dearly for it. Attempting to scale a bluff well covered by German defenders, more than 2,000 GIs were killed or wounded. By nightfall they had secured it, and joined the 156,000 Allied men on their way to liberate France.

Despite its astonishing success, the invasion of Normandy was a messy affair. German mines (nicknamed "Bouncing Betties") made the waters treacherous, and red with blood. After penetrating the corpse-laden beaches, the soldiers ran into the Normandy *bocage*, a maze of hedgerows in which the Germans had stationed small groups of machine gunners, invisible to the Allies until they were virtually on top of them. Still the British and American losses were nowhere near those anticipated. The total number of casualties suffered in the operation's first day was under 5,000, considerably less than the 75,000 some planners had feared.

Around the beginning of July, the Allies had landed more than one million troops, 566,000 tons of supplies, and 171,000 vehicles. By August, they had freed Paris and turned east. But the Germans were not ready to give up. They mounted one last strike at the Allies through Belgium in what became known as the Battle of the Bulge (because it pushed a forty-five-mile-wide dent into Allied lines). When Eisenhower's forces broke that offensive, too, the march to the Rhine was easy.

By early 1945, the Nazi strategy had been reduced to the bizarre. In an attempt to stiffen German morale, the high command unveiled an epic movie on the resistance of a small German town to the invasion of Napoleon in 1807. *Kolberg*, which had been created at Goebbels's insistence, was a film with Hollywood flair. It included 187,000 soldiers, who had been borrowed from the front to serve as extras. And at a time when the rail lines were under siege, hundreds of train cars had been commandeered to transport salt to the set where it became the "snow" of winter scenery. Even the director was appalled at the excess. "Hitler and Goebbels must have been obsessed with the idea that a film like this could be more useful to them than even a victory in Russia," he said.

Hitler was surrounded, his nation rapidly disintegrating. From the East, the Russian army pushed through Poland (conveniently pausing outside Warsaw so that the Germans could finish off the city and make it easier for the Soviets to hold it in their palm after the war) and marched toward Berlin. From the West,

On August 25, 1944, French army units rolled into Paris and liberated the capital after four years of German occupation. Despite Hitler's orders to reduce the city to a "blackened field of ruins," the German commander opted to surrender to avoid senseless destruction.

In Namering, Germany, the Allied military government displayed exhumed bodies as proof of the atrocities performed by the SS. Townspeople were paraded before them, and then ordered to bury the victims.

the Allied forces moved deeper into Germany, their eyes on the Elbe River. His nation was a landscape of ruins: Dresden, Essen, Düsseldorf, Nuremberg, Frankfurt, Hamburg, all reduced to rubble. Hitler retired to a concrete bunker at the center of the German capital, the only place where the myth of his destiny remained intact, and waited for a miracle.

The German leader first put his hopes in a home army composed of teenagers and old veterans — the only men who had not yet been drafted; later in the death of Roosevelt on April 12, which he received as his last bit of good news. Perhaps now, he thought, his fortune will change, just as it changed for Frederick the Great in 1762 when his rival, Tsarista Elizabeth of Russia, died, shifting the momentum back toward the House of Brandenburg. But of course the transition to Harry Truman was smooth, and the Allies remained solid.

By April 30, even Hitler's fanatical optimism had failed him. After a quiet lunch of spaghetti and salad, the führer and Eva Braun (he had married Braun, his longtime mistress, only two days before) walked into his underground suite, closed the door, and proceeded to swallow lethal doses of cyanide. An aide, following Hitler's instructions, waited until the poison had taken effect and shot him once in the head (to be sure that he was dead), then helped carry the two bodies upstairs where they were laid side by side in a garden, soaked with gasoline, and set on fire. Shells from the guns of the invading Russian army were bursting around them while a small group of mourners stood and raised their arms in a final salute. Within days, the Germans had surrendered.

Crowds in Red Square, Times Square, Picadilly Circus, and along the Champs Élysées erupted in celebration. But the news from Berlin failed to slow

Revelers in Times Square, New York City, celebrate the end of the war in Europe, May 1945. Fighting in the Pacific remained vigorous, but there was a sense of an ending in the air. The most murderous conflict in history was racing to a conclusion.

the pace of warfare on the other side of the globe, where the savagery of the Pacific war had been becoming increasingly surreal.

When the Marines landed on Saipan in 1944 (the tiny island was strategically important because its airfields would put American B-29s within striking distance of Tokyo), they battled fiercely against the Japanese banzai attacks, losing more than sixteen thousand men, then encountered a surprise: wave upon wave of Japanese civilians coming at them in a suicidal orgy. While the conquering Americans assured the people from loudspeakers that they would be treated well as captives, mothers threw their children from the edge of cliffs and then jumped after them; others pulled the triggers on grenades, then hugged them close to their bodies.

Reclaiming Guam the same year, Marines encountered desperate enemy soldiers armed only with pitchforks and baseball bats, bottles and rocks. Some took sticks, attached knives to the ends of them, then came hurling at the Americans in an unrelenting suicidal barrage. And even after the island was securely in American hands, thousands of Japanese refused to capitulate, taking to the hills instead, where they continued to attack guerrilla style for months.

But the stories of the fighting at Peleliu (pronounced Pell-ee-loo) are surely among the most bizarre, and tragic. The island was considered a stepping-stone to the recapture of the Philippines and an easy one at that. Admiral Chester Nimitz expected the Marines to work for three or four days and encounter minimal casualties. In fact, the fighting would last for two months and end the lives of 1,262 Marines and nearly 10,000 Japanese.

A preinvasion bombardment was thought to have weeded out most enemy troops at Peleliu. But when the Marines hit the beaches on September 15, 1944, they discovered thousands of Japanese hiding in a series of interlocking caves. Safe from attack, the enemy troops then undertook a deadly game of hide and seek, popping open the camouflaged steel doors of the caves, firing at the Marines, then disappearing again into the earth. The terrain, too, proved an obstacle. The Americans had brought shovels with them to dig out their protection, but the island's tough coral surface was impossible to penetrate, forcing them to lie exposed to deadly accurate mortar and artillery fire, or to crouch behind their own dead. In the end, the Marines would need almost two months to root out the enemy, and only much later would they learn that the island fight had probably been unnecessary: the Philippines were in easy grasp whether they had Peleliu or not.

The battle for Okinawa had already begun when news of the end of the European war arrived. The island was a critical target for the Americans — just 350 miles from Kyushu, the southernmost of Japan's four main islands, it was a natural step before the invasion of Japan itself. But a wave of suicide bombers, numbering in the thousands, was making it hard for the Americans. Off the coast of the island, a Japanese Zero crashed onto the flight deck of the U.S. aircraft carrier *Bunker Hill*. Thirty seconds later, another *kamikaze* fell from the sky ripping a forty-foot hole in the side of the *Bunker Hill*. The Americans won at Okinawa (at a price of fifty thousand casualties) but the Japanese resolve showed no signs of easing.

> "We come from a nation and a culture that values life and the individual. To find oneself in a situation where your life seems of little value is the ultimate in loneliness. It is a humbling experience. Most of the combat veterans had already grappled with this realization on Guadalcanal or Gloucester, but it struck me out in that swamp."
>
> *Marine Eugene B. Sledge,*
> *writing of the invasion at Peleliu*

Survival and surrender on Okinawa: "I followed trails of ants that led me to food in dead soldiers' knapsacks"

When the battle of Okinawa started, I was six years old and living with my family near Shuri, Okinawa's ancient capital city. My father was a farmer, and my mother had died the year before. I knew about the war because my brother had gone away to fight in it, but I didn't know that we were losing. Then the war came to Okinawa, and they put up a communication unit near my house with a lot of soldiers coming in and out. When the war reached a critical point, food started to get scarce, so we gave the soldiers all of the big potatoes from our farm and kept the smaller ones to eat ourselves. Soon, though, we had killed all of our livestock and run out of food, and my father had to leave to get some more. He said, "If I don't return for some reason, you must escape."

When the bombing got really bad and my father still hadn't returned, many of the people around us started to flee and my sister decided it was time for us to go as well. So we headed south, hiding during the daytime and moving only at night. My sisters' arms were full of things they had brought from the house, and I held hands with my brother, who was three years older than me. We were able to see clearly at night because of all the bombing and the flares. I saw a lot of dead people — we were tripping over bodies as we went along. I remember a baby trying to suck at her dead mother's breast. One night we were getting ready to sleep on a beach called Komesu, and there was shelling and gunfire

all around us. We dug out a little hole to sleep in that was barely deep enough to cover our bottoms. I was sleeping next to my brother when a soldier came and told us that the war was going to get worse in that area so we had to go. I shook my brother, but he didn't wake up, even though his eyes were open. That's when we saw that there was blood all over the back of his head. But he was still warm and I just didn't think he was dead, so I didn't want to bury him. My sisters insisted.

With my brother gone, there was nobody to hold my hand, so I held onto my sister's clothing instead. But that night as we walked along, the moonlight shone on this person's face and I realized I was holding on to somebody else's clothes. I called out my sisters' names again and again, but nobody answered. I feared that they might have died as well, and for a while every time I saw dead bodies with hairstyles like either of my sisters I would look at the face to see if it was one of them. There were mountains and mountains of dead bodies all over, and I kept looking but I just couldn't find them. My sisters had been carrying everything, including the food, so I was alone and I had nothing.

I remembered some of the survival skills my father had taught me on the farm, so I was able to find a little bit of food. Sometimes I followed trails of ants that led me to food in dead soldiers' knapsacks. I felt bad, but I figured that they were dead, so I would pray for them and say, "Thank you for the food." I also remembered

my father telling me not to always do what everyone else was doing, so I kept to myself instead of traveling with other people. It was like a game of hide and seek, and I hid alone so that no one would find me. Once I met up with a family with a child my age, living in a cave. I stayed around for a little while, until the mother said to me, "Do you want to die with us? If not, you better run away now because we are going to stack up all the rocks at the entrance of the cave, and set off a bomb to kill ourselves." I didn't want to die, so I ran as hard as I could, and I heard the blasting sound behind me.

One day a few weeks later I was really thirsty, and I had just about lost my strength to live. I found a little hole that I thought was a spring, but it turned out to be a cave. I stuck my face in, and it was very dark but I could smell miso soup, just like my mother used to make. I could see a little bit of light and I heard an old man say to me, "Come down." I also heard a woman's voice, saying, "Who is here?" And when I looked into her eyes I could tell she was blind. They said, "You must be very hungry, where have you come from?" I told the story about my sisters and my brother and that I had no one. And so the old man said, "Stay with us." I was so grateful because all of the other adults I had seen in caves had shooed me away. But they gave me food and water, and let me stay with them, taking care of their wounds and helping them however I could. I grew to love them and the beautiful cave, and I never wanted to leave.

One day, the American forces came close by the cave, and we could hear a voice on a loudspeaker. A man was saying, in very strangely accented Japanese, that it was safe to come out — that the war was over on Okinawa. A few days before, I had told the old couple that I wanted to stay with them forever. They had cried, and told me that they were fated to stay in the cave. The man had told me, "Life is a very precious thing. You have to go on living." So on the day that the Americans came, the old couple made me a white flag, which I tied to a tree branch, and they sent me out of the cave. When I got outside, I noticed it was very quiet — no more bombs or gunfire. I began to run, and soon I saw some American soldiers pointing a black box at me. I thought it was some new kind of weapon, and that they were going to kill me. Then I remembered my father's voice saying, "If the time comes when you are killed by the enemy, just remember, don't cry. It's your last day. Greet death with a smile on your face, and wave good-bye to the enemy." So I waved to the Americans, and I tried to smile but I couldn't really smile — just a little bit. I saw the Americans' faces and I thought they looked so kind. They were smiling, too. And they didn't kill me. I just walked right by them, and followed the sound of the voice coming from the loudspeaker.

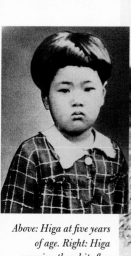

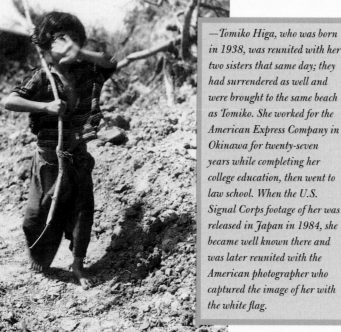

Above: Higa at five years of age. Right: Higa carrying the white flag as she approaches American soldiers.

—Tomiko Higa, who was born in 1938, was reunited with her two sisters that same day; they had surrendered as well and were brought to the same beach as Tomiko. She worked for the American Express Company in Okinawa for twenty-seven years while completing her college education, then went to law school. When the U.S. Signal Corps footage of her was released in Japan in 1984, she became well known there and was later reunited with the American photographer who captured the image of her with the white flag.

By early summer 1945, the Japanese had just 800 functioning aircraft; the Americans, 22,000. American fliers were finishing the last of hundreds of fire-bombing sorties over Tokyo, Osaka, Nagoya, Kobe, Kawasaki, and Yokohama, obliterating every military target, and killing hundreds of thousands of civilians, too. Yet their devotion to Emperor Hirohito forced the people of Japan to fight on. Expecting an invasion force even larger than the one which hit the beaches of Normandy (in fact, fifteen divisions were in the blueprints for Operation Olympic, as the Allied invasion was to have been called, versus the nine that crossed the English Channel), civilians on Japan's main islands were mobilizing to repel the enemy with anything they could find: rocks, sticks, bamboo. Throughout the Pacific, the American forces were dreading the coming weeks, if only because they had seen the tenaciousness of the Japanese and feared that an invasion of the main islands could only create a gruesome battle fought to the last man, another Stalingrad.

The precious few who knew that America was testing a secret weapon in the summer of 1945 never referred to it as a bomb. To the boys at the assembly plant in Oak Ridge, Tennessee, it was Project S-Y; to the Joint Chiefs, S-1; to the head of the Department of War, only "X" (though Secretary Stimson's diary entries also include references to "the thing" and "the dreadful"); to the scientists at the Los Alamos, New Mexico, test site, the ones with the best vantage point to the weapon's awesome power and destructive potential, it was "the gadget," "Thin Man," and "Fat Man." Such was the peculiar, humbling atmosphere

Even though Japan was on the brink of defeat, the nation still refused to surrender. Bracing for an expected Allied invasion, the country's leaders ordered the military training of civilians. Here, an army officer instructs Japanese housewives on how best to resist the enemy with bamboo spears.

Hiroshima: **A powerful flash and then "the sound of a whole town crying"**

It was a beautiful day. I had just finished breakfast, and my mother told me to go water the front yard. I went outside and saw a friend in the street and went to greet her. We started talking, and then we heard a B-29. It was a sound we knew well. I called it the angel, because it had never dropped a bomb to hurt us. Up in the sky we saw the beautiful airplane, just like a ballerina, dancing against a blue sky. I told my friend to wave at the angel, and then it was gone. The only difference was that this time it left a white spot up in the sky. I thought it was the parachute of an American pilot coming down in enemy territory. Then suddenly there was a very, very powerful yellowish-orange flash — like when you're taking a picture and you use the flash — only a hundred thousand times more powerful.

The flash was over in a second, and I was already on the ground. When I woke up, I knew something was wrong, because when I tried to move, I couldn't. The house across the street had collapsed on top of my body. I crawled out and made my way back to the middle of the street where just a moment ago I had seen the angel dancing the sky. Where the blue sky had been, there was only a grayish fog, and everywhere a red color — blood.

The very first voice I heard was that of my father saying, "Help me, help me." Gradually, my other neighbors came into the street. My mother was a real surprise to me. Early in the morning she had fixed her hair nicely, but now her hair was standing on end, a grayish mess. Everybody was saying, "What happened? What's going on?" We thought an individual bomb had been dropped on our house or on one of our neighbors' houses. I knew that in other cities, almost every single day a B-29 or a different plane would come and drop individual bombs. But in Hiroshima, we didn't have that kind of tragedy. The B-29 that used to come every single day had never dropped a bomb, never hurt us.

> *—Kaz Suyeishi was born in 1927. Despite their serious injuries, her immediate family members survived the bombing. In 1958, she came to the United States to marry and has, since then, dedicated her life to teaching the public about the horror of nuclear weapons.*

In the summer of 1945, I was sixteen years old and a junior in high school. August 6 seemed like any other day. All my classmates and I were working in a munitions factory, as we had since we were freshmen. I had just stepped out of the factory and walked behind a two-story building when I saw this big ball of orange fire. The whole building — and the earth itself, it seemed — moved once to the left and once to the right, and then everything started to fall on top of me. I hit the ground immediately. After everything settled down, I found that

In one of only five known photographs taken in Hiroshima on the day the bomb was dropped, a bandaged policeman certifies victims for emergency aid.

I was covered with glass, boards, rocks, and sand.

I walked to the nurse's office to find bandages and medications and whatnot, as we had been trained to do. When I found the nurse she couldn't speak. She was bleeding, and she pointed to her mouth, in which a large piece of glass was wedged. I just went over and pulled it and other big fragments of glass out of her mouth. Then I broke the medicine chest open with a bat and carried some first-aid supplies to my friends.

A while later, we went out into the street only to discover that the entire town of Hiroshima was ablaze. We could see the smoke of those famous mushroom clouds, and the skies were all dark. We started to walk toward the bridge, which was only about a quarter of a mile away, but we couldn't cross it because it was covered with people. They were all hurt, all burned. Some were dead. A lot of people were floating in the river; some were swimming, but some of them were dead, drifting with the current downstream. Their skin was red and their clothes were nothing but strips of cloth hanging from them. Our teacher decided we should go back to the factory to spend the night. All night long we watched the town burn.

Early on August 7, some of us left the factory and started to go toward my high school. We walked through the town. Since the town was still burning, you had to be careful where you walked, tiptoeing to keep from stepping on people. When we got to my school, we found that about 285 out of the 300 students died. I tried to help some of the kids out of the swimming pool, but they just rolled right back in, their skin peeling right

off from their arms. I walked back to the dormitory where I stayed for about two days more. People began to fear typhoid, and they wanted to start cremating bodies. Someone had to do it, so I helped cremate some of my fellow students.

On the third day, I went back to where my mom lived in the countryside. The train was full of wounded people, dying people. When I finally made it to my house my mother couldn't believe I was still alive. I remember she hugged me so hard that I told her I couldn't breathe. The course I had taken, walking through the town, trying to help people and cremating some of my friends, that was a really terrible thing. I actually took a step through hell and returned.

> *—Junji Sarashina, born in 1929 in Hawaii, went to Japan in 1937 to study and remained there until after the war. He fought in the Korean War for two years, then settled in Orange County, California, where he worked for Northrup until his retirement in 1987.*

At about eight-fifteen in the morning, the bomb came. I came into the kitchen of my dormitory, and all of a sudden this purple, severe light just came right through the house. I tried to get out the door, but the door fell outward, and I fell with it. Up in the sky, this black cloud was getting bigger and bigger, as if it would swallow you. It kept on moving, and just watching that movement would drive you nuts. You could see it far into the distance, a very strange and scary cloud. I knew this bomb was something different.

I left my dorm, which was right near the epicenter, and tried to get back to the city. I went as far as the Hiroshima station and found that the town was wrapped up in a big wave of heat and flames that were whirling around and around, like a wave gushing at you. There was a terrible whirring sound. The fire in the city went way high over your head, so you couldn't walk in it at all. The city looked like a construction site filled with lumber. Dead people were everywhere, and throughout the town was the echo of people moaning; it sounded like an animal shelter. When I found out that eight of my school friends were dead, I almost went berserk. It couldn't happen this way, I thought, it shouldn't. I said to myself, "Why Hiroshima? Why did they do this to us?"

> *—Irene Nakagawa, who was born in 1925 in Fresno, California, went to Japan for an operation during the Depression and remained there during the war. In 1947 she moved to Los Angeles. She goes to Japan regularly for the medical checkups that are provided to Hiroshima survivors.*

around the first atomic weapon that the closer it came to reality, the more childish the appellation those near it gave it.

On August 5, 1945, "Little Boy," which was the name that stuck on the one that mattered, was loaded onto the bomb bay of Lieutenant Colonel Paul Tibbets's B-29. Seventy-five crack fliers had been waiting for months for this moment, having volunteered for an assignment about which they knew only one thing: they would be doing "something different." During maneuvers, the fliers had been instructed to wear welder's goggles and never look back in the direction of their target (peculiar enough) but when they were told they would be dropping one bomb and only one bomb, they took the news as both perplexing and demeaning.

On August 5, the night before the historic day, the members of the 509th Composite Group learned that their "one bomb" would be delivering a destructive force of twenty thousand tons of TNT. By that time, it was obvious that something *very* different was at hand. The military's top brass had arrived on the island. Still photographers and a movie crew stood ready to record the mission's departure, the runway so bathed in light it prompted one scientist to compare it to the grand opening of a Hollywood drugstore. Tibbets posed next to the plane he had christened *Enola Gay*, after his mother; so did co-pilot Robert Lewis and the eight crew members. With the escort planes waiting to take off behind them, it seemed like the only thing not in the official picture was "the gadget."

At 2:45 A.M., the B-29, overweight at sixty-five tons, lumbered down the runway and lifted off into the darkness, its mission nothing less than a quick and sudden end to the Pacific war. If it worked, the bombing would provide a symmetrical counterpart to the invasion of Pearl Harbor, with Tibbets as America's own Mitsuo Fuchida, and to that end the cabin was loaded down with various charms and talismans: silk panties, a nude picture of a woman known well to the boys at the training base in Wendover, Utah, six prophylactic kits, and a lipstick kiss imprint on the plane's nose signed "Dottie." But until they were airborne, not even the crew realized that an end to the war was only part of what this mission would accomplish. Seven minutes after the flight began, ordnance expert William Parsons retreated to the bay to begin arming "Little Boy" and Tibbets took the opportunity to provide full disclosure to his men. He asked if any of them knew what was below. "A chemist's nightmare?" said tail gunner Robert Caron. Tibbets told him to try again. "A physicist's nightmare," said Caron. Then the truth dawned upon him. "Colonel," he said, "are we splitting atoms today?"

The crew flew onward, into the dawn, exchanging little conversation. Co-pilot Lewis, writing in his journal, noted that Bombardier Tom Ferebee, the man who would actually pull the trigger sending the world into the nuclear age, seemed "very quiet," as if he were "mentally back in the midwest part of the old U.S.A." Over Honshu, Parsons finished his work assembling "Little Boy" for detonation. "It is a funny feeling," wrote Lewis, "knowing it is right in back of you." Then, at 8:15 A.M., with the target point of the Ota River in the crosshairs of his bombsight, Ferebee squeezed once, releasing "Little Boy" over the city of Hiroshima.

It descended in forty-three seconds. And when it exploded, not on contact, but actually, as planned, two thousand feet above Hiroshima, it produced a column of fire and then a huge cloud, like a gigantic mushroom. Only Caron looked back at first. Despite the goggles, he felt blinded for a moment, but then the scene emerged and it looked to him like "lava or molasses," a seething mass of red and purple fire. The *Enola Gay* and its escorts banked over the site while crew members took pictures, then prepared to flee, the most dramatic hit-and-run in history. But first Tibbets turned the B-29 to bring the ruined city into view. The image of devastation was stunning. "My God," wrote Lewis, "what have we done?"

The bombing of Hiroshima (below) and, three days later, the industrial city of Nagasaki, brought history's most destructive war to a close.

7

An Uneasy Peace
1946–1952

An Uneasy Peace 1946–1952

Previous spread: In 1951, when the government begin a series of atomic tests in the Nevada desert, mushroom clouds became a regular part of the Las Vegas skyline. Aware of the public's curiosity about the A-bomb, the government heavily publicized the tests and one explosion was broadcast live on local television. Forty-six years later, the government would admit that fallout from these and subsequent Nevada nuclear tests may have caused up to seventy-five thousand cases of thyroid cancer.

The most popular attraction of the 1946 Christmas movie season was a film depicting the story of three men returning home from the war. The ironic masterpiece entitled *The Best Years of Our Lives* had been inspired by a photograph that appeared in *Time* in 1944, showing a group of Marines looking back from a train car. The men were on furlough, and they had painted the words "Home Again!" across the side of the train, but their true feelings were more complicated, a mixture of joy and bewilderment. One corporal described why he couldn't sleep ("I just lay there all night grinning"); another jumped off at a whistle-stop to grab a piece of ice from a passing wagon ("Boy, what we would have given for ice on Guadalcanal"), but mostly the men sat in silence, staring off at the fields and the weather-stained buildings, wondering what it would feel like to be home again.

In the movie, the three veterans return to the fictitious Midwestern town of Boone City. Fred Derry, played by Dana Andrews, is a B-17 bombardier; Al Stephenson, played by Fredric March, is an infantry sergeant; and Homer Parrish, played by Harold Russell, is a Navy seaman who lost his hands in the war and has to cope with prosthetic hooks. Eager to portray the life of the returning soldier as honestly as he could, director William Wyler used costumes bought off-the-rack in department stores and ordered the cast to wear them for weeks before the shooting began so the look of newness would be gone. Wyler even opted for a real-life amputee in the role of Homer (Russell, no actor, had lost his hands in a military training accident). But his character was largely symbolic: Wyler's larger point was that home was at once a welcome and cruel sight for the returning veteran, neither the place he knew before the war nor the one he dreamed it might be on the coldest nights abroad, and a common feeling was one of uselessness.

As the men settle into their postwar lives, Al Stephenson takes a job as a loan officer but he is scolded by his superiors when he bends the bank's rules to give a veteran a break. Fred Derry discovers that his shotgun marriage,

Euphoric veterans arrive back in New York aboard the Queen Elizabeth. *In the period following the end of the war, the army shipped home GIs at a rate of up to one million per month. Each veteran was given a physical exam, fifty dollars in cash, and the coveted "White Piece of Paper," discharging him from service. At Fort Dix, New Jersey, the chaplain offered this advice: "Take it easy. Have confidence in God. Help build a better America."*

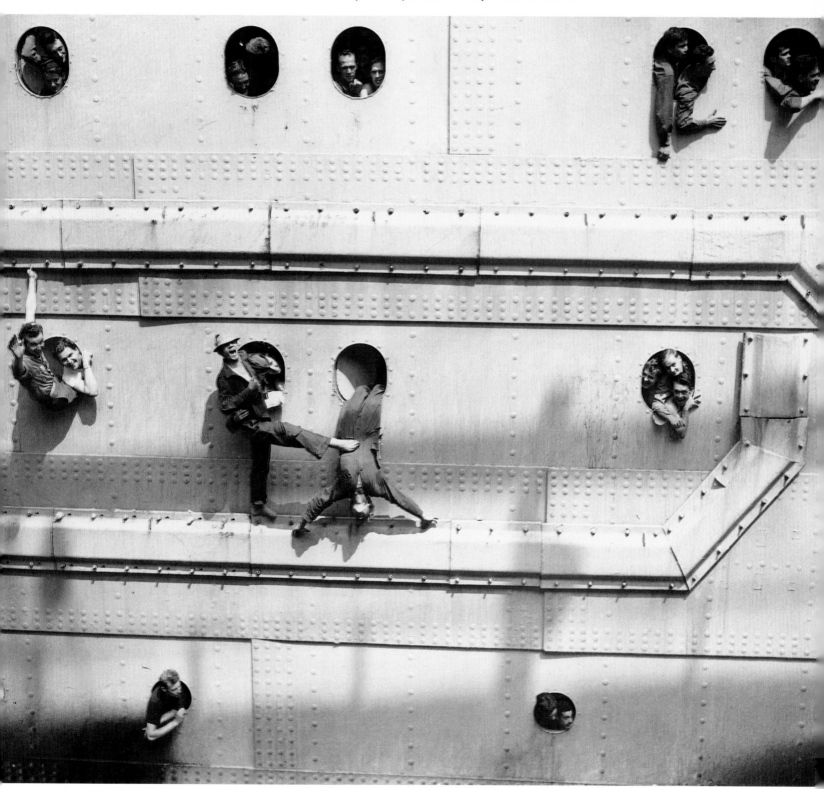

interrupted by the war years, is a failure and, assuming a menial job as a clerk in a chain store (the local owners had been bought out), spars with a customer who criticizes the war as pointless. Fired for his belligerence, Derry ends up with a job sorting through discarded war planes, looking for scrap metal that could be used for the building of prefabricated houses. Homer Parrish provides the movie's most emotional moment. Convinced that his girlfriend will not want him now that he is flawed, he tries first to avoid returning, pleading with the others to go with him to a bar for "a couple of drinks." Finally confronting her, he declares, "You don't know, Wilma. You don't know what it would be like to live with me, to have to face this every day — every night."

Director Wyler had turned down the more obvious postwar story, a dramatization of the life of Eisenhower, the war's biggest hero. And he had refused Samuel Goldwyn's pleas that he consider making a silly Christmas fantasy movie starring Cary Grant, something — anything — to help people forget the war. But *The Best Years of Our Lives* turned out to be an enormous hit anyway, a movie that touched the audience profoundly even as it entertained. The film won nine Academy Awards (including two for Russell, the amateur) and played to millions precisely because it so accurately captured their mood, particularly at the moment when Stephenson, arriving home for the first time, surprises his wife, played by Myrna Loy, with an embrace as passionate as any in film. After fifteen years of Depression and war, there was nothing quite like coming home and yet home seemed so different these days.

It was a complicated victory that emerged from the ashes of the Second World War, and how could it not be? The war had opened so many wounds so

"Raise babies and keep house!"

A navy petty officer in Seattle, asked about his plans for the future

deeply, the mere cessation of hostilities could not possibly bring an end to the pain. The familiar images from the moment of triumph — the drunken soldiers and civilians dancing in the streets of London and Paris, the couples kissing in New York's Times Square, the looks of delirious exaltation on the faces of people everywhere — are genuine, to be sure, but they fail to capture the enormity of feeling attached to that event. Just how, for instance, does one acknowledge the end of a war that had killed sixty million, with glee that it is over or despair that it has happened at all? Is a victory a victory when it is achieved by force of a weapon so horrible, mankind is paralyzed at even the thought that it might be used again? What of the emaciated camp victims? The fortunate few who escaped Hitler's killing machines felt joyous (if joy can be felt without benefit of nourishment), but were they to now embrace a world that had made possible the genocidal monsters of Nazi Germany? No wonder that one European survivor when asked what victory meant to him uttered the less than satisfying comment: "one was not dead."

The delirium lasted longer, and felt less confused, in America, where the end of World War II was followed by years of breathtaking energy and ambition. Americans had won not one, but two world wars now, their presence being a decisive factor in the conclusion of each, and in the process they had licked the worst economic crisis to befall them in their 170-year history. Both capitalism and democracy had been redeemed and with the clearing of the dust of battle, the future of the nation most identified with both seemed, quite suddenly, limitless. In many ways, and to many people, the late 1940s felt like one of those unique points in time, when a single people stands astride the world. Publisher Henry Luce had predicted an "American Century," rivaling the epochs of history's

The contrast between European and American fortunes in the postwar era was undeniable. Homeless Germans were crammed into Quonset huts supplied by the Allied armies (right) while new cookie cutter suburban developments addressed the housing demand in the United States (opposite page). Housing starts in the United States jumped from 114,000 in 1944 to 1.7 million in 1950.

"Turned loose": **Peace, prosperity, and disappointment for returning vets**

When the atomic bombs were dropped, I was a prisoner of the Japanese, working in a little town several hundred miles north of Saigon called Tuy Hoa. I think I weighed about eighty-five pounds. For weeks we had been put to work at nighttime fixing the same bridge, only to watch it get bombed out again the next day. But one day, all of a sudden, the Japanese attitude toward us changed. They stopped beating us for doing the slightest thing wrong. We knew something was up, but we didn't know what, and we couldn't get too excited for fear that the Japanese would start banging us around again. Then one day, they just told us to stop working, and a native went by on a bicycle chanting, "The war is over! The war is over!" There were no great expressions of jubilation in the camp, we all just felt, "Oh, thank God it's over." I guess after three and a half years of starvation and brutality and beatings, we had kind of become devoid of emotion. But thank God, it *was* over, and we were going home.

Things were different in those days, and the United States didn't quite know how to handle returning prisoners of war. My rehabilitation, if you can call it that, consisted of this: About two weeks after getting out of the prison camp, I arrived in Washington one night at about eleven-thirty. I made a telephone call home and was sent to bed, and then at six o'clock the next morning, they "processed" me and gave me a new uniform. They gave me a cursory physical examination and my back pay, and by three o'clock that afternoon I was on a train going back home to Newark, New Jersey. That was my rehabilitation.

I think that my return home was one of the most traumatic experiences of my life. Because even though I was coming home to my family, I was leaving my real family — all of us guys who had stuck together in the camps and helped each other through sickness, beatings, and all of that. When I got into Newark Penn Station that night and walked into the empty waiting room, it was the first time I had been alone in five or six years — I mean, really alone. I stood there and I didn't know what to do. I was really fouled up — turned loose too soon.

In my frustration I looked around, saw a soldier sitting on a bench, and went over and started talking to him. I asked him what he was doing and he said that he was trying to get home to Nutley, New Jersey, but he didn't have cab fare, and there were no buses running. So I said, "Don't worry about it, I'll get you home." I hired a cab and I took him all the way to Nutley before I could even think about starting to go home. I couldn't shake the strangeness of being alone — I was in shock.

Eventually I went home at about one o'clock that morning. My sisters and my mother were there waiting

A veteran of the Pacific war is doted on by his mother and fiancée after returning home. This Marine was one of the six soldiers featured in the famous flag-raising photograph shot at Iwo Jima.

up for me because I had told them I'd be home that night. We had a very joyous reunion, but I still felt restless. I couldn't possibly go to bed, so I went to the post office where my stepfather was working, just to avoid trying to sleep. For the next 120 days I was on "rehabilitation leave," but I spent all of it tavern hopping. I would close the taverns in Newark at two in the morning and then come over to New York for more. I just didn't know what to do with myself.

> *—Otto Schwartz, born in 1923, was a seaman second class on the U.S.S.* Houston *when it was torpedoed in the Pacific. He was captured by the Japanese and spent three years in labor camps. Upon his return to the United States, he went to work for the post office, and after thirty-two years there he retired from a position in labor relations. He lives in Union, New Jersey.*

I am no war hero. I was very fortunate in the service because I never really was in direct combat. But I saw things — walking along railroad tracks I'd seen guys right in front of me or behind me step on a mine and get killed. Even when the war was damned near over, there was still the residue that was left there, which meant that every day we were taking our lives in our own hands. So I was happy to make it back alive. When I got discharged and sent home from Europe at the end of the war, they flew me down to Burbank where my family was. My wife met me at the airport. She was beautiful, as usual. She didn't normally wear a lot of makeup, but she had makeup on that day, and it was running down her face. I just didn't want to let go of her. And that was the first time I'd seen our daughter since she was a little over a year old, and there she was, almost four. My wife told me that during the war, whenever my daughter saw a photo or a film of a man in uniform, she would say, "There's Daddy." Coming home, it's a joyous occasion.

You're filled with tears, but you're so happy.

In Southern California at that time, things were booming. Jobs were plentiful, and salaries were better than they were in other parts of the country. It seemed to me that everything was moving more rapidly than it had been before I left. Cities were growing, big highways were popping up everywhere, even the cars seemed faster. I felt excited by it all, and also determined to succeed and make something of myself. Suddenly I felt very confident about my future. I was assistant delivery manager for Western Union when the war broke out. When I came back, they gave me a raise of twenty-five cents more an hour, and I thought I had the world by the tail. I thought, "My gosh, I'm set for life. I've got a place to live, I can support my family, and hopefully even have more kids."

My wife had bought a duplex in North Hollywood while I was in the service, but it was kind of small, so I got us a VA loan and bought a bigger house down the street. Somebody had bought up an old strawberry field, divided it up into lots and built forty-two houses. They looked a little different on the outside, but they were all pretty much the same floor plan on the inside. I believe we paid $850 down for a $12,000 house, brand new. I had to work overtime to help pay for it, but oh, how wonderful it was. And there was a great camaraderie between all of the young families in the neighborhood. We used to have barbecues and parties, play golf together, and our kids ran around together. In fact when my wife was pregnant with our second daughter, I think there were ten or twelve other women in the neighborhood who were pregnant at the same time.

In the early days after the war, we used to think we were struggling, but we were really having a wonderful time. We were just doing all those kind of things that young families do, trying to make up for those years that we didn't have together, and everyone was having fun. It was a very happy time.

> *—Walter Girardin, who was born in 1919, was a battalion sergeant major in the U.S. Army. He eventually became the president of Western Union in 1976. Retired since 1981, he lives in Southern California with his wife of fifty-six years.*

Throughout the war, we were fighting a battle on two fronts: one was against Hitler in Europe, and one was against racism in the United States, and many of us had illusions that, as a result of our efforts in the war, the whole system of second-class citizenship and discrimination against blacks would be ended. I was in the 92nd Division, along with ten or twelve thousand other black troops. In Europe, the men of the 92nd were regarded as heroes. We liberated a number of Italian towns, including Lucca and Pisa, and when the Italian people saw these brown troops coming into their community, they just hailed us as conquering heroes. So when we came back to the United States, we expected to be treated as if we had made a contribution; we didn't like coming back into a Jim Crow scene. Being from a predominantly black community in New York, I was treated with respect when I returned. But that was not true for most of the black troops. Most of the enlisted men in the 92nd were from the South, and it was ironic for them to return to a country for which they risked their lives, and they still had to go to the back of the bus, could not sit downstairs in the movie theater, and could not leave the plantation except with a pass from the owner.

A number of us got together and decided that it would be a good thing for us to form a black veterans' organization. One of the first things we took on was the issue of terminal leave pay. Each veteran was entitled to anywhere from $100 to $300 for having served in the U.S. Army. In the South, plantation owners attempted to prevent many of the returning veterans who worked on their plantations from getting into town to apply for their terminal leave pay. You see, blacks could only leave the plantation with a pass and the passes were usually given for Saturday noon until Sunday evening; you couldn't leave the plantation during the work week. The application blanks for terminal leave pay were at the post office, which shut down at noon on Saturday, so it was impossible for a black veteran to pick up the application blank. So our group went to the War Department and got them to agree to release terminal leave pay blanks to our organization so we could distribute them through the Baptist Church, NAACP, and the Negro Elks Clubs. A number of our GIs went onto the plantations, sometimes dressed in blue overalls and things like that. It was almost an underground operation. We helped veterans throughout the South to get their terminal leave pay.

We also organized early bus boycotts and marches of veterans to county courthouses, to get their ballots to vote, because they had been denied the right to vote prior to World War II. We organized picket lines against job discrimination. We organized black and white tobacco workers in Winston-Salem, and got tobacco workers in a union for the first time. All of these activities laid the basis for the civil rights movement of the late fifties and sixties. It was a direct outcome and carryover of the goals of World War II. The war was still being fought, in a sense.

—Howard "Stretch" Johnson, born in 1915, received two Purple Hearts for injuries suffered while fighting with the 92nd Division.

greatest empires, would follow the end of war. By 1946, the world was witnessing one.

It seemed to be so naturally America's moment, if for no other reason than that America was the one major country among a world of belligerents which emerged from the war stronger and more confident than it had been before the conflict. Indeed, when measured by personal comfort and economic well-being, the war proved to have been a blessing for Americans, delivering to the years that succeeded it an economy that accounted for half the world's manufacturing and more than 40 percent of its income, an unemployment rate of just 4 percent and a plethora of fresh consumer goods. While Europe was in ruins, America in the late 1940s was a nation of abundance, a society comfortably ensconced in new tract-housing suburbs where the war veterans and their wives settled down to the good life. They also made babies, many babies. Using the statistics of sex researcher Alfred Kinsey (himself a late forties icon), historian William Manchester calculated that in the postwar period, a woman — somewhere, someplace — became pregnant every seven seconds, adding a city the size of Los Angeles to the census roles each year.

No problem was too big for American energy and brainpower. If American manufacturing had earned the world's respect and admiration during the war, then American science, led by the reaction to the atomic bomb, now equaled it, choosing this moment to unveil the world's largest telescope in Mount Palomar, California; and the first civilian forms of penicillin and other "broad spectrum" antibiotics so powerful, they seemed to promise a cure for all infectious diseases. American pilot Chuck Yeager broke the sound barrier, scientists at America's Bell Laboratories discovered the transistor, and others at the University of Pennsylvania assembled the world's first electronic computer, a thirty-ton monstrosity roughly comparable in power and capability to a handheld calculator of the 1980s. There was even progress, it seemed, in social affairs. In 1947, when Jack Roosevelt Robinson strode to the plate in his first appearance for the Brooklyn Dodgers, baseball became integrated; a year later, with the signing of an executive order by President Harry S. Truman, so, officially, were the armed forces.

"This is an American child. This is an American home. Lucky young American. No child in the world has so bright a future."

Ipana toothpaste advertisement

Life was good. After years of Great Depression deprivation and the deferment of pleasures to the emergency of war, this generation had come to feel that it deserved to curl up with a blanket and wallow in the warmth of domestic bliss. The song most requested of Bing Crosby, touring U.S. military bases at the end of the war, was not, as one might expect, a treacly romantic ballad nor an inspirational marching tune, but a pop version of Brahms's Lullaby (complete with Hollywood's own lyrics). It felt great to be home, rocking in the hammock on a sleepy sunlit afternoon, and it felt great to be an American, looking down from the mountaintop of achievement and prosperity, confident in having just beaten back evil in the name of the good.

But even America's self-satisfied image soon began to fade in the heat of

When Jackie made the major leagues: Suddenly "anything was possible"

Above: Sharpe James, at age twelve.

*Jackie Robinson as a
Brooklyn Dodger, 1947.*

I was born in the South, but my mother and I moved up
North to escape from my stepfather, who was very
abusive. In 1944, we moved to 43 Emmett Street in
Newark, which was in a predominantly Irish American
neighborhood. Now, in Newark at this time, race relations were pretty much based on neighborhood —
whites lived in white neighborhoods, blacks lived in
black neighborhoods, and if you went into other neighborhoods, you'd get beaten up or threatened. But my
mother bought this house, right in there with the
McGuinnesses and the Healeys, and we were the only
black family. At first all the kids ignored me, but what
saved me was stickball. I'd be sitting on my stoop,
watching the kids play, and eventually they'd let me play
with them. Soon I played baseball with them, too.

　　Being the only black kid in my crowd, I used to
hear my white buddies say things like, "Let's get them
blacks, run them blacks out of the neighborhood." But
then they would always add, "We don't mean you,
Sharpe." To them, "good blacks" were those that lived
in their neighborhood and participated with them. Bad
blacks were those in other neighborhoods. So I was a
"good black."

　　When you're poor, you've got to have a vehicle that
you believe in, some kind of dream. And for all of us

> —*Sharpe James, who was born in 1936, was a
> public school teacher and athletic coach, and then a
> college professor for eighteen years. After entering
> local politics in 1970, he was elected mayor of
> Newark in 1986. He is currently serving his fourth
> term, and lives in Newark's South Ward neighbor-
> hood with his wife and three sons.*

playing on that street, baseball was it. We all dreamed
that someday we would grow up and be major league
players. The key to getting out of the ghetto for us kids
was not to be a movie star, or a football player. Baseball
was our game, because we could wake up, go out on the
street, and get a game going, which is something you
coudn't do with basketball or football.

　　When I went to Ruppert Stadium to see the Negro
League games, I got to see teams like the Newark Bears
and the Newark Eagles and players like Monte Irvin and
Satchel Paige. That was the best of black baseball. And
watching that, I felt that might transform my life if I
could just make a high school team and then eventually
perhaps go into the Negro Leagues. But before 1947,
major league baseball was white only. So here you had

thousands of black kids like me playing baseball, but the
ones with superior talent could never hope to get the
same recognition that the white players would get. So as
a black kid I knew I didn't have the same opportunities
that the whites did, and that was really a frustration.

　　Then one day we got the news about Jackie Robinson. I remember all the folks in the black neighborhoods
sitting around playing their card games, and saying,
"Did you hear? [Brooklyn Dodgers general manager]
Branch Rickey's going to bring Jackie up to the majors."
Everywhere you went, people had their newspapers out
and they were talking about it. It was the talk of the
black community because it gave hope and spirit to the
downtrodden. Once Jackie broke the color barrier, I
guess the thinking was that if you could break it in
baseball, anything else in the world was possible. People
said, "Here is a man of color who's going to make it." So
suddenly everybody took him on as part of their family
— everyone became a cousin of Jackie Robinson. And
everyone had some weird story about how they were
connected to Jackie.

　　But to everyone in my neighborhood, white or
black, Jackie Robinson was a hero. He was our role
model. When we played baseball, suddenly everybody
was saying, "I'm fast as Jackie Robinson," "I can catch
like Jackie Robinson," even the white guys would say
that. We all used to go over to Mrs. Hooper's house and
watch Jackie Robinson on her fancy color TV. You
know what color TV was then? You had a black and
white television with a piece of see-through colored
paper that you put over the screen — that was it. Jackie
was a thrill to watch because he was such a great athlete;
his skill and aggressiveness changed the game of baseball. He was the first player who could save a game with
his glove or with his bat; he could steal any base and
create more excitement than any player before or since.

　　Jackie's success started to affect my self-esteem,
because my friends started to see my skills a different
way. These white guys realized that my playing could
really take me somewhere. Before, I was one of the
accepted blacks. But I think when they realized that a
man of color had made it into the major leagues they
suddenly became aware that they had this good baseball
player living in their community, that someday maybe I
would make it like Jackie did. They would say things to
me like, "Hey, Sharpe, you going to take us with you?"
So I spent more time playing ball than I ever had before;
around that time I don't remember doing anything but
baseball seven days a week. And when I look at what
people wrote in my high school yearbook, they all
wrote, "Good luck in your baseball career. We'll see you
in uniform at the Polo Grounds." Because I was going to
be next.

In 1947, Kiwanis International published a series of leaflets celebrating "the American Way of Life."

Lullaby and goodnight!
Those blue eyes close tight,
Bright angels are near,
So sleep without fear.
They will guard thee from harm,
With fair dreamland's sweet charm.

Words written to Brahms's Lullaby, a late 1940s favorite.

"You're a lucky fellow, Mr. Veteran," announced a 1949 advertisement for Levittown. William Levitt's houses proved so popular that he once sold 1,400 of them in a single day.

reality. For if, as so many believed, the war had been nothing more than a morality play, with virtue residing exclusively on the side of the Allies (a view which seemed further confirmed when the Nazi death camps were opened and the treatment of the Jews became more widely known), then the United States, as the Allied nation which suffered the least, could little afford to retreat to its shores. To many, the United States now represented nothing less than the hope of the world, an awesome responsibility made even more frightening by the presence of atomic arms. When, in short order, a challenge to the peace then emerged from a new enemy — a nation that only months before had been a critical partner, perhaps the *most* critical partner, in the defeat of the Nazis — a prolonged period of international tension, pitting East against West, began.

There were those who still wished for an isolationist America, heartland folk who recalled fondly the days when the problems of Europe remained Europe's, when there was no radio voice reciting to them from London or Berlin, no airplanes ferrying people across the country and around the world, and no threat that an atomic bomb would be dropped on the cornfields in Kansas. But the forces of inevitability were against them. America's destiny was to reconstruct the war-torn world and defend civilization from yet another totalitarian menace, one presumed to be motivated by a sense of ideological superiority and dedication to a world revolution that aimed to destroy Western capitalism. If there was a degree of paranoia wrapped up with that view of the Soviet Union, it only matched the paranoia emanating from the Soviets at the same time regarding the intentions of the West. And in the ensuing "Cold War," when families began building bomb shelters in their backyards and looking suspiciously at their neighbors, few could pretend that international events did not put his or her interests very much at stake.

Thirty-eight-year-old William J. Levitt was serving in the Pacific with the U.S. Navy when the Japanese surrendered in 1945. A builder by trade, he had spent a good part of the war working for the U.S. government, erecting some two thousand homes for defense-industry workers in Norfolk, Virginia. Finding the work too slow for his taste (and his ambition), Levitt arrived at a monumental idea: after determining that there were twenty-seven separate tasks involved in building a house, he decided to divide them among twenty-seven separate teams of workers and build simple, low-cost suburban homes the way that Henry Ford built simple, low-cost automobiles. There was, of course, one key difference between a car and a house — a car could be assembled as it glided along a conveyor belt, a house had to be constructed on site — but Levitt figured out a way around that, too: he would build his houses in large numbers next to each other on enormous flatlands and simply shuttle the workers from plot to plot, the foundation team arriving one day, the sheetrock team the next.

Levitt had little doubt that he could sell houses. A home of one's own was the dream of nearly every navy man stationed with him, and since the construction industry had been largely inactive during the Depression, it seemed a safe bet that afford-

Levittown attracted young, first-time homeowners eager to settle into domestic bliss. Virtually all its residents were married, under thirty-five years old, and had children under the age of seven.

able housing would be in big demand upon the return of all of America's thirteen million veterans. Levitt and his brother Alfred bought twelve hundred acres on Long Island, about thirty miles east of New York City (the deal was struck while Levitt was still in the service). Then, following Alfred's rudimentary design, they began building identical 750-square-foot Cape Cod–style two-bedroom residences, a size and design that potential buyers often described, admiringly, as "cute." During the Depression, builders were content to construct two houses each year. By 1948, the Levitts were assembling thirty of theirs each day.

The first "Levittown" included seventeen thousand houses and, priced at just $7,990, every one of them sold almost as fast as it was finished. Soon, imitators were springing up nationwide, the construction industry answering to the housing scarcity the way that other industries had so successfully responded to the needs of war with ships and tanks and ammunition. The new housing dramatically changed American life. Before the war, the American suburb had been the domain of the well-to-do; now Levitt and others like him achieved the dream of home ownership for millions in the lower income brackets. But the shift of demographics came at a price: Levittown and other middle-class suburbs were built for white homeowners exclusively (Levitt refused to sell to blacks), and just as the construction of Levitt's homes had been dictated by strict specifications (even the planting of trees was uniform, one appearing every twenty-eight feet), so was uniformity demanded of those who lived inside them. Washing, for instance, was to be hung to dry on weekdays and only weekdays, lawns were to be mowed regularly (the deed demanded it), and fences were strictly forbidden. Social critic Lewis Mumford decried Levittown as an attack on individuality, a place where the spirit would languish, he said, conforming as it must "in every outward and inward respect to the same common mold." But even more disturbing was the effect that the new suburbs would eventually have on the American city. Abandoned by the middle class, the nation's largest urban centers would eventually fall into a precipitous decline from which they would never recover.

In its regimentation, Levittown mimicked life in the service (the houses even had the look of Quonset huts), but the appeal of the coddling suburb was the break with the war years it seemed to offer, its promise of a green-grass haven separate from the worries of the world. People had seen enough of the drama called war. They wanted to leave the theater, now, and enjoy the good life, cooking barbecues, forming Little League teams, listening to Frank Sinatra.

Unfortunately, the century's second big conflagration, and its peculiar horrors, pursued them. At issue was the haunting way that the war had ended, with the intrusion of venal science in the form of the A-bomb, and the feeling that civilization had entered a new and terrible epoch, undeniable and unavoidable. At first, most people had approved of the use of the bomb on Hiroshima (and a second bomb, a few days later, on Nagasaki). They agreed that it had hastened the end of the war and, in so doing, saved many more lives on the American side than it had taken from the Japanese. Most people had looked upon the bomb much as President Truman and the majority of the members of the nation's defense establishment looked upon the bomb, as an extension of modern weapons technology to its next logical degree. There had even been some early giddiness about the atomic age (after Hiroshima, the bar at the Washington Press Club served an "atomic cocktail"; the General Mills cereal company offered an "atomic ring" in exchange for box-tops; and jewelers sold an "atomic earring" in the shape of a mushroom cloud), but the joking masked a paralyzing anxiety that was slowly developing throughout the culture. For in the months after it ended the war, the bomb also began to effect an extraordinary philosophical reassessment, and generate a penetrating level of guilt and fear.

The entire August 31, 1946, issue of the *New Yorker* was devoted to a thirty-thousand-word article by John Hersey called, simply, "Hiroshima." Inside, the writer described the lives of six survivors before, during, and after the dropping of the bomb: a young secretary; a tailor's wife; a German Jesuit missionary; two doctors (one old, one young); and a Japanese Methodist minister. The power of Hersey's reporting (which was delivered devoid of melodrama, in an unaffected style) was to bring human content to an unimaginable tragedy and the response, in turn, was overwhelming. The magazine sold out. A book version became a runaway best-seller. Albert Einstein bought a thousand copies himself and distributed them to friends. And an audience of millions tuned in to hear the piece read, in its entirety, over the ABC radio network. After Hersey's article,

"For years the playground in Washington Square has resounded to the high-strung anh-anh-anh of machine guns and the long-drawn-out whine of high-velocity shells. Last Saturday morning, a great advance was made. We watched a military man of seven or eight climb onto a seesaw, gather a number of his staff officers around him, and explain the changed situation. 'Look,' he said. 'I'm an atomic bomb. I just go "boom." Once. Like this . . .'

Report in the New Yorker *describing children at play after Hiroshima*

American business wasted no time in taking advantage of the bomb's commercial possibilities. In the late forties, nearly 750,000 children mailed in fifteen cents and a Kix cereal box top to get an "Atomic 'Bomb' Ring."

with its explicit description of the atomic horror ("their faces were wholly burned, their eye sockets were hollow, the fluid from their melted eyes had run down their cheeks"), it was impossible to ever again see the bomb as just another weapon. Hiroshima had cut the years passed from the years to come so sharply, it was as if humanity had closed one book and opened another.

For now, there was comfort in the fact that America, and only America, possessed science's terrible secrets. But it soon became clear that it was only a matter of time (five years, ten years?) before the knowledge would spread and atomic warfare between nations would become possible. When early stabs at sharing the atomic research peacefully were scuttled, the imagination reeled. Considering the likelihood of a World War III (given that world war had developed twice over a twenty-five-year period, it seemed a fair assumption that it would happen again) and the level of destruction that atomic weaponry would cause, people confronted for the first time the very real possibility of human extinction. The next war, they understood, would indeed be what Woodrow Wilson had dreamed the First World War would be — a "war to end all wars" — though only because it would likely end life itself.

If that final tragedy were to come soon, and many believed that it would, there was little doubt which nation would serve as America's primary adversary. In their mutual desire to defeat Hitler, the United States and the Soviet Union had reduced their differences to a deep blur. Indeed, photographs of the meeting at the Elbe River, when the American soldiers and their Soviet counterparts greeted each other, one coming eastward, the other westward, are among the most indelible images of the war's triumphant end. But once the glow of victory had faded — and it faded fast, as Russia's soldiers, in the role of "liberators," continued to rape their way through defeated Germany — the communication passed between sides became an intense display of international suspicion.

From American shores, the vision was clear: The Soviets were a nation of evildoers, intent on spreading their godless ideology throughout the world, but particularly in crippled Europe, Turkey, and the oil-rich land of Iran. From Moscow, it was equally focused: The Americans were the new imperialists, ready to deny Russia the spoils of a war that had extracted a significant price from the Russian people and prevent them from gaining a buffer defense against another invasion of their western border, the frontier over which so much Russian blood had been spilled.

Both perspectives were informed by recent history. Just as they had balked at the Versailles conference following the end of the First World War, Americans found themselves bristling at the conclusion of this war, as the trading of war booty was again carried out like the dealing of so many cards across a table. The American negotiators had pleaded that democratic principles be used to reorganize the ravaged nations of Europe, but the Russians were committed to holding those lands where the Red Army stood, and gaining ground elsewhere, too. Many in the United States blamed the American negotiators at the 1945 Yalta Conference for their present predicament; eager to retain Soviet assistance in concluding the Pacific war, they had conceded too much to the Soviets and were now paying the price. Fearing another Munich-style appeasement would lead to another Hitler-like march through Europe, America's leaders determined that the

DIRECTION OF
HEAT FLASH

If you are caught outdoors in a sudden attack, a hat will give you at least some protection from the 'heat flash'.

Even as awareness of the unprecedented power of the atom bomb was growing fast, government recommendations for protection in the event of an attack were laughably inadequate. One civil defense poster proposed that people be ready to "jump in any ditch or gutter . . . drop flat [and] hide your eyes in the crook of your elbow" while a government-sponsored book, How to survive an Atomic Bomb, *included the suggestion, above, that men wear wide-brimmed hats to protect against the "heat flash."*

As Stalin solidified his grip over Eastern Europe, one British diplomat declared, "Our relations with the Russians . . . are drifting into the same condition as that in which we had found ourselves . . . with Hitler." Here, the Soviet Union flexes its military muscle during a traditional May Day celebration in Red Square, 1952.

"When wolves are about, the shepherd must guard his flock, even if he himself does not care for mutton."

Winston Churchill, defending the need for U.S. involvement in Europe

time to stop Stalin was now and, knowing that there was little enthusiasm among their people for a return to war, hoped that the atomic threat alone would do their bidding.

The Russians, on the other hand, their population and industry spent by battle, felt that their battered nation faced a hostile world. They resented the Americans for their refusal to start a second front earlier in World War II (Stalin had pleaded for a D-Day invasion in 1942, thinking that it would take the burden off his troops, but Roosevelt felt, correctly, that it was too early) and for not sharing the atomic secrets with them or, for that matter, even telling them they were going to drop the bomb (though Stalin knew there was a bomb, having planted spies at the Manhattan Project). They worried, too, about the future of Germany. If that nation were to be reconstructed by forces unfriendly to the Soviet Union, would the Soviets then be left to face another Prussian invasion, the third of the century? They saw the postwar years as a historic opportunity to build an impenetrable defense around their beleaguered land, like a moat around a castle.

With each side sweating in the cause of its own precious virtue, the world seemed on the edge of another suicidal holy war. In February 1946, Stalin declared that "monopoly capitalism," more than Hitler, had been the force that created World War II and added that it must be replaced by communism. His speech, which seemed dangerously close to a declaration of war, shocked even those American liberals who had been arguing for a conciliatory tone toward Moscow. Then, on March 5, 1946, Winston Churchill mounted the podium at tiny Westminster College in Fulton, Missouri, and, as Harry Truman sat behind

Espionage in occupied Vienna:
"We [got] our information from . . . broken codes, tapped phone lines, and, of course, from secret agents"

During World War II, I was in the OSS, the Office of Strategic Services, which was a predecessor of the CIA. Now, some people in the intelligence world are little more than mercenaries, especially the spies. But I believed in what I was doing. I believed in Western democracy, and I was certainly morally opposed to Hitler, and I thought the Soviet Union was a mess from day one. After the war, it was apparent that the Soviet Union was not going to disarm and that they had no intention of giving up the lands they had taken in the course of the war. And so with Germany out of the picture, suddenly our intelligence efforts were focused on our former ally. There was this ongoing sense that the war wasn't quite over.

When the CIA was formed in 1947, I, like many other OSS members, just slid along into the new organization. The impetus for Central Intelligence came from Pearl Harbor. Not too long after the attack, people in the government and military realized that they had had all of the data needed to predict the Japanese strike. But there was no place in the government where the information could be brought together, analyzed, and collated with other pertinent information. The CIA was formed to prevent another Pearl Harbor, which, of course, became much more important with the atomic bomb.

In 1951, I went to Vienna to become the chief of operations in the CIA installations in Austria, which meant I was in charge of espionage and counterespionage. At that time, Vienna was a hotbed of intelligence activity. When I briefed people about it, I would always start by pointing to a map to show them that Vienna is actually east of Prague and that Austria sticks right out into Eastern Europe. Austria was divided into French, British, American, and Soviet zones. Vienna, which was deep in the Soviet sector, was also divided into five segments, one for each of the occupying powers and a fifth called the *Innere Stadt*, which was an international sector. There was no wall in Vienna; once in the city you could circulate freely.

I was nominally an officer in the embassy, a first secretary I think or an attaché; that was my cover. And I lived a pretty normal life. My efforts were aimed at monitoring Soviet activity in Austria, in the Soviet Union, and in the Soviet central group of forces headquartered in Hungary. There was a tremendous interest in Soviet armor and Soviet military plans in the Eastern Euro-

pean satellite countries. We would get our information from various sources: from broken codes and ciphers, monitoring open radio broadcasts, tapping phone lines, following diplomats, and, of course, from secret agents. Sometimes information came from just pure luck.

One day I was at the office when I took a call from the wife of one of my colleagues; she had called her husband, but he was not in. She drew a deep breath and whispered into the phone that some Russians were burying a bomb in the woods behind her house. She had just happened to look out the back window and had seen four Russian-looking fellows bury something and then camouflage the hole before walking back into the woods. I thought it was just the imagination of a nervous wife. There had been some tensions in Vienna, and people tended to see things in strange ways. But I decided to send a couple of people out to look, and low and behold something had been buried there. So they dug it up, rather gingerly, and found a Soviet agent's radio. They carted it back to me and I sent it off to Washington. It turned out to be a new model Russian radio set we had never seen before. I think that the Russians must have stopped for a vodka for breakfast and then probably used a bad map of the woods around Vienna and had gotten lost. I suggested to headquarters that they code name the radio "Harriet" after the woman responsible for finding it, but they never answered me on that one.

We kept a very careful eye on the Soviet intelligence officers in Vienna to the degree that we could. Our biggest breakthrough came when a sealed envelope was found in an American diplomat's car. The American had been in downtown Vienna sight-seeing with his wife and young son. And on the way back the boy wanted to sit in the front seat, so the wife jumped into the back and

Hood during his OSS days, 1945.

—*William Hood was born in 1920 in Maine. He was drafted into the army in 1941, where he served in Army Intelligence before crossing over to the counterespionage section of the OSS. After the war he worked for the CIA until he retired in 1975. Hood is now a writer living in Maine and New York. His books include the nonfiction* Mole *and three novels:* Cry Spy, Spy Wednesday, *and, most recently,* The Sunday Spy.

found an envelope addressed to the top American Embassy official in Vienna. Had the kid sat back there, it might have been a week or two before anyone found the envelope.

The letter was brought to us. And although the introduction was in very bad German, the rest of it was in absolutely fluent Russian. This man specified a place in the *Innere Stadt* where he would be on a specific night. Vienna was quite dark and after checking out the site, I felt it was a fairly safe place to meet. That night, I put a couple of chase cars nearby, in case it was a setup, and then I sent in a Russian-speaking agent to make contact. Sure enough, there was a Russian in civilian clothing waiting for us.

The Russian turned out to be Pyotr Popov, a major in the GRU, which is ostensibly the Soviet's military intelligence service — a parallel organization to the KGB — and he was willing to trade information for money. This was an incredible break, the CIA had never before been able to recruit a Russian intelligence officer. There were two reasons why Popov contacted us. The thing that triggered it was that he dipped into his official funds and had spent some money in a couple of nightclubs in Vienna. He felt he had to replace it or else his tail would be in a ringer. But beyond that, Popov was ideologically motivated. He detested Stalin. He was from a peasant family in the poorest part of Russia, and he couldn't believe his eyes when he got to Vienna. Contrary to what he had been told all of his life, the peasants in the West — even in occupied Austria — were much better off than his family was. Stalin had made promise after promise that the peasants' lives were going to be better, but as far as Popov could see, none of these promises had ever been met.

Over the next eight years, in Austria and then later in Berlin, Popov gave us a very good view of Soviet military strength from the inside, as well as information on Soviet spies traveling in the United States. Someone in the Pentagon once told me that the information Popov provided saved them a half a billion dollars. Eventually Popov got careless, and he was caught. The Soviets realized that military information was leaking, and they eventually came down on him. He was arrested, tried, and then later executed. In the years that I dealt with Popov, I never actually met him face to face, yet I felt that I knew him, and I was saddened when he was killed. Popov was a hero, and he was a very, very brave man. He could have defected at anytime, but he said he didn't want to leave Russia. It was his home, and why should he let Stalin and that gang drive him out of it? He said, "I'm a Russian, and I will remain a Russian, and I will die a Russian."

him, delivered perhaps the most significant speech of any leader since the war had ended. With his left hand gripping his lapel, Churchill intoned that an "iron curtain" had descended upon Europe ("From Stettin in the Baltic to Trieste in the Adriatic . . ."), a barrier that could be lifted only by the power of the Anglo-American alliance. Churchill went on to claim that no less than God himself had divined that America be the one nation to carry the responsibility of the bomb, a statement that prompted Stalin to retort that the British and the Americans were being led by the same kinds of racial theories that had inspired Hitler.

Stalin moved to solidify Russian control throughout Eastern Europe, beginning the pattern of deportations, intimidations, and outright corruption that would lead to "People's Democracies" loyal to the Soviet Union in Poland, Hungary, Bulgaria, Rumania, East Germany, and Czechoslovakia. The story of Czechoslovakia, where the moderate foreign minister, Jan Masaryk, leaped to his death (or was pushed by Communist hit men) in 1948 rather than serve as a Soviet lackey was especially tragic. But the subjugation of Poland to a Soviet-style regime may have hurt most. It was to preserve Polish independence that the West had originally gone to war.

George Kennan,
1904 –

Their vision obscured by the saber rattling, Americans struggled to understand the precise nature of the threat. Was Russian communism a single international force to be resisted everywhere, a virus as evil in its way as Hitler's fascism had been and as intent on destroying everything that Americans held dear? Or was Stalin more accurately a tsar by another name, warding off invaders and blustering about in an attempt to keep his nation on a war footing (and, in turn, under his thumb) but little interested in engaging the West beyond those areas he deemed essential for his nation's security? How could the map of postwar Europe be drawn in a way that would both preserve the ideals for which the Allies had fought, while at the same time satisfy the Russian need for security? And if it could not, just what cause was vital enough to American interests that it justified going to war again? Or, worse, using the bomb again?

American intellectuals argued, principally, from two perspectives. From inside the American embassy in Moscow, diplomat George Kennan wrote that the Soviets were in the spell of an ideology as deeply felt as any religion. Like religion, it was accepted on faith, and defended at all costs. Kennan felt that there was no chance of a *modus vivendi* with the Russians, for they saw the capitalist democracies of the West as inconsistent with their vision for the world. But the Russians were not likely to undertake any undue risks, either; in short, they could be dealt with by holding them to their present sphere, and "containing" their expansionist tendencies by resisting them at every new aggressive move.

Walter Lippmann,
1889 –1974

Columnist Walter Lippmann took a different track. He saw Kennan's thinking as a "strategic monstrosity." If the United States followed a "containment" theory, he said, it would soon find itself running about the globe pursuing Communist insurgencies and propping up corrupt non-Communist regimes, stretching the nation's military resources and making Americans more like the invading imperialists the Russians were claiming them to be. To Lippmann, the Soviets were not leaders of an international Communist conspiracy, but frightened nationalists (Stalin, the modern-day equivalent of Ivan the Terrible), whose hostile intentions were largely defensive. The columnist suggested that instead of "con-

taining" the Russians, America should calm their fears by suggesting a joint withdrawal of forces from Europe and the demilitarization of Germany.

Lippmann's thinking would prove to be amazingly prescient (as America's experience in Vietnam would demonstrate), and Kennan himself would later insist that the Truman Administration's interpretation of his theory as a posture of global military defense was a distortion of his words (he favored a moderate containment policy, focusing on Western Europe and Japan); but a strong and worldwide Allied military resistance was the idea that won this day, and it set the course for American foreign policy over the next forty years. Building off Kennan's "long telegram," as the diplomat's initial policy cable from Moscow was called, the State Department created what became known as the Truman Doctrine, mandating American support for "free peoples" resisting "subjugation by armed minorities or by outside pressures." And suddenly the ante had been upped. Within months, the National Security Act was signed, establishing the Central Intelligence Agency, and American aid had replaced British aid in Greece, fighting a Communist insurgency on behalf of the king.

Almost simultaneously, Stalin began a new propaganda campaign against the West. Fearing that democratic ideas might contaminate the minds he held sway over throughout the Soviet Union, the Soviet leader had already banished to the gulags thousands of Russians whose war experiences had brought them into intimate contact with societies freer than their own (including those who, from their years inside Nazi prisoner-of-war camps, had witnessed the "freer" world under Hitler). Now, he ratcheted up the pressure on historians, musicians, economists, poets, and writers, demanding that they reject Western decadence and put their efforts to building the myth of Soviet supremacy.

In the new Soviet canon, everything was suddenly reassessed. That which glorified Russia was good; that which was foreign was bad. The work of some contemporary Western writers was, naturally, banned; so, too, was that of some Soviets now deemed out of favor. Sergei Prokofiev and Dmitri Shostakovich, the two Russian composers who commanded the most respect outside Soviet circles, were condemned for writing "bourgeois" music too arcane for workers' ears. Boris Pasternak, hard at work on *Dr. Zhivago*, watched while his pregnant wife was shipped off to a labor camp as punishment for writings of his deemed disrespectful to the revolution (in shock, she lost their child). Nothing, it seemed, was spared reexamination. Even the story of Leningrad's wartime resistance, which had brought the Russians so much pride, was suddenly hushed, the "Defense of Leningrad" museum closed. Deluded by his fever of distrust, Stalin, it seemed, had come to believe that Leningrad thought itself too independent.

If there was a common feeling crossing this postwar world, cutting through the barriers of language and ideology, and connecting the American family, in its evident abundance, with its Russian counterpart, struggling for the merest crumb, and both of them with the destitute families of Europe, it had to be fear. The Russians were frightened, both of the terror that ruled them and the terror, so they were told, that aimed to conquer them. The Americans, too, were horror-struck, convinced that the barbaric forces of the Soviet Union represented nothing less than undiluted evil. Caught between them were the shivering Europeans.

Despite emergency shipments from the United States, 125 million Europeans were still not getting enough to eat. Here, Greek children sing while waiting for rations of powdered milk in 1948.

Once the center of Nazi power, Berlin was a wasteland after the war.
Desperate Berliners rummaged through the refuse of the Allied occupation forces
looking for scraps of food, cigarette butts, or anything they could barter.

While their future prompted heated debate across vast conference tables and occupied the full attention of earnest emissaries from two opposing civilizations, Europe's people remained in shock from their recent trauma. The Second World War, finishing the work of the first, had wasted and ruined them. What the fighting men of 1916 did to the soil of Verdun had been repeated now across the span of a whole continent. Europe's cities were in chaos, its bridges broken, its roads torn, its economies devastated. The Continent had gone from being the source of man's most advanced creations to serve, pathetically, as the evidence of his most perverse. And still the nightmare had not reached morning.

It was this landscape that the Russians and Americans now argued over, convinced that the combination of Europe's poverty, its war-weariness, and its disappointment with its own shattered political traditions made it open as never before to Communist insurgency. The poverty, in fact, was spreading. Farm production was considerably lower than its prewar levels. And industrial production was minuscule. Many factories had been destroyed during the war; and those that hadn't were now so overused, they were in desperate need of repair. While its leaders pleaded with people for the time necessary to put their houses in order, Europe had to import most basic goods from America, leaving it with little cash with which to pay its mounting debt.

The winter that bridged 1946 to 1947, the worst of the century, sounded a death knell. With the weather creating a shortage of fuel, many of the Continent's few remaining industrial plants were forced to shut down. Train lines, clogged by snow, were impassable. Able neither to produce nor move goods, workforces fell idle, with unemployment rising to Great Depression levels. Rations, already tight, were reduced again. And still there seemed to be no end in sight. Billions of dollars of American aid were provided and then spent, with Europe's starving children only left crying out for more, and the more they cried the more likely it seemed that the future would include revolution. The Communists were already strong in France, Italy, Belgium, and Greece. How long would it be before Moscow would step in to help them tip the balance?

On June 5, 1947, General George Catlett Marshall climbed the steps of the Memorial Church in Harvard Yard to address commencement exercises. The American Armed Forces Chief of Staff throughout most of World War II, Marshall was a man of impeccable reputation. Recently named Secretary of State, he had chosen a sunny afternoon in Cambridge to unveil the dramatic policy plan that would make his name synonymous with American beneficence for a generation. Over the next four years, Marshall announced, America would spend billions to reconstruct Europe. There would be direct aid in the form of fuel and food, whatever was necessary to ease the Continent through its most immediate crisis. But the bulk of the Marshall Plan's $13 billion effort would be spent re-tooling industry so that Europe could once again compete.

This assistance would be offered, Marshall said, "not against any country or doctrine, but against hunger, poverty, desperation and chaos." Aid was to be provided to any who would accept the conditions (with the exception of fascist Spain), the most important of which was that the money would be distributed not as a blank check, but according to common plan, agreed to by all parties. Even the Soviet Union could participate (for his proposal, the secretary had de-

Getting by in devastated Germany: "If you want your baby to live, you steal"

When I first saw the pictures of people dancing in the streets at the end of the war, I was shocked. I thought, "How could anyone have danced?" But that was happening on a different continent. In Germany we experienced nothing like that. First of all, how do you even know when the war is over if there is no electricity, no radio? Here's how it was for me: One morning I woke up and felt strange. I realized this was because I had slept all night long — no air raids or bombs had woken me up. That's when I knew the war was over. And at that moment, I felt a great sense of relief that the killing had stopped. But then other cares came up, because I was a refugee, and I didn't have anything.

My hometown of Danzig on the Baltic Sea had been 95 percent destroyed. We had heard about what was happening in Poland and East Prussia when the Russians invaded those places. People were killed and women were raped, even children of eight years. It was part of their philosophy, I guess, that women were a part of the loot. I was all alone with my baby because my husband, a naval architect, was off at war. I knew what would happen to us if we stayed, so in January of 1945 my baby and I set off to escape toward the West. It wasn't easy because it was winter, and the Russians had taken over many of the roads. But people were still walking through Europe seeking safety, melting the snow and feeding it to their children to keep them alive. Very small babies could never make it; they usually died on the road. I knew there was only one way we could survive, and that was to get out by boat, so we joined the other two million women and children trying to get on the ships docked at Danzig. My parents had to stay behind, because they were sixty-two years old, and they did not think they could survive the journey.

I got onto a small ferry that was carrying a few hundred women and children, but after two or three days, nothing was happening — the ship wasn't leaving. I couldn't stand it anymore, so I took my baby and left the ship. Luckily I soon saw a young sailor in the same naval architect's uniform that my husband wore, so I went to him and said, "I'm Eva Krutein. Do you know my husband?" He said he did. Just then, a small motorboat came to take him to his ship, and I yelled to the sailors, "Wait! Take me and my baby, also." They just assumed I was this young sailor's wife, so they took me, too. I didn't have a permit, though, so when the guards came toward me I pretended to trip and then just kept saying, "Oh, it hurts so much," while everyone else was showing their permits. And so I made it onto this huge ship, which had a capacity of 1,600 people and was carrying 6,000.

I got out at the ship's first stop, which was a German port city on the Baltic called Kiel, in the province of Schleswig-Holstein, not far from Hamburg. I had left everything behind — I couldn't take anything except my baby. Fortunately the Nazis, still in power at that time, could force people to take us in, so we were given a place to stay. With so many buildings bombed out, housing was very crowded; two-bedroom homes had

Left, Eva Krutein in 1942; above, her mother, Emma Lehnert, in 1944, with Krutein's first child, Lilo.

—*Eva Krutein, who was born in 1921, immigrated to Chile in 1951 with her husband and children. After nine years, they moved to Southern California. Eva, her husband, and their oldest daughter have revisited Gdansk and Kiel, and have hosted several Polish students from Gdansk, one of whom, Aleksander Kwasniewski, became the president of Poland.*

five to seven families living in them. Our main problem, though, was getting food. Luckily, somebody had told me before I left to put on three dresses and three sets of underclothes. I looked very fat, but at least I could take one or two things off and exchange them for food. That only lasted a little while, though.

The hunger was the worst part of it because it never left you. My baby was sick for a long time, so I took her to a doctor who said, "That's malnutrition. You have to feed her more protein." And I said, "Okay, if you can tell me exactly where to get that, I'll feed it to her." And she said, "Steal it. If you want your baby to live, go and steal it." So I went to the black market where people were selling food for money or cigarettes. I didn't have any of those things, but a woman offered to give me ten eggs in exchange for my kid gloves and shawl.

We also had to resort to looting. Once we looted a German Air Force warehouse, and I got a lot of shirts, which I traded for a full sack of potatoes. I was very proud and I thought we could live off them forever. But then a policeman stopped me and confiscated it, so that was the end of that. And the hunger continued. You got used to it, but it was very difficult when your little child would say to you, "Mom, I'm hungry," and you had absolutely nothing, not a crumb.

Toward the end of the war my husband had found my daughter and me fairly easily, but we were still having trouble finding out anything about my parents. So for the first six months or so, we just waited for them to show up. Then one day I found out about them the way many people found out about their families. Someone from Danzig came up to me and said, "I can tell you what happened to your parents."

Shortly after I had left Danzig, when the Russian soldiers came into town, my mother and some neighbors went to hide in a cellar. A few hours before the Russians arrived, a pharmacist who was down there with them told all the women, "If it becomes unbearable and you don't want to live anymore you can take this, potassium cyanide. It takes a fraction of a second, and it's a painless death." My mother was gang-raped, along with the rest of the women, but she was the only one who used her cyanide. She died immediately. There was no grave for her, and no funeral.

When Russia then gave Danzig back to Poland and it became Gdansk, everyone who was German was told by the Poles that they had to leave. Germans were put in stock cars and sent on a five-day trip to Berlin with no food or water. Bandits came into the train cars and robbed these "expellees," as we called them, of what little they had, including their clothes. My father was on one of those trains, and the bandits left him with nothing but his underpants. He got very sick from exposure, and he made his way to a hospital. Some months later, the hospital contacted me and told me that he had stuffed some money in his underpants that no one had found. He told someone at the hospital that he was going to give this money to his daughter and her family to build up their life. He died there of typhus fever.

For me, that was the hardest thing about that time, finding out about my parents. I knew they hadn't deserved to die, and all I could think of was how terrible it must have been for them. The Germans were punished very, very severely. Very seldom were the right people punished, of course, but you can't help that. That's the way it was.

fined Europe as including "everything up to the Urals"), though Marshall and his advisers had conceived their idea in part as a way to disarm Moscow.

Aware that his plan committed the nation abroad as it had never committed itself in peacetime before, Marshall then left the green elms of Harvard and set out to sell the concept to the American people. The European Recovery Program, as the Marshall Plan was formally known, represented a dramatic shift in American thinking and for it to work, the American people needed to be persuaded to shed their isolationist traditions. While Congress debated, Marshall visited chambers of commerce and women's groups; spoke to cotton and tobacco farmers and to newspaper editorial boards. He contended with not only the deeply held suspicions many Americans had toward foreign entanglements but also with their sense of thrift. America had already given Europe so much — hundreds of thousands of the nation's young in two devastating wars; billions of dollars in postwar relief already spent — so why should it now give more?

Marshall never had a better answer to that question than he did when seven Cub Scouts from Troop 232 in Bethesda, Maryland, arrived one day in his Washington office. Wearing neatly ironed uniforms and earnest expressions, they told him of their idea for a "Junior Marshall Plan." They would raise money on their own, the group's nine-year-old chairman offered, and then send it abroad to suffering children their age. "Mr. Secretary," said the boy, "we want to do everything we can to help the children of Europe." Marshall, clearly moved, saw an extraordinary opportunity to make his case. With his press secretary scribbling notes and a cameraman shooting pictures of the event, the general expressed admiration for the Scouts and then explained that their magnanimous gesture was in the spirit of the times. In his day, said Marshall, no boy would have been so inspired. He was halfway through college before he knew much more about the world than he could read in his rudimentary school texts. Now, with greater communication and the effects of two world wars, the world had changed and American responsibility had changed with it.

The Marshall Plan began its life in June of 1948, a whirlwind of energy and commitment that carried with it a feeling reminiscent of the first years of the New Deal, except now the setting was Paris, not Washington, and the do-gooders were out to save a Continent. American economists, bankers, businessmen, and diplomats poured into the program's makeshift offices (which, among other amenities, included a snack bar offering hot dogs and hamburgers to the thousands of Americans who were still too timid to try French food) and proceeded to turn theory into action, doctrine into practice.

In a matter of months, Europe was showing signs of recovery. Malnutrition was eased. Factories were restarted. New deliveries of fuel ensured that people would not have to go without heat. At the height of the plan, every day 150 ships were either bringing cargo to Europe or unloading it on her ports. In February of 1950, journalist Teddy White surveyed the coast of France and discovered the S.S. *Godrun Maersk*, three weeks out of Baltimore "butting through the heavy seas of the Channel to dock at Rouen and unload Marshall Plan tractors, chemicals, synthetic resin and cellulose acetate"; the S.S. *Cape Race*, sixty miles downriver, docked with a load of general cargo; and the S.S. *Gibbes Lykes*, five hundred miles to the south of that, at the port of Marseilles, bearing 3,500 tons of sulfur. Ten more American ships, wrote White, would land at France over the next three

George Marshall,
1880 – 1959

The first Marshall Plan shipments were food supplies. Subsequently, aid shipments included raw materials and capital goods that helped restart Europe's sputtering economies. But Congress demanded that every Marshall Plan shipment be marked to clearly indicate who was providing the assistance.

days, bringing tires, borax, aircraft parts, drilling equipment, farm machines, chemicals, oil, and cotton. The delivery of cotton alone would save the jobs of 170,000 French textile workers.

There was, regretfully, a bit of American self-righteousness attached to the moment, the feeling among the savior bureaucrats that American business would wave its wand over the cauldron that was Europe and turn it from bad to good, sickness to health, weakness to strength. Yet the effects of the program, generated by a people known for their energy and idealism, were overpowering and undeniable. Just as the New Deal had saved America for capitalism, the Marshall Plan would save Europe for democracy.

The Russians were indeed disarmed. They had rejected the offer to participate in the Marshall Plan when it became apparent that they would have to share too much information about their internal affairs with the plan's administrators (a stroke of luck for Marshall, really, since Soviet participation would probably have doomed the plan's chances for passage in Congress). And they had summoned the leaders of their new satellites to Moscow, arguing that the Marshall aid was an American Trojan Horse, designed to infiltrate Europe, and insisting that they reject it, too.

In some ways, the Russians were right. The massive delivery of American money was a humanitarian gesture of enormous magnitude ("the most unsordid act in history," said Churchill) but it was not without selfish motives. If the plan worked, it would carry two distinct side benefits for America's Cold War position: a healthy non-Communist Europe preserved international markets for American goods; and it joined American and European economic interests in a way that made a political and military union that much more natural. If Marshall saved Europe, it thus also increased the heat on it, "containing" communism just as Kennan had wished, and dividing the Continent more distinctly now between those nations loyal to America and those loyal to the Soviet Union.

Just as it had once seemed absurd to Americans that their boys be asked to die because someone had murdered the Austrian archduke, so, now, it seemed equally absurd to Europeans, noted Teddy White, that they might be annihilated because of the tension between the two newest players on the world's stage. But the Europeans' position left them little choice but to lean East or West. The world no longer belonged to them.

Germany remained Europe's most vulnerable spot. It had been agreed among the Allies before the war's end that the defeated nation would be divided into four zones of military occupation, governed by the British, the Americans, the French, and the Soviets. And though Berlin fell deeply within the Soviet zone, its importance as the capital city required that it be divided into four separately governed quarters itself. Germany, and Berlin, existed under this awkward arrangement while leaders of all four countries argued bitterly over how to resolve the German question.

The Russians' hope, thinly disguised in conference talks, was to wait until the Anglo-American occupation forces grew weary and went home, then seize the country much as they had already seized Poland, Rumania, Hungary, and Czechoslovakia. Their greatest fear was a reconstituted Germany allied with the West. Hoping to both defang the Germans and take advantage of their technical know-how at the same time, Stalin had ordered the dismantling of numerous factories and armaments plants in the Eastern zone and their transport and reconstruction on Soviet soil. But now the Marshall Plan, suggesting as it did a profound commitment by the Americans to Europe, and the specter of an economically revitalized Western Germany (the Eastern zone, like the other Soviet-controlled states, had refused the American aid) prompted Stalin to assume an even more aggressive stance.

Berlin was the setting for the first Cold War showdown. The clumsiness of that city's occupation arrangements meant that the Western powers were dependent on Russian cooperation for the access that would allow them to provide supplies to their forces and to the two and a half million Germans living within their sectors. In June 1948, while the Marshall Plan was beginning to take effect, Stalin, claiming that urgent "repairs" to the autobahn were needed, simply cut off Western passage to Berlin.

The American response was cautious. Stalin had determined that Truman did not wish to risk war over Berlin and he was right. But the West's strategy in Europe also required that it maintain the confidence of the Europeans. And that meant standing firm against any Russian threat. The American military governor in Germany, General Lucius Clay, lobbied hard to push an armored column

Europeans, like the designers of this French poster, were grateful for Marshall Plan assistance, which they saw not as a handout, but as an aid to future development.

Postwar Berlin: "The smell of death was in this town. The sweet smell of corpses was everywhere"

—*Jack Bennett, born in 1914, first went to Berlin in 1937 on a Rockefeller Scholarship to study aeronautical engineering at the Berlin Technical University. Upon hearing of young Bennett and his flight experience, Hermann Göring grew suspicious, requested to see him, and accused him of spying on Nazi air technology. He never was able to convince Göring of the contrary and returned to the United States in 1938. He began a long career in various facets of the air industry, traveling frequently between Germany and the United States, and in 1958, when Khrushchev threatened to turn control of West Berlin over to East Germany, he built a home there in protest. His book* Forty Thousand Hours in the Sky *achieved wide acclaim in Germany.*

Jack O. Bennett in the cockpit of one of the first planes to land in Berlin after the war.

As an American pilot and engineering student I had studied in Berlin on a scholarship for a few years before the war. And when the war ended, because I was in the right place at the right time, I got to fly the first American airplane into Berlin. I was working as a pilot for American Airlines, and the president of the company wanted me to go over there and start an airline. I asked him when, and he said in about eight months. But I said, "How about today?" and he gave me the okay. So I took off from New York in a DC-4, a civilian airplane with big American flags on the side. As I circled around where I thought Berlin used to be, I couldn't find the city. There were no navigational aids. Even though I knew Berlin well I damn near flew into the North Sea. And when I landed, I couldn't believe it. The city was nothing but a rubble pile.

Around this time the city was being divided into four sectors: the American, the Russian, the British, and the French. Jimmy Forrestal, the Secretary of the Navy, was on board the plane with me, and we were landing into chaos. The first thing we saw when we landed at Templehof Airport was a woman having a baby on top of a junk pile, right there amid the wrecked planes. Then all of the sudden the Russians started to lob rockets over our heads. I figured they had seen the American flag painted on the tail. A few of them came out onto the airstrip carrying these stubby machine guns. They tried to get me to take off and leave, but I wouldn't do it. I looked around and saw that the Russians were shooting the windows out of the airport with artillery shells, and was totally confused. I wondered,

"Why the hell are they doing that to this magnificent airport?" Then I realized that the airport was going to be in the American sector, and they didn't want to leave the Americans anything.

I tried to get a Jeep that afternoon. There were only two or three American officers in the whole town, and when I got in touch with them, they said, "Sure, we'll lend you a Jeep, but you're not going to be able to go downtown. There are no bridges any more." I said, "Listen, I know Berlin well." So they gave me a Jeep, but I couldn't even get a thousand meters from the airport. I had no sense of orientation, no way to navigate. So I came back, and the officer laughed and said he would give me a German driver the next day.

The following day when my German driver picked me up, he said, "I've heard you were here, before the war." I said I was, and he said, "You're not going to like this. First I have to show you how to get to Pragerplatz." It turned out that every main thoroughfare was piled up five stories high with rubbish, wrecked tanks, and wrecked airplanes. We made our way to Pragerplatz and then walked a ways to find the street where I used to live. There was no apartment house there at all, and I sat down and had tears in my eyes. My driver had tears in his eyes as well. I said, "They'll never rebuild this city." He said, "No, they never will."

As we drove around the city, the Germans would run right across the street, in front of our car, as though they wanted to be killed. I called it the death syndrome. They just had no reason to live anymore. And all around the wrecked apartment houses were posts in the ground,

which said things like, "Herr Schmidt doesn't live here anymore; he lives at such and such address." And the smell of death was in this town. The sweet smell of corpses was everywhere. So I said to my driver, "Let's get the hell out of here," and we headed back to where I was staying.

The dangerous people in the city were not the Germans. No, the dangerous ones were the displaced persons, or D.P.s, as we called them — the Poles, the Slavs, and the Gypsies. They'd kill you for a piece of bread. You could not go ten feet out of Templehof Airport without carrying a gun — you had to have a .45 in a holster. And of course you stayed off the streets at night, unless you could speak German. The Russians did not behave very well here either. More than once I saw a truckload of Russians with maybe ten German girls in the back, and the Russians were raping them as the truck drove through town. So the Russians really sent some pretty rotten, profane people to Berlin.

In the first days after the war, cigarettes were $1,000 a carton in Berlin. Then in a couple of days, the price dropped to $100 and stayed there. Germans were strictly forbidden to have any American money; in fact we Americans weren't even allowed to have it. We were using military scrip — little, tiny dollar bills that looked like clown money. Most everything was exchanged using the barter system, and cigarettes were the main form of currency. You could get almost anything with a pack of cigarettes. And a lot of foreigners were getting rich off the situation. There was one man, a captain, whom we called Camera Dan, because he was buying expensive Leica cameras for one pack of cigarettes each and sending them home by the thousands. I'm sure he became wealthy.

The American rules and propaganda generally told us to stay away from the Germans because they were our enemy. American soldiers were not allowed to fraternize with the German girls. In the commissary out in Templehof, there were big signs up, saying, "Don't associate with German girls." They showed a naked fraulein with maggots all over her body. But I was surprised to see that the Germans were very happy to see the American soldiers come into their country. I thought there was going to be lots of hostility, but there was very little. I said to people, "Where are all the Nazis I used to know?" "Well, there aren't any Nazis anymore," I was told. A young German woman I knew before the war said to me, "Jack . . . they deceived us. Hitler deceived us." And a considerable number of Germans agreed with her; they felt that Hitler had wrecked the country. Which he did, no question about it. Defeat is very hard to accept, you know. And people don't like defeat, especially the Germans.

straight through the border, dare the Russians and come what may, but cooler heads understood that such an aggressive move might indeed lead to war. And with the Red Army vastly outnumbering America's shrunken force in Europe, war, as far as the United States was concerned, would most likely mean their resorting to their growing atomic arsenal. It was an ironic moment, the first of many, for the world was adjusting to the reality of the atomic age, when the two new superpowers, knowing the devastation that atomic warfare would bring (even if only one of them actually had the bomb), competed like cat and mouse, probing and testing but never attacking, reaching the precipice of all-out war, and then recoiling at the horrors that possibility brought to the imagination.

Truman decided on a more peaceful course. He would simply ignore Stalin's blockade and supply Berlin by air. But just to keep the Soviet premier guessing, he ordered a group of B-29 bombers to England, and let Stalin think that each of them was prepared to be moved at a moment's notice to drop an atom bomb on Moscow (the planes were, in fact, empty).

It was an enormous gamble. To keep Berlin functioning normally, Western officials calculated, American C-47 aircraft would have to land a minimum of eight thousand tons of supplies each day at the impossible rate of one planeload every forty-eight seconds. For the city to simply survive, they'd have to provide four thousand tons, or one planeload every three and a half minutes. Still, it was worth a try. After a duplicate of Berlin's air corridor approach paths was built in Montana as a training site for fliers, American and British air force planes began landing supplies around the clock.

At first, the plan was a resounding failure. Barely a thousand tons were making their way to the German capital city in the early summer. Then came a breakthrough. Larger planes stationed in the Pacific were routed into service at Berlin, and the British and American airmen — flying on little sleep, their planes weighted down with excess cargo, well beyond the limits of safety — became more proficient at their assignments. Most important of all, the people of Berlin responded to the crisis themselves, mustering twenty thousand volunteers to build a third airfield in a remarkable display of willpower.

For the next several months, Berlin went to sleep at night and rose the next morning to the steady rhythm of American and British airforce planes droning overhead. The schedule was grueling: pilots would arrive, unload their freight, then climb in their cockpits and fly back for more. Adrenaline flowed. Only a few years before, Americans and Germans had been mortal enemies. Yet here were the same two peoples, standing shoulder to shoulder, both under siege, both confronting and, it appeared, beating the same enemy.

By December, 4,500 tons were being flown in each day; by the spring, 8,000, then 13,000, the American pilots dropping bags of candy over the rooftops as they arrived, the German children eagerly running to greet them. Berlin, giddy with victory, was beginning to look like Western Europe's other cities, brimming with Marshall Plan vitality. By the middle of May, the blockade was finished. Convinced that he could do nothing to interrupt the flow of cargo, Stalin backed down.

The airlift seized the imagination of the world. And when it was over, for one brief moment, the balance of favor in the battle between the West and the

To keep deliveries moving as fast as possible, Berlin Airlift flight crews were ordered to remain in their planes between landing and takeoff. Food was brought out to them, and the planes were refueled and serviced as they were being unloaded.

"Stalin cutlets"

Berliner's name for warmed-over toast

Children in Berlin called American airlift planes "chocolate bombers" because pilots dropped candy tied to miniature parachutes as they flew into the city.

Soviet Union appeared to rest decidedly with the West. But a Cold War, fought as it is by gesture and statement, by covert network and proxy, by symbol and suasion, does not end as quickly nor as definitively as a hot war. Its battles are not as easily understood and its sides are not as easily drawn. America may have won in Berlin, but with the world still adjusting to its postwar shape, the East-West conflict simply continued now in dozens of other venues.

One of the most far-reaching consequences of the Second World War was the abrupt end that it brought to colonization. The finish came at the urging of the United States, which had long argued that colonial empires were inconsistent with its belief in democracy, and at the expense of the crippled European powers, particularly Britain, whose rule had dominated the map for centuries. But the change was inevitable: if they had done nothing else, the century's wars had confirmed the illegitimacy of the dusty old order and its subjugation of the masses (though the surge of the world's population would probably have forced the issue if war had not). Even the Moscow-led Communist insurgencies, seizing power sometimes with little popular support, cynically claimed the mantel of democracy.

Three young survivors of the Buchenwald concentration camp head for the British colony of Palestine, June 1945.

At the same time that the Marshall Plan's ships were sloshing through the Atlantic waters and the airlift planes were gliding safely into West Berlin's airfields, Jewish refugees were making their way to the former British colony of Palestine, where the recently formed United Nations had established the state of Israel (one decision reached with the agreement of both the Russians and the Americans) despite continuing hostility between the new settlers and the Arabs they displaced; French soldiers were battling Ho Chi Minh's Communists for control of French Indochina; and the populations of the world's two biggest nations, India and China, were wrestling with new identities. The Indians were emerging from under the cloak of the British raj into a bloody civil war, pitting Muslims against Hindus and Sikhs, while the Chinese Communists, led by Mao Zedong, were coming to the end of their decades-long struggle for power by defeating the American-backed Nationalists of Chiang Kai-shek.

Mao's victory stunned Americans, and erased much of the sense of triumph that had accompanied the Berlin story. The China they knew, the one that resided happily in their minds, was the China of Pearl Buck's *The Good Earth* and the China of Chiang, a convert to Christianity and supporter of America. Both the United States and the Soviet Union had considered a stable China under Chiang so important to world order, they had agreed to include it as a member of the "Big Five" that made up the United Nations Security Council. Now those benign images of a friendly ally had been replaced by the sweep of a short, stout Hunanese with a circular, cheeky face, a man with a curiously serene demeanor that Westerners read as diabolical. When Mao then followed up his victory with a two-month visit to Moscow, sealing a Sino-Soviet friendship treaty, it could only confirm the West's worst fears of a Communist world revolution. With China in the Red column, communism was now in control of 40 percent of the earth's population and 20 percent of its geography.

China's Communists were, in fact, a vastly different brand of revolutionary from their Soviet neighbors, and they were led by a vastly different kind of

Shanghai, 1949: "I was sympathetic to the Communists because I knew China was in such a mess"

My husband and I went back to China from Australia in 1948 when he was asked to work for Chiang Kai-shek's government in Shanghai. We came home to a very unstable country. The Communists were camped out on the banks of the Yangtze river, ready to take over. The chaos throughout the city made it clear that Chiang Kai-shek's Nationalist government was crumbling. For example, in the cold October weather the policemen directing traffic were shivering in their light, summer uniforms because the government couldn't give them winter uniforms. But much worse than that, wounded soldiers back from the frontlines of the civil war were left lying on the sidewalks, bleeding and groaning, with nobody caring for them.

It was clear to me right away that order in the city had completely broken down. Inflation had made everybody poor, because their wages were not worth anything after one or two days. There were bandits all over the place, many of whom were just ordinary people dislocated by the war. When my car came to a red light, the chauffeur turned around to me and said, "Wind up the window! Wind up the window!" I wasn't quick enough, though, and one of the refugees passed his hand through the window and begged me to give him money, which I did. When we checked into the hotel that first night, we had to pay cash in advance. And the hotel people immediately took that local money outside to an illegal money changer and traded it for American dollars, because if they held the local money overnight, it would depreciate dramatically. When I went to have some Chinese clothes made, I had to carry a bag full of banknotes to the shop with me. The shop people didn't count each note — they just counted the bundles.

Of course we were full of curiosity about communism. Naturally, the Nationalists forbade any writings of Mao Zedong to be published in Shanghai because a war was on, but when a Communist victory started to seem inevitable, everybody was curious to find out what Mao advocated. Many of our old school friends in Shanghai were professors, and they passed along to us some of Mao's writings, which were circulating through the Communist underground. My husband and I read quite a lot of these writings, and they were very misleading because the Communists deliberately circulated only quotes that would be acceptable to liberal-thinking Chinese people like ourselves. There were stories about how honest the Communist officials were and how good their soldiers were when they entered a village — how they would help peasants to harvest and work, and never take anything from the people. So naturally I was not afraid of a Communist takeover, mostly because I was brainwashed, you might say, from reading all of that propaganda.

Soon it became apparent that the Nationalists were going to lose their hold on Shanghai. At night we heard the sporadic gunfire on the outskirts of the city, but then one night in May of 1949 the fighting seemed much closer. I was awakened by my cook at about six in the morning, and he said, "The Communist soldiers are here." I went downstairs with him to the front door, and outside on the sidewalk we saw a lot of really young-looking soldiers — they couldn't have been more than fifteen

—Nien Cheng, who was born in 1915, is the daughter of a Chinese navy official. She studied at the London School of Economics, and married Kang-chi Cheng, a diplomat and businessman. After his death in 1957, she worked for Shell Oil until she was imprisoned by Mao's Red Guards in 1966. Her memoir, Life and Death in Shanghai, *chronicles her imprisonment and the six years she spent in solitary confinement as an "enemy of the State."*

or seventeen years old. They wore khaki uniforms and straw sandals or just their bare feet, and they looked very worn out, but they were standing very erect with their guns beside them, as if they were at attention.

Some people from the neighboring households had already come out and offered the soldiers cups of water, cookies, and things like that, but they had all refused. I was very puzzled. I learned later that when they were marching into the city, each soldier had a piece of paper pinned on his back with Mao Zedong's orders written on it, and the first order was that they were not to take so much as a needle or a thread from any of the citizens. They had to show that they were strict and well behaved to contrast with the behavior of the traditional Chinese soldiers, who would loot and rob people.

The new Communist soldiers created a very good impression when they first came into Shanghai. It was an eye opener to all of us that they could be so well disciplined. And of course, most of these soldiers were just peasants — young people from the countryside who had never been in a city. They were billeted in high-rise, European-style hotels with flush toilets, and we heard many funny stories about them using the toilets to wash their clothes and so on. But it seemed to me that the Communists might be able to organize China, and make it a proper, law-abiding country. They certainly were on the side of the people.

The soldiers set up booths at all the crossroads, and grabbed any passersby to give them injections for

Above: Nien Cheng with daughter Mei Ping after returning to China, 1949.

Left: Chinese Communist troops in Nanjing, June 1949.

cholera and other epidemics that were common then. Their goal was to immunize every citizen, but instead of doing it in an orderly way, going from house to house, they would just grab people. They didn't give you any documentation, though, so at the next street corner you could get grabbed again, and you would have to say, "I already had it! I already had it!" All of this was very refreshing, though, because Chinese people were so used to bad government, a government which didn't care for the people.

Of course, there were restrictions. All of the bookstores that sold English language books closed down. No Western publications were allowed in China, and that was inconvenient for us, because we were used to reading magazines like *Time* and the *New Yorker*. Also, when I went abroad, I had always brought back records, mostly classical. But under the Communists I had to hand over the records I bought, and they would play them to make sure that it was classical music and not jazz or rock and roll. After a while, we really lost touch with what was going on in the world.

Still, I wasn't opposed to the Communists at all. They got rid of the inflation very quickly, and organized the economy. I didn't feel threatened by the regime, either, because at that time, Mao's policies did not oppose the upper classes. Above all I felt curious to see whether their methods would work or not. I observed the Communists very closely, and I read up on Marx and Engels and their theories of communism and socialism to enable myself to understand what was happening. I was sympathetic to the Communist cause, because I knew Old China was in such a terrible mess. I thought maybe this was what China needed, after so many years of war and chaos. When a country becomes very chaotic, a strong government is sometimes necessary to pull it together. That's what I thought then, anyway.

*Highly dedicated and well tested after waging a
guerrilla war against the Japanese during World
War II, Mao Zedong's Communist army was able to
defeat Chiang Kai-shek's Nationalists despite being
outnumbered five to one.*

patriarch. The peace treaty aside, Mao had more suspicion than affection for Stalin; and the hordes who followed the Chinese leader came from villages so primitive it was unlikely that they knew of the Soviet Union's existence, much less thought of themselves as committed allies in a quest for world domination. Hungry and determined, having tasted little food and even less liberty, they were attracted to communism because it offered them the chance, small though that might be, of something more. And that, in a nation where half the people died before the age of thirty.

Chiang may have been a friend of the United States, but he presided over a corrupt society made ungovernable by China's decade-long occupation at the hands of the Japanese and by the growing strength of Mao. Inflation was rampant. So was starvation. Meanwhile, Chiang's police crushed the opposition, Communist or not. No manner of American pressure would change him (in 1946, George Marshall had made a valiant but fruitless attempt to join Chiang and Mao in a governing coalition), and yet caught in a Cold War conundrum, Americans saw their own security at stake by doing anything less than supporting the anti-Communist. The new Chinese revolution came to power with an ardent hatred of all things American and was followed, in September 1949, by more grave news. Even as the last of the Chinese Nationalists fled the mainland for a safe haven on the island of Formosa, a squadron of United States Air Force B-29s, flying over the North Pacific, photographed traces of radioactive material, irrefutable evidence that the Soviets had successfully exploded their first atomic bomb.

Americans were disillusioned. This was not the way things were supposed to go. Right was supposed to triumph over wrong. Good over bad. Freedom over oppression. God over the godless. Hadn't the Allies just finished proving this on the beaches of Normandy and in the waters of the Pacific? And hadn't God, surveying the postwar world, determined that Americans alone possess the atomic secrets to keep the forces of evil in check?

Mao's victory and Stalin's bomb (the Americans had code-named the Soviet's first atomic experiment "Joe I," the "Joe" for Stalin, the "I" to reinforce that there would be more) forced a reconsideration of plans for occupied Japan, for now the line between East and West had been drawn even more firmly and every American decision had to be viewed through the prism of the Cold War. The initial strategy, as it had been for occupied Germany, had been to halt the nation's capacity for future aggression, to disarm the former enemy and slowly introduce democratic values. But just as the Russian actions in Eastern Europe had changed the pace of "reeducation" in West Germany, so the victory of the Chinese Communists made it essential that Japan be immediately strengthened against the spread of the "red tide" through Asia.

General Douglas MacArthur, the commander of American forces in the Pacific in World War II, who had become the supreme commander of occupied Japan, had personally written the new Japanese constitution which, among other restraints, banned the formation of an army ("Land, sea, and air forces, as well as other war potential, will never be maintained.") or the development of a military industry. Just three years after the end of the war, that ban was now lifted, creating a "self-defense force" of seventy-five thousand.

*Whittaker Chambers,
1901 – 1961*

> *"When I took up my little sling
> and aimed at communism,
> I also hit something else. What
> I hit was the forces of the great
> socialist revolution, which in
> the name of liberalism,
> spasmodically, incompletely
> and somewhat formlessly, but
> always in the same direction,
> has been inching its ice cap over
> the nation for the last two
> decades."*
>
> *Whittaker Chambers*

In this tortured international environment, set in a sharp relief defining everything and everyone as "for us" or "for them," Whittaker Chambers was a rarity — a man who had dug in at the foxholes of both sides, a true "witness," as he described himself, to the "two great faiths of our time." Once a dedicated Communist, during the idealism of the 1930s, and an admitted spy, Chambers had since renounced his party affiliations and, in a drama that transfixed the nation throughout the fall of 1948, sat before the House Committee on Un-American Activities to name the names of his partners in espionage.

As a spokesman for freedom, Chambers made an unattractive appearance. He was slovenly and his past was shady. In his life in the Communist underground, he had assumed nearly a dozen aliases and as many life stories. His agenda, to act as an informant on his former co-conspirators, was undignified. And listening to him there was always the nagging feeling that if he had once been a spy, living a life of deceit, and plotting against his own country, who was to say that he was telling the truth now? Still, there was something riveting about the man as there always is to the criminal who has gone clean, the air of a poor soul who, having spent time in purgatory, emerges with clearer vision and a message from the heart.

Chambers's most dramatic claim was dramatic indeed: He asserted that Alger Hiss, the head of the Carnegie Endowment for Peace, had, as a member of the State Department in the late 1930s, been part of a Communist spy ring and had personally passed critical documents to him. At any other time, the charge might have been laughable, but not in the dense fog of intrigue that blanketed American life through the Cold War.

When Hiss himself entered the picture, the plot only thickened. Handsome, distinguished, well bred, Alger Hiss was everything that Chambers was not. His professional career spanned the century, including stints as a clerk to legendary Supreme Court Justice Oliver Wendell Holmes and as a low-level diplomat at Yalta. He had been educated at Harvard and had served in the New Deal. He was articulate, well spoken, and charming. So charming, in fact, that after an initial appearance in which Hiss denied Chambers's charges, the committee seemed ready to dismiss the issue. But a young congressman named Richard Nixon, being fed incriminating documents on Hiss by the FBI, insisted that Hiss and Chambers, then a writer at *Time*, face off against each other and prove which one was lying.

Over the next year and a half, while it made its way through additional committee hearings and then two well-publicized trials, the story of Alger Hiss and Whittaker Chambers grew to become the symbol of American domestic turmoil in the postwar era. There were plenty of tantalizing parts to the tale. Hiss lied to the committee when he first said he had never known Chambers. In fact, he had known Chambers well and had even loaned him his apartment. But why had he lied? Was it to protect his wife, whose Communist leanings were more clearly evident than his own? Or to hide an affair? Chambers, a homosexual, seemed to have an extraordinary fixation on Hiss. The case reached a climax when Chambers announced with great fanfare that he could prove his testimony by revealing several of the documents which had been typed on Hiss's typewriter and then handed over to him for delivery. They were still in his possession, said Chambers, squirreled away in a hollowed-out pumpkin on his Maryland farm.

Finally convicted of perjury in 1950 (the statute of limitations had passed on his alleged espionage), Hiss was sentenced to five years in jail, insisting he had neither been a Communist nor spied for them. But the importance of the story lay less in Hiss's innocence or guilt than in the way that Chambers's charges reverberated with the tensions of the times. It was not just Alger Hiss on trial but, as Alistair Cooke wrote, an entire generation and the ideas that it embraced.

The passage from the 1930s to the late 1940s had been an extraordinarily jarring one for American domestic culture. After all, only a few short years separated the rabid anti-Communism of the present moment from the era of the New Deal, when liberal ideas were ascendant, and communism, while not popular, was hardly the abhorrent demon religion it was to become in the minds of so many Americans a few years later. The memory of that earlier time now haunted the nation. To Chambers, whose 1952 book *Witness*, became a best-seller, and, increasingly, millions of others, communism was more than a system of government; it was a campaign for the absolute control of men's minds. According to them, too many Americans, particularly the powerful, elite class of educated Americans, had fallen victim to it by spending the 1930s in awe of the "Soviet experiment." Infatuated by its promise of economic egalitarianism and unaware of the crimes of its authoritarian leadership, they had been "soft," leading America, and the world, into its present predicament.

Chambers was an intellectual and a gifted writer, but the anti-Communists were to find their most vocal champion by accident, and he was a buffoon. Senator Joseph McCarthy of Wisconsin, a hard-drinking, coarse man who, it was later said, knew so little about his pet subject, he would find it hard to distinguish Karl Marx from Groucho, made a reference in a 1950 address before a group of Republicans in West Virginia, to a list of 205 known Communists working in the State Department. McCarthy had no list (and in subsequent speeches, he changed the number to 57, 81, and then 4), but, with self-aggrandizement his only real professional goal, he soon realized he had hit upon something and when reporters asked him for more information, he decided to play along. By the time he was done, some four years later, a pitiful alcoholic mess, thousands of lives had been ruined, "McCarthyism" had entered the language as a word describing "the use of indiscriminate allegations," and the nation was embarrassed, exhausted, and frayed.

There were, no doubt, plenty of Communist agents in America, but it is unlikely that McCarthy or his followers ever found any. What they did accomplish was to reduce all manner of modern frustrations to the menace of communism and its "sympathizers," exploiting the vulnerabilities of a frightened and insecure people. McCarthy became anti-communism's most captivating spokesman because he was able to simplify a complex series of confusing international developments into language and ideas that tapped deeply into historic divisions in the American culture. If things had indeed not turned out the way that Americans had hoped or expected they would, then McCarthy helped them find someone to blame.

By suggestion and innuendo, diversion and outright attack, McCarthy pointed his finger at labor and liberals, at America's well-bred elite and its dominant educational institutions, at FDR and the New Deal. In one broad sweep, he

"It was quite a different atmosphere in Washington then than today."

Alger Hiss, explaining his leftist associations of the 1930s to a court trying him for espionage

*Alger Hiss,
1904 – 1996*

The fact that Communist agents could not easily be identified by race, sex, ethnicity, income, dress, language, or religion helped to fuel American paranoia. This series of U.S. Navy stills warned servicemen not to be fooled by a pretty face; that new girlfriend might be a Red spy.

"[The Democratic Party has] bent to the whispered pleas from the lips of traitors . . ."

Senator Joe McCarthy

was able to draw a line of resentment that stretched from the present back to World War I, insisting that America's sin had been in going to Europe in the first place, when the Germans and the Bolsheviks should have been left to fight it out on their own. In his bluster and populism, he was the worthy successor to Huey Long and Father Coughlin and, in fact, his campaign, like theirs, had less to do with politics than with turning up the heat on the class and culture wars that simmered throughout this century. When McCarthy complained that the State Department was stocked with "bright young men . . . born with silver spoons in their mouths" and posed for photographs looking as disheveled as the town drunk, he was appealing to that bitter nativist part of American society that had felt left out for too long.

McCarthy's strategy was to smear first and investigate later, though the fun of smearing usually kept him from ever getting on with investigating. In Congress he had his supporters and some were as vocal as he was; more often, his fellow lawmakers privately condemned what he was doing but, fearing his poison darts, cowered rather than confront him. The "evidence" that led him to make a charge was almost always suspect and sometimes completely fabricated, as when he arranged for the creation of a composite picture joining Senator Millard Tydings of Maryland and Earl Browder, the American Communist Party chief, in what looked like a friendly encounter. When it appeared in the Washington *Times-Herald* (journalists were often McCarthy accomplices, if for no other reason than that he made a good story), few people read the fine print that acknowledged the composite and Tydings, a Senate fixture for thirty years, went down to defeat.

McCarthy was, without a doubt, the most destructive anti-communist of his time, but he was not the only one ruining careers and smearing reputations. Around the country, thousands of civil servants, schoolteachers, trade unionists, and scientists were driven from their jobs by witch hunts equal in viciousness to those mounted by the Wisconsin senator. Thousands of other citizens remained silent for fear that they, too, would be attacked. The hysteria had the quality of the ridiculous. Schools banned "Robin Hood" for its "Communist" themes. The Cincinnati Reds baseball team changed its name to the "Red Legs" for fear that anyone would receive the wrong idea. Mickey Spillane, author of the sensational Mike Hammer adventure stories, had his tough private eye go after agents of Communist subversion instead of the gangsters he had shot up in the early 1940s. And two years after he had broken baseball's color barrier and earned the respect of the nation, Jackie Robinson was called before the Un-American Activities Committee to testify about Communist influence in the black community. Only in 1951, when McCarthy dared to challenge the character of George Marshall himself (claiming, absurdly, that the general had in his postwar policies joined "common cause" with Stalin) did McCarthy's reputation with the public finally begin to sour.

Even as McCarthy pestered him with lists of suspected Communists hiding under desks at the White House, Truman decided to go to war in Korea in June 1950. In fact, the president had little choice. The success of the Communists in China had people in America and Europe fearing a domino effect for the whole of Asia; the American commitment to defend Europe militarily had been met skeptically by people there and needed to be backed up by the display of

A young actress is blacklisted: "I felt the floor rush out from under me"

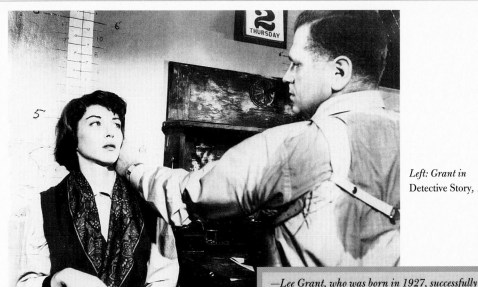

Left: Grant in Detective Story, *1951.*

—Lee Grant, who was born in 1927, successfully campaigned to abolish the practice of blacklisting in the television union. For seventeen years, she earned only minor roles in films, until her name was officially "cleared" with the help of an attorney in 1969. Her first motion picture role after the blacklisting period earned her another Academy Award nomination, and in 1976 she won an Oscar for her supporting role in Shampoo. *She has also directed numerous documentaries, including the Academy Award–winning* Down and Out in America.

When I was young, I had very few talents. One of them was acting, and the other one was fighting for what I believed in when I thought something unfair was being done. In 1951, the first play I was ever in, *Detective Story*, was made into a film, and I got my first Academy Award nomination. Around that time, I was asked to speak at the memorial service for an actor I had been working with named J. Edward Bromberg, who had been questioned by the House Un-American Activities Committee as a suspected Communist. I got up there and said that I felt he was hounded to death — that his constant appearances in front of the committee had contributed to his death. The next day, at an Actor's Equity meeting, somebody turned around to me, and said, "Congratulations. You made it into *Red Channels*." This was a weekly periodical that listed the names of the people who were to be blacklisted. I felt the floor rush out from under me and my heart drop, and I said to myself, "That's it."

Of course there really weren't very many Communists in Hollywood. And they were not a paramilitary group — they were writers and composers and actors posing no real threat to anyone. But once the anti-Communists had taken care of the real Communists, they started picking on people who had given money to certain organizations, people who had shown up at the "wrong" party, or people who voted for the "wrong" person — people who weren't even political at all, like me. And the entertainment industry buckled under the pressure. A grocer in Syracuse, for example, ran a successful campaign against actors. He filled his super-

markets with signs that said things like, "If you buy Colgate Toothpaste you are buying a product that sponsors this program with this actor, who is a Communist." And when people started contacting the networks about it they would just take those actors right off the programs.

Red Channels became the bible of the television industry. It was easy to make it in there — all you had to do was stand up at a union meeting and ask, "What are you trying to do about blacklisting?" Then somebody from the union board would write your name down, and the next day you'd be on the list. The Screen Actors Guild, run by Ronald Reagan, did the same thing. And once you were blacklisted you were out of work, unless you got up in front of the union and said, "I'm sorry that I gave money to that," or, "I'm sorry I showed up at that party. I am a good American. I never meant to do it." You had to humiliate yourself in front of your peers, or maybe give some money to *Red Channels* as a way of showing that you supported their patriotic effort. Luckily, the Broadway producers got together and they made a pact that nobody in the theater would be blacklisted. So those of us actors who were blacklisted for TV and film could work on Broadway.

When I got the subpoena from the House Un-American Activities Committee asking me to testify against other actors, it was very frightening. I was in a Broadway play at the time, and I went to the producer, and said, "I'm going to take the Fifth Amendment. And I understand if you want to replace me in the part if you're worried about audiences not coming to the theater." But he said, "No, absolutely not. You do what you have to do, and you've got a job here." And so I went. They asked me lots of personal questions, things that could have put other people in jeopardy, because I knew all the other people in the union who were fighting blacklisting. And I could have hurt them if I talked. There were other people, though, who succumbed to the pressure. And I wouldn't talk to them once they did. Because not only did they cave in, but they also wanted other people to come along and to join them in being informers. Being an informer meant placing your fellow actor, fellow friend, or fellow director in jeopardy. It meant that a person didn't work anymore. So taking that step was about the worst thing that you could do to anybody.

When I made a choice not to give names, and therefore took my place in society as being outside it, I never really knew if the whole thing would ever end. It seemed like it might go on forever. Fighting the blacklist became my career. If somebody said at that time, "It's okay, we have a job for you," I'd say, "I can't do that, I'm fighting." All around me I could see the victims of this war, because there were many suicides, many early deaths. My husband, Arnold Manoff, whom I was separated from at the time, died at age fifty-one from heart disease while being investigated. One of the residual problems that I developed during that time was a "name block." The fear of saying a name and putting somebody out of work became so enormous, that my brain blocked out people's names. When I went on stage, I would have to write down names on my palm or I'd never remember them.

As the years went on, I really felt terrible for a lot of the people who named names, especially the ones in their forties and fifties. They were faced with the threat of losing everything, and the pressure was so powerful that they did what they didn't want to do. They didn't know, either, that the cycle was ever going to end; they, too, felt that it might go on forever. So now those people have to cope with a kind of terrible guilt. For me, it was simple. If I had given names, they would have had to put me in an asylum — it's as simple as that. For other people, it meant losing everything — losing their positions in the industry, losing their power, losing their homes. And they had a lot to lose. I was just starting out.

Senator Joseph R. McCarthy signs autographs for a group of adoring students, 1950. At the height of the McCarthy hysteria, six detention camps were readied to handle the anticipated arrest of Communist agents, but Mc-Carthy was unable to produce enough legal evidence to support a single charge.

A Minnesota-based religious group printed and distributed four million copies of this Red scare publication.

action; and the 38th Parallel, which separated Communist North Korea from the non-Communist South, was one of two places — Berlin being the other — where the cold warriors stood face to face and where the offer of a challenge by either side had to be answered with force, or so it seemed. (The demarcation line was chosen arbitrarily by the American government to keep the Russians, who had been the first to liberate Korea from the Japanese, out of the strategic areas in the South.)

There were, also, the real stories of Communist penetration in the West, the ones which stood separate from the fabricated news reports pouring out of Mc-Carthy's office, and which, in their legitimacy, tended to lend substance to the twisted creations emerging from the senator's imagination. Stories like the arrest of Klaus Fuchs, who, as one of the primary physicists at Los Alamos in 1945, had been funneling information on the bomb to Soviet agents. And Fuchs's own revelation that he had not worked alone, but in a spy ring that included nine others, among them Julius and Ethel Rosenberg. At the Rosenbergs' trial in 1951, which resulted in a death sentence for each of them, the prosecutor offered that the Russians would never have "started" the war in Korea if traitors had not helped them to the information that allowed the building of a Soviet bomb.

There was no evidence to back up the prosecutor's claim; still, there was plenty to suggest that the Russians meant to press communism on a growing portion of the world's geography, that Korea might be just the first of several

Escape from North Korea: **An American POW's harrowing tale**

On the twenty-eighth of November 1950, I was in a convoy in the Chosin Reservoir that was completely surrounded by Chinese troops, who were aiding the North Koreans. We all hopped out of our trucks and got into the ditches, and the Chinese were all over us. We fought them off for twelve hours, but we had an awful lot of dead and dying in the ditches, so we eventually had to surrender. At just about dawn, I was breaking my carbine over the bumper of my truck, smashing it to ruin the mechanism (we did this to avoid giving them to the enemy), and I felt a tap on my back. I turned around and this little Chinese guy — he couldn't have been more than five foot two or three — was standing there with a submachine gun slung over his shoulder, and he stuck his hand out to congratulate me for surrendering.

We had heard about the North Koreans, that they were just as apt to execute a prisoner as they were to imprison him. But the Chinese fighting with them were different. They had the idea that they were going to put us through a political indoctrination course — what some people called a low-power brainwashing course — and actually convert us to their cause. They rounded up 123 of us and started us off on what was to be a 120-mile walk to another camp on the northwestern border of North Korea. It took us almost twenty days to get there and we didn't have much to eat but boiled potatoes. A lot of the men were getting stomach problems or severe colds, but they just kept marching us. When we got to the camp, there were only one hundred of us left.

They let us rest for about two days. Then, on December 24, they threw us a Christmas party. They had actually gone and cut down a pine tree and decorated it with pieces of colored paper. They handed each of us a few pieces of candy, five or six salted peanuts, and a tailor-made cigarette — these were our Christmas presents. And then they started this bit where they wanted us to get up and make confessions. This was a big deal in Communist brainwashing, to confess your sins.

After about a week or two, they started giving us English editions of Chinese newspapers, with certain articles circled in red. We had to read these articles and make sure we understood them, because later the Chinese would test us on them. And they were so ridiculous — stuff about Chinese soldiers who jumped on the back of an American tank, ripped open the hatch with bayonets, and threw grenades down there and killed the crew, and you were supposed to believe it. There were also stories about the terrible situation that we had in the United States. I remember one about how people were dying of starvation on the streets of Bakersfield, California. Of course, we all knew this was rot, but when we told them so, we had to listen to long-winded lec-

—Len Maffioli, who was born in 1925, served with the Marines in three wars: World War II, the Korean War, and the Vietnam War. After thirty-three years in the service, he retired as a master gunnery sergeant. He has returned to Korea numerous times and visited some of the sites where he fought. He is the co-author of Grown Gray in War: The Len Maffioli Story, a memoir of his time in the Marines.

Maffioli, the day after his escape, holding cigarettes, candy, and toiletries given to him by the Red Cross.

tures in a barn, which meant three or four hours of freezing to death. So eventually we got the idea. They never interrogated us much on military matters; what they were more interested in was our family life, our social life. They couldn't believe that a lot of the people captured, me included, owned our own automobiles. I remember one of them saying one morning that in China he could have an egg every morning for breakfast if he wanted. And somebody laughed and said, "God, we could have a dozen if we wanted, every morning." Well, he refused to believe that food was so plentiful.

The Chinese put out a little camp newspaper and encouraged us to write articles for it. You got two cigarettes if you wrote an article, which of course had to be a confession of some kind. Of course we were thinking up all kinds of crazy things to write. Once I wrote, "When I was being interrogated they asked what party I belonged to in the United States and I said I was never in a political party. But I have to confess, I was a registered Republican and I voted for Thomas Dewey." And that was worth two cigarettes.

We were on a diet of soybeans and sorghum seed, the seed that they would thrash off the sorghum cane and boil until it swelled up to about the size of a grain of rice. Coping with hunger wasn't our primary worry — we were more concerned with frostbite and the wounds that hadn't healed. There were quite a few guys who died of gangrene. But there was something else in Korea that U.S. troops hadn't been faced with before. It was called "give-up-itis" for want of a better term. I had a young trooper die in my squad. It seemed there was nothing we could do for him. When he was captured, he had been waiting to hear news about a serious operation his mother had to undergo back home. Now he didn't know if his mother was dead or alive, plus he had seen a lot of his buddies killed in action, so he just went into a state of depression. And unless you had somebody to keep an eye on you, you could crawl into a corner, throw

a blanket over your head, and be dead in a period of twenty-four hours.

One day they called out the names of nineteen of us, and told us we were going to welcome some Marines as they brought them into the prison camp. They drove us in a truck and we had no idea where we were, but we could hear the sound of Allied artillery. Our Chinese guards took off in fear, and, surprisingly, some Korean civilians helped us hide out in a house. We were in Chinese uniforms — those Chinese hats with the earflaps — and we had no weapons, so we were in quite a predicament. But we couldn't figure out why these Koreans were helping us. Early the next morning we saw an Allied spotter plane, and somebody got the idea to take down some of the hut's wallpaper, which was peeling from the walls, and cut it into strips that would spell out "POW" and the figure nineteen. So we laid this stuff out on the rice paddy, and with some shell casings we spelled out "rescue" and ran back into the house. A few minutes later the spotter plane came down real low and looked at it, and we were waving our old dirty skivvy shirts at him. He wagged his wings and flew away. About fifteen minutes later he came back and dropped a message in a streamer saying he'd sent for help. And soon three tanks came around the bend. Luckily one of us had the idea to take the hats off, because later, the tank lieutenant said he had almost mistaken us for Chinese troops. Then, we asked where we were and found out that we were in South Korea. We had crossed the 38th Parallel and didn't realize it, that's why the Koreans were so friendly.

We were just overjoyed to be back with the Allies. I think every man had tears in his eyes, overwhelmed with joy. We realized we were going home. I weighed one hundred pounds. All of us were malnutrition cases. But we were the only group ever to escape from the enemy in Korea. And we were the first Allied troops to come home as graduates of the political indoctrination course.

Asian nations on the Soviet wish list, and that only America was in a position to stop them. As such, the Korean war would mark a turning point in American life, the initiation of the nation into its new self-appointed status as the free world's protector. How times had changed. Wishing to avoid foreign commitments, Americans had argued vigorously before entering the century's two world wars. Now, seizing their new identity, they left the serenity of their prefabricated homes and marched off willingly to defend a nation most of them had never even heard of.

The Korean War began when the North, with the blessing of Stalin, invaded the South, but it took a bloody turn for the worse when the Chinese Communists joined in, led by some of the same fighting men who had defeated Chiang only months before. The attitude of the American soldier was naive, at best. Many figured they would be but a week in Korea, "settle the gook thing," then head home. They believed Truman when he described their mission as a "police action," as if they were going to Asia not for war, but to bang the heads of a few delinquents discovered breaking into the corner drugstore. In fact, three years would pass before the fighting in Korea was done, leaving that nation ravaged, but divided politically much as it had been when the conflict began. And for that outcome, fifty-four thousand Americans and over two million Koreans would die.

MacArthur's motorcade makes its way through downtown San Francisco. Enterprising merchandisers cashed in on the MacArthur hysteria by offering buttons, pennants, and replicas of his familiar corn cob pipe.

Korea presented Americans with an odd dissonance. Because it was the first hot flash of the Cold War, there were fears, the longer the war drew out, that the fighting had become the preamble to the dreaded World War III. Contemplating the coming atomic exchange, people imagined a world of Hiroshimas, each one of them as ugly as the one described by John Hersey in the *New Yorker*, and began to construct bomb shelters (the newest addition to the local hardware store's merchandise) next to the swing sets in their backyards, cinder-block caves where they would huddle until the next civilization emerged. Yet, because, in the end, it did not expand and in fact became America's first limited war, fought only to a draw, Korea also frustrated them. They feared the atomic possibility, but felt cheated by a war which was to be ended short of its natural conclusion. If the issues at stake were worth fighting for, why, many people asked, were they not worth fighting all the way to victory?

General Douglas MacArthur, the commander of the American forces in Korea, agreed. He saw something unmanly, unprincipled in a war of limited aims. MacArthur had fought valiantly in World War I and had served as the commander of American forces in the Pacific during World War II. In Korea, he had entered at a moment when that nation seemed lost and, against all odds, reversed the tide, driving the Communists back above the 38th Parallel. But when the general announced his desire to go deeper, through North Korea and across the Yalu River into mainland China, and suggested that the Nationalist Chinese join him, the president ordered him back, fearing a deadly confrontation with Mao. This was the era of containment, not liberation, and in the Administration's view anything more than the restoration of a divided Korea risked the launch of World War III.

When MacArthur, in a display of extraordinary bravado, then resisted Truman's orders, he was called home, whereupon the nation, in a gasp of nostalgia for the old kind of war, supported the fired general over the more pragmatic view of the White House. How was it, people asked, that American boys should die to free the people of South Korea, but not the people of the North? And why was it that the Koreans deserved to be fought for, but not the Chinese?

MacArthur had been fired, but his return was, paradoxically, like one long, confetti-filled victory lap and the egotistical general loved every shred of it. He started in Japan, where over 400,000 turned out to cheer him, then flew to Hawaii, where another 100,000 met him on the tarmac. From there, he went to San Francisco, where 500,000 welcomed him en route to give a speech at city hall, and finally landed in Washington, where a defiant Congress invited him to address the nation. The enthusiasm was overwhelming. One congressman said he "heard the voice of God" in MacArthur's thundering tones; former President Herbert Hoover discovered in him "the reincarnation of Saint Paul." A ticker tape parade followed in New York City, even larger and louder than the one that had greeted Lindbergh in 1927. Then, oddly, the ovation stopped. People still respected the "old soldier," as he called himself, but MacArthur, making his case as he toured the country, sounded more and more like a man whose time had passed. The world the general described, the world in which his kind of war could be fought, was a world untouched by the light of the atomic bomb, the world as it would never be again.

Respect for the flamboyant general ran high and talk of a MacArthur presidency persisted. But in the end, America would turn to the general's former deputy, the more cautious Dwight Eisenhower, to take them forward through the rest of the fifties.

8

Mass Markets
1953–1961

Mass Markets 1953–1961

On July 24, 1959, tens of thousands of curious Russian citizens began filing through Moscow's Sokolniki Park to view an exhibition of American consumer goods. Models wearing America's newest fashions strutted down hastily constructed runways; a television camera recorded interviews with the Russian visitors, then broadcast them, in color, to the crowd's evident glee; a robot named Ramac 305 delivered written replies to any of 3,500 questions on life in the United States (with Russians most interested in those requesting information on American material success); and a never-ending film loop displayed idyllic views of American society to the jazzy accompaniment of Leonard Bernstein's music.

The show, which also included samples of American shoes, lingerie, and cameras, and featured a beauty salon where Russian women could opt for a new Western hairdo (and then pause for a "photo moment"— or Polaroid — photograph), would have been unthinkable a decade before when the Cold War was just beginning. But after Joseph Stalin's death in 1953, and the ascension of the bulky but charming Nikita Khrushchev, a momentary thaw in East-West relations ensued. Khrushchev denounced Stalin, loosened Soviet reins on the Eastern bloc (with the notable exception of Hungary, where he eventually tightened them), freed thousands of prisoners from the gulags, and encouraged cultural exchanges with the West. A similar exhibition, featuring the achievements of Soviet society (and a model of the new *Sputnik* rocket), had recently opened in New York. Yet, the outstretched hands of the two rising superpowers were not to be confused with those of long-separated friends. The Cold War had simply shifted to a new arena.

The American vice president, Richard Nixon, saw the Moscow exhibition as an opportunity to promote both American ideological supremacy and his own personal ambitions for the White House. Given the assignment to go to the Soviet Union and officially open the show, he spent weeks studying Russian history (encountering, for the first time, the work of a brilliant young Harvard scholar named Henry Kissinger) and poring over State Department and CIA documents.

Nixon learned Russian phrases and consulted with leaders who had met Khrushchev before. Ready for a fight, the man who had built his reputation combating communist influence inside America then headed for the source.

Nixon was met coolly at the Moscow airport. The American Congress had passed a bill declaring "Captive Nations Week" only days before, a direct slap at the Soviet Union's control of Eastern Europe (Americans were told to spend the week praying for those living under the tyranny of communism), and the Russians were unhappy. "People should not go to the toilet where they eat," Khrushchev scolded Nixon privately. "This resolution stinks." Later that day, when they were filmed before the exhibition's new television cameras, the two men's spat evolved into a lively piece of international theater.

"How long has America existed?" chided Khrushchev as they made their opening remarks. "One hundred and fifty years," replied Nixon (in fact, it had been 183 years). "Well, then, we will say that America has been in existence for one hundred and fifty years and this is the level she has reached. We have existed not quite forty-two years and in another seven years we will be on the same level as America. When we catch up with you, in passing you by, we will wave to you." Nixon smiled nervously as Khrushchev continued his barrage. Referring derisively to the Captive Nations resolution, the Soviet leader looked around him at the men and women who were still finishing the construction of the exhibition hall and asked, "You know who this man is? He is the vice president of the United States. He says you are slaves. Are you slaves?"

Like actors after a first take, the two men then watched the replay of their exchange on the color television monitors. Nixon was disappointed; the Soviet leader had clearly bullied him. But there would be more opportunities to push his case. Examining the exhibition's model kitchen, the proud vice president declared that it included many appliances dedicated to easing the burden on American housewives. Unimpressed, Khrushchev pronounced that the Soviets do not confine their women to the stove. And, anyway, the new devices were merely gadgets — unnecessary and, no doubt, prone to disrepair. "Don't you have a machine that puts food into the mouth and pushes it down?"

Undeterred, Nixon said the kitchen could be found in a home costing about $14,000, a price affordable even to the average American laborer. Khrushchev scoffed. And it has been built to last "not longer than twenty years, so builders could sell new houses at the end of that period . . . We build firmly, for our . . . grandchildren." But the vice president, and capitalism, would have the last word. Before the end of his visit, Nixon would deliver a thirty-minute television address to the Russian people — unedited — and, fulfilling a promise to a Pepsi executive, coax the Russian premier into posing for a photograph sipping (what else?) Pepsi-Cola.

For Americans, the remaining years of the 1950s were a period of enormous physical and psychic transformation. Home life changed. Where they had once been a rural people, and then an urban people, they now became a decidedly *sub*urban people, the tentacles of some metropolitan areas reaching out so far they interlocked, like the roots of neighboring trees, with those of the next sprawl. Work life changed. Sometime between 1950 and 1960, the number of people employed to shuffle paper around desks or sell things in stores exceeded

U.S. farm population, 1950: **4,393,000**

U.S. farm population, 1960: **2,780,000**

the number of people who made things with their hands or operated machinery that made things, and those employed by large corporations far exceeded those who worked for themselves. Even farmers, once the backbone of the nation's economy and the symbol of American self-reliance, left the soil in large numbers to join the commuting hordes, the hands that once cupped the earth between their fingers now more likely to rest on the keyboard of a Smith-Corona electric. Shopping changed, making room for a burst of new chain stores and the first suburban malls. Supermarkets began to replace grocery stores; McDonald's started to push aside the diner; and the Holiday Inn was making the downtown hotel obsolete. Even baby care changed. Isolated from her own parents and increasingly dependent upon the advice of experts, the fifties mom scoured Benjamin Spock's *Common Sense Book of Baby and Child Care* for answers to questions on everything from diaper changing to breast-feeding (and felt cheated when he repeatedly counseled them to follow not some new scientifically proven route, but their own instincts).

The postwar economy continued to purr, but the engine was fueled not so much by bigger and better products as by bigger and cleverer campaigns to sell products. In this sense, the fifties picked up where the twenties had left off, and, in fact, many of the emblems of the twenties — the seductive advertising, the appeal of credit, the lively popular culture — came roaring back in the fifties, delivered now at an even more demanding volume. If the twenties had radio, the

Americans were getting married younger and having babies sooner than ever before, leading the birthrate to a twentieth-century high by mid-decade.

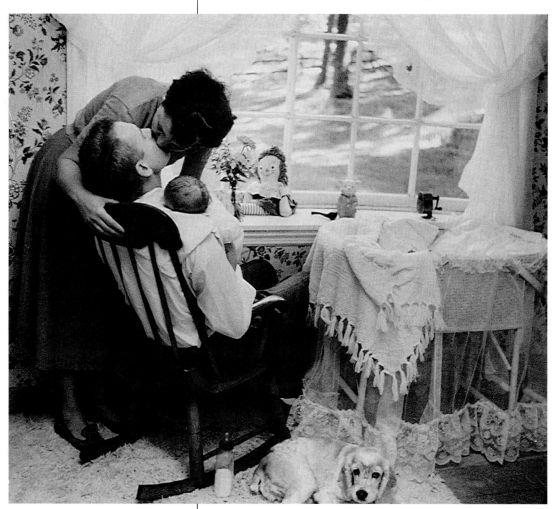

> *"These are the days in which even the mildly critical individual is likely to seem like a lion in contrast with the general mood. . . . when men of all social disciplines and all political faiths seek the comfortable and the accepted; when the man of controversy is looked upon as a disturbing influence; when originality is taken as a mark of instability; and when, in minor modification of the scriptural parable, the bland lead the bland."*
>
> *Economist John Kenneth Galbraith*

fifties had television. If the twenties listened to jazz, the fifties danced to rock and roll. If the twenties built roads, the fifties built interstate highways. If the twenties consumer bought "on time," the fifties consumer flashed a credit card. The patron saint of the new economy was the 1920s General Motors chairman, Alfred P. Sloan, whose innovations in marketing — creating consumers where there were none simply by convincing people that they needed to buy a new car each year even if their old one worked fine — now held sway over much of American commerce. In the fifties, new markets were made daily, by the lilt of a clever jingle or, more likely, the rush of beguiling imagery contained in a brash new television campaign (television being the one home appliance that could be used to sell other home appliances to its owner). Advertising, said sociologist David Potter, had now become an American institution, exerting as much, if not more, influence on human behavior as the school, the church, and city hall.

More people than ever before shared in the abundance brought by America's unprecedented economic growth, a fact that served as a potent piece of propaganda in the continuing rivalry with the Soviet Union. There was even an air of patriotism attached to all the buying and selling, to the uplifting suburban life, and to the devotion to the corporate organization: the sense that a healthy and robust American economy was itself a more powerful demonstration of the supremacy of Western ideas than could be produced by all the bluster of all the Cold War's politicians and generals (though there continued to be plenty of that) and that the happy, smiling suburban families, with their gleaming new appliances, would serve as an advertising-obsessed society's advertisement to the world, the slogan "come join us" glittering beneath them.

But along with the contented life of the suburbs, the fifties also contained a growing undercurrent of rebellion — both earnest and angry. The plentiful society inspired many of those deprived of the American promise to stand up and demand more. And the competition inherent to the Cold War prompted some in the broader population to question whether America, flaunting the virtues of democracy, had closely examined its own house. If the world was really looking to the United States for leadership, asked some in the generation that rose to power in 1960, then would not America lead best by example? And if the nation's presence needed to be felt outside her borders, should it not be in the form of peaceful volunteers, doing good works, rather than men of war? These were the ideas of wide-eyed youth, arriving at the same time that a vigorous youth culture, at once playful and visionary, appeared ascendant across the nation. With one of youth's own in the White House — the youngest and most glamorous president ever to be elected to the throne of American government — the nation would enter the new decade flush with the enthusiasm born of idealism.

It was perhaps inevitable that the population shift that deposited so many Americans into the "crabgrass frontier," as one historian described the suburbs, would bring upon the nation a fresh way of life. Millions were making the transition to suburbia, now, stepping up the ladder from tiny urban apartments, eager to enjoy the sense of satisfaction offered by home ownership and a plot of land, a modest flower garden and a backyard swing. The cities they left behind were in decay; with so little new building they felt more like the relics of a bypassed civilization and, in a sense, they were. For the future belonged to the suburbs, featur-

In the fifties ideal, women dedicated their lives to becoming good home-makers, mothers, and loving wives. Often isolated inside their suburban communities, housewives, such as these, relied on each other and the ubiquitous television for social inter-action and companionship.

"a device that permits people who haven't anything to do to watch people who can't do anything"

Comedian Fred Allen, describing television, which hastened the demise of his radio program

ing larger houses now than had been built for the Levittowns of the late 1940s, in multiple styles and colors, erected near shopping centers — some of the first — containing all the essential retail businesses and services (and a few unessential ones, too).

Thanks to the postwar economic boom but also to the redistribution of income achieved by the success of union wage demands and the progressive income tax, the middle class was now rapidly swelling. Many Americans were for the first time enjoying the fruits of success: health insurance, vacations, savings accounts, and freedom from landlords. And they came to the suburbs to live their lives of abundance, settling in places with names that suggested rustic Edens — Park Forest, Victorian Woods, Ivy Hills, Crystal Stream — all the while dreaming of California, the state that looked from a distance to be nothing more than a suc-cession of suburbs, each one sunnier than the next, and where everything — jobs, money, and even one's neighbor — seemed to be headed.

Wherever they were, the suburbs were now much more than a new place to live: they offered a whole new method of being, stressing openness (as symbol-ized by the ubiquitous picture window), safety, conformity, and belonging. Per-haps because suburbanites were in some cases forging communities where none had existed before, and where they were often many miles from the nearest urban center; or because many of them had left parents and grandparents and extended ethnic communities to come to places where they knew no one; or because their situations were so transitory, their jobs often sending them packing to other regions of the country where they had to quickly reassemble themselves in new

Making a new life in suburbia: "Coffee klatches" and "flying flags on the holidays"

My husband, John, and I were living in Massachusetts in 1953. John had just come out of the service, and work was scarce. We were wondering what to do when my mother-in-law saw an article in the *Saturday Evening Post* about the suburban community of Levittown offering five swimming pools and land for churches and schools. She said, "I think you guys ought to look into this." Since we had no concrete future plans at the time, John moved in with some of his family in Princeton, New Jersey, and while he was down there, he picked out what would become our home. It was so easy. We didn't have to worry about any kind of property settlement or picking out land. The whole community was there waiting for us.

Moving into the suburbs was an adventure. We traveled twelve hours from Boston with a truckload of furniture. We piled a garbage can and my son's crib on the back of the truck, and I sat in the front with the goldfish, the plants, and my son on my lap. We lived too far away to prepare our new home before our arrival. In fact, we hadn't even seen the house. We arrived and took our first steps through the back door and into our new home. I remember it took me five hours to get from my back door to the bedrooms because of the parade of salesmen waiting to greet us on our arrival. They were selling gravesites, landscaping, storm windows, and milk and bread and diapers. It was really something. One day after we were all moved in, the property was landscaped.

One of the most important things about suburban life was forming a bond with your neighbors. Our town was a veritable melting pot with people coming from all over upstate Pennsylvania, New Jersey, and Philadelphia. I think we confided in each other to alleviate the loneliness of coming from different sections of the country. Mothers and dads and grandparents weren't there. Sisters and brothers weren't there. We shared the same problems of trying to build a home, raise children, and find work. Everybody was the same age, and everybody wore the same clothes. If you ever had a disaster in your family, there'd always be an outpouring of help from your neighbors, and I think it all stemmed from that fact that each and every one of us came here alone.

The woman's role was to keep the home fires burning. We were expected to keep a clean home, to look after and discipline our children, and to take care of our husbands. It was very easy, really, yet we were all a bit lonesome. There were many, many get-togethers. Around ten o'clock in the morning, we'd sit out and have coffee klatches, and there'd be kids running all around and you'd be watching this child and that child. We'd baby-sit each other's children when need be. There were plenty of home demonstration parties. Even

though they were commercial, they still brought us together.

The suburbs was the perfect place to raise children, and children were our primary focus. The statistics said that every home had at least two and a half children. When we first moved to our town there were only three obstetricians. As the birthrate rose, the obstetricians extended their office hours to 2:00 A.M. Our hospital and nursery were enlarged. Many times in the newspaper we'd see at least three columns of names listed in the birth announcements for the week. There was much emphasis placed on babies and bringing them up during their first year of life. We used Dr. Spock's

> —*Harriet Osborn, born in 1928, has played an active role in Levittown community affairs throughout her life. She worked for thirty-two years at the local newspaper the* Courier Times, *serving as advertising secretary and then assistant to the major accounts manager. She was a charter member of the town library, which had its beginnings in the basement of a neighborhood pharmacy. She participated in the planning of Levittown's twenty-fifth and fortieth anniversaries and in many fund-raising drives over the years. Her son, Frank, is what Harriet calls a "second-generation Levittowner," residing, with his wife and son, close to the home where he grew up.*

Top: *The Osborn family — John, Harriet, and their son, Francis, Christmas, 1955.*
Above: *John Osborn checking the camping equipment in the back of the family station wagon, summer, 1956.*

guide religiously, and we would compare notes all the time. Once in a while we'd hear a seminar on how to raise children. Everything in the stores was geared toward children. It was always, "What do children want and what will parents buy for their children?"

The television also served as a baby-sitter. You could just put your children in front of the TV and while they watched *Davy Crockett* and *Ding Dong School,* you could make supper. TV taught our children things that we couldn't teach them. It taught them right from wrong. TV was our information box and our link to the outside world, and, of course, it entertained us. My family always loved the dramas and the variety and comedy shows. We saw Elvis from the waist up on *The Ed Sullivan Show.* We loved the programs that focused on family like *Ozzie and Harriet* and *Leave It To Beaver.* We identified with these pictures on the television screen, and they became an integral part of our lives. Appointments and outings were sometimes canceled because our favorite shows were on. We'd say, "I can't go to the doctor on Monday. *I Love Lucy* is on Monday." On Sundays we had to see *The Ed Sullivan Show.* It was a "have to" situation.

Funny things happened when the TV shows were done live. I remember when Betty Furness was promoting the Westinghouse refrigerator and she tried to open the door but the door stuck, and she pulled and pulled and pulled. There was a live drama we used to watch starring Ed Begley, Sr. At one point he fell over and had to crawl across the front of the stage set. A cameraman accidentally caught him, and so we saw him crawling across the front of our TV screen. Sometimes we'd be sitting around the TV and the set would look great and then all of a sudden the picture would get a little dimmer and a little dimmer, and I'd ask my husband, "Is there something wrong with the lights, dear?" And he'd say, "No, it's the TV again." And we had to wait until things were adjusted in the studio. These were common occurrences, and we took them in stride.

People seemed more patriotic back then. We flew our flag on almost every holiday. If somebody had a flag of a certain size, you'd go out and buy a bigger flag. We were just keeping up with the Joneses. But regardless, we'd be flying the American colors on patriotic holidays and even on birthdays, anniversaries, and get-togethers. As I saw it, patriotism is just a love of country, and a love of country is a love of home. In those days, we were just trying to have a good home in a good country. There were few worries. We could afford the house, and we could afford to clothe our child, and everybody else clothed their children. It was a good life. It was the American dream that we experienced, and we experienced it firsthand.

surroundings, they lived lives that put a high value on social skills. They were, in the language of sociologist David Riesman, who first charted the phenomenon, more "other-directed" than "inner-directed," more concerned with blending in than standing out. Suburbanites joined PTAs, held Tupperware parties, and did (mostly Republican) political party canvassing. They resisted privacy (a common house floor plan had no interior doors, save those for the bathroom) and frowned upon behavior out of the norm.

Riesman saw this as a marked (and regrettable) shift in American culture, the rejection of the time-honored focus on individuality and entrepreneurial spirit that had characterized much of the nation's history in favor of the sense of harmony experienced in the collective. Human motivation was redirected from the self to the group, and a big emphasis (with Cold War implications) was put on being part of the team. At home, this took the form of shared values as well as shared experience (Riesman compared the suburb to "a fraternity house at a small college"), the masking of ethnic differences and the embracing of a common religion, less important for the meaning of its scripture than the opportunity it provided for yet another place to meet and agree. (Not coincidentally, "one nation under God" was added to the Pledge of Allegiance in 1954, "In God We Trust" to American currency a year later.)

But the modern workplace, as experienced in the 1950s, may have required even more other-directed skills than the home. Small businesses were disappearing while Americans went to work for large and impersonal bureaucracies. Not only did local ownership give way to chain stores but an ever-increasing segment of the workforce represented men who worked at the behest of other men in enterprises controlled distantly by someone (or group of someones) whom he would most likely never meet. The new white-collar employee who emerged at this time was easily caricatured: he rode the commuter train to work (or drove one of the fifties' brash new cars, big as a yacht and full of chrome and fins), wearing a gray flannel suit, and once there participated eagerly in work of a paper-pushing variety, which he fervently undertook to promote the interests of the firm (be it business, law, government or some other "organization") and his place in it, never questioning authority, subsuming his wishes to the larger needs of the company, in return for the security and perquisites that guaranteed a continuing life of affluence.

The new enterprises were part of a profound shift taking place in the American economy. To please others, to conform to superficial niceties, to be congenial and easy to get along with — these were the requirements of a society whose principal focus had turned from work as production to work as the manipulation of demand. What mattered most to the fifties businessman was not the product as much as the expansion of the sales volume for that product. The innovator had been replaced by the marketer — just in time to exploit an exciting new medium.

By 1956 there were, for the first time, more white-collar workers in the United States than blue-collar, and large corporations seemed to influence just about every aspect of their employees' lives — from issuing company neckties to training the spouses of junior executives to be good corporate wives. Here, corporate recruiters interview college seniors at Michigan State University.

The new corporate culture: "An impressive-sounding title" and "a job for life"

My first big job offer out of college was from the Portland [Oregon] Gas and Coke Company, with a beginning salary of $500 a month, and that was pretty good money in 1958. When they hired me, my wife was very happy that we'd have a steady paycheck to support our family, and I was glad to be working for a growing, established company with excellent benefits and a certain amount of prestige. At that time, once you made the decision to take a job, you pretty well figured you were going to stay there the rest of your life. I know I felt that way, so I was feeling rather excited about my new job and my new, impressive-sounding title, which was market research assistant or some such thing.

—*Jack Trachsel was born in 1931. He eventually remarried his wife, Sally, and brought his family to London, where, determined now to resist the pressures of corporate life, he worked for Exxon. The family returned to Portland in 1973, and Trachsel eventually went back to work at Portland Gas, which had adopted a new name, Northwest Natural Gas Company. Now retired, he lives outside Portland.*

Trachsel, fourth from right in black suit, at a corporate meeting for Portland Gas and Coke, 1959.

During my first month at the company, I was put in an orientation program, and unfortunately, I was a little shocked by the corporate culture; people just weren't very productive. I was right out of school — really an eager beaver ready to accomplish all sorts of great feats of marketing, but at the gas company, nobody worked real hard. On my very first day I was introduced to a sales supervisor. He was a tall, good-looking guy in his late forties — he looked like an executive. He didn't look terribly pleased when our supervisor said, "Jack's going to tag along with you today and sort of find out what you do." After we drove around for a while and took a long coffee break, he looked at his watch and said, "You know, I've got a bunch of things I got to do this afternoon, of sort of a personal nature, so I'm just going to drop you off here in the parking lot. My suggestion is you just go on home. Nobody will ever know." And this was my first day on the job! I started watching this guy, and I noticed that every morning he'd have a sales meeting at about 8:30. And then at about ten o'clock, he'd grab his briefcase and charge out of the office, taking very long strides. Everyone thought, "Boy, what a go-getter — he's out to get the market." Well, it turned out that he had another full-time job! He had worked it out very carefully. He was only discovered when his two bosses met at a cocktail party.

Now, that was certainly an extreme case, but the daily routine for the rest of us was not all that taxing. The two-martini lunch was *de rigueur*. All of us in management were just expected to have a couple of drinks in the middle of the day. And if you went and had three or four, that was okay, too. My boss was a member of the Arlington Club, an all-male social club, and he used to take me and the other marketing people to lunch there a few times a week. We would go into the bar, and if you

got there anytime after twelve, there would be men three deep at the bar, and bartenders mixing the drinks just as fast as they could. Of course, we talked about business at these meetings, but after several martinis you wonder just how effective these meetings were. Some people would come roaring back into the office about four o'clock in the afternoon just long enough to check their phone messages and get ready for the happy hour. I guess all of this drinking was considered kind of macho and also sort of sophisticated. It was almost a guarantee that if you declined cocktails at lunch and didn't go out in the evening with the other management people, your career was pretty much dead in the water. You wouldn't be fired, of course, but you'd probably be subject to some not-so-subtle ostracism.

There was a certain amount of conformity in the atmosphere at the office. Our dress code was pretty rigid, so we were always expected to wear conservative business suits, with conservative ties and white shirts, and polished shoes. Just about everybody in the office had a gray flannel suit — at least the younger crowd. I had two of them. It just didn't do your career any good at all to wear, say, a checkered sport coat. Or if you came to work without a tie, you might face some discipline. But I really didn't mind the dress code or the drinking. I think most people liked to be dressed alike and to follow the same sort of social customs.

The office was staffed entirely by white men, except, of course, for the secretaries, who were hired for their good looks. At that time, you could write an ad for a newspaper saying "Must be between 18 and 30 years, and attractive . . ." and though the newspaper ads didn't say it specifically, of course, to apply you had to be white. As a matter of fact, one of my supervisory responsibilities at that time included the administration of the office, so the office manager reported to me. He was a

bit of an old fuddy-duddy, and his main interest in hiring secretarial and clerical help was that he get the most qualified person for the job, so I gave him a bit of leeway. He would interview perhaps twenty applicants and, at my direction, pick three. Then he would send them to me for the final interview, and I would simply just pick the best-looking one.

I think there was a tacit understanding that if you were going to be a secretary or a clerical person in this particular business organization, you were expected to — if not necessarily fraternize — at least enjoy yourself at all of the office parties. And it was definitely bad form for a secretary not to come to a party — that just didn't happen. There were not a lot of company functions that involved wives, certainly the Christmas party didn't. We usually had it on the last working day before Christmas, which was often Christmas Eve, so instead of being with our families we would be at these wild parties. And on the next working day the boys would meet and compare notes as to how many of them had scored with the secretaries.

After working for a while in this environment, I started to defend this way of life to my wife. The two martinis at lunch, the happy hours, the office parties, it just seemed like the way to go. I got promoted a number of times, and I was pretty pleased with myself. I had my company car, a Chevrolet, and I enjoyed going out every evening after work to the local watering hole with the other people of my rank in the company, which meant getting home rather late most evenings. I used to lecture my wife that if I were a shoe clerk I wouldn't have to do this. "But," I'd say, "I'm not a shoe clerk and we have the material advantages that come with the job and you have to accept some of this."

After eight years of this, though, I was ready to leave. My wife had divorced me, and my boss, who had a drinking problem, was getting more and more out of control. He had appointed me to be in charge of the company liquor locker and was ordering large amounts of alcohol which he would then just drink himself. I knew this would show up on the expense account records sooner or later, and I didn't know what to do about it. So when I was recruited by a firm for a job overseas, I took it, even though that violated company loyalty to a certain extent. When I look back on that time, I think it certainly would have taken a person with a great deal of character to have actively opposed a lot of the things that were going on in that company; to take a moral stand and say, "I'm not going to a Christmas party because it's Christmas Eve, and I want to be with my family and I don't want to seduce my secretary." It would have doomed your career. I didn't have the moral character, I guess. But I was certainly happy to be leaving.

Television had arrived shortly after World War II, a faded, flickering black-and-white picture so streaked through with evenly spaced white lines that it made the viewer feel as if he were watching through venetian blinds. No matter. Most people saw the medium as a miracle — a miniature theater tucked into a highboy — and even though sets cost an average of $500 (at a time when the average family earned less than $3,000 a year), more than 7 million of them were sold before the decade was out and many to people in places where there weren't yet any stations to watch.

There was something irresistible about television, and while few understood just how important it would become (more a new environment than a new mass medium, as inescapable as the weather, wrote Richard Reeves), they wanted to be there when it took off. In the medium's early years there was Howdy Doody and the World Series, but only when the rectangular cathode-ray tube was perfected in 1950 and the price of the average DuMont and Philco dropped to $200 in 1953 did the age of television truly descend upon the nation. By 1960 more than 45 million television sets had found homes, not only in the suburbs, where their elaborate wood cabinets fit quite nicely into the family room or the den, but also in inner-city taverns (where bartenders complained that patrons spent too much time watching and not enough time drinking).

More often than not, programming conformed to the new white bread standards. Ethnic and working-class radio shows like I *Remember Mama* and *The Goldbergs* were unsuccessful at making the transition to television; suburban dramas like *Father Knows Best* and *The Adventures of Ozzie and Harriet* took their place. And while the popular *I Love Lucy,* in which Desi Arnaz portrayed Cuban-American bandleader Ricky Ricardo and Lucille Ball his madcap redhead wife, was set in a New York City apartment, a sometimes theme was Lucy's wish to flee the city for the more relaxed life in Long Island or Connecticut (in the series' last season, she and Ricky finally moved to Connecticut, their friends the Mertzes in tow).

By the end of its first year on the air more than 30 million viewers tuned to CBS to watch I Love Lucy *every Monday night, making Lucille Ball, above, one of the most popular stars on television.*

Comedy, too, was different. Radio's focus on words had encouraged the dry joke, the kind of ironic turn of phrase at which comedians Jack Benny and Fred Allen excelled. Television, by contrast, thrived on the sight gag and was better suited to old-fashioned vaudevillian slapstick. Catskills comic Milton Berle had a mediocre career before joining NBC. On television, in skits where he dressed up as a woman and pranced bucktoothed before the camera, he became one of its biggest stars. *The Today Show* picked up viewers after it added a monkey, J. Fred Muggs, to the lineup of hosts. And the rubber faces of Red Skelton, Sid Caesar, Imogene Coca, and, of course, Lucille Ball gave those comedians careers that would have been impossible on radio.

I Love Lucy was an enormous hit, with as many as 45 million people watching some episodes. Even more than most shows, *Lucy* had a dizzying way of blurring the line between reality and entertainment. Arnaz and Ball were married in real life, and when Lucy got pregnant, her condition became material for the show's plot (though the puritanical times dictated that her swelled stomach be hidden from view and that she be referred to only as an "expectant mother"). Viewers so believed the couple's on-screen performances that their real-life divorce in 1960 was received as if Ricky and Lucy had split. By then, Americans were spending a third of their waking hours watching television, and many

were more involved with its dramas than they were with those of their own friends and family.

The confusion between artifice and truth was part of the magic of television. Viewed "in a ceremonial space," on a "screen populated by giants," movies, wrote Robert Hughes, had always been understood by viewers to be another reality, not their own. But since television resided in the living room (Bob Hope called it "that piece of furniture that stares back at you"), on a domestic-sized screen, it had a different effect, the feeling of looking through a peephole at something going on somewhere, someplace, and watching it happen *as* it happened.

Of course, the important thing about television was that people were looking at all. For what separated the new medium from the medium it seemed destined to replace was the simple fact that TV had pictures and radio didn't. While it was true that many families in the thirties and forties sat in a circle around the radio, listening to the evening fare, they could also listen during the day while cleaning the house or being otherwise engaged. Radio required only that listeners' ears be attentive, leaving the rest of the story to be filled in by the imagination. Television demanded their eyes.

The difference was significant because it meant that people had to give up so much more in order to be physically there for the medium. Even in the fifties, viewers were organizing their lives and daily habits around the television schedule. Studies showed a marked increase in toilet flushing at the precise

In the fifties most new television programs were geared toward young middle-class families with small children. "We're after a specific audience," said one network executive, "the young housewife . . . with two to four kids, who has to buy the clothing, the food, the soaps, the home remedies."

Writing for TV in the early days:
"We hoped the audience would see something of themselves in what we were doing, and laugh"

In the 1950s I think people liked television so much because it was about them. They would see things on television that would remind them of events in their own life — when they went out on a date or out to a show. That was the key to the success of *Your Show of Shows*: we always wrote sketches about things that happened to normal people. Quite often it was drawn directly from things that happened to us. If it happens to you, that's firsthand experience, and you know what you're talking about. Then the audience will always have immediate recognition. When we would write a sketch, the most important thing was how does this affect the people — the people that have to wait in line, that have to park the car. Writing for television, you had the feeling that you were communicating with the people.

Most of the time we had little choice but to write from our own experiences. We had an hour-and-a-half-long show to write every week. So we needed new ideas, as well as things we could always go back to. If we did a certain kind of sketch — like a husband and wife sketch — and it went well, then we'd do another husband and wife sketch. If we did a satire of a movie, we'd say, "Hey, we can do more movie satires." So you'd have something that you've tried before. It gave you something to hang your hat on. One time, the writers and I went into a delicatessen for lunch and it was so crowded you couldn't move. They seated us at this table by a swinging door that led to the kitchen. So I'm sitting there eating my sandwich and, "bang!" the door keeps flying open and hitting me on the back. The next week we wrote a sketch about that very same thing. There's this guy who gets seated next to a kitchen door, and every time the waiter tries to serve him, the door comes flying open and he gets smashed all around. So, in taking our sketches from things that happened to us first-hand, we hoped we were giving the audience something they could see themselves in, and laugh at.

One day, while we were rehearsing, my secretary came in and said, "Mr. Caesar, Dr. Einstein wants to talk to you." Of course, I didn't believe her. I looked at the guys and said, "All right. The joke is over. We're stuck here, and we gotta rehearse. We gotta get this thing going. No more joking around."

And she said, "No, no, no, Mr. Caesar. Dr. Einstein . . ."

And I just said, "Hey, the joke is over. Come on, let's not fool around. We don't have time for this."

But she was persistent, "No, it's not a joke. It really is Dr. Einstein's assistant. She said that he wants to talk to you." I still didn't really believe her, but I went up to my office and got on the phone anyway. This

Left to right: Carl Reiner, Sid Caesar, and Howard Morris in Your Show of Shows.

—Sid Caesar, born in 1922 in Yonkers, New York, started out as a musician, studying saxophone and clarinet at the Juilliard School of Music and playing in various bands before turning to comedy in the World War II service show Tars and Spar. *After successful appearances in nightclubs and in the Broadway hit* Make Mine Manhattan, *Caesar made his mark on television, costarring with Imogene Coca in the 1950s landmark hit* Your Show of Shows *and then* Caesar's Hour. *After appearing in nineteen motion pictures, Caesar returned to Broadway in 1989 in* Sid Caesar and Company. *He lives in Beverly Hills, California.*

Your Show of Shows *boasted one of the finest teams of writers and producers in television. Left to right: Mel Brooks, writer; Mel Tolkin, head writer; Hal Janis, NBC representative; Sid Caesar; Pat Weaver, president of NBC TV; Mark Harris, Sid's dresser.*

woman said, "I am with Dr. Einstein. He would like to set up a meeting with you to talk." I was so shocked I almost dropped the phone. Einstein wants to talk to me? I mean, how did he know about me? When you're doing a show, you don't really think about people actually watching. Let alone Albert Einstein. It was like Copernicus calling up and saying, "I'd like to talk to you." I mean, what am I gonna say to Einstein? "You know, I think you made a mistake in there. I don't think it is *E* equals *MC* squared; it is *EM* squared, to the umda-eighteen power, not the numbers here." You know, what am I gonna tell him? I knew I would just sit there like a little boy and listen — just to be in a room with him, my God.

Apparently, Einstein liked the character I did called the Professor. I later learned he called him the buffoon. The Professor was a big bluffer. He had this German accent and he pretended like he knew everything. We would always interview him about mundane things like food, and he would just go on and on: "Food is very important. It's vat keeps you going. It's the combination of foods that are important. You take spaghetti

and meatballs. They get along wonderful. The spaghetti would say, 'Well, here's my old friend the meatball. I'm going to surround you and we'll have a good time.' But then you get something like ice cream and pickles. They don't like each other. And when you swallow them together, they fight all the way down. . ." And he would go on and on like that. The fact that Einstein enjoyed that character was a tremendous thing for me.

Unfortunately, he passed away before I actually got to talk to him. But a little over a year later, I was up at Columbia University to give a lecture when somebody stopped me in the hall and said, "Pardon me. You're Mr. Caesar, aren't you? Allow me to introduce myself. I'm Robert Oppenheimer." We spoke for a minute and then he said, "Albert always liked you. He always talked about you. He wanted to meet you. He said that he had solved the physical equation, and he wanted to talk to you about the human equation." I was left speechless. We shook hands, and he walked away. The fact that Albert Einstein knew who I was, was so gratifying. It was one of the most beautiful moments of my life.

Swanson's first TV Dinner, above, featured turkey, corn bread dressing, gravy, peas, and whipped sweet potatoes in a package designed to look like a television set. By 1955 the company had added three other entrées and was selling 25 million TV Dinners a year.

"Should the room in which you are viewing television be darkened to resemble a movie theater? Answer: Definitely not!"

Early ad for television

moment that the most popular television shows went to commercial, and in 1954, noting how television was wreaking havoc with the family meal patterns, Swanson created the "TV Dinner," a frozen individual meal, tidily packaged in a little tray, that could be heated up and rushed to the living room.

Marketers promoted television as a way of bringing the family together. Baseball, vaudeville, and the movies all took people out of the home, they said. Television kept them there. And it was also recommended as a domestic helper. "Relax with a second DuMont," said one store display aimed at fathers who needed "a well-earned rest" from the rest of the household; and while Dad was enjoying his moment of privacy, read the same ad, Mother could be watching her own show, picking up new ideas for fashion and cooking.

Yet it was the advertisements *on* television more than those selling televisions that proved to be so revolutionary. Never before had there been as captive an audience and, as writer Earl Shorris has pointed out, never before such a flawless way to pitch products to it. Like no other sales medium in history (including, the oldest one, the sales*man*), television could present an advertiser's wares to their perfection. Automobiles always started, purred like kittens, and gleamed like freshly shined silver. Washing machines never overflowed, cleaned clothes spotlessly, and made mothers smile at their chores. Temperamental children could be quieted by a bowl of morning cereal. Tonic water never lost its fizz; frozen food was cooked to gourmet perfection; and vacuum cleaners made all rugs look like new.

Before, advertisers could only describe a product. Now the viewer could actually see it, or, more precisely, a televised representation of it, and because television was so believable, people tended to accept the television image, blended with an elaborate sales pitch, over the real one. The Marlboro Man, rugged and alone when most of the male world was manicured and suited, deeply embedded in the cocoon of a corporation, helped men believe that smoking a certain brand of cigarettes was a way for them to reclaim their masculinity; a Clairol commercial directed at the overworked mother suggested that she could reclaim her youth with a quick color rinse, leaving friends and neighbors to wonder "Does she or doesn't she?" Through television, Americans now led a mediated life, interrupted by the gentle (or not so gentle) urgings of advertisers, helping them to see their lives in special ways, requiring special needs.

Intellectuals worried about the effect television would have on society, that it would destroy reading and cheapen the culture. The word had been sacrificed, they said, at the altar of the image. Would children, excited by this endless stream of noisy pictures, ever find their way back to the exacting silence of a book? With so many people spending so many hours in passive submission, would the art of conversation wither? What was one to make of the new ceaseless sales pitch, repeated like a rosary into the ears of the nation? Had we succumbed to a gross materialism? Observers also fretted that television would take on the power they recalled from wartime propaganda; used by the wrong forces, they asked, could this seductive medium lead people astray, the way that Nazi imagery had encouraged the Germans to goose-step for Hitler?

Some of their concerns seemed fantastic. Television was fun, and if the main thing it appeared to be encouraging was buying, then who was to deny a

As automobiles became larger, fancier, and more expensive, commercials
for them became louder, livelier, and employed more visual tricks. Ads like the
one for Ford being filmed below, for instance, were less about cars than the
dream of an auto-centered suburban life. Using such techniques to great effect,
the Big Three automakers pushed new automobile sales to $65 billion in 1955
alone, a sum that represented 20 percent of the gross national product.

Advertising in the golden age of television:
The "perfect medium" to "show off the virtues" of any product

Ned Doyle, Bill Bernbach, and I founded the advertising company of Doyle Dane Bernbach on June 1, 1949. Ned and Bill had worked together at Grey Advertising, and when they decided to break off from Grey, they asked me if I wanted to come in as well. We were a very close, intimate group at Doyle Dane Bernbach. Bill Bernbach, who was the creative nucleus of the agency, once said, "Nothing will ever get between us, not even punctuation."

Our first location was on Madison Avenue. The office was on the top floor; I guess you could call it the penthouse. The only problem was, the elevator stopped at the floor below. So our people had to be young enough and sturdy enough to climb up a long flight of stairs. Of course, our clients and prospective clients also had to climb that flight of stairs if they wanted to do business with us. In a way, this was good. We were looking for clients who wanted to be different, clients who were willing to take a chance. And that meant that they had to subscribe to our approach to advertising, which was to try and be more creative than anyone else. We wanted our ads to tell the truth, but to do it in a way that spoke to the strength of the product and in a way that really made people take notice.

One of our first accounts was with Ohrbach's department store. Just about all of Ohrbach's ads appeared in New York newspapers. We knew that people didn't buy newspapers to read the ads, so we had to figure out how to attract the reader's attention, not just from the other ads, but from the newspaper articles themselves. We had to have something to say which was memorable and credible, and if you could inject some humor into it, so much the better. One Ohrbach's ad actually had a headline that said, "I hate Ohrbach's!" It featured a small, sad-looking dog that, as the copy explained, felt neglected because its owner was always running off to Ohrbach's to buy shoes, or a hat, or a dress.

When we first started the company, we relied primarily on print advertising with some radio sprinkled in. Then as the fifties wore on, television came into its own and really changed things. Suddenly you had this visual medium where you could reach millions of people — coast to coast — all at one time. And you could control exactly what the people would see and what they would hear. Like radio, you could have scripted action, but television also included the visual. It was a very powerful medium. No advertising agency could ignore television. One of our earliest and most successful major television campaigns was for the Polaroid Land camera, which took pictures that developed instantly. Of course, live television was the perfect medium to show off the virtues of an instant camera. We developed a series of live sixty-second commercials featuring extremely popular personalities, such as Steve Allen, Garry Moore, and Jack Paar, demonstrating how the camera worked and what great pictures it took. The viewers actually got to see the picture develop before their eyes. Since it was live television, we had no control when things went wrong. Once one of our spokesmen, I think it was Steve Allen, took a picture that didn't develop properly. Being the professional that he was, he just simply took another photograph and said, "See? You know instantly whether or not you've got the shot."

Another early client was Jack Dreyfus, who had developed a small mutual fund as part of his brokerage business. Now, Jack Dreyfus was one of the new breed of businessmen who were willing to take chances and try different things. So he was excited when we proposed doing some sixty-second television spots. At this time, no other mutual fund or brokerage business had ever used television advertising. The most famous of those ads was one that showed the Dreyfus lion going through the subway turnstile. Dreyfus had been using the lion as his company symbol for some time, but now with television, you could actually see the lion move and hear it roar.

Left to right: Dane, Bill Bernbach, and Ned Doyle, 1950.

—Maxwell Dane was born in 1906 in Cincinnati, Ohio. After his family moved to New York City in 1923, Dane — who was still in high school — began his advertising career as an office boy for Gillman, Nicole, and Rothmans. He went on to work in the advertising departments of various companies, including Stern Brothers, the New York Evening Journal, *and* Look *magazine, before founding Maxwell Dane, Inc., in 1944. Five years later he cofounded Doyle Dane Bernbach, where he remained until retiring in 1971. He then served on the board of directors of DDB until 1986.*

Throughout the 1950s, Europe was still rebuilding and American companies were thriving, and helping to set the economic ideal. America was the principal supplier to the world, so our economy was becoming more global. As American companies expanded overseas, advertising agencies had to develop ways of handling them. London, Dusseldorf, France, these were major areas for our clients' advertising in the later 1950s. In addition to handling American companies overseas, we also acquired a few foreign clients — Volkswagen being our most famous. When we first landed the Volkswagen account in the early fifties, they were selling very few cars in America. This was the era of the big American car. The Volkswagen was unique in its smaller size, lower cost, and low fuel consumption. It was a simple, reliable, honest, and very unusual car, so Bill Bernbach developed an advertising campaign that reflected that. His ads stressed the quality and reliability of the car and were aimed at people looking for an affordable second car, as well as at the growing youth market looking to buy its first car. Appearing on both television and in magazines, the Volkswagen ads were a sharp departure from all of the other automotive advertising. People read them, laughed at them and believed them, and by the early sixties, sales for this unusual car were booming.

Doyle Dane Bernbach started in 1949 with about $500,000 in billings. In four or five years it had grown to $5 million, and by 1960 it had reached $20 million. And it wasn't just DDB; advertising in general enjoyed substantial growth during that period — thanks largely to the postwar economy, greater competition among manufacturers and the growth of television as a viable advertising medium. But in addition to the strong economic growth, advertising seemed to have a subliminal influence on people that I was not immediately aware of. One year when my wife and I were on vacation in Palm Springs, we visited a synagogue where we met a French Jew who had recently emigrated to the United States. In the course of our conversation, we asked him what made him decide to live in the United States. He said he had been visiting New York when he saw an advertisement on the subway. The ad, which was one of DDB's most famous, read, "You don't have to be Jewish to love Levy's real Jewish Rye." The ad made him laugh, made him feel welcome, and made him decide that America was where he wanted to live. I never thought that advertising could have such impact on people's lives.

prosperous nation that? Commentators also pointed out that the new medium was doing a great deal to knit the country together, blending differences in a *positive* way that reflected consensus, not forced conformity. Not everything on the tube was junk. Television pictures let people see how other people lived and introduced them to culture, albeit a lowbrow variety. For many blue-collar families, the "theater" they saw on the box was the only theater they would ever see. And anyway, television was only part of a richly developing mass culture. If the overall feeling was one of superficiality, then perhaps that was less the fault of the medium than the times.

Indeed, the fifties were the backdrop for an avalanche of production in popular entertainment, much, but not all, of it fleeting. Movies, seeking to compete with television, moved to the drive-in and tried experimental formats like 3-D, Cinerama, and stereo sound. Music now appeared on long-playing records. And a new kind of amusement park, the "theme park," opened around the country, led by the establishment of Walt Disney's Disneyland in California.

Billed as entertainment for both children and adults, and built across 160 acres formerly used as an orange grove, Disneyland was an improvement on traditional amusement parks like Coney Island (which, like the cities where they were built, now were largely neglected). It had more than roller coasters and Ferris wheels (rides in the Disney lexicon were "attractions"; customers were "guests"). Wanting to educate children as well as thrill them, Disney created within Disneyland a "Tomorrowland" set, which borrowed from the popular theme of the 1939 World's Fair; a "Fantasyland" area, which brought Disney cartoon figures to life; a "Frontierland," which revived the pioneer spirit of the Wild West; and a "Main Street," responding to the creeping nostalgia across the country for a simpler time, which re-created America's forgotten Main Street as it might have looked at the turn of the century.

To bring his $17-million Disneyland dream to reality, Walt Disney put together an "Imagineering" team to design a park that would seem larger than life. In Sleeping Beauty Castle, below, larger stones were used at the building's base followed by smaller ones toward the top in order to make the seventy-five-foot spires appear even taller.

When it opened in July 1955 (coinciding with a Disneyland television special hosted by Ronald Reagan), the event attracted so many people it was nearly a disaster. Traffic jammed the Santa Ana Freeway, food ran out, a gas leak shut down Fantasyland, and the day's blistering heat caused women's high heels to sink into the freshly laid asphalt on Main Street. Still, a million visitors pushed through the turnstiles in the first seven weeks, nearly 4 million within the first year. If Disney's re-creations tended to sanitize history (and they did, like everything else in this immaculate wonderland), well, then, it only fit the idealized past that people preferred to remember. Disneyland was a monument to the wholesome, and, opening in the most wholesome of times, it became an instant symbol of American optimism. Even

In Disneyland's Fantasyland all of the attractions were based on cartoon characters, such as Dumbo, above. "What youngster," reasoned Disney, "has not dreamed of flying with Peter Pan over moonlit London, or tumbling into Alice's nonsensical Wonderland?"

Nikita Khrushchev, on his visit to the United States in 1959 for a Camp David summit, asked that Disneyland be included on his itinerary (and was outraged when the State Department informed him that security considerations would prevent his visiting there.)

Disney promoted the new park on television, to the millions of viewers who tuned to the studio's regular Wednesday night show. And both Disneyland and the Disney television series helped, in turn, to popularize Disney television, feature film, and cartoon character merchandise. The most popular Disney character, for a time, was Davy Crockett, the martyr of the Alamo. Disney's Crockett, as one might have suspected, lacked the outrageousness of the original, who had been a bit of a drunk and a scoundrel, but scoundrels don't sell merchandise and television's Crockett sold a lot: in 1955 alone, millions of Davy Crockett guns, Davy Crockett lunch boxes, Davy Crockett records, Davy Crockett sweatshirts, and Davy Crockett (fake) coonskin caps. During the craze, coonskins were in such demand the price leaped to eight dollars a pound and, as historian William Manchester has reported, a retailer stuck with an oversupply of pup tents simply stenciled the words "Davy Crockett" on them and sold them all within two days.

The 1950s were an era filled with such "stuff" — Frisbees, Wiffle balls, Hula Hoops, and Mickey Mouse ears all took their turns as the merchandise of the moment, and the market that responded to them was the nation's youth. The postwar boom had brought an enormous number of children into the world (more in the years 1948 through 1953 than had arrived in the last thirty years). Now those babies, as young children, joined with teenagers, born during the war, to form an enormous youth population. They, too, reaped the benefits of an affluent society and became the focus of intense advertising and marketing campaigns.

The term "teenager," used to denote a separate phase of life between childhood and adult years, had only come into common use in the 1940s. In the years before World War I, most children went to work (and hence, adulthood) by the age of fifteen. But since then, with the extension of secondary education in the 1920s and the lack of jobs during the Great Depression, the experience of youth had been extended. Now the new American prosperity had slowed adolescence even further, fattening allowances and encouraging children to live their version of "the good life." Business, sensing a market (and teenagers, inexperienced at buying and driven more by hormones than reason, were an unusually *vulnerable* market), then directed advertising into the path of this new emerging consumer, using the medium that the baby boom children knew better than any other: television.

More than 90 percent of mothers in one study reported that their children had asked for something they had seen on television; another recorded that words repeated in commercials entered the vocabulary of infants before they could even read. Sensing a target demographic, whole industries retooled to attract the youth dollar, and they succeeded. In the fifties, billions were spent by parents on children and by teenagers on themselves. By the end of the decade, the American teenager, as a group, was spending more than the gross national product of some minor European states.

Comic books, particularly horror comic books, abounded. Movies became

In 1958 the Wham-O Manufacturing Company started one of the biggest fads of the decade when it introduced the Hula Hoop, a three-foot plastic ring that children rotated on their hips. In less than six months, Wham-O and dozens of imitators had sold nearly 30 million hoops, both in America and abroad.

Born on a mountain top in Tennessee,
Greenest state in the Land of the Free,
Raised in the woods so's he knew ev'ry tree,
Kilt him a b'ar when he only was three.
Davy, Davy Crockett
King of the wild frontier!

"The Ballad of Davy Crockett,"
which sold 4 million copies
throughout 1955

"If you want to know the truth, they're all a bunch of goddam phonies . . ."

Teenager Holden Caulfield, speaking of adults, in J. D. Salinger's Catcher in the Rye

dominated by teenage themes, most of them, like the enormously popular *Gidget,* silly and pubescent; others, like the classic *Rebel Without a Cause,* filled with adolescent angst. One of the most significant novels of the time, J. D. Salinger's *Catcher in the Rye,* portrayed the restless life of a teenager so colorfully that it was banned in the high schools of fifteen states (making it even more of a must read among those under twenty). Radio, finding its way in a world won over by the television, turned its programming over to the disc jockey (most radio music pre-1950 having been live), whose bread and butter was teenage music, promoted now as "the Top Twenty" and "the Top Ten" and sold on records at a rate that made up nearly half of all record buying in America.

Much of the teenage culture was fleeting, but what separated the fifties from past periods was that there was a teenage culture at all, and as the baby boomers grew older, so would the power and vitality of their expressions. In the fifties most of the serious rebellion came from the "Beat Generation," a relatively small group of poets and writers in their twenties who glorified the spirit of alienation (the word "beat" referred to their "weariness" with the traditions and conventions of the time). Still, even now there were plenty of signs that the younger crowd intended to shake things up, and music was one way they were going to do it.

The era's most important "teenager" passed into his twenties in 1955, the year that the world began to notice him. Elvis Aron Presley was a forty-one-dollar-a-week truck driver for the Crown Electric Company in Memphis, Tennessee,

The new teen culture included fresh fashions (ducktails, poodle cuts, rolled-up sleeves, "pop-it" necklaces), slang ("cool," "blast-off," "square") and, left, dances (the stroll, the circle, the hand jive, the bop).

Dancin' to the Bandstand: **"I would stand in front of the television, the refrigerator door my partner"**

I was about ten years old the first time I heard Elvis. I was walking past this little soda shop and I saw all of these teenagers inside having fun. So I went in, stood by the counter, and tried to pretend like I was older and more mature — like I belonged there. All the kids were talking and laughing and having a good time when all of a sudden this music came on the jukebox. Well, everybody immediately stopped what they were doing and started dancing and jumping around. I'll never forget the energy in that place. It was fantastic. After the song ended, I turned to the girl next to me and asked, "Who was that?" She looked at me as if I was from another planet and said just one word, "Elvis."

When I saw that Elvis had the kind of courage to dance and love his music and shake his hips, it helped me, because if he could feel free inside and dance and shake around, so could I. I think that every teenager in the country wanted to be like Elvis. The rock and roll of guys like Elvis and Chuck Berry was the first music that belonged to the teenagers. Our parents called it the devil's music, but rock and roll wasn't the demon. It made you feel good, it made your heart smile, it made you laugh, and it made you just jump around and dance.

American Bandstand was kind of like the first televised revolution of teenagers in this country. We could watch the show and see our peers dance and then we could go out and buy records of the music that we heard. That show brought all the teenagers together. It's the first time that we could identify with other teenagers that were on TV. When I was growing up in Darby, Pennsylvania, I would run home from Catholic school every day to watch *American Bandstand*. I couldn't wait to turn on the TV — Dick Clark, the music, and all those kids having a good time. When I watched the show, I felt liberated. It made me forget about my problems at Catholic school and the difficult life I had at home. I would watch the kids on the show dance, and I would dance along. I would spin around and do all the steps using the banister or the refrigerator door as a partner. I got pretty good with that old banister. I figured, if I could dance that well alone, imagine how I would be with a real partner. So I decided to go down there and try and get on the show.

One day I stole fifty cents from my mother's purse, played hooky from school, and hopped on a bus downtown. I tried to look older by putting on lots of makeup and making my breasts look bigger. You see, I was only thirteen and the minimum age for *Bandstand* was fourteen. I was so nervous while waiting in line to get in. I was sure somebody was going to tap me on the shoulder

Top: Bunny with Don Travarelli, whom she eventually married. Right: Dick Clark (with microphone) and dancers on the Bandstand *set.*

—*Bunny Gibson was born in 1946 in Jersey City, New Jersey. She was a dancer on* American Bandstand *from 1959 through 1962. In 1963 she married Don Travarelli, her* Bandstand *admirer, and the couple eventually had two daughters, Angel and Maria. Bunny moved to Los Angeles in 1983 to pursue an acting career. In 1997 she appeared in the film* No Ordinary Love. *She currently lives in Los Angeles and is working on a book about her* Bandstand *experience.*

and say that I was too young. But the minute I walked through those green doors, I knew I was at home. And that little studio became my home for the next several years. It was really the first place where I felt like I belonged. Every day after Catholic school, I would go in the back of the bus with my little bag full of clothes, and I would tease my hair into a big bouffant. I'd replace my oxfords with penny loafers and get into my little *Bandstand* outfit. When I got off the bus the driver would always do a double take because I would be dressed like this totally different person. I changed on the bus because I didn't want to miss one minute of that dancing.

One time Dick bused us up to New York City for a Saturday night show. When we got off the bus, people were pulling and tugging and screaming our names. This one lady went up to Frankie, one of the other dancers, and asked, "Who are you?" And he just looked up and he said, "Nobody." And that was probably the most significant thing, because we were nobodies. We were just street kids, who watched the show, and had the courage to break out of the conformity of the times and go down there and dance. I think because of that, kids all across the country loved us and could relate to us. We would get thousands of fan letters and kids would come from all over to see us. One boy saw me on the show and became infatuated with me. He came down to the studio one day to try out for the show, but they wouldn't let him on because he was too old. He was twenty and the maximum age for dancers was eighteen. Even though he couldn't get on the show, he was determined to meet me, so he had one of the other dancers, who he knew, introduce us. He was this dark, macho Italian type, who I fell for immediately. Four years later we got married.

Even on *Bandstand* we had to conform. We had a strict dress code. The guys all had crew cuts and wore ties and jackets. All of the girls' dresses had to come up high on the neck and could not reveal too much. Dick wanted to cultivate a real clean-cut look. I think that really helped change the image of rock and roll. How could rock and roll be the devil's music when all of the kids on *Bandstand* looked so nice and clean? I think the show really helped to smooth over the image of rock and roll and to bring it into the mainstream.

In the fifties we were supposed to listen to our parents and not really have a lot of thoughts of our own. We were supposed to do what we were told, which didn't really allow for much freedom. But like me, a lot of teenagers wanted to be able to find things out for ourselves: who we were inside, what we liked, what we wanted to do. Rock and roll was music from the heart and the soul that gave us a feeling of freedom. And once we got that freedom, it was like the parents really lost their control over us. Little by little, we got more and more freedom. The parents didn't have a chance.

Shopping Elvis before he was Elvis:
"All the white DJs thought he sounded too black, all the black DJs too hillbilly"

Phillips, far right, at the Memphis Recording Service, 1954, with, from left to right, Elvis Presley and his band, Bill Black (bass) and Scotty Moore (guitar).

In the early 1950s, rhythm and blues was considered the music of black people. It was even called race music, which meant that it was black music played by and for black folks. At Sun Records, I recorded primarily black rhythm and blues artists. And in talking to my distributors and friends at radio stations across the country, it was evident that a lot of young white kids were listening to black rhythm and blues. A lot of the adults I talked to were worried about that. They thought their sons and daughters were falling in love with black people. I would always just look them straight in the eye and tell them, "Your kids aren't falling in love with black or white or green or yeller. They're falling in love with the vitality of the music."

From very early on, the biggest thing that I hoped to achieve was to find a white person who could help broaden the base of rhythm and blues music and to help us get over this black and white thing. To me, Elvis Presley was the perfect person to take black rhythm and blues and combine it with white country blues into something interesting. Now, I was criticized plenty by people saying, "Hey, man, you have been recording our black artists, and now you're going to steal it and give it to some white kid." But I never set out to steal anything. I just wanted this exciting music to be heard by the widest audience possible.

When I sent a copy of Elvis's first record to Paul Ackerman, the editor of *Billboard* magazine, he said that I had to either be a damn fool or a genius to have Elvis sing a blues song written by Arthur "Big Boy" Crudup on one side ("That's All Right, Mama") and Bill Monroe's country bluegrass anthem ("Blue Moon of Kentucky") on the back side. Nobody had ever combined a black rhythm and blues song with a white country hit;

you just didn't mix things up like that. Also, Elvis's versions of these songs were unlike anything ever done before; they were fast, exciting, and powerful. I headed out on the road to try and push the record to my distributors and to the radio stations across the South. I first hit Shreveport, Louisiana, and visited my dear

> —*Sam Phillips was born in 1923 in Florence, Alabama. He began his career in music in 1942, first working as a radio station engineer and then later a disc jockey. In 1950 he founded Phillips Records and the Memphis Recording Service in Memphis, Tennessee, where he recorded rhythm and blues artists such as B. B. King and Ike Turner. Phillips opened Sun Records in 1952, in order to record both rhythm and blues artists and country and western acts. The small Sun label turned out to be a major influence in the creation of rock and roll music by recording not only Elvis Presley but also Jerry Lee Lewis, Carl Perkins, Roy Orbison, and Johnny Cash. Phillips still lives in Memphis.*

friend at KCIJ, Tommy Cutrar. But as much as he wanted to accommodate me and play the record just on the basis of friendship, he told me, "Oh, my God. Sam, if I play just the 'Blue Moon of Kentucky' side, I'll be run out of town." He was sure that his white listening audience would view Elvis's rocked-up version of Bill Monroe's classic as near sacrilege. So, next I went over to another Shreveport station, KENT. There I talked to Fats Washington, a black disc jockey who had a very popular show. He told me, "Mr. Phillips, I tell you, I've played all of your records in the past, but this guy is so white sounding. Man, he is so country. There's no way I can play this." I left Shreveport and drove on to Houston to see Paul Berlin, another old friend from WREC in Memphis who was now the number one disc jockey in Houston. And it was the same story: he couldn't possibly play Elvis Presley's record. All the white disc jockeys thought Elvis sounded too black, and all the black disc jockeys thought he sounded too hillbilly.

I left Houston with my tail dragging and headed for Dallas. And wouldn't you know it, all the bad luck I'd been having trying to push this record just kept going, and I ran into something that seldom ever happens in middle and eastern Texas: a dust storm. You have plenty of them in West Texas, but they just don't usually happen between Houston and Dallas. Even though the storm had kicked up pretty good, I decided to try and push on. I got about one hundred miles out, almost halfway there, and I just had to turn around and

go back because I thought I was going to suffocate in my car. By the next morning, the storm blew through, and I finally made it to Dallas. My first stop was the Big State Distributing Company, where I talked to a woman named Alta Hayes. Alta had a great ear for music and was just a master at selling records. As soon as I walked in, she motioned to me to come over and said, "Sam, you look like hell. Why don't we go out and have a cup of coffee?" We went to this little restaurant on the corner that had anything you wanted, as long as it was a doughnut. She sat down, looked at me, and said, "Sam, what is your concern?" Well, she knew damn well that this record was out. She had the samples on it. I said, "Well, Alta, I am concerned that this record is not going to make it." She shook her head and said, "You have got a hit record." After all I had been through the last few days, I was still really upset. I said, "Don't kid me, honey. I mean, you know what's going on." She said, "Darling, it's a hit. You've just got to give it a little time. These people don't hear this like you and me do. You ought to know that."

Well, it turned out that Alta was right. I kind of understood why people were hesitant to take a chance on it; it was so different. It wasn't fish and it wasn't fowl. It was something all its own, and I don't care how smart or how rich or how poor, we're all creatures of habit as to what we like and don't like. By it being something that was rejected to a great extent on the front end, it turned out to be the greatest thing probably that could have happened to the record, because then I guess I didn't expect too much out of it. At the same time, I was so much in hopes that it would be a big record, not just for the sales, but so that I could say to myself, "Man, we're making progress here on this black and white thing." We had been criticized in so many ways about Elvis sounding too black or too white or just too wild. But with all the preachers and people preaching about the horrors of this kind of music, it created a momentum of discord and divergence of opinion that actually helped that first record become a hit. There was so much said about it — a lot of bad things and some good things — that it created a kind of inertia for other disc jockeys to listen and say, "What's all of this about?" When "That's All Right, Mama" and "Blue Moon of Kentucky" turned the corner and became hits, that was the defining moment when people began to feel the music and not think about whether it's black or white, or whether it's sophisticated or rude. Once word got around about what was happening with Elvis, it opened the doors for a lot of other singers, and it ultimately helped change the way people felt about music and about race.

when he first walked into a recording studio, uninvited, and in a baritone, alternately mean and sweet, laid down the simplest of tunes. He said the record would be a gift to his mother, to whom he was unashamedly devoted, but Gladys Love Presley was one of the few parents to happily greet the arrival of "the King."

Presley's lyrics were innocent enough, silly rhymes about tutti-frutti and hound dogs mixed up with the occasional mellow love ballad, but his music and performance style were not. To the fledgling art form known as rock and roll, a black music, really, derived from rhythm and blues, he brought a country and western beat and even more important, a white face. To the tradition of pop performance, he added attitude, sinking eyelids, a curled lip, sideburns, and a husky voice that rose from somewhere below the waist. Rock and roll had already established itself as a more overtly sexual music; Presley's manner retained the libidinous message even as he softened it with some sugar.

Onstage the King affected a performance style that borrowed something from the tradition of the entranced rural preacher, only Presley's god was a more lustful fellow than Billy Sunday's and his trance was orgiastic, not spiritual. Hips gyrating (his other nickname was "The Pelvis"), his feet aquiver, the singer so offended parents that the producers of the Ed Sullivan television show finally decided to show him only from the waist up. The shirt was open and the hair, modeled in a ducktail, swung freely despite ample coats of grease. "I don't know what he does," said Sullivan, introducing him for the first time, "but it drives people crazy."

For America's largely white teenage population, many of them entering the period of their own sexual awareness, Elvis provided a sense of identification. Soon it seemed that every boy was crooning "Love Me Tender" into a mirror and fashioning his hair like the singer's (with neighborhood barbers charging an extra quarter for all the fuss). Rock and roll, heretofore known as race (or Negro) music, was now theirs, and if the parents objected (and they did), that was only more reason to embrace the thumping rhythms and electric squeals as their own.

Rock had youth's energy and simplemindedness. Musically, it was essentially a variation on the blues. A twelve-bar format dominated, delineated by the most unsubtle of drumbeats and lyrics that defied poetry. But what mattered to its teenage fans was less the quality of the sound than its volume, less poetry than crudity, anything to puncture the sweet suburban mood of their parents which to many adolescents hung in the air like the family lie. When a *Time* writer groused in 1956 that rock did for music "what a motorcycle club at full throttle does for a quiet Sunday afternoon," youth could nod in approval, for that was precisely the point.

In 1958, when Elvis Presley was inducted into the army, legend spread that he drove to his physical in a big Cadillac convertible, a showgirl cooing beside him. His appointment with a military barber was front-page news, and as the singer's famous locks were shed, a *Life* photographer recorded the event. Later, rock critics would view that moment as significant: the adult culture had won, taming youth's wild boy, and, in fact, critics also noted that around that same time Presley's music became complacent and overtly commercial. The sense of danger and spontaneity was gone.

They were right about Presley, wrong about the adult "triumph." By 1960, when he appeared in a television special with Frank Sinatra, wearing a tuxedo

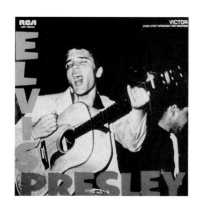

Released March 13, 1956, Elvis Presley's first album, above, became the first album in history to sell 1 million copies.

"... an unrelenting, socking syncopation that sounds like a bull whip; a choleric saxophone honking mating call sounds; an electric guitar turned up so loud that its sound shatters and splits; a vocal group that shudders and exercises violently to the beat while roughly chanting either a near-nonsense phrase or a moronic lyric in hillbilly idiom ..."

Time, *June 18, 1956, in an article announcing the "arrival" of rock and roll*

"I'm not kidding myself," a candid Presley once told an interviewer. "My voice alone is just an ordinary voice. What people come to see is how I use it. If I stand still while I'm singin', I'm dead, man. I might as well go back to drivin' a truck." Here, he performs at the Municipal Auditorium in New Orleans, Louisiana, August 12, 1956.

and singing sedate duets with the older generation's heartthrob, the King was no longer a revolutionary. Rock and roll, on the other hand, had only begun to inflict its damage on the establishment. By the succeeding decade it would lead the charge for an unprecedented youth revolution.

Elvis Presley was one of two mass media figures who came of age in the fifties. The other was Marilyn Monroe. That the age of television should have produced one of the biggest movie stars in history would seem to be a paradox, but just as Elvis was more than a musician, Marilyn was more than a movie star. She was Marilyn, the object of mid-century wish fulfillment for men, of envy for women, and of fascination for quite nearly everyone with eyes.

There is still considerable debate about Marilyn Monroe's theatrical talents, but even those who praise her as one of film's more charming performers, with a knack for self-parody, acknowledge that the core of her appeal was less acting than presence, the way that she seemed to vibrate the screen with a wiggle and an innuendo, and apply steam to windows with a simple parting of her famously luscious lips. To the naked eye, said director Billy Wilder, who made one of her most celebrated movies, *Some Like It Hot*, her performances were nothing special. You could not detect any magic on the set. But when she went up on the screen, Marilyn glowed like neon. "Celluloid," said Wilder, "loved Monroe."

Marilyn's screen personality accented what movies still had over television, size, for she was all exaggeration and excess — lips and buttocks, breast and cleavage out of proportion (her measurements were 37-23-36) — and to American men, in particular, the arousal was powerful. Marilyn Monroe gave a dramatic boost to the ailing motion picture industry, leading the way as movies, confronting television's competition, ventured into more blatantly sexual topics. She was best when she played a vulnerable young woman, both seductive and needy, naughty and innocent, which is to say when she played the cultural icon the world came to know as Marilyn Monroe. And the fact that she played her over and over again, both on screen and in photographs, suited the age. When, in 1962, pop artist Andy Warhol reproduced Marilyn's face fifty times across a canvas, each face identical to the next, making the viewer feel as if he were looking at a row of "Marilyn" soup cans in a grocery store, he got it right: mass culture was the experience of repetition, whether it be a television commercial or a movie star. In the glut of imagery making up the fizzy consumer economy, Marilyn was just another object of desire, a logo for sex.

In 1953 a nude photograph of Marilyn Monroe appeared in the first issue of a new magazine. The picture had been taken years before (it was then that Norma Jean Baker chose to sign "Mona Monroe" on the model release form, beginning her transformation), and the rights to it had been bought for $500 by a Chicago publisher named Hugh Hefner. Up to now, nudity had been the province of the underground press, but Hefner was in search of a wider audience. After flirting with the name *Stag Party*, he landed on *Playboy*, a title that suggested the bacchanalian lifestyle of the hedonist, the kind of pleasure seeking reader whom Hefner hoped to capture with his publication. Still, Hefner was so uncertain that his magazine would succeed, he refrained from putting a date on the first issue's cover, for who knew when he might be able to publish a second?

"We like our apartment. We enjoy mixing up cocktails and an hors d'oeuvre or two, putting a little mood music on the phonograph, and inviting in a female for a quiet discussion on Picasso, Nietzsche, jazz, sex."

Hugh Hefner, writing in the first issue of Playboy

"You mean you didn't have anything on?" a female reporter asked Marilyn Monroe about the photo session that produced pictures published in the first issue of Playboy, *above. "Oh yes," replied Monroe. "I had the radio on."*

As it turned out, the robust postwar economy had produced plenty of hedonists. Drawn by the promise of a peek at Monroe's flesh, 53,000 of them bought *Playboy*'s first issue (nearly double what Hefner himself had predicted). And by 1956, when circulation reached 600,000, *Playboy* was on its way to becoming an American institution.

Monroe received no payment from *Playboy* for use of the picture. After all, it didn't belong to her any more than the thousands of other "Marilyn" photographs and celebrity detritus did. But she became all too familiar with exploitation, suffering it from men and from Hollywood producers throughout her unhappy life. "That's the trouble," she said once. "A sex symbol becomes a thing. I just hate to be a thing." Her marriages were publicist's dreams (baseball star Joe DiMaggio, playwright Arthur Miller), but they failed nearly as miserably as did her affairs (apparently, Frank Sinatra and Bobby Kennedy, if not President John F. Kennedy himself). When she died a suicide at age thirty-six in 1962, in an event still shrouded with controversy, it seemed somehow darkly fitting. Marilyn would now never grow old, never depart from the extravagant fantasy pose she struck at her peak, never lose her mysterious celluloid luster.

Marilyn is greeted by a crowd at Ebbets Field in Brooklyn, 1959. In her first screen test, she walked across the room, sat down, and lit a cigarette. After seeing the rushes, one studio executive exclaimed, "I got a cold chill . . . Every frame of the test radiated sex."

Rosa Parks, 1913–

"If you will protest courageously and yet with dignity and Christian love, when the history books are written in future generations the historians will pause and say, 'There lived a great people — a black people — who injected new meaning and dignity into the veins of civilization.'"

Martin Luther King, speaking to the Montgomery boycotters, 1956

On December 1, 1955, after a long day at work, a forty-two-year-old seamstress named Rosa Parks boarded the Cleveland Avenue bus in Montgomery, Alabama, and, being a "Negro," took her place at the back. Montgomery, like most southern cities in the fifties, operated segregated buses — the first rows were for whites, the remaining rows for blacks — and Parks sat at the front of the black section. But when the bus reached the next stop, enough whites got on to fill the white seats, leaving one white man standing, whereupon the driver turned around to request that Parks and three other blacks give up their seats, as was the practice when the designated white area was filled. "Y'all better make it light on yourselves and let me have those seats," he said. The three others complied; Parks sat stone-faced. The driver again asked her to move. "No," she said quietly. "Well, I'm going to have you arrested," said the driver. Parks was calm. "You may do that," she said.

Her resistance was spontaneous. Though an active member of the NAACP, Parks had not, as some later claimed, been sent by them to force a confrontation with the white establishment. In fact, as she sat there, waiting for the police to arrive, she refused to even allow herself to think through the consequences of her action. "If I had," Parks later said, "I might have gotten off the bus." The police came, Parks was arrested, and after her bond had been posted, she was released from prison. But within hours an elaborate network of civil rights leaders in Montgomery had met and determined that they would use Parks's arrest to both challenge the constitutionality of the city's segregation laws and rally black commuters to a boycott of the city's bus system. By saying no, Rosa Parks had triggered one of the most dramatic demonstrations of nonviolent protest in the history of American race relations.

To lead them, the Montgomery organizers chose a twenty-six-year-old minister. Born Michael King, Jr., his name had been changed at age five by his preacher father (who changed his own similarly at the same time) in order to pay respect to the Protestant religion's most powerful leader of reform and defiance. Martin Luther King, Jr., had been in Montgomery less than a year when the boycott began, yet he seized the opportunity to put into practice the principles of nonviolent protest he had learned from the writings of Mohandas K. Gandhi, the Hindu leader whose fasts had brought the era of British rule in India to an end.

King joined Gandhi's method of passive resistance with the Christian doctrine of love to create a form of nonviolent protest he referred to as "Christianity in action." The Montgomery demonstrators would force their opponents to justice not by confrontation, nor by submission, but by embrace. They would court their own arrests, and, if convicted, said King, they would "enter jail as a bridegroom enters the bride's chamber." King told his followers that they must commit no violence, raise no fist, no matter how powerful the provocation. "Blood may flow . . . before we receive our freedom," he said, "but it must be our blood."

To keep the Montgomery boycott going, more than twenty thousand black citizens formed car pools, drove bicycles, hired taxis, or simply walked to work. ("Not since the First Battle of the Marne," wrote a supporter to the local newspaper, "has the taxi been put to as good use.") Their cars were stopped regularly by police in search of a violation — any violation — so much so that most car pool drivers crept along the roads at a snail's pace, signaling turns well in advance, so that police would not have reason to ticket them.

E.L. POSEY. PARKING LOT

During the boycott, Montgomery's black citizens relied on an efficient car pool system that ferried people between more than forty pickup stations like the one above. Support for the protest came from within the black community — workers donated one-fifth of their weekly salaries — as well as from outside groups such as the NAACP, the United Auto Workers, Montgomery's Jewish community, and sympathetic white southerners.

After two months, King himself was arrested for going thirty miles per hour in a twenty-five-mile zone. The police deposited him at the Montgomery city jail, but he was released when an enormous crowd of his supporters surrounded the prison. Then, shortly thereafter, King's house was bombed. It was his most serious challenge to date. Arriving on the scene, he discovered a barricade of white police officers standing guard while a group of angry blacks, holding guns and knives, threatened a riot. After checking on the safety of his family, King reemerged on the front porch and raised his hand. "Don't get panicky," he told the mob. "If you have weapons, take them home . . . We want to love our enemies. Be good to them. This is what we must live by. We must meet hate with love." The crowd dispersed.

The protest went on for over a year, and always with the same dependable rhythm: the white establishment would challenge the protesters, the protesters

Fighting segregation in Montgomery: **"It was providence"**

At the time of the Montgomery bus boycott, I was the assistant editor for the black edition of the *Montgomery Advertiser*, the local paper. In those days, the paper had what was called a branch office, which was the generic name for any black group within a white organization or business. We had our own editor, advertising person, and sports editor. The white paper had a page devoted to stocks and bonds — something we weren't supposed to know anything about. On the pages where the financial news would have been, we had our own church news, our theater listings, and our school programs. To distinguish it from the white edition, the black edition had two stars on the front page.

I took the bus to work every day. Our bus system was segregated just like practically everything else. There was no specific line of demarcation separating seats reserved for white and black passengers. It was usually at the bus driver's discretion, and it varied depending on time of day and the driver, but you were just supposed to know. One thing was for certain, when a white person occupied a seat, even if it was one man to an entire long seat, blacks had to walk right on past. About six o'clock one evening, I received a phone call from a friend's mother telling me to go to the Dexter Avenue Church. That's where I heard about Rosa Parks's arrest. I had first met Rosa Parks during the time that I was a member of the NAACP. She had always impressed me. She was just an angel walking. When things happened that would upset most people, she would just give you this angelic smile, and that was the end of that. When I arrived, a small group of people were gathered in the church basement, and they were already talking about boycotting the local bus system and spreading some leaflets around about it.

News of the boycott spread pretty quickly between the leaflets and the headline in the Sunday morning *Advertiser*. Plus, the telephones were ringing off the wall all over town. I was wondering how many people were going to get on the bus in the morning, because some of us had to travel five or six miles to get to work. But when Monday morning came, there were empty buses wherever you looked. That night a mass meeting was held at the Holt Street Baptist Church. It was not a large church, but it was packed to the rafters with people from all walks of life. We were all waiting for Dr. King, who had just been chosen as our spokesperson. There were people singing the Negro spirituals. You just don't need an organ and a cathedral the size of St. Peter's when a thousand black voices are singing with all their feelings and pathos. Everything was coming out in these songs. Dr. King finally arrived and came in through the side door while everyone was singing. There was first a hush, and then the whole place exploded. This was the

first time this crowd had seen him since he had been asked and accepted the position of our spokesperson. Martin Luther King spoke in a very soft, rich voice, and as he was going along, you'd get the feeling that this was not just something on paper, but rather that here was a person who really cared. He looked right at us when he spoke. He was able to make all of us — the washer-woman, the domestic, the teenager — feel like he was talking directly to each of us. "I feel your pain. I know what you have been going through," he said.

I remember one particular day during the boycott when everyone was asked to walk to wherever you had to go. From where I lived to my office was approximately eight miles, and it was drizzling and it was cold. As we walked, we just kept conversing and singing, but by the time I was halfway to work, the singing and conversation weren't helping me very much because I was damp and cold. But then I heard that an older woman had said, "My feets is tired, but my soul is resting." There were plenty of elderly persons walking with us and when you saw them walking, singing, and smiling, you knew you just had to go on. I thought, "If they can do it, so can I."

All the people who were against us knew exactly where to hit at the heart of the black race. They started bombing our churches. You have to know something of the culture of the black man to know that the church is our place of comfort and our place of solace. It's a place where even the most incorrigible kids in the community don't play pranks. Going from one bombed church to another, covering the story for the paper, it seemed as though it wasn't me at the sites. This wasn't me smelling this business from these bombs. When you pull up to a churchyard where the dust has yet to clear, you get a strong smell from the explosives. The church is like an open wound, and if you let yourself begin to feel at a time like that, then you lose sight of what you are supposed to be doing. One night they bombed five churches, bless their hearts, but that action only streng-

Baskin riding a bus after the end of the boycott, with Reverend Ralph Abernathy (to her right), Martin Luther King, Jr. (second row, left), and Reverend Glenn Smiley, a white minister from New York.

—*Inez Jessie Baskin, born in Alabama in 1916, left the Montgomery Advertiser in 1963 to attend Seminary School at Selma University, followed by graduate study in religion at Southern Christian University. She was a social worker for the Alabama State Health Department until her retirement in 1973, and has remained active in Montgomery community activities, serving on the board of the Alabama Legal Services Corporation since 1988 and working with the Montgomery Community Action Agency.*

thened enough of us to support the weaker. You don't fight a man using his tactics. You have to fight back with something that your enemy does not have, and what we had was a theory of nonviolent practice. Some of us, of course, had to be spoon-fed with it, but then Dr. King made us know that it made sense. If we were ready to die and stand up for our rights, let the enemy be the one to do the killing.

The night the boycott ended, I had been out on a story with the paper's photographer and had just come in. I was thinking about getting a little sleep when the telephone rang. It was a friend saying, "Get up. I'm picking you up. The buses are running." Well, that opened my eyes. We went right over to the bus stop in front of Dr. King's house on Jackson Street, just as the bus pulled up. There were several ministers over there standing around in all of this. I got out of the car and waltzed up to the bus. I stepped on to the bus, and the bus driver held out his hand for the bus fare. I looked directly at him, all the while knowing that I had only two things in my hand: a pencil and a piece of paper. I didn't have a dime in my pocket. I glared at the bus driver, and I guess he glared back at me because I was wondering why he was asking me for bus fare. I said to myself, "You're lucky to have a job." (The drivers hadn't been working as much during the boycott.) Fortunately, one of the ministers gave me bus fare, and so I got on the bus with Dr. King and Dr. Abernathy right up in front.

I had been living in Montgomery most of my life, and up until then, you couldn't even get three people to stay together for two hours. And here we had all come together as one for 381 days. It made me feel that there was more to this cohesiveness. There was more than Dr. Martin Luther King and Rosa Parks involved in this. It was Providence. I still believe that.

would stand firm. King and his followers were on trial for another infraction — this time it was for "running a business without a franchise" (the "business" was the boycott car pool) — when news arrived that the Supreme Court had ruled in the protesters' favor. Soon after, King boarded a Montgomery bus. "Is this the reverend?" asked the driver. "That's right," said King. After depositing fifteen cents into the coin slot, he then sat down in what had only recently been a "whites only" seat. The boycott had lasted 381 days.

Martin Luther King, who would go on to have every bit as significant a fifties (*and* sixties) media presence as Marilyn Monroe and Elvis Presley (only King was selling justice, not movies or records), arrived on the scene at an extraordinary time for the black race. The Great Migration, which began around 1910 and flourished during the time of the First World War, had, by the time of the Second World War, delivered roughly 1.5 million black people up the Mississippi to the great cities of the North. There would have been more if there had not been so much resistance from the southern cotton planters, who depended upon black labor to harvest their crop. But when the mechanical cotton picker, a device that did the work of fifty people, became more widely available around 1944, their resistance let up. As far as the southern planters were concerned, the machine was a more reliable worker than a human any day, particularly since the black sharecropper had begun to get "funny ideas" in his head. Since returning from World War II, he had become less willing to take orders, appeared more brazen, and demanded a higher wage.

Now unimpeded by the cotton planters of the Old Confederacy, and urged on by the promise of manufacturing jobs paying as much as four times the highest sharecropper wage, the flight of black southerners to the North took up fresh speed. Chicago was still a popular destination. The city's black population increased 77 percent in the 1940s, another 65 percent in the 1950s. For a while, 2,200 southern blacks, their lives packed into bulging suitcases or wrapped in cloth sacks, were entering Illinois Central's railway stations every week. But almost all the great northern (and western) cities received thousands of new black citizens, so many that by the time the second, postwar wave of migration slowed in 1970, it would add nearly 5 million people to the northern urban centers — without a doubt the largest movement of population in American life since westward-bound settlers first packed covered wagons and headed toward California.

Blacks were coming to New York, Chicago, Detroit, and Los Angeles at roughly the same rate that whites were leaving for those cities' suburbs, and the cultural shift they experienced was as dramatic. Though it was now nearly a century since Americans faced off against each other over slavery and half a century since Booker T. Washington and W. E. B. Du Bois argued over how blacks should best respond to the humiliation of Jim Crow, southern blacks still experienced a segregated society and not only when they boarded their buses. Southern bathrooms, beaches, drinking fountains, and housing were still divided between facilities for whites and (vastly inferior) facilities for blacks. Blacks were

"Listen, nigger. We've taken all we want from you. Before next week, you'll be sorry you ever came to Montgomery."

Late-night caller,
addressing Martin Luther King

Prior to leading the Montgomery boycott, Martin Luther King, Jr. (seated), had been reluctant to take a leadership role outside of his own congregation. Even after spearheading the civil rights movement of the 1950s and 1960s, King modestly referred to himself as merely a "drum major for justice."

rarely allowed to vote, addressed as "boy" or, in the case of women, "aunt," and subjected to other insults intended to remind them that the Civil War may have ended the practice of indentured servitude, but not the practice of discrimination.

In the North, blacks found a freer (though far from equal) life. They settled into working-class ethnic neighborhoods, prompting even more whites to move to the suburbs, but while they could freely vote in northern election precincts (even sending some black politicians to Congress) and were enjoying in somewhat lesser terms the boom that white America was enjoying, their lives could hardly be called an improvement upon those they had lived in the rural South. The shift from rural to urban society put enormous stress on black families. Illegitimacy rates soared. And the spread of a drug called heroin (or "horse" in street parlance) increased crime and juvenile delinquency.

Meanwhile, those blacks who remained in the South began to challenge the white power structure. Through their service in World War II and the growth of mass communication, they, too, had come to witness a basic fact — most of the world was nonwhite — and watched enviously as colonial peoples (most recently, citizens of the black African nations) fought successfully for release from the bonds of white imperialists. On television and in print, they witnessed the abundant life being enjoyed by white consumers and wanted to taste it themselves.

Progressive-minded white Americans were sympathetic. Far from being simply the submissive "subhuman population" exploited by southern racists or the "nation within a nation" that black nationalists sometimes held out as an alternative to integration, black America was seen by many as an ill-treated member of the vast American family. Awakening from their moral slumber, some white citizens felt the need to extend the promise inherent to an egalitarian nation, if for no other reason than the shame they felt witnessing the sins of their own country even as it enjoyed unprecedented prosperity and basked in the light of noble certitude that came with the defeat in World War II of an evil regime built upon its own theories of racial superiority.

In its competition with the Soviet Union, America had spoken up for the right of self-determination and against the subjugation of the peoples of Eastern Europe, yet it could be argued that America's own colonialism occurred *within* its borders, against men like Oliver Brown, a black welder in Kansas. Forced to send his eight-year-old daughter to a black school a mile away even though a white school was considerably closer, Brown sued the Topeka Board of Education, and in 1954 the Supreme Court ruled with him, making white-only schools a violation of the law. The justices, being sensitive to the enormous social implications of their decision, granted states and municipalities time to integrate their schools, but as far as education was concerned, integration was now the law of the land, and the implications of the Supreme Court's decision were obvious: it would not be long before other racial injustices would be struck down as well.

The Montgomery bus boycott was only the first of many incidents to follow the Court's decision on *Brown v. Board of Education,* each of them recorded by the unblinking eye of television. On radio, or in print, the issue of civil rights could be muted by the polite quality of words; in court decisions it could get waylaid by abstract constitutional arguments over states' rights. But on television

The siege at Little Rock: "Like the Civil War revisited"

My family were just ordinary, salt-of-the-earth people. My dad was a hardworking man who lived day by day, week by week. Although we were very poor, I didn't really know it. I felt as though I was the luckiest person in the world. Our life was very typical. Every day, I went off to school, my dad went off to work, and my mom worked hard at home. My parents' main concerns were making a living and raising their family.

Segregation was simply the way of life; we never knew anything else. As it was in most southern cities, the blacks had their part of town, and the whites had their part. I can't remember ever going into a restaurant and seeing blacks there. I never really thought about it. My parents were wonderful people, but they were also a product of their society. We were all taught that you just don't mix. We were very ignorant about segregation and integration. It wasn't even an issue until we found out that they were going to integrate Little Rock Central High.

I was a fifteen-year-old tenth grader when they made the announcement. At first, many of the parents refused to believe that it was actually going to happen. Some parents formed groups and committees to try and stop it, but my parents didn't really take part in any of that. It's not that they weren't interested; they just didn't know what to do, or where to go. Ultimately, they just decided that their child was not going to an integrated school, and that was that. I don't think it was really out of hate for anyone. I think it was out of ignorance and fear of the unknown. "What would this lead to?" "What would be next?" That was the mind-set; people just didn't know what to expect. And we couldn't understand why they would ever want to leave their black school and come to Central in the first place.

The day the black students arrived, there was a circuslike atmosphere around the school. There was fear and there was anger, but there was a lot of excitement, too. It was almost as if something fun was about to happen. There were all of these cameras and reporters, and all the parents were there, urging us on and telling us to get out there and not let them in. The parents gathered in this vacant lot directly across the street from the school. There was so much electricity and tension coming from that vacant lot that something big was bound to happen. Every now and then fights would break out among the parents. There were things said and done over there that frightened me much more than these black students did. At one point an elderly black man in a blue and white Chevrolet drove up Fourteenth Street alongside Central High School. Suddenly, all of these white parents surrounded the car and started yelling. I was so afraid they were going to turn that car over with the elderly black man in it. I honestly believe

Above: Thompson at age sixteen. Right: Thompson (left, carrying books) and schoolmate Hazel Bryant (center background, with mouth open) shout epithets at Elizabeth Eckford. In 1956, a sympathetic white citizen paid to have this photograph published in the Little Rock newspaper along with the line, "If you live in Arkansas, study this picture and know shame. When hate is unleashed and bigotry finds a voice, God help us all."

—Anne Thompson was born in England, Arkansas, in 1942. After the integration of Central High School, she transferred to North Little Rock High School. She has lived in Arkansas for most of her life and has two children and two grandchildren.

that had the parents stayed away, there wouldn't have been a problem. The whole thing was at their insistence. We were all thinking, "Well, we're just doing what our parents want us to do." We almost felt like we didn't have a choice; we had to get out there and protest.

At first the National Guard was there, but they didn't really tell us what we could or couldn't do. As far as we knew, we were doing the right thing. None of the guard told us to get back or that we couldn't say certain things. The students felt as though they had a free reign. Some of the girl students were even flirting with the boys in the guard, and they would flirt back.

When the federal troops came in, things changed. I remember thinking, "Here are these young men, just a little older than me, and they're here to protect blacks? Why would they do that?" I was afraid of the federal troops, of what they might do. It was like the Civil War revisited. It was as though the federal government was taking over Little Rock, and we were going to lose control of our lives. We all had this vision of Little Rock under siege by federal troops.

I honestly can't remember exactly when I first saw

Elizabeth Eckford (one of the black students). Everybody was milling about and looking around, wondering which way they were going to come from. I knew immediately something was happening when the noise picked up from the parents and the students. All of a sudden Elizabeth was walking down the sidewalk and there was this rush. We had to let her know that she couldn't come to our school. So we ran up behind her and started chanting and jeering, "Two-four-six-eight. We don't want to integrate!" And, "Go back to your own school!"

Throughout it all, Elizabeth was absolutely stoic. You couldn't tell that she heard anything. She held her head slightly downward and just walked. Even as I was jeering, I couldn't help but feel sorry for her. I realized then that this must all be very hard for her. I don't know that I felt empathy, because I don't know that I could really feel what she was feeling. But I did feel sorry for her, and I was saddened. That day when the black students entered the white school, we felt as if they beat us. They won; we lost. We knew then that Little Rock would never be the same, just because nine black students walked through the front door of Central High.

the issue was made plain and simple through the power of images: while much of the nation watched, peaceful demonstrators asking for the most basic elements of respect were greeted with fire hoses and police dogs. The subtleties of the law mattered little here; on television, villains were villains and victims were victims.

Like few others in his time, Martin Luther King understood this. As a religious leader, he was familiar with the power of the well-chosen symbolic story. And the nonviolent strategy he employed worked not only in fact but also in theater, for to most people watching the story of Montgomery on television, the black boycotters were the essence of heroism, self-sacrifice, and principle, the white lawmakers small-minded, irrational, and backward. Americans had become familiar with black athletes like Jackie Robinson and entertainment stars like Duke Ellington, but the television footage of Martin Luther King leading the struggle helped make him the first black *political* leader to capture national attention and drew unprecedented attention to the civil rights issue.

Barely a year after Montgomery had been settled, the decade's most frightening civil rights struggle erupted in Little Rock, Arkansas, and once again the cameras were there. Nine black children had been chosen to integrate Central High School in a working-class neighborhood of Little Rock, and Governor Orval Faubus, a populist otherwise known for his liberal policies, remained adamantly opposed. Faubus had grown up in a poor rural county in one of the nation's poorest and most rural states. By his own family's admission, he had not laid eyes on a black man until he was an adult, but his opposition was more political than personal: he felt that his campaign for a third term would go down in defeat if he dared to defy Arkansas's segregationists.

Starting with a list of eighty volunteers, Little Rock school officials carefully interviewed both parents and children before selecting three boys and six girls, above, to become the first black students at Central High School.

On the pretext that the admission of the Little Rock Nine would incite violence, Faubus stood up to the courts and ordered his National Guard to turn away the black students when they came to school. In fact, the only threat to the peace that morning was the National Guard itself, which confronted the students with rifles pointed and a chorus of racial slurs. If there had been no violence brewing before Faubus's order, it was brewing now.

Having watched the confrontation on television, segregationists arrived in Little Rock in droves. Then, while the governor fought the federal courts with homilies on states' rights, the battle was joined. Mobs roamed the school, assaulting reporters and pushing cops. The black students returned home; had they stayed at the school, there is little doubt that they would have been the target of considerable violence. The Little Rock mayor, fearing a total breakdown of order, telegrammed Washington for help, and after agonizing over the issue, President Eisenhower agreed to send the 327th Battle Group of the 101st Airborne to restore peace. A staunch advocate of states' rights, the president paused at the idea of ordering federal troops into Arkansas, tasked with defending against American citizens (a scene that may have recalled, for him, the federal attack on the Bonus Army marchers of 1932, which he and General MacArthur had led), but he had little choice. For the first time since the days of Reconstruction, the federal army would be employed to seize control of a southern society.

Central High was occupied territory now, rimmed with jeeps and tents and

Even though plans for the desegregation of Central High School had been advancing smoothly, Arkansas Governor Orval Faubus virtually ensured unrest by falsely announcing that the city was on the brink of a riot and that the city's stores were selling out of guns and knives (sold "mostly to Negro youths"). He then encouraged one of his closest friends — a local athlete and professional strikebreaker — to stir up trouble outside the school. According to an assistant police chief, "Half the trouble-makers were from out of town."

In November 1957 an Atlanta restaurant tried to cash in on America's fascination with the Russian satellite. Their "Sputnikburger" was garnished with Russian dressing, caviar, and a large "satellite olive" pierced with three toothpicks for "antennae."

a makeshift command station every bit as serious as those constructed on the run in Europe a bit more than a decade before. When the black students made their way to school next, there were at first a few violent skirmishes. Faubus, claiming the South's fabled literary license, declared that the federal government's paratroopers were "bludgeoning innocent bystanders . . . the warm red blood of patriotic Americans staining the cold naked unsheathed knives." But, in fact, the crowds complied with the show of force and, guided by the protection of the Constitution, the Little Rock Nine entered classes.

In the early evening of October 5, 1957, Americans stood in the twilight and looked up from their backyards, squinting. They were trying hard to distinguish the night's many stars from what they hoped to see: a satellite — the first — orbiting the earth at a speed of 18,000 mph. Space travel had been a subject of serious study for most of the century, and spaceships had long been a staple of science fiction and fantasy. But what was traveling above now, etched against the darkening sky, was the real thing: a polished metal ball launched the day before, weighing 184 pounds and equipped with a rudimentary radio transmitter. It was hard to believe and even harder to see (the satellite followed a path that blocked it from view to North Americans for all but a few minutes in the early morning and early evening), but, failing to catch a glimpse, people could always return to their homes and radios to hear it: the transmitter gave off a faint beep-beep audible on most home sets.

The excitement was palpable. Surely people were witnessing the dawn of a new era, when they would go to the moon for dinner and back again before midnight, when space colonies would become homes to the adventurous and explorers would tap secret worlds in distant parts of the universe. But the fact that the satellite carried the name *Sputnik* (Russian for "fellow traveler") made them also, alternately, suspicious, anxious, and outraged. Was the spacecraft real or some elaborate Soviet hoax? Were the audible signals innocent or some dastardly code? Were the Russians really that smart? And why had America's exalted scientists not succeeded at it before them? The first satellite's beeps faded by the end of October (the batteries had run down even though the ball itself continued to orbit), but within weeks there was *Sputnik II* loaded with over a thousand pounds of sophisticated radio instruments and space's first passenger, a dog named Laika. Now there was no doubt about it: *Sputnik* was real, and the implications that came cascading from that fact were nothing less than terrifying.

The news fell hard on American sensibilities. Nuclear scientist Edward Teller called it a technological Pearl Harbor, and it did shock almost as rudely. While, in a sense, America's own exploration of space reached back to Kitty Hawk and the first tentative steps toward the airplane, its latest stage had been inaugurated by the departure of Germany's most brilliant scientists to the West. Their experience building the German V-2 rockets, which had terrorized London at the end of World War II, would now be put to use for America. There had been much discussion and competition over which of the three American armed services should administer the American space effort, but it had always been taken as an article of faith that democracy's encouragement of the free exchange of ideas would catapult its science ahead of communism's and deliver Americans into space first.

A Russian learns of Sputnik: **"Who did it? We did it! The Soviet Union is first in space!"**

Looking back, life in the Soviet Union in the 1950s was miserable, but at the time, we just didn't realize it. Since the first responsibility of Soviet teachers was to create the perfect Soviet citizen, our political education was stressed above all. It wasn't a special discipline or subject, rather it was prevalent in everything we studied, from math to drawing to literature. All over the country, Soviet children studied the same subjects from the same textbooks — all of which were approved by the higher authorities. We were taught that the Soviet Union was a country of workers and peasants, and that because of this, it was the best country in the whole world. According to our text books, the workers of the world looked to us as sort of a shining star, because the Soviet Union was the only country in which the government really cared about working people. We were taught that *they* were the hungry, the persecuted, and the exploited and that *we* were free.

We weren't really afraid of America in the usual sense of the word, because in Russia fear was a shame. We didn't think we had anything to fear, anyway, because we thought that we lived in the best and mightiest country in the world. We were taught, however, that America's main intention was to wage war against us, and for that we had to be prepared. Most of my classmates and I were members of a communist organization for children called the Young Pioneers. As members, we had to give an oath of "readiness" to the cause of Lenin and Stalin, which meant that we had to be strong so that we could fight the Americans. We were just young kids, but if we ran one hundred meters within a certain time limit, we were entitled to a special badge signifying our preparedness in the fight against the American capitalists. This was the focus in the classroom and at all of our children's organizations.

It was absolutely unimaginable to us that Stalin could die. And when he finally did die in 1953, it was such a shock. He was kind of a living god to all of us and there was a feeling that he would always be with us, that he would live forever. It was irrational and even untenable, but somehow he existed in the atmosphere and climate of the country. And then, when Nikita Khrushchev, who had been appointed the new head of government, made his speech in 1956 denouncing Stalin and saying that the Communist Party had not always taken the right path, it was absolutely revolutionary. Stalin had died just three years earlier and here Khrushchev was saying that this god had made mistakes, he had actually steered the country from the right path of Leninism. This was terribly shocking, because we had to reevaluate our ways.

Khrushchev went on to say that because this was the age of nuclear arms, in a future war between the Soviet Union and the United States there would be no winner. Prior to that, we had been absolutely brainwashed into believing that in a war between East and West, only the socialist East could win. History just moved in that way. At the same time, however, he told us that there could not be an ideological coexistence. We learned that the ideological war would go on and we would eventually win peacefully, because *their* people, the workers exploited by the capitalists, would want to be like us in the Soviet Union. But this victory was to occur in the distant future.

One of the reasons that scientific progress took on such importance during those years was our belief that through technological progress, the Soviet Union would be victorious over the United States. I myself loved science and

Reznik (left) with two friends at the Moscow Civil Engineering University, 1958.

believed in scientific progress, because it would move history forward faster, just as the Marxists claimed it would. Science and technology would make our production more efficient, making life easier for us, the workers. I thought science would make our society better in a moral sense and a social sense and that science would put our nation back on the right path of Leninism. So I was very excited about the fact that the Soviet space program was advancing so rapidly.

The day our satellite *Sputnik* was launched, a special voice came over the radio to announce it to us. Traditionally, in the Soviet Union a few of the radio announcers were hired to read only the most urgent news on the radio. We always knew when something extra special was coming over the airwaves, as we would hear a special signal, "ta ta toe, ta toe, ta toe" and then one of those readers with a deep voice would begin speaking. And if your radio wasn't on at home, a neighbor would let you know immediately. It was pure genius on the part of Soviet leaders to create this kind of a show. You'd forget about everything at this moment — about your problems, about your spouse and your fam-

ily. This was like a kind of religious performance.

On an October morning in 1957, we heard one of those voices announce, "Attention. All radio stations of the Soviet Union are broadcasting . . . Our satellite *Sputnik* is in space." I felt so proud. Who did it? We did it! The Soviet Union is first in space! I was in my second year of college and just couldn't imagine that this could happen in my lifetime. In my mind, space travel only existed in science fiction. We didn't even know that the project was in the works. We weren't told the names of the people working on the project for years

—*Semyon Reznik was born in Moscow in 1938. He spent much of his career in the Soviet Union working as a freelance journalist in science and wrote two novels dealing with anti-Semitism in Russia, neither of which was permitted to be published. In 1982, after a long struggle with the Soviet authorities, Mr. Reznik, along with his wife and son, defected to the United States. In 1985 he moved to Washington, D.C., to work as an editor, writer, and broadcaster for the Russian Service of Voice of America. He is the author of* The Nazification of Russia: Anti-Semitism in the Post-Soviet Era.

afterwards. We only knew of the "general constructor," as he was called. He became kind of a mythical figure. It didn't really matter, because we were the first in space.

By the early 1960s, I had become somewhat skeptical of the Soviet government and its propaganda. Khrushchev had announced that we would overcome American production of milk and meat in twenty years, and that then we would reach our communist paradise. I thought, "Wait a minute, so they actually produce more food than we do. How could this be, when in Marxism the highest step of societal evolution was socialism?" But then something happened that in my mind was the perfect example of Soviet superiority: on April 12, 1961, our radio stations announced that Yuri Gagarin was the first man in space. As soon as he returned to earth, he was brought to Moscow. There were spontaneous demonstrations everywhere. This just never happened in the Soviet Union. Usually, mass demonstrations were organized by the government, but this time everything closed down and everyone headed to Red Square to see Gagarin. I rushed to the square and passed within five meters of him. He was so charming and so happy, and he was just a few years older than me. I even sent him a note inviting him to my university for a student dance. We had organized a show, as well, and by pure coincidence, it was entitled, *We Are Going to Space*. It was kind of a satire. Of course he didn't come, but we still felt like he was one of us.

By the end of the decade, the U.S. had formed the National Aeronautics and Space Administration (NASA) and named the first seven American astronauts, shifting the focus of space exploration well past the simple orbiting of unmanned satellites, as pointed out by this August 1959 issue of Popular Mechanics.

The failure of American science was disappointing, but the success of the Soviet rocket was chilling, for *Sputnik* had been launched by an intercontinental missile, and if the Soviet rocket had been capable of flinging radios and dogs into space, it seemed safe to assume that it could also fling an atomic or hydrogen warhead onto American soil. When, in short order, an American missile, rushed to the launchpad, then collapsed in flames, the United States, so recently revered for its technological expertise, became the target of jokes. The Russians had their *Sputniks,* went a familiar line, the Americans, *Kaputniks.*

Blame fell on American material self-indulgence. Surely the United States could have beaten the Russians; the nation had simply lost its edge, grown fat and besotted with its own abundance. If only the children had been learning more science and mathematics in school, this would never have happened. Eisenhower administration officials played down the news, reminding people that American supermarkets were superior to those anywhere in the world and that it was only a matter of time before the American system would produce a better satellite. To Senate Majority Leader Lyndon Johnson, that had the hollow ring of advertising. "The Roman empire controlled the world because it could build roads," he said, hoping to ride the issue to his own election to the White House. "Later, when men moved to sea, the British Empire was dominant because it had ships. Now the Communists have established a foothold in outer space. It is not very reassuring to be told that next year we will put a 'better' satellite into the air. Perhaps it will even have chrome trim and automatic windshield wipers."

There were now two challenges to American self-satisfaction: the moral confrontation contained in the growing impatience over civil rights and the competitive life-and-death struggle symbolized by the space race. Both informed the emerging presidential election. Perhaps because it involved the departure from the White House of the esteemed general, hero of the last war, or because the two men who competed to replace him were young enough to be his sons; or perhaps because the issues at hand, both domestic and international, seemed so complicated and dangerous, or because the newest medium, television, put the campaign for the presidency into a new arena before an audience of millions, the 1960 presidential election was an American classic, a turning point in the nation's political and cultural history. Being there was like being there for a great sporting event, and long after it was over, as it lingered in the mind, people talked about it that way.

The election involved two titanic American political figures, each of whom would leave his mark on the history of the century. From the Republican side, Richard Milhous Nixon, the vice president, forty-seven, aimed to succeed Eisenhower; the Democrats nominated Massachusetts Senator John Fitzgerald Kennedy, forty-three. They differed little on the issues (each was a Cold War hawk and a domestic affairs moderate), but, as became most evident in the campaign's high point — the televised debates — the two separated markedly in manner.

Conceived by the networks as a way to circumvent the awkward "equal time" provision in their licensing agreements with the federal government, the debates were at the same time an earnest and exciting use of the new medium. No longer could a candidate hide himself behind red, white, and blue bunting and loud brass bands, saying one thing to voters in one region and the opposite to those in another. Now he had to speak to everyone at once, knowing that the slightest duplicity could be caught. Anyone who owned a television set would be able to watch the two aspirants to the highest station in the land challenge each other point by point, and size them up, if not in person then in what felt like the closest thing to it, for the television lens did allow the viewer the remarkable experience of being able to sit in his living room and look as closely into a man's eyes as he could if the candidate had stopped by for dinner. Television had taken part in the 1952 and 1956 presidential campaigns, as a medium for advertising, but the candidates had never appeared live in the same studio. The Great Debates of 1960 would be held in a space no larger than a high school auditorium stage, yet they would be seen by an audience of 70 million, the most powerful mass experience of the political process to date. Surely democracy could only gain, even if, as Walter Lippmann opined, there was something demeaning to the office of the presidency in the image of a moderator interrupting a candidate to tell him that he had but only so many seconds longer to finish his point.

Arriving in Chicago for the first of what would be four encounters, the two men went into their separate corners: Kennedy to prepare in his hotel room with three-by-five index cards; Nixon to a campaign visit at the offices of the United Brotherhood of Carpenters and Joiners. Nixon was sure that he had the upper hand, having already shown himself capable of performing well on the screen. His television speech in the 1952 campaign, defending his ethics when they were under attack, had saved his spot on the ticket with General Eisenhower, and his

Believing that their young, handsome, well-spoken candidate would outshine the gruff, awkward Nixon on live television, Kennedy campaign officials wanted to schedule as many debates as possible. "Every time we get those two fellows on the screen side by side," said one adviser, "we're going to gain and he's going to lose."

sparring with Khrushchev over the modern American kitchen in 1959 had made him a folk hero to some. But he was still no match for Kennedy, whose looks and manner were glowingly suited to the medium. (On another occasion, the witty senator quipped that "Mr. Nixon may be very experienced in kitchen debates, but so are a great many other married men I know.")

Handsome, tan, clever, Kennedy displayed a nimble mind and a fountain of confidence. On TV he crackled. Nixon, recovering from an illness in which he had dropped a few pounds, was wan, nervous, and off his game. His suit blended into the gray background (even though, at his aides' demanding, the studio had been repainted twice to darken it), and his shirt was loose around the collar, making him look a trifle scrawny. His complexion was dark and pasty, owing to a last-minute application of Lazy Shave, a product intended to hide a five-o'clock shadow.

On substance the debate was a standoff, and those who listened to it on radio came to that conclusion. But for those who were watching it, the picture took over. It was not a debate over the missile gap between the United States and the Soviet Union, the future of the two Chinese islands of Quemoy and Matsu, the recession of 1958, or the "loss" of Cuba to Fidel Castro and the communists. It was which pixelated version of a presidential candidate best represented the image of the presidency held most dear to the nation at that moment. And on that score, Kennedy was the clear victor. Media philosopher Marshall McLuhan pronounced that he was like a young and earnest sheriff in a television western; Nixon, the insensitive lawyer come to impose the will of a distant corporation on a small town.

The concern of many regarding Kennedy had been that he was all splash and no substance. The debates remedied that. Yes, he had pizzazz, but the mere sight of him, holding his own with the well-informed vice president on subjects as weighty as foreign policy, gave him the heft he needed and excused his arrogance, for what was wrong with a little splash if you could back it up? Though most observers agreed that Nixon did better in the succeeding debates than he had done in the first (and won, by nearly all accounts, the third encounter on international issues), it no longer mattered. Their first meeting had given Kennedy the momentum that would take him to victory, and permanently changed the nature of American politics, the era of the big political bosses now giving way to the world of television and television advisers.

The Massachusetts senator's other big liability had been his religion. No Roman Catholic had ever been elected president, and a sizable part of the South, in particular, remained distrustful. Even Martin Luther King, Sr., the civil rights leader's father, admitted to having trouble voting for a Catholic, though he eventually came around. ("Imagine," said Kennedy, "Martin Luther King having a bigot for a father.") Throughout the campaign, Kennedy dispensed with this issue by appealing to the nation's better instincts. Visiting the Alamo, he noted that the list of the dead included several Irish-Americans, like himself. No one knew if they were Catholic, he admitted, building up to his punch line, because religion was not seen as a requirement for defense of one's country. The appeal worked.

Another crucial turning point of the campaign involved Martin Luther King, Jr. The two had never met before Kennedy began his campaign to become the thirty-fifth president, yet Kennedy probably owes his election to King, who was originally leaning to an endorsement for Nixon, and only switched after Kennedy, persuaded by the urgent pleas of a political aide, made a historic phone call to Coretta King, the civil rights leader's wife, in which he offered to help secure King's release from a Georgia jail cell. King was serving a sentence for participating in a sit-in at an Atlanta snack bar when the Kennedy camp convinced the presiding judge to free him, impressing untold numbers of black voters. After that, King didn't endorse Kennedy in word, but his aide, Ralph Abernathy, announced to King's followers that they should "take off their Nixon buttons." And on November 8, 1960, in the first election in which the "Negro" voter,

"We wouldn't have had a prayer without that gadget."

JFK, speaking of the television's role in his 1960 campaign for president

The thrill of JFK:
"The idea that this guy, who looked like your cool older brother, might be President was really exciting"

If you were a teenager in the 1950s, the president, Dwight Eisenhower, looked a lot like your grandfather. In fact, he was old enough to be your grandfather — the oldest man ever to have served as president at that time. By the late fifties he'd been through a heart attack and a stroke, and he was never particularly good with the English language. To my parents' generation, he was the guy who won World War II. But to my generation, he just looked like a somewhat befuddled elderly gentleman.

So along comes the 1960 campaign, and John Kennedy, the youngest man ever elected. And the idea that this guy, who looked like your cool older brother, might be president of the United States was a really exciting proposition. Kennedy came to my college, the University of Wisconsin, and I had a seat several miles high up in the bleachers. There was this impossibly tanned, impossibly energetic young guy, giving a rousing speech about our generation and what it meant. And it connected, because we were not cynics then. It was possible to listen to somebody running for president of the United States talk about our responsibilities as the next generation, and believe it.

I watched all the debates in the common rooms on campus, and they were absolutely packed. And then after Kennedy was elected and his press conferences were televised, you could go into the student union, and there would be a huge crowd watching them. I think we all felt a sense of identification, and it wasn't just that he was young. Kennedy's presidency seemed to suggest that there was some role for us in the world. When the Peace Corps recruiters came to our campus, the line to apply went around the block. Hundreds upon hundreds of people lined up to see whether they could sign up to spend two years of their life thousands of miles away at subsistence wages. That to me is the most memorable measurement of how much we did believe there was something for us to do.

The idea of a White House run and staffed by younger people suggested that government and politics was not simply the province of people impossibly older than we were. There was the feeling that, well, if they're running the political system, surely we can be somehow involved in it. It gave us a sense that we were entitled to be part of the political process, even as naysayers and protesters. Because, after all, look who was running the country.

—Jeff Greenfield, born in 1943, was a legislative aide to Senator Robert F. Kennedy and a speechwriter for Mayor John V. Lindsay of New York, before becoming a columnist and a political media analyst.

John and Jackie greet reporters from the balcony of their Georgetown home.

John F. Kennedy came to our campus during his campaign, and he drove down Euclid Avenue. I can still see him there in the car, smiling. Just the excitement of standing there and watching that has always stayed in my mind. I didn't really know much about him, but it was a thrill to see him go by. And there were lots of students out there, so there must have been some sense among the student body that he was the guy for them. There was also this undercurrent below the surface of our lives, about sexuality, about politics, even feminism. All of these things were percolating and suddenly we felt that we might be able to do something in the world and make changes. And the things that Kennedy said made us truly believe that he was the one who would help us make a change.

—Marnie Mueller, born in 1942, went to Ecuador as a Peace Corps volunteer in 1963. She is the author of Green Fires, *a novel set in the Ecuadorian rain forest.*

I went with a friend of mine to Columbus Circle in New York to see John F. Kennedy speak. We got as close as we could, which was about two blocks away where you could just see this little dot, which was him. There were a lot of what we used to call bums hanging out near us, and they were saying, "Everything's going to be all right once he gets in there. Our lives are going to change." These guys, who lived in a world where there was plenty of reason to be cynical about politicians, heard in this guy's voice and saw in his persona that something was changing. And that was my sense as well. A lot of Kennedy's appeal was superficial. He was young. But in my mind, he embodied something new. And in a world which felt encrusted in outdated values, something new spoke to me. He was like a beacon, affirming certain things that were happening in the society, but that up until that time hadn't been being acknowledged. It wasn't like he was showing us how to be idealists, but rather like he was saying, "It's okay to be an idealist."

—Stuart Ewen, born in New York City in 1945, participated in Freedom Summer in 1964 and joined the Student Nonviolent Coordinating Committee (SNCC) shortly thereafter.

The 1960 campaign was the first campaign in which I was able to vote. Everybody in my family had always voted Republican, and I voted for Nixon. I didn't find him nearly as appealing a candidate, but I found some of his stands on the issues a little more like mine. Kennedy was such an unknown. He seemed to represent a whole lot of ideas that were new and different, and I was sort of a traditionalist at that point. Having grown up in New England where a lot of the lines are drawn on religious and ethnic lines rather than racial lines, I think I was very much aware of the whole Catholic issue. And I was really surprised that he succeeded, because some of those feelings ran so strong in the environment that I grew up in. I was a political science major in college, so I was tuned into political behavior, and I followed the election with great interest. The day after the election I went into a coffee shop, and there were three or four women sitting around. And their comments were, "Didn't we elect a cute president?" "Isn't he gorgeous?" "Aren't we glad that we elected him because he's so adorable?" And I was sitting there thinking, you know, the reasons they voted for him had nothing to do with the issues. It had nothing to do with the different stands of the parties. But then came Kennedy's inaugural speech. Particularly the famous line about, ask not what your country can do for you, ask what you can do for your country. I think it had a lot to do with the things our generation was raised with, the idea that you had an obligation to give something back. I had been ambivalent about Kennedy and probably even a little bit negative, but I was very inspired by that speech. I felt a real sense of excitement, because it was a wonderful moment. And I don't think there's been one like that since.

—Martha Naismith, born in 1938, returned to university in 1981, earning a master's degree in Public Administration in 1983 and going on to serve in various positions in the field of health and human services in Washington, D.C.

enfranchised in the freer northern cities, is believed to have made a difference, the Massachusetts senator won 70 percent of the black vote, the election by a mere 120,000 ballots.

With King, Kennedy shared the flame of idealism. In his inaugural address he spoke eloquently with phrases that are perhaps even more memorable than anything he accomplished in office. The torch, he said, had been passed to a new generation, born in this century, and he defiantly claimed that his administration would "bear any burden, meet any hardship, support any friend, oppose any foe to assure the survival and the success of liberty." His most famous utterance was the very essence of mid-century grassroots idealism. "Ask not," he implored Americans, "what your country can do for you, ask what you can do for your country." Yet what John Fitzgerald Kennedy did for his country was more style than substance, more rhetoric than program. "He gave the country back to its best self," said historian Arthur Schlesinger, "wiping away the world's impression of an old nation of old men, weary, played out, fearful of ideas, change, and the future." In one of the more telling pictures of the time, Kennedy is seen from behind as he sits in the Oval Office, the camera capturing only the back of the chair and the famous Kennedy hair: mounds of it and not a follicle of gray.

Asking Americans to look deep into their consciences and find a better self was a big part of the Kennedy message. In the debates, Nixon, as the sitting vice president, was forced to ally himself, more or less, with the status quo; Kennedy, as the challenger, could appeal to a new vision for the nation, and he did. His ideas on foreign policy were, in some respects, even more hawkish than Nixon's, but Kennedy refused to accept America's righteousness on principle. He felt it crucial that the nation bolster its own economy, improve its own practice of civil rights, erase its own poverty, for "if we do well here, if we meet our obligations, if we are moving ahead" (the repeated-phrase structure was a Kennedy staple), "freedom will be secure around the world." His inaugural address looked to extend American assistance around the world through peaceful means — not guns or dollars, but a helpful hand offered to "those people in huts and villages . . . struggling to break the bonds of misery."

The combination of pragmatism and vision recalled the era of the New Deal, and, indeed, Kennedy and his aides did a great amount to attach themselves to the memory of Roosevelt (even inspiring reporters to refer to the new president by his initials, JFK, in the way that Roosevelt had been known as FDR). In truth, Kennedy had shown little affection for FDR until it served his purposes, and like many liberals, Eleanor Roosevelt, the president's widow, had initially been a Kennedy skeptic; still, there were plenty of similarities between the two men: both had gone to Harvard, both came from patrician backgrounds (though Kennedy, as an Irish Catholic, could also appeal to Americans as the rejected outsider who blazed a path to power), and both saw public service as a responsibility of wealth. Roosevelt had been the first president to use radio effectively, Kennedy the first to master television. But where cataclysmic world events, notably the Great Depression and World War II, had given shape and direction to the earlier era, the sense of urgency around Kennedy's time was born from frustration with the complacency of the prosperous fifties.

Television had fused the nation together as never before, diluting the states

---

" His crowds had been growing for a full seven days before the debates, but now, overnight, they seethed with enthusiasm and multiplied in numbers, as if the sight of him, in their homes on the video box, had given him a 'star quality' reserved only for television and movie idols."

Theodore H. White on John F. Kennedy,
The Making of the President

as centers of separate and distinct opinion and uniting the marketplace as a single entity coast to coast. Yet, while Americans were now joined together more than ever before, they lacked a clear sense of national identity. The fact that they bought the same soap or listened to the same music didn't satisfy. The country was fat and comfortable, but just as its most dynamic leaders seemed to believe that responsibility came with success, so, increasingly, did its people.

Kennedy attracted some of the most talented people of his time to serve in his administration ("the best and the brightest," as David Halberstam's book by that name so aptly — and sardonically — called them), and the nation looked to them as an elite force of intellectuals dedicated to crafting America a more noble vision. His wife, Jacqueline, equaled them in style and poise — if not the most admired First Lady, certainly the most alluring. Yet it was the president himself who best personified the new era, a time in which many Americans believed that not only youth but intelligence and breeding, style and élan, ebullience and vigor (a favorite Kennedy word, pronounced with Bostonian flair) would see the nation through.

Not only was Kennedy young, he inspired the nation's young, too, like this crowd that greeted him on the campaign trail in rural Wisconsin and thousands of others who now jumped at the chance to work for the government. "Young people running for office explained that Kennedy had made politics respectable," wrote historian and Kennedy aide Arthur M. Schlesinger, Jr. "What perhaps they more often meant was that he had made it rational."

9

Into the Streets
1961–1969

Previous spread: In a prelude to the more violent protests of 1968, thousands of Vietnam War demonstrators besieged an army induction center in Oakland, California — pulling parked cars into the street to block traffic, overturning trash cans, fighting with police — during Stop the Draft Week in October 1967.

In the turbulent sixties the Soviet Union tested America's resolve by sealing the border between East and West Berlin and by building nuclear missile sites in Cuba, bringing the two superpowers to the brink of war. "What is in danger of being destroyed here," reported Edward R. Murrow, "is that perishable commodity called hope." In the picture below, children play at the West German side of the wall, 1962.

Into the Streets 1961–1969

On August 17, 1962, eighteen-year-old Peter Fechter and his friend Helmut Kulbeik skipped out of their East Berlin place of work and, devouring a quick meal of bacon and boiled potatoes as they ran, made their way toward the city's latest fascination: a twenty-eight-mile "wall" erected by the East German authorities to separate communist East Berlin from the city's Western sector. The barrier had been built, to the horror of the world, under the secrecy of night exactly one year before, ostensibly to keep westerners out, but in reality to stanch the flow of East German refugees who had left that nation desperately short of workers. Nearly 3 million people had fled East Germany since 1949; 30,000 alone in the month before the erecting of the wall.

Fechter, who had been born during the last furious days of the Third Reich, had never known any life but the rather limited and oppressive existence allowed him under communism. Engaged to be married, he had worried that his meager fifty-dollar-a-month mason's salary would never be enough to support the family he hoped to create. His only chance for the life he wanted lay in defection to the West, where his fiancée could later meet him and together the two could reconstruct their lives. But to do that, he had to somehow find his way past the "antifascist protective barrier," as the East German authorities euphemistically labeled the wall.

Shortly before 2:00 P.M., the young men approached a sawmill that backed onto the sandy area separating East Berlin from the barrier at Zimmerstrasse. They made their way to a back window of the mill and quietly removed the barbed wire and boards covering it. They then took off their shoes and stepped through the window, slipping into the sandy open-air area immediately preceding the wall, a place known to all Berliners as the "death strip." Above them, in the bricked-up windows of the sawmill's upper floors, stood East German police, their guns aimed in an ironic mission: Germans ordered to shoot Germans trying to leave one German homeland and go to another German homeland.

With shouts of "Come on, Peter," Kulbeik made a sudden rush toward the

> *"America's need in those years was to take an existential turn, to walk into the nightmare, to face that terrible logic of history which demanded that the country and its people must become more extraordinary and more adventurous or else perish."*
>
> *Norman Mailer*

bulwark and flung himself over its six feet to freedom. Fechter followed, but, stunned by the sight of a policeman only a few feet away, he hesitated just long enough to dim his chances. As he reached the top, a burst of machine-gun fire tossed him back on the sand.

What followed was a scene tragically descriptive of the limits of power in the nuclear age. While Fechter lay pleading for help, his hands gripping the ground in desperation, authorities on both sides of the wall stood motionless, waiting for orders, aware that any interference could initiate an international incident. West Berlin police threw Fechter packages of bandages, but he was already too weak to apply them. His body drained of blood and began twitching. Then, after forty awkward minutes had passed, the boy succumbed, a martyr to freedom.

History does not usually distribute itself neatly into ten-year episodes any more than it distributes itself neatly into century-long episodes, yet no decade in the twentieth century more determinably describes an era than does the sixties. The prosperity and the signs of an emerging shoot-for-the-moon idealism were there a few years before, as was a more benign form of the music; the fifties' beatniks may have prefigured the sixties' hippies, and the war in Vietnam didn't end until midway through the 1970s. Yet it was the cascade of events contained between the years 1961 and 1969 and the social metamorphosis that arrived with them that put this decade in stark relief to what came before and after it. Nothing can challenge the status of the Second World War as the century's most dynamic event, but while it is harder to measure its impact, the sixties were nearly as transforming, if only for the sheer quantity of conventions overturned, battles joined, and ideas put forth.

The decade was unusual for the degree to which it contained both parts of its own story, exposition *and* development, introduction *and* conclusion, antecedent *and* consequence. In the sixties man set his sights on the moon and in the sixties he got there. History's most significant popular singing group, the Beatles, introduced their first single in 1962 (the sweet and simple "Love Me Do"), helped lead the youthful rebellion with their long hair, mid-decade forays into hallucinogenic drugs, and fascination with Eastern mysticism, then as if on cue, promptly disbanded as the calendar turned onward to the next decade. The sixties contain both liberal apotheosis *and* conservative backlash, Eugene McCarthy *and* George Wallace, Lyndon Johnson *and* Barry Goldwater. So much happened so fast that conservatives could later claim victory (the wave that brought Ronald Reagan into office in 1981 began with Goldwater's nomination in 1964) even as liberals looked wistfully back at the time as *their* moment of triumph.

Most of the period's stories outline a tragic arc: the civil rights movement that proceeds in earnest in the early years of the decade, endures the burning of Watts and Detroit in the mid-sixties, and then nearly collapses with the murder of Martin Luther King in 1968; the war in Southeast Asia that many at the outset believed was both winnable and necessary ("to avoid another Munich" went the mantra in the halls of the Defense Department), escalating abruptly in the Lyndon Johnson years, killing tens of thousands of American boys, rupturing families, and tarnishing the trust Americans held for their government; the

Thousands of mourners lined the tracks as Robert Kennedy's funeral train traveled south from New York to Washington, D.C., in 1968. "Some stood at rigid attention, hand over heart," observed Arthur M. Schlesinger, Jr. "Some as if in a daze followed the train down the roadbed." This latest assassination, coming just two months after the murder of Martin Luther King, Jr., left many Americans wondering how the United States had become such a violent society.

expressions of a culture of significance, as represented by the hope contained in early-sixties folk music building to mid-decade outrage and finally ending in the despair and defeatism ringing out in Jimi Hendrix's sardonic electric rendering of "The Star-Spangled Banner" at Woodstock.

Not only did the decade witness the flagrant division of Berlin into East and West, free and captured (a kind of cruel irony, forcing the people responsible for Treblinka and Auschwitz into what felt like one big concentration camp, run, effectively, by their historical enemy, the Russians), but so, it seemed, was a great divide brought upon everything else. The champions of peaceful protest who held sway through the civil rights struggles of the fifties competed now with those who saw violence as the only effective way to change an entrenched system of injustice. Throughout Europe and the United States, the "establishment" generation fought with the "counterculture," adult with student, old with young. In America, parent fought child over music, hair length, the war in Vietnam, and the viability of the nation's oldest principles and institutions. And within the ranks of the rebellious young, those who wanted to work within the system for change clashed with those who wanted nothing less than revolution. Even man and woman were split: it was during the sixties that the divorce rate, which had languished in the previous decade, began to climb, and it climbed rapidly.

*"Before the Peace Corps, the only
Americans the poor Venezuelans
ever saw were riding around in
Cadillacs. They supposed them
all to be rich, selfish, callous,
reactionary. The Peace Corps
has shown them an entirely
different kind of American.
It is transforming the whole
theory they have of the United
States."*

Allan Stewart,
U.S. ambassador to Venezuela
during the Kennedy years

The contrast of a few powerful images from the era tells this story: Martin Luther King standing at the Lincoln Memorial in 1963, imploring 250,000 Americans, the people of the March on Washington (and millions more watching on television), to dream as he dreamed, of a time when black and white children would form one tolerant and loving nation; and King, just five years later, lying on the cold concrete of the balcony of a Memphis motel, a bullet having cut life from him only minutes before. The freshly scrubbed volunteers who undertook the first Peace Corps missions eagerly arriving in Ethiopia and Colombia and Iran and the Philippines in the decade's early years, bringing with them the unbridled energy of youth and the will to conquer disease and illiteracy and poverty, and thousands of similar-aged protesters gathered in Chicago during the 1968 Democratic convention, facing off in an angry and violent confrontation with Chicago police intent on interrupting their demonstration over the war in Vietnam. And of course, perhaps most significant, the scenes of the young president who christened the decade with an incantation of hopeful phrases, and his beautiful wife — one charming, the other elegant, the two of them together a riveting regal presence for a nation of immigrants — captivating America in their "thousand days" and the same president on November 22, 1963, slumped in the seat of a shiny blue Lincoln convertible motoring hysterically through Dealey Plaza, Dallas, while the First Lady, her raspberry-pink suit covered in her husband's blood, irrationally climbs backward in pursuit of parts of his cranium ruptured by a bullet fired from the Texas Book Depository but in reality from where? Russia? The CIA? The mob? Like no other divide in a decade of divides, the assassination split American life between what was and what came to be. And it begged the question that nagged at the mind about so much throughout these years of tumult: what if? Would the sixties be the sixties if the nation (indeed the world) had not suffered the very public murder of its dashing prince?

To be alive in the sixties was to feel exhilarated, present, not necessarily happy but at least fiercely awake. To be young in the sixties was to be all this and more. Along with "consciousness-raising" and pleasure (particularly sexual pleasure, freed from the fear of pregnancy when the Food and Drug Administration approved the birth control pill in 1960), the sixties glorified youth and freedom; the years also maligned old age and tradition, discipline, and the conformity that had been a hallmark of the most recent decade. If the gray-suited businessman had been the icon of fifties' life, the university student filled that role now. The throng that arrived on campuses in the early sixties represented the largest population of college students in the history of the nation. America was now the first society to possess more college students than farmers, as historian Todd Gitlin has pointed out, and by the end of the decade, when students the world over were in loud revolt, there would be fully three times as many American men and women in the halls of academe as there were tilling the earth.

A college education had become a proud by-product of the nation's overwhelming prosperity. It was also fast becoming a necessity in an economy more and more devoted to service jobs and less to manufacturing. In theory, at least, the sixties student had been sent to college to *become* the gray-suited symbol of managerial success that had defined the earlier years. That he might have other ideas for his future, revolutionary ideas rejecting the world that had conceived and nurtured him, repudiating the university itself as a bastion of corruption and evil, was in those early days unthinkable.

Youth's man at this time was John Kennedy, which, in retrospect, also appears ironic, for long after his death, when the myth of his life had worn thin, Kennedy was believed by many to have offered no "new torch" to follow, but a decidedly traditional, even bellicose, cold warrior foreign policy, responsible in part for the American debacle in Vietnam, and a remarkably passive attitude toward domestic affairs, particularly slow in its response to the pressing issue of civil rights. Still, Kennedy's influence, which continued to reverberate long after his death, vastly outpaced his achievement. And in the early sixties, when the largely unformed visions of the young could yet coexist with the broader population's belief in the status quo, the president's focus on a government of action, his quoting of poets and wooing of such unfamiliar Washington types as writers and artists and historians (the first administration since Franklin Roosevelt's, wrote Teddy White, to have the air of a court), his words of encouragement to youth, and the overall sense of expectation that he fostered were seductively powerful.

One of the administration's most public attempts to include the nation's young was the Peace Corps. The idea, originally proposed by rival Hubert Humphrey in 1957, was seized by Kennedy during the campaign as a romantic approach to diplomacy. Kennedy had long admired the capacity of communists to rally the young and idealistic to their cause, the way that Cuba's Fidel Castro, for instance, had mobilized thousands of young teachers to go out to the countryside and campaign against illiteracy; now he wanted to find a font of idealistic youth to do the same kind of tasks, but in the name of democracy.

His timing was perfect. Studies of the class of 1961 described a population possessed of an emerging impatience, a keen yearning for adventure. And one of the most popular novels of the time, *The Ugly American*, had recently embarrassed the nation

President Kennedy greets Peace Corps volunteers on the White House lawn, August 9, 1962. While nearly eighteen thousand people signed up in the first year, skeptics abounded. "Who but the very young themselves," wrote the Wall Street Journal, *"can really believe that an Africa aflame with violence will have its fires quenched because some Harvard boy or Vassar girl lives in a mud hut and speaks Swahili?"*

with its portrayal of Americans living the life of luxury in the Third World, feeding off the indigenous population. The book illustrated the need for a class of engineers and technical experts to help the undeveloped peoples (the word "ugly" in the title referred to these unglamorous sorts, not, as many thought, to the colonial parasites). When, three months into office, Kennedy announced the formation of a Peace Corps dedicated to just such a purpose, hundreds, then thousands jumped at the chance.

The Peace Corps was a benevolent way of executing an interventionist foreign policy in parts of the world where ignorance and poverty would likely make the appeal of communism strong. But the Kennedy administration had some less genial strategies for the Third World, too, centered, for the moment,

In Latin America with the Peace Corps: "We were adored and we were resented"

When Kennedy was elected there was definitely a feeling that he was going to somehow lead the country in a different way than Eisenhower. He was young and handsome, and he talked a language that I could understand. When I heard his inaugural speech, and he said, "Ask not what your country can do for you, ask what you can do for your country," it struck a very profound chord in me. I was a junior in college when he announced the formation of the Peace Corps and I immediately thought, "I'm going to get an application, and I'm going to join the Peace Corps." I was going to go and help the poor people of the world do something better with their lives. The idea was to go there and help people to help themselves. That was the slogan of the time, and I truly believed it. I felt that this was a way that I could give something back. I don't think that any of us who joined the Peace Corps really had an international view of the world. We just thought that the United States was the best and that the Peace Corps was a way in which we could bring the best of our nation to these floundering countries.

I originally wanted to go to Africa. Then I got a notice that said I was going to Ecuador, but I didn't have the slightest idea where Ecuador was. I just thought, "Oh, okay, I'll go to Ecuador." After about three months of training, I boarded a plane for South America. My destination was the coastal city of Guayaquil. It was a place like I had never seen before, this very exotic, tropical city built on a swamp. It was like something out of *Casablanca*. The first shock that I experienced was when I opened my mouth and what came out didn't sound like Spanish. After three months of Spanish training, I realized I couldn't really speak the language.

I was assigned to an extremely poor barrio on the northern side of Guayaquil, on a very picturesque hill, full of cane shacks. The running water only went up to a certain place on the hill. Beyond that, water had to be carried in buckets up to people's houses. Many of the houses had dirt floors and none of them had windows. There were holes in the roofs. There was garbage and sewage overflowing down the hill. It was a pretty big shock to me. My job was to organize activities for a new community center, which was built by previous volunteers. You have to understand, I was a twenty-one-year-old girl. I not only had to live twenty-four hours in a very rough-and-tumble community, but I then had to try and work some miracle within the community. I was alternately thrilled, moved, excited, terrified, and filled with the desire to go home. There were so many emotions. I thought, "Am I up to this? Am I ever going to be able to do this?" Then I thought, "Well, of course, I can do this. I'm strong."

The way I saw my role in the community center

Mueller, left, at home in Hempstead, New York, 1960, and, below, three years later during her second day of Peace Corps training in Puerto Rico.

—*Marnie Mueller, born in 1942, worked as a Head Start organizer in East Harlem, New York, after leaving the Peace Corps. She has subsequently worked as the director of Summer Programs in the New York Deputy Mayor's Office and as program director of Pacifica Radio. She currently runs her own business, producing events in New York City, and is the author of two books,* Green Fires *and* The Climate of the Country.

was to first find out what people wanted. Even if it was something as frivolous as cake decorating, I would say, "Okay, that's what you want, that's what we're going to do." We had a library in the community center. We had mechanics classes in there. We organized football teams for the boys to play. Whatever the community wanted we developed. Out of that grew more serious projects such as a preschool for the youngsters in the community. Out of the sewing classes grew an economic development project where the women made mosquito nets and sold them to CARE to make money. On the one hand, I was very accepted in the community, almost accepted too well. Many people adored me and almost thought of me as a star. On the other hand, whenever you're a First World person working in the Third World there is always a certain anger and resentment toward you. The people accept you and resent you at the same time. I knew that at any moment, if I stepped out of line in a certain way, I would be in trouble with the community. I also knew that if people adored me too much, that, too, could be unhealthy.

The Ecuadorian Small Business Organization helped to fund the community center. Every month I would go downtown and the president of that organization would give me a check. When we were doing the kindergarten and cake decorating classes, and all of those things, everything was fine. But out of the activities at the center grew a notion that the community could begin to demand bigger, more fundamental changes. And when we began to deal with the true needs of the community, we got into some trouble. One of the first indications that something was wrong occurred at a

party I threw at my house. The president of the Small Business Organization pulled me aside and pointed to somebody in the room and said, "What is he doing here? He's a communist." And then sometime after that, when the people in the community marched on the *municipio*, the city government, to demand a new sewerage system, the money for the center disappeared. This man told me, "Sorry, Marnie, there's no more money. The money dried up." And then the U.S. ambassador called me in and warned me not to enter into the politics of the country. It wasn't until years later that I heard reports that the center was funded by CIA money filtered through the Small Business Organization.

When I hit the glass ceiling on how much I could do in the community, I was very frustrated. I knew that the only way to make true change was to press the *municipio*. I think I understood at the time that something was amiss in the Peace Corps. Many of us suspected that there was something else going on, that there was another purpose for our being there that we weren't told about. There was something wrong with young, inexperienced kids coming like gangbusters into these Third World communities as though we knew everything about the world — as though we knew how to help these poor people. There was a certain arrogance about our being there, and it was very disturbing for us to find that out. What evolved out of my Peace Corps experience is that I realized that, in fact, we shouldn't be fooling around in other people's countries. I felt that we did more harm than good whenever we did that, and I felt that we were in there for other reasons than doing good. We were in there to set things up to exploit natural resources. We were in there to have control over those countries. We were not in there to help the people. The Peace Corps became both a radicalizing and a disillusioning experience for me. And I think that the two went together to completely change the way I saw the world.

American attempts to topple Fidel Castro only served to bolster Cuban nationalist sentiments against the United States and to increase the fiery dictator's popularity, especially among Cuba's rural and urban labor classes. Here, an enthusiastic supporter pulls playfully at Castro's beard, 1964.

around Cuba. The small island-nation had been a source of great pain to Americans ever since the bearded, baseball-loving Fidel Castro Ruz emerged from his hideout in the mountains of the Sierra Maestra, marched six hundred miles over seven days down Cuba's Central Highway, arrived in Havana to seize the reins of power left vacant by the fleeing dictator Fulgencio Batista, and then declared himself a communist and enemy to the United States.

In the spring of 1961 Kennedy approved a CIA plan that had a group of Cuban émigrés (some of whom would later be linked to the Watergate break-in) storm the coast of Cuba at the swamp-filled Bay of Pigs, 150 miles south of Havana. They would then run to the mountains, inspire a revolt of anti-Castro movements already on the island, and call on the United States for support. But, aware in advance of the plan (word of an American-backed coup had been circulating for months throughout Central America), Castro's modest air force simply met the émigrés and quickly cleared the beach of them.

The invasion was more than a failure; it was a fiasco. It had been too limited to succeed, and yet those very limits were essential if the United States were to maintain the myth that the invasion was an indigenous uprising, springing from the hearts and minds of anti-Castro Cubans. Kennedy took four days to admit to the American people what much of the rest of the world already knew: that the Bay of Pigs was an American operation, conducted in secrecy without even the benefit of congressional sanction. And by then, much damage had been done to the American image, both at home and abroad.

Had there been no Bay of Pigs invasion, or had the invasion been a success instead of a humiliation, had it been the first sign of President Kennedy's skills at international affairs instead of a dangerous display of incompetence, the world may never have faced the terrible events that were to follow, events that would bring humanity to the edge of Armageddon and serve as the defining moment of the Cold War. Sensing from the Bay of Pigs episode that Kennedy was weak, and prone to blunder, the Soviet leader, Nikita Khrushchev, embarked upon a series of challenges to the young president that included the building of the Berlin Wall, the testing of new and more destructive nuclear devices (three thousand times more powerful than the Hiroshima bomb), and, finally, in an attempt to discourage another American invasion of the island, the arming of Cuba with nuclear-tipped missiles aimed directly at the United States.

While each event raised the temperature of international affairs and brought anxiety into nearly every home in the developed world, the discovery of eight ballistic missile launchpads in Cuba, by American U-2 reconnaissance planes on October 15, 1962, was the most terrifying. The U-2 photographs, taken in what had become routine flyovers of Cuba, showed the beginning stages of a Soviet medium-range-missile base, but critically, they did not show a missile in position ready for launch. Choosing the least aggressive of the options he and his advisers considered, Kennedy then ordered a "quarantine" of all ships

U.S.
NO
U.S.S.R.
WAR
OVER
CUBA
NOT CROS
WE O
ALL

"My thinking went like this: if we installed the missiles secretly and then . . . the United States discovered [them], the Americans would think twice before trying to liquidate our installations . . . I knew the United States could knock out some of our installations, but not all of them. If a quarter or even a tenth of our missiles survived . . . we could still hit New York and there wouldn't be much of New York left."

Soviet leader Nikita Khrushchev,
recalling the strategy of the Cuban missile crisis

Although terrified at the prospect of nuclear war, most Americans supported Kennedy's handling of the Cuban missile crisis. Others, such as these demonstrators in New York City, took to the streets to protest what they viewed as senseless saber rattling between the two superpowers.

headed from Soviet ports to Cuba (the president chose the softest term he could for it, knowing that a "blockade," which is what it was, would be seen as an act of war) and waited to see what the Russians would do.

For thirteen days, while the two leaders faced off "eyeball-to-eyeball," the world sat dumbstruck by the imminent danger of nuclear destruction. On October 22, Kennedy explained his decision to mount the blockade to more than 100 million Americans in a remarkable seventeen-minute television address. He told them that the medium-range missiles being constructed in Cuba could conceivably destroy Miami and Cape Canaveral, Mexico City, and much of Central America. They could even reach as far as Washington, D.C. Longer-range missiles now on the way to Cuba could reach to New York City, Boston, indeed as far as Hudson Bay, Canada.

This was surely the most frightening speech ever delivered by an American leader to his people. And yet the danger had less to do with the presence of the missiles in Cuba than in the injury they brought to American pride and to the stature of Kennedy, as leader of the free world. In the complex sphere of atomic diplomacy in which Khrushchev and Kennedy now operated, missiles in Cuba would be a great boon to Russian prestige; for Kennedy, they could be crippling.

From the Vatican, Pope John XXIII pleaded with the two leaders to consider their obligations not only to the interests of their respective states but to humanity, which hung in the balance. The *Los Angeles Times* reported that students at local high schools were breaking down in class and sobbing, "I don't want to die." But the preparations for war continued. American ICBMs at silo bases across the West were loaded and cocked for delivery; fleets of the American Polaris submarine, armed with nuclear missiles, were set on an approach to Soviet waters. The nation's air force was put on DEFCON 2 (an acronym standing for Defense Condition 2, DEFCON 1 being a state of war), the highest alert in the post–World War II era, while sixteen navy destroyers and three cruise ships formed a five-hundred-mile arc interrupting access to the east coast of Cuba. Still, twenty-five Soviet merchant ships headed there stayed on course. Kennedy was pushing forward plans for an air attack on Cuba, followed by an invasion, when Khrushchev cabled an offer: he would dismantle the missile bases in return for an American promise not to invade Cuba. Though he would later tack on an additional demand that the United States withdraw its own missiles from Turkey (and the administration would quietly agree to do just that), war had been averted.

Kennedy was now a hero, the man who had saved the world from nuclear chaos, even as he had preserved American dignity. Gallup had the numbers: the president who had only squeaked by his opponent in the 1960 election now carried a 77 percent approval rating. And yet, the dark residue of the Cuban missile crisis would linger. With Cuba, the sixties had become the "crisis years," as one book so titled later called them, when life seemed darkened perpetually by the clouds of a storm that always threatened but never quite arrived.

These were "crisis years" on the domestic front, too, as the nation continued to struggle with the challenge of civil rights. The nonviolent campaign of the 1950s, driven as it had been by the power of the black church, had established the activists as morally superior to those defending the entrenched system of white power, but little else. The protesters of the Montgomery bus boycott had won the right to sit wherever they chose; the students at Central High School had been forced to accept the Little Rock Nine; and the Court had endorsed integration with the 1954 decision on *Brown*. In February 1960 four black college students had broken the whites-only policy at a Woolworth lunch counter in Greensboro, North Carolina, and within weeks, sit-ins had forced the desegregation of hundreds of lunch counters and restaurants across the country. But these victories, dramatic though they were, only stoked the fires of impatience in the black race. If segregation was wrong in one place, it was wrong everywhere. And if the courts had ruled it wrong, why must black people risk their lives to have that wrong righted?

A mounting bitterness infected the ranks of civil rights activists, directed not only at the resistant white establishment but also at the movement's own leadership. Many began to feel that the campaign of nonviolence, while winning them admiration, had been a failure and that Martin Luther King and other moderate leaders had been too willing to settle for the small victory at the expense of the large. They became cynical, too, about the support of the federal government. The string of rulings civil rights activists won in the Supreme Court had brought comfort that their claims of injustice were supported by the Constitution, yet so long as local authorities refused to enforce the principles the Court now recognized, these victories were hollow. Only the intervention of federal authorities could ensure justice, and on that score, the Kennedy administration, absorbed in international emergencies like Cuba, quickly proved to be almost as cautious as the regime it had replaced.

Some of Kennedy's reluctance was political: his narrow victory in 1960 owed as much to the votes of conservative southern Democrats as it did to northern liberals and urban blacks; similarly, the president's success with Congress depended upon his maintaining friendships with a coterie of southern Democratic senators, most of them die-hard segregationists. But even more significant was the conundrum that civil rights posed to those hoping to preserve order in an increasingly fractious society. Racism was so deeply a part of the social fabric of the South, so ingrained in local custom, gesture, and speech, that undoing it was tantamount to disassembling one society and building another one in its place, and doing it against the will of a militantly defensive majority population.

In 1961, after the Court ruled that segregated interstate bus terminals were unconstitutional, a group of activists calling themselves Freedom Riders rode buses into southern strongholds, hoping to be arrested and force the Justice Department to act on their behalf. But to the increasing number of skeptical activists, the campaign only seemed further proof that no matter what the law said, they were on their own. In Anniston, Alabama, a mob apprehended one of the buses and set it on fire. In Birmingham, Alabama, a group of Klansmen set upon another bus with the full support of Police Commissioner Bull Connor, who told them to keep up their attack until the riders "looked like a bulldog got ahold of them." And in Montgomery, home of Rosa Parks, a waiting mob set upon the activists with metal pipes and baseball bats while that city's police chief declared that his department had "no intention of standing guard for a bunch of troublemakers coming into our city."

When Martin Luther King showed up at Montgomery the next day to lead

Black students take a stand: "They could kill us, but they couldn't segregate us any longer"

I grew up on the South Side of Chicago, and while there was segregation there, I didn't really notice it that much. I always knew things were much worse in the South, because my father was a dining car waiter, and he would often come home and tell us about how hard it was to find a hotel down there that would accommodate Negroes, as we were called at that time. While I ran into some discrimination growing up, it wasn't until I went to school in Nashville, Tennessee, that I experienced real segregation. When I arrived at Fisk University, I spent the first month or so on campus. When I did venture out, I visited a few of the places near campus that were available to blacks, but everything else was segregated. After a few weeks, when the novelty was wearing off, I really started to feel limited. I resented not being able to go downtown to the Woolworth's and have lunch with a friend. Also, when I was downtown, I saw lots of blacks sitting out on the curb or on the ground

Nash (far right) at an integrated lunch counter.

eating their lunches because they weren't allowed to sit in the restaurants and eat. It was so demeaning. The first time I had to use a women's rest room marked "colored" was pretty humiliating, too. I was at the state fair with a young man, and when I came back from the rest room I was really fuming. This man was from Tennessee, and he said something like, "Are you really that upset?" And I said yes, I really was.

Pretty soon I started looking for an organization — someone, somewhere — that was trying to do something to change segregation. I heard about a series of workshops conducted by Reverend James Lawson, a conscientious objector who had spent some time in India and was extremely versed in nonviolence. So I went to these workshops, and I listened very carefully. After a

few weeks, I decided this nonviolence couldn't possibly have any impact. But because they were the only group in Nashville that was trying to make a change, I kept going. I learned that you can respect a person, and at the same time, not tolerate oppression and the actions that person is doing — that you can attack the philosophy without attacking the person.

In the fall of 1959 we started going to restaurants downtown and trying to get served. When we were refused service, we would ask to see the manager, ask him why we were being refused service, and then tell him we thought it was morally wrong. We called that testing. In February of 1960 we heard on the radio that sit-ins had begun in other southern cities — Greensboro, Orangeburg, Knoxville. We jumped up and down and applauded, and then we decided to have our sit-ins at the same chains that the students were targeting in other cities.

—Diane Nash was born in 1938. Committed to her belief that nonviolence could effect social change and to the cause of peace in Vietnam, she went to Hanoi in the winter of 1966 and as part of a delegation sponsored by the North Vietnamese Women's Union and the peace movement in the United States, was received by Ho Chi Minh. Since then, she has continued her involvement in social affairs, holding positions in welfare advocacy, tenant organizing, and serving as director of a Chicago housing agency. She has two children and two grandchildren.

As the sit-in movement spread, the executive director of the Southern Christian Leadership Conference, Ella Baker, decided it would be a good idea to bring the participating students together in one place for a conference. Over the Easter weekend in 1960 we all gathered at Shaw University in Raleigh, North Carolina. At the conference, we discussed the need for a central place to gather and disseminate information and the value in coordinating some of our activities on a South-wide kind of basis. We also decided not to become the student arm of an older organization, because we did not want to be taking orders from a distant board of directors. The Student Nonviolent Coordinating Committee was formed, and we distinguished ourselves from the older organizations, because in SNCC, the

people who did the work and took the chances were the ones who made the decisions.

By 1962 I had left Fisk University to devote all my time to the civil rights movement. In May I was in Mississippi, where the bus system was still legally segregated, encouraging black young people to sit at the front of the bus and conducting workshops in nonviolence to prepare students for the things they needed to know in order to join in the Freedom Rides. I was twenty-three at the time, and since I was encouraging these minors to do something illegal, a warrant was issued for my arrest, charging me with contributing to the delinquency of minors. I faced a two-and-a-half-year jail term, and I was about six months pregnant with my first child. My husband drove me down to Jackson and I surrendered to the sheriff, and the following Monday I surrendered to the court. I sat in the first bench in the first row and refused to move to the rear when the bailiff ordered me to do so, so I was put in jail for ten days for contempt of court.

Those ten days were really hard. The jail had so many cockroaches that I soon learned to sleep during the day so that I could sit up at night and dodge them as they dropped off the ceiling onto my cot. One night there was an insect that was so large I could actually hear it walking across the floor. I had taken a toothbrush, comb, and my vitamin pills (since I was expecting), a change of underwear, and an extra skirt and blouse, because I knew I was going to jail. But the prison officials would not let me have anything, not a toothbrush, not toothpaste, nothing. I was determined not to be demoralized, so I worked out a little schedule. I had clean clothes every day because I would wash my underwear and my outerwear at different times and they could dry while I was asleep. I remember combing my hair with my fingers and working out a way to brush my teeth. I emerged from the experience even stronger because I learned that I could get along with nothing if I had to — except food and water perhaps. I never got to the point where I felt like I had to quit, because when the officials would do oppressive things, it deepened my resolve and made me angrier.

When you are faced with a situation of injustice or oppression, if you change yourself and become somebody who cannot be oppressed, then the world has to set up against a new you. We students became people who could not be segregated. They could have killed us, but they could not segregate us any longer. Once that happened, the whole country was faced with a new set of decisions. I think most of the students that were participating were confident that we could change the world. I still think we can.

a rally at a local church, bottles, stones, and firebombs broke through the sanctuary's windows as he spoke. With shards of stained glass raining down upon them, many in the group held hands and sang. Finally, federal troops, in the form of U.S. marshals, arrived to drive the white mob back. But in its pattern of reluctance and indecision, the Kennedy administration seemed to be indicating that federal intervention would be available to back up civil rights activists only as a desperate last resort. Attorney General Robert Kennedy, the president's brother and the administration's point man on civil rights, responded to the violence at Montgomery by advising King and his colleagues to observe a "cooling-off period." Frustrated, organizer James Farmer responded with a blistering retort: "Please tell the attorney general," he said to reporters, "that we have been cooling off for three hundred and fifty years."

The founding of the Student Nonviolent Coordinating Committee (known as SNCC or Snick), composed of activists in more than fifty high schools and black colleges throughout the South, was a turning point toward a more militant, if still peaceful, brand of protest. The idea to bring students into the movement in the first place had been King's, but almost from the beginning, the group began to distance itself from him. SNCC's organizer, Ella Baker, grew to see King as arrogant and glory seeking, too interested in the spotlight of television and in making deals with the rich and powerful to address the real needs of his followers. She hoped the newer group would embrace a less centralized form of authority, where the decision making would rise from the bottom up. But, in the end, the principal difference between SNCC and King's Southern Christian Leadership Conference would be style. SNCC members saw the older organization as emanating from the more docile, deferential black spirit personified by the clergy that ran it, while their group reflected the raw rebelliousness and impatience of youth.

After Freedom Riders were beaten and their bus set on fire outside of Anniston, Alabama, above, segregationist governor John Patterson called the riders "a bunch of rabble-rousers" and warned them "to get out of Alabama as quickly as possible . . . The state . . . can't guarantee the safety of fools."

In the fall of 1961 SNCC focused its energy on a massive demonstration aimed at integrating the bus stations and other public places of Albany, Georgia. The Albany campaign was as lively a moment as the civil rights movement had yet known, a triumphant expression of pride and principle best remembered for the powerful singing it inspired. Rekindling a sense of biblical righteousness, protesters regularly broke into choruses of old slave spirituals as the police herded them off to packed jails.

But while Albany seemed to enliven the spirit of the movement, its failure to establish any political result only brought more doubt upon the strategy of peaceful protest. Here the police responded to nonviolence with nonviolence, jailing the demonstrators but resisting the kind of club-wielding incidents that had brought condemnation upon the South in so many other instances. Against the wishes of many of its members, SNCC finally turned to King to save them, but while he came to Albany, spoke, and was arrested with the rest of the activists, this was not the platform he needed now. Albany's civic leaders had shown that Gandhian methods of social protest could be resisted effectively. In

The awesome power of protest music: "If I sing, you stand in my sound"

I spent my youth in Albany, Georgia, which is in southwest Georgia. It was a singing black culture with a strong choral tradition, and many of us knew the same songs. Black people just did not get together without singing. When I went to Albany State College in the fall of 1959, I initially went into music, because I thought I was going to be a singer. At college, I sang spirituals as I had done my whole life, but was also introduced to Western choral classics, Italian *arias* and German *lieder*. My professors placed a high value on music literacy, but I had some trouble with the idea of reading songs off of paper. In my mind most of the music in the world was transmitted orally, just as it had been in southwest Georgia. I had even thought about majoring in something else, but then I got swept up in the changing tide of the civil rights movement, and that threw all those troubles I had been dealing with in college right up and out of the window.

Song was essential to the civil rights movement in Albany. When students would get together for a rally, they would come in and sit down, but their presence alone did not create the community. It wasn't until we raised a song and everybody put their part into making the song happen that we could start our meetings. Initially, the songs we sang were from a stock of songs that were in the black church, many of them coming out of slavery. We moved back and forth with traditional songs and spirituals that we put new words to and a few new songs.

In Thanksgiving of 1961, several students were arrested for attempting to purchase bus tickets at the "whites only" counter of the Trailways bus terminal in Albany. A march was organized in protest. We walked around the jail and back to the Albany State College campus and then to the nearest black church to end the rally. After the march I was asked to sing a song. And I chose the spiritual "Over My Head," which goes, "Over my head, I see trouble in the air . . ." But as I sang the first line I changed "trouble" to "freedom," and by the time I got out of the first line everybody was singing. I was trying to make the song fit the moment, and it was one of the first times that had happened to me as a song leader. It was really my first *freedom* song.

I remember one particular demonstration at this time during which some two hundred people were arrested. I had been taking a test that day (which I didn't pass) and thought I had missed my chance to be arrested and my chance to be in the movement. All across the South, freedom fighters were being arrested, and I myself was so caught up in the movement that I knew that if the movement was going to come to Albany, Georgia, I did not want it to be over before I had done everything I could. If freedom fighters were going to be

Reagon (center) performing with the Freedom Singers, 1963.

—*Bernice Johnson Reagon was born in 1942. Although she was suspended from Albany State College in 1961 for her participation in the civil rights movement, she would go on to receive a Ph.D. in American history from Howard University in 1975. In 1973 she founded Sweet Honey in the Rock, a world-renowned a cappella music group. Ms. Reagon has served on the faculty of several universities and as curator emeritus of the Smithsonian Institution National Museum of American History. She resides in Washington, D.C.*

put in jail, I was determined to be put in jail, too. The next day, I went to another rally and then I was arrested. So I was very, very pleased.

Once you get in jail, it's a sobering experience. I was put into a four-person cell along with eleven other women of all ages, from high school students to senior citizens. For the most part, we would just try to deal with getting through the minutes and the hours. It was in jail where I began to be asked to sing a lot, and it became very clear to me that that's where I was supposed to be. For others, however, the purpose of this time in jail was not so absolutely clear. Some people would get into prison and cry as soon as they heard the sound of the cell doors clanging. Others felt that they should pray. Teenagers wanted to do rock and roll or talk about their boyfriends. It was really a microcosm of a community that was penned in too close, but one of the things that gave space in that community was singing. We sang almost all of the time, and people told stories and in between the stories, we sang and prayed. The experience was incredible because it really crossed the generations. I thought about how Jesus was crucified on the cross with those other two thieves, and how he was innocent. It seemed to fit. From the jail cell, his cross looked like a lynch tree to me.

Little by little, people began to write about the singing in Albany. The people from the Student Non-

violent Coordinating Committee (SNCC), who had recently come to Albany to encourage voter registration, would come out of our mass meetings and say, "Man, those people can sing." The leaders of SNCC started to talk about using the singing to organize support outside the South. They saw music as a way to get publicity about our voter registration drives. It was Cordell Reagon who formed the Freedom Singers, and I was an alto in the group. We called ourselves the Singing Traveling Newspaper, because we traveled all around the country singing songs and telling stories of the organizing in the South. We helped organize food and clothing drives to assist people who had actually lost their jobs trying to register to vote, and we formed committees all over the country to support the activities of the freedom movement in the South.

There is no difference between singing at a mass meeting, singing in jail, singing on a march, or even singing when the authorities tell you not to. Singing gives you the power to be heard, because if I sing, you stand in my sound. I remember being in a church at a mass meeting in Terrell County, Georgia. The sheriff and deputies walked in, completely changing the atmosphere there. Then somebody started singing, and the music of the song was carried back to where they were standing, and the uneasy air they had created with their presence and their guns was somehow transformed. Singing really extends you beyond your physical body, because people have to walk into the sound of your voice before they get to your body. You are not protected by singing; it does not save your life or keep people from shooting or arresting you, and singing will not set you free. Nonetheless, I knew that my part in the civil rights movement would be in song, and that song was the sound of the movement.

Police Chief Bull Connor ordered the use of high-pressure fire hoses on black protesters, above, as they attempted to march on Birmingham's City Hall in 1963. While many of the marchers were forced to retreat, one small group braced themselves against the onslaught and repeatedly chanted the word "freedom," inspiring the remaining marchers to continue on.

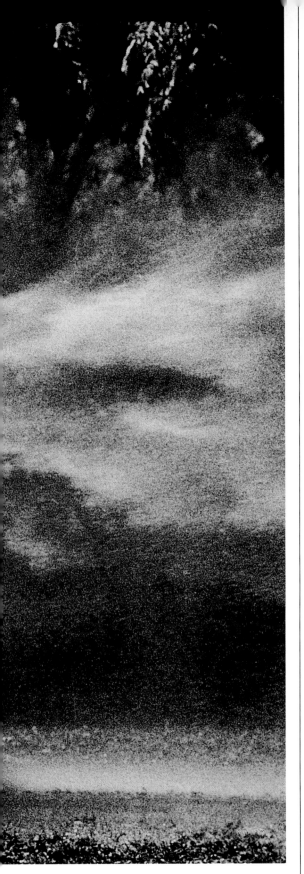

Albany it was finally the black protesters who succumbed to violence, at one point going on a bottle-and-stone-throwing rampage against the town's police that sank King into a deep expression of grief. This was just the kind of incident he had worked so hard to prevent.

Still, there were soon so many challenges to the old segregated order springing from so many sources and so many lines drawn in the Dixie "dust" to defend against them, it was hard not to feel that the nation was reaching a critical juncture. The Kennedy administration's hope for a smooth and peaceful transition away from segregation and toward a more just society was unrealistic. There was no room for compromise; the issues of civil rights were so fundamental to both sides, they would forever resist political brokering. Either the Old South would defend itself, at a considerable price, or it would die.

In the fall of 1962 James Meredith, attempting to become the first African-American to enroll at the University of Mississippi, came up against the full weight of white intransigence, precipitating a standoff between Governor Ross Barnett and the president, and the assignment of federal troops to Oxford, Mississippi. A few months later, delivering his inaugural address as the governor of Alabama, George Corley Wallace declared that he would fight for "segregation now, segregation tomorrow, segregation forever" and, if necessary, position himself "in the schoolhouse door" to stop integration. Then came Birmingham.

The Magic City, as it proudly called itself, carried also (and also quite proudly) the appellation as the most segregated city in America. There were 220,000 whites in Birmingham and 140,000 blacks, two populations living side by side, equal only in the brimming reserves of rage that each carried for the other. Given the choice by minor-league baseball to integrate its local team or give it up, Birmingham had chosen to go without; ordered to integrate its local parks, Birmingham officials chose instead to close them.

Unlike Albany, Georgia, this was a city made for racial drama and, in choosing to make a stand here, Martin Luther King was aiming high, hoping, in what could be his last stand, to create the kind of spectacle at which he so excelled. Under such challenge from within the ranks of his own movement, King hoped that a confrontation at the country's most notoriously segregated community might finally make clear to the rest of the country and the world that segregation was so insidious it could not simply be chipped away by grass-roots demonstrators; it needed to have the full force of the nation brought down upon it, in the form of outrage and condemnation.

In the end, Birmingham was indeed a remarkable story. It had a villain (Police Chief Bull Connor, who, ousted in elections the year before but in power until his successor could be installed, hoped to resurrect his reputation by taking a brutal stand against black activists); poetry (King's "Letter from a Birmingham Jail," written in the margins of a newspaper while he was incarcerated by Connor for violating an injunction against marching on Good Friday, is a gem, perhaps the greatest piece of literature produced by the civil rights movement); pictures (the scenes of Connor's police dogs and pressure hoses attacking the demonstrators were so powerful they did rally much of the nation to examine its commitment to equal justice); danger (in a final, desperate act that could have cost him his reputation, King sent children — some as young as six years — into the streets to face arrest and jail); and results (after announcing that a picture of a police dog

Martin Luther King, Jr.,
1929 – 1968

attacking a black woman had made him "sick," President Kennedy increased the pace and scope of civil rights legislation he planned to now put before Congress). Birmingham lit a fire across the map of the nation. Almost a thousand demonstrations, in over one hundred cities, followed. Fifteen thousand people were arrested. But the much-vaunted southern white power structure had finally cracked.

On a steamy summer night in August 1963, nearly a quarter of a million people, most of them, as one speaker noted, the great-grandchildren of slaves, boarded trains and buses, drove cars, and hobbled along by foot on their way to the nation's capital. They would go first to the Washington Monument and then, proceeding in execution of the grand gesture that they had come to make, march to the Lincoln Memorial, singing "We Shall Overcome" and reveling in a peculiar, giddy kind of confidence born of the righteousness of their cause.

The March on Washington, as it was called, was one of the crowning moments of the civil rights movement, and certainly the high point of the career of Martin Luther King. Much disagreement had been evident in the event's planning, reflecting the continuing split in the movement's ranks, and much of official Washington, fearing violence, had left town before the march began. Yet the demonstrators proceeded as one, with "deep fervor and quiet dignity" (President Kennedy's words), on a distinctively American mission: to lay claim to the most explicit rights offered them in the Constitution. "If I had to pick one day in my public life when I was most encouraged democracy would work, when my spirit soared on the wings of the American dream," said Senator Hubert Humphrey, who was one of the few politicians to join the march, "it was that day."

The president had originally discouraged the event's planners, worrying that a march now could only damage the chances that his civil rights legislation would pass, and FBI Director J. Edgar Hoover, a conniving enemy to both King and the Kennedys, tried hard to scuttle it through more subversive means. But there was no stopping an occasion of this magnitude. The March on Washington was the first massive display of sixties "people power," loud and undeniable, and as it played out, it had the feeling that destiny was directing it. Folk singer Joan Baez opened the ceremonies with her rendition of "Oh, Freedom"; Odetta, Marian Anderson, Mahalia Jackson, Bob Dylan, and Peter, Paul, and Mary followed (their rendition of Dylan's politically charged "Blowin' in the Wind" was then the second most widely played recording in America). When it was announced, shortly after Odetta sang, that W. E. B. Du Bois, the legendary black leader whose ideas had inspired generations of African-Americans to push for justice, had died in Africa, it almost seemed as though he had timed his passing to be a part of the gathering, to initiate the ceremonies that owed so much to people like him.

With an international audience watching on television (the march was one of the first events to be broadcast live via the communications satellite Telstar), Sammy Davis, Jr., Ossie Davis, Lena Horne, Harry Belafonte, and Josephine Baker all made appearances onstage. But this was a rally that belonged to Dr. King. From the pulpit of the Lincoln Memorial, underneath the brooding marble visage of the Great Emancipator himself, King offered one of the most compelling speeches in American history, not so much by addressing the injustices of America as it was, but instead by repeatedly invoking the image of Amer-

*The choice of the Lincoln Memorial, above, as the rally site for the
March on Washington was a profoundly symbolic one, particularly since
1963 was the centennial of Lincoln's Emancipation Proclamation.
The D.C. police liked the site as well, but for a more cynical reason: with
the monument grounds surrounded by water on three sides, any violence
among the demonstrators could be easily contained.*

ica as it *could* be, indeed as it *should* be, as the American founders in establishing this nation hoped it *would* be. "I have a dream," he said to the assemblage of tear-filled black and white faces in front of him, imploring them and the millions tuned in at home to join with him. And then, in rhythms known only to a man of the cloth, he repeated it again and again. "I have a dream . . . I have a *dream . . .*"

In Harlem, where, like many northern urban areas, the separatist ideas of the Black Muslims were gaining large numbers of recruits, leader Malcolm X mocked King by calling it "the farce on Washington." And even within the crowd that day there were mumblings of despair. "[Forget] the dream," shouted one angry attendee. "Now, Martin, now!" But to most of those watching, King's words were electrifying. Listening to him, many white Americans understood the movement for the first time. Far from being rebellious upstarts, the civil rights workers were patriots, jogging the conscience of the nation to come alive to its best traditions, and King himself was like Kennedy, challenging them to listen to their better selves at a critical time. Thanks to King's speech, the March on Washington was lifted to its place as one of the grandest of democratic spectacles. And the euphoria was still ringing in the ears when, two weeks later, a bomb exploded in Birmingham's Sixteenth Street Baptist Church killing four young girls as they donned choir robes for a morning service.

News of the shooting in Dallas spread quickly throughout the world via television, radio, news wires, and word of mouth. Above, stunned New Yorkers in Times Square anxiously wait for word on the president's fate.

Anyone alive and aware on November 22, 1963, when the news from Dallas arrived across radios, televisions, and phone lines, in the form of frantic voices of neighbors calling over suburban lawns and the somber tones of tearful school principals speaking to their students from loudspeakers, remembers in sharp detail where they were and what they were doing. More interesting are those who can recall what they felt. For most, the information struck like a poison-tipped dagger, delivering to the system equal amounts of grief and disbelief. Surely the newsman was wrong; this was some *other* president of some other *distant* country that had been killed, the leader of a place where things like that happened, not the president of the United States, the nation of death-defying hope and possibility. The writer William Styron, rummaging through the refrigerator at his Connecticut home in search of a lunchtime beer when the phone rang, remembers the sense that he was suddenly shrinking and becoming aged beyond his years. Riding a taxi through the dense and chaotic traffic of Washington, D.C., Daniel Patrick Moynihan, then assistant secretary of labor, became consumed with fear. Worried, like many were, that Kennedy's death was only the first blow of some international plot against the nation, he opened his wallet and retrieved a map containing the route to a West Virginia cave where he and other government officials were to go in the event of a nuclear attack. Moynihan considered handing it to the driver, then reversed himself. With the traffic, he thought, he would never arrive there.

The assassination of John Fitzgerald Kennedy on the second day of the eleventh month of the third year of his presidency was at once a story of drama, pathos, horror, dread, mystery, trauma, suspicion, and tragedy. The president had gone to Texas to heal a rift in the state's Democratic Party and, in anticipation of the 1964 presidential election, begin repairing his image in the South, where he had been perceived as too eager on civil rights. He did not expect to be greeted warmly in Dallas, in particular; only two weeks before, United Nations Ambassador Adlai Stevenson had been heckled there by right-wing demonstrators. But the crowd meeting him at the airport was warm and the parade route was lined with outstretched hands. Then, beginning with what observers called a "cracking" sound at 12:30 P.M., central standard time, came the series of events that would be played and replayed, analyzed and reanalyzed for generations.

An eight-millimeter film, barely thirty seconds long, shot by a local garment manufacturer named Abraham Zapruder, showed the assassination in vivid color. Though amateurish and without sound, it was as remarkable a document as any in history, as if someone in the audience at Ford's Theatre one hundred years before had brought a motion picture camera and directed it toward the Lincolns' box at precisely the moment that the pistol-carrying John Wilkes Booth intruded upon the evening. Zapruder caught the delight of Kennedy's penultimate moment, the majesty of the police motorcade escorting his limousine around the bend; the president, smiling and waving, his right hand rising to push back a shock of the famous Kennedy hair. Then, suddenly, he bends forward, clutching his throat, and is almost immediately thrown by a second impact, his head exploding in a bright orange spray.

The nation's shock was overpowering. Just twenty-five minutes after the first news flash, the television audience tuned to any one of the three major networks had doubled; by the time the president's body arrived back at Andrews Air Force Base (the new president, Lyndon Johnson, having been sworn in on the plane), 70 percent of the nation was watching. And by Monday, the day of the funeral of the first slain American president since McKinley, a full 93 percent of American homes were tuned in, joined, thanks to the Telstar satellite, by millions abroad.

The rush of images that bombarded the mind those four days took life as many in America then knew it and split it, like a jigsaw to cardboard, into too many pieces to ever again form a coherent whole: the arrest on Friday afternoon of the presumed assassin, Lee Harvey Oswald, in a Dallas movie theater (he was watching a double feature, *Cry of Battle* and *War Is Hell*); the arrival in Washington later that night of the coffin carrying the president's remains, moved awkwardly (as all coffins are) to a waiting black limousine by the men who had only recently formed the president's sturdy team of close advisers; the rain of Saturday, an ugly Washington downpour, as the body of the president lay in the East Room of the White House; the transfer of the coffin, on Sunday, up Pennsylvania Avenue along with a riderless black horse, reversed boots in the stirrups; the murder on live television of Oswald, by a nightclub owner named Jack Ruby, later

No novelist's imagination could have created an assassin better suited to early-sixties fears than Lee Harvey Oswald, below at Dallas police headquarters. Oswald had connections to the Soviet Union (his wife was Russian and he had once lived in Moscow), Cuba (the pro-Castro Fair Play for Cuba Committee), and the mob (he had tenuous links to a New Orleans godfather).

During the Kennedy era, I was a journalist working as the L.A. bureau chief for *Life* magazine. Even though I tried to remain objective about Kennedy, deep down I thought he was the most exciting politician to come along in some time. He was a young, vibrant man, who came out of World War II and who represented an idealism that was rampant in the country at that time. There was just so much political excitement and glamour associated with him and his family. He was truly *the* politician of our generation.

On November 22, 1963, one of my colleagues, who was watching the AP ticker, suddenly shouted to me that Kennedy had been shot in Dallas. I got on the phone to the New York office, and they told me to get to Dallas as fast as I could. A reporter named Tommy Thompson, two photographers, and I jumped in a car, headed to the airport, and were on a plane heading to Dallas about forty-five minutes after we heard the news. We arrived in Dallas by around 4:00 P.M. that Friday. By that time, Lee Harvey Oswald was in the Dallas jail, and the town was swarming with reporters from all over the country.

Tommy and one of the photographers went down to the jail, where they uncovered a lead as to where Oswald's family might be staying. While they tried to hunt down the Oswalds, I set up a bureau office in a downtown hotel. At about six o'clock, I got a phone call from a *Life* stringer. She had heard from a cop that a Dallas businessman had been in Dealey Plaza with an eight-millimeter movie camera, and had photographed the assassination from beginning to end. She wasn't sure of the name, but she sounded it out phonetically. When I hung up the phone, I thought to myself, "Now, what the hell do I do?" If that film actually existed, I just knew I had to get it, but I wasn't sure where to look. So I picked up the Dallas phone book, and just ran my fingers down the Z's, and, God, there it was, just the way she had pronounced it: "Zapruder," comma, "Abraham." I called the number every fifteen minutes for about five hours, but no one picked up. Finally, late that evening, around eleven, this weary voice answered, and I said, "Is this Abraham Zapruder?" He said, "Yes." "Is it true that you photographed the assassination?" "Yes." "Have you seen the film?" "Yes." "Did you get it from beginning to end?" "Yes." And then I said, "Can I come out and see it now?" And he said, "No. I'm too upset. I'm too tired. Come to my office at nine."

I got there at 8:00 A.M. Saturday. Zapruder was slightly annoyed that I was an hour early, but he let me come in anyway. Zapruder owned a garment factory, which was only about one block away from Dealey Plaza. He led me through a large room full of sewing machines and into a much smaller white room that he

Stolley in 1963 with a copy of Life's *special issue on the assassination.*

—*Richard Stolley, born in Pekin, Illinois, in 1928, started working for* Life *magazine in 1953. After the weekly* Life *magazine closed in 1972, Stolley launched* People *magazine and was its editor for eight years. He then served as editor of the monthly* Life *magazine and as editorial director of Time Inc. He currently is senior editorial adviser for Time Inc.*

probably used for showing samples to buyers. Inside that room were four, very grim-faced Secret Service agents who had also come down to see the film. Zapruder got out this creaky old projector, with, of course, no sound, and he beamed the film up on a plain white wall. Within just a few seconds, I knew that I was experiencing the most dramatic moment in my entire career. I was sitting there with these Secret Service agents as they watched a film of their failure at their number one job, which was to protect the president. We watched the motorcade snake around onto Elm Street around Dealey Plaza. It went behind a sign and Kennedy was briefly out of the scene. The next time we saw the president, his hands were up around his throat, and Connally's mouth was open and he was howling in pain — they had both already been shot. Jackie turned her head and looked quizzically at her husband. Less than two or three seconds later, without warning, the whole right side of President Kennedy's head just exploded in pink froth. Everyone watching the film in the room, including the Secret Service agents, just went "Ugh!" It was like we had been gut-punched. Zapruder, who had already seen the film, turned his head away just before the image of Kennedy getting shot appeared on the screen. It was an absolutely astounding moment. There was Jackie crawling up onto the trunk, and Secret Service Agent Clint Hill leaping up onto the car, pushing Jackie back in, and holding on for dear life as the limo sped away to the hospital. The camera ran out of film just as the limo disappeared under the underpass. Zapruder got the

whole assassination, in perfect focus and steady as a rock.

As soon as I saw the film, I realized that this truly was a scoop of global magnitude, and *Life* had to have it. I knew that other reporters would eventually show up at Zapruder's office, and, indeed, before too long they did. People from newsreels, magazines, and wire services all got to look at the film, and then we all gathered in the hall to see what Mr. Zapruder would do next. I was standing quietly in the background when Zapruder came out and said, "I know you want to talk with me, but Mr. Stolley there from *Life* was the first to contact me, so I'm going to talk to him first." Well, the others just went nuts. They started screaming at him, "Promise you won't sign anything. Promise, promise!"

I walked into his office to start negotiating. I knew how high I could go, but I first had to test whether he knew what he had, so I said, "Mr. Zapruder, I think first of all you know *Life* magazine will treat this material in a tasteful manner and we will not exploit this. I think you can trust *Life*." And he said that that was very, very important to him. He was a big fan of Kennedy, and was quite distraught about what had happened, so he didn't want to see his film used in a garish way. Then I said, "These are unusual pictures. You know, we might even pay as much as $5,000 for pictures like these." And he just gave me this little smile, and I immediately knew that he had an idea of what this film was really worth. We then quietly negotiated for the print rights to the film, never raising our voices. Meanwhile, the other

Left: Zapruder (with glasses) on local television the day of the assassination. Above: The opening spread of the Life *story. Right: Packaging for the film when it began to be available in video stores in 1998.*

reporters were going nuts out in the hallway. They were banging on the door, screaming through the door, going outside to the pay phone, and calling in to harass Zapruder's secretary. I finally got to $50,000, and I said, "Well, truthfully, I cannot go higher than that without calling the editors in New York." And he just looked at me and he said, "Well, let's do it." I sat down at his typewriter, and I wrote about a five-line contract which he and I signed, and his partner witnessed. He gave me the original and the one extra copy that he had of the film. I said, "Boy, do you have a back door to this place? I really don't want to go back out into that hall and face those guys." I went out the back door and immediately shipped the film to Chicago. Black-and-white stills from the film appeared in the next issue of the magazine.

After leaving Zapruder, I went back to our hotel, where I got a call from Tommy Thompson. He said, "I've got a terrific story. And I've got Oswald's family. I think I'm going to bring them back to the hotel so I can keep them away from other reporters." In about a half an hour, the door opened, and in walked Tommy along with Oswald's Russian wife, Marina, clutching a very young child, Lee's nutty mother, Marguerite, clutching the other young child, and Lee's brother, Robert Oswald. A few minutes after they had come to our hotel, the phone rang, I picked it up, and an angry voice said, "Okay, you son of a bitch, where are they?" I said, "I beg your pardon?" He said, "This is Agent So-and-so of the Secret Service, where is the Oswald family?" And I tried to bullshit him, and he said, "Look, don't do this to me.

I'll make a deal. If you'll tell me where they are I promise you I will not reveal their whereabouts to any of the press. Sooner or later, we are going to find where they are, and we're not going to make it very pleasant for you." So I told him, and he kept his bargain.

Tommy interviewed the Oswalds on Saturday afternoon and submitted a two-thousand-word story by that night. The next day Tommy and I went down to the county jail, the jail to which Oswald was supposed to be transferred. Since the city jail was such a madhouse, we figured we'd have a better chance of seeing Oswald when he arrived at county. There was a television crew there with a soundman who was monitoring what was going on back at the city jail through a pair of earphones. All of a sudden, the soundman jerked his head and said, "God, what is that?" Then he looked at me and said, "Oh my God. Oswald's been shot." Tommy and I immediately ran out to try to get to the city jail. We went up to cars and tried to get people to roll down their window, but most people just took one look at us and shook their heads. Finally, one young guy did roll down his window, and I threw a twenty-dollar bill through it and said, "Can you take us to the jail?" He tried to take us, but the police had cordoned off the area. Then we headed back to the hotel, only to find that the Oswald family was gone. By that time, the Secret Service had become concerned that there was some sort of conspiracy, so they came and took the Oswalds away.

During that whole weekend, the gravity of what had happened never really hit me. We were so busy

chasing our stories that we had almost no sense of what the country was going through. Occasionally, we'd catch a glimpse on television of what was happening around Dallas, or in Washington, but things were happening so quickly for us — the film, Oswald's family, and, finally, Oswald getting shot — that we didn't have time to grieve, or to think about anything except how we were going to have to change the magazine, yet again.

When I finally got back to L.A. the day before Thanksgiving, nobody wanted to talk about what had happened. Everybody there was already cried out at that point. I think those of us that were covering it in Dallas never really understood what the country went through. It wasn't until twenty-five years later when *Life* did a retrospective issue on the assassination that it really hit me. For that issue, we interviewed a lot of people, and looked at a lot of photographs and film of Kennedy that I had never seen before. In a very strange way, it was not until then that I got the sense of, not so much the personal trauma, but the national trauma, and what the country had gone through after Kennedy was killed. In 1996 I was asked to give a speech at the museum they have established at Dealey Plaza, and describing my delayed reaction to the assassination, I suddenly stopped, broke down and cried. I guess I was still coming to grips with the grief that I had put aside. It's like T. S. Eliot writes in one of his poems, "We shall not cease from exploration / And the end of all our exploring / Will be to arrive where we started / And know the place for the first time."

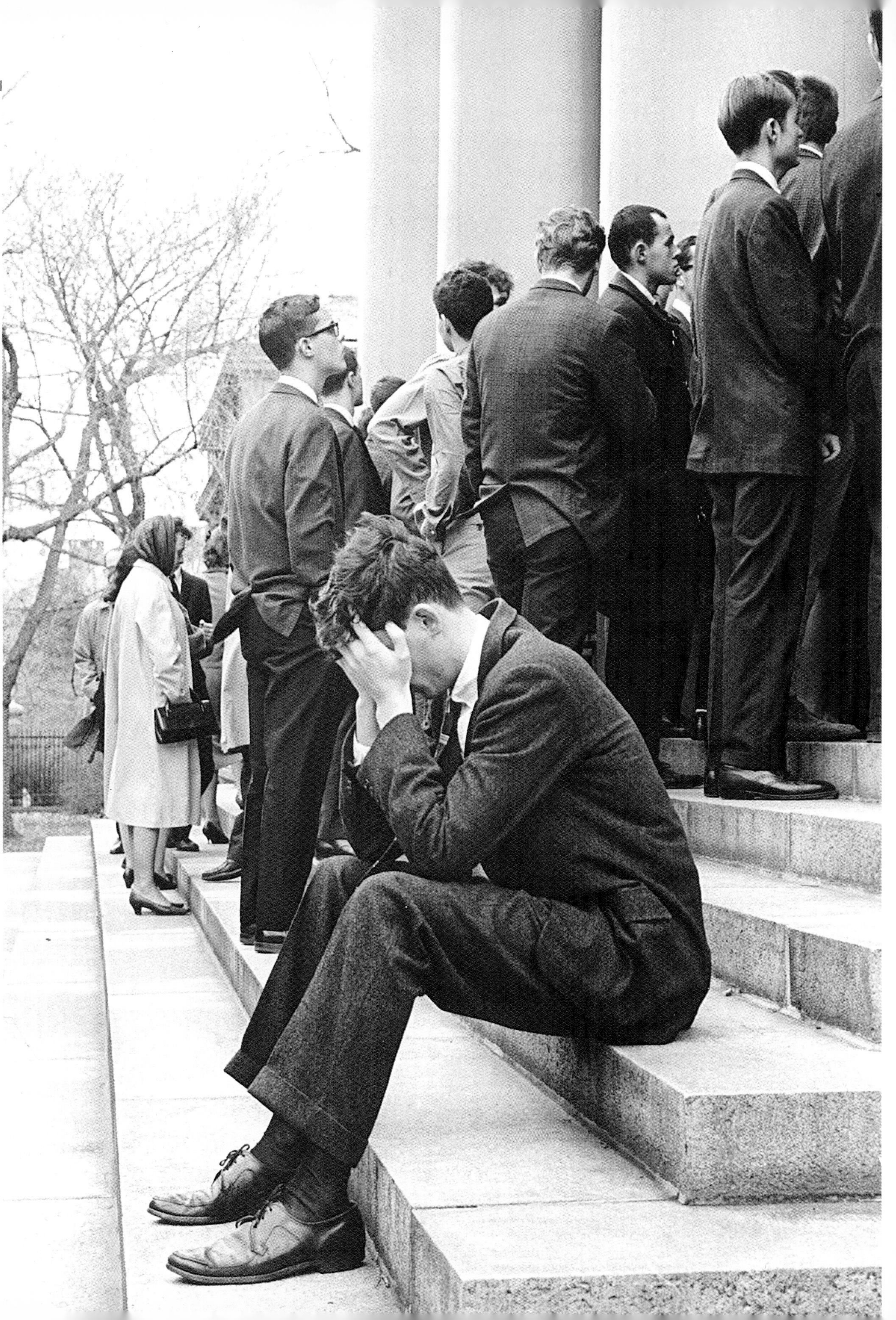

that same day; the funeral procession, on Monday, with the three-year-old John, Jr., saluting his father for the last time; and, finally, the lighting of the eternal flame at the president's Arlington gravesite by his young widow.

A commission headed by Supreme Court Chief Justice Earl Warren issued its report on the Kennedy assassination in 1964, asserting the theory that Oswald had acted alone, but in time few were willing to believe it. Deeply wounded by these events, Americans wanted a conspiracy large enough and bizarre enough to match the crime. They simply did not want to accept the unsatisfying conclusion that it had happened for no reason but the whim of a misfit lunatic gunman whose ordinarily poor marksmanship turned lucky one fateful day.

Certain images from that tragic weekend were burnished into the collective psyche of the nation, among them the sight of Kennedy's widow, Jackie, and their daughter, Caroline, kneeling beside the president's coffin.

Among those most traumatized by Kennedy's death were America's young people. Arriving at Andrews Air Force Base the night of the assassination, author Teddy White remembered enormous numbers of them, gathered "on every autumn hill, sitting in the brown fall grass" waiting, in quiet respect, for the body of the president to pass by, their "bubble and laughter . . . stopped in sorrowing stillness." The presidency had succeeded to Lyndon Johnson, but the decade itself now passed even more completely to them, the way that a father's death forces both freedom and responsibility upon his children. Had he lived, it is unlikely that Kennedy would have remained a role model very long, particularly among the considerable number of young people who had begun to find their identity in ideas hostile to Cold War hawkishness and to the material fruits of prosperity; now his death only encouraged their emerging picture of a senseless adult world, caught up in random violence and petty feuds.

These mid-decade years were a fertile time for the youth movement, primarily because it was now that the idea of a counterculture, led by the young, began to gel. Purely by virtue of their youth and the emerging sensibility that youth had begun to embrace as its own, millions of young people were beginning to regard themselves as a class separate from mainstream society. They had been told since childhood that their generation was different, that they were the inheritors of the free world that the previous generation had fought to create, that they would grow up in prosperity, with the best that humanity could provide them, and that they, too, would become great. Now they were about to turn that idea on its head.

Never before had a single event instantly summoned so many Americans together in mourning. Hastily organized memorial services for President Kennedy were conducted nationwide, allowing many, like these students outside a ceremony at Harvard University, to share their grief.

Rock and roll was the driving force of the youth culture, and the driving force of rock in the sixties was the Beatles. Fewer than a hundred days after the nation sat gripped before pictures of the funeral of the murdered president, the four mop-haired Liverpudlians arrived in New York, beginning a six-year creative spree that is unrivaled in popular music history. Like Elvis Presley before them, the Beatles appeared on *The Ed Sullivan Show*, their sweet harmonies setting off paroxysms of excitement among the hundreds of squealing teenagers in the audience. Over the next two years alone, they would issue no fewer than twenty singles and nine LPs, holding at one point all five top positions of the *Billboard* Hot 100 list.

The Beatles were not overtly political; in fact, their rebelliousness was

Not since Elvis Presley had a musical performer or group garnered such frenzied adulation as the Beatles did when they arrived in New York City on February 12, 1964. Thousands of screaming fans greeted them at the airport and then shadowed their every move throughout the city. Here, a group of "Beatlemaniacs" wait across the street from New York's Plaza Hotel hoping to catch a glimpse of the Fab Four.

Seventy-three million people watched the Beatles in their U.S. debut on Ed Sullivan's television show, above. "You really do believe they can see you . . . when they're up on stage," explained one of the fans. "That's why you scream, so they'll notice you."

sweetly innocent, particularly at first. Where Presley had swiveled his hips, the Beatles merely wanted to "hold your hand." Yet, led by them, rock soon began to articulate that separate sensibility that youth wished to express, a worldview that rejected the values of the establishment and embraced a new "consciousness," open to mystery and mysticism, spontaneity and fun, sensuality, and, in a direct affront to the emphasis on private satisfactions that typified the fifties, the virtues of communal spirit. The civil rights movement had already established the power of camaraderie in the interest of change. With songs like "All You Need Is Love," the Beatles helped youth, too, conclude that the route to happiness lay in seeking a little help from their friends.

Those friends sometimes included drugs, both marijuana and hallucinogens like LSD, which, particularly in the early years of the youth culture, were seen less as a vice than as simply another way to raise consciousness. Together with "head" groups like the Grateful Dead and Jefferson Airplane, the Beatles were a major influence behind the spread of drugs. With albums like *Sergeant Pepper* and *Revolver*, the Fab Four, as they were affectionately known, bent harmonies into weird, otherworldly shapes and put psychedelic imagery onto their album jackets. Some of their late-decade music suggested that it could not be fully appreciated unless the listener was stoned, ready to turn off this world and float quietly into another.

Even if the Beatles were not very political, much of the rest of youth culture was, and the subject on which they would most vocally attack the established order was the Vietnam War. It was only natural that a counterculture built around a set of vague notions emphasizing peace and love would object to an aggressive American policy in a distant Asian nation populated by peasants and consisting mostly of rice paddies and jungles. The American government's position in Vietnam had been shaped from the harsh realities of postwar geopolitics and the equally harsh realities of American domestic politics, neither of which was carried out in the language of romance.

Just as Kennedy had inherited America's sticky relationship with Cuba from his predecessor, Lyndon Johnson had inherited the mess in Vietnam from Kennedy. Indochina's war for independence from France had ended in 1954, with the partitioning of Vietnam into what would become the American-supported government in the South, and the communist North, led by the legendary Ho Chi Minh. The agreement to end the war had mandated that both Vietnams hold elections addressing unification within two years and abide by the result, but with the support of the Eisenhower administration, the South had put off the referendum; the unpopularity of South Vietnam's corrupt and aristocratic president, Ngo Dinh Diem, who was to Vietnam what Batista was to Cuba, had made it clear that the communists would win. After a few years of calm, Ho's forces then began to gradually infiltrate the South until an intense guerrilla war, fought throughout the jungles and villages, had begun.

Like Cuba, Vietnam was, for America, an issue of perceptions. The nation was of little direct importance to the United States except as its fall to the com-

"Critical mass" in Haight-Ashbury: **"We acted as if the revolution was already over and we had won"**

When I moved to San Francisco in 1964, my first apartment was at Haight and Clayton, right at the hub of the Haight-Ashbury district, which was then just a quiet working-class neighborhood. One day this place called the Psychedelic Shop opened up. It was run by two brothers. They were two purebred, Eagle Scout types of boys who had discovered psychedelics and wanted to spread the word. They thought that psychedelics were part of a spiritual, psychic, and consciousness evolution. So they opened this store to disseminate information and sell different kinds of trinkets and paraphernalia. By chance, I had a friend in Kansas City who made the world's most beautiful candles. I went into the shop, told the brothers about my friend's candles — pure beeswax, beautiful dyes, really nice. We got to talking, they decided to sell the candles, and we soon became good friends.

As the 1960s wore on, kids from all over the United States started moving to the Haight. These kids were expressing a very different sense of honor and ethics. They didn't care so much about money and about material wealth. They got to the Haight, and, bingo, it was like a nuclear fission when you have critical mass. You know a certain amount of plutonium will explode on its own. Well, Haight-Ashbury achieved critical mass, and the neighborhood was transformed into an environment where your personal history did not matter. Nobody cared who your parents were, whether you were rich, whether you were poor. It was an opportunity to find yourself and define yourself on your own terms. Make your own music. Live your own life.

The counterculture was beginning to blossom in the neighborhood. Haight Street was soon lined with alternative shops, coffee shops, and bookstores that sold psychedelic gear, posters, drug paraphernalia, hip clothes, and books with information about transcendental experiences, LSD, and mushrooms. "Revolution" was interpreted differently by different people. For some it meant political overthrow. For some it meant change of consciousness. For some it meant change of style. For some it meant long hair and dope at the office.

You would get up every morning and you had no idea what the day would bring. You didn't need money; you could get food without it. You could crash at anybody's house. You didn't need to look good or wear your hair a certain way. It didn't matter if you didn't look like Tab Hunter or Debbie Reynolds. There was a sense of adventure, random combinations. You could catch a woman's eye and offer her your arm and without a word walk away and spend an afternoon making love.

I let my hair go, and after a while it was so long I could sit on it. My girlfriend brushed it and tied it up like a Navaho with a red velvet ribbon. She sewed silver studs on my pants and made me these great velvet shirts. The thing was to be a stud peacock. Haight Street was the stage. It was the place where you danced out your identity and said, "This is how I feel. This is who I want to be." People were not buying into the majority culture's values and style. They were inventing their own. The styles came out of Goodwill stores, but what made them stylish was that people were looking at them with new sophisticated eyes, eyes that had been washed clean by marijuana.

During this time, I became part of a group called the Diggers, after a seventeenth-century English religious sect that practiced communal living. These were people who were inventive, imaginative and had great humor. They thought about ideas and cared passionately about things. For the Diggers, revolution meant re-creating the culture. We felt that the problem in the United States was not a political problem. It was a cultural problem. People so associated their jobs with their identity — I'm a plumber, I'm a stockbroker — that they lost track of their inner wilderness, which is the imagination. We began to look around for things to do that would alert people to other ways of living. We were also afraid that we were products of this culture and that we might unconsciously act out values that we'd inherited with our mother's milk, so we did things anonymously and without money — "free." We felt that if you weren't getting either rich or famous for what you were doing, then you probably meant it. We started by feeding people in the park.

There were a lot of kids crashing on the streets, and the Haight was becoming a problem. So the Diggers fed them. We would go to the farmer's market and get surplus food and donations and then pass them out. We were feeding maybe seven hundred to a thousand people a day at these "Digger Feeds." The only thing we asked was that, to get their food, they step through a six-foot-by-six-foot yellow frame, called the "free frame of reference." After they stepped through that yellow frame, we gave them a little yellow frame on a cord to hang around their neck, so that they could then look at the world through their own free frame of reference. Our feeling was that if we created enough alternatives that people loved, people would defend them. And they would have revolutionary import.

After we established the Digger Feeds in the park, we opened a store where everything was free. The world was awash in stuff, so we lined the shelves with things that many people viewed as castoffs. The machinery of society was able to build a television set for every man,

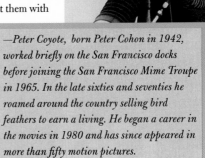

—Peter Coyote, born Peter Cohon in 1942, worked briefly on the San Francisco docks before joining the San Francisco Mime Troupe in 1965. In the late sixties and seventies he roamed around the country selling bird feathers to earn a living. He began a career in the movies in 1980 and has since appeared in more than fifty motion pictures.

Coyote on the first day of a cross-country motorcycle trip, 1967.

woman, and child on the planet. If you didn't have a television because you didn't have the money, it was the money that was scarce, not the television. The money was a valve for creating scarcity. If you didn't care if your television was brand-new or not, you could have a TV. If you didn't care if your clothes and furniture were brand-new, you could have clothes and furniture. Why spend ten hours of your day working to get the money, when that was just a way of creating scarcity?

The Diggers were never really a big part of the antiwar movement, although we ran our own kind of draft resistance out of the free store. We had a number of draft cards and stamps from various draft offices. Soldiers would come into the free store, hang their uniforms on a rack, take other clothes off the rack, have a couple of conversations with someone in the store, and Billy from Nebraska would leave as Frank from Kansas. There is no question that what we did was illegal. But those kids didn't kill anybody. They didn't get their arms and legs blown off. And they got a chance to redefine life on their own terms. Most of us felt that the war was a logical outgrowth of capitalism, an imperialistic culture that had to get cheap labor and raw resources. We felt that rather than attack the war, which other people were doing honorably and well, we wanted to attack the root causes of the culture and change that. We wanted to create revolutionary change in the United States, nonviolent change. The United States owned the option on violence, so we knew we couldn't win that way. But we could get into the imagination of the United States. We tried to create new alternatives. We acted as if the revolution was already over and we had won, and we just lived our lives that way. We assumed freedom.

In June 1963 a Buddhist monk burned himself to death in downtown Saigon to protest the cruelties of South Vietnamese President Ngo Dinh Diem, leading many Americans to begin to question U.S. support of the repressive leader.

munists might demonstrate, like Cuba's fall to the communists, American weakness, and there were many who believed that Vietnam's fall might lead to the precipitous fall of neighboring Asian nations — like the tumbling of a row of dominoes — in a further demonstration of American impotence. But in their quest to assert the sense of national purpose and moral consistency that Kennedy had asserted as his administration's goal, the nation's expert foreign policy makers had effectively dissolved distinctions between situations where American interests were at stake and those where they were ambiguous. Vietnam was important primarily because it became a test of Kennedy's inaugural pledge to "bear any burden" in the pursuit of liberty.

There was, however, a tragic flaw to such a policy. Just as Kennedy had sent armies of Peace Corps volunteers into the Third World, eager to provide technocratic expertise to people in underdeveloped societies, so his foreign policy involved the export of *government* technocrats ready to put forward their ideas on how to build democracy and promote economic growth. By following the American model, Kennedy's men believed they knew how to produce a prosperous commercial world free of communist influence even if that put them in opposition to the established history or cultural tradition. From 1961 onward, under Kennedy's leadership, American Green Berets came to the aid of the South Vietnamese army in their battles with the Viet Cong, while teams of American social scientists descended upon the nation ready to institute the wrenching reforms they felt were necessary to make the transition to a successful democracy, among them the forced removal of Vietnamese people from their ancestral villages. In the end, America imposed a different kind of imperialism than had been imposed upon Vietnam when it was a French colony, but it was imperialism nonetheless. And, despite their nation's strong anticolonial traditions, the American people initially supported it, believing the Third World to be the stage upon which the forces of freedom needed to defend against the communist menace.

Only in June 1963, after they saw the gripping pictures of the self-immolation of Buddhist monks opposed to South Vietnam's Diem, and learned of Diem's assassination, in a successful November 1963 coup (the coup — but not the assassination — had the tacit approval of the United States, which hoped that a more reform-minded government would follow), and of the street celebrations that ensued after the death of the man American dollars and personnel had so fervently supported, did the American public receive its first hint that Vietnam was more complicated than had first been suggested, that not every noncommunist leader was a democrat, and that not every people wished to cast aside their own firmly entrenched traditions and nationalistic spirit to uncritically follow the American experience.

When Lyndon Baines Johnson, who had less interest in foreign affairs than his predecessor, became president, he found Vietnam to be a nuisance. Like most postwar politicians, the former Texas senator believed in the policy of containment, but in contrast to Kennedy he hoped to establish America's sense of national purpose not so much on the international stage as at home, by committing the government to the creation of a more just and equitable society, a *Great* Society, as he called it, every bit as transforming as FDR's New Deal. It was Johnson who pushed for the passage of the landmark 1964 Civil Rights Act (originally proposed by Kennedy) and then followed it with the 1965 Voting Rights Act, the two most significant pieces of civil rights legislation this century; Johnson who declared a "war on poverty" and created Medicare; Johnson who established the National Endowments for the Humanities and the Arts; and Johnson who increased the nation's commitment to a domestic imitation of the Peace Corps known as VISTA. As far as the new president was concerned, the war in Vietnam could only serve to disrupt the execution of his grand vision.

Yet, like all leaders, Johnson served by the light of the (sometimes inspiring, too often burdensome) lamp of history. Over the five sad years of his tenure, he would attempt earnestly to follow the example of his hero, FDR, while dodging the ghosts of Joe McCarthy, Neville Chamberlain, Douglas MacArthur, and John Kennedy. He would serve with the phrase "Who 'lost' China?" ringing in his ears and the map of the divided Korea, symbol of stalemate, not victory, ever present in his mind. Fearful that conservatives would label him soft on communism if Vietnam should collapse, yet worried that an all-out war in Vietnam would rob him of the congressional support he needed for domestic programs; convinced that not going to war now risked World War III later (for Vietnam, in Johnson's mind, was surely analogous to Czechoslovakia, where the West's appeasement of Hitler had given him the opportunity to march on Europe), and yet worried that going to an all-out war also risked World War III, and risked it now (for how could Communist China sit by and watch?), Johnson would try to have it all ways. And he would work his ambitious domestic program with one hand as he surreptitiously brought the nation to the battlefield with his other, hoping to mimic the maneuvering that FDR cleverly used to move America gently into World War II and in so doing apply the "slow squeeze" to Ho Chi Minh and the communists.

"We are not about to send American boys nine or ten thousand miles away from home," Lyndon Johnson declared in the 1964 presidential campaign, "to do what Asian boys ought to be doing for themselves." But by the time Johnson left office in 1969, he had delivered 500,000 GIs to do just that.

Using the now-controversial 1964 Gulf of Tonkin Resolution as his license to commit the nation to wage war without actually asking Congress to declare war, Johnson responded to calls from the desperately weakened South Vietnamese government by moving America deeper and deeper into the mud of Southeast Asia. In the end, Vietnam would indeed be a war, America's longest and costliest, a feverish hallucination of a war, more gaudy than anything imagined under the most intense drug high, and certainly more lasting. More than 58,000 Americans would die, more than 1 million Vietnamese, leaving both countries, America *and* Vietnam, scarred forever.

All wars are alike, the stench and fear of death the same, the same essential and interchangeable messy horrors involved in an activity that is never better described than as men hunting men for reasons essentially unknown, really, to any of them. Still, this war was also different. American soldiers had fought in the trenches of World War I, run bombing missions over Europe in the battle against Hitler, clambered over the seawall at Inchon in Korea, and yet never encountered anything quite like the monstrous scenery of Vietnam, a place where the enemy was everywhere and nowhere at once, appearing and disappearing into the foliage, sucked into the swampy undertow. Imagine, if you will, Stalingrad played

An American in Vietnam: "Those were the first men I ever killed and I remember each of them"

I arrived in Vietnam in July of '65. I landed with a group of soldiers on an airstrip just outside Saigon. Walking out of the airplane, the heat hit everyone in my entourage instantaneously, and everybody started to sweat. The roads into Saigon were dirt, and en route we passed homes which were nothing but tar paper and aluminum shacks with pigs and chickens in every yard. I thought, "*This* is the Third World." After an hour and a half, the school bus crossed a bridge into the teeming capital of Saigon. There were two traffic lights, and only one was functioning, so it was absolute bedlam between the jeeps, the trucks, the taxis, the buffalo carts, and the people on bicycles. Just before we pulled into headquarters, someone smashed a bottle against the corner of one of the windows on the bus. This person obviously didn't care about Americans and really didn't want us there. It was my first indication that maybe our presence wasn't quite as welcome as we had been led to believe.

After a week, I was posted in the Mekong Delta. Flying in, I looked out and saw the airport overflowing with Americans and Vietnamese stockpiling weapons and planes taking off with their bomb loads. I thought, "Oh wow, there is a war going on over here." It grabbed me, but then life got very serious after that. I initially worked with the South Vietnamese army battalion monkeying around in the rice paddies and rolling up and down in canals trying to clear roads — basically getting my feet wet. I was struck by the behavior of the Vietnamese I had been sent to work with. They seemed to be little kids just playing at this game, and they didn't seem serious about defending their country. Many times out in the middle of the rice paddies I wondered why we were there. I was very happy when I received orders to go to the 1st Cavalry Division.

I was sent to a base at An Khe to prepare for the arrival of fifteen thousand troops in mid-September. The troops arrived, and by early October had con-

structed a defensible perimeter around the base, and then we began our operations. On the afternoon of the fourteenth of November, we heard that the first battalion was engaged in heavy contact at a landing zone [L.Z.] code-named X-ray in the Ia Drang Valley. My company was quickly sent in, in three waves of six helicopters each. I remember running to my helicopter and looking back at the landing zone and seeing our troops running to their helicopters, and feeling this incredible sense of pride. These guys knew what they were heading for, yet nobody hesitated or skedaddled. We lifted up over the tall trees of our L.Z., and we could see the clouds of smoke drifting from the Chu Pong Mountain where we were headed. I thought, "Oh my God, we're not going to fly into that mess, are we?"

The helicopter set me down in the midst of chaos. There were air strikes against the mountain and the *pop, pop, pop* of rounds in the air sounded like firecrackers. I saw three or four Americans huddled around a tree saying, "Get down, get down, man, they're all around us." I had been on the ground for all of ten seconds when a fellow jumped up next to me and said, "I'm hit, sir." Carrying our wounded guy, we dodged and weaved forward for about a hundred yards until we got to where we could see the battalion commander's post. In between there was nothing but burnt grass, where napalm had killed some people, stacks of empty ammo crates, and bent and broken weapons scattered around. There was a row of American dead covered with ponchos, but we had to sprint past it and report and get ready to fight.

On the morning of November 17 we received orders to move to another landing zone about three

Gwin (left) with a fellow marine in Vietnam, 1965.

—*Larry Gwin, who was born in 1941, returned from Vietnam in 1966 and taught history as a ROTC officer at Northeastern University before heading to law school at Boston University. Graduating in 1970, he began a career at a large Boston law firm, but remained haunted by the memory of his tour of duty in Vietnam. In 1982 he left his job and went into seclusion to write about his experiences during the war. In 1996 he was awarded a Silver Star for his "extraordinary heroism" in Ia Drang.*

miles due north. We knew there were North Vietnamese in the area, so we had to move tactically. We took a slightly different route, five miles through the jungle. The temperature was maybe a hundred, and everybody was exhausted because we'd been awake for two days and were weighed down with our equipment. When we got through the jungle, we ran into some North Vietnamese scouts. For some reason, our colonel wanted to interrogate them, and he talked to them for twenty minutes, giving their compatriots twenty minutes time to run back and tell their bosses that we were heading their way. Meanwhile, we set up in a clump of trees, waiting for the other platoons to go around and secure the area. All of a sudden, we heard some shooting from the vicinity of our first platoon. After two or three single shots, the whole jungle opened up in one massive crescendo of fire. It seemed that everybody I knew and everybody behind us was firing every weapon they had. We had run into the North Vietnamese, and they had attacked us immediately.

I remember jumping up to go to a tree for some cover when the firing got bad, and as I was looking at the tree, right in front of my eyes, this chunk of wood came out at me, and I realized it was a bullet and that it had almost taken my nose off. I crunched down in the grass and ran back to where my company commander and radios were. The guys I was with were all down in the grass, hugging the dirt, because there was so much fire coming in. Basically, if you stuck your head up you were dead. Since I was lieutenant and had to know what was going on, I stuck my head up and saw about forty North Vietnamese soldiers coming across the grass at us. All I did was say, "Here they come," and start shooting at them. Everybody got the message and we cranked out a lot of fire, killing all the North Vietnamese. I remember those were the first men I ever killed, and I remember each one of them very distinctly. But if we hadn't killed them, they would have killed us. The Vietnamese came back that night and killed a lot of our wounded lying in the grass. Most everybody I knew was dead, and the stench of the battlefield was just unbelievable. It took us two days to clean up our dead and wounded and get us out of there.

We lost 70 percent of our men in the battle, but, in the end, we were the winners, so to speak. General Westmoreland came down for Thanksgiving a week later to congratulate us on what he called our "distinguished victory," and as he did every one of us looked around and counted our losses. We thought, "Is *that* a victory, General?" I don't believe Westmoreland yet knew just how many men we had lost. On the other hand, who could have mustered up the courage to tell him? I honor my brothers in their memory by saying,

"Yeah, we won. We took on the North, and we held our own." But there is a joke amongst the veterans. When we're asked, "How does it feel to be in the only war the United States lost?" every veteran I know says, "We were winning it when I was there." Ultimately we did what we had to do, and then we decided it was not a good place for us to be, and we left. Looking back, I think if the boys in Washington had done their homework, they wouldn't have sent us there in the first place.

The Battle of Thanh Son 2 in May 1966 was a turning point for me. On the morning of May 6, we attacked a village complex surrounded by trees. We didn't really know what was behind the trees, because we followed a walking artillery barrage. It wasn't until we got to the site that we realized we had devastated a village, killing many civilians. We saw children and little kids with their legs blown off and old couples under smoking wreckage. It broke my heart and it broke the hearts of the guys I served with. I know after we left that village, none of us could talk and none of us could look back. It was my job to get the wounded civilians medevacked back to some help. Putting a thirteen-year-old girl whose leg has been amputated above her knee onto a medevac is just another example of how unbelievably horrible war is. We killed those civilians in the morning, and that afternoon we flew to another hot landing zone and lost 30 percent of our men. I myself was wounded. You could call it retribution. The next morning I was medevacked out and was enjoying clean sheets and a nice cot to sleep on, but I couldn't help but think of what had happened the morning of the sixth when we butchered that village.

There was no point during my year in Vietnam when I realized that the U.S. had made a mistake and that we shouldn't have been there. But I also know in my heart that any American soldier who went to Vietnam didn't have to stay there long before he knew that there was something wrong with our presence there, either by the look in the Vietnamese eyes or the way that we were treating them or what we were doing in the countryside. I remember sitting with a good friend and my father a few years after I had returned from Vietnam. President Johnson had just announced that he would not run for reelection. My friend turned to me after Johnson's speech and said, "Well, Larry, we just lost the war." I just shook my head, for I just couldn't quite grasp it. We had worked so hard that year, as had the thousands and thousands of troops who had been fighting there since my tour had ended, and here, the president was quitting. It was appalling. I had also recently read an article saying that American national interests were not being served by our presence in Vietnam. Suddenly, I realized that everything that we had done over there was a waste.

out in the jungle *and* played out over decades.

In some ways, the war was America's own experience with the kind of shock and disillusionment that greeted Europeans on the western front. Like the British in 1914, the American soldier came dutifully to battle, unclear as to why he was fighting other than the vaguest sense that this was the traditional knightly procession of good against evil, freedom against communism, right against wrong. In this scenario, the guerrilla war then provides the trauma that the World War I trenches provided: an evil game that the American soldiers were not prepared for, that defied the more delineated logic of enemy and friend that they were accustomed to, and that, again like the trenches, destroyed the mind. Just how was one to fight a war that featured smiling children concealing grenades behind their backs and an army of snipers that dissolved into the villages by day, serving tea and bowing to the very soldiers they then returned to the treetops to pick off from the early-morning shadows? No wonder journalist Michael Herr, noting what he saw on the faces of American soldiers as he arrived to cover the war, compared the scene to "a walk through a colony of stroke victims."

The odd relationship between the American home front and the Southeast Asian battleground was also peculiar to Vietnam. Almost from the moment Johnson began to escalate American participation, forces opposed to the war began to escalate their attacks upon his policy ("Hey, hey, LBJ, how many kids did you kill today?") until, eventually, they were among the loudest voices of the decade. And because the antiwar movement became subsumed with the youth culture, most particularly the culture of rock and roll and drugs, and because those fighting in Vietnam were America's youth, too, and they, too, existed on rock and dope, there was the tragic irony of soldiers marching to war, not with the sounds of marching bands encouraging them, but with the angry electric twangs of the *anti*war culture, the culture that attacked and reviled them, playing out in their heads.

If that described one intolerable, dissonant, and suicidal relationship, there were others. There was also the soldier's experience with his government which he gradually came to disrespect, usually for different reasons than the protester's. To the GI, Washington became the great liar, fighting a war that the Pentagon refused to call a war and fighting it not to win. There seemed to be nothing but the most tragic logic at work. Washington had sent him there to fight a limited war, of dubious aims, against a people dedicated to absolute war, in a fight for their very survival. The GIs were, ostensibly, the soldiers of democracy, and yet it was not at all clear that the government of South Vietnam, in whose interests they were fighting, had anything more than minority support from the South Vietnamese people. If the people of Vietnam wished for any future, it seemed to be most importantly a future free of colonialism, benevolent *or* hostile, making many of them see the Americans as no better than the French and, in some ways, even more of an enemy than the Viet Cong. And then there were the Pentagon lies, the inflated body counts, known to most on the scene as inflated, that were issued to bolster support for the war at home, to suggest that the war was a winning proposition, with the end in sight, when most soldiers knew otherwise.

All of these factors, taken together, brought a remarkably dark psychological condition down upon the fighting man. The traditional rites of war are traditional for a reason: they help men do the intolerable (killing) and survive. The

American soldiers rush their wounded to safety during a firefight in one of the northern provinces of South Vietnam, 1966. Despite vast logistical and firepower superiority, the U.S. forces were unable to make substantial gains against the guerrilla and ambush tactics adopted by the North Vietnamese.

The North Vietnamese credo: "We thought we were one nation; the Americans wanted to divide us into two"

Life was pretty peaceful in Hanoi until 1964, when the American bombers came. I lived there with my family; my father worked and my mother stayed home and took care of us children. I knew that a war was under way in South Vietnam, but that seemed very far away, and we children heard very little about it. When the bombing started, suddenly the war became something real, something very close to us that was threatening our lives. My brother and I had to evacuate to the countryside to study. My parents stayed in town, and continued to work.

Nearly every afternoon during our first summer in the countryside, we would look back toward town, where our parents still lived, and watch as hundreds of American airplanes bombed the neighborhoods of Hanoi. But we weren't safe in the country, either. Our school had a big bunker under the ground, because we had no idea when an airplane might fly right over us and drop a bomb on us. We spent a lot of time studying in those bunkers, listening to planes flying overhead. In school we learned about how our ancestors had defended Vietnam against major invasions in the past; four thousand years of fighting against foreign domination came across vividly to us because we were under attack ourselves, and I think this had a very powerful effect on my whole generation. We also learned about the history of mistrust between Vietnam and the United States government that had begun after the Second World War. Since the Americans had come in to help the French try to take over our country, we saw no difference between the terrible French colonialists and the Americans. In fact, we called them the American imperialists.

In 1967, the bombing in the North of Vietnam reached a climax, and the Americans were intensifying the fighting down in the South as well. Ho Chi Minh went on the radio and called on the whole nation to resist the American forces. He said that the war may last five, ten, twenty years or longer. Hanoi and other major cities in Vietnam may be bombed and destroyed, he said, but the Vietnamese are not frightened — we will carry on this war to the end. He told us that Vietnam was one country, that the rivers may run dry, and the mountains may collapse, but the truth will never change. This statement was right in line with the mind-set of the North Vietnamese. We were one nation, with one language, and suddenly somebody had come in and said, "Vietnam should be two." The weight of history on every Vietnamese person wouldn't allow us to accept that kind of division at all. So we were determined to fight for our freedom.

The constant bombing had made my whole generation so angry with the Americans that the government didn't have to draft people into the army — most young,

Hung, in 1974, just before a 1975 spring offensive.

—*Nguyen Hung, born in 1949, lost his brother and seventeen cousins in the war. He spent six years in combat and was among the North Vietnamese troops who marched into Saigon shortly after the South Vietnamese surrendered. In recent years he has been actively involved in efforts to bring American and Vietnamese veterans together for reconciliation. He has traveled around the United States to speak with American veterans about their experiences during the war and collaborated on a Vietnam war memorial in Wisconsin with veterans from that state.*

able-bodied men volunteered for the service. When I was eighteen years old, I volunteered, but the government told me, "You did very well at school, so go on to college. The war will end very soon, and we will need people to rebuild the country." So I went on to college. Many of my friends and classmates went to war; some of them came back, some never did. The ones who returned told us all about the Tet Offensive, and how bloody the war had become. Soon the losses suffered by our army were so heavy that I was drafted. I didn't really want to go because I was very happy at school, but of course I went anyway.

I went into training where I learned how to handle an AK-47, antitank weapons, bayonets and hand grenades. Army life was very different than student life, and at first it was hard for me to catch up with the guys from the countryside who had been used to farmwork and were very strong. But gradually I became a tougher person, and a more responsible person as well. For us, the army was like a family, because unlike American soldiers who came to Vietnam for one year and then got out, in Vietnam we had to go on fighting until the end of the war. The only way we could live together for that long was to treat each other like brothers, so we became very close.

I was an infantryman, and I saw a lot of combat. We were not fighting a conventional war, because the Americans had such superior firepower, so we had to be clever and design our own techniques of outsmarting the enemy, like ambushes and surprise attacks. The Americans had many helicopters and it was pretty scary to encounter one if you were with a small, defenseless group or totally alone. One day I was walking along a

highway by myself and I saw a helicopter flying very low. I couldn't resist trying to shoot it down, so I aimed my AK-47 at it and opened fire. Nothing happened, but they spotted me and chased after me, barraging me with rockets and gunfire. The intensity of their firepower was terrifying, and I had to figure out a way to escape from it. Luckily, there was a whole grove of tall plants nearby, so I took a huge rock and rolled it down the hill to make a visible trail toward the river. The helicopter dived after the rock, and I escaped to the other side of the road and ran for my life. It was a terrible experience but that was the kind of thing you had to do to stay alive.

The B-52 bombings that the Americans did were horrible also, because there was no way for us to fight back. So we would look up into the skies and see the bombs coming at us, and the only thing we could do was just to lay down and wait. I remember one very beautiful, sunny day in 1971 in southern Laos; we knew that B-52s were coming, but we didn't know exactly where. I was talking to a friend about what we would do after the war, and he was saying he would study civil engineering so that he could build houses. I told him that I wanted to become a teacher to share with the younger generation my experience in this war. Then a few minutes later, we saw three huge B-52s coming in, and then we saw the bomb coming right down on top of us; it was like a layer of golden cloth, falling from the sky. We knew that we were right under it, and we couldn't run so we just laid there, waiting for death to come and greet us. I somehow survived, but my friend was blown up. I was beyond feeling anything by that point because I had seen so much death and so many bombs that it had just taken everything out of me.

> "*I was a coward...I don't believe in heroes...A buddy was still on fire and I carried, I crawled with him twenty-five feet. It had nothin' to do with heroism. It was because I did not want to be alone. Everybody else was dead and I was sittin' there cryin'.*"
>
> *Vietnam combat veteran*

> "**You go into a local market in Watts. Besides the rats and the roaches, the food was rotten. There would be some Jewish guy or a white guy standing there saying, 'The Hell with you, you're going to have to buy this anyway.' Those are the first places people went, to burn down the store. What we didn't have in Watts wasn't civil rights. It was jobs, housing and education. It was a positive image of ourselves. We didn't know what they were complaining about in the South.**"
>
> *Paul Williams*
> *Watts resident and rioter, 1965*

marching bands, the supportive home front cultures, the clearly defined objectives, the sense of a righteous purpose backed by authority, all work to smooth the transition when man is called upon, as he is in war, to leave civilization temporarily, commit barbarous acts, and return to function in civilization again. Absent that supportive structure, the American soldier in Vietnam often lived with a sense of self-loathing, believing that he killed alone and killed for no reason.

In late 1964 Martin Luther King was awarded the Nobel Peace Prize. In early 1965 he led a dramatic march through Selma, Alabama, protesting that city's stringent voter registration rules, which effectively denied the black vote, and, in part because it was marred by white violence, Selma helped convince Congress to pass Johnson's Voting Rights Act. Yet the act was, in some ways, too late and King's Nobel more like the proverbial gold watch, for a critical moment had already passed in the civil rights movement, and the once-revered leader and his ideas of nonviolence and integration were about to enter a rapid decline.

Less than a week after the Voting Rights Act became law, rioting broke out not in the South, with which the nation long associated events of racial confrontation, but in the West, in Los Angeles, in the black ghetto of Watts. And the fact that Watts was by no means the worst of America's urban slums, but instead an unusually quiet neighborhood of simple stucco houses and bungalows, only made the riot doubly perplexing. On the issue of racial integration, Los Angeles ranked high. Blacks held a quarter of city jobs and were well represented on the city council and in the state assembly. Yet in one of the sixties' many ironies, it was the *success* of the civil rights movement in the South that seemed to inspire violence in the North, the landmark legislation having given license, in a peculiar way, to the expression of a century of repressed rage and frustration.

Rioters in Watts, their fuse lit by what they perceived to be police brutality in the arrest of a young drunk driver, looted and burned stores (including those displaying signs that declared black ownership) and pelted police with bottles and cans. Thirty-four people died, almost all of them black. More than nine hundred were injured and more than four thousand were arrested. Watts quickly inspired rioters into the streets of other cities, too, including Chicago, Hartford, San Diego, Philadelphia, and Springfield, Massachusetts, leading to the pattern of urban rioting that would dominate the middle sixties in America. Altogether, between 1965 and 1968, there would be over one hundred riots in American cities, in which more than eight thousand people were either killed or injured. Times had changed. Noting that Martin Luther King, walking through the litter of Watts, was greeted with hostility, William Manchester wrote that the torch had been passed to a new generation, only in this case the torch was no image, it *was* a torch.

America's new urban violence was an act of despair, for it targeted no unfair laws, laid claim to no long-denied rights, and held up no grand ideal. If anything, it seemed to be nothing more than a deeply cynical statement, a message from northern blacks directed as much to their brothers in the South as it was to whites, offering that all that work at removing the legal representations of prejudice and attacking state-sponsored segregation was for naught; for in the North, where blacks could more easily vote and travel as they pleased, they were

In Selma on "Bloody Sunday":
"We crossed the bridge and saw a blue sea of troopers, carrying nightsticks and bullwhips"

In the summer of 1964, the Civil Rights Act was passed and signed into law by President Johnson. While that act dealt with discrimination in places of public accommodation and employment, it dealt only in a secondary sense with the whole question of voting rights. Throughout the South, people were still being denied the right to register to vote based on the color of their skin. Blacks who attempted to register were being harassed and intimidated and were required to pass literacy tests. One county between Montgomery and Selma was more than 80 percent black and there was not a single registered black voter.

We decided to spearhead an aggressive effort to fight for voting rights in Selma, Alabama. Selma was the center of an area of Alabama known as the Blight Belt, which had a heavy concentration of blacks. Yet, only about 2 percent of blacks of voting age in Selma were registered to vote. Early in 1965, a young black man named Jimmie Lee Jackson was shot and killed during a demonstration in Marion, Alabama, about thirty-five miles from Selma. So we decided to march from Selma to Montgomery to petition the governor and the state officials and to dramatize to the nation and to the world that people have been denied the right to participate in the democratic process simply because of their color. On Sunday, March 7, 1965, almost six hundred of us gathered at the Brown Chapel African Methodist Episcopal Church in downtown Selma. We lined up in twos and started walking. It was a silent march; no one said a word. We walked through the streets of Selma to the Edmund Pettus Bridge, which crossed the Alabama River. As we started over the bridge, I felt this gentle breeze come up off of the river. It was so peaceful and so quiet, yet something didn't feel right. When we got to the apex of the bridge, we saw a sea of blue on the other side. It was a sea of Alabama state troopers. The night before the March, Jim Clark, the sheriff of Dallas County, had issued a request for all white men over the age of twenty-one to come down to the Dallas County Courthouse to be deputized. So waiting for us on the other side of the bridge were Sheriff Clark and his posse, carrying nightsticks and bullwhips — some of them riding horses.

When we were within hearing distance of the posse, a man identified himself as an Alabama state trooper and said, "This is an unlawful march. It will not be allowed to continue. I give you three minutes to disperse and return to your church." We decided that we should kneel and pray, but before we could get word back through the crowd so that people could start kneeling, the man with the bullhorn called out, "Troopers advance!" Very few of us had thought that we would actually make it all the way to Montgomery; we fully

Lewis in 1964, during the Birmingham campaign.

—Congressman John Lewis, born in 1940 in Troy, Alabama, participated in the Freedom Rides in 1961 and was the chairman of the Student Nonviolent Coordinating Committee (SNCC). He was one of the planners and a keynote speaker at the March on Washington in August 1963. Despite forty arrests, physical attacks, and serious injuries, Lewis remained a devoted advocate of the philosophy of nonviolence. After leaving SNCC in 1966, Lewis became the director of the Voter Education Project. He was elected to the Atlanta City Council in 1981 and then to the U.S. House of Representatives in 1986. He is currently serving his fifth term in Congress.

expected to be arrested. I was even carrying a knapsack with an apple, an orange, and a toothbrush in it. But none of us anticipated the reception we got on the bridge that day. The state troopers shot off tear gas, charged toward us, and started beating us and trampling us with their horses. A trooper grabbed me by the arm, held me down with one hand and beat me in the head with his nightstick. Then he just left me lying there bleeding in a cloud of tear gas. I thought I was going to die. To this day, I don't know how I made it back across the bridge and through the streets of Selma to the church. I do recall being back at the church, where thousands of people from all over the city had gathered. At one point, someone asked me to say a few words. I stood up, gave an account of what had happened and said something like, "I don't understand how President Johnson can send troops to Vietnam, and cannot send troops to Selma, Alabama, to protect people whose only desire is to register and to vote." A few minutes later, I was put in an ambulance and transported to the hospital for treatment.

That day became known as Bloody Sunday. When people watched the news that night and saw what had happened, they couldn't believe their eyes. They couldn't believe that their fellow citizens could be so mistreated because of their desire to register and to vote. People saw these young people, these brave and courageous people, literally putting their bodies on the line. They saw the blood. They saw the violence. They saw people who believed in the philosophy and discipline of nonviolence, who were just trying to exercise their constitutional right to petition their government.

Bloody Sunday had an unbelievable impact on Lyndon Johnson and the whole of Washington. President Johnson was angry. He called George Wallace to get assurance that he could protect the marchers if they decided to march from Selma to Montgomery. Wallace said in so many words that he couldn't. That he wouldn't. So President Johnson federalized the National

Guard of the state of Alabama, and called up part of the United States Army. One week after Bloody Sunday, Johnson went on national television to speak to a joint session of Congress. That day Johnson made one of the greatest speeches any American president ever made on the question of civil rights and voting rights. Johnson started off by saying, "I speak tonight for the dignity of man and for the destiny of democracy." And he went on to say, "As it was more than a century ago at Appomattox . . . so it was last week in Selma, Alabama." And in that speech, Lyndon Johnson condemned the violence and introduced a Voting Rights Act. He said over and over again, "And we shall overcome. And we shall overcome." I was with Martin Luther King, Jr., that night, watching the speech on television. And, as Johnson spoke, tears started streaming down Dr. King's face. I knew then that we would make it from Selma to Montgomery. I knew then that the Voting Rights Act would be passed and signed into law.

On March 21, 1965, we left Selma, thousands strong, and marched toward that same bridge that had seen such bloodshed only two weeks earlier. As I crossed the bridge, past the spot where I had been beaten, I was filled with exhilaration and pride. We were involved in a holy crusade, and we were finally going to make it. We marched the fifty miles of Highway 80 from Selma to Montgomery over a period of four days. The army and the National Guard protected us the entire route. By the time we arrived in Montgomery, we were more than 25,000 strong. It was the largest demonstration ever in the history of the state of Alabama. There were blacks and whites, senators' wives, statesmen, and celebrities, even the cousin of Nelson Rockefeller. But there were also the poor sharecroppers and tenant farmers, people from the Blight Belt of Alabama, whose only desire was to register and to vote. And we stood on the same spot that Jefferson Davis of the Confederacy had stood a century ago, and we demanded a Voting Rights Act.

Detroit, above, erupted in violence after police raided a black nightclub for a liquor violation. For six days rioters ransacked stores, overturned cars, smashed windows, and set fires. Frightened Michigan national guardsmen frantically tried to quell the violence while snipers shot at them from above.

nonetheless hampered by more subtle and more insidious forms of racism, the kind that deprives jobs and housing through the wink of an eye and an elbow to the ribs. Watts and Detroit and Newark were declarations that there were really two levels of racism at work in America, the kind of legal barriers that southern blacks had begun to remove and the more elusive economic and social barriers that were the bane of the urban North, where discrimination declared itself more through class distinctions than laws. And while it was relatively easy to address conditions where Americans were being denied the right to eat in the same restaurants, use the same rest rooms, and vote in the same elections, it would be much harder to legislate away economic inequalities and disparities in the quality of life.

The voice that spoke most clearly to the young rioters of Watts (and their counterparts in Newark, Chicago, Detroit, and elsewhere) was that of the Black Muslim leader who called himself Malcolm X. Born Malcolm Little, in Omaha, Nebraska, in 1925, he was, like Martin Luther King, the son of a Baptist preacher. But that is where the two men's similarities ended. Malcolm X's father, who believed in the purity of the black race and the destiny of the black man to return to Africa to attain true freedom, independence, and self-respect, was brutally killed when Malcolm was six, and Malcolm himself (the "X" was something he added later as his way of refusing the name bestowed upon his ancestors by white slave-owners) would go on to become, successively, a hustler, a burglar, a convict, a member of a prison debate society, a Muslim, a Muslim minister, an author, and, finally, one of the century's most influential proponents of black nationalism. Long after he died in 1965, the victim of a bullet fired by a Muslim rival while Malcolm was speaking at the Audubon Ballroom in New York City, Malcolm X's influence continued to spread to larger and larger numbers of frustrated African-Americans grappling with their sense of identity.

Malcom X (right), 1925–1965

In the mid-1960s, as the writings and teachings of Malcolm spread throughout the streets of Harlem, Watts, and the South Side of Chicago, more and more African-American people began to see nonviolence as an option, not a moral imperative, and integration, the ideal to which King was so dedicated, as impractical or even destructive. The assimilation of the black race into white society might represent the purest form of democratic idealism, yet it was on another level deeply unsatisfying, even threatening, for an assimilated black person was, in essence, no longer black and certainly not white. If King had dedicated his life to making black Americans more a part of America and the ideals to which the nation was dedicated, then Malcolm, put simply, wanted black Americans to feel more black and embrace their African heritage. Viewed his way, the great American melting pot was a sinister image, a cauldron brewing a form of cultural genocide. And blacks in America's cities could relate directly to that experience, since most of them had left tightly knit communities in the South (over 90 percent of black America lived in the South at the turn of the century) in the hope of leading freer lives in the North and had discovered after living there for a while that they had neither the comforts of community *nor* the benefits of freedom. Unlike other populations, for whom the urban life had provided the first step up the ladder of mobility, the black peasantry streaming into the cities after World War II had arrived at precisely the time that the demand for unskilled labor was fast disappearing. And their arrival had coincided with the departure of much of the immigrant white population (even, in many cases, inspiring it), forming a parallel to southern segregation, in fact if not in law.

If nothing else, Malcolm X was provocative. He saw southern whites as morally superior to northerners, for, as he said, at least they were *honestly* racist, while northern racism hid behind a liberal exterior. He mocked the image of the North as free. "I'm not going to sit at your table and watch you eat, with nothing on my plate," he declared in a mordant voice, "and call myself a diner." Preaching separation of the races, he urged Americans to adopt the vernacular usage of "black" to denote African-Americans instead of the then more common term, "Negro," knowing all along that even the word "black" would declare itself as opposite to and incompatible with "white."

Yet for whites, the most disturbing message in Malcolm X's many diatribes was his contempt for King's strategies of Christian nonviolence, his description of the "human combustion" that was packed into the ghettos, waiting to explode, and his references to the "social dynamite" that was America's black population. And they listened fearfully in 1966, as his separatist ideology evolved in the hands of SNCC leaders Stokely Carmichael and H. Rap Brown and the newly established Black Panther Party, led by Huey Newton and Bobby Seale, into the slogan "Black Power." King and other moderates chose to interpret "black power" as black pride, but to many people (including many of those who began chanting the phrase angrily in America's streets) black power meant nothing short of a black revolution overthrowing the white establishment. Despite all the hard work of so many committed people, it was hard not to feel that the ultimate racial clash Americans had long feared might finally come to pass.

There are years in this century, single 365-day episodes divided just like all the other 365-day episodes and featuring the same meteorological patterns,

The appeal of "black power": **"You do your hunger strike; we'll be throwing blows"**

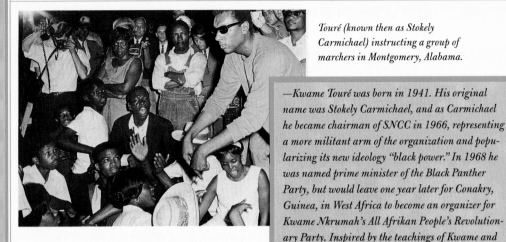

Touré (known then as Stokely Carmichael) instructing a group of marchers in Montgomery, Alabama.

—*Kwame Touré was born in 1941. His original name was Stokely Carmichael, and as Carmichael he became chairman of SNCC in 1966, representing a more militant arm of the organization and popularizing its new ideology "black power." In 1968 he was named prime minister of the Black Panther Party, but would leave one year later for Conakry, Guinea, in West Africa to become an organizer for Kwame Nkrumah's All Afrikan People's Revolutionary Party. Inspired by the teachings of Kwame and Guinea's late president Sekou Touré, he changed his name to Kwame Touré. He still resides in Guinea.*

I was born on the island of Trinidad and Tobago on June 29, 1941. When I was about ten, I came to the United States and lived in the Bronx. Moving here was a shock in every sense. Although Trinidad was a British colony at that time, and we were certainly oppressed victims of colonialism, the British only sent their own to fill the highest official positions. The civil servants were all of African descent. All those in immediate authority, like policemen and teachers, were African. In the United States, however, all in immediate authority were white. I knew that Africans were capable of doing these jobs, and I immediately understood, almost instinctively, the racism in America.

I was a senior at Bronx High School of Science in 1960 when the sit-in movement caught my attention. By spring of that year the Student Nonviolent Coordinating Committee (SNCC) was being formed to coordinate the rapid growth of the sit-in movement. I was thrilled by SNCC and got involved because in my mind the older organizations, like King's Southern Christian Leadership Conference (SCLC) and James Farmer's Congress of Racial Equality (CORE), were holding back the students and the youth. My freshman year at Howard University, I was indoctrinated in nonviolent discipline on the battleground. I took it seriously, very seriously, and it called for a lot of philosophical study and understanding and debate.

I was with the first group to take trains from New Orleans as part of the Freedom Rides in 1961. It was a rough ride, because we were confronted by segregationists breaking train windows at every single stop until we got to Jackson, Mississippi, where the police arrested us for refusing to leave the white waiting room. We were sent to Hinds County Jail, and then, just to increase the pressure on us, a group of us were transferred to the Parchman Penitentiary on death row. My cellmate and I were the youngest, at eighteen and nineteen, respectively. We occupied the first cell, so whenever trouble

started, it came to us first, and being the youngest we responded the most arrogantly and aggressively — all the while staying true to nonviolence. The police were beating us and torturing us every night, and part of our group called for a hunger strike. I thought, "They want to kill us, and you want us to get weaker." We screamed, "No, no way. Y'all can do your own hunger strike." I respected Martin Luther King for sticking to the nonviolence under all conditions, and I believed in it as long as it was effective, but if it wasn't working, then I decided that I would be throwing blows. By the time I walked out of Parchman Penitentiary, I was prepared to carry a gun in my work.

When I was growing up in Harlem, Malcolm X was there all the time, so I knew all about him and the Nation of Islam. I had been to the mosque several times, like all the young people of my age who were serious and seeking ways to help alleviate the suffering of our people. Malcolm X presented a clearer, more direct political analysis, stripped of sentimentality, that saw the reality of the enemy we were fighting. Since Malcolm X aimed his message directly at African-Americans, he could touch us more deeply, while Martin Luther King's message also had to speak to white society. King would say, "What we need is morality," while Malcolm would say, "what we need is power." To Malcolm, nonviolence just meant that you're giving your cheek left and right to a man who has no conscience. He thought we needed an eye for an eye.

Malcolm X's assassination had a profound effect upon us, especially those of us in SNCC. In all revolutionary movements, once the leader is assassinated, the movement intensifies. It doesn't disintegrate. After his assassination in 1965, those of us in SNCC who really understood him made a conscious decision to pick up

Malcolm's points and to build on them. We wanted to keep his philosophy alive.

We decided to go into Lowndes County, Alabama, bordering Selma and Montgomery. Our goal was to use the vote as a means to organize the people. There was not one single black registered to vote there in 1965, yet 80 percent of the population in the county was black. We followed the Selma to Montgomery march to Lowndes County and stopped there, and then we contacted all the people from Lowndes who had come and given their support to the march. With these names, we planned to create our own independent political party, a party with arms. In the state of Alabama at that time, the Democratic Party was run by Governor George Wallace. The official emblem of their state chapter of the Democratic Party was a white rooster with the words "White Supremacy for the Right." It would have been difficult for us to tell Africans to come and vote in this party. We formed the Lowndes County Freedom Organization and came up with the symbol of the black panther, and the people just loved it. The press saw it and wrote that terrorists were coming — SNCC is here, and they have a black panther party. The press called our party the Black Panther Party (Bobby Seale would adopt the symbol for his own Black Panther Party in Oakland, California) in the hopes that somehow by making us sound negative, we would back down. But instead of weakening us, the people said, "Have you ever seen a panther and a rooster in a fight?"

For three months before the arrival of election day, white terrorists sent out word that if any Africans went to vote, they'd be left there for dead. Young men and women from across the country volunteered to assist SNCC. In order to encourage Africans to get out and vote, we let them know that young brothers and sisters were coming, armed, from the big cities to help out. I remember the Justice Department sent somebody to see me who said, "You know, your people are bringing in guns. What are you gonna do?" I said, "We're gonna vote." He said, "The whites are very upset about this." We had already decided that we would not fire the first shot, so I said, "You tell them they've got the first shot, but we're voting." When election day came, the people turned out to vote and not one shot was fired.

Even though we didn't win, for the first time, black citizens of Lowndes County felt they had exercised their political rights, and they began to feel like dignified human beings. They began to understand the power of politics. With their voting bloc, they could get rid of the sheriff who was terrorizing their entire community; they could get a school superintendent who would at least listen to them; and they could enter a courthouse without being afraid.

*In October 1967 nearly fifty thousand protesters assembled in Washington, D.C., for what
organizers called the March on the Pentagon in protest of the Vietnam War. For the first time since the
Bonus Army descended on Washington in 1932, the federal government deployed troops to protect the
Capital from its own citizens. "Saturday night's confrontation at the Pentagon was a last sit-down
for us," warned one activist who felt it was time that the protests turn violent. "Why the passivity?"*

the same requisite spring, summer, winter, and fall, that are yet somehow different. Nineteen sixty-eight was that kind of year, a standout annual in a standout decade, composed, to be specific, of 366 days, being a leap year, and yet in fact made up of nothing less than the whole shimmering fiber of the human spirit, in at once its darkest and brightest forms, welling up and crisscrossing like a pattern of nerve endings bristling with fever. It was now that all the forces of the sixties came together, a fitting climax to a powerful drama. There was the pulsating music, crammed with rage and grand moral pronouncements ("This is the dawning of the age of Aquarius," sang the cast of the iconoclastic Broadway musical *Hair*); the continuing battle over the Third World, twisted into a new and even more grizzly shape with the arrival of the Tet Offensive, the Viet Cong's lunar new year onslaught against South Vietnamese cities the American soldiers felt they had long ago secured; the deadly patricidal attacks upon America's leadership, including the murder of Martin Luther King and the pounding on his grave that was delivered by the massive street violence it inspired, an incendiary send-off for the man who had dreamed, Christlike, of a world governed by love and died, Christlike, with those who were once his followers betraying him with riots across the nation. Then, too, there was the assassination of another Kennedy, presidential candidate Bobby Kennedy, played out, like the first assassination, before the unblinking eye of the television camera; and, finally, the full boil of the long-simmering student rebellion, not only in America but also in Paris and Mexico City and Prague, and wherever students responded to the clarion call urging them forth. Sixty-eight was the decade's proud and pagan closing parade, led by a thousand marching bands.

Tet, which began in January, resulted in enormous losses for North Vietnam, but in laying bare several of the war's most difficult facts, it proved to be an enormous blow to home front morale. By demonstrating the weakness of the American position (Viet Cong commandos invaded the American Embassy, took a major Saigon radio station, and attacked the presidential palace), the offensive showed that the administration had either been wholly incompetent in analyzing the North's position as one of dwindling strength or, worse, that the Pentagon had simply lied to the American people by implying that victory was imminent. The end of the Vietnam War was not at hand, nowhere near. And the myth that it was to be a quick act of military expertise executed by the world's greatest power upon the unruly factions of a backward people was now exploded in living color across American televisions. The desperate American troops seemed hopelessly dazed by their predicament, never voiced better than by the officer who announced that the town of Bentre had to be destroyed "in order to save it." And by prompting the Pentagon to request even more troops, Tet demonstrated the American high command's continuing befuddlement over how to conduct a guerrilla war. "Half a million American soldiers with 700,000 Vietnamese allies, with total command of the air, total command of the sea, backed by huge resources and the most modern weapons," said an incredulous Bobby Kennedy as he prepared to challenge Lyndon Johnson for the Democratic nomination, remained stymied by "an enemy whose total strength is about 250,000." And still, the ships bringing the wide-eyed boy soldiers continued toward Asian shores.

One family's tragic conflict: **Dad helps run the war; son marches against it**

Throughout the 1960s, my father was the director of the Defense Intelligence Agency, which was sort of a military version of the CIA. During the Vietnam War, the DIA gathered intelligence on the numbers and condition of the enemy, what areas should be targeted for bombing, what happened after the bombs were dropped, and how much the bombing affected the Vietnamese. My family lived at Bolling Air Force Base on the east bank of the Potomac River in Washington, D.C., on what was called General's Row. Every day my father would be chauffeured down to a dock on the Potomac River, where he and the other air force generals would get on a very posh cabin cruiser that would ferry them up the river to the Pentagon.

One of my first ambitions was to join the air force. I loved the idea of the air force: the glory of the victory against Germany; the triumph of the Berlin airlift, where air force pilots were true humanitarians, bringing food and fuel to a besieged city. It was an irresistible image, manly and virtuous at the same time. I completely accepted John F. Kennedy's vision of the American mission: "We will go anywhere, pay any price, to keep the light of freedom alive." I even went as far as to join the ROTC when I was in college, but I eventually realized that the air force wasn't for me. After a couple of years of college, I decided to enter the seminary, to become a priest.

Although I didn't understand it then, I was in some way taking my father's place in the priesthood. As a young man, he had entered the seminary and prepared to be a priest for many years; that's how he got his education. I think that in part I was unconsciously acting out his dream. But I was also a very religious person. And once I acknowledged that about myself, it seemed that trying to build a life around my belief in God was the most important thing I could do.

I started studying to become a priest around the same time that Kennedy sent the very first advisers to Vietnam. As the war grew, during my years at seminary, I pretty much accepted that it was a just war. I still believed in the idea that communism was evil and had to be opposed. I would go home and listen to my father defend the idea of the war, and I would come away convinced. My father knew more about this than anybody. He was a good man, and he told the truth.

In 1965, several things happened that gradually started to change the way I felt about the war. First Pope Paul VI — the avatar of my ambition — came to New York for the United Nations' twentieth anniversary. The pope addressed the United Nations General Assembly with a resounding speech that ended with two lines that were forever seared in me because it was such a rejection of what I had grown up believing: "War No More. War

Never Again." About a month later, a young man named Norman Morrison went to the Pentagon, where my father's office was, and set himself on fire as an act of protest against the war, and he died. A month after that a man named Roger Laporte went to the United Nations, and he set himself on fire. His last words were "I am antiwar, all wars. I did this as a religious act." As a seminarian, I was trying to understand my religious faith and my identity as an American, and to have these things happening in those years changed everything.

Since the Norman Morrison immolation happened within sight of the window of my father's office, I had to talk to him about it. My father's opinion was very simple. He knew that people like Norman Morrison and

Right: Carroll being carried off by police during a demonstration at Hanscom Air Force Base in Lexington, Massachusetts. Left: Carroll's father in the late 1960s, when he was director of the Defense Intelligence Agency.

—*James Carroll, born in 1943, took his vows and became a priest in February 1969. His father resigned from the Pentagon in September of the same year. Carroll left the priesthood in 1975 and is now a writer living in Boston with a wife and two children. His books include* An American Requiem, The City Below, Memorial Bridge, *and* Madonna Red.

other serious war protesters were acting out of good intentions, but he seriously disagreed with them. He was convinced that the issue in Vietnam was to get the North Vietnamese to understand that they had to bend to our will. He was appalled by the peace movement, because it gave the North Vietnamese reasons not to negotiate, not to surrender, not to do as they were told.

By 1966, I was still defending the war, although my doubts were growing. And I could see changes occurring during my visits home. My one younger brother, Dennis, had grown his hair long and declared himself a vegetarian. Although Dennis and I didn't see each other very often, we had learned to find each other's eyes during our increasingly charged family gatherings. At holiday dinners, my father would try to convince me that he was right about Vietnam. But as I listened to his arguments, I was continually haunted by the memory of

Norman Morrison and Roger Laporte. And I was sickened by the grotesque film footage I saw night after night on television, the brutal use of venal weapons against civilians. It was clear that the traditional illusion about warfare — that we can distinguish between the enemy and innocent civilians — simply didn't apply in this war. That same year I read an article in the *New York Times* that described American bombs blowing up the Bach Mai hospital, which was primarily a pediatric hospital. I went home armed with this to see what my father would say. I no sooner said the words "Bach Mai" when my father became livid. He threw his napkin down on the table, poked his finger in my face, and yelled, "If I found out that an American pilot had deliberately dropped a bomb on a hospital, what do you think would happen?" And I said, "You would see that he was court-martialed." And he said, "You're damn right I would. And I don't want to hear Bach Mai from you again." I

realize now that the energy and emotion with which he responded to me was a signal of his own distress. Bach Mais were happening all over Vietnam. It was the true meaning of the air war. It was a war against civilian people, and my father was in denial about that. He didn't want to admit it, and, believe me, neither did I. During that whole period of my life, I felt this sickness in my stomach, this nausea caused by my conflicted feelings about the war. I wouldn't recognize until much later just how depressed I really was.

In October 1967, a massive antiwar demonstration was planned for Washington. As I heard about these plans, it became unthinkable to me that I not somehow be part of it. At this point, I had accepted that the war was unjust, but I still hadn't openly declared myself about it. It was a very radical act for me to attend an antiwar demonstration. I was stepping away from being a well-behaved American, and stepping into the circle of people who, in my parents' terms, would have been bad company. And I wasn't raised to be in bad company. When I made the decision to attend the demonstration, I had still not told my father about my true feelings about the war. I couldn't stand an open confrontation with him. Not just because I feared his disapproval, but because I feared facing the truth about what he was doing.

I decided to go to the march with the only person I knew who felt both sides of the struggle the way I did: my brother, Dennis. The two of us rendezvoused near the Washington Monument and then joined some fifty thousand other demonstrators at the Lincoln Memorial. There were speeches, but we never got close enough to hear them. There were banners everywhere, banners for groups I should have identified with, like the Catholic Peace Fellowship, but we stayed clear of every group. Dennis and I moved through the experience that day, not as observers, but quite clearly as participants. We wanted to be counted against the war, but we didn't want to be seen. At one point, about twenty thousand demonstrators broke off from the main group and headed across the Memorial Bridge and toward the Pentagon. Dennis and I decided to follow. The Pentagon was sacred territory for us. It was where Dad had worked all these years, and it's where he was that day. We were quite aware of his presence. We knew exactly which window was his, and we stood staring at it, watching for any movement of those curtains. Dennis and I stayed very close to the crowd, so that if he were looking, he wouldn't see us. Part of me was wishing that he would see us. Then I'd have said what Martin Luther King said. "Here I stand. God help me, I can stand no other place."

As it turned out, it would take almost two years for me to have that moment with my father. It was Christmas, 1968. At dinner that night, I brought up the subject of Philip Berrigan. He was a priest, a leader of the Catholic antiwar movement, and, by then, a serious influence in my life. A few months before, he and several other people had stolen draft records from a draft board in Baltimore, taken them out into the parking lot, and poured blood all over them. Of course the act enraged my father. He denounced Philip Berrigan as a "kook." It was by then a favorite word of my father's, and it was a word I had grown to detest. I banged my fist on the table and said, "Philip Berrigan is not a kook." Then I turned to my mother and said, "Tell him. Philip Berrigan is a priest." I left the house that night knowing that I wasn't coming back. Not to that house. Not at Bolling Air Force Base. Not with the generals. As I left, I looked back and again caught eyes with my brother, Dennis. And as I did, I couldn't help but feel as though I was betraying him by leaving him behind.

Like much of America, Bobby Kennedy was undergoing a transformation — over Vietnam, civil rights, the moral vacancy of the abundant society — and as he did, his metamorphosis gave encouragement both to the growing mood of skepticism over the war, penetrating now beyond the universities and the liberal community into the mainstream of American life, and to the persistent feeling that this all wouldn't have happened if there were still a Kennedy in the White House, for surely John Kennedy would have had the good sense to get out. The coming presidential election gave opponents a chance to challenge Johnson, and they did. At first, the opposition to the president and his policies formed behind the long-shot, antiwar candidacy of Minnesota Senator Eugene McCarthy, who received a big boost from the reaction to Tet. After Tet, even conservative Democrats responded to McCarthy's appeal, hoping to cast a protest vote against the administration's ineptly executed, limited war (60 percent of those voting for McCarthy in the New Hampshire primary described themselves as hawks). Yet it was the army of young student liberals who put in hours of hard work for McCarthy (shaved and neatly combed, they called themselves "Clean for Gene"), marching door-to-door, landing in the living rooms of America to teach the nation that the war was evil, even as many of them, seeing McCarthy as a one-issue candidate, waited patiently for the magical name of Kennedy to reappear on a presidential ballot.

March brought the government-sponsored Kerner Commission report, describing what most people had already begun to see, a nation in the grip of a growing racial divide, only, to the surprise of many, the document came down decidedly on the side of the rioters, declaring, as Malcolm X had, that America was at core a racist society, needing to address equality not only in the form of legal recognition but in result. Johnson promptly ignored it. Later that same month, Bobby Kennedy entered the race, and, stunned by McCarthy's showing in New Hampshire, the president withdrew his name from consideration for the Democratic nomination, a deeply broken man. It was a historic moment. The last time there had been a serious challenge to an incumbent president from within his own party was 1912, when Teddy Roosevelt took on President William Howard Taft and split the Republican Party.

Johnson's surrender was a victory for democracy. He had failed, and the forces of public opinion, from both the Right and the Left, had told him so, but 1968 seemed to match each triumph with tragedy. The same week as the president's announcement, Martin Luther King took a break from his other activities to appear in Memphis, Tennessee, in support of striking sanitation workers. He had been booked into a twenty-nine-dollar-a-night Holiday Inn, an extravagance noted by the local newspapers, and switched at the last minute to the seedy thirteen-dollar-a-night Lorraine Motel, adjacent to where the sanitation men were planning a march. And it was there in the early evening of April 4 that America's greatest prophet of nonviolence leaned forward from the cinder-block balcony outside room 306 as an assassin's bullet fired from a rooming house 205 feet away bit through the night air.

The bright orange flames that streaked through many American cities over the next few days were as hot on Fourteenth Street, just a few blocks from the White House, as they were in Harlem and Detroit, Chicago and Kansas City,

Baltimore and Atlanta. With the smoke of seven hundred fires pouring from the Capital, Washington looked more like a Third World city, even a little like Saigon during Tet, the fifty thousand national and federal guardsmen rushing to bring control across the nation more like an invading army than protectors of the peace. Over a hundred cities were marked with a violence that included not only arson and looting but also the exchange of gunfire. In Oakland, the Black Panthers entered into a shoot-out with police. In Chicago, Mayor Richard Daley gave his officers the order to shoot to kill.

Some looters described their destructive escapades as "early Easter shopping," and from inside shattered Washington storefronts, a few others were heard shouting, "Take everything you need, baby," as if the death of the nation's greatest civil rights leader could be salved by the pleasures of an unanticipated shopping spree. Yet the riots were really the flames of an indescribable grief, the smoke choking the cherry blossoms around the still-sturdy Lincoln Memorial the symbol of anguish over the nation's lost connection with the picture of harmony King had so eloquently drawn there only five years earlier. Even the most violent black power advocate understood the debt African-Americans owed to the man they sometimes mockingly called "de Lawd."

Robert Kennedy was boarding a plane for a campaign stop in Indianapolis, including a rally in the city's black ghetto, when he heard the news that King had been shot, and on his arrival, he was informed by the Indianapolis chief of police that the city could not guarantee him protection if he decided to go ahead and speak there. Kennedy ignored the warning (and advice from some in his party who wanted him to cancel) and ordered his driver to take him to the rally anyway, riding silently through the city's empty streets, then turning to an aide to mumble quietly through his despair, "What should I say?" When his car arrived in the ghetto, the police escort peeled away. Now Kennedy was on his own.

The crowd of nearly a thousand waiting for him was unaware that King had died and as the candidate told them the people gasped. Some, in disbelief, continued to cheer: they had not heard him or they had not wanted to hear him. He quieted them down and repeated himself. Then he appealed to their best instincts. "You can be filled with bitterness, with hatred and a desire for revenge," he said, speaking in the glare of searchlights, a black overcoat protecting him from the cold. "We can move in that direction as a country, in great polarization — black people amongst black, white people amongst white, filled with hatred toward one another. Or we can make an effort, as Martin Luther King did . . . to replace that violence, that stain of bloodshed . . . with an effort to understand, with compassion and love."

For his campaign, Kennedy had employed some of the best speechwriters in the business, many of whom had once served his brother, yet here, in what may well have been the most powerful oration of his young life, he spoke extemporaneously, asking the people to reject division and lawlessness and to pray for "our country." The senator even found time to quote the Greek poet Aeschylus. "In our sleep," he said to his rapt audience, "pain which cannot forget falls drop by drop upon the heart until, in our own despair, against our will, comes wisdom

"When white America killed Dr. King, she declared war on us . . . We have to retaliate for the deaths of our leaders . . . in the streets."

Black power leader
Stokely Carmichael

The riots that followed the assassination of Martin Luther King, Jr., charred America's cities, like Washington, left. In one last cruel irony, the plane carrying the body of the apostle of nonviolence is given the salute of black power advocates, above, while an armed guard stands watch: the victim of violence, protected by the tools of violence, mourned with a symbol of violence.

" And it's one, two, three,
       what are we fighting for?
Don't ask me, I don't give
       a damn
Next stop, VIETNAM!
And it's, five, six, seven
       open up the pearly gates
Ah, there ain't no time to
       wonder why
Whoopee! We're all goin' to die!"

"I Feel Like I'm Fixin' to Die Rag"
Country Joe and the Fish

Approximately five hundred student radicals seized five buildings in the 1968 Columbia University protests, even occupying the president's office, above. The group was protesting military research on campus and the building of a university gym in a Harlem park (which the students sarcastically called Gym Crow).

through the awful grace of God." While the rest of America burned, there were no riots in Indianapolis that night or the next or even the night after that. There the people took their grief home quietly and they grieved again when, two months later, after winning the California primary, Kennedy, too, became the victim of an assassin's bullet.

The nation was killing its heroes, and an air of the absurd and the perverse was moving into the void. On television, Rowan and Martin's *Laugh-In* tweaked establishment sensibilities with fast cuts of irreverent humor interspliced with a go-go dancer in body paint (Goldie Hawn). A twenties throwback named Tiny Tim crooned "Tiptoe through the Tulips" accompanying himself on a ukulele. On radio, rock and rollers like Country Joe and the Fish sang irreverently about the war in Vietnam ("Be the first one on your block to have your boy come home in a box!"). And the folk duo Simon and Garfunkel offered a plaintive response to it all in the form of a vibrating question, pining for a time when life was simpler: "Where have you gone, Joe DiMaggio?" they sang. "A nation turns its lonely eyes to you."

The campuses were in revolt. Less than three weeks after King was assassinated, a group of radical students began an uprising at Columbia University in New York City, seizing five buildings and even breaking into the president's office. There they smoked his cigars and sat at his desk, in a gesture reminiscent at once of a banana republic coup and of a group of scruffy teenagers who had discovered an open liquor cabinet while Mom and Dad were out for the evening.

The Columbia University insurrection was among the more colorful, but it was not unique. All over the world, students seemed to be responding to the same herald. In Paris what began as a protest over sex-segregated dormitories ended in a general strike, including massive industrial walk-outs, and the near collapse of the government of World War II resistance leader and French hero Charles de Gaulle. Anger over British support for the American position in the Vietnam War galvanized students in London to mount a massive march to the American Embassy, including participants from France, Germany, Sweden, Belgium, and the rest of continental Europe. Then, in August, 650,000 Soviet troops marched into Czechoslovakia with orders to thrust a chill upon the "Prague Spring," as leader Alexander Dubcek's "Socialism with a Human Face" had been dubbed. Mobs of Czech youths emptied into the streets where they defiantly climbed the Russian tanks and chanted "U.S.S.R. go home," a scene that many of America's young saw less in terms of *Soviet* brutality than as a parallel to their own situation: "old people killing young people." Indeed, the common ground on which most of the world's students were joining forces seemed to be more generational than ideological. And if youth had already grown to think of itself as exceptional, it now determined that exceptional youth's exceptional moment had arrived in 1968.

The most notable American uprising came with the Democratic National Convention in Chicago (or "Czechcago," as some preferred to call it). With the death of Robert Kennedy, the fading of McCarthy as a viable candidate, and the political bosses' virtual anointing of Johnson's vice president, Hubert Humphrey, as the nominee (Humphrey had not entered a single primary), youth had lost its enthusiasm for working "within the system." Led by absurdist figures like Abbie Hoffman and Jerry Rubin (whose Yippie — as in Youth International — "political party" compiled a preposterous mock agenda that included seducing the delegates' wives, slipping LSD into the city's water supply, and seizing the Nabisco headquarters and distributing free cookies), 10,000 demonstrators came to the City of Big Shoulders to wreak havoc. Unfortunately for them, 23,000 police and national guardsmen awaited them.

Played out on a national scale, Chicago was the moment of confrontation every dysfunctional family dreads, the ritual dinner when son finally challenges father and the long-suppressed oedipal rage breaks free across the table sending the potatoes flying and the rest of the family running for cover. Only the ritual here was a national ritual, a political convention, as old a national ritual as the nation itself, and the family watching the blood flowing was the family of America, at home in front of its television set.

The incongruity of the scene was not lost upon the nation. At the podium, politician after politician droned on about the greatness of America, of the Democratic Party, of Roosevelt and Truman and Kennedy and Johnson, of the New Deal and the Great Society, even as the cameras were flashing outside to the violence in the streets. "The whole world is watching!" the demonstrators chanted at the police and, in fact, much of it was. By midweek the convention itself took on a confrontational tone. From the podium, Connecticut Senator Abraham Ribicoff denounced the "Gestapo tactics" of Mayor Daley's police, and Daley, standing barely twenty feet away on the floor, cupped his hand to his mouth and shouted an expletive-filled retort. A group of antiwar delegates joined hands and sang "We Shall Overcome," enraging other delegates who attempted to shout them down. By the end, as Humphrey stood up to accept the nomination, the Democratic Party was a shambles, the election effectively lost to them already, and not so much because Americans disapproved of the violence being committed on the youthful rioters, but because it had happened at all, that there *was* a Chicago, and that the whole bloody mess was shameful. In one of the more powerful demonstrations of that disappointment, a surprising percentage of blue-collar voters who had supported Bobby Kennedy in the primary rejected the Democrats entirely in the fall election and voted instead for the third-party candidacy of segregationist George Wallace, who by then had made himself the most vocal supporter for imposing strict order on America's streets.

Sixty-eight had been a weird nervous breakdown of a year — all the dirty rioting and assassinations, the cold-blooded killing, and the absurd, nihilistic campaigns — and when it ended not with a revolution, but with the election of Republican Richard Nixon, the man whom the decade had sent to the showers so long ago, it had the feeling for many, particularly the vocal young, that all the idealism had failed, its spear carriers murdered or otherwise silenced — and the power had not gone to the "people" in that energetic sixties rallying cry, but to the kind of establishment figure from whom it was supposed to have been taken.

If anything, the year had demonstrated just how deep the divide through

When Soviet tanks rolled into Prague on August 20, 1968, they clashed head-on with a population determined to hold on to their nation's recent modest democratic reforms. The fiercest fighting erupted when the Soviets tried to storm the national radio station, which had vowed to continually play Czech composer Bedrich Smetana's "My Country" as long as the station remained free. Early in the morning of August 21 the station went silent, signaling the end of the "Prague Spring."

416

Students and police clash in Chicago: "We knew this thing was going to be huge"

I had been active in the student Left throughout the sixties, but by 1968, I was so alienated from the political system that I was not following the processes of the Democratic candidates very closely. I remember many people saw Bobby Kennedy and Eugene McCarthy as hopeful forces for change, but after Martin Luther King's assassination, I began to feel that there was a rottenness at the core of the political system of this country.

I was a marshal out in the streets during the Democratic National convention in Chicago. We expected a police riot at the Chicago Convention because we had heard that was what the police were gearing up for. We taught the demonstrators to link arms and make an arc to keep the police from charging them. From what I could see, there was very little provocation on behalf of the students. Sometimes students ran around, and they would get arrested for simply playing. There were students who were clearly provocateurs, and we disarmed most of them. There were others who were maybe just hotheaded youths who had bricks to throw or bats, and we would take those things away from them.

My most vivid memory of the convention was at the demonstration down at the hotel where the McCarthy campaign had its headquarters. A crowd of thousands of people gathered outside, and the police were pushing us closer and closer together. Those of us who had experience protesting kept saying, "Stand up, stand up, stand up." Because we knew the police were gonna charge and were gonna go in and slaughter them. After the police charged in, I saw this young man in a suit and tie and a woman who looked like she was a sorority girl, very well dressed, and she had blood pouring out of her hair. This young man had picked her up and was trying to push her in the door, and he was hysterical. I was so furious, because these kids were doing nothing.

When Humphrey was nominated, I was in the YMCA watching it on TV. I ran out in the streets, and armored personnel carriers with barbed wires on the front of them moved into position. The young people chanted, "The whole world is watching," which really meant that the whole world is watching this massive injustice that's going on here, the ripping-off of our democracy from us.

—Jane Adams, born in 1943, was an active member of SDS (Students for a Democratic Society) until its dissolution in 1969. She is currently a professor of anthropology at Southern Illinois University in Carbondale. She is the author of The Transformation of Rural Life: Southern Illinois, 1890–1990.

Chicago police beat back protesters attempting to reach the convention headquarters in the Conrad Hilton hotel.

In 1968, we went through what we in the Chicago Police Department like to call the long, hot summer. I was part of a special task force of two hundred detectives created during the riots following the assassination of Martin Luther King. Even after the city had finally quieted down, with antiwar protests and the black power movement in full swing, and with the Democratic convention coming up, the administration decided to keep the task force active.

A couple of weeks before the convention started, we were briefed about several known "agitators" that would be coming to Chicago for the purpose of disrupting the convention. We were shown pictures of people like Abbie Hoffman, David Dellinger, and Rennie Davis. In the meantime our two-hundred-man task force was split in two, and a hundred officers were sent to patrol the West Side, and the other hundred, myself included, were assigned to the Lincoln Park area, where the students were expected to congregate. There were all these kids — flower children, Yippies, and hippies — arriving in Chicago with their backpacks. The task force was working days, and we were meeting with these kids and having lunch with them. At this point, I didn't feel any animosity toward the protesters.

Within a few days, we witnessed the arrival of kids who had been identified as "troublemakers" by the department. I saw Abbie Hoffman walking down Lincoln Avenue, and he had an obscenity painted on his forehead. The students stopped talking to us, and started talking about killing the "pigs" and passing out literature showing how to make snake lines and self-defense lines against us. They even brought in their own medics. I was thinking what the hell's going on here. We're here to have a convention and they're here to start problems.

The night before the convention, there was a peace

rally in the southwest part of the park, and for whatever reason the kids started a bonfire, using park district benches. Even at that time some of our bosses said, "Just let them do their thing." But this bonfire got to be many feet high, and a resident living near the park called the police to report the blaze. I was just watching the rally from afar, and when this uniform car drove into the park area, and these kids started throwing bricks at it, busting the lights, we had to clear the park.

I had a lot of things thrown at me. The students had fashioned weapons out of rubber balls with spikes poked in them, and they had bags of urine to throw at us. I also remember seeing people who were taking balloons or bags filled with animal blood and smacking themselves over the head with them. The way I see it, the whole thing was staged by the so-called agitators. Nobody bleeds profusely from a ding in the head with a nightstick. The Supreme Court said that as a police officer, you have to take verbal abuse, but as a human being, there's a limit to the amount of abuse you can take. When you've got people walking up to you and making references about your mother and things they'd like to do to you, it's hard to take. I probably whacked a few people in the head, but if you were in the Lincoln Park area and you had a group of several hundred people yelling, "Charge! Get the pigs," and people throwing things at you, I don't think you'd stand there and say, "Wait a minute! Time out."

I think overall the focus of the media was on the reaction by the police. But I saw many times where police officers were harassed. I remember seeing a guy run up to a police lieutenant and punch him in the face. In response, three other officers took the guy out. What's more sensational, a policeman getting punched in the face or a policeman picking some guy up and throwing him into a paddy wagon? The media made a big story out of it, and thirty years later I'm still hearing about the police riot that week.

—Larry Evans, born in 1936, retired in 1991, after thirty years with the Chicago Police Department. He has four children, two of whom are police officers in Chicago.

When LBJ went on TV and announced he wasn't going to run for president again, I saw it as vindication. I thought that we — the counterculture, the students, and the blacks — had stuck our feet in the cogs of the war machine and brought it to a halt. But then, in April of '68, Martin Luther King was shot and the cities broke out in violence. People went wild on campuses across America, and then one month later Robert Kennedy was killed. All this craziness was kind of brought to a head for me when a friend and I went to Chicago for the Democratic National Convention that summer. We decided to pretend to be newspeople at the convention and to go around interviewing people. We thought it would protect us by distancing ourselves from the participants a little.

As soon as we got to Chicago there was a sense that this thing was going to be huge. The National Guard was there, and there were jeeps going through the streets, and barbed wire was being put up all over the place. You just couldn't help but get caught up in all the violence. Most of the time I couldn't finish any of my interviews, because halfway through them suddenly everyone would start running. Cops were all over the place, banging people on the head and shooting off tear gas. I remember standing in front of the Loop in a big demonstration when the cops came and pushed us through a plate-glass window, and there was glass all over and people were screaming, and their heads were bleeding.

Along with the student protesters, Ralph Abernathy and the Poor People's Campaign marched into Chicago with their mules and horses and signs, and they were also getting knocked around. In the park, the protesters were giving speeches and folks were saying, "We're not going to let this pass. This convention is not going to go down the way they want it." Meanwhile, Mayor Daley was calling all of us a bunch of un-American pinko subversives.

I left Chicago with very little faith in the government's ability to change. I started to see people like Mayor Daley, President Johnson, Robert McNamara [the former secretary of defense], and even the president of my college as a separate class of people that were part of an impenetrable system. I always felt that the violence the police and the National Guard had shown toward us students and to Abernathy's protesters was a part of the violence of the whole machine — the machine of war in Vietnam, the machine of Bull Connor in the South. To me, there was no comparison between a war that was killing millions and millions of people and decimating a whole country and what was happening right here at home. I decided to go back to college and get my degree, because it seemed like the one tool I was going to get that would help me to be part of turning this whole system around.

—John Field, born in 1947, graduated from Oberlin College in 1969. In the early seventies he moved to New York, where he worked as an oxygen technician at a hospital in the Bronx and as an organizer for the Young Lords, a Puerto Rican political group similar to the Black Panthers.

the American people had become. Campaigning, Richard Nixon had spoken of America's "silent majority," a conscious appeal to the American constituency that, as he described it, still believed in the flag and the family, in individual initiative and the need to stand strong in the world against the communist threat. They had watched the Chicago convention, too, and seen not only the collapse of order but much more: because the demonstrators were, by and large, the children of affluence and the police were blue-collar, much of middle America saw the fighting in the streets as a class war; because the demonstrators mocked so many traditions and conventions, they were the children of permissiveness, in need of the swift discipline they were getting from the police; and because the young dissenters challenged American policy in Vietnam, and did so not in the reasoned voice of civilized argument, but in the streets and on television, they were traitors, "communists," more deeply endangering the boys who had dutifully and patriotically gone to Southeast Asia, the soldiers who were much more likely to have been the brothers and cousins of the lower-middle-class Chicago policemen than relations of the demonstrators.

There was also, in Chicago, a classic clash between the messenger and his audience. Many of the television correspondents and print journalists covering the convention abandoned their oaths of objectivity to speak and write of the outrage taking place on that city's streets. It had seemed to them to be that kind of moment, when a reporter's sense of justice dictates that he leave the gallery and join the crowd. But, ironically, most of the people at home disagreed with them. They watched the same pictures and came to opposite conclusions. And because so many people saw the demonstrators as destructive, as rich, spoiled, and ungrateful, Chicago was, for many of them, the moment when the sixties became the sixties of modern conservative dogma, to be reviled as the root of all later twentieth-century ills.

On the night of July 20, 1969, thousands of people descended upon Central Park, New York City, and other public venues around the country to bear witness, collectively, to the greatest technological achievement in the history of mankind. In New York, and elsewhere along the eastern seaboard, a heavy rain fell, creating enormous mud puddles which the park gatherers carefully negotiated, though some, in the spirit of the age of Aquarius, simply tossed their shoes, shucked their jackets, and opened themselves up to the elements as willing victims. This was, after all, no ordinary night. For in the heart of Central Park, at the long stretch of green known as the Sheep Meadow, stood three nine-foot-by-twelve-foot television screens. And on those screens and the screens of billions of other television watchers around the world, at precisely 10:56 P.M. EDT, the fuzzy image of a man in a space suit would emerge and, under the transcendent light of a lunar morning, move carefully down a ladder until the moment when his size 9½B boot struck the fine-grained surface of the moon.

Apollo XI was the amazing coda of the amazing sixties. The story of the astronauts — Alan Shepard's simple arc, the dramatic orbit of John Glenn, the tragedy on the launchpad that killed Grissom, White, and Chaffee — had run parallel with the decade's other dramas, yet as the early feeling of "gee whiz" gave way to late-decade cynicism, the long series of space shots began to feel routine, and even many who agreed that the landing of a man on the moon would be a

When astronaut Neil Armstrong radioed earth, "The Eagle *has landed," a relieved Mission Control in Houston replied, "You've got a bunch of guys [who were] about to turn blue . . . We're breathing again." Below, "Houston" celebrates the successful completion of the lunar landing mission.*

remarkable achievement had begun to question the priority of space discovery in a time of so much domestic strife. Apollo XI turned the lights back on. Child and parent, Republican and Democrat, hawk and dove, all sat together as kin, united by curiosity and wonder, and above all by their sense of awe. Particularly for those who took the opportunity to join large outdoor public gatherings, there was the unmatchable feeling that came with breathing the night air, watching a picture transmitted across 240,000 miles, showing man — man! — bouncing and tumbling and playing like a child on the cratered surface, at the same time that they could divert their eyes from the large-screen televisions and look up at the powdery sphere itself, the very one that had occupied the imaginations of poets and lovers since the beginning of time. Newspaper publishers ordered up their "Second Coming" type, as *Time* described it, for this was no mere piece of news; *this* was history, big enough and splashy enough to challenge some of the best stories of the Bible.

The plan to go to the moon had been hatched in the conference rooms of the Cold War, and the mission's pilots were the kind of straight arrows who were devalued in the funky sixties, "organization men" who had been set upon their tasks way back when *Sputnik* embarrassed American science in 1957 (they moved into high gear in 1961, when President Kennedy audaciously promised a moon landing before the end of the decade). Yet in an odd way Apollo XI belonged not only to America as it once was but to America as it had become, to this era, too, and its abundant sense of free spirit. Potheads and acid freaks watching Neil Armstrong and Buzz Aldrin bounce along like kangaroos in the gravity-free environment had to feel at least a trifle envious: no drug was powerful enough to take them *there*. And watching the astronauts navigate their lunar module until it touched down in the Sea of Tranquillity (even the name of their destination seemed to suggest a narcotic high), there was also the liberating feeling, however fleeting, that at least they had discovered an antidote to the malady created by the naggingly incompatible emotions of the sixties, for they had escaped. The people of earth may be in chains, but they, *they* were free.

Among those at the crowded Apollo XI launch site, looking skyward with the rest at liftoff, was the heroic 1920s pilot Charles Lindbergh. Lindy was sixty-seven now, in the evening of his distinguished life, his hair gray, his face lined, yet it would have been interesting to have stood next to him and listened to his reactions as the courageous aviators of another age were propelled skyward, not simply across an ocean, as he had been, but flung violently with the force of a bullet toward the stars. A mere forty-two years separated the two feats, Lindbergh's and NASA's, and yet the world had changed so much. His had been an individual accomplishment, theirs the work of billions of dollars of taxpayer money and more than 400,000 people in assembly plants and control rooms; he had navigated his own craft through near disaster, their journey was programmed by computer, with hundreds of ships, planes, doctors, and technicians standing by waiting to rescue them from error; and while Lindy had flown across an ocean, in the overused phrase of explorers, "because it was there," Armstrong and Aldrin and Collins arrived on the moon largely because the government that funded them wanted to settle a score with its superpower opponent. Only the solitary experience of the mission itself, an apt metaphor for man's own essential loneliness, seemed to directly compare. "You have experienced an aloneness unknown

> **"The surface is fine and powdery. It adheres in fine layers, like powdered charcoal, to the soles and sides of my boots. I only go in a fraction of an inch, maybe an eighth of an inch, but I can see the footprints of my boots and the treads in the fine, sandy particles."**
>
> *Neil Armstrong*
> *July 20, 1969*
> *The Moon*

to man before," wrote Lindbergh in a letter to Michael Collins, the one who didn't get to walk on the moon, who stayed in the orbiting spacecraft, an idling car waiting for the kids to get back from the playground. "I believe you will find that it lets you think and sense with a greater clarity."

Whatever it was for Collins, the moon landing proved, for most Americans, to be a temporary high, and while there were many then who thought that Apollo XI would lead to a shuttle service delivering adventurers regularly to the newest terrestrial tourist locale, the program, like other artifacts of the sixties, swiftly evaporated. Like a middle-aged marathoner, NASA, having proved it could do it, searched elsewhere for a sense of purpose. In all, just twenty-four men would walk the surface of the moon, so few that even thirty years later, the footsteps of Aldrin and Armstrong remained crisp, the flag of the United States, staking the nation's claim to a kind of Fourth World, held erect by metal supports in an atmosphere devoid of wind.

Still, like Lindbergh's feat in the twenties, the three astronauts' mission had provided a balm for the pain of their own crazy decade, perhaps most importantly in the views their lunar cameras captured when they were directed back toward earth. At home, no matter where you stood, the sixties looked messy and unreadable, like a painting viewed too close to make out anything but the texture of the brushstrokes and the smudge of color. Yet from out there, in the dark eternity of the universe, the planet projected a picture of harmony, an essentially beautiful orb, ordered and still.

The lunar module, Eagle, *returns to the mother ship,* Columbia, *after the first lunar landing. With Apollo XI, the American space program made good on President Kennedy's promise to put men on the moon by the end of the decade, and it did so with six months to spare.*

10 Years of Doubt
1969–1981

Years of Doubt 1969–1981

Previous spread: For the first time since World War II, Americans had to learn "to live with less" as an oil shortage, inflation, and high unemployment brought the U.S. economy to a grinding halt. By the time the decade hit its midpoint, 7.8 million Americans, such as these unemployed Detroit autoworkers, were out of work.

Left: No single event darkened the mood of the seventies more than the crisis that forced a president from office. Here, the Army One *helicopter ferries Richard Nixon, disgraced by the Watergate scandal, from the White House for the last time. "To leave office before my term is completed is abhorrent to every instinct in my body," declared a defiant Nixon in his farewell speech. But he hoped his resignation would start "the process of healing that is so desperately needed in America."*

Katherine Boudin, a twenty-six-year-old *magna cum laude* graduate of exclusive Bryn Mawr College, was one of five members of the radical Weatherman faction of the Students for a Democratic Society (SDS) holed up in a Greenwich Village town house on March 6, 1970. The home, one of those elegant Federal-style buildings that line the streets of Old Manhattan, belonged to James Wilkerson, an advertising executive, and his wife. Off on an extended vacation in the Caribbean, the Wilkersons had given over the keys to their 1845 brownstone to his twenty-five-year-old daughter, Cathlyn. And there, surrounded by expensive antiques, including a 1790 square piano and John Wilkerson's pampered collection of china and wood-carved birds, Boudin, Cathlyn Wilkerson, Ted Gold, Diana Oughton, and Terry Robbins, all of them children of privilege, plotted violent revolution against the government of the United States of America.

Shortly before noon, Oughton and Robbins were in the basement, delicately wrapping pipe bombs with supplies of flesh-shredding nails, the better to destroy their dozens of targets at Columbia University and military installations around New York. Gold was returning from a quick trip to the drugstore. He had been assigned to find cotton to wrap a small alarm clock that would serve as the timing device for a bomb they planned to deposit at Fort Dix, New Jersey. Just as Gold entered the house and was opening the basement door, Robbins crossed two wires by mistake, delivering an explosion so fierce it collapsed the entire building into a pile of smoldering debris. A beam from the house landed on Gold's chest, killing him instantly; Oughton had to be identified by one of two severed fingers found in the dust; and Robbins's body was so obliterated, it took months to confirm that he had been killed, too (a mole on the lower left side of his back became the sole identifying characteristic). Only Boudin and Wilkerson escaped. The two fled to a neighbor's house for clothes (the force of the explosion had blown Boudin's from her body) and then into life underground.

Of the two survivors, Boudin was the more dedicated radical, the prized daughter of Leonard Boudin, a noted attorney who, along with his partner, defended more targets of Joe McCarthy's witch-hunt than any other member of the bar. She had grown up with a parade of distinguished American liberals traipsing through her family's living room and had seen their frustration as they pushed for change through the traditional democratic methods. In this sense, Boudin was like many another young activist. "[We] are affirming the values which you have instilled in us," declared radical activist Meldon Levine, as he delivered the English Oration at Harvard in 1969, "and we have taken you seriously." Boudin had spent her senior year of college at the University of Moscow (which she found disillusioning) and worked for SNCC. She had demonstrated at the 1968 Democratic National Convention in Chicago and in 1969, as a member of the SDS, visited Cuba, which she found impressive. Then, as the SDS, like everything else in the sixties, splintered into rival factions, she elected to go with the most violent, the Weatherman (the name came from a Bob Dylan lyric, "You don't need a weatherman to know which way the wind blows . . ."), joining them at the windshield-smashing "Days of Rage" demonstration in Chicago, where she boldly carried a Viet Cong flag.

The town house explosion cooled the enthusiasm many had felt for the New Left, for how could a movement whose tactics included murder and mayhem seriously claim that it stood for peace? Yet it did nothing to dim Boudin's radical aims, nor those of her many remaining Weatherman colleagues. If anything, it added a level of mystique to the cause, its very own Memorial Day. "Ted Gold died for our sins" read a sign in a Greenwich Village store shortly after the event. And for years afterward, a handful of radical sympathizers would gather outside 18 West Eleventh Street on the anniversary of the explosion to leave flowers and observe a moment of silence.

Over the next eleven years, Boudin lived the life of a spy novel, skipping from one safe house to the next, placing coded phone calls from public telephones and living off the generosity of friends. She changed her name, dyed her hair, used altered driver's licenses to establish new identities, had a child and collected welfare, all the while continuing to spout revolutionary rhetoric even after the Vietnam War had ended, Watergate had ousted Nixon from office, and the fashion for the Left had faded from American life.

Then, on October 20, 1981, Boudin's bizarre life took a tragic turn. In the small town of Nanuet, New York, a Brink's truck collecting cash from a local bank was attacked by robbers who opened fire on the armored car's guards and took off with $1.6 million. Thirty miles away, the robbers encountered a police barricade and with that, the career of the revolutionary who dreamed of defeating the "imperialist mother country" came to an end in a hail of gunfire. Two policemen, including the only black officer on the Nyack, New York, force, were fatally wounded before Boudin and the others finally surrendered. "Don't [shoot]," she screamed as the apprehending officer leveled his gun at her. Then, implicating one of her coconspirators, she shouted, "I didn't shoot him, *he* did."

The years that followed the sixties were like the proverbial "morning after": some of the previous night's hot blood still flowed through the system, yet to the mind it offered no energy or clarity of purpose, just a sense of disorientation and the throb of pain. The cupboards were bare, the once-mighty passion for public acts now spent, along with much of America's heretofore indefatigably

> **"In five years, from 1971 to 1975, I directly experienced est, gestalt therapy, bioenergetics, Rolfing, massage, jogging, health foods, tai chi, Esalen, hypnotism, modern dance, meditation, Silva Mind Control, Arica, acupuncture, sex therapy, Reichian therapy, and More House — a smorgasbord course in New Consciousness."**
>
> *Sixties activist Jerry Rubin*

optimistic spirit. Even more important, the unequaled postwar economic boom had now expired, victim of a nagging virus known as stagflation that was characterized by simultaneous high unemployment and high inflation and experienced as an intractable misery.

There was, particularly in these economic ills, the feeling that American civilization had entered into an irreversible decline, and indeed, in almost every aspect, the seventies stood as antonym to the heady days in the 1940s and early 1950s when the boom began: the sense of invincibility born of the victory over fascism contrasting with the humiliation brought by defeat in Vietnam thirty years later; the feeling of unlimited abundance and top-of-the-world power then dislodged by the seventies' tussle with double-digit interest rates, economic dependence, and scarcity; and the rosy afterglow of the "Good War," leaving America flush with the spirit of community, now replaced by a desire to look inward and seek personal fulfillment, even if it was at the expense of the public good. In the seventies, there would be no movies titled *The Best Years of Our Lives*, unless they were written by cult members retreating to awaken their "inner bliss" in one of the many interchangeable self-awareness disciplines that occasionally left the air humid with guru righteousness.

Gurus notwithstanding, most people found these to be years of doubt, and who cannot see why? The foundation under America's house had not only been cracked open by an unpopular war but vandalized by the crisis of authority that was only most publicly demonstrated by Watergate. It had been further injured by the vicissitudes of the Western economy and quite literally undermined by the growing awareness that our industrial form of capitalism had contributed significantly to the deterioration of the place environmentalists liked to call "little Spaceship Earth." In fact, it was in this sense of an impending apocalypse that the late-forties and seventies worlds agreed, except that whereas postwar families feared their lives would evaporate in an atomic vapor, people now contended with a Baedeker of routes leading backward to the Dark Ages, among them overpopulation and pollution, inflation and recession, even (as a growing number of social and economic conservatives began to claim toward the end of the decade) permissiveness and taxation.

On July 4, 1976, bicentennial celebrations, such as this lackluster one in Valley Forge, Pennsylvania, ranged from the tacky (in the town of George, Washington, celebrants dined on a sixty-square-foot cherry pie) to the magnificent (fifteen tall ships sailed up the Hudson River in New York City). Yet, no amount of red, white, and blue could cover up America's uncertainty about its future.

Americans celebrated their bicentennial, yet this most patriotic of moments came at a time when the nation felt decidedly unpatriotic, confused about what it meant to be an American and not so sure that was such a great thing to be anyway. The institutions that had served to define national character for so long — business, government, church, family — were all now in retreat. And with their decline, the sense of an American identity had come loose. More and more people described themselves in terms that separated them from the national body, so much so that by the time pollsters began to assemble the 1980 census, they departed from past practice by allowing people to now declare themselves not simply as black or white but according to every conceivable ethnic background (with the notable exception of the mixed-parentage ancestry that was perhaps the most "American" of all).

"What used to be a statistical account is now [becoming] a social accounting of our society ... we've moved to a more pluralistic society where people are now spending more time identifying themselves with their various heritages and seeking from that either an inner or outer strength."

Vincent Barabba,
director of the 1980 census

Millions of Americans danced their troubles away amid the flashing lights and throbbing sounds of the discotheque. By decade's end, there were ten thousand discos in America and the industry as a whole had earned over $4 billion.

The broader population had only just begun to accept the need to incorporate blacks more fully into the promise of the Constitution when it was challenged by "me, too" campaigns from women, homosexuals, American Indians, the elderly, and the disabled, all of which resulted in the institutionalizing of some of the ideas of the Left, even if the movement itself had disintegrated. But while each group could mount an impressive case for having endured the pain of oppression, their claims were expressed at a time when the opportunity to more fully join the great American fabric seemed less attractive than the need to extract one's rightful share from it. This was, after all, "the Me Decade," as writer Tom Wolfe declared in a much-cited magazine article, a time when America exhibited "The Culture of Narcissism," as historian Christopher Lasch announced in a landmark book; and the need to keep "Looking Out for Number One," as a popular paperback implored, was, for some, quite nearly overwhelming.

The preoccupation with the self made this, for Americans at least, the century's most hedonistic decade. Perhaps it was because they felt such guilt about the behavior of their institutions and their leaders (or, at any rate, powerless to affect them with moral direction), and so suddenly confined by limits to their once-dependable postwar bounty, but the need to feel "guilt free" in one's private life, to act *without* a sense of limits, became, for many, paramount. Thus, the age of no-fault insurance and no-fault divorces included, the Catholic Church reported, fewer trips to the confessional (though decidedly more visits to psychotherapists), freer attitudes toward sex, and a new vocabulary entry that described just about anyone with a private conscience as possessed of "hangups."

Around the world, the reputation of the United States had suffered mightily, thanks to the experience in Vietnam (and the proliferation of a kind of international guerrilla warfare expressed in the form of terrorism), and even America's

The Age of Experimentation: **God, running, disco, and the "Zen" of just about anything**

At the beginning of the seventies, I felt as though I had a very deep void in my life; I was looking for something, but I didn't know how to find it. I needed a purpose, a reason for being. I was just looking for something to give me direction. These were the days when cocaine started to become really popular. My husband, Glen, worked in the film industry so we were part of this Hollywood scene; not the upper-echelon scene, but the one with the grips and technicians and camera people. We went to a lot of parties and there were a lot of drugs and people having these sexual flings. People didn't even care if you were married or not! Thank God we never got into that. But Glen and I did smoke some marijuana. Luckily, we avoided falling into the worst of it.

The moral landscape of America seemed to turn drastically in the seventies. Everything was in an upheaval. Young people were tired of their parents' traditions, and they knew there had to be a better way. But instead of taking some of the old with some of the new, they just shoved out all the old and said, "We're going to make our own rules. We're going to do it our own way." It was around that time that the family unit began to break down in America. This was the most crucial thing. Because your first form of government is the family. If that breaks down, America's going to break down.

I looked into transcendental meditation, astrology, Eastern religions, anything where I might find the truth — that true thing that would really fill the void in my heart. One day, I was meditating, and all of a sudden, the Lord just came. And he spoke to my spirit and he said that Glen's and my questions would all be answered. And the void got filled. I became alive to God. It wasn't a church or a religion. It was Christ.

That was February 1976, our bicentennial year. And I began to believe that America was part of my destiny. I had this tremendous, patriotic call to the nation, and I felt it was inspired by the Lord. America was my nation, and I wanted to see her straightened up, and I was going to do what I could to help. I've always been patriotic. Even as a little child when I learned all those wonderful songs, "America the Beautiful" and "God Bless America," my heart would just swell up with pride. After I was born again, well it was just magnified. My calling was to help transform and change America.

> *—Marilyn Noorda, born in 1942, was actively involved in the 1976 movement to pass Proposition 13, a petition against rising property taxes in California.*

When I was at college in Southern Illinois, a lot of people were experimenting with LSD, marijuana, and other drugs. There was free love and sex. And I, like many other women, was trying to find out where I fit into all of this. It was a real time of confusion. People were saying, I don't want to be like my parents, but on the other hand, I really don't have any other role models to look up to. The Vietnam War also really disrupted our society. Once it ended, I think people wanted to find a way to come back together again, but they had a hard time doing that. No one was too sure where they wanted their life to go, so they started experimenting.

Kathy Smith in 1975.

Along with the social and political uncertainty of the time, I had some family tragedies to deal with. My dad died of a heart attack in 1969, and then two years later my mother and my stepfather were both killed in a plane crash. It was a very traumatic time for me. I was very depressed, and I didn't know what direction I wanted to go in. Luckily, a friend of mine who was a runner asked me to go out jogging with him. I found that all of this depression, all of this worry, all of this fear, just left, at least for that brief period of time — forty-five minutes to an hour — that I was out there running. I would just get out there and put one foot in front of the other. And I would get into a repetition and my mind would either wander into a brainstorm of ideas to solve my problems, or I would just completely zone out. And with it all would come this calmness. After I was done, I'd feel as though I'd washed my brain.

Of course, a lot of people didn't understand anything about running back then. I remember one Christmas telling my relatives that I was going to go out for a run, and they thought I was completely nuts. They'd say, "Now come, Kathy. That's not very feminine." Or "People don't do that." But people were doing it. They were beginning to understand how exercise affects your soul, how it affects your being. People started getting into the "Zen" of things: the Zen of tennis, the Zen of working out, the Zen of motorcycle repair, the Zen of running. I, like many others, started connecting physical activity to the spiritual side. People also started looking at some of the Eastern disciplines like yoga and tai chi, and not only the stretching aspects of these disciplines but the mental aspects. Now they were working the body, the mind, and the spirit.

> *—Kathy Smith, born in 1952, ran her first marathon in 1975. After graduating from the University of Hawaii, she moved to Los Angeles and began teaching fitness classes. She made her first video,* Ultimate Video Workout, *in 1984.*

When I was in high school in Bay Ridge, Brooklyn, the Vietnam War was like this giant sword of Damocles hovering over us. It was the only thing we could focus on. We became involved in politics and in civil rights and in trying to get a peace candidate elected even when we couldn't vote. We were very socially conscious, but basically we were worried about dying. Then the war ended in 1973 and we no longer had to worry about going to Vietnam. We felt we were immortal. Now we weren't going to die. And that's when disco came out. Right when it was the perfect time for us to go out and celebrate the fact that we were going to live forever.

Dancing to disco provided me with this incredible release. The music had this fast beat with a great melody behind it. When I danced, I wasn't just moving my legs up and down, I was flowing with the music. Disco had such a distinctive sound that, if you loved to dance the way we did, the music could just carry you away almost into another world. We would go to the discos several times a week, but the weekends were always the best. Getting ready to go out was sort of a ritual, especially on Saturdays. During the day you would go buy that shirt, or that belt, or those platform shoes, all of which seemed incredibly important at the time. You had to have a particular type of look. And we all dressed the same way. We would call each other up to coordinate what color suits everybody was wearing — who's wearing the powder-blue suit, who's wearing the white suit, who's wearing this, who's wearing that. And then we would carefully iron everything so it was just so. Even though most of us were used to having our mothers iron our regular clothes, they couldn't go near our disco clothes. Once you made sure that everything was right, then you waited around for whoever had the car. More than anything, we wanted to be cool. We wanted to look like someone that women would like to meet. Image was everything back then. We were in the middle of a tribal ritual where we met people depending on how we looked, not from talking to them. So it was very important to have a cool image to attract that pretty blonde or redhead.

> *—Gus Rodriguez was born in 1955 in Puerto Rico and moved with his family to Brooklyn, New York, when he was one year old. He currently manages BKNY, a nightclub in Bay Ridge, Brooklyn.*

I'm OK — You're OK

Looking Out for Number One

Your Erroneous Zones

Pulling Your Own Strings

Power!

Success!

How to Be Your Own Best Friend

1970s best-sellers

Can we control our world?

Is America in retreat?

Can love be reinvented?

How will the pie be cut?

Is America getting mean?

Is equality possible?

Can we find more oil?

Can less be more?

Can we keep hoping?

Questions asked by a
Newsweek *panel of historians*
at the end of the 1970s

position as the engine of the Western economy had been threatened by the rise of the Middle Eastern oil-producing nations to positions of crippling power (the Middle East becoming the preoccupation that Cuba and the Far East had been the decade before). But perhaps the greatest challenge offered by the 1970s, both privately and publicly, was a philosophical one, a rude awakening to the finite, complex nature of life itself and, with it, the rejection of some of the century's most dearly held, open-ended beliefs: that progress comes inevitably with the passage of time and shows itself with the unfolding of greater and greater freedoms, that nature is a limitless resource capable of supporting the indefinite expansion of industrial civilization, and that the time-honored institutions of modern life, the once-mighty agents of the liberal tradition, can be trusted to guide society into a difficult future.

There was no one event, like the 1929 Crash, that announced the economic uncertainty of the 1970s and no one measure to explain all the economy's obvious maladjustments. Instead, the misery of what turned out to be the most disruptive decade since the Great Depression crept up on America, like a raccoon in the storeroom, and confused economists who struggled to describe the nation's shrinking growth according to traditional theory. In the widely accepted postwar model, unemployment goes down as inflation rises, and over the years, economists had watched that happen with the same certainty that they watched the sun rise. But in the early years of the seventies, the inflation rate mounted *with* unemployment, prompting Federal Reserve Chairman Arthur Burns to announce (in one of the leaderless decade's more frustrating statements of leaderlessness) that "the rules are not working the way they used to"; or, put simply, that the doctor doesn't have a clue.

Since then, many economists have determined that the economic malaise Americans suffered in these years was a result of their nation's own generosity toward Western Europe and Japan (now rebuilt, both offered significant competition to American manufacturing); an outgrowth of American labor's growing position as a "have" instead of a "have-not" (which drove up the cost of production); and a nasty by-product of the policies of Lyndon Johnson and Richard Nixon, both of whom conducted an expensive war in Vietnam and an ambitious social policy without raising taxes. In this sense, the blame for American troubles in the seventies could actually be laid at the door of the fabled American postwar hegemony. For both Johnson and Nixon had become locked in a vicious cycle, pressed upon them by their continuing faith in the policy of containment (and America's responsibility for carrying out that policy) even as they tried to maintain prosperity and effect a social transformation toward a more equitable (and stable) society at home.

Still, if there was a representative image that hung in the mind from this time, and that lingered throughout the decade, it was the picture of lines of automobiles at filling stations (soup kitchens for the mobile class) accompanied by another one showing the faces of smiling Arabs in kaffiyehs standing in back of

As the price of crude oil climbed, the combined earnings of the OPEC nations rose from $23 billion in 1972 to $140 billion in 1974. The Saudis used the new profits to modernize their desert country. Here, King Khalid, center, examines a model of the $8.5-billion King Khalid Military City, a garrison town for seventy thousand being built near the Iraqi border.

"Eventually all those children of well-to-do families who have plenty to eat at every meal, who have their own cars, and who act almost as terrorists and who throw bombs here and there will have to really think of all these privileges of the advanced industrial world and they will have to work harder."

The Shah of Iran

models of new expensive desert cities to be built somewhere on the sandy edges of civilization, paid for with crisp American dollars. And, indeed, not only the most visible but, for Americans, the most humiliating sign of the West's economic troubles was the sudden dearth of cheap oil that forced the United States, once capable of producing nearly all of its own reserves, to pay the Arabs' price.

Particularly in 1973, when the Arab states punished the West for its support of Israel in the Yom Kippur War by creating an oil embargo, Americans found their standard of living held at the mercy of what felt like obscure border clashes in strange parts of the world. For at the same time that diplomats representing the once-mighty United States were being frustrated by the Vietnamese at the bargaining table in Paris, a new kind of Arab, a *modern* Arab—often Harvard-educated and familiar with the ways of the West even as, in the example of Saudi Arabia, he represented the interests of a feudal state—was standing up to the American oil companies that had once held his nation in a vise grip. And who could not see the irony? Not long before, John Kennedy was establishing a foreign policy based in part on Americans as benevolent teachers, introducing the ways of the West to undeveloped societies. And yet here, just twelve years later, it was Hanoi and Riyadh that were teaching the Yankee a lesson in the traditions of the Third World, and making him pay mightily for it, too.

*During the 1973 OPEC oil embargo, many filling stations, such as this
one outside of Boston, simply ran out of gas. Even after the embargo ended,
Americans saw little relief at the pumps. The OPEC nations had raised the
price of crude oil to $11.65 per barrel, an increase of 387 percent.*

Oil is the American lifeblood. Every plane, tank, and car needs it. Every skyscraper and industrial plant. Its presence in fertilizer helps farmers produce the bumper crop; in drugs it aids the fight against disease; and in synthetics it helps clothe a nation. But even more important, oil is mixed in with the soil of the American character. Like no other raw material, it has contributed to the American ethos, most notably for its propulsion of the American dream machine, the automobile.

Since it became readily available to the middle class in the 1920s, the car had become nearly as fundamental a symbol of American prosperity as the dollar. And particularly in the postwar period, when the growth of the suburbs made mass transit a near anachronism (or at the very least, one of the burdens of poverty) and when General Motors ran up revenues larger than the GNP of most countries, the car had become an extension of the American character. As General Motors went, an executive trumpeted in 1958, so went the nation, and particularly since GM had signed a labor agreement that made the United Auto Workers a near-junior partner, ensuring a generation of peace with its assembly workers, it was hard to argue with him.

GM made big cars after the war and people bought them according to their status: the bigger the car, the bigger the sign of success. One's automobile was part of one's statement to the world, a chrome and steel declaration of self that spoke to the twin American obsessions of speed and power, and, in the clichéd image of the American male, was often doted upon like a love object. But with the oil crisis of the 1970s, a new mind-set was demanded of consumers, a quite nearly "un-American" mind-set that forced them to think small and conserve, to curtail their freedom of movement, to anticipate and plan.

The embargo, which came at a time when 85 percent of American workers drove to their places of employment each day, set the nation on a course of voluntary rationing. President Nixon called upon homeowners to turn down their thermostats, companies to trim their employees' working hours, and governors to enact ordinances reducing the speed limit to fifty miles per hour. Gas stations were asked to hold their sales to a maximum of ten gallons per customer, and drivers were requested to get along on those ten gallons (enough to drive the average car of that time just 110 miles) for the entire week.

By March of 1974, the five-month boycott was over, and all the dimouts, slowdowns, and middle-of-the-winter chills came to an end. But the event had left its mark and not only because the high (and climbing) price of oil encouraged inflation. American prosperity had depended in part on what the Shah of Iran described as "the mystical power of the oil companies," or, put only slightly differently, the arrogance with which the industrial world, in the role of colonial power, claimed dominion over the planet's natural resources. Now, with smaller foreign cars taking a bigger part of the American market and Detroit itself looking at plans for scaled-down, economical models, the era of the gas-guzzler and much of what it represented about the American spirit was in eclipse.

Perhaps it was this loss of the auto industry's unquestioned position of dominance in the world economy or, as United Auto Workers Chairman Douglas Fraser concluded, merely the trickle-down of the sixties generational split, the passing on of the culture of impudence from the upper-class children who had

Detroit's blind faith:
"We wondered, 'When are they gonna get the message that we're not in love with those big cars?'"

LaNita Gaines speaking at a UAW convention in 1975.

—LaNita Gaines, born in 1950, took a position at Chrysler's Jefferson Plant in 1981. She has continued her involvement in her local union, serving as a guide, employee assistance plan director, and financial secretary, the position she currently holds.

In the late sixties, Detroit was in this golden age. There were plenty of jobs and plenty of opportunities. I was working as a nurse's aide at Grace Hospital in Detroit, and looking for something that paid a little better. People were saying that if you could get a job in the automobile industry, you could really have anything you wanted. A friend of mine suggested I go and take Chrysler's employment test with her. I took the test, and I got a job, but my friend didn't. When they brought me into the plant on my first day, I really didn't know what was expected of me. I saw the cars rolling down the assembly line and wondered if I could fit in such an environment. They brought me over to my position on the line and said, "You are going to be doing the emergency brake cable job, and no one that we've brought in has accomplished that job, so you'll probably be gone in thirty days." This kind of scared me because at that time I had quit my job at the hospital, and I needed this paying job, so I got real busy and learned the job real fast. The world seemed to open up for me from the minute I received my first paycheck. For the first time, I actually

had the means to do something. It really gave me a chance to think about living the American dream. I could own my own house, buy a new car, and maybe even go back to school and do some real things for myself.

When I first started working at the plant, Chrysler was manufacturing these giant-sized cars. At that time, of course, America was in love with big cars, and Chrysler was building the Imperial and the Newport. They had gigantic gas tanks and got little mileage, but they were big and comfortable. It seemed as if people were changing cars every two years, and they weren't really going for the quality of the car, they just wanted to keep up with the latest model. I swear at one point they were moving down the assembly line so fast that we'd sometimes miss a screw.

In 1973, we began to see a downturn in the industry as a whole. We workers would read about the oil crisis in the papers, and we didn't quite know what to make of it. All we knew is that people were waiting on seemingly endless lines to get a tank of gas, and Chrysler just kept building those huge cars. The public started paying closer attention to gas mileage and began turning to smaller, more fuel-efficient cars from abroad like the Germans' Volkswagen Beetle and Japanese cars. We had a Chrysler Imperial at that time, and it was a real gas-guzzler. We were getting eight miles to the gallon on it, and it seemed as if you could barely get from one gas station to the other before you had to fill up again. I used to pull it up in my driveway and go in the house and I would listen, and I'm sure that car'd still be drinking gas while it was parked. Eventually I had to say good-bye to it because I couldn't afford to keep gas in it.

The American companies were refusing to change to what was now going to be the new road for the auto industry. We workers just kind of looked at that and said, "Well, why don't they change? When are they gonna get the message that we're not in love with those big cars anymore?" We'd try to tell them that *we* were the ones that were buying those little cars, but the company didn't want to listen. We were looking for companies that made smaller cars, of course, that were American-made, but if America was not making those cars then you had to buy what you could find. We had to get to work; we had to get our families around; and with gas prices climbing much faster than our wages, we had to do something. The UAW taught us to buy what we make, but we had to buy what was economically feasible for our families, as opposed to being company loyal and

buying a product that the company makes. If you brought a foreign car onto the lot during those days, the guards would turn you around and not allow you to park there to come to work. That gave you an incentive next time, don't buy a foreign car.

I worked at Chrysler until around 1974. I had bought my first home and started a family. At that point, everyone in my family, even my mother and brother, was dependent on me, because I had the automobile job. That November they came around and told us that we were permanently laid off. I was terrified. I thought, "What does this mean? I've had a job for all these years, and now I'm being put in the street." They said, "Well, you're gonna collect unemployment and substitutes, so don't worry about it." But the bliss, the high standard of living, did come to an end, because all of a sudden there was not enough money for the mortgage note and the car note. We could barely keep food on the table. I thought I could rely on unemployment for a while, but the industry had recently changed some of its policies in the cutbacks, so the sub fund, which was to help laid-off workers, was depleting quickly, and I realized there was just one step between me and the welfare line.

A lot of people picked up and left the city of Detroit, and to me that was the downfall of the city. There was a sentiment of despair everywhere. These were very shaky times, and we just didn't know what to do. I would go to restaurants or other social spots and talk to people, and everyone was worried. We all had the same fear — What was happening? What are we gonna do? Are we gonna have jobs tomorrow? It seemed like everyone was losing their homes and cars, and there sure were a lot of divorces at that time. We were trying to break free of any debt that we had.

I was let go and rehired a couple of times, and each time my anxiety worsened. It seemed by 1979 that Chrysler was gonna go right down the drain. Everyone, I mean all of us workers, had to put in an effort to keep Chrysler's doors open and to save our jobs. Even though we were earning $9.50 an hour and our counterparts at Ford and General Motors were earning $12.50, we had to live out our contracts without any raises or bonuses. And when Chrysler was on the verge of declaring bankruptcy, thousands of us mobilized and went down to Washington, D.C., to convince Congress to guarantee a loan to help bail out Chrysler from bankruptcy. We weren't gonna sit back and allow the industry to go under. We had some pretty tense times waiting on that loan guarantee back in Detroit. When Congress finally gave the okay, we left the factory floor and went to the nearest lot for a beer or two. Finally, things were gonna get a little better.

My name is William Calley
I'm a Soldier of this land
I've vowed to do my duty
    and to gain the upper hand
But they've made me out a villain
    they have stamped me with a brand
As we go marching on . . .

    "The Battle Hymn of Lieutenant Calley"

In a photograph that became emblematic of the violence that now accompanied the American divide over the Vietnam War, a young woman grieves over the body of a twenty-year-old man, one of four shot and killed by national guardsmen during a protest at Kent State University in Ohio, May 1970.

rioted in the streets to the working-class men and women that represented the UAW's next generation, but whatever the reason, Fraser and others began to notice, among his group's youngest members, a loss of respect for the union and its leaders, a higher rate of absenteeism, and a cynicism about their own futures. In fact, what Fraser was seeing was pervasive and not only among the nation's young. American morale was at a postwar low.

In the 1930s, when the Depression struck, many people had felt that they themselves were responsible for their sorry lot. But decades of big (and then bigger) government had made people place more responsibility for the state of their lives with those in authority, and now that things were going so badly, the sense among many was that authority had failed them. Inflation was the latest calamity, but the disappointment in the nation's leadership had really begun with Vietnam and the domestic strife that it created, destroying Lyndon Johnson, and after a brief lull, when President Nixon's "Vietnamization" program (whereby the South Vietnamese would become more responsible for their own defense) was bringing American soldiers home, it stretched to the new administration, too. The civilian massacre by a U.S. infantry company at My Lai, unveiled in 1970, the illegal American invasion of Cambodia the same year, and the National Guard's deadly attack on protesting students at Kent State rent the nation all over again, with youthful protesters seeing the tactics of a police state and vigilante hard hats seeing the youth, in turn, as agents of a traitorous conspiracy coddled by an American system gone soft.

In mid-1971, the *New York Times* began publishing excerpts from a secret Defense Department study, "The History of U.S. Decision-Making Process in Vietnam." Better known to the public as the Pentagon Papers, it became a best-seller in book form. While few people were able to penetrate its arcane language, they knew what it revealed: that the government had been lying to them on both its motives and its conduct in Vietnam. The study had been leaked to the press by a former Defense Department analyst named Daniel Ellsberg who, joined by his ten-year-old son and thirteen-year-old daughter, photocopied its seven thousand pages, snipping the words "Top Secret" off the uppermost part of each. By playing David to the government's Goliath, Ellsberg soon became the kind of folk hero to the Left that Lieutenant William Calley, the American commander who was prosecuted by the Pentagon for the slaughter at My Lai, had become to the Right. It seemed that the only thing Americans could agree upon was their disappointment and growing distrust of their own government.

On television, a new situation comedy made light of the persistent enmity between the generations. *All in the Family* was a sharp break with tradition. Despite enormous domestic turmoil, television's portrayal of American homelife had remained remarkably consistent since the days of *Lucy* and *Leave It to Beaver*. Now the openly bigoted Archie Bunker and his brood changed all that, giving voice to bitter attitudes many felt, but few dared utter publicly. Bunker actually reveled in his display of rudeness and intolerance, belching at the dinner

With cries of "America: love it or leave it," about two hundred New York City construction workers, equipped with American flags and lead pipes, descended on a group of peace protesters holding a memorial for the slain Kent State students.

table, barking at his wife, tweaking the sensitivities of his feminist daughter and liberal-minded son-in-law, and they, in turn, loved directing their wrath back on him. The satire was all in good fun (Bunker still seemed lovable, despite his abhorrent attitudes) and all parties were caricatures, yet they offered a release to very real emotions boiling throughout much of the country, where resentment raged.

Still, by early 1973, the preoccupation of the moment, the one that added a philosophical turn to all the rancor, was not the war or the sad economy or even the continuing split between the generations, but the constitutional crisis that carried the name of a Washington luxury apartment and office complex. Watergate was an odd moment in American history, as much a lesson in hubris and the arrogance of power as had been taught to American industry in the oil emergency and yet more profound and far-reaching, for it attacked one of the institutions central to Americans' respect for their system, the presidency, and in terms so elemental that even a schoolchild could see that something had gone desperately wrong and that the man in the Oval Office, the man the nation looked to for spiritual and moral leadership, was to blame.

When the break-in at the Watergate offices of the Democratic National committee was first revealed, in June of 1972, Presidential Press Secretary Ron Ziegler described it as a "third-rate burglary," hardly worthy of reporters' attention, and indeed few newspapers other than the *Washington Post* pursued it.

When the hard hats reversed the tide: "We descended on the protesters like a herd of bulls"

I grew up in Brooklyn, New York. We were pretty patriotic back then. I can remember throwing homecoming receptions in my neighborhood for the veterans returning from World War II. We'd have kegs of beer and sandwiches and stuff, and the celebrations would go into the wee hours of the morning. In those days you never saw a military uniform or the American flag defiled. Uniforms were well-kept and worn with pride, and military personnel were never hassled, and I was living in a pretty rough part of the city. Whenever you'd see a veteran walking around in uniform, you always raised your shoulders up a bit, and even gave a little salute. On the Fourth of July, if you didn't have a flag, it would not be uncommon for somebody to knock on your door or window and say, "Where's your flag?" And you'd be pretty embarrassed and would go and put it out, but you'd always bring it in before the sun went down.

I had always wanted to become a soldier. I'd seen all the war movies and watched my heroes like John Wayne charging up hills in battle, and I wanted a taste of what life was like in the service. When I reached the age of seventeen, I sat down with my father and explained to him that school was not for me and that I wanted to join one of the armed forces. Eventually, I went to Korea and became a paratrooper in the 187th regiment. In 1953, I returned home with the pride in my country that I had carried around with me when I'd see the World War II veterans. I'd had enough of the service, but I still saw it as America's duty to defend the world.

Even though I was a veteran, in the beginning the anti–Vietnam War stuff didn't phase me. It was fairly harmless, and if anything, I thought watching the protesters would give me a chance to open my eyes up about dissension. But as the movement intensified, I had a hard time believing what I saw on the television and read in the papers. What really brought me to my boiling point was the fact that the majority of the protesters were college-educated people. To me, these people had to have been educated to know about what had gone on in this country just a few decades before, and yet here they were urinating on statues, burning American flags, and carrying Cong flags, and desecrating the memories of the people who went and fell in combat in the name of democracy. I took the insult personally.

In the spring of 1970, I was doing some construction work in the Wall Street area. A lot of the construction workers were veterans of the Korean or the Second World War, and many of them had been in the construction business since they had left the service. From the heights of the new buildings you could see very clearly what was going on below. One afternoon in May, we saw this raggedy-looking mob of people carrying flags and singing songs and knocking the war in Vietnam. Some

Tommy Burns in 1979.

—Tommy Burns was born in Brooklyn in 1933. During his forty years as an iron-worker, he has assisted in the construction of such notable projects as the Verrazano-Narrows and Tappan Zee Bridges and the World Trade Center. He is an active veteran, marching annually with his regiment in New York City's Memorial Day parade and assisting in the fund-raising for several Korean War memorials. He has nine children and twenty-one grandchildren.

of the protesters were wearing parts of military uniforms and fatigues. I had never seen anyone wearing uniforms like that. The people I knew wore them with dignity, but these people were wearing them as rags. I would say four out of ten of the protesters were carrying Viet Cong flags. It seemed to be their symbol; to me it was comparable to seeing someone coming down Broadway carrying a Japanese or German flag during World War II. And along with that they were spitting at, stomping on, and ripping up *our* flag.

I was on Water Street, and I came down with my hard hat on and headed toward Broadway. It seemed as if every worker came down from these buildings, and as word spread to other parts of the city, carpenters, elevator operators, plumbers, electricians, and other laborers all came downtown to see what the fuss was about. We descended upon those protesters like a herd of bulls coming down the street in Spain. All the protesters were running like mad and looking back to see if we were catching up to them. People were cheering for us through their office windows, saying, "Go on, go on! Get 'em! Get 'em!" and pointing out the ones we could get at, whether it was the tall one urinating on Washington's statue or the short one over there with the shirt on that's torn.

I only got really heavily involved with one incident. My friend Jimmy had lost one of his brothers in Nam, and he had a very deep-seated anger toward the antiwar kids. He caught one guy and started punching him, and then he picked up a trash can and started beating him with it. After seeing so much blood, I think a little bit of fear came over me, and so I jumped in with a couple of other fellas and pulled Jimmy right off. But I understood how he felt, because we were all in such a rage, defending something that was very sacred to us. Most of the

blood was shed on one side, but thank God, nobody got killed.

When we went back to work, there were loads of people, white-collar workers and restaurant workers, who congratulated us. And for a few weeks afterward, when we stopped in to get our morning coffee before work at some restaurants, we'd get it on the house. Some of these people couldn't even speak fluent English, and they were very proud of what we were doing. They even went further to say we were defending the flag. "We're not citizens yet, but we will be," they'd say. There were comments like that all the time at the restaurants where we had lunch. I think from that day on we were branded with the name "hard hat." Prior to the protest, we'd always distinguish ourselves as "electricians," or "carpenters," but from then on we were one group, we were the hard hats. And from the way I saw it, we carried the feelings of so many people who hadn't had the chance to be heard.

We all walked away with mixed feelings. I'm sure there are many who felt we should have hung those protesters up from lampposts. We had served our country and seen some pretty heavy-duty stuff, and we had been carrying around a lot of hurt for so many years that we just exploded. Yet with all the protesting around, we couldn't help but wonder if it had been right to serve the country the way we did. I began to wonder if I'd have been drafted for Vietnam if I would have turned my tail and run to Canada. But after witnessing the behavior of the antiwar protesters on that day, I knew where I stood. I decided we had finally met the challenge of the protesters and actually settled what we had fought over. We rallied around the flag, and down the road we went, and all you could hear was shouting of "let's get them . . . let's finish this once and for all."

(Later, when the president was caught in one of many lies, Ziegler, in an even better spin, insisted that Nixon's words were merely "inoperative" — in other words, as historian Christopher Lasch pointed out, a lie that didn't work — rather than acknowledge that he had been willfully incorrect.) Still, the early dispatches did contain some tantalizing information. Seven men, five of whom were wearing surgical gloves, had been arrested. Four of the seven had taken part in John Kennedy's Bay of Pigs fiasco of 1961. And one of those four was a writer of spy stories. When it was then discovered that all of the burglars were on the payroll of the Committee to Re-elect the President (CRP), the slow and steady pace of hearings and subpoenas and trials and judicial decisions that would captivate the nation began. Over the next two years, as the tentacles of a complicated story reached higher and higher, the president would labor to keep his administration afloat, lightening ship by throwing subordinates overboard, until finally the dirty water had reached high enough to threaten the highest office in the land.

For sheer longevity, not even the reign of FDR can compete with Richard Milhous Nixon's amazing public career. From his time as a Red-baiting congressman in the late forties, pursuing Alger Hiss, through his years as Eisenhower's vice president, his own failed campaign for president in 1960, and then the dramatic comeback that brought him to the Oval Office in 1968 only to face an ignominious departure six years later, Nixon compiled a twenty-eight-year run at or near the center of the world's stage, a political chameleon who defied the conventional logic about him time and again, yet even among many of those who supported him, seldom raised his image above that of a power-hungry and highly secretive man, self-destructive and psychologically flawed.

Nixon described himself as a conservative, and the political constituency that he drew from saw him as a bulwark against what they perceived to be a leftward drift of the country. Yet in fact he was more pragmatist than ideologue and more interested in keeping his hands on the reins of authority ("The important thing is to win" was one of many locker-room phrases he delivered with abandon) than in pulling them in any particular direction. Lyndon Johnson may have conceived the Great Society and identified his tenure with the entitlement programs that would in later decades receive such critical abuse, but in fact it was the Nixon administration's sweeping innovations that institutionalized many liberal ideas: Nixon who tied Social Security benefits to the cost of living; supported programs giving minority businesses preferred access to federal contracts; established wage and price controls in a futile attempt to control the economy; reduced military spending and proposed a guaranteed annual income for the nation's poor (which the Senate defeated). And it was Nixon, the staunch anticommunist, who pursued détente with the Soviet Union and stunned the world by recognizing the People's Republic of China in 1972.

Still, wherever Nixon's public actions led, his private obsessions followed, and the president's need to maintain power against all adversaries, real and imagined, would in the end be his undoing. "He wasn't a little boy you wanted to pick up and hug," said a family friend to biographer Stephen Ambrose. And indeed, even before his tenure became mired in scandal, few voters warmed to Nixon personally. Then, as Watergate unfolded, the president's jowly face, born to caricature (where it inevitably sported a dark beard, a Pinocchio nose, and the crystalline shine of nervous perspiration), soon became associated in the public mind with deceit, his pronouncements of executive privilege reminiscent of Samuel Johnson's description of patriotism as "the last refuge of a scoundrel."

It is unlikely that Nixon knew about the break-in itself, but in the end that was unimportant. For it was what Watergate revealed about the Nixon White House that turned the public against him. The cover-up, as an act obstructing justice, was the error that forced Nixon from office, sparing the country the misery of impeachment, but as the investigations leading up to his resignation went on, it became clear that dirty tricks were far from an aberration; for Nixon, they were a way of life.

The issue that Watergate presented was, at heart, a constitutional one. The three branches of American government had been created, as every grade school history text describes, to check and balance each other. Yet, owing to the need for strong and responsive leadership to tackle first the Depression, then the Second World War, and finally the ambiguities of the Cold War, the executive branch had grown in size and power to where by the early 1970s, as historian Arthur Schlesinger wrote, "the American President had become on issues of

Nixon's awkward public demeanor made him an easy target for ridicule. Here, a protester sporting a Nixon mask mocks the president at an early-seventies peace march.

Watching Watergate unfold:
"One morning, I heard Liddy say, 'My boys got caught last night' . . . It got me thinking"

I started working in the White House as an assistant to the president's appointment secretary during Nixon's first term in office. It was all pretty standard junior-level stuff, but I was very young and driven and it was exciting to see the inner workings of government. While I didn't have much contact with Nixon on a personal level, I did see him as a man with a probing legal mind and a strong inquiring intellect, and I believed in his vision for the country. When election time neared I was put on a team to help organize the Committee to Re-elect the President. I was to organize the finance side, while a man named Jeb Magruder was to set up the political side. We were responsible for renting space, hiring the initial staff, setting up bank accounts, that sort of thing. It was always understood that, as the election got closer, the president was going to ask Attorney General John Mitchell and Secretary of Commerce Maurice Stans to step out of their cabinet roles to run things, and once Stans moved over to finance chairman I assumed the treasurer's role for the committee. Working on the campaign was even more exciting than working at the White House. Every day was extremely high-energy. And at the time, I had the energy to burn. We were all working for a cause and by and large we were all believers, so there was a lot of enthusiasm around the office.

One morning, I was in the office and I saw G. Gordon Liddy, who was in charge of campaign security, hurrying down the hall in a bit of a panic. As he ran by, I heard him say something like, "My boys got caught last night. I told him I'd never use anybody from here. I made a big mistake." I didn't know exactly what he was talking about at first, but it got me thinking. Then I read in the papers about the Watergate break-in, and I saw that James McCord was one of the people arrested. I knew McCord; he was directly involved in the Committee to Re-elect the President. The pieces fell together pretty quickly in my mind. It was obvious by the way everyone was acting around the office that the campaign was somehow involved in the break-in. The men who were arrested had a fair amount of cash on them, most of it new hundred-dollar bills. I suspected that cash might have come from money that I had given Liddy, purportedly for campaign security. I remember thinking that the expenditure was kind of peculiar at the time. It had been requested by Jeb Magruder and it was to be given to Liddy in cash and in high denominations. When it came out that the hundred-dollar bills the Watergate burglars were carrying had consecutive serial numbers on them, I realized that, in fact, it was the same money that I had given Liddy. All of a sudden I started wondering whether the investigators would be able to pick my fingerprints off of those bills.

As the Watergate situation ballooned, the atmosphere around the office became very bizarre. I couldn't get straight answers about anything. I went to Stans to talk to him about what was going on, but his point of view was basically, "You don't want to know about it, and I don't want to know about it. It's their problem. Our job is to raise money for the campaign." Of course, that wasn't particularly helpful to me. It didn't take a lot of thought to know that one of the first things the investigators would ask would be who paid for this thing.

I told some people at the White House that there were real problems over here at the committee and that they needed to do something. But their reaction was to just turn their backs on it. They said, "If you need a lawyer we'll help you, but the main thing is to get through the election." Once the subpoenas started being issued and it became obvious that I would eventually be called, I tried to get to Mitchell. At this point, both Magruder and Fred LaRue, who was Mitchell's right-hand man, talked to me and they both suggested that I say that the money was for campaign security and that I paid out $40,000 instead of what was actually close to $200,000. They obviously felt that the size of the disbursement would affect their credibility. I told Magruder that I had no intention of committing perjury. And he replied, "Well, you may have to."

Next I talked to the two attorneys who had been hired by the campaign committee. They said that if what I was telling them was accurate, then they'd been lied to by other people in the campaign. They were worried that I would be subpoenaed before they had time to deal

with this, and they asked if I had any legitimate reason for being out of town. When I got home that night, Fred LaRue called me and said that I should fly to California to help raise money for the campaign. He wanted to know if I could be on the morning plane from Dulles Airport. And then he said, "Oh, by the way, could you spend the night at a motel near the airport so you won't be subpoenaed in the meantime?" So I did.

The next day on the flight I had a long time to think. Everything started to seem so crazy to me. Here I was, fleeing from the authorities. It was like I was a character in a movie. The lawyers for the campaign were there to protect the more senior people, and they weren't concerned about what happened to someone like me. Obviously I was in the chain of command that paid all of these people to do something that was illegal. The question was would anybody know that I was not part of the conspiracy in the first place? Also, my wife, Deborah, was pregnant at the time, and she was very upset by what was going on. Carl Bernstein and Bob Woodward, two reporters from the *Washington Post,* practically lived on our doorstep.

It was during that flight to California that I decided I could no longer work every day with people that were clearly trying to abort the investigation and, in essence, cover it up. I thought it would be easier to cope with things on my own. I knew I would have to testify, and I felt an immense pressure to be as accurate as possible because I knew my testimony was going to have an impact on people's lives. I think the tragedy in all of this was that I saw a lot of young enthusiastic people make terrible mistakes and get chewed up in the gears. Particularly people who had no direct involvement, but who perjured themselves to protect more senior people. So many people went to jail because they lied about the cover-up.

The night Nixon resigned I felt truly sad for the country. This was the first president ever driven from office. And I always thought that it didn't have to happen that way. If Nixon had acted early and asked his entire campaign staff to resign, a lot of the mess could have been avoided. But he was an individual who obviously had some flaws, and he really brought this thing on himself. I felt a personal disappointment in what happened. I had had the opportunity to work for the government and to serve the White House and it all came to a tragic end.

Hugh Sloan and his wife, Deborah, who worked for Pat Nixon, stand with the president in the Oval Office.

—*Hugh Sloan, born in 1940, worked for the Budd company, an automotive parts manufacturer, after resigning from the Committee to Re-elect the President. In his first year with Budd he had to take more than fifty days off of work to testify at Watergate-related hearings and trials. He later moved to Canada for nine years, during which he worked for Budd, and then the Woodbridge Automotive Group, another automotive parts company. He currently lives in the Detroit, Michigan, area, where he occasionally speaks at local high schools about Watergate.*

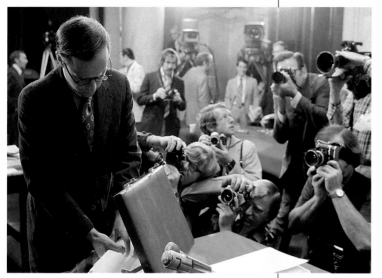

The Watergate hearings, televised gavel-to-gavel, were already a national habit when the testimony of White House Counsel John Dean III, anticipated for months, directly implicated the president in the cover-up.

war and peace the most absolute monarch (with the possible exception of Mao Zedong of China) among the great powers of the world."

Schlesinger called this new, more muscular executive "the Imperial Presidency," and while he had seen its beginnings in the administrations of other leaders, it was Richard Nixon who seemed to him to have taken the arrogance of power to a new level. After all, it was one thing for a president to claim executive privilege in the conduct of war, but Nixon had extended the definition of national security to encompass much of his domestic decision-making, indeed as a justification for any and every executive act. "When the president does it," he said, famously, "that means it is not illegal."

There was also, in the shift of power that began with Roosevelt and the New Deal, a growing sense of the presidency as the office of Supermen, bestowed with the responsibility of correcting the flaws of the nation. The quantity of mythmaking tools available to a politician had grown enormously over the century; so had the number of people around a president dedicated primarily to preserving his image with the public. Noting how awash the nation had become in the activist rhetoric of John Kennedy, a Chicago journalist expressed concern in 1962 about the precedent that was being set. "It boils down to government by intellectual elite," wrote Lawrence Fanning. "[But] what happens if the elite is replaced by a venal, arrogant or power-mad cabal?"

The cabal arrived with Nixon, who gathered around him a small coterie of advisers whose experience had been in campaigning, not government — advertising men, out of the tradition of the consumer culture, preened by corporate organizations to do what good corporate men do: follow orders, please superiors, and hold individuality to a minimum. Aghast at the abuses testified to by Nixon's men, many people wondered how it was that so many at such a high level of public service had gone astray. Yet, as Hugh Sloan, who had served as treasurer of the CRP finance committee, testified, "there was no independent sense of morality there." The men around Nixon had been bred to believe that "if you worked for someone, he was God, and whatever the orders, you did it."

In the interest of serving the president, Nixon's people faked cables to distort the image of John Kennedy (they wanted to suggest that he had ordered the assassination of Vietnam's Diem); broke into the office of Daniel Ellsberg's psychiatrist (looking for dirt on the Pentagon Papers leaker); and planned to set a fire at the Brookings Institution, a liberal think tank (in order to pilfer documents). Watching as these and other abuses were revealed, many people found it hard not to conclude that the man who wanted to be known as the law-and-order president had little respect for the law himself and that their nation was being run by a team of gangsters who espoused the principles of democracy even as they willfully violated them.

On the morning of August 9, 1974, the thirty-seventh president of the United States, his eyes red, his voice shaky, addressed his staff in the East Room of the White House, imploring them, in a mawkish nineteen-minute ramble, to

"Had I but served my God with half the zeal I served my King, he would not in mine age have left me naked to mine enemies."

Senate Watergate Committee Chairman Sam Ervin citing Shakespeare's Henry VIII, *to scold the Watergate criminals*

DING DONG, THE WITCH IS DEAD

Sign on the White House fence,
August 8, 1974

Richard Nixon bids farewell to the White
House staff and members of his cabinet in
the East Room of the White House.

never "hate" those who "hate you," lest "you destroy yourself." Then, exiting to applause, Richard Nixon and his wife, Pat, walked through the mansion doors and down a freshly laid red carpet to the helicopter known as *Army One*. In a last incongruous gesture, the man who had just relinquished the most powerful single office in the world threw up his arms in a sign of victory, the fingers of each hand split to form his signature "V," then disappeared from view inside the chopper. Nixon was a private citizen seated in a California-bound 707 somewhere over Missouri when Vice President Gerald Rudolph Ford stood in the same stately, chandeliered room — right hand raised, left hand on a Bible opened to the book of Proverbs — and recited the oath of office as the new president.

With a swiftness that restored faith, at least temporarily, in the system, the forced exit of one leader and the entrance of his successor had been carried off smoothly. Around the country, champagne corks popped, and across from the White House, protesters, mocking Nixon, chanted "Jail to the Chief." But the most common reaction was not so much joy or residual bitterness as it was relief. When all was said and done, a crisis had been met, and met peacefully. Just after swearing in the new executive, Chief Justice Warren Burger, sounding like a nervous inventor whose contraption had finally been put to the test, turned to Senate Republican Leader Hugh Scott. "It worked, Hugh," he said of the system. "Thank God, it worked."

Ironically, in succumbing to congressional pressure, Nixon, announced *Time,* had finally delivered on the 1968 campaign pledge he had taken from a little girl holding up a sign that said "Bring Us Together." For, as with most divorces, the pain and suffering had come in getting to this point, and despite Nixon's claims that Watergate was at root the work of political adversaries, the decision over his fate had drawn together people who otherwise stood apart. Republicans and Democrats, liberals and conservatives, young and old, agreed that the president had to go.

Unfortunately, the crisis of authority lingered. Because Nixon's resignation had been preceded by that of his elected vice president, Spiro Agnew, who had been taken down by a separate scandal, and Gerald Ford had been appointed, not elected, to succeed Agnew, Ford was now the first American president to serve without a national mandate of any kind. And when, four weeks after he ascended to the nation's top post, the new president issued a "full, free and absolute" pardon to Nixon — the man most Americans saw as having brought shame upon the national house — he squandered much of the goodwill people had provided to both him and his attempts to establish a more humble presidency.

Finally, just six months later, Vietnam fell to the communists, the end coming in a humiliating spectacle that included looters rifling through the American Embassy and Marine helicopters evacuating the remaining Americans off the tops of Saigon buildings, while desperate refugees clung to the choppers' landing gear. Few scenes in American military history can match the image of betrayal those pictures delivered to an already disheartened American population. For while the last American troops had departed with the truce at the end of 1973, the United States had maintained its commitment to the freedom of South Vietnam, providing it with a $5-billion arsenal and millions in related aid to hold off attacks from the North. Nixon's program of "Vietnamization" had appeared a

With the North Vietnamese army descending on Saigon, the U.S. Armed Forces Radio station played "White Christmas" to signal the beginning of a massive helicopter airlift of one thousand Americans and five thousand South Vietnamese from the U.S. Embassy. Thousands of other desperate South Vietnamese frantically tried to storm the compound in the hopes of gaining a place on a helicopter.

success, the handing off of the burden of South Vietnam's defense to the South Vietnamese seeming at first glance to be one of those solutions that offered comfort to both sides of America's home front debate, for even with the soldiers returning, America could be said to have not given up the fight.

Now, with the South's defeat, the program had to be viewed a failure and the fifty thousand American boys as having perished for nothing, for not even American honor could be said to have survived the debacle in Southeast Asia. In one last crowning insult to the people Americans had ostensibly come to help, 420 loyal Vietnamese, eager to depart with their American friends, were left waiting in the American Embassy compound when Ford issued the order to end the evacuations. Anguished, the U.S. Army captain supervising the mission simply told the Vietnamese that he was going to the bathroom, presumably to return, and instead climbed to the roof and the safety of the last departing helicopter.

The end of Pax Americana, the disappearance of the energy abundance, and the collapse of faith in American leadership all combined now to force apart the body politic. Faced with disappointment, Americans responded in a distinctively American way: they migrated, declared new identities, searched for alternative heroes. And as they did, one could almost feel in the narrowing of loyalties the dissolution of one society — federal, urban, optimistic, socially committed — and the emergence of another — regional, exurban, suspicious, detached.

It was, in fact, the beginning of a movement that would last well into the next decade and beyond: the slow disintegration of the liberal experiment that had begun with the New Deal and the sense of community that surrounded it. The campaign that had invested itself in government and in an immutable belief in progress appeared ready to collapse now that faith in both government and progress had likewise seemed to collapse. But in some ways, it could also be said to reach back to the time before the New Deal when, in the 1920s, Americans faced that epic struggle between the modern and the traditional. Then it had appeared as if the city and its newer values had won out over the more stolid country, but now, as the seventies came into their own, the "country" began to even the score.

Evangelical religion, that of the variety once preached by the twenties' own Billy Sunday, returned in force; indeed, in 1976, Americans elected their first "born again" president, former Georgia governor Jimmy Carter. And while there was no marked reemergence of the kind of reactionary thinking represented by the Klan, which had thrived in the twenties, more and more people began to feel that progressive-minded ideas, like the push for racial integration, needed to be reexamined, particularly when, as in the case of the use of school busing to correct racial imbalances, the solution actually seemed to exacerbate the problem.

Finally, there was the very clear decay of the city itself. America's great urban centers had been in a long decline, and by the mid-seventies it became clear that many of the liberal solutions for urban blight were failures; indeed the massive housing projects that had been erected with Great Society promise were now festering eyesores, breeding grounds for crime, juvenile delinquency, and drug addiction. In 1975, New York City entered a dramatic fiscal crisis, and Washington, at first, rejected all appeals for help, prompting the *New York Daily News* to run its now-famous headline "Ford to City: Drop Dead." Yet the decision not to aid New York was one in which Ford had properly gauged the national mood: many Americans were gleeful to see the nation's premier metropolis in trouble, for they had come to see the city in general (and New York in particular) as a symbol of excess and waste, a monument to failure. And they had declared their new loyalties with their feet, moving away in large numbers from the Northeast, which most represented this rusty, discredited urban view of the world, and toward the "Sun Belt" states of the South and West.

In Boston, during the mid-decade years, the argument over school busing reached a frightening impasse that seemed to symbolize this changing mood. The city had long had a reputation as being among the more liberal communities in the nation, the once-reliable New Deal coalition that had governed it for decades held together by a union of old-line Yankees, working-class ethnic voters, and blacks. Yet starting in 1974, when a federal judge imposed a desegregation plan upon Boston's schools, ordering the busing of nearly half of all students to schools outside of their neighborhoods, the glue that held the city together began to come undone. The "Athens of America," home to Harvard and the Kennedys, rapidly began to resemble Bull Connor's Birmingham. By the time school opened that year, the city's neighborhoods were in a siege mentality that reminded Irish residents of yet another battle zone: the streets of Belfast. "If they can tell you where to send your kids to school," said one irate mother, "they can tell you anything, they can take anything away from you."

In a scene reminiscent of Little Rock, Arkansas, in the 1950s, riot-helmeted Boston police stand guard over black students as they are bused to a white school district in 1974.

The most public confrontation came between two of Boston's oldest neighborhoods, the predominantly black district of Roxbury and the mostly Irish community of South Boston (or Southie, as it is commonly known), with white parents viewing the black district's housing projects across the bay from them as nothing less than the encampments of an army preparing for an invasion. "Being able to stand on that hill and see the [Columbia Point housing project] is . . . like seeing your enemy before they attack," said a white mother of four. Others were even more blunt. "I was born here and Southie [high school] is my alma mater," said one truck driver. "My kids go to Southie, too. Why should I send them off to Amazonland? It's getting so the coloreds gets everything."

As buses transporting black students into Southie arrived, they were greeted with racial insults and rocks. But the violence went in both directions. Blacks in Roxbury hurled bricks at passing cars carrying white passengers, and

As bystanders shouted "Get the nigger!" South Boston students beat a black passerby who unwittingly stumbled upon an antibusing demonstration. "Violence which once focused on the schools and buses is now engulfing the entire community in racial confrontation," wrote Boston Mayor Kevin White in an appeal for help from federal marshals.

Boston police informed whites that while the buses carrying their children would receive protection, they could not guarantee any other whites safe passage through the black neighborhood. In what was the crisis's worst episode of violence, South Boston High School had to be closed in 1974 when a black teenager stabbed a white classmate and a mob of fifteen hundred angry white parents trapped the black students inside the school for four hours. But even when the schools were calm, there was an ever-present air of hostility.

The working-class Irish felt betrayed from all corners, for the church, supporting the courts, refused to allow people to enroll their children in Catholic parochial schools simply to avoid the buses, and some of Boston's mostly Irish politicians stood in support of the integration plan, too, including Senator Ted Kennedy (who, offending what was once his most loyal constituency, was pelted with raw eggs at one appearance) and Mayor Kevin White, who became known among embittered Southies as Mayor Black. But the situation in Boston represented more than simply a coarse display of racism: it was also a demonstration of just how complicated the question of racial integration had become. For while it was simple to see that no black child should be denied the opportunity to attend a nearby school with whites in, say, Little Rock and Topeka (where the landmark case leading to the Supreme Court's 1954 decision on integration had been brought), it was much harder to see the virtue in busing either black or white children many miles outside of their neighborhoods in the interest of achieving a racial balance. Boston, as journalist J. Anthony Lukas wrote, had put the nation face-to-face with the tragic clash of two worthy principles — equality of opportunity, as dictated by the Constitution, and the call to community, as represented by the neighborhood school — and in the attempt to protect each of them, both were lost.

Finally, Boston revealed another ugly side issue to the push for integration: class. It grated upon the city's blue-collar community that the elite ranks of the city's population were those pushing hardest for integration, the very people who would always remain buffeted from its effects (in the heart of the crisis, someone scrawled "Bus Teddy" on the sidewalk outside the Kennedy family home); to them, it rekindled the feeling that had for generations made the Irish and Italian immigrant feel unwelcome in a city run by Boston's Brahmin class. Why was it, they asked, that progressive experiments had to be carried out on the backs of the poor? Years later, in a much-acclaimed book, journalist Lukas looked at Boston's integration crisis from three different perspectives: through the life of a fatherless black family of seven on public assistance; an Irish Catholic family composed of a widow and seven children living in public housing; and an upper-middle-class WASP family whose interest in the crisis was motivated by liberal compassion. Ironically, both the Irish and the black families felt victimized by busing, while the white liberals, representing in a sense the ruling class, became frustrated by the clash of reality with their ideals and, leaving South Boston in a shambles, eventually returned to the comfortable life of the suburbs.

In the end, the Right would gain most from the growing numbers of people who now questioned government solutions to social problems, and it would carry that mandate into power throughout the next decade and onward, but in the seventies many groups picked fruit from the same vine, and thus, also in part because they had lost faith in traditional institutions, people from all sides of the political and social spectrum began to see themselves in opposition to established institutions and identify instead with any of a long list of special interests. Ideology, it seemed, no longer mattered. Far more than declaring themselves as Republicans or Democrats, liberals or conservatives, people now saw themselves first as "women" or "gay" or "gray" (as in elderly) or "green" (as in environmentally aware) or "Latino" or "Asian" or "Native American" or as members of any number of flourishing religious cults. "All the isms," explained an influential art critic who saw the same attitude emerging in culture, were now "wasms." And to the degree that politics remained an enthusiasm, it was to further the interests of a bloc hoping to extract new or unrecognized rights.

Women were by far the largest and, in terms of legislative and social achievement, the most successful of the groups now making up what was sometimes described as a "Balkanized" America. Feminist claims to equal rights had been heard ever since Betty Friedan issued her groundbreaking book, *The Feminine Mystique,* in 1962, and in light cast by the civil rights movement of the six-

"They're taught to hate us. How can you learn anything if you're afraid of being stabbed?"

Student, on plans to integrate all-white South Boston High School with forced busing

Stonewall and beyond:
"'Gay is good' sounded preposterous, even to our own ears. But the more we said it, the more we began to believe it"

The Stonewall was a gay bar and a dance place on Christopher Street, in Greenwich Village, New York City. It was really two large rooms with a long bar that ran down one side. To call it a disco was a stretch, because in those days you didn't have a disc jockey blending one record into another. What you had was a jukebox and people who fed it with quarters and played their favorite songs. It was a place where a lot of gay Puerto Rican and black kids went.

It was also a hangout of mine. At the time, I was living in New York working as an editor at a very conventional publishing company. I would go to Stonewall because I liked to dance, I liked the crazy, liberated atmosphere of the place, and there was a guy that I fancied who I would occasionally meet there. In those days there weren't very many places in the Village where gay men could go to dance. It was still technically illegal for two men to dance together in New York City, but by the end of the sixties the police began to look the other way. Gays had become much more conspicuous on the streets in the West Village. The neighborhood had basically become a gay precinct where you would see gay people walking up and down the street, even hand in hand. Gays felt they had one street of their own, Christopher Street, in this whole vast city. It was our turf.

One summer night in 1969, a friend of mine and I were walking down Christopher Street toward Sheridan Square when we saw this commotion going on at the Stonewall. When we got to the bar we found out that a mammoth paddy wagon, as big as a school bus, had pulled up and about ten cops had raided the place. All of the patrons of the bar had been shooed into the street, and the cops were hauling away the people who worked there. As my friend and I joined the sizable crowd that had already gathered outside of the bar, the cops told everyone to disperse. But we didn't. When they hauled about ten people away in the paddy wagon the crowd started jeering and yelling at the cops. People started chanting "gay is good." It was like a form of street theater. The funny thing is, we all had big smiles on our faces. It was like we were saying to ourselves, isn't this ridiculous, aren't we being silly? It was obviously an echo of "black is beautiful." But whereas we could respect "black is beautiful" as a valid concept, to say "gay is good" sounded preposterous, even to our own ears. But the more we said it, the more we began to believe it.

At first I was kind of nervous. I thought that everyone should disperse. I thought that we should be law-abiding. I had never done anything like this before. I was this mild-mannered, do-good type boy who had never

expressed any kind of violence; I was probably even wearing a coat and tie at the time. This whole event felt quite kooky and daring. I was worried that my picture would be taken and it would be in the paper and I'd lose my job. But there was also this rage boiling up inside me. Like a lot of other gay men, I was tired of people thinking I was pathetic or pathological. I started to feel that I wasn't the one who should have to adjust to society, but maybe society should change in order to accommodate me. It wasn't too long before I was shouting myself hoarse, along with everyone else.

The police really picked a bad time for their raid. It was very hot and people's tempers were short. Also, Judy Garland had just died and she was a gay heroine. The day before, everyone had filed up to the Riverside Memorial Chapel to pay their final respects to her. So nerves were on edge. At one point, there were a few cops and a few employees barricaded inside the bar. Christopher Street was completely blocked off and there were about a thousand people outside. Suddenly this one kid pulls up a parking meter right out of the pavement and starts using it as a battering ram on the heavy wooden doors of the Stonewall. Then people started smashing the windows of the place to cries of "Liberate the bar!" and "We are the Pink Panthers!" When the door gave way, people emptied trash cans full of paper and set them on fire. This was extremely wild behavior for a group of people who usually fled into the woodwork whenever they were challenged in any way. Soon more cops came and fire engines pulled up, and the crowd eventually dispersed. But it still wasn't over. The next night the crowds were back and the riot continued. Kids were turning cars over, they were breaking windows in the whole area, so the police sent the riot squad out. We looked up and saw this great phalanx of cops in riot gear

marching down Christopher Street. But what they did not realize was that we understood the layout of the Village a little better than they did. So we dashed down a side street called Waverly which connected to another small street curiously enough called Gay Street, and we came out behind the cops dancing in a chorus line, kicking up our legs, and singing and yelling "yoo hoo!" It was all great camp. We were trying to infuriate these policemen by being frivolous and yet very spirited. My one friend turned to me and said, "You know, this may be one of the first funny revolutions in history."

It was a completely exhilarating weekend. For the first time gays, instead of running away when they were challenged, stood their ground and fought back. Gay student organizations and academic unions sprang up all over the country. Gays organized sit-downs and be-ins and other protests for gay rights. As the seventies wore on, the movement managed to get a lot of pro-gay ordinances passed in different cities across the country. . Then Anita Bryant came along and fought against that. She was a pop singer, orange juice spokeswoman, and born-again Christian who led a "Save Our Children" campaign against gays. Her reasoning was that gays, especially in the schools, were dangerous role models. She campaigned to have the pro-gay ordinance in Miami revoked and she won, but she awakened a militancy in the gay movement. Gays led a boycott against drinking orange juice, and Anita Bryant's sponsors dropped her. She had become too controversial for them. Eventually she herself became aware of how much suffering her campaign was causing to individual gays, and I think she also began to perceive gays as being real human beings. Of course, it was Stonewall that set in motion this entire political movement; it really changed the whole world for gay people.

Edmund White in 1972, a few years after he joined in the Stonewall riot.

—Edmund White, born in 1940, is a writer whose books include A Boy's Own Story, The Beautiful Room Is Empty, Forgetting Elena, Nocturnes for the King of Naples, *and* Caracole. *In 1983, he received a Guggenheim Fellowship and the award for literature from the American Academy and Institute of Arts and Letters. He was made a Chevalier de l'Ordre des Arts et Lettres in 1993 and was awarded the National Book Critics Circle Award and the Lambda Literary Award for his book* Genet: A Biography *in 1994. He lives in Paris.*

ties, many people had grown to believe that not only blacks but women, too, had been leading lives short of the promise contained in America's highest ideals. Still, by the late sixties, the movement had been confused by a radical leadership grown more angry than it was productive. Only by the mid-1970s, when the economy had brought an enforced enlightenment on family life (a working spouse becoming a necessity in many homes) and when the quality of leadership demonstrated by white males had come under such severe attack (prompting many to consider the need for "feminine" qualities at the highest level), did the ideas of the women's movement begin to take hold in the broader population.

Friedan, who in the end was more moderate than those who succeeded her, had taken issue with what she called "the problem that has no name," the powerful, but unarticulated, feeling so many women of her day had that motherhood and housework constituted an unfulfilling life. She established the National Organization for Women (NOW) in 1966, and within a year the group had focused upon two primary goals: the Equal Rights Amendment and the right of women to "control their reproductive lives." By the late sixties, they had been joined by other, more radical organizations, some of them seeing heterosexual intercourse as oppressive and advocating nothing short of war with the male sex. (Not wanting to be corrupted by male influence, a group called the Feminists allowed only a third of their membership to be involved with men.)

In 1972, Congress passed the Equal Rights Amendment and sent it to the states for ratification, and in 1973, with _Roe v. Wade_, the Supreme Court ruled in favor of abortion rights, handing victory to the feminists on both major issues. While those victories would come under severe attack (and the ERA would never achieve the ratification of the states), the psychological shift that the women's movement had brought to American society became almost more important than what it had achieved in the courts or the legislatures. By the mid-seventies, women could be said to have made greater strides toward a social transformation than were achieved by blacks.

Even the "date," that ritual step in courtship that had remained informed by so many age-old customs, was affected, with the presumptions that the man would initiate the encounter, pay for it, open the door for his partner (being the weaker sex, she had to be spared exertion), and maintain the exclusive right to ask her out again, all now disappearing. And for the fewer and fewer couples choosing marriage (the single life and cohabitation emerging as socially acceptable alternatives), there now emerged confusion over household chores, even if many men conveniently interpreted liberation as extending a woman's responsibility to include both a paycheck _and_ the vacuuming of the rugs.

The need to see men and women as equal prompted many people to reassess the gender stereotyping that had long characterized attitudes toward child rearing. Why were girls enrolled in "home economics" and boys in "shop," they asked, when true equality would suggest that boys should be taught to be just as ready to cook dinner and that girls could just as capably operate a lathe?

Do you feel yourself to be a victim of discrimination?

(asked of a cross section of American women)

	No	Yes
1962	66%	33%
1970	50%	50%
1974	33%	66%

> _"By the time my husband walked in the door all hell would break loose . . . He was responsible for all the evils of the world and especially responsible for keeping me trapped."_
>
> Woman recalling the onslaught of feminist ideas across radio and television in the 1970s

Fifty years after the ratification of the amendment that gave women the vote, feminists across the country held rallies and marches, such as this one in New York City. The protesters demanded reproductive rights, equal opportunity, child care, an end to violence against women, and approval of the Equal Rights Amendment (which was first submitted to Congress in 1923).

Why must the woman raise the children and the man go out in the world, when true equality would suggest that those roles could just as easily be switched? And yet, in the topsy-turvy seventies, it was the fears that rippled from such vigilant attacks on tradition that also helped to temper the popular mood and give voice to those who called some aspects of feminism into question. For even as the advancement of career opportunities and the adjustment of some of the more archaic social conventions gained broad acceptance, antifeminist leaders — complaining that the trend, if unchecked, would lead to unisex toilets and homosexual marriages, the destruction of the family and the glorification of the self — awoke a late-seventies backlash that questioned much of the more aggressive feminist agenda.

Anti-feminists wrapped their campaigns in tradition. Adopting many of the same arguments that had been used to counter suffragists in the earliest days of the century, they declared themselves as defending nothing short of the family itself, and by extension from that, civilization. To them, the movement for women's rights was at heart an attempt to undermine the collective spirit in the interest of serving the needs of the individual. Feminists, they claimed, valued self-fulfillment as a goal above all others. And the issue that best articulated their drama, and the one that brought the emotions of both sides to a fever pitch, was abortion.

Many feminists saw abortion as the most fundamental of rights, the one that mattered before all others, for it spoke not so much to a woman's relationship with society as to a woman's relationship with herself. "None of the other [rights] means a doggone thing," said one activist, "if we don't own the flesh we stand in, if we can't control what happens to us, if the whole course of our lives can be changed by somebody else that can get us pregnant by accident, or by deceit, or by force." By contrast, antifeminists saw abortion as one more attempt to subvert the family for the will of the individual, to replace God with man. Abortion smacked of eugenics, it valued the quality of life over the sanctity of life, and because it allowed for the undoing of the consequences of sexual behavior, it encouraged moral decay.

Yet at the heart of the matter was that classic clash between the modern and the traditional. The mostly middle- and upper-class population that wanted to protect the right to abortion still saw life in terms of rising expectations and the pursuit of greater and greater human freedoms; in short, the modern promise of a world made to conform to human needs and desires. The largely working-class Catholic antiabortionists, on the other hand, placed their faith in the whims of nature; indeed, in a God who operates beyond human understanding. To them, the termination of a fetus was an act of human arrogance less politely described as murder.

The healthy, even lusty cry that emanated from a delivery room in a British mill town hospital at precisely 11:47 on a summer night in 1978 brought joy to Gilbert and Lesley Brown and why not? Ever since they married in 1969, the couple had wanted a child of their own and now they had one, thanks to the $1,500 Gilbert won betting on football and the brilliance of two British doctors who, after no fewer than eighty tries, had just become the first physicians to create what was being popularly called a test-tube baby.

The burgeoning women's movement: "My feminism came straight out of my own circumstances"

I never read *The Feminine Mystique,* but in the early 1960s, I lived it. I was quite certain that after college I'd marry, have children, stay at home and have this great life that I saw in the Betty Crocker ads. But I was living in a very interesting time, sort of on the cusp between two eras. Half of me wanted to do something different, but half of me felt loyal to this vision of life as a wife and mother. So when my boyfriend proposed to me in 1962, I decided to drop out of college and marry him, but then I immediately changed my mind and canceled the wedding, deciding to go to graduate school instead. Just as suddenly, I changed my mind again and had the wedding after all. Within nine months I was pregnant with my first child.

I felt like things had gone badly for my mother because she had to work outside the home; but it would be different for me, I thought, because I would stay home and be a happy, loving, perfect mother. Of course, things didn't happen that way. My husband and I moved around a lot and I didn't have a very good support system, so I was home alone with the baby quite a lot. I started to feel like you would feel on an airplane when they tell you the mask is going to drop, and that you should just breathe normally. You can't breathe normally with a child in an apartment, without a lot of money, without friends and family. Children aren't meant to be raised in a home with just one adult who never leaves the house. I didn't like it. And I was also disappointed with myself for not absolutely loving this motherhood experience.

I got pregnant again — my fourth time in four and a half years. I had been sick a lot during those years — my body was just worn out — and I remember sitting in the bathtub and crying. I asked myself, "What am I gonna do? I really can't deal with having that many children, and the only alternative is abortion. Can I risk getting an illegal abortion?" There was a good chance then that I could die from it, and I didn't want to leave my children motherless. It suddenly hit me that something was wrong with this picture. For the first time, I realized I had been working for African-American rights, for peace in Vietnam, but that I still had no choices, nor any peace, in my personal life.

The push for women's rights in this country really was a kitchen-table movement, started by women like me who needed changes in their lives. I found a number of women out there who felt the same way I did, and we started working together in our homes. Everything we wanted in life — whether it was to choose how many children to have, to go back to school, to get involved in the workforce — we were determined to go out and create in the world. So we gathered around kitchen tables and pieced together legislation, wrote petitions and

planned events while our children ran around the room. We figured out who to write to in the legislature in order to pass the Mondale child-care bill in the early seventies. We decided which one of us was charming enough to successfully lobby at the statehouse. We figured out what to do about the guys who put their hands on our legs while we were lobbying them. I remember working on the Mondale bill, talking to a labor economist in my kitchen; I had a child in one hand, and I was stirring spaghetti sauce with the other.

Meanwhile, the media was creating a movement that was unrecognizable to me — people who burned bras, who hated men and all of that. I had no idea who these people were, what they did, what they looked like. In 1970, I heard about some kind of march, but that branch of the movement was never something I could identify with. My feminism came straight out of my own circumstances. I needed to space my children, so I worked on choice. I needed child care in order to work, so I worked on child care. I needed a better job, so I worked on creating good work for women. It wasn't about a national movement. It was simply something that was happening to me, to my friends, to my community. That was feminism.

—Marie Wilson, born in 1940, joined the Ms. Foundation for Women as president in 1984. During her tenure with the foundation, she has led such projects as Take Our Daughters to Work Day and the Reproductive Rights Coalition Fund.

In 1965, a friend of mine was raped at knifepoint in her bed in the off-campus housing at my university. A group of friends and I went with her to student health services to get her a gynecological exam and some support, but she was refused assistance. She wasn't given an exam because they weren't covered by our student health plan, and to make matters worse, she was given a lecture on her promiscuity. We refused to leave the clinic until she was given an exam. In effect, this waiting became a sit-in for women's rights, though it's not what we realized at the moment. That event over a rape at the university was just a reflection of how women were treated as nearly invisible characters, even on campus.

A group of us did a study in one of my sociology classes to analyze what I call "significant responses." We would compare the responses of professors to female versus male students. It seemed like whenever a woman would respond to a teacher's question, the teacher would say, "That was nice." But when a man would raise his hand a teacher might say, "That's a stupid idea" or "That was brilliant." Even if the comment was negative, at least the teacher was engaged in what the male student was saying. It was as if the female student's answer

Left: Heather Booth speaking to a group of grassroots activists, 1978. Right: Jane Adams with her daughter Dawn, left, and niece Arwen, 1971.

didn't exist. We counted something like four to one significant response from men versus women. It was just one more part of realizing that women weren't treated as full participants in society — even at a university that prided itself on that kind of equal treatment.

I was a member of SDS, and I noticed there was even a double side to the way in which we were treated there. We were certainly taken more seriously than we were in general society and were able to act out our beliefs. But we also had a sense of a woman's place. The leaders of the organization were typically men, and the women were typically the workers. Eventually we created this women's organization out of SDS called WRAP, or Women's Radical Action Project. During our first public meeting we put up some signs and had a small meeting room. We thought if we had ten or fifteen people show up, that would be fine. There was such a great response to come and discuss the women's issue that the meeting was standing room only. We had discussion groups where we would go around and talk about our situation and then there would be this click of recognition, a realization that the problems that you had felt were your personal problems were shared by other women, and if they were shared by others, it was a social problem and, therefore, needed a social solution. What propelled us was a sense of justice and mission, and also the sense of community with other people.

—Heather Booth, born in 1945, is the founding director of Mid-West Academy, created in 1972 and dedicated to the training of leaders in mass-based citizen organization. The group has provided such assistance to, among others, the National Organization for Women and the Children's Defense Fund.

I wasn't involved in any of the conventional politics of organizations like NOW. I always had a very particular, radical view of the women's struggle. I always saw issues of poverty and those kinds of inequalities as being really important. Whereas the mainstream women's movements were focusing on legal rights, I thought the emphasis should be on transforming the whole system and creating a greater equality for all people. The tradi-

tional women's groups and the media dealt mainly with the middle-class mom, who was supposed to be like June Cleaver in *Leave It to Beaver*. But poor women weren't part of that. As a member of SDS, my work often involved assisting poorer women, who were really down in the trenches. I could never quite relate to the struggles of the middle-class woman.

In the summer of 1969, when SDS fell apart, my partner and I packed the car and headed out to the Northwest. But we ran out of money and our tires were bald, so we landed in one of those shared communities in San Francisco's Bay Area by default. We were living communally and were faced with the nuts-and-bolts problems of daily life in that kind of situation. It seemed that women were stuck doing all the housework. We always had big fights over who washed the dishes, and who swept up, and who picked up. But the deeper thing we were struggling with was really sexual politics, because that's where men and women meet most intimately. We discovered that when the bounds were broken and women became sexually active and liberated, men were still acting in predatory ways. It was very clear that men and women had completely different ideas about what sexual liberation really meant. Men were bringing all that old cultural baggage to what was supposed to be a revolutionary situation. They were still calling us "chicks" and dishing out the same lines they had been before.

Some women within the community began to see men as the enemy. If you were in a relationship with a man, you were, in effect, sleeping with the enemy. There was a real pressure to become a lesbian. In the really radical organizations, it became obligatory to declare yourself a lesbian. Now, I always thought that was pretty silly. We do, after all, have to procreate. We all have fathers who contributed to our upbringing in some way. One of the things about those sorts of what you call communal identities is that people decide that you're the enemy if you don't toe the line. It was somewhat demoralizing, but I didn't fight it. Some women did, but I just figured I would get bruised.

—Jane Adams, born in 1943, was a protester at the Democratic National Convention in Chicago in 1968. Disenchanted with the feminist movement, she turned to teaching, leaving the Bay Area in 1976 to pursue studies in anthropology.

The Supreme Court's 1973 decision in Roe v. Wade, *which established abortion as a "fundamental right," galvanized the antiabortion movement and intensified an emotional debate that would escalate for decades to come. On January 22, 1979, sixty thousand antiabortion protesters held a rally in Washington, D.C., right, on the sixth anniversary of* Roe.

Of course the more official term for the method that produced little six-pound Louise was "*in vitro* fertilization" (literally, "in glass"), but the image of a test tube better fit the imaginations that were running wild the world over. With the news of the arrival of Louise, people had begun to recall the pages of Aldous Huxley's 1932 thriller, *Brave New World,* and Huxley's vision of a society where "babies are mass-produced from chemical solutions in laboratory bottles." In fact, Louise was nothing of the kind; she represented the union of Gilbert Brown's sperm with Lesley Brown's egg and she had been carried to term by her mother just as other babies are. Only the actual joining of the egg and the sperm had been done in a laboratory, the incipient embryo then transferred back to Lesley Brown, where it implanted itself on the wall of her hormone-prepared uterus.

Still, in an atmosphere already hot with the abortion debate's argument over the moral and legal status of the human embryo, the news from Britain was incendiary. And the fact the story broke not in a medical journal, but in a tabloid, the kind of publication that thrived on tales of the bizarre (the Browns had sold their account to the *Daily Mail* for half a million dollars), only took the news that much further into the realm of science fiction. "The potential for misadventure is unlimited," said one wary Los Angeles obstetrician, for what was there to ensure that the Browns' baby would follow normal development? "What if there was an otherwise perfectly formed individual that was a Cyclops? Who is responsible? The parents? The doctors? The government?"

Clergymen focused the discussion on ethical misgivings. To the Catholic priest, it was simple: *in vitro* fertilization was contraception turned backward and therefore immoral (interfering with nature to *encourage* conception being no less abhorrent than interfering with nature to prevent it). To Protestant and Jewish leaders, it was more complicated. Most agreed that medical science was entering a thorny territory. Yet if the end result of the obstetrician's work was a child, *life,* in all its glory, who was to say that it was any less an expression of God's will than other babies? And if a couple was unable to conceive through traditional means, who could justify denying them the benefit of science to do so? Still, to most people, the questions raised by the arrival of Louise Brown were a matter of degree. Just how far should man go into what had always been presumed to be nature's

"We could get baby farms, mass produced kids, 1984 six years early!"

London Daily Express *editor Derek Jameson, on the arrival of the first "test-tube baby"*

domain? And just how much was he to be trusted dabbling in such a sacred realm?

By coincidence, the news of the Browns' baby came at the same time that a $1.5-million lawsuit brought by a couple that had once expected to be the first parents to an *in vitro* baby was being heard in a New York court. Back in 1972, a doctor at New York's Columbia Presbyterian Hospital had fertilized an egg from Doris Del Zio with sperm from her husband, John. But upon hearing of the experiment, the doctor's supervisor destroyed the specimen. He apparently saw the work as too risky (he later claimed that he had no ethical objections to *in vitro* work) and was disturbed that the doctors who performed the operation had done so without the hospital's approval. Now the couple, in their suit, turned the ethical question around. For while those objecting to *in vitro* might believe that the doctors performing the operation were "playing God," the Del Zios felt it was the doctor who destroyed their fertilized egg who had "played God," for he, after all, had "killed" a "potential baby." Their heads swirling, the New York jury eventually came out on the side of the Del Zios. But they still managed to straddle the more fundamental issue of what the fertilized egg represented. Apparently deciding that it was something more than a chemical solution and yet less than an embryo, they awarded the couple just $50,000.

The argument over the future of the environment represented an even more tangled crossing of loyalties than did the battles over feminism. Like feminism, environmentalism had its roots in the questioning sixties. In 1962, Rachel Carson had written *Silent Spring*, which unveiled the dangerous side effects of the pesticide DDT, and by 1970, awareness of industrial abuse of the environment had grown to where the nation's first Earth Day brought millions into the streets to declare their concern. At issue was the growing belief that American postwar prosperity had so fouled the nest that it risked the health of the earth itself. A wealth of legislation addressed some of these worries in the sixties and early seventies, yet many people still believed the day would soon come when fossil fuels would so destroy the atmosphere that Americans would have to wear gas masks to breathe and when an environmental catastrophe might deliver life to a new Dark Age, shorn of industrial progress.

There was even doubt cast on that most fundamental symbol of optimism, procreation. After a late-sixties study predicted mass starvation flowing from overpopulation, many among the generation that had produced the postwar baby boom (and even more of the babies they had produced) began to see the large family as another kind of abuse of resources, a statement of selfishness that in this age of limits could no longer be tolerated. Environmentalists were also questioning science. They believed that it had lacked a social conscience, had pursued knowledge for knowledge's sake with little concern for the consequences of that knowledge. And they felt it had been co-opted by the forces of materialism and mass consumption, made to address the need to maintain Western prosperity at the expense of all other societies and, indeed, of the future itself.

But what would a seventies movement be without a countermovement? And that which targeted environmentalists joined voices from many different sectors. There were, of course, the businessmen (and business*women*) who saw environmental regulation as a threat to profits, joined now in many instances by

Life at Love Canal: **"Don't go in the basement, don't eat from your garden," and still they insisted "it's perfectly safe"**

When I moved to Love Canal, in 1972, I felt I had achieved the American dream: I had a husband with a good job, a healthy one-year-old child, a station wagon, and my very first house, which even had a picket fence. I was living in a thriving young community directly across from the mighty Niagara River. It had two elementary schools, a drug store, two churches, sidewalks everywhere, and lots of young families fixing up these small starter homes. Every time you looked out the window you would see a kid riding a bicycle or a mom pushing a baby buggy. Near one of the schools was an open field that was supposed to be turned into a park, with baseball diamonds and drinking fountains and big playgrounds and picnic tables. Everything in Love Canal seemed to be meant for families. We felt it was just the perfect neighborhood — perfect families, perfect little houses, a perfect stepping-stone in our lives.

Then my son Michael got very sick. When we moved into our house, he was one year old and perfectly healthy. Then he developed skin problems, asthma, epilepsy, a liver problem, an immune system problem, and a urinary tract disorder. It was just one thing after the other. When I asked the pediatrician what was going on, he told me, "You just must be an unlucky mother with a sickly child." My second child, Melissa, who was conceived and born at Love Canal, at first seemed to be perfectly healthy. Then one Friday, I noticed bruises on her body. On Saturday the bruises were larger. And by Sunday the bruises on my little girl's body were the size of saucers. She looked like a child abuse victim! I took her to the pediatrician, but he didn't know what was wrong. He just took a blood test and sent us home. Later that afternoon he called and said, "Mrs. Gibbs, I believe your daughter has leukemia. Her blood count is critical, and we need you to quickly take her to Buffalo Children's Hospital." We had no family history of any of these types of illnesses. It just didn't make any sense to me why my kids were so sick.

Around that time articles started appearing in the *Niagara Falls Gazette* that talked about hazardous waste in dump sites all across the city of Niagara Falls. I read them with a sort of passive interest. Then I read one article that talked about a dump next to the 99th Street Elementary School, the school where my son attended kindergarten. In this article, they listed the chemicals that were buried there and what could result from exposure to these chemicals. I literally checked off every single one of my children's diseases and said to myself, "Oh my God. It's not that I am an unlucky mother. My children are being poisoned." I couldn't believe that somebody would build a school next to a dump site.

I decided to move my son from the elementary school. The board of education told me that I needed statements from two doctors saying that Michael had to move. At first, neither my pediatrician nor my family doctor would sign such a statement, but I was very persistent and they eventually wrote notes saying that there could be some relationship between the school, the dump, and Michael's illnesses. But when I went back to the school board they said, "Well, let's not say that it's dangerous for Michael. If it's dangerous for Michael then it's dangerous for all 407 children who go to that school, and we're not about to close a school because of one hysterical mother with a sickly child." I was flabbergasted! I decided to go door-to-door with a petition to close the 99th Street School. Nothing in my life had prepared me for this. I was a housewife. Before all of this, my biggest concerns were whether my sheets were white, whether my floor shined, and what I was going to fix for dinner. I wasn't active in the community at all. I was a shy person. The first door I came to, I knocked on very lightly, so lightly, in fact, that their dog didn't even bark. And then before anybody answered, I just ran back home and started crying. I was so afraid that people would think I was nuts.

Then Michael came down with pneumonia and had to go to the hospital. That's when I decided that the only person who was going to protect Michael and Melissa was their mother. So I went back out, knocked on the door, held my breath, and waited for somebody to explode at me. But it never happened. Instead, I found out that other people were going through the same thing I was. One person had a thirteen-year-old daughter who had to have a hysterectomy due to cancer.

—Lois Gibbs, born in 1951, moved with her family to the Washington, D.C., area in 1981, where she founded the Citizens' Clearinghouse for Hazardous Waste (now known as the Center for Health, Environment, and Justice), an organization dedicated to public education and awareness about a variety of environmental issues. She returns to Love Canal several times a year for work on the Love Canal Medical Trust Fund, set up to assist families still battling with health problems related to Love Canal. Her children, Michael and Melissa, have recovered from their illnesses, and she has since had two sons.

There were eight other epileptics living in houses that practically encircled ours. And it wasn't just children who were sick, adults were getting sick as well. People would walk me down to their basement and show me orange goo coming up from their sump pumps. In some homes, the chemical smell was so strong that it was like walking into a gas station.

In the spring of 1978, the state department of health came in and did some tests around Love Canal. And then they denied, denied, denied, and denied from that point on. They told the people living closest to the canal, "Don't go in your basement. Don't eat out of your garden. Don't do this, don't do that, but it's perfectly safe to live at Love Canal."

We did our own house survey. And we found that 56 percent of the children at Love Canal were born with birth defects. And that included three ears, double rows of teeth, extra fingers, extra toes, or mentally retarded. The state came in and said, "No, no, no, no, no. That's useless housewife data, generated by people who have a vested interest in the outcome." Through some pressure we forced them to do their own study. They confirmed the birth defect rate, but said it wasn't related to Love Canal. They said it was related to a cloistering of genetically defective people in this community. How can you have 20,000 tons of toxic poison and fifty-six percent birth defect rate in the same community and say that the two of them are not connected?

Before Love Canal, I believed that if you had a problem you could just go to your elected officials and they would fix it. I now know that that's not true. The state didn't do anything until we forced it to. Eventually nine hundred families were evacuated from Love Canal. But what outraged me the most was that a state health department knew people were sick, knew people were dying and decided to do nothing about it. They turned their backs on us. They put dollar signs on our foreheads and dismissed us like we were pieces of trash. And we were the backbone of America. We were the workers in the plants, the people who paid the taxes.

Above: Lois Gibbs in the office of the Love Canal Homeowners Association. Left: One of hundreds of abandoned homes at Love Canal.

working-class people, who similarly accused environmentalists of promoting their cause at the expense of a healthy economy; if business were made to conform to the strict environmental standards, labor argued, the workers would be the ones who would feel the pinch first. Yet, just as often it was working-class people speaking in *favor* of the environment and against its abusers (usually, a polluting factory) if only because, as in the tragedy at Love Canal, it was the working class that was most likely to live closest to the offending source and thus become its victim.

Finally, where a fealty to a natural order had been claimed by the traditionalists in almost every other cause, here that was just as likely to be a loyalty embraced, after a fashion, by the reformers, too. The image of earth seen from the 1969 moon landing had provided an important turning point for mankind's relationship with his planet. Just as the construction of the Eiffel Tower for the Paris Exposition of 1889 had provided millions with a new image of their world — climbing its nearly one thousand feet, they looked across Paris and into a century of air travel — the view of the universe delivered to living rooms by Apollo XI and its cameras had given a new perspective on the earth itself, a sense of the planet's vulnerability and the feeling that the exquisite harmony in which it had been conceived had been contaminated by man and his interfering ways.

In late March 1979, with the nation's attention riveted on the enormous, hourglass-shaped cooling towers of a nuclear power plant on the banks of the placid Susquehanna River, the environmental calamity that everyone had so long feared appeared to be finally at hand. One of many giant power plants that spoke to the hope that nuclear energy might eventually free Western culture from its dependence on oil, Three Mile Island sat nestled among the farms and hamlets of Pennsylvania Dutch country — a nineteenth-century setting, if ever there was one. Yet when, at 4:00 A.M. on March 28, an inoperative valve released thousands of gallons of coolant from the plant's reactor, prompting half of the 36,816 exposed fuel rods to melt in temperatures soaring above five thousand degrees, the region became the setting for a modern nightmare.

The molten material burned through the lining of the reaction chamber, sank to the vessel's floor, and then stopped there. But as a nervous nation soon learned, the plant had come dangerously close to a meltdown. Had the mass gone on to burn through the floor itself and burrow into the soil, it would have released unknown quantities of radioactivity into the atmosphere, particularly if it had hit a water table and thrown back a deadly radioactive geyser. People had only recently watched just such a catastrophe in a suspense movie thriller called *The China Syndrome* (the phrase implied that the molten material would burn a hole through the core of the earth all the way to Beijing). But Three Mile Island was the real thing, and the sense of science gone awry filled the mind with images of birth defects and crippling cancers, and with the irrational yet understandable fear that the reactor would explode like a bomb, leveling Pennsylvania and delivering fallout across the nation. Even without that ultimate calamity, the lower levels of radiation that did escape from the plant prompted locals to file claims of personal injury (later dismissed), and, while the company operating the reactor insisted that no harm had been done, over the years, tales of giant mutated vegetation, livestock peculiarly unable to give birth, and unusually reddened skin persisted.

"Guards gave out Hershey bars at the doors. Concession stands disgorged free potato chips, hot dogs and sodas. A preacher created a de facto day-care center … leading games, doing magic tricks, acting out the story of Jonah and the whale. Grownups played cards and watched television and shared their anger at 'them' — the people who let the accident happen. 'I guess I'll just sit here,' said Bonnie Morgan, nineteen years old, nine months pregnant and utterly bewildered. 'I don't think they know what they're doing.'"

Newsweek, *April 9, 1979, reporting on the scene at a makeshift shelter holding evacuees from Three Mile Island*

Both feminism and environmentalism — and a growing grassroots rebellion against taxation — demonstrated a newfound popular allegiance to cause, but the loss of confidence in established forms of authority (and the general feeling of rootlessness that flowed from that) also led many Americans in this time to search for surrogate truths — new religions embracing new messiahs. The proliferation of cults and alternative "theologies" like Scientology, Sun Myung Moon's Unification Church, Synanon, Erhard Seminar Training (est), and the "church" of Guru Maharaji demonstrated the need many felt for a spiritual port in the midst of a secular storm, at the very least a new "system" by which to organize their lives and provide meaning, and for many, something more: a father, a family, a transcendent experience, a god. In 1978, just a few months before Three Mile Island, the tragedy at Jonestown became the chilling parable of fanaticism, paranoia, moral righteousness, and empty devotion that suggested that quest was yet another symptom of a society in deadly crisis.

When, in late November, the pictures of the mass suicide of the Peoples Temple cult began to appear in newspapers and magazines (and as moving images in the camera work of an NBC photographer who had himself been killed in the ambush that began the tragedy), they had the quality of an allegorical painting from the brush of Hieronymus Bosch or Pieter Breughel, gruesomely

The antitax revolt: "More grassroots than the Boston Tea Party"

One morning in 1976, I opened my paper and read that property taxes in California were going to double. I just couldn't believe it. It would have made our property taxes higher than our house payments each month. At the time, I was part of the Homeowners Association in Sherman Oaks, California, so I knew that something had to be done. This was just before the real estate boom in California, and a lot of the homeowners had bought their property at a very reasonable price, so while they could afford to make their house payments, they couldn't afford exorbitant taxes. There were also a lot of people who had inherited their property and had it for years, and a lot of widows who were trying to hold on to their homes after their husbands died. These people would risk losing everything if this tax hike went through. Even for middle-income people, which was how my husband and I were classified at the time, it would have been a crunch.

I guess the cities felt they needed more money, but what they really needed to do was cut back. Back then the government was just out of control. Anybody with any sense of money — a housewife who can handle a checkbook — knew that the government was spending way too much. We were spending so much money on so much foolishness. I'm not talking about the police department, fire department, or the National Guard. We're all thankful for those agencies. But when you are working and half of your salary is supporting someone that's not working — that's what aggravates people.

The week after I read about the tax hike, I saw this little ad in the paper that said, "If you want to lower your property taxes, call this number." And so I called and was put in touch with a gentleman named Howard Jarvis. I met him, we hit it off, and he gave me this petition — which became known as Proposition 13 — and asked me to get some signatures. The gist of Proposition 13 was to make it so California would not be able to charge more than 1.25 percent of the property value of your home. Well, I'm not a type of person who can go out and just stand on a corner and get signatures, so I wrote a letter to the editor that told people about the petitions and that we were trying to fight the property taxes. That was all I had to do. All of a sudden my phone started ringing, and people just started coming out of the woodwork. There was a real sense of desperation; people were afraid they were going to lose their homes, and they were fed up by all of these taxes. I seemed to draw an army of retired elderly people and widows on fixed incomes. Wonderful people. They would come to my home and they would get petitions, and we would work together, and plan our strategy. At one meeting someone suggested dropping the petitions from an airplane, but the president of the Homeowners

Marilyn Noorda with her one-year-old daughter, Tiffany, at home in Sherman Oaks, California, during the Proposition 13 heyday, 1976.

—Marilyn Noorda, born in 1942, was so inspired by the teachings of Pastor John Hinkle that she was "born again" in 1976. In 1979, she participated in Pastor Hinkle's prayer meeting of 35,000 in Washington, D.C., which she and her husband documented in a film entitled America Under God. *In 1990, she was ordained, and after a year as associate pastor of her church, she became a pastor-at-large, organizing prayer groups around the state of California.*

Association, who was a lawyer, convinced us that that wouldn't be such a good idea.

At this point, the calls were coming in so fast that we couldn't handle them all. The demand for the petitions grew so great that on some days hundreds of people would come to my house to pick them up. There would be lines of cars four blocks long! I knew my neighbors would quickly get fed up with this, so we had to find another way to get the petitions to the people. Then someone came up with the idea of posting the petitions with the real estate companies. We knew they would be sympathetic, because if the property taxes doubled, it would make it harder to sell houses. We ended up putting petitions in every real estate office in the valley. The people in each neighborhood could go to their local real estate office and pick up petitions and, boom, they'd be disbursed. People went door-to-door through their neighborhoods, they took them to their churches, their club meetings. In Sherman Oaks, we set up tables in malls and in front of busy stores, anyplace where there was heavy foot traffic. It became a very easy, efficient system. Eventually the petition spread throughout the entire state.

I didn't really plan on any of this. It was one of those things that just evolved, and once it got rolling, it was like spontaneous combustion. One day, I was content to be at home, taking care of my second child, and the next thing I knew I was part of a tax revolt — a tax revolt that went on for more than a year. The beautiful thing about Proposition 13 was that it was a totally grassroots movement. It didn't begin with any people in politics who were looking for votes or looking to get their names in the paper. It started with people who stood up to the government and said, "You're not going to get away with

this." It was retired senior citizens, mothers with their children in tow, who would come up and grab a handful of petitions and go out and give them to their neighbors.

It was just simple, down-to-earth, everyday people who had had enough. It was even more grassroots than the Boston Tea Party. I had learned that even that first great tax revolt had been set up by the Founding Fathers; they had planned the entire action.

I had never been involved in politics before and I didn't know how the system worked, but one thing I found very interesting was the way that the politicians reacted to us. The majority of them were very favorable to what we were doing. They saw that we were a loud voice, and they wanted to be on the side of that voice. It seemed that a lot of them were afraid to come out against us. One government official who I talked to said, "You know, if you get this Proposition 13 through you're going to be hurting a lot of poor people. You're going to be taking food right out of their children's mouths." I just looked at him and thought to myself, "That's just not true." I, like many other people, believe we do have a responsibility to the poor, but the government cannot force us, as a people, to take care of them. It's the charities that are supposed to take care of the poor, not the government.

We easily got the 350,000 signatures needed to get Proposition 13 on the June ballot, and when election day finally came, I just couldn't wait to vote. I just knew it was going to pass. It was one of those magical days. When I got on the Ventura Freeway to drive downtown, these two police cars just happened to pull in front of me, and it was like I had a police escort all the way to the voting booth. After voting, a friend and I hit a couple parties that were being thrown in honor of the day, but we eventually settled at this little restaurant in Van Nuys where a lot of the original grassroots people were gathering. There was a bigger, fancier party downtown at the Biltmore where Howard Jarvis and a lot of the more political people were celebrating, but we decided to stay in Van Nuys to watch the results. All of a sudden the news came through that we had won. Everybody started jumping up and down, and hugging and grabbing each other. And before long we were in a big circle doing the Hava Nagilah. It was spontaneous, wonderful joy. There I was with all of these other people who had worked so hard. We were just common people — nobody famous or rich — just a group of dedicated citizens who banded together to make something happen.

detailed photographs showing hundreds of dead bodies lying across a flat plane and next to them an enormous vat of purple liquid — cyanide-laced Flavour-Aid (a Kool-Aid competitor) — from which the cult followers had ladled their own deaths. No, this was no ordinary story of sacred rapture gone wrong; this was a tale for the ages.

The cult had been built around an eccentric minister named James Jones, the son of an Indiana railroadman who rarely worked after a gassing in World War I left him impaired and who was rumored to have joined up with the Klan in the twenties. The younger Jones's religious history was eclectic. As a teenager, following the lead of a neighbor, he had attended the services of the Church of the Nazarene; at matriculation from Butler University in Indianapolis, however, he declared himself a member of the Unity Church. There was a brief association with the Methodists, and when he finally founded his own church in 1956, he called it the Community Unity Church. Jones's church, which directed its ministry at the poor, eventually raised enough money to buy an old synagogue in a black neighborhood, and, in a demonstration of their commitment to aiding other races, Jones and his wife, who were both white, adopted several black and Korean children.

"We'll all fall tonight, but he'll raise us tomorrow."

Jonestown cult member, moments before committing suicide

Bodies lie by a vat containing a drink laced with potassium cyanide at the Jonestown commune in Guyana, November 1978. "Hurry, my children. Hurry," implored cult leader Jim Jones as his followers drank the deadly poison. "Lay down your life with dignity."

In 1961, possessed by visions of a nuclear holocaust, Jones abandoned the congregation to move his family to Brazil (he had read in a magazine that his new home would be one of the best places to avoid nuclear war). But then, a little homesick, they returned to the States, where he was ordained by the Disciples of Christ (a denomination with 1.3 million parishioners) and moved his church, now called the Peoples Temple, to northern California, where it met with enormous success. Drawing parishioners again from the black community, Jones expanded the church's reach to include the services of an infirmary, a food kitchen, and programs of liberal political activism. He also initiated a regular schedule of pilgrimages to sites that by 1974 included the 27,000-acre plantation Jones had bought in the jungles of Guyana, South America.

By now, however, Jones's "services" had become the bizarre rantings of a madman, scenes where he would profess to "heal" parishioners by withdrawing "cancers" from their bodies (and display bloodied chicken gizzards, which he claimed to be the diseased cells he had extracted). No longer a minister of Christ, he now declared that he was God himself, and, so licensed, ordered harsh physical discipline upon his followers, insisting, too, that they empty their bank accounts into church coffers. But the merely bizarre became a scene of tragedy when California Congressman Leo Ryan, concerned over reports of the death of a constituent who tried to leave the cult, determined that he should look into the activities of Jones, and visited Guyana.

Although fearing that it was the first step toward an American invasion of his compound, Jones reluctantly let Ryan and a handful of reporters examine Jonestown (140 miles northwest of Georgetown, the Guyana capital) and even

speak to those living there. But after becoming suspicious of the congressman's questions and, in particular, his insistence that he take home with him several Jonestown residents who asked to return to the States, Jones ordered Peoples Temple guards to kill Ryan and his entourage. The original plan was that an agent for Jones would request to leave with Ryan; then, once the congressman's plane was in the air, he would kill the pilot, forcing the plane to crash. But the plans got bungled and Jones's gunmen opened fire on Ryan and his entourage on the tarmac of the airport. While newsmen watched in horror, Ryan and four others were shot dead at point-blank range.

Now Jones was certain that an invasion would follow the news of Ryan's death, and, hastily organizing a town meeting, he ordered his group to employ the plan for a "White Night," the code for the sect's much-rehearsed suicide plan. "We must die with dignity," he told them. The mothers were directed to bring the youngest children forward first, and syringes were used to squirt the poison into their throats. Then, while the babies went into convulsions, the adults and older children took paper cups of the Flavour-Aid and lay down in neat rows to await their deaths. Half of the 913 who would die at Jonestown had already expired when Jones himself, sitting on a throne amid them, put a gun to his own head and pulled the trigger.

No piece of theater, no overwrought novel, no tabloid tale of horror, no stirring vision issued from a pulpit, could have better summed up the profound tension of the seventies than the unpredictable drama that enveloped a Middle East nation in 1979 and, for Americans, closed out the decade with a new and ferocious attack upon their pride and sense of well-being. The charge was issued from a most unlikely source, an ample-bearded, humorless Muslim cleric — born in 1900, he was as old as the century itself — who had spent fifteen years in exile from his native Iran, the last of them in Neauphlé-le-Château, outside Paris, preaching the seventh-century lessons of the *Shari'a* (Islamic law) and campaigning for the ouster of the most Western of the region's Muslim rulers, Iran's shah.

> **"All Western governments are just thieves. Nothing but evil comes from them."**
>
> *Ayatollah Khomeini*

In early 1979, the Ayatollah Ruhollah Khomeini succeeded at his life's goal, the shah's Pahlavi dynasty crumbling under the weight of an Islamic revolution that installed Khomeini himself as the *de facto* head of a modern theocracy. As he did, the enthusiasm that his insurrection released fanned flames of anti-Western fanaticism throughout the Muslim world.

After centuries in which they were guided by conservative mullahs little removed from the Middle Ages, Iranians had been wrenched into the twentieth century by what the shah described as a "white" (or bloodless) revolution. The son of an army officer who had seized control of Iran in 1921, he had come to power during the Second World War, was deposed in the late forties, then reinstalled by a CIA-led coup in 1953 and gradually, over the years since then, pressed dramatic reforms on his people. The shah divested the clergy of their vast landholdings, declared radical new rights for women (including the right to vote and to attend universities), dramatically increased urbanization and industrialization and in the process struck a dependent relationship with Western

Millions of ecstatic Shiite Muslims took to the streets to celebrate the return from exile of the Ayatollah Khomeini in February 1979. The seventy-six-year-old religious leader promised to create the nation's first "government of God."

DEATH TO AMERICA IS A BEAUTIFUL THOUGHT

GIVE US THE SHAH

Banners held by Iranian students as they seized the American Embassy in Teheran, 1979

Outraged and frustrated by the events in Teheran, many Americans turned their anger toward the forty thousand Iranian students living in the United States, calling for their deportation at rallies such as this one in Washington, D.C.

democracies, which coveted his country's oil and saw Iran as a strategic bulwark against the advance of the Soviet Union, with which it shared a border.

As it became the West's favorite Muslim nation, Iran made stunning advancements, the once-backward desert state now sporting steel mills and nuclear power plants and an outsize army stocked with American artillery. Yet the shah was always more popular outside of Iran than he was with his own people, most of whom did not want to abandon their rich heritage to join the developed world with all its problems. They found inspiration in the sermons of Muslim leaders who denounced the material pleasures of the West and the colonial pressures brought to bear on their nation by American industry and government. "What does this Westernize-or-bust program give us?" asked an Iranian newspaper editor at the height of his country's tension. "Western banks, Western guns, Western secret police, Western buildings. They are supposed to solve our problems, but do they? I don't think so." Increasingly, the only way the shah could maintain control over his people was through harsh repression and brutality (tactics that only increased resentment toward him), and by 1979, not even that could resist the popular mood.

For Americans, the collapse of the shah's regime was yet another lesson in hubris. Once again, a Third World nation had examined the American system and rejected it, and, unlike Vietnam, here there was no Communist China or Soviet Union upon which to pin the blame. Even more important, the event seemed to embody all of the more philosophical challenges that confronted Americans throughout the decade: the crisis of authority persisted. Jimmy Carter had only recently achieved a stunning success by bringing together the leaders of Israel and Egypt at the Camp David summit. Now, as he and Khomeini confronted each other in mutual incomprehension, Carter's appeared to be just another in a succession of failed presidencies. There was the continuing struggle over the economy, for with Iran's oil fields in the grip of a hostile power, prices rapidly rose, forcing interest rates to record levels and impressing upon people just how dependent the American system had become. And finally, there was the abrupt affront to progress itself, for if any message was to be gleaned from the revolution in Iran and the many reverberations it set off elsewhere, it was that industrial capitalism, indeed liberal democracy itself, had become suspect to a significant part of the emerging world's population, even to the point where the certainties of the seventh century — divined long before the Enlightenment, even before the Renaissance — seemed preferable. In the penetrating stare of Iran's Khomeini could be read the harsh denunciation of American life as a culture absent of moral fiber, a civilization grown fat and weak.

Early on Sunday, November 4, 1979, while most of America was fast asleep, a mob of 450 demonstrators — students rabid with enthusiasm for Khomeini and his revolution — cut the chains that barred the iron gates of the American Embassy in Teheran and surged across its twenty-seven-acre compound. The students pushed past the marine guards, took sixty-six members of the U.S. Embassy staff as hostages, and demanded the return to Iran of the shah, who was at that moment undergoing treatment for cancer at a New York City hospital. They intended to try their former leader for the excesses of his rule. But with Khomeini pronouncing the American Embassy as "a nest of spies" and a

One hostage's story: "I wanted to be a good American, but I also wanted to survive"

In the months before the shah left Iran you could see a tremendous deterioration of the government's power. The Iranian people were up in arms. Every night I would hear shouting on the rooftops, *"Allah hu Akbar. Marg bar shah!"* "God is great. Down with the shah." I loved to go outside to see what was going on. There were troops on the streets everywhere, but the Iranian people would walk up to them and put flowers in their rifles. I would walk around and then report what was going on back to the United States Embassy. Sometimes, of course, I'd get rifle butts stuck in my back and people would tell me to move on. But I could feel it, sense it, smell it — the regime was falling. The day the shah finally left was one of the most potent and vivid days imaginable. I never thought it would happen, not in my lifetime. It's difficult to fully understand just how much the Iranian people hated him. And then when Khomeini returned, ecstatic crowds carried him through the streets of Teheran. It was as if the Messiah had landed. The months following Khomeini's return were the most jubilant in contemporary Iranian history.

Of course things drastically changed for those of us in the United States Embassy. To me, November 4, 1979, seemed like just an ordinary gray, rainy Sunday in Teheran. But to the Iranians it was the one-year anniversary of an uprising at Teheran University in which some students were shot. If we had been a little bit more perceptive about things, we might have been ready for what was going on. I was at work at ten o'clock that morning. All of a sudden I heard marching sounds coming from the main avenue in Teheran. I looked out my window and saw Iranian students climbing the gates and jumping over the walls of the embassy. They had photographs of Khomeini on their chest and they were yelling *"Marg bar Amrika!"* "Death to America!" The students banged on my door, and then came storming in with clubs and some small arms. My main instinct was preservation; preservation for everybody who was with me.

We were taken to a library in the embassy, where the hostage takers interrogated me and my Iranian coworkers. They eventually let all the Iranians go; they had enough problems trying to round up the rest of the Americans in the chancery. I had become good friends with the Iranians in my office, and I cried because I was happy that they were being let go. They cried because they were sure that I was going to be executed. I was tied up and blindfolded and then led out of the library and into the courtyard, raindrops hitting me on the head, a bleak day now turning even bleaker. That's when I started to think about my family, and I began to wonder, "Will I live through the rest of the night?"

My captors dragged me into the cook's quarters,

Below: Barry Rosen being examined before his release from captivity in Iran. Left: Rosen (with beard, waving) and the other former hostages, with their families, at Andrews Air Force Base, Washington, D.C., 1981.

—*Barry Rosen, born in 1944 in Brooklyn, New York, first went to Iran as a member of the Peace Corps in 1967. After getting a graduate degree in Central Asian studies, he went to work for the Voice of America for Central Asian broadcasts in Washington, D.C., before being hired as a press attaché at the U.S. Embassy in Teheran. He is currently the executive director of public affairs for Teachers College at Columbia University and is the author of* Destined Hour: Iran Since the Revolution.

where they took off my shoes and started searching them, trying to tear the heels apart. They thought that I had some secret message machine in the heels of my shoes. They were convinced that we were all CIA agents and would do anything to escape. That's why they tied us up day in and day out.

One of the most wrenching moments in my captivity was when the students tried to get me to sign a letter indicating my crimes against Iran. This young man held an automatic weapon to my head, and started to count down from ten to one. It was then that I realized that I would do anything to survive. I wanted to be a good American, and I didn't want to sign something that would state that I was not, but I knew that the best thing to do to survive was to sign whatever needed to be signed; so I did. What made it worse was that I felt so strongly about the Iranian people, in a positive way. I really cared about the culture.

The worst pain of it all was brought on by the length of captivity. Not the boredom, but the fear that grows inside of you over a long period of time. The fear of death. A fear that creeps into the subconscious. That, and just not being able to go outside, to see a bird fly, or to take a walk. The physical cruelty, getting beaten up or being pushed around or being blindfolded, was less of a

potent force than the lack of freedom.

One morning, some other hostages and I were dragged out of the embassy into a van. We were then dispersed to different sites throughout the country. I had no idea why they did this until one day I found an Iranian newspaper that one of the guards had left in the bathroom. It said that Americans had been killed in a rescue attempt. I translated it to my cellmates and we all just sat there glassy-eyed. We couldn't even speak. We knew that other people had died trying to save us, and we felt incredibly guilty about it.

Inertia is what kept me going. There was no other alternative but to live. I spent several months sharing a room with a lieutenant colonel named Dave Roeder. He was a man who knew how to survive. He taught me to get up and exercise and to meet each day with purpose. We learned to make small things beautiful. For example, for whatever weird reason, the Iranians gave me the classifieds from the *Washington Post* boat section. Not great reading, but something. Dave actually knew something about boats, so he would describe the different types and we would both lie down on the floor, and we would take a trip on the Chesapeake Bay. Just escaping in our imaginations like that made life worthwhile.

One morning in January, a guard came in and said, "Pack your bags. You're leaving." Just like that. Once again, we were bound and blindfolded and then marched to a bus. I had no idea if indeed we were going to be released, or if we were just being moved to another location again, or if they were just playing a cruel joke on us. We traveled on the bus for what seemed like an interminable amount of time. When it finally stopped, they ripped off my blindfold and pushed me out of the bus. I stumbled past this long line of Iranian guards who spat on me. I was just soaking wet from spit. But I saw this light and an arm waving toward me. It turned out to be the entrance of an Air Algiers plane, so I ran toward it. Even after the plane took off, everyone was worried that the Iranian air force might shoot us down or something. It seemed so unreal. It was as if we were in another world altogether — very blurred, but once we realized we were free, also very beautiful.

Back in the United States we were greeted as heroes. We were so isolated that we didn't realize that we had become the center of the American news; that we had been their purpose for the past 444 days. In some ways, I think the people were celebrating what they believed was American power. They were trying to make a bad situation into something great. I remember seeing this sign that said, "America 52 — Iran 0." But I honestly think that both countries lost. There was a lot of hate on both sides that didn't need to happen. I don't believe we were winners. I believe it was a period of great sadness.

"center of intrigue" looking to stir up a counterrevolution against him, the United States was just as vital a target of the students' wrath. "Death to America," the invaders shouted as they burned American flags and paraded blindfolded hostages before Western television cameras. And with that began the Iranian people's slow and cruel 444-day declaration of vengeance against the nation they liked to call "the Great Satan."

The seizing of the American Embassy in Teheran was a crisis of unusual dimension, for it placed the United States in a diplomatic confrontation with a foe disinterested in diplomacy. Indeed, the act of compromise itself was antithetical to Iran's theocratic rule, for Khomeini saw himself not as a politician, but as a messenger from God, and who can broker a deal with the Almighty? For fourteen and a half months, while the hostage dilemma became a daily staple of the evening news, the American people were delivered to a dungeon of despair. Amid threats to try the hostages as spies before kangaroo courts and — after the expected guilty verdicts — sentence them to death, the students offered up flagrant acts of insult, posing for photographers while carrying out garbage in an American flag and daring the United States to intervene. "Why should we be afraid?" asked a defiant Khomeini. "We consider martyrdom a great honor."

The students — and Khomeini — displayed an inspired level of intransigence. When Carter pushed the United Nations to condemn Iran, Khomeini shrugged that his struggle was not just against the United States but against all "infidels." American journalists were expelled for unfriendly reporting. And Iran's foreign minister, Sadegh Ghotbzadeh, announced that his country was prepared to keep the hostages "more or less forever." In April 1980, the United States did intervene, haplessly, the attempt to rescue the hostages called off in midraid, leaving aircraft wreckage and the bodies of eight U.S. servicemen behind, where, picked over with knives by Iranian authorities, they became objects of derision. Not even the death of the nearly forgotten shah on July 27 affected the standoff, the Cairo funeral of the disgraced Iranian leader attended by just one notable American, the disgraced American leader Richard Nixon.

In yellow ribbons tied on trees across the nation (a simple symbol of remembrance taken from a pop song) Americans invested their last shred of optimism, the hope that the ordeal would still — somehow — end peacefully and with its resolution would return not only the hostages but the sense of pride that had been so long absent from their lives. There was no obvious course of action, neither with the crisis in Iran nor with the many other dilemmas facing the nation, but symbols helped. Indeed, as America underwent the 1980 presidential campaign, the need to hear stirring phrases of national purpose was so great, the desire to shed the politics of gloom so powerful, the will to believe again in something — anything — so present, the country rejected the more introspective Carter and handed the presidency instead to a sixty-nine-year-old former actor who, brimming with can-do confidence and a dewy-eyed nostalgia, vowed to return America to her Golden Age.

It was a tall promise, but the inaugural that installed Ronald Reagan as

> *"At about 200 pulls, I thought I'd never make it. Then at about 300 pulls, I got my second wind and kept going all the way."*
>
> Barbara Deffley, wife of a Holmer, Illinois, Methodist minister who, at the news of the hostage release, rang her church bell 444 times, once for each day of captivity

America's fortieth president in 1981 was perhaps the most emotional since Kennedy's, and not only because Reagan, his voice thick with portent, asked Americans to believe once again in their capacity for great deeds but also because, as he spoke, the weary hostages were being dragged into the night and placed aboard a white bus with drawn curtains. They were driven to Teheran's blacked-out Meharabad Airport, where, forced to disembark, they were grabbed roughly and shoved through a gauntlet of taunting militants. At the end of the gauntlet, in the moonlit runways, sat a Boeing 727, and one by one, the haggard and dazed pawns of America's long-running ordeal were pushed aboard. Their send-off was certainly not a friendly one, but it was a send-off nonetheless. In one stunning gesture, the runway lights came on and the plane taxied ahead before rising in a graceful arc and penetrating the starry skies over Teheran. The long national nightmare was over.

With the hostages finally back on home soil, Americans, such as these at a welcome rally at Chicago's Daley Center, January 1981, looked forward to what the newly inaugurated president, Ronald Reagan, promised would be "an era of national renewal."

11

New Morning
1981–1989

New Morning 1981–1989

Previous spread: The collapse of communism was the most significant story of the eighties by far. While Mikhail Gorbachev's reforms in the Soviet Union led the way, the drama was perhaps even more intense throughout Eastern Europe, where brutal tyrannies fell under the weight of the freshly energized public mood. Here, Czech revelers tear through the streets of Prague, late 1989, in anticipation of their long-awaited freedom.

America's own transformation began early in the decade, with the election of the most conservative chief executive since the 1920s. Ronald Reagan unified the Right, wrote journalist Sidney Blumenthal, by animating its theories with "images of idyllic small town life, enterprising entrepreneurs whose success derived from moral character, and failure induced only by federal bureaucrats." A campaign worker cheers her hero, opposite, at the 1984 Republican National Convention.

Maya Ying Lin was an undergraduate student in architecture at Yale University in 1980 when she was directed to participate in an unusual classroom exercise: with the newly formed Vietnam Veterans Memorial Fund soliciting designs for a monument to honor the American troops who had served there, Lin and each of her fellow students were assigned by their teacher to come up with their own plans for a memorial and, if so inclined, submit them to the competition.

To the memorial's organizers, most of them veterans, Vietnam remained all too real, an unsettling memory they now wished desperately to transform with the powers of ritual; but to Lin, and the others in her class, it was simply "history." The child of Chinese immigrants who had fled the communist takeover of China in 1949, Lin was born and raised in Ohio (her own mother described her as "a modern American"), and yet at just twenty-one years of age, she was too young to have anything but the most superficial awareness of the war's divisive effect upon American society (she had been eight during the Tet offensive; ten when the students were killed at Kent State), too young even to understand just how controversial a monument to America's Vietnam experience could be. And on this she had, notably, received little help. Throughout the seventies, the soldiers returning from Vietnam had been greeted coldly by a nation that felt humiliated by the events in Southeast Asia, and when plans to develop a Vietnam Veterans Memorial in the nation's Capital were initiated by a private group in 1979, the idea was greeted inhospitably. Vietnam, it seemed, was a war most people would sooner forget.

Still, since beginning her studies in professor Andrus Burr's class on funerary architecture, Lin had thought long and hard about the nature of memorial environments. In her travels to Europe, she had noticed that the older war memorials, those of previous centuries, tended to reflect the now archaic vision of battle as noble enterprise, while those that remembered the losses on the western front, for instance, were decidedly more muted. In Thiepval, France, Lin was

"Hush, Timmy, this is like a church . . ."

Father speaking to his young child
at the Vietnam Veterans Memorial, 1985

moved by a walk through the memorial honoring the soldiers who died at the battle of the Somme, a great arch framing two tunnels in which the names of 73,000 were etched. And closer to home, in a wall carrying the names of the Yale students who perished in American wars, Lin had become aware of the way that a memorial space becomes integrated into the life of a community. The names at Yale, she observed, were not high up, heaven-bound in the aerie of a grand Gothic dome, but down below where they could be read by the eye, touched by the finger.

Lin's proposed design for the Vietnam memorial incorporated this experience. It was to be a simple monument composed of two symmetrical, black triangular walls positioned at a 125-degree angle to each other and joined by a common hinge at their highest point. The whole monument was to be sunk into the sod near the reflecting pool on the Mall so that one side of it would remain completely out of sight, abutting the dry earth. Then, as if walking into a grave, visitors would move downward into the memorial space and, along the way, meet a list of the dead etched into the rock in chronological order — from Dale Buis, an adviser killed in 1959 (ironically, the year of Maya Lin's birth) to Richard Vandegeer, one of the last Americans to perish, just days before the war's end in May 1975.

To her surprise, Lin's design, officially number 1,026 of the 1,421 entries, was the unanimous choice of the organizer's expert panel (she later admitted that her professor had awarded her only a B in the course). Yet, shortly after the plan was unveiled, opposition to it started to build. For if this was the place that would tell future generations what had happened in Vietnam, then just what *had* happened? A dishonorable act of American imperialism, carried out in the form of massive atrocities against a nation of innocent peasants? Or an earnest and honorable effort to save a people from the tyranny of communism, tragically undermined by a traitorous antiwar movement at home? "History can be re-evaluated," wrote former marine officer James Webb, who opposed Lin's design. "But a piece of art remains as a testimony to a particular moment in history and we are under a solemn obligation to get that moment down as correctly as possible."

Some charged that Lin's choice of the color black suggested shame, to which proponents countered that the much-revered Iwo Jima memorial was the same color, and besides, as one African-American veteran declared, when had the nation returned to thinking that "black" denoted something disgraceful? Others, objecting to the abstract quality of the design, derided it as a "degrading ditch." They saw the idiom in which Lin worked, and the modernist ideology from which it sprang, as a paean to leftist thinking ("a wailing wall for liberals") and demanded that a work of figurative realism, with its attendant conservative symbolism, be built instead. There were even those who felt suspicious of Lin herself for her Asian heritage, racistly suggesting that the "yellow enemy" was still among us. "Too bad it wasn't a simple war," sighed veteran Jan Scruggs, who had originated the idea for a memorial. "Then we could have put up a heroic statue of a couple of marines and leave it at that."

In fact, when the argument finally found its compromise, it was to erect the memorial as planned, then later add a flag and a traditional sculpture of three foot soldiers nearby. But that was before November 1982, when the sleek granite structure was finally dedicated, leaving a nation in awe. No one, maybe not even

The dedication of the Vietnam Veterans Memorial in 1982 marked a turning point for the men who had served in Vietnam. "[We] used to be like cops," offered one former pilot. "No one was comfortable around us. People are now more willing to listen."

Maya Lin, had quite understood the power of her design. For all at once, in the melding of elemental geometry with the chemistry of a well-polished stone, in the joining of the nation's collective history with the intimacy of a personal encounter, the Vietnam Veterans Memorial transformed a plot of land into a national shrine, as powerful as a cathedral, absorbing people from all political denominations and preaching a simple, unifying liturgy: the names.

From its first day onward, the "wall," as it was soon known, became the most popular tourist attraction in Washington, more popular even than the Washington and Lincoln memorials, to which its two narrow arms pointed, courageously joining this most difficult piece of American history with the memory of the nation's most revered leaders. It turned out that the placement of the memorial belowground only emphasized its sacredness: one entered it as if in a solemn procession, leaving the temporal world behind, falling silent in respect. The "list," too, had a mesmerizing effect upon the visitor: many, standing before the wall, recited its names out loud, as if in a trance; some snapped photographs, others took rubbings. Mothers stood arm in arm with their dead sons' former comrades, wives with other wives in tears. And all, it seemed, reached out to touch, to connect with the memorial's grave majesty, if only to leave the humidity of a fingerprint. They had lost friends and husbands and children and fathers to a war that had posed more questions than it answered, and they had been left, until now, with no place to contemplate the episode's one undeniable truth: in Vietnam, people, *real* people, had died.

History is a photograph, a picture framed this way by one lensman, that way by another. And like a print, it changes color with the years. By the time

> "The only reason people want to be masters of the future is to change the past."
>
> *Czech novelist Milan Kundera*

Americans entered the 1980s, still worn and disheartened by the events of the previous decade, the picture of bright promise that had served as the national identity through much of the postwar period, surviving (some would say even encouraging) the turbulent sixties and seventies, the one that had helped them not only to understand their present and future but to give meaning to their past as well, had become so faded and frayed around the edges that now, quite suddenly, the nation was ready to do something radical: shake off the dust, shift the frame to the right, and declare a new, more conservative orthodoxy.

In fact, it would be hard to imagine a time more devoted to historical revisionism than this decade, when symbols of the Left were co-opted by the Right and, in time, those of the Right embraced, in near concession, by the Left; when glories of the past were derided as failures and past failures ennobled with the shine of courage; when reinterpretation, it seemed, was in style across the world; and when in America, in particular, feelings of nostalgia for less complicated times ran so high it felt occasionally as if the society had been transplanted to the grounds of an elaborate theme park where a tidied-up, even cinematic, version of the past could be lived out in comfort. One could sense, for instance, in the renewed feelings of prosperity and unchecked ambition, the mulch of fifties suburban grass underfoot ("meaningless years, yes, but were we any better off in the meaning*ful* sixties and seventies?"); hear the rush of the Roaring Twenties bull market calling forth from the buzz on the Wall Street trading floors ("and what's really wrong with making money?"); even, in the wealth of images emerging from the new occupant of the White House, himself a man of the movies, detect something of the air of a revered Roosevelt — either one of them. Was that Teddy, in cocked Stetson, we saw in the chief executive astride a horse, brandishing a big stick toward Latin America? Or was it Franklin we heard in the mellifluous sounds so suited to mass communication, the tenor of confidence, the vocabulary of certitude?

The decade had a neat balance between issues of domestic and international concern; between two dynamic political figures of nearly equal historical weight, in Ronald Reagan and Soviet reformer Mikhail Gorbachev; and between a period witnessing the most seriously threatening Cold War competition since the early sixties and, with the dissolution of the Soviet empire, the collapse of the Cold War itself. The hinge fell somewhere around 1985, when Gorbachev came to power and the "revolution" brought to pass by Reagan, who had been re-elected the year before by a landslide, could be said to have finished much of its work. But ultimately, the victorious forces emerging from either half of the eighties (and from either side of the world) shared much the same philosophical foundation, and, at least for the twentieth century, it was an extreme one: statism (whether the vicious kind represented by Stalin or the more benign form associated with the legacy of FDR) was now in retreat, the individual spirit ascendant; communism was spent, capitalism refreshed; the forces of totalitarianism defeated, those of democracy on the rise. It seemed that the American suspicion of authority, grown now to become a wholesale cynicism toward government itself, had coincided with a worldwide frustration with the state as the agent of a positive social change, a disappointment so deep it had even penetrated the granite facade of Soviet bureaucracy itself. And with that, the era of the government solution — be it the Great Society or the Five-Year Plan — was finished.

When the Polish government moved to squash Solidarity, the trade union had already assembled 10 million members — more than four times the rolls of the Polish Communist Party — and the charismatic yet rough-hewn Lech Walesa, a simple electrician with uncanny political instincts, was an international hero. Above, Walesa addresses striking workers in 1980.

Much of the old establishment remained hostile to the changes roaring forth: the new era was not, after all, theirs. Whether in Poland, where the Solidarity trade union (which had represented the first significant crack in the hegemony of the Soviet empire) was shut down for a time in 1981 by a period of martial law encouraged by Moscow, or in the Soviet Union itself, hard-liners worked desperately to protect the system that had been their benefactor. And particularly in the early eighties, American liberals, clinging to the hope that this moment, too, would pass, derided the new atmosphere in their own homeland as superficial, greedy, materialist; its Cold War threats as barbaric; its economics as indifferent, even primitive.

With time, in America, this view appeared to be redeemed by a different set of "theme park" images: the growing homeless population reminding many of the Hoovervilles that followed on the collapse of the Republican prosperity of the twenties; the 1986 Iran-contra scandal recalling the embarrassment of Watergate, even as it represented in the end an even more dangerous abuse of power than had been demonstrated in the Nixon years; and the 1987 stock market crash, the first since 1929, looking like the comeuppance so many wished upon the wildly successful investment bankers, yuppies (as in "young urban professionals") so young they had come to believe that the stock market only went in one direction, up.

Finally, with the deepening of the chasm separating America's rich and poor, the arrival of AIDS and a drug epidemic in the inner cities, the soaring deficits encouraged by Ronald Reagan's ambitious defense spending, and the insider trading scandals that brought down two of Wall Street's most outrageous billionaires, it was hard not to feel that the nation was just pretending to be in

Martial law in Poland: **"I awoke to a voice saying, 'Civil rule is suspended. The military has taken over.'"**

—Maciej Wierzynski, born in 1937, fled to the United States in 1984 and enrolled in a journalism program at Penn State. In 1989, he returned to Warsaw to cover the liberalization of Eastern Europe and stayed on until 1991, when he returned to the United States and became a reporter for the Eastern European service of the Voice of America in Washington, D.C.

Wierzynski in Warsaw with his taxi.

I grew up believing that Poland was really a Western country at heart, especially in the spiritual and intellectual sense. The time before the German invasion in 1939 was later looked upon as a sort of lost paradise, because at that time Poland was an independent country. And the experience of war, with the memory of the invasions of Poland from both the East and the West, was always fresh in my memory. When I graduated from high school in 1954, I chose to study geology at university, because the liberal arts were so infected by Marxist and Leninist ideology. But in the late fifties and early sixties, when Khrushchev gave the Eastern bloc a taste of freedom, I decided to switch to journalism. Unfortunately, I learned quickly that the whole notion that the press was freer under Khrushchev was simply a fantasy.

In early 1980, the Polish government was running into financial difficulty and decided to raise the prices of basic foodstuffs. This sent a wave of protest throughout Poland. At that time, I was covering the summer Olympic Games in Moscow for Polish television. Of course, none of these protests were reported in the Polish press. I learned about them from reading Western newspapers available to us reporters in Moscow. But as word got out, journalists descended on the mining sites and shipyards of Gdansk, where the labor unions, led by Lech Walesa's Solidarity movement, had united to strike against the price increases. Poland was in turmoil. As word of their success spread, other groups began to demand rights as well.

Solidarity had asked for access to television, and after some consideration, the government agreed to discuss several issues with the leaders of the Solidarity movement in an open forum on television. I was to be the moderator of these discussions. State television would not be so extravagant as to let the debates air live, and so it was my job to edit them down to a version acceptable to all sides. This experience brought me much closer to the high-rank Solidarity people. They were very suspicious of a guy like me, and in some respects I did feel as if I had to compromise my beliefs to appear neutral, but in reality I was with Solidarity all the way.

The very fact that the government had accepted the existence of Solidarity was so unusual it was like a miracle. If you thought about it logically, you knew that the government could not tolerate what was happening in Poland for very long. But we weren't thinking logically at that time. I remember talking with an American correspondent from *Time*, in early fall 1981. "You know it's impossible," he said. "This liberalization will not last longer than another three to five weeks." I said, "No, you are quite wrong."

On the evening of December 12, 1981, I was working the night shift at the TV station. At about midnight, we received a call from the Polish television bureau telling us to stop the broadcast of the movie we were showing. I was wondering, "What's going on? Whose order is this?" I went back to my office and tried to call my wife, but the line was dead. At first, I thought this was just routine. The authorities were constantly disconnecting things — especially for people who were involved in politics in one way or another — just to make life a little miserable. But when I talked to my colleagues, I discovered their phones were also disconnected. We all went down to the lobby of the building to leave together, and there we were confronted by a group of fifteen military people. We were sent into a room near the entrance and told to wait until the building had been completely searched. A half an hour later, we were allowed to leave, one by one. My wife was in the last month of her pregnancy, and I wanted to buy some gas on my way home in case of an emergency. I drove from one gas station to another, and they were all closed down. I noticed some tanks and military vehicles in the street. I was starting to get a little bit scared. Oddly enough, the prevailing feeling for me was still that this was just a demonstration of force in order to intimidate people. I didn't know it was the first step to the imposition of martial law.

The next morning I awoke to the voice of [Prime Minister and Communist Party chief] General Wojciech Jaruzelski on the radio declaring, "Civil government is suspended, and now the military has taken over." I turned on the TV to get more news, and they were rerunning the general's speech. An army man in a military uniform read several very tough military rules. We were told to stay inside between the hours of 11:00 P.M. and 5:00 A.M., and communications were entirely cut off. I got into my car and drove back to the television station to get more information. All along the route, the streets were eerily empty. People were afraid to leave their homes. When I pulled up in front of my building, it was surrounded by troops blocking the entrance. They informed us we were all on "forced leave."

A few weeks after the crackdown, journalists were called to the television station for "special talks." It was a sort of political investigation. I was brought into a room where a team of four military and security police lined up to interrogate me. They took out a file on me and began asking about my political activities over the past two years. I felt my career as a journalist was over. I accepted that with ambiguous feelings, with sadness and some relief as well, because the ambiguity of my own personal situation had ended. I felt I had to compromise myself somewhat with the editing of some of the debates. I just couldn't be a journalist again. I became a cabdriver. As a driver I knew I would have access to gasoline and that this would be the best way to help Polish people during the crackdown. The government had imposed even stricter rationing of absolutely everything and raised prices drastically, distributing coupons for food and rationing gasoline to keep people under control. There were military checkpoints on the outskirts of most cities.

I used my cab to distribute food and clothing sent to Polish churches from abroad, and I drove around distributing papers from the underground press. After spending all that time on TV during the debates, I had become sort of a local celebrity. Government officials knew what I was doing, and they would try to intimidate me. Plainclothes police, pretending to be regular passengers, would hire my cab. Then they'd start talking to me and telling me that I was too good for such a job and that I was wasting a great education being a cabdriver. They actually wanted me to come back to journalism. But I wouldn't budge.

I felt a tremendous amount of anger and hatred towards the government. How could they cut a movement short that was only intended to improve upon the lives of Polish people? The military was on the air with their official propaganda saying that they had *saved* Poland from falling into the hands of the enemies, the Solidarity movement. We all knew it was just a bunch of nonsense. Here were young soldiers, knowing nothing, coming from the same country as we were, threatening to put their own people in jail if we were out in the streets after eleven. It was very similar to what the Germans did in Poland during the war. We were in a state of occupation, but instead of being occupied by foreign armies, we were occupied by an army in Polish uniforms. Fortunately, the Solidarity movement refused to die. Little by little, their voice would be strengthened, and in 1989, Poland was freed for good!

better times, distracted by the fizz and bubble of its new wealth, tolerating the worst kinds of ethical and moral abuse, pushing aside bad news or, worse, delaying its full impact for future generations. Even Vice President George Bush, running for the White House in 1988, felt compelled to promise a "kinder, gentler nation" than the one he would inherit from his boss. Still, Iran-contra came and went, hardly denting the Reagan legacy, the stock market shook off its fall and began a new climb, the criminal traders served their time and returned to society, and the rightward tilt of the times continued. This was no blip.

By 1989, with the world positively giddy with its sense of a new beginning, the moment for ceremony was at hand, and the place to hold it all too obvious. There were many who saw in the collapse of the Soviet empire an end to what could be called the "short" twentieth century. It had begun in 1914, with the guns of August, and played itself out over the next seventy-five years as a struggle between East and West, and it would end with the sound of pickaxes landing on concrete and the sight of cheering East Berliners, the light of freedom shining from their eyes. Thousands of cameras clicked as that *other* Wall — the one that had stood as the ultimate symbol of cruelty and oppression for nearly thirty years — came down piece by piece, and at least here, no matter where one stood, the frame captured the same emotional view: the indomitable human spirit reaching out in triumph.

The scene at airports, bus stations, and car rental counters in August 1981 was near bedlam. With airline schedules running at just 70 percent of capacity, terminal lobbies had become makeshift campsites housing tens of thousands of people who waited desperately for transportation. Meanwhile, up in the control towers, nervously policing the nation's skies, were many rank amateurs — armed forces personnel with just one week's training in civilian airports. The sense of gamble surrounding the 1981 strike of the Professional Air Traffic Controllers Organization, or PATCO, was extraordinary. Unlike a walkout of automobile workers or steel miners, this one was less a threat on the economy than on the safety of the nation's innocent travelers — lonely salespeople out to meet quotas, families on the way to see Grandma, children on field trips — and should the tense standoff between the union and its employer, an emboldened new federal government, lead to a crash, there were many people who would have blood on their hands, including the president himself.

At issue was PATCO's claim that its members deserved something more than the modest raise offered them. And, arguing that the stress of the job demanded a shorter workweek and earlier retirement opportunities as well as more money, the union had reason to believe that the country would stand behind it. Since the classic struggles of the thirties, Americans, with a few exceptions, had projected a sympathy for labor, and after all, among the many workers who claimed that they suffered from job stress, who could deny that these were among the most deserving? A mistake of judgment by an assembly line worker was one thing; a mistake by someone charged with safely landing a four-hundred-ton Boeing 747, carrying 420 pas-

The public's decision to support President Reagan in his 1981 dispute with the striking air traffic controllers, seen below, was the first sign of a dismal decade for labor. Ironically, the controllers' union had been one of the few to support Reagan in the 1980 election.

sengers, was quite another.

Still, in walking off their jobs, PATCO's members were, critically, in defiance of the ban on strikes by government employees. Indeed, each worker, when hired, had taken an oath not to strike. And now, claiming extenuating circumstances, the PATCO workers were willing to go back on their promise. To the new president, fresh from victories in Congress, and a remarkable recovery from a bullet wound suffered in an attempt on his life, that was unacceptable, and he framed his position with an idea that was radical, if only in its simplicity: people who commit oaths should be held to them. In an era fond of examining life with the forgiving eye of moral relativism, a word, Ronald Reagan seemed to be declaring, is a word.

As a precedent for presidential intervention, Reagan could have cited Democrat Harry Truman's firm stance against railroad and coal workers in the late forties (frustrated by their stubbornness, Truman broke the unions by threatening to draft railroadmen into the army and force them to work), but he reached back instead to recall a leader as little remembered as he was rarely quoted. When he assumed the Oval Office the previous spring, Reagan had declared to the amusement of many that "Silent Cal" Coolidge was his favorite chief executive if only because he had been *so* silent, keeping the hand of the federal government out of the conduct of society and allowing business to prosper throughout the twenties. Reagan even had a portrait of Coolidge brought out of the attic and hung in a position of reverence in the Cabinet Room (where it replaced a painting of Truman).

Coolidge's had been the last successful presidency to precede the New Deal — but even more important, the Republican had been, in some ways, the last of the premodern chief executives, the last to adhere, unapologetically, to the old maxims of an American mythology. Coolidge believed in hard work, frugality, and piety (ideas, mocked twenties historian Frederick Lewis Allen, that had long ago been left in "some Vermont attic where *McGuffey's Reader* gathered dust"), and he had come to national attention when, as governor of Massachusetts, he had turned the National Guard loose on a strike of Boston's policemen. "There is no right to strike against the public safety," said Coolidge, "by anybody, anywhere, any time . . ."

Inspired by Coolidge, Reagan stood firm against PATCO, and the nation, surprisingly, did too. If he wanted to "jut his jaw out," as one adviser described the president's stance, then people would "jut" along with him. PATCO's leaders predicted an imminent air disaster, and even some of the president's advisers worried that he was being too harsh with the union. But soon air travel had returned to its prestrike regularity, schedules were running more smoothly, the nation's fears of a disaster had subsided, and PATCO, abandoned now of even the support of its sister unions, had gone bankrupt. Ironically, the training of new, nonunion controllers had cost more money than it would have cost to give the union workers what they had originally demanded, but, more important, what the president had sought, and won, was a symbolic victory, and the extent of that was immeasurable. For with one stroke, the balance of power in labor disputes had clearly shifted toward management (be it the government or a corporation), and this president's image as a leader courageous enough to make the tough decisions and stand by them had been firmly established.

Ronald Wilson Reagan was the most significant president in forty years. When, in 1980, he was elected to the nation's highest office, catapulted by anger over Carter-era interest rates and the humiliation of the Iranian hostage crisis, some had feared the former California governor for his simplistic and extremist rhetoric, particularly on issues of foreign policy. Still, most people assumed that an old maxim would apply — the one that said that the office had a tendency to smooth the edges, turn all men into moderates — and that Reagan's would ultimately be a presidency like that of his two recent Republican predecessors: conservative, yes, but unchallenging either to the long-established principles of containment as regards foreign policy or to the consensus on social policy that had been in place since the time of Roosevelt and the New Deal. They could not have been more wrong.

In the end, it is hard to determine whether Reagan created the times or the times created him, whether he rallied the public will or simply mirrored it, whether communism collapsed under the weight of his bellicosity or imploded coincidentally at the time of his leadership. But this much is certain: like no other president since FDR, Reagan presided over a dramatic transformation of Ameri-

In the suspicious eighties, much of Reagan's popularity derived from his portrayal of himself as a Washington "outsider," which, of course, he was. And he achieved his legislative triumphs by playing more to the public, below at an outdoor market in Philadelphia, than to Congress.

The Celluloid President

The Teflon President

The Great Communicator

The Great Manipulator

The Gipper

> *Nicknames for America's fortieth*
> *president, Ronald Reagan*

can life. To look back at the world he inherited and compare it with the world as it was when he departed Washington in 1989 is to see the difference between despair and an emerging new confidence, decline and affirmation, decay and renewal. Fans described it as a "revolution," critics as the work of a master illusionist, both of them overstatements, but it is fair to say the pendulum swing was reversed during Reagan's tenure and that many long-accepted tenets of modern American life were left on the other side of the balance.

He was, in some ways, the anti-FDR. Like the thirty-second president, Reagan was a master communicator, a font of good feeling and assertive spirit, of whom much was expected at a time of national desperation. Like Roosevelt, he worked imaginatively on both the domestic and the international stages at once. Both men pursued foreign policy in a close alliance with the leader of Great Britain (Roosevelt with Churchill; Reagan with Margaret Thatcher) in suspicion of an unpredictable Soviet Union led by another titanic historical figure (Stalin; Gorbachev), and it could be argued that, ironically, both preserved the American system for the constituency that most consistently and fervently opposed them: Roosevelt rescuing the practice of business by tempering the excesses of frontier capitalism, Reagan saving the welfare state by restraining its growth. Even the way that the two men appealed to the bedrock middle American population, whose following they largely shared, could be compared, for both men's programs were presented as givebacks to working people: Roosevelt's in the form of public assistance; Reagan's as tax cuts. Yet the philosophy that each etched so clearly into the American ethos could not have been more opposite. While Roosevelt saw a regenerative social tool in the power of the state, Reagan found a crippling and corrupting force sapping the individual will, punishing the creative spirit. Or, to put it most simply, Roosevelt wanted to save people *with* government, while Reagan wanted to save them *from* it.

The comparison to FDR is an important one, for as Reagan himself knew well, Roosevelt's name still resonated deeply with the American public, even fifty years after he was first elected. After all, it was not Roosevelt who had fed and nurtured the people's present cynicism; that was the making of those who had inherited the government from him, both Democrats and Republicans who had presided over twenty years of assassination and social strife, over an unpopular and ill-fought foreign war, over an international humiliation, and, finally, over a bafflingly unresponsive economy. Roosevelt's was the last presidency to have proposed an activist course and adhered to it to the point of success; to have promised the country a transforming episode and then delivered on that promise; and the last for whom the epitaph could be stated simply and admiringly at once: he had seen us through the Depression and marched us to victory at war.

Ironically, Reagan, too, added his voice to those who still praised the memory of FDR, though he usually followed it with a strikingly self-serving interpretation of FDR's place in history. Indeed, Reagan claimed, amazingly, that he, no Democrat, was the truest inheritor of the Roosevelt mantle, citing often that he had voted for Roosevelt, that in his youth he had been an ardent Democrat, and that in the end (in a phrase he delivered with a devilish grin) he had not deserted the Democratic Party, the Democratic Party had deserted him. Yet Reagan's larger goal in this was to connect himself with the Roosevelt majesty and to let people feel that to reject the progeny of the New Deal was not to reject its father. In fact, it was to embrace him. Reagan would selectively recite from Roosevelt's first platform, focusing on those parts that called for a reduction in the national budget and a restoration of states' rights and claim that it was not Roosevelt, but the people *around* Roosevelt, who had pushed for the expansion of the federal government, and, even more so, that it was those, like Lyndon Johnson, who, seeking to follow Roosevelt's lead, swelled the size of the state well beyond anything FDR had envisioned.

Of course, the record read otherwise — Roosevelt's 1932 platform, a throwback, represented a small part of the FDR chronicle, and while impossible to know for certain, it is likely that Roosevelt would have approved of Johnson's Great Society. Still, Reagan seemed to be convinced of what he said (like the actor that he was, he knew that sincerity was the route to believability), and at any rate, it was the stuff of brilliant politics. For by claiming that the source of the nation's present predicament lay in its having strayed from the path it once occupied with one of its greatest leaders, Reagan was inviting people to go back with him through the woods to a clearing, to a spot where the air was clean and the animals friendly, and from there start their journey all over again, on a *different* trail.

While the Vietnam Veterans Memorial was being constructed, the proposal for another memorial, one dedicated to FDR, continued to be debated. It had been approved by Congress back in 1955, and yet, appropriately for those who saw Roosevelt as the initiator of an immovable federal bureaucracy, it was still mired in discussion twenty-some years later. Not even the imminent arrival of the centennial of Roosevelt's birth in 1982 had pushed the plan along any farther. Still, when the birthday moment came, there was a lavish fete arranged by an enthusiastic president. It was Ronald Reagan who stood in black tie at a gala affair praising the leadership of FDR, even as he scuttled his legacy. And six months later, it was Reagan who signed the directive finally authorizing the construction of the FDR memorial.

Reagan's ideas may have sounded simplistic to his critics, and in the press and popular culture he was often portrayed as a kind of amiable idiot, a "child monarch," as one writer declared, whose schedule was composed under the consultation of an astrologer (it was), whose public appearances were carefully orchestrated by political "handlers" (they were), a lazy president who started work late and quit early (he did), and who baffled even his own aides by his complete indifference to details (at the 1983 economic summit, Chief of Staff James Baker was astonished to discover that Reagan had spent the night watching *The Sound of Music* on television rather than studying the briefing book Baker had carefully prepared for him). But for his many fans, simplicity was Reagan's strength. To them, Reagan's solutions correctly cut through all the baffling complexities of the seventies — the seemingly unanswerable questions that left people in a conundrum over the economy, over America's place in the world, over its relationship with the Soviet Union, and over a social contract that seemed to have failed the nation's poor and broken the population into squabbling precincts of special interests. Reagan brooked no moral ambiguity; tolerated no tantalizing intellectual diversions; sought no brokered solutions. To him, there was just right

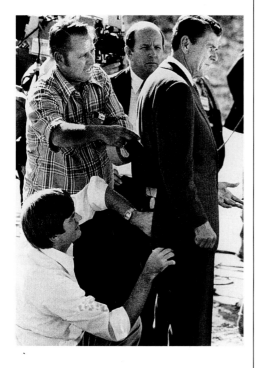

Though many people complained of a stage-managed presidency, Reagan was a leader well suited to an image-driven culture. He believed he was "not really a politician at all," wrote biographer Lou Cannon, "but simply an actor on loan from Hollywood." Here, technicians ready candidate Reagan for a speech to Missouri farmers.

"We can lecture our children about extravagance until we run out of voice and breath. Or we can cut their extravagance by simply reducing their allowance."

Ronald Reagan, justifying a reduction in the federal government, in terms which attempted to appeal to the nation's common sense

Reagan roundup: **A "bold" leader with a "simple" message**

The scene at the 1984 Republican National Convention, where Reagan was nominated for a second term.

Ronald Reagan was the epitome of America. He was an optimist and a "can-do" type of leader. He believed that today is great, but tomorrow's going to be better. In times of crisis, Reagan was able to reach out to the American people and put his arms around us and bring us all together. He was always recognized as "the great communicator." And, yes, he obviously was a very effective speaker; he was an actor. Well, Hollywood has thousands of actors and actresses, but not one of them can speak like Ronald Reagan. The reason Ronald Reagan was such an effective speaker was because he had a message that resonated with America.

I believe you make your own luck, just like you cause your own problems. And it was no accident that, literally a few minutes after Reagan became president, the hostages were freed. I think that if Carter had been reelected, those hostages would have been there throughout Carter's presidency, because Khomeini knew he had somebody that he could move around like a puppet on a string. But Ronald Reagan had sent a very clear message — which is the old New Hampshire state message — don't tread on me. The Iranians weren't 100 percent sure of Ronald Reagan and they weren't gonna take any chances.

Ronald Reagan moved boldly and decisively. The major world leaders saw that they were dealing with a man of strength and that the rules had been changed from the Nixon-Ford-Carter days. They were now dealing with an administration that was going to stand up for its beliefs and its rights. Mr. Reagan had an agenda, and he knew where he was going.

—*Richard Viguerie, born in 1933, created one of the first political direct-mail lists in the 1960s. He is the publisher of the New Media News Corporation and is the author of* The New Right *and* The Establishment vs. the People.

What was discouraging to me about President Reagan was that he was the first style-over-substance president. He had great style in front of the public up there, but he was lacking in substance. For example, he talked about church values, but he never went to church. He talked about family values, yet he had an incredibly dysfunctional family and his children didn't talk to him. He was a president who talked about the pro-life issues, but abortion rates were higher in his tenure than at any other time. He spoke out against drugs, but we saw cocaine wars in South Florida. He wanted to reduce government spending, yet the deficit skyrocketed. President Reagan introduced something very detrimental, and that is this photo-op kind of candidacy: setting up the image over the substance. It dumbed down the political debate and made everybody more interested in good sound bites and creative commercials than in real issues that affect the country.

Also Reagan's economic policies made life very difficult for a lot of people. The theory behind Reaganomics was that the rising tide would lift up all the boats. If the already well-to-do started making more money, then it would trickle down to the less well off and everyone would do better. But in reality that was not the case. I lived in Bristol, Connecticut, in the 1980s. And under Reagan, Bristol, like a lot of New England, experienced this huge boom. I mean, it was great. Everyone was saying, Aren't things wonderful? Aren't things just spectacular under President Reagan? He's our man. He's lowered interest rates. I'm making money hand over fist. But that was for people who owned property and who were already fairly well off. For people who didn't have money — for the poor — it was a horrible time. Property values in Bristol doubled or tripled, but so did the rents. And as the rents went up, the wages of the working class stayed the same, and suddenly many

people couldn't afford to live in their own homes anymore. In Bristol, as in a lot of America, entire families found themselves without a home. These were not lazy people. They were not sluggards or substance abusers. They were committed, dedicated men and women who were trying to make a difference in their own life, and suddenly they couldn't afford a place to live.

So when I hear about the legacy of Mr. Reagan, and I hear of the good times of the Reagan years, I can say that I personally benefited — the value of my home more than tripled — but the same factors that allowed for me to make money turned out to be very hard on the working class. The trickle-down theory just stopped at those who already had money, and many of those who were already struggling to make ends meet were forced out into the streets. It was tragic.

—*Reverend Patrick Mahoney, born in 1954, is a longtime spokesman for the antiabortion group Operation Rescue. He currently heads up the Christian Defense Coalition.*

One afternoon, I was home and turned on the TV and all of a sudden Dan Rather interrupted with this special announcement saying that Reagan had been shot and the word from George Washington Hospital was that he may not live. My first reaction was "Oh, dear Lord, not again." The memory of the Kennedy assassination was still very fresh in my mind. I was no great Ronald Reagan fan. In fact, I had voted for President Carter. I just felt that, as a people, we should not do this to ourselves. We're a civilized country. We shouldn't be killing our leaders. We shouldn't have this, this evil streak in us.

Later I heard the press reports about Reagan in the hospital, hovering in a critical state, on the verge of death, and that he was making jokes about it. I couldn't believe it. Here he was, lying on death's door, and he was able to meet that terrible crisis with a great deal of courage, and also with a great deal of humor. He was actually trying to relax the people around him. I thought to myself, "That guy's got a lot of guts." And my opinion of Ronald Reagan really went up after that.

— *Malcolm McConnell, born in 1939, is a journalist specializing in scientific and military history. He is a contributing editor to* Reader's Digest.

New Yorkers, like myself, were mostly Democrats and there was something about Reagan that creeped a lot of us out. He was a B-movie actor — and not a very good one — who had done very well for himself in California as governor. But then again, the movie industry was out there, so they sort of elected one of their own. Then he became president. Here was this man, whose job his whole life had been to act, and now he was running our country. And the whole time he was in office, it seemed as if he was just acting. He did a very good job for one segment of the country. But for people who were poor, or people who were being devastated by things like HIV and AIDS, it was a different story. He just didn't seem to have compassion for people who were suffering. The man couldn't even say the word "AIDS." It just wasn't on the script. They didn't have their cue cards written big enough so that he could say the word. You know, we're talking about the beginning of one of the major health crises of the twentieth century that had already caused millions of deaths, and the man couldn't say a four-letter word? That was really disturbing to me.

—Victoria Leacock, born in 1963, is a filmmaker who shot a feature-length documentary film on AIDS produced by Jonathan Demme and directed The Dead Speak, *a series commemorating the fiftieth anniversary of Hiroshima. She is also the author of* Signature Flowers, *a collection of famous people's drawings of flowers.*

I always found Ronald Reagan to be very courageous. He reminded me of an American West cowboy. He was that strong, silent type who made you feel that everything was going to be fine. And he always lived up to that image, especially in crisis situations. I admired him quite a bit. He was, I think, a very wise man. He made people feel good about being American. He made people feel good about our country, that it was strong economically, and strong in defense. He would stand up against the Russians and any other countries that would threaten us.

I was a social worker in the inner city, so I knew things weren't quite as rosy as he said. I had issues with him and his politics, but I still admired his charisma and the way he put the country at ease. Ronald Reagan harkened back to my grandparents' generation. He appealed to people who thought of America as the protectors of the world, a country with Christian values, the defenders of the weak. Ronald Reagan brought back these feelings about our country, and he made people very proud.

—Lisa Donegan, born in 1963, worked as a medical technician specializing in sudden infant death syndrome (SIDS) at Harvard Medical School and George Washington Medical School before becoming a social worker in Virginia.

and wrong. And for too long America had not only been wrong but *un-Americanly* wrong.

The essence of Reagan's economic approach was the tax cut, and the simple philosophy that went with it was this: those who make money should be allowed to keep it. The root of his appeal to business was deregulation, and the slogan was equally elemental: government should encourage, not hamper, the entrepreneurial spirit. Just as the regulators had intruded on the free conduct of business, so, in Reagan's mind, had social engineers (in the form of quotas and busing in particular) intruded upon the average man's sense of control over his own life, and here the answer, too, was simply to "get the government off our backs." Even the often enigmatic arena of international affairs was best understood when viewed without complication: the Soviet Union, Reagan declared, was an "evil empire," and evil should not be coddled.

Besides his attacks on the welfare state, Reagan, with his "supply side" approach to economics, defied the Keynesians who had presided over the federal budget since the thirties and, with his posture of insult toward the Soviet Union, challenged Nixon-era détente as well as Truman's policy of containment. But the fact that the new president was tearing the nation from the intellectual foundation it had occupied during much of the twentieth century was unimportant to most of his followers. For Reagan expressed his ideas in comforting anecdotes that people quickly understood, and he described his as a *counter*revolution aimed not at realizing some untested vision of the future, but at returning America to her glory days, the safe society of Coolidge and McGuffey, Norman Rockwell and the *Saturday Evening Post*, a premodern fantasy society that resembled not so much the past as it was, but the past as one wished it might have been. And yet it would be unfair to dismiss his vision as only that, for Reagan was also clearly tapping into the very real feeling many Americans had that the nation had lost touch with the self-reliance and resourcefulness that had been the essential characteristics that put it on the path to greatness. Onetime Reagan aide Dinesh D'Souza recounts that years before Reagan became president, he confronted a group of hostile students who discounted him for having grown up in "a different world," one that left him out of touch with modern needs. "Today we have television, jet planes, space travel, nuclear energy, computers," said one of the students condescendingly. "You're right," replied Reagan. "We didn't have those things . . .We *invented* them."

In the end, Reagan's leadership would prove to be less pure than his rhetoric. He would, for instance, drastically cut social programs that had benefited the poor, but leave much costlier middle-class entitlements like Social Security and Medicare — the biggest geography of the welfare state — untouched. He would challenge the Soviets in proxy skirmishes in Central America and the Caribbean and through a dramatic increase in the size and power of the American nuclear arsenal, but fail, to the relief of many, to risk a direct confrontation with them over Poland. And his economic policy, while dominated by a large 1981 tax cut, would be joined by both a strict control of the money supply — breaking inflation, but only through the tough medicine of a brutal 1982 recession — and prohibitively restrictive deficits, created, in large part, by his increased defense spending, that put a balanced budget (another of his campaign promises and a hallmark of conservatism) well out of reach.

The "yuppie" may have been the paradigmatic eighties success story, but older money flaunted its jewelry, too. These people at a party in New York demonstrated the new dress code: jeans were out, tuxes in.

"Go back to the heyday of Venice. Why did people put Titian paintings on the ceiling? It was to show they had money to burn. You could not be too ostentatious in Venice and . . . and there has been a lot of that spirit today."

Writer Tom Wolfe, on eighties excess

Still, by 1984, it could be said that to judge only by results, Reagan had largely done what he had set out to do: the economy was on the mend, the mandate for new social spending had been broken (the budget deficits had proved a valuable, if backhanded, way to restrict new initiatives simply by squeezing the amount of money available to fund them), and thanks in part to a dramatic 1983 American invasion of the Caribbean nation of Grenada, reasserting American power in the Third World, national confidence was, so to speak, back in the saddle.

Like no other time since the 1920s, America in the mid-eighties embraced a culture of money and glitz. The yearly income of the top 20 percent of American families rose only about $9,000 in the Reagan economy (after adjusting for inflation), but so many people also dramatically exceeded that number that wealth and its excesses became a public fascination, a raucous burlesque show paraded across the national stage. Starting with the end of the recession in 1982, more than 100,000 new millionaires were created each year, so many that the title lost its significance. Millionaire? Try decamillionaire, centimillionaire, even billionaire. There were now, quite suddenly, many more of each (and fully *fifty-one* billionaires), the largest upsurge of riches, wrote political analyst Kevin Phillips, since the late nineteenth century, when the Morgans and the Vanderbilts

The wild life of a Wall Street "golden boy": **"Our mission is commission"**

In 1979, I was two years out of high school and working in a local bar in Manhasset, Long Island, a bedroom community for people who work in Manhattan. And probably about 80 percent of those people worked on Wall Street. A lot of these Wall Street guys were regulars at the bar and they were always saying things like "What are you doing here? Come down and work on Wall Street with us. You have what it takes." They made it all seem very glamorous, and I was lured in. In 1980, I went down to work on the floor of the New York Stock Exchange. Wall Street was just heading into a big upswing, so things were pretty exciting down there. Suddenly there I was, a twenty-year-old kid with a high school education, and I was starting out at $40,000 a year. Most of my friends were still in college, and they didn't even have beer money.

I was a clerk for a specialist house that traded in about eighty big stocks like TWA, Delta Air Lines, things like that. This was before they used computers, and every order had to be handwritten. They had a dot system where you fill out these little cards with a number 2 pencil. It was like being in second grade. I stood behind a counter, and outside the counter was the broker I worked for. Surrounding him were ten to twenty guys just screaming and yelling, buying and selling. And I'd have to record all of these orders. Hectic isn't the word. It was overwhelming. It takes a certain kind of person — perhaps not a well person — to do this every day. I wasn't really aware of the size of the transactions that were taking place. It was all funny money. And of course, there were a lot of QTs, questionable trades — out trades, error trades — which were mostly human error. But you didn't have time to worry about it. If you stopped to think about anything, you would get so backed up. We ripped our hair out of our head for the entire day every day.

When the bell rang in the afternoon, we cleaned up, and then it was cocktail time. I went out every night with the guys that I worked with and our immediate bosses. And we never spent a penny. Everything was on an expense account. We would go to this same restaurant a couple of blocks from the stock exchange. There'd be about fifteen guys. And we'd head right for the bar and just start pounding drinks. Then we'd sit down at the table. And we'd never even see a menu, the food would just start to come out and it seemed like it would never end. It was obscene. Platters and platters of food and bottles and bottles of wine. We never thought once about what anything cost. Not at all. Just like at the exchange, it was all funny money. Never your money. So you didn't think about it.

I stayed on the stock exchange for about two years, but I was working for a small firm and if your last name

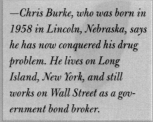

Burke, left, in 1985.

—*Chris Burke, who was born in 1958 in Lincoln, Nebraska, says he has now conquered his drug problem. He lives on Long Island, New York, and still works on Wall Street as a government bond broker.*

wasn't one of the names on the letterhead, you were only going to go so far. In 1982, I switched over to the government bond market. I guess I had a knack for that end of the business. By the mid-1980s, the government bond market was booming and I was making good money with a nice bonus every year. I bought a new house, new cars, new clothes, and I became so entrenched in the lifestyle that I was spending tons of money. When your whole life revolves around money, pretty soon your value judgments come into question. My buddies and I would literally be stepping over homeless people on our way to work, and we'd snicker about it. We certainly didn't want to get our shoes scuffed up by their burlap pants. "Get a job" was our attitude. It didn't matter what your politics were. My personal beliefs and politics leaned a little more to the Left, but I just kept that to myself. Wall Street was Republican and it was conservative and if you wanted to get ahead you carried the party line. "God bless Ronald Reagan. Screw the poor."

We spent unheard-of amounts of money entertaining clients. It was very competitive in the government bond market, so your relationship with your customer was everything. You would do whatever was asked, whatever was required: women, drugs, you name it. You'd be surprised what you could put on an American Express card, and when the statement came back at the end of the month, it all looked pretty up-and-up. "Don't leave home without it." That was our living motto. There was a lot of money down there and from five o'clock on, nobody was spending their own. I also used to take clients on special trips. My favorite was going out to see Notre Dame football games. The games were always on Saturdays, but I'd need to do a little recon, so I'd fly out with a couple guys to Chicago on Wednesday. We'd stay at the Ritz Carlton and tear up Chicago for a couple of days, going to nice restaurants, bars, clubs. Then we'd hop in a fully stocked rented Winnebago and drive down to South Bend on Saturday for the game. We'd tailgate, go to the game, and then it was back to Chicago by Saturday night, where we would rip it up all

night long, before hopping on a plane back to New York. I'd be back at my desk on Monday morning, my client would be happy, and he would continue to do his trades with me.

There were countless nights when I wouldn't even make it home because I was out too late. I'd just go back to the office at about 4:00 A.M. and sleep under my desk for three hours. A lot of guys kept blankets under their desks. And it took its toll. My first marriage ended up in divorce. But I just kept on rolling along. A lot of guys got burned out and ended up in rehab. Wall Street kept the rehab clinics in business. Your friend would be at his desk one day and the next he would be gone and you wouldn't see him for four weeks. We called it "going to computer camp."

It was bad the day the market crashed, but it wasn't as bad as most people think it was. First of all, there was a lot of volume. There was a lot of business done from Wall Street's standpoint. So in many ways it was just another opportunity to make money. It doesn't matter if people are buying or selling, we still make our commissions. "Our mission is commission." The investors were the ones who lost money, not the firms. Plus we all believed that it would eventually go back up. Good news, bad news, as long as there was news, we would make money. So what was horrifying on the front page of the papers across America was not nearly so horrifying inside the culture of Wall Street.

At one point, I covered just one big account. It was my meal ticket. I had to give away all my other accounts so I could focus full-time on this one. Then all of a sudden the firm blew up and all my good buddies who I was doing business with were suddenly scattered to the wind. One day I was a golden boy with two phones to my ear taking more orders than I could handle. And then boom, I wasn't doing anything. I felt useless. I was burnt-out. I had a drinking problem and a drug problem. Finally, I just had to quit.

Wall Street in the 1980s was like nowhere else on this planet. It was a culture of greed and back-stabbing and partying. Your best buddy is the one who's gonna stab you in the back tomorrow if it means some more greenbacks in his pocket. It wasn't a good way to live, but it was the only way I knew. And there were plenty other people clamoring to get in the doors. After about six months off the Street, I realized that I couldn't make it in the real world, so I called up some of my old customers who had regrouped at different firms, and I got right back on the horse. If the right guy sitting in the right seat supports you, all he has to do is make a phone call and say, "Hire this guy." Bang, the next day you're signing a contract for a lot of money. It doesn't matter what your problems were. You're right back in business.

"You can have it all . . ."

Michelob beer slogan

While the big money men and women of the eighties were ensconced in nondescript offices, making millions over the telephone and the computer, the trading floors were buzzing in reaction to what they did. Here, a man in the pit at COMEX, New York's international metals exchange, demands to be heard.

and the Rockefellers built their fortunes. Even more important, the enthusiasm for the newly moneyed, the desire to be them or, at the very least, act like them, became surprisingly contagious. After years of contemplating an end to their prosperity, a limit to their abundance, Americans jumped to the thrill of conspicuous consumption.

The financier — whether broker, trader, raider, or arbitrageur — became the quintessential eighties character, the decade's "organization man," and not only because the markets enjoyed unprecedented success in the new era but also because money men and women best represented the new shift of manners that the culture encouraged. Now it was okay to crassly pursue the dollar ("Greed is not a bad thing," said arbitrageur Ivan Boesky; "Greed is *good*," echoed Michael Douglas as corporate raider Gordon Gekko in the movie *Wall Street*), and each night on the evening news the graphic showing yet another day's jump in the seemingly unstoppable Dow Jones Industrial Average appeared layered over video of the frenzied Wall Street trading floor, a picture, as writer Tom Wolfe saw it, of "well educated young white men baying for money."

America, declared enthusiastic Republicans, was in another Gilded Age, a "Roaring *Eighties*," and in a way it was. Yet there was significance to the fact that the new rich were making money differently than their predecessors. Where the Vanderbilts built railroads and the capitalists of the twenties built automobiles or sold them with new techniques of advertising, the eighties were the decade of the "paper entrepreneur," of lawyers and investment bankers who made their income not by building or selling anything, but by shifting and manipulating deeds of ownership, by repackaging or remortgaging or even dismantling companies — dealmakers interested not so much in making things as, in a sense, *un*making things, *rearranging* things and *putting things back together*.

At the time, there were many who criticized an economy that seemed in a sense to be feeding off itself, yet looking back later, experts would agree that it was a streamlining that American business desperately needed. Unlike past periods of Republican prosperity, this economy was fueled not by the pursuit of the better mousetrap or even the better advertisement to sell an existing mousetrap (as might have been the goal, perhaps, in the fifties), but by organizing a leveraged buyout of a mousetrap company and merging it with a company that made something of related importance, like, say, cheese. And while it was unclear then, much of the reorganization and remortgaging of the nation's businesses was itself a kind of retooling of the economy for a high-tech future. Ironically, while Reagan was trumpeting a return to older, simpler values, his economy was dismantling the manufacturing plants of the old Rust Belt and replacing them with shiny, futuristic software firms in Silicon Valley.

In part because the activity of the paper economy was that much less visible and because it coincided with the departure of so many American manufacturing jobs to the Third World — the kinds of jobs where workers made things you could actually point to or even hold in your hand — the nation's new prosperity felt abstract, sort of unreal, a "smoke and mirrors" economy consisting of little more than people making money from money and then spending it lavishly. Still, all the financial maneuvering of Wall Street, all that "paper," represented the reconfiguration of enterprises where real people worked and where the lives of

Junk Bond

Poison Pill

Leveraged Buyout

Golden Parachute

Triple Witching Hour

White Knight

Financial terms that entered the vernacular in the high-stakes eighties

Pursued by a corporate raider: "He was the hunter and we were his prey ..."

Strykula, right, in 1985; above, one of his family's convenience stores.

—*Keith Strykula was born in 1959 in Rochester, New York. After leaving his father's company, he entered Fordham Law School, where he received a degree in 1991. He has since worked as a securities attorney for C.S. First Boston, Salomon Brothers, and, most recently, Warburg Dillon Read.*

In the mid-1980s, a few years after I graduated from college, I moved back home to central Pennsylvania to go work for my father, who had built a successful business from two smaller dairy processing companies that had nearly gone bankrupt in the 1970s. What my father did was build a chain of convenience stores and make them part of the larger company. The idea was that these convenience stores would provide a natural outlet for the local dairy farmers and milk processors. He devoted years to building this company up and turning it into a viable contributor to the community. Dad would work six, seven days a week, building a business, managing customer relationships, trying to build a platform for his coworkers to be able to succeed. He always said that his main responsibility was seeing that payroll was met so that everybody would get their weekly paycheck.

I felt good about coming back and working for my father. Then about three months after I started working, I opened the morning paper and saw an advertisement announcing that a group of investors were bidding for all the shares of the company. And that the group was headed up by a man who had recently been elected to our board of directors. This man, it turned out, was a professional corporate raider from Philadelphia who was launching a hostile bid to take over our company. He had been conspiring with a group of other investors who set up separate accounts and had accumulated enough company stock to get this guy elected to the board. We knew from the beginning that he was a dissident shareholder who was always proposing all sorts of self-interested business practices. But we had no idea that what he was really doing was using his position on

the board to gather information that would help him seize control of the company, so he could break it apart, sell off the most profitable parts, and earn a few million dollars in the process.

Well, I was infuriated. It seemed so unjust that someone could come in, anonymously, and try to tear down everything that had been built up over decades. This man's idea of success was to actually co-opt someone else's hard work, the sweat of someone else's brow, and to somehow use that as a commodity or a trade. He treated corporations as objects that he could buy on the cheap, break apart, sell each part for a much higher value.

A little while after the takeover bid was announced, this corporate raider came to our office, unannounced, to meet with my father. This just happened to be the first day of hunting season, which is like a state holiday in Pennsylvania. So in walks this man completely decked out in his hunting duds. It was a very peculiar thing just for him to be in the office. I mean, sure, he was a board member, but in reality, we thought of him as the enemy. And in he walks wearing full hunter's gear. It was like he was a big-game hunter who came into the office to scout out his prey. And I think it really was just a big game to him. Here he was tweaking around with other people's livelihoods and all he cared about were the numbers — the ink on the sheets.

News of the takeover bid spread quickly throughout the community, and people were very worried. The milk producers didn't know if they would continue to have an outlet for their milk, and the people who worked in the stores didn't know if they were going to have jobs. This part of Pennsylvania used to make its livelihood from coal mining and other heavy industries that had pretty much shut down in the previous decades. There was already a lot of poverty in the area, and if our company went out of business, a lot of people would be put out of work. People were constantly coming up to my father and me — whether it be at church or at the country club — and they would ask, "Is everything okay? Is everything going to be okay?" They were very concerned for the company and they were very concerned for my father. We would put on a good face, and say that everything was going to work out, but we really didn't know whether or not we would prevail. This kind of financial hocus-pocus was completely mysterious to us.

We knew that we had to get help, so we hired a high-powered law firm from outside the area. I'll never forget going into that law office and sitting in on our first meeting. There were all of these lawyers in nice suits sitting around this huge oval table in a conference room.

And we had this long meeting going over every aspect of the takeover bid. It felt good to lay everything out on the table, but I was concerned because we hadn't even met the lead lawyer on our case; he hadn't even come into the meeting. And then, just when we were about finished, this kind of gruff-looking man in his late thirties or early forties, comes strolling into the room smoking a cigar. The man just exuded confidence. He shook our hands, smiled at us, and said, "We're going to kick some ass here. This is going to be fun. Roll up your shirtsleeves, it's going to be a good ride." Now, I knew that this guy was just posturing, but, at the same time, after all of our worries and concerns, it felt really good to know that we had a hired gun who knew this game. He immediately identified ways that this hostile raider would be vulnerable. "Who is providing his financing? Has he done all the requisite filings with the state? With the FCC?" I quickly learned that there *was* a game being played here, and it was being played on a level that I never even imagined before. This lawyer brought us up to that level. I also realize that it was the lawyers that were, in fact, ruling this game of the 1980s. Our opponent may have had some good attorneys, but we were able to hire an attorney who was going to come in and save the day. He would come up with a plan to fight this takeover. He would find that "poison pill" that would save our company. These guys were moving the big levers of society. Here I was, with a college education, coming back to my father's company to try and help things, and there was nothing I could do except just sit back and watch others take control of the situation.

Even with all of our expensive legal help, there eventually came a point when it seemed like the hostile raider might prevail. Fighting the takeover was a huge financial strain that consumed the company for an entire year. The shareholders were getting antsy and were leaning toward selling out to this guy at a 20 percent profit. We managed to bide enough time to work out a plan. Ultimately, the lawyers introduced us to a third party that was interested in buying the company, a "white knight" who would buy everyone out, but without dismantling the company and selling off the parts. This acquirer came in, bought the controlling interest in the company, and was able to protect all the constituencies while still maximizing shareholder value.

When it was all finally resolved, the company that my father had worked so hard to build continued to exist, and the people who worked for it were able to hold on to their jobs. But it taught us all a lesson about the changed nature of business in the 1980s. And ironically, the corporate raider was happy with the way things turned out. He ended up selling the stock he had accumulated for about four times what he had paid for it.

real people were being affected by all the wheeling and dealing, sometimes dramatically.

Whole towns, many of them the kind of middle American outposts that seemed so well matched to Reagan's image of the ideal American life, the life he wanted the nation to strive to return to, suffered dramatically as the mergers-and-acquisitions activity roared like a fireball through the national marketplace, terminating career employees, liquidating whole divisions, and evaporating grand old American companies even as it arranged for "golden parachutes" (one of several financial euphemisms that in the eighties became part of the American vernacular) for executives.

While it was true that more and more people were benefiting from the expansion of the economy and even joining the stock market themselves (the percentage of Americans owning stocks in the eighties far exceeded even that of the boom market of the twenties), just as significant were the great numbers of people whom the nation's new wealth never reached, the underclass roaming jobless through America's continuingly decaying cities, and especially the "homeless," as they had begun to be called, an increasingly visible street population that seemed, to many, to put the lie to claims that the nation was back on its feet. For how could a great and affluent people conduct its business indifferent to those who slept on subway grates, in abandoned automobiles, or in cardboard boxes?

Throughout the eighties, there were hundreds of thousands of them at any given time, challenging the prosperous on street corners, marring the self-satisfaction of diners who emerged into the night from hundred-dollar feasts only to be confronted by an insult or a plea, by the odor of an unbathed body or the soiled and weathered skin of an extended palm. And yet exactly who were the homeless? Middle managers who, discarded by the new economy, had entered into a pathetic downward spiral or opportunists who had for too long squeezed the "system" for its generosity? The descendants of the hard-luck cases who stood on soup lines in the thirties or a wholly different, less sympathetic population? Roosevelt's "deserving poor" or Reagan's "welfare cheats"?

Reagan adviser George Gilder commented, chillingly, that the destitute needed the "spur of their poverty" to succeed and raise themselves out of despair. But in fact the homeless problem was a complicated one, in which the administration's welfare cuts shared the blame with a handful of other causes: the deinstitutionalization of mental patients which, beginning in the late 1950s and accelerating in the seventies, had tragically landed many incapable of independence onto the streets (in part a liberal idea, intended to recognize the insane as no less deserving of civil liberties); an inner-city drug epidemic centered around a sinister new form of cocaine known as crack, which had created addicts who desired a drug hit more than a warm bed; a shortage of affordable housing; and the decline of marriage, a development that meant that more people struggled, and failed, on their own, for even in the eighties the married hardly ever became homeless. More profoundly, as sociologist Deborah Stone asserted, the arrival of the street people also focused Americans on the nation's evolving attitude toward the very concept of "home." Poet Robert Frost wrote that "Home is the place where, when you have to go there, they have to take you in . . ." But he was from another generation, another America, and by the eighties fewer and fewer families served as the destitute's last resort.

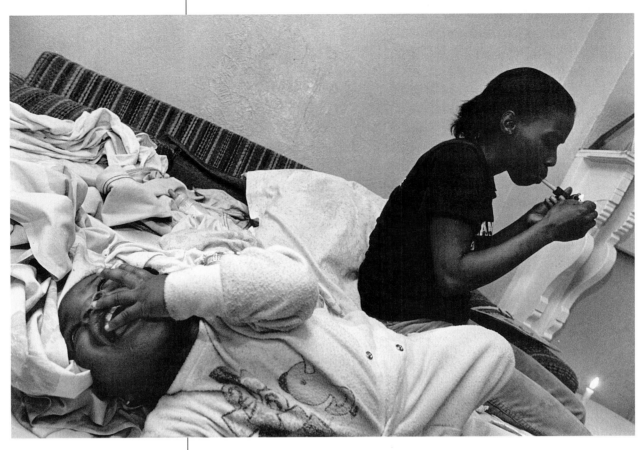

Crack appeared around 1985, as a cheaper version of the upper-class drug cocaine. But the dependency that the drug fostered forced many into lives of crime and desperation. New York's addicts spent as much as a thousand dollars a month on their habit, and one study found traces of the drug in two-thirds of single men and women occupying the city's shelters.

Tom Wolfe's *The Bonfire of the Vanities* was the best-selling novel that confirmed him as America's Balzac, a writer of acute observation, whose look back at this period captured the essential chaotic spirit of American life in the eighties through a description of the raw anxiety that separated America's arrogant haves and resentful have-nots. In Wolfe's eighties, the rich lived buffeted from the rest of society in fear of a confrontation with the "other half," of the poor uncle who might emerge from the closet, embarrassing the host and ruining the party. *Bonfire* was admired for its satire, criticized for its use of stereotypes, yet its crazy-quilt image of American society was undeniable to those who had lived through it: no matter the old-fashioned rhetoric issuing forth from the White House, America felt like a colder, crueler place.

The signs of an incipient class war were everywhere — in the ceding of public parks and plazas and transportation depots to drug addicts and pushers; in the graffiti-marred building walls and subway cars and the wanton desecration of other symbols of public authority; in the so-called revitalization of America's once-grand urban centers with building-enclosed developments for the rich like New York's Battery Park City, places one architect described as "defensible space" as if he were designing not apartment buildings, but moat-protected castles for the ruling class, which in a sense he was. Historian Fred Siegel noticed that in an attempt to recapture the lost urban dream of the twentieth century, architects began drawing up plans for "City Walk," a new suburban San Fernando Valley shopping mall which was to be "an exact replica of Venice Beach and Sunset Boulevard" absent the assaulting graffiti, crime, and homelessness that

488

> *"We were wards of the state. Imagine, belonging to the state? What the hell is that? How can you belong to something so big and vague? Can you come home to the state? Can it hold you and make you feel safe?"*
>
> Homeless woman

America's many homeless were a powerful reminder that the new economy defied that age-old proverb: these rising tides did not lift all boats. In 1987, one out of every five Americans lived in poverty, a 24 percent increase over 1979. Here, an eleven-year-old boy sleeps in the front seat of the family car in 1985.

When "crack" betrayed New York's neighborhoods:
"Everyone's sister was addicted . . . and then even their mothers"

I grew up on the treelined streets of Hollis, Queens, in New York. Most of the parents in my neighborhood were hardworking people with nine-to-five jobs. They were schoolteachers and nurses and engineers. In spring and summer, you'd see people outside watering their lawns. In winter after a big snowstorm, it was like payday for us kids. We'd go around door to door, and our neighbors were waiting for us saying, "All right, I'll give you fifteen dollars just to shovel the driveway and the walkway." We'd go around and clear up practically all of Hollis. And everyone knew each other. You knew everybody's parents, every kid, every uncle, the name of every dog and cat on the block, and the TV repairman, the oilman, and the mailman. Hollis was really a close-knit middle-class community.

My friends and I were too young to go to the discos around the time of *Saturday Night Fever* and the Bee Gees, but we loved music. We'd take a bunch of old records and some old stereo equipment and drag them to the park and hook them to an electrical current of a nearby shop. If the store didn't let us use its power, we used to bust open a lamppost and plug the system in there. Almost every Saturday in the summer, the whole neighborhood would come into the park, and a DJ would be there, and the rappers and the emcees from the neighborhood would come on the set and we'd rap and we'd party and we'd DJ and we'd play music and have fun until the police came and said, "Somebody called the cops on y'all. Y'all gotta go home."

When we weren't hanging out in the park, we'd be at the White Castle hamburger restaurant. It was the neighborhood mainstay. If you were coming to Hollis to buy some burgers, you might stop at our drugstore or grocery store on your way. All the businesses benefited from it. But times were changing in Hollis. In the early eighties, I started noticing neighborhood businesses were closing down. Our favorite candy store and deli, where we'd go as kids to read comic books, closed. The supermarket kept closing and reopening under a new name. It went from Dan Supreme to Met Food to Key Food and then some other name we'd never heard of before. The crime level was going up a little bit. People, particularly older people and well-educated people, started moving out of Queens, too. Even when we'd DJ in the park, fewer and fewer people were coming.

One morning, we woke up to discover the whole White Castle was gone. I mean gone — there was just a vacant lot sitting there. A lot of people in the neighborhood felt that this was like an omen. You'd hear people talking about this guy getting killed or that one in jail. It was really crazy, but once the White Castle was demolished, everything else went down with it.

So the neighborhood was already starting to go

—Darryl McDaniels, born in 1964, is "DMC" of the rap group Run-DMC. In 1984, they were the first rappers to earn a gold album for Run-DMC/Profile *and went on to earn platinum and multiplatinum albums for* King of Rock *(1985) and* Raising Hell *(1986), respectively. In 1988, McDaniels moved his family from Hollis to a suburban community in Long Island. When he is not on tour, he lives in New Jersey with his wife and son.*

McDaniels, in center above, with his mother, far left, and a friend; at right, the family home in Hollis, Queens.

downhill when I left to do a tour from 1984 to 1986. My rap group Run-DMC had made it big with our first single, and we had been making a name for ourselves for a few years. Everywhere we went on tour, and especially in the South, people were talking about this new drug called crack. We'd hear stuff like "They cook cocaine and make rock and you put it into a pipe." And we'd see crack fiends on the road and we could see how it hooked people. But we didn't realize crack had penetrated so deep into our own neighborhood.

I came off the tour in 1986 and went home to Hollis. I remember walking around and noticing how desolate everything had become. I looked at the playground, and the bleachers were gone. The park house was all boarded up and looked as if somebody had set it on fire. All the signs were ripped off and there were holes in the fence and glass and rubbish and garbage all through it. The place looked like a war zone.

I was walking around one afternoon when I heard a woman say, "Darryl!" I turned around and I couldn't figure out who this person was. "It's me," she said. She said her name, and I realized she was my good friend's sister. She may as well have pulled out a gun and shot me, I was so stunned. It was obvious she was using crack, but she was trying to hold on a regular conversation as if nothing was wrong. How was I supposed to react when she looked like she weighed about ten pounds? She had lost all her teeth and her clothes were dirty. She asked me for money, and I gave it to her. I didn't think she'd turn around and buy crack with it. I thought she might have gone and bought something to eat. The whole effect was just devastating. I had held her as a baby. But now to see her like that it was really scary.

Everyone's sister seemed to be getting addicted to crack. But when I started hearing about people's mothers, I just couldn't believe it. They'd be saying, "Yo, his mom's illing. She's smoking and she's bugging out, and she's not paying the bills." You'd look at the babies and wonder why they were like that. And it was because the parents were cracked out. I never knew that a drug could have such an impact on a community or a society.

Nobody hated the drug dealers because they had two things: money and power, which some used to make things better for the neighborhood. It wasn't like everybody out in the neighborhood selling drugs was Scarface saying, "I'm taking over the world and I'm getting all the money. "In Hollis, selling drugs was about making money, period. Some dealers would take groups of people to Atlantic City or to the amusement park, Great Adventure. Others would give money to local churches or foster homes or homeless shelters. If you're not looking at the downside, some of the stuff was positive from our point of view. Because at the time, President Reagan's economic policies dictated that federal programs aimed to help us would shut us down. You couldn't hate the drug dealer because he put money back in the community, which a lot of prominent people and the government weren't doing.

But crack did bring a lot of violence and guns into the neighborhood. Once there was no property and material stuff to attack, people started messing physically and mentally with the human beings in the neighborhood. Every week something happened, whether it was somebody getting killed or arrested or dying. It was as if the whole neighborhood started disappearing. It became like a ghost town.

At the time everything in the neighborhood was falling apart, a lot of billboards saying "Say No to Drugs" were going up. I remember thinking how much money it cost to put up those signs each week. To me, they were spending money on the wrong thing. I knew perfectly well that people weren't gonna look at a sign like that and say, "All right, I'm gonna just say no to drugs." The way I see it, the mayors of the big cities were looking at the statistics and seeing crime levels rising in the inner city, and the murder rate going up, and then Nancy Reagan was probably hearing about this, too. Of course, Washington, D.C., had its problems, too. Every state was being affected by this. I found out that just telling people not to do drugs doesn't work. Besides, that saying came a little bit too late. Don't you think, Mr. Reagan?

greeted those who ventured to the real thing. It seemed that if America's cities truly worked anymore, they only worked in such oversterilized memories.

Out of this social powder keg emerged the "subway vigilante." Bernhard Goetz's uncommanding appearance made him an improbable hero or villain, yet on a Saturday afternoon in late 1984, just three days before Christmas, Goetz, while riding a Manhattan subway, fired a .38 revolver at four youths who had approached him menacingly, and forthwith became the subject of an intense national debate on crime and self-defense. Had he committed his act of violence in another time — even as recently as the seventies — Goetz would probably have been roundly vilified, particularly after it was reported that he had shot two of the youths in the back and finished off his spree with a challenge worthy of the Clint Eastwood movie tough man, Dirty Harry. ("You don't look so bad . . . here's

another," he growled at his last victim as he pulled the trigger, crippling him for life.)

But Goetz claimed that he acted out of fear, certain that the youths, who had approached him asking for five dollars, intended to attack him, and the situation he described resonated darkly with much of the American population. Nearly half of those polled in the days after the incident said they thought Goetz's rampage was justified. And while there were many who also condemned the attack, the loudest voices praised Goetz for his courage, for doing what many others wished they could, but never would. "The Goetz incident is just symptomatic of what's going on everywhere," declared a South Carolina judge. "People are just sick and tired of being pushed around by punks."

Indeed, while Goetz was not part of the emerging prosperous class and his victims were not homeless, the story of his attack assumed an immediate us-versus-them kind of symbolism that was driven by the social divide. Goetz was white, the youths were black; Goetz was employed, the youths were drifters; Goetz had been mugged before and had armed himself precisely for this moment when he could exact revenge, the youths were frequent troublemakers whose "weapons" were screwdrivers they used to break into video game machines and steal quarters. And in fact, the root questions of the case went right to the awkward social manners of the time, to the difficulty interpreting the meaning of gesture and posture, language and dress, in a society where the relationship between the classes (and the races) had become so fundamentally hostile: When is a request for five dollars a request for five dollars, and when is it a veiled threat? Does it become more of a threat if the request crosses an invisible social barrier; that is, if the person asking is black and poor, the person receiving white, middle-class or moneyed? Does the interpretation of class (or race) as an element of threat deny civil rights? Does the rejection of class (or race) as an element of threat deny common sense? If a threat, at what point in such an encounter is it deemed reasonable to act in self-defense? And at what point does self-defense cease and an unprovoked attack begin? In the end, Goetz was to be convicted on only a minor weapons charge (for which he would serve 250 days in prison), but years later he would be retried in a civil case brought by one of his victims, and ordered to pay $43 million in damages.

The eighties were the decade of "Fortress America," as one writer called it, when even many middle-class homeowners sought out communities protected from the "other half." The security industry burgeoned (tripling the number of armed guards in Los Angeles alone), and gates and security fences, like the one erected to define the space around Los Angeles's Hidden Hills, above, disrupted areas formerly open to pedestrian traffic.

"There are no more liberals . . . They've all been mugged."

Harvard government professor James Q. Wilson

Watching Challenger: **"Someone asked, 'What's happened?' And I said, "They're dead. We've lost them.'"**

Left: The astronauts on the morning of their fateful mission. McConnell, right, on assignment at the Kennedy Space Center.

— Malcolm McConnell, born in 1939, is the author of a number of scientific and military histories including Challenger: A Major Malfunction *and* Men from Earth *with Apollo astronaut Buzz Aldrin. He is currently a contributing editor to* Reader's Digest.

In the early 1980s, I was assigned to cover the space shuttle program for *Reader's Digest*. By that time the dark days of the past two decades seemed to be behind us and the space shuttle symbolized America's new, bright, optimistic future. For the first time since the moon launches, NASA had back that old can-do spirit, and after only four test flights, this very complex spacecraft was ready to provide routine access to space.

Before I witnessed my first shuttle launch, NASA officials escorted several other reporters and me down to the launchpad to see the shuttle up close. I felt like an ant walking around a stepladder. It was virtually the size, length, and weight of a World War II destroyer. Now, imagine a World War II destroyer turned up on its tail and then light a fire under that thing and expect it to take off and rise into the sky. I felt awed and dwarfed by this huge machine. When you're three miles away in the press grandstand, and that huge assembly lights itself on fire and takes off, the feeling is overpowering. There is a bright flash from the solid rocket boosters, and then you see an almost volcanic burst of steam from the main engines. Immediately after the flash this huge vehicle begins to rise away, and it's all silent. A second or two later, you are literally assailed by the shock waves. The press grandstand has sort of a tin metal roof that begins to bounce up and down and your chest is hit by this cacophonous pounding. The first time I saw it, I was virtually speechless. I felt proud that my country, my civilization, had put together this wonderful machine which was so powerful, so complex.

By the mid-1980s, NASA had pretty well convinced most of the world that it could not only run the space shuttle economically, but that the shuttle could actually pay for itself on a commercial basis. NASA wanted to prove that the shuttle was so safe that even a common person could ride into space. So Christa McAuliffe, a high school social studies teacher from New Hampshire, was to encourage an interest in space for millions of schoolchildren.

Before each launch, NASA goes through a ritual called Astronaut Arrival, in which the astronauts are formally presented to the press. On the day of Astronaut Arrival for the *Challenger* flight, the shuttle crew, including Christa McAuliffe, marched across the runway in sort of Tom Wolfe *Right Stuff* style to greet the assembled press corps. I noticed that the regular NASA astronauts had their little flight suits on and they were all wearing shining black aviator's boots. But Christa was wearing a pair of gray running shoes. After the formal interviews, I happened to slip in beside her and I said, "I like your shoes." And she laughed and she said, "Well, next time they're gonna get me some real boots." In retrospect, I realize there was a great naïveté on her part in the sense that she trusted NASA to provide for her safety and for all of her needs. She had great confidence and trust in the space program, as did most of the American people.

The morning the *Challenger* was launched, very few of us who had covered the space shuttle program thought it was going to fly that day. It was bitterly cold. One reporter pointed up at one of the monitors and said, "Look at the ice." The launch tower looked like a frozen waterfall. But we got our coffee and we sat around and waited. As it got light, the launch control people began saying, "Well, it's looking better and better." Several reporters who had never covered a shuttle launch before rushed out into the cold weather to the grandstand. Most of us old-timers stayed in the dome, nice and warm, and said, "Well, they're gonna scrub it at T minus 10, and we'll wait for a better day." Well, at T minus 10 we were quite surprised to hear that the countdown was proceeding. We gathered up our notebooks and cameras and we went out to the press grandstand. NASA had somehow pulled this thing off. And then the countdown reached 5, 4, 3, 2, 1, and that glare lit up from the solid rocket boosters. I had a sense of great pleasure and satisfaction.

As the shuttle cleared the tower and the first shock waves of sound began to pound the press grandstand, I had my first sense of foreboding. Because the air was so cold and dense, the pounding sound was much louder than I'd ever experienced. I thought, "That does not sound right." But I quickly shrugged it off as the shuttle rose. All of us on the grandstand were screaming our heads off, yelling "Go! Go!" Any sense of professional composure was lost; we were all caught up in the euphoria of the moment.

The pillar of smoke with the little tiny shuttle had turned to the degree so we could no longer see the shuttle itself. We could just see this rippling cloud of white and orange smoke coming back toward us. From our vantage point, it still looked like a normal flight. Then there was silence. For a long time. I would say ten seconds, which is a long time during a launch. And we began looking around at each other. And then the voice came over the loudspeakers. In a very dry, almost emotionless voice, "Obviously a major malfunction. We have no downlink . . ." And then there was a pause. "The flight dynamics officer reports that the vehicle has exploded." I felt this terrible cold drenching doom pouring over me. I could almost feel ice water pouring down over my head and chilling me deep into myself. Looking around me, I saw people who had been standing and cheering a moment before sink back down to their benches. Many people put their hands over their faces as if to blot out the sight. Other people put their hands to their throats, as if they themselves were being physically assaulted. One of my colleagues looked at me and asked, "What's happened? Where are they?" I said, "They're dead. We've lost them, God bless them." And she got angry. She kind of pushed me and said, "Stop kidding, what happened, where are they?" And I said, "They're dead. They're dead." And at that moment we looked up again, and the pieces of the *Challenger* began tumbling out of that pillar of smoke. That massive vehicle had been shredded into tiny little pieces that were falling like confetti out of the sky. Although people all around me were running off to file their stories, I was rooted to the ground. I couldn't make my legs move.

As that terrible day progressed we began to sort it out in our own minds, what this meant. For me, the sense of the tragic loss of the astronauts — people whom I had known and liked — gave way to a sense of anger and frustration. I felt like I had both been deceived and that I had allowed myself to be deceived. I felt a sense of personal failure that, as a journalist, I had not done my job. We took NASA at their word and what we had been told was false. This was not a fail-safe spacecraft. In fact, it was a very vulnerable machine that could be blasted, in an instant, into thousands of twinkling pieces of debris. And if what we were told about the space shuttle was not true, then perhaps other things that we had been told and had let ourselves believe were not true as well.

The shuttle disaster, above, set back hopes for a revival of the American space program, which had been floundering since Apollo XI landed the first man on the moon in 1969. "More than the Challenger exploded in the blue sky over the Atlantic Ocean," wrote New York Times science correspondent John Noble Wilford. "We [were] left full of doubts . . . about the very fundamentals of our national space policy."

"We will never forget them nor the last time we saw them this morning as they prepared for their journey and waved goodbye and 'slipped the surly bonds of earth to touch the face of God.'"

President Reagan, addressing the nation

Fear *was* a driving emotion of the eighties. As much as greed, it was fear that propelled the yuppie dreams of the decade, fear not only of crime but of poverty, of failure, of living at a standard below that of their parents, of living a life without meaning. The Reagan administration had weakened the "safety net" for those under public assistance, yet in the eighties, safety was an elusive goal in so many ways and to so many people. The regenerated superpower arms race had renewed fears of a nuclear Armageddon (the 1983 ABC movie *The Day After*, detailing the aftermath of a nuclear war, recorded a viewership of 100 million). And, after an explosion destroyed the reactor at the Soviet Union's Chernobyl power plant in the spring of 1986, unleashing a radioactive cloud for miles, there were renewed fears of a nuclear power accident. After all, Chernobyl was, in a sense, just Three Mile Island without the "happy" ending.

Still, the most paralyzing single event of the decade, and one that would imprint itself upon the mind in much the same way as the Kennedy assassination had a generation earlier, appeared in the pictures of the cottony tendrils of smoke forming in the sky over Miami in late January 1986, the vaporized remains of Shuttle Mission 51-L. The explosion of the space shuttle *Challenger* demonstrated the vulnerability of even the most sophisticated technology, for a $1.2-billion spacecraft had been felled by the malfunction of a $900 synthetic O-ring — a piece no more complicated than the washer on the faucet in a bathroom sink. Yet even more important, it did so in front of the full, wide-eyed anticipation of the nation's schoolchildren, destroying a dream.

The *Challenger* crew represented a remarkable cross section of American life and, in a sense, at least one admirable by-product of the reform movements of previous decades. While space travel had begun in the Kennedy era with the heralding of the Mercury Seven astronauts, white men all of them, the *Challenger* crew — also numbering seven — included two women, a Jew, a black, and a Japanese-American. Among the mission's goals were the establishment of a $100-million NASA satellite and the deployment of instruments that would record the ultraviolet spectrum of Halley's comet, but the flight's greatest significance, as far as the public was concerned, was that it would inaugurate a new era of civilian space travel, for the *Challenger*'s seventh passenger had been chosen from over eleven thousand volunteers to become the first private citizen in space, an ebullient and charismatic thirty-seven-year-old social studies teacher from Concord, New Hampshire. With Christa McAuliffe aboard, Shuttle Mission 51-L would demonstrate that space belonged not to NASA or the Pentagon, but to everyone.

Plans called for McAuliffe to conduct two fifteen-minute classes from "out there," beamed by closed-circuit television to millions of students back home. In one, she would guide the cameras through a tour of the spacecraft; in the other, she would address the history and future of the space program, describing "where we've been, where we're going, and why." NASA dubbed it "the ultimate field trip," and on the morning of January 28, 1986, televisions were wheeled into the nation's classrooms so that children could watch their courageous teacher, the *nation's* teacher, and her six copassengers begin their journey.

The air at Cape Canaveral was unseasonably cold, but not cold enough to cancel, administrators determined, and indeed liftoff appeared to go smoothly. But in fact the critical O-rings, sealing the joints between the rocket boosters, had failed (they had frozen in the chill), igniting the spacecraft's main fuel tank. Seventy-three seconds into flight the sleek white "bird," as space engineers had affectionately called *Challenger,* erupted into a fiery red ball. "Flight controllers are looking at the situation," announced NASA's Stephen Nesbitt to the television audience. ". . . Obviously, a major malfunction . . ." But the millions watching needed no confirmation. The pictures they were watching were this event's Zapruder film, and they were graphic enough to tell the story. Over the next few days, as the film was run and rerun on television, viewers could watch the seven crew members in uniform on the morning of their mission, smiling for the cameras, then marching confidently to their fate, and in shots of the spectators' gallery, where the crew members' families were gathered, they could see faces taut with excitement dissolve into grief at the sudden realization of the horror before them.

In fifty-five manned missions, NASA had never experienced such a catastrophe. But while the blow to the space agency was devastating, the trauma for the children was immeasurable. Across the nation, teachers and principals, parents and guidance counselors, searched for something, anything, to help America's youth make sense of a tragedy that was, in a special way, theirs. "Someone they admired and loved has been taken away," said the principal at McAuliffe's Concord high school of his own students, ". . . [and] they have learned that nothing in this life is certain."

By 1986, fear had even penetrated the nation's bedrooms. For years, medical science had been scoring success after success, so many that there was the feeling that disease was about to become an anachronism. Along with technology, medicine had been society's best advertisement for progress, boasting an uninterrupted flow of accomplishments leading to the bettering of human life. Then came the deadly pandemic known as AIDS. The acronym (for "acquired immune deficiency syndrome") stared out from the page ominously, like a finger of fate resurrected from the time when plagues like the Black Death ravaged whole populations in medieval Europe. Now AIDS appeared capable of wiping out as much as a quarter of those alive in our own time, an Old Testament kind of scourge spread primarily through sexual contact, which in itself represented a cruel piece of irony, for now man's most intimate act, the one that conceives life and gives pleasure, could also take life away.

When AIDS was first detected in the early eighties, it was believed to be a disease confined to specific segments of the population. Initially reported in the *Morbidity and Mortality Weekly Report,* a publication of the U.S. government's Centers for Disease Control, as a curious pattern of opportunistic infections found in gay men (the original acronym was GRID, for "gay-related immune deficiency"), it was then noticed among increasing numbers of intravenous drug users, prostitutes, hemophiliacs, Haitians, and Africans. Yet since so little was known about AIDS, including the method of its transmission, its rapid spread set off an epidemic of hysteria and hatred. By early 1983, there were thirteen hundred cases, and health authorities were predicting that greater numbers of heterosexuals would soon join the ranks of the infected.

Much of the goodwill that had been projected toward homosexuals as the movement for gay rights gained respect throughout the broader population now

By the late eighties, Americans had become used to pictures of the AIDS-ravaged patient, on his or her way to an ugly death. They had also begun to read the obituary page with a new awareness: the rising numbers of young people, many of them gifted, now lost in the prime of their professional lives. Above, twenty-four-year-old Steve Brown lies dying at Bailey House, a New York residence for HIV-positive patients.

vanished as people worried whether a handshake or a polite kiss, a public swimming pool or toilet seat, could become the agent of death. And, predictably, the divide that already separated America's underclass from the rest of the population became even wider, for sadly, the more people learned about AIDS, the more it seemed to reinforce racism and classism, and not only in the growing numbers of IV drug users who were rapidly making this a disease of the powerless but also in the discovery that the virus's place of origin was most likely in the Third World, perhaps even an African beginning, associated with green monkeys, a notion that arrived with Darwinian overtones. Susan Sontag has written that, historically, the diseases that gain the title of "plague" (like leprosy or syphilis or even Black Death) are those that transform the body into something alienating, and in the need to see it as more a product of "them" than "us," the disease is almost always described as an invasion from "somewhere else." In the way that it ravaged the bodies of its victims with a virus thought to have first appeared in the "dark continent," AIDS had undeniably met both criteria.

The disease was riveting in its elusiveness. Because it was believed to have a long incubation period of ten or more years, a person carrying it might appear healthy, even robust; particularly before the licensing of what came to be called the AIDS test in 1985, a person could even be unaware that he or she was a

I was sitting on Jones Beach in New York with my friends Burt and Jimmy in the summer of '82. They were reading about a so-called gay cancer in a magazine, and once I heard the details from this report, I thought to myself, "Oh my God. This is monumental." I sensed this disease was not some anomaly that would blow over fast, but rather it was going to affect the whole gay community. We all just sat there stunned and with the premonition that something terrible was coming.

My first boyfriend, Gerald, died of AIDS pretty early on. Another ex-boyfriend of mine had started volunteering at the Gay Men's Health Crisis (GMHC). A group of gay men had founded the organization as a means to raise funds for biomedical research on AIDS. It housed the very first AIDS hot line. GMHC's first headquarters was literally across the street from where I live. I could see it from my bathroom window. This friend urged me to go and volunteer with him. He became the first GMHC employee to die of AIDS, so there were two boyfriends gone. And he went really fast too. He died while I was marching in the Gay Pride Parade.

One month after I started volunteering at GMHC, I became a "buddy" to an AIDS patient, helping him out with chores at home that he was too weak to handle on his own. Certain boundaries must be observed between buddies, which is very difficult because they get attached to you. For instance, you must not allow them to put you in their will. You know there's some conflict of interest there. And you should not have sex with your clients, not only because of the risk involved but also because of that boundary. It's very easy to fall in love when someone is very, very needy and vulnerable and starts confiding in you their greatest fears and deepest, darkest secrets. Sometimes they fall in love back with you. And that's doubly tragic because, at least in those days, inevitably you were going to lose them.

I tried hard to keep this distance with my buddy, Martin Davis. He was a wonderful, rare bird. I would have never met this man in my own social circle. He had studied art and was the head of the art department at the Strand bookstore in Manhattan. He was a real child of the seventies, had been on the fringe of that Andy Warhol crowd. His apartment was painted entirely black.

In the beginning he was okay, but every time he bent over he would get very dizzy. I would come in once a week to vacuum and mop his entire apartment, and we would chat. Toward the end, as he got sicker, Martin got a little paranoid. He was so eccentric that it took me a while to catch on he was getting dementia. At one point, he was lying in bed with the checkbook trying to pay his bills, but he couldn't do it right. He kept voiding them and tearing them up. So I said, "Would you like me to help?" I didn't realize it at the time, but by offering to help I was taking away the one thing he could control that he had. He didn't have control of his bowels, but until then, he could at least pay his bills.

There wasn't much I could do for him at the end, and I tried to stay detached. But I couldn't. My response was to throw myself even more into my work, doing twice as good a job mopping or vacuuming. The irony was that it made less and less of a difference. A spotlessly clean apartment was not going to save him. I was anticipating the end, but at the same time, trying not to think about it. He went within a year. After he died, one of his good friends gave me a sweater that Martin had knitted. I call it my *Starry Night* sweater, because it has all the colors of a Van Gogh painting, deep blues and bright yellow spots. I have that to remember him.

By then, GMHC had hired me on full-time to work with Jerry Johnson on the AIDS hot line. What I didn't know at the time was that I had changed careers forever. Jerry Johnson was an early gay activist. His claim to fame was that he had been in the clothing business and he had invented the T-shirt dress. Jerry was not a mental health professional. We were all nonprofessionals back then, working by the seat of our pants and just trying to get GMHC's name out there. His instincts were what we call "client-centered" and "nondirective," which means that you accept the caller where they are, and you support them where they are, and you do *not* judge them whatever you do. And you don't tell them what to do. You ask them what *they* want to do and you ask them how *they* think they can do it and in the end you help them figure out the options. For example, if you're talking to a woman and she says, "I can't ask my boyfriend to use condoms. I'm afraid he'll hit me," then you say, "What do *you* want to do?" And then you ask her how she thinks she could take baby steps toward that goal.

One of the great challenges of a hot line is that you get one chance to make a difference in the lives of the callers. In our case, we had to do that in under ten minutes (the proscribed time limit on most calls), and you have to maintain your anonymity (another requisite). It's really the only way to stay emotionally distant from the caller, although there are calls I carry around with me to this day. People called who were bed-bound, crying and sad with no hope. They'd start talking about how they used to be young and beautiful and had a future and how they had lost their identity, independence, and pride. A lot of people called and said, "I'm not afraid of death. It's getting there that scares me." Being stripped of all your dignity and losing half your body weight and having friends turn away just because they're in such pain they can't stand to see you that way is just horrible.

The level of ignorance and homophobia from some of the callers was just amazing. And the indifference was overwhelming. When I first started, prank callers would just say, "All you faggots should die!" Click. Thank you for sharing. You didn't even have enough time to tell them where to go, which, of course, we weren't allowed to do anyway. It was bad enough all these people were dying and there was nothing that we could do about it, and then you've got people hating you for being sick or for helping sick people. Of course, you wanted badly to be able to say, "Where's your compas-

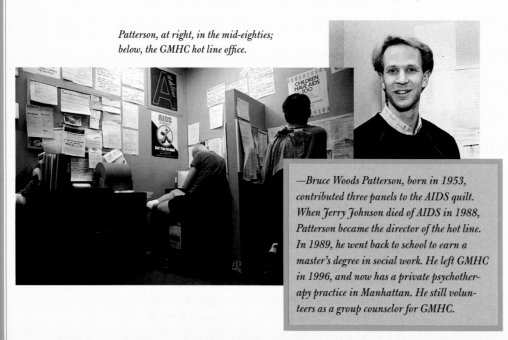

Patterson, at right, in the mid-eighties; below, the GMHC hot line office.

—*Bruce Woods Patterson, born in 1953, contributed three panels to the AIDS quilt. When Jerry Johnson died of AIDS in 1988, Patterson became the director of the hot line. In 1989, he went back to school to earn a master's degree in social work. He left GMHC in 1996, and now has a private psychotherapy practice in Manhattan. He still volunteers as a group counselor for GMHC.*

sion? Who do you think you are? What's wrong with loving someone?"

I remember one afternoon a woman called to ask for an HIV clinic for her husband. He had tested positive for HIV. He had a job, but it didn't offer medical insurance, and he made too much money to be on Medicaid. She was looking for a public health clinic that knew HIV medicine and wanted to find one convenient to where she lived in lower Manhattan. I suggested a few hospitals, and then I said on the East Side there's Beth Israel. She had this really strong reaction, "No! Not Beth Israel!" I said, "May I ask why you seem so adamant against Beth Israel?" Then the truth came out: "My daughter died there two months ago." She had a five-year-old adopted daughter who had died of AIDS there.

She and her husband had been through the ringer with her. This little girl sounded really exceptional. She was going in and out of the hospital periodically, and she would be like a little angel to the other terminally ill patients her age. She would console her mother by saying, "Don't worry, Mommy, because you know they're gonna be with the angels, and when I'm with the angels, I'm gonna look over you." She was trying to talk out her feelings with her friends and they were saying, basically, "Get over it. You've got to move on." The fact is the mother was still so upset she couldn't even open the door to the little girl's room when she walked by it in her apartment. Compounded by the fact that she was worried about her husband's health. We both kinda cried on the phone.

The limits of the hot line are such that you can really only do so much in one phone call. She had established herself as HIV negative at the beginning of the call, and I didn't want to ask her how her husband had got HIV. Clearly she was grieving and that's what I needed to attend to. I ended it by giving her a couple of clinic referrals that she had requested when the call began. I myself learned the hard way that you've got to work through it, and you've got to talk about it, and you've got to let yourself feel all the emotions. Bereavement is not just about sadness. It's about rage, remorse, and regret.

My friends and I often talk about the community of infected and affected people. I am HIV negative, but have been affected deeply. We're all living with AIDS. I often wonder why I have been so lucky, when so many of my friends and colleagues have died of AIDS. When I look back at the pictures of the early days at GMHC, it hits me every time that the majority of the people in them are no longer living. In the end, I have to be philosophical about it. I guess my job is to be there for everyone else. The best thing that I can do is just stay HIV negative.

carrier. Similarly, the virus eluded researchers, for it was remarkable in its ability to mutate, a murderer with a million costumes, capable of morphing into different shapes and sizes. And in part because it was so undefinable, indescribable, and undetectable, nearly any definition, description, or system for detection could be made, in panic, to fit.

Almost as if on a stage cue, a chorus of moralists emerged from every corner, declaring AIDS as representative of the moral bankruptcy of modern society, a pandemic caused by permissiveness, God's revenge on the licentiousness of the modern world. As such, it returned to America a feeling not unlike that which accompanied the Red Scare of the 1950s. Then, as now, the society began to condemn behavior that had been commonplace in the previous decade (the leftist experiments of the thirties; the sexual experimentation of the seventies); then, as now, people recoiled in fear of a deadly invasion of a silent killer (the fifties Red Menace was sometimes described as a virus); then, as now, people were encouraged to look upon their neighbor distrustfully ("Are you or have you ever been . . . ?").

When, in 1985, the news emerged that the movie actor Rock Hudson, the quintessential fifties leading man, was dying of the disease, AIDS, like the Red Scare, had even begun to assemble its own Hollywood profile. Hudson's death raised awareness of AIDS substantially, but it also fed suspicions, for while there had long been rumors among insiders that the actor was gay, he had never revealed that information publicly. Instead, in the conformist fifties, his studio had encouraged for him an image of rugged all-American heterosexuality endorsed by a willing popular culture ("He's wholesome, he doesn't perspire . . . he smells of milk . . . the boy is pure," gushed *Look* magazine in 1958). Now, prompting irrational fears for the leading women Hudson had kissed in a career of 37 years in film and television, it appeared that he had all along been leading a secret, double life. And if Hudson was a carrier, who else might be?

Curiously, AIDS had timed its appearance well. In the charged atmosphere of the eighties, it could be utilized as the tragic medical counterpart to the myriad attacks being flung at modernism: just as Ronald Reagan was scolding lawmakers for their freedom with the nation's tax dollars, so disease was scolding the sexually promiscuous for being too free with their bodies. Modernity had been under a crippling attack since the mid-1970s, and as Sontag points out, the signs of a return to premodern conventions were already emerging everywhere: in music's rediscovery of tonality, in art's return to realism, in the newfound joys of church weddings and careers in investment banking. To all of that could now be added the virtues of monogamy.

Indeed, there were many, and not only the fire-and-brimstone moralists, who saw in AIDS nothing less than the rescinding of the sexual revolution that had brought such dramatic changes in American mores over the past twenty-five years. It was, in part, the advances of medicine — birth control, antibiotics — that, by reducing the consequences of sex, had encouraged freer behavior in the first place. Now it was, in a sense, the failure of medicine to combat a new deadly disease that was changing them back. At the very least, AIDS was altering courtship, urged on by this chilling warning: "Remember, when a person has sex," declared the secretary of health and human services, "they're not just hav-

"It's hard enough to find attractive single men without having to quiz them on their history of bisexuality and drug use, demand blood test results and thrust condoms into their hands. Wouldn't it be easier to give up sex altogether and join some religious order?"

Novelist Erica Jong, on the AIDS epidemic

Hate crimes increased with the AIDS epidemic, which some extremist religious groups saw as God's revenge on "sinners."

ing it with that partner, they're having it with everybody that partner had it with for the past ten years."

Private discussions of sexual histories became a common part of dating, frank discussion of techniques for sexually transmitted disease prevention a common part of public discourse. Debates over the issuing of free condoms to high school and college students and free needles to drug addicts (the sharing of needles was discovered to be a primary mode of the virus's transmission) occupied government panels and television talk shows. So, too, did astounding statistical studies predicting the cost AIDS would inflict on the nation's insurance industry.

Yet too often lost in the middle of all the finger-pointing and high-minded moral pronouncements, in all the hand-wringing over dollars and cents, was the fact that it was the loss of humanity that was wreaking the most devastating toll on American life. The arts were particularly hard hit, but, as Americans gradually began to understand, the sad truth was that AIDS was striking broadly throughout their society, including AIDS *babies* to whom the virus had been passed by infected mothers in a seemingly endless chain of misery. When, in the late eighties, the death toll climbed toward 100,000, just about everyone in America knew someone — a colleague at work, a neighbor, a friend, a classmate, a family member — whose life had been affected by the disease.

Shortly after Marvin Feldman died in late 1986, his friend Cleve Jones hit upon an idea by which to remember him and others. Marching in San Francisco to honor the slain gay councilman Harvey Milk (Milk and Mayor George Moscone had been murdered in a sensational spree by a resentful rival), Jones noticed a group of cardboard placards affixed to a stone wall, commemorating the lives of people who had died of AIDS. "I thought it looked like a quilt," he recalled later. "And when I said that, it evoked powerful, comforting memories." Within a year, Jones and others had organized the NAMES Project, a campaign dedicated to a singular task: constructing a massive patchwork memorial, composed of three-foot-by-six-foot panels, each designed by a friend or relative to honor a single life lost to AIDS. The AIDS "quilt" grew rapidly to hundreds, then thousands of panels which, when sewn together, took up the size of a football field. And when it appeared on display for the first time in Washington, D.C., in 1987, it had its intended effect: as one strolled among its many pieces, it was impossible not to see that because of AIDS, people, *real* people, had died.

On July 7, 1987, a forty-three-year-old ramrod-straight marine lieutenant colonel walked into the Caucus Room of the Russell Senate Office Building, raised his right hand for his swearing in, and proceeded with a performance that would etch his name onto the short list of twentieth-century American folk heroes. The appearance of Oliver North before the Senate committee charged with investigating what would become known as the Iran-contra affair had been anticipated for months, ever since the sensational

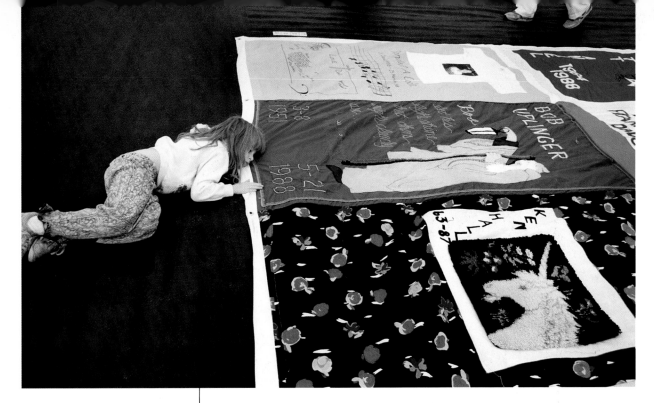

"Nick was my neighbor.
 He liked art.
 He was a computer programmer.
 We rode the El to work together
 almost every day.
 He was a loner.
 He never said he was sick.
 He died alone.
 I'll miss you . . ."

A message from the AIDS quilt,
a memorial to the dead

discovery that the Reagan administration had concocted a bizarre plan by which American arms (ammunition, spare parts for tanks, jet fighters, missiles) would be shipped to Iran in a scheme designed to gain funding for the contra rebels fighting the Marxist government of Nicaragua.

The plan was in violation of several laws. The arms sales themselves were illegal, and Congress had recently passed a ban on military aid to the contras. Even more important, as far as the public was concerned, the trades seemed in direct contradiction of the morally direct philosophy that had been such a large part of Reagan's appeal. It was Iran, after all, that had only recently humiliated Americans with the protracted hostage crisis that brought down the Carter government. Reagan officials eventually offered that their overtures were intended, in part, to gain confidence with Iranian moderates there who might work to reduce hostilities between the two countries and to aid in the release of other hostages now being held by pro-Iranian guerrillas in Lebanon. But those arguments fell flat: after all, to many in the know, an "Iranian moderate" was a misnomer; Khomeini would never have tolerated any drift from the firmly dictated principles of his theocratic state. And Reagan himself had long insisted that negotiation was never to be pursued over hostages; it only rewarded the hostage takers.

Attorney General Edwin Meese and others initially blamed North, an aide with Reagan's National Security Council, for directing the operation. But North appeared to many to be a scapegoat for a policy supported by more powerful Reagan officials, maybe even Reagan himself. The comparisons to Watergate were tempting, even if Nixon's "cover-up" seemed tame in comparison to the charges here. Searching for an easy name by which to identify the whole affair, journalists tried "Irangate," "Khomeinigate," and "Contragate" before settling on Iran-contra. A few, watching as the Senate committee was chosen, even began to treat the story as if it were a Hollywood remake of the Nixon panel, with Senator Howell Heflin of Alabama, a font of old-fashioned wisdom, playing the role of "country lawyer" created by the Watergate committee's Sam Ervin, and Chair-

In the spring of 1984, I was working in the international division of a public relations firm called Gray & Co. One day my boss called me in and said, "Hey, I got an interesting assignment for you. One of our people was approached by the [Nicaraguan] contra rebels, and they want to employ our firm to help them. Do you know anybody in the White House, or the CIA, or the State Department, who can give us some guidance?" I said, "Well yes, I know a guy; his name is Ollie North."

I had met Oliver North less then a year earlier when I was working for then Senator Dan Quayle. Working for Quayle, I had traveled extensively in Central America to see firsthand what the goals of the Sandinistas were and what effects they were having on the country and on the region. And what I saw was a flood of refugees fleeing communism. Under the Sandinista regime, if you were not for them, you were against them. And if you were against them, then you were gonna pay a price. And that price was fear and intimidation.

The contras had come to Gray & Co. because Congress was cutting off all of their aid. They had hoped that an American public relations firm could help improve their image and influence public opinion. I was very sympathetic to their plight. While I was in Nicaragua, I had met many people who were fighting against the Sandinistas. These were people who felt that the only course of action for their country and their future was to take up arms. And they looked to the United States for guidance and for help. We had been supplying them with beans and bullets and blankets and Band-Aids and boots. And now with the signing of the Boland Amendment (which abolished covert actions "for the purpose of overthrowing the government of Nicaragua"), the U.S. Congress was about to walk away. We had said, we believe in you. We believe in your cause. And then we went and cut everything off. It just didn't seem right to me. At the same time, the Soviet Union was feeding the Sandinista regime with military advisers and weapons. I didn't believe that the United States could just let this happen. We had to try and make some effort to alter Nicaragua's course.

At the Jefferson Memorial, inside the circumference of the rotunda, there's a saying, "I have sworn upon the altar of God eternal hostility against every form of tyranny over the mind of man." And I truly believe in that. So after Gray & Co. rejected my proposal to help the contras, I decided to leave the firm to work directly with Oliver North. He and I had agreed that we needed to provide pressure, both political and military pressure, to deviate the course that the Sandinistas were on. Even so, I still had to ask him, "Before I get into this I just want to know, are we doing the right thing?" And he said, "Look, my boss knows, and my boss's boss knows.

Owen, top, with his wife, Beth, and above, crossing the Honduras-Nicaragua border with a contra official in 1985.

—Rob Owen, born in 1953, eventually went to work for Dr. Robert Schuller's Crystal Cathedral Ministries in California. Two years later, he moved his family to Florida and became a fund-raiser for a local private grade school. Unable to quell his zest for international life, in 1996 he took a position as manager of two apparel manufacturing plants in El Salvador.

I've been told to keep these guys alive. Heart, mind, body, and soul. And that's what I'm gonna do." That was enough for me. After all, his boss was Bud McFarlane and his boss's boss was Ronald Reagan.

When I was working for North, I traveled back and forth between the United States and Honduras, El Salvador, Costa Rica, and Nicaragua. Here I was, this preppie-looking guy, who didn't really know squat about what he was doing. I didn't even speak Spanish. I had no formal training. I just improvised the whole way along and I learned from experience. I acted as a facilitator, a coordinator, and a liaison with different factions within the resistance. At times I was a courier, taking information back and forth between Washington and Central America, which included everything from intelligence information to arms to money. Sometimes I felt like I was a character in a spy novel. Once, I was sent to this little Korean grocery store in Manhattan where I gave a password to the man behind the counter. It was so surreal. I was looking around and asking myself, "Where's the FBI? Where is the sting on this operation that's going to send me to jail?" This man reached down, rolled up his pant leg, and pulled out a wad of cash. He counted it out — there was $9,900 and change — put it in an envelope, and handed it to me. I just walked out, went directly to the airport, and hopped on a plane for Washington, D.C. We usually worked with amounts less then $10,000, because if you moved $10,000 or more you were supposed to report it to the IRS. Even in what we were doing we tried to stay within the law as much as we could, so as not to draw attention to ourselves.

Another time, I flew to Colorado to meet with a retired army general who was brokering an arms deal for

the resistance. At one point during our meeting, he reached out and gave me a grenade. Now this particular hand grenade was no longer live — it had been turned into a lighter — but it was a type of Argentinean grenade that was pretty widely available on the arms market at the time, and the general wanted me to show it to my contact in the resistance. I put the grenade in my bag and forgot about it until I was at the airport and had already put my bag on the belt for the X-ray machine. My heart just jumped up into my mouth. Even though it was not a live grenade, I didn't really want to draw too much attention to myself. Fortunately they never saw it. I just walked on the plane with my hand grenade and said, "Thank you, Lord."

From Colorado, I flew to San Francisco, where I met with Adolfo Calero, who was one of the leaders of the resistance. We rode around town in the backseat of a car, putting together this list of weapons. At one point, I pulled out the hand grenade to show him, and I noticed the driver look into his rearview mirror and then sort of gulp. I don't know what he thought was going on. We stopped at a pay phone, I called up Ollie North, gave him the list of weapons, and that was that. I often played the role of facilitator in deals like this. North didn't want contact with certain people and so I would be his contact for him.

In October of 1985, my presence was becoming known to reporters who were trying to track me down. At the same time, Congress had approved humanitarian aid, which was going to be distributed through the Nicaraguan Humanitarian Assistance Office (NHAO). North wanted to legitimize my activities, so he arranged for me to become part of the NHAO. I guess you could say I was forced upon them in a way. So, under their auspices, I continued to travel back and forth but this time we were taking planes loaded with humanitarian goods out of Miami and Washington. We sent down medical supplies, boots, uniforms, all sorts of things. Congress and the State Department had this whole laundry list — yes, this is humanitarian, no, this is lethal, you can't do that, yes you can do that.

At the same time that I was running these humanitarian supplies down there, I continued to do things on the side for North and for the resistance. We were trying to set up a southern front in the war. I talked to a lot of the Nicaraguan opposition leaders as well as a few, I guess you would call them "internationalists," who were helping the cause. I worked very closely with a Panamanian by the name of Hugo Spadafora. He had come up to help fight against the Sandinistas, and he became a very close friend of mine. One day he was caught by the Sandinistas at the border. Later, his headless body was found stuffed in a U.S. mailbag. Most of his bones had been broken and he had been castrated. Things like that really brought it home to me that this was much more than a game. I guess I was always in danger of being caught, but I was no hero. I was just a guy who was trying to help. The heroes were the guys who were out there every day living in the jungles and doing the fighting. They were the ones who were bleeding and dying.

By the summer of 1986, word of our activities had begun to leak out and Ollie and I both agreed that I should take a low profile. Then one day I saw on television that both North and Poindexter were fired, and in essence the proverbial shit hit the fan. I managed to track Ollie down and he told me to go find myself a good lawyer. He also said, "Whatever you do, tell the truth, tell the truth, tell the truth, because anytime in the past when these things have happened, people who have lied have really gotten burned." A few days later I got my first subpoena.

I had made my choices, and I was ready to accept whatever the consequences were. But I had a good lawyer and he managed to get me immunity. At first I didn't want immunity, but my wife and my lawyer talked me into taking it. I had a deep abiding faith that what I did was the right thing. In those days there was still very much a Cold War mentality and there was a strong feeling that the Sandinistas might spread communism throughout the region. I had a faith and belief in the goodness of my country and what democracy and freedom meant. I thought, if I could convey those feelings, then the American people would understand and even accept the actions of all of us who were involved — from foot soldiers to the generals and the politicians. And I still stand by the righteousness of what we did.

The Iran-contra affair did temporary damage to Ronald Reagan's popularity, for its very deviousness contradicted the essence of his appeal. Said one observer: "[It was] like suddenly discovering that John Wayne had secretly been selling liquor and firearms to the Indians." Here, Lieutenant Colonel Oliver North testifies before Congress.

man Daniel Inouye playing the role of, well, Daniel Inouye, for the Hawaiian senator had the historical distinction of appearing on both committees. Certainly when North arrived to tell his story, he had already become the "John Dean figure," the little guy who would finally cut the doublespeak and tell the truth. Even Dean himself, sent by *Newsweek* to report on North's testimony, declared that it felt like he was watching "history unfolding through a rearview mirror."

Still, the bureaucratic-looking former Nixon aide never achieved the star status afforded this marine, who, one reporter declared, "somehow embodied Jimmy Stewart, Gary Cooper and John Wayne in one bemedaled uniform." While North would tell the committee that he believed that he was operating "with authority from the president," he had not come to Congress to bring Reagan down and certainly not to disown the actions for which he was being tried. In six days of testimony, nearly every minute of it impassioned, North made the case for behavior that, while perhaps illegal, was pursued with a moral certainty. "Lying does not come easy to me," he said, referring to the covert nature of his work. "But we all had to weigh in the balance the difference between lives and lies."

To some, North was little more than Goetz in marine green, a "loose cannon" whose willingness to operate outside the law represented an arrogance worthy of punishment, no matter his intentions. But there were also many who were charmed by North — not only by his candidness but also by his catch-in-the-throat expressions of patriotism, and by the sense he portrayed to the national audience that he did what he did not for power or money, but out of frustration with Congress and loyalty to his commander in chief.

As such, the appeal of Oliver North went to the heart of the nation's frontier mentality, to that part of the American personality that likes men of action, particularly when they show up men of inaction. And while North was no MacArthur, you could hear in the way the no-nonsense warrior challenged the "suits" of the civilian Congress the same kind of in-your-face machismo that the general once brought to bear on Washington, winning him great popular support, the kind of attitude that said in essence, while you study your briefs and

"*What crashed was more than just the market. It was the Reagan Illusion: the idea that there could be a defense buildup and tax cuts without a price, that the country could live beyond its means indefinitely. The initial Reagan years, with their aura of tinseled optimism, had restored the nation's tattered pride . . . But he stayed a term too long.*"

Time, *November 2, 1987*

write your laws, *I'm* out there in the jungle, and the truths *I* learn, the ones that guide *my* behavior, are elementally more significant.

Ultimately, the most commanding comparison to Watergate came in Iran-contra's central question: "What did the president know and when did he know it?" And while the answer remained unclear even after hundreds of hours of testimony from dozens of people in the National Security apparatus, that hardly spared Reagan. For even without evidence of a direct link to the Oval Office, Iran-contra had portrayed the president as either a figurehead in a rogue government or an impotent and forgetful leader whose lack of attention to detail had finally caught up with him and the nation. To the problems of homelessness, AIDS, the skyrocketing budget deficit, and a frightening arms buildup could now be added a morally suspect foreign policy. And this, from the man who had made a return to an old-fashioned moral ethic central to his national plan. Of the first-term Reagan accomplishments, only the economy, it seemed, remained firmly on track. And on October 19, 1987, Black Monday, even that appeared to come apart.

Some called it the "market meltdown," and certainly the scenes of traders standing helplessly before their computer terminals, watching millions of dollars

Inspired by the October 1987 Wall Street Crash, a self-proclaimed oracle declares the "end of capitalism" — prematurely, of course. Like so many fearful eighties moments, the panic that hit the financial markets came and went, proving little more than the resiliency and flexibility of an evolving economy.

evaporate before their eyes, had the feeling of a Three Mile Island or a Chernobyl. A seemingly irreversible decline had taken hold, pushed onward by uncontrollable technology (much of the selling-off had been the work of computer "program trading" scheduled to respond to drops in the indexes). And as with those nuclear accidents, here, too, there was the panicky feeling that one was witnessing something dangerously apocalyptic, the end of capitalism or Western society or, at the very least, the recent prosperity. For too long, the stock market had been daring the gods, climbing dangerously high, and now, well, the gods had struck back. By day's end, the Dow Jones Industrial Average had lost 508 points, or 22.6 percent, a blow that represented $500 billion in the "paper" of the "paper economy," a value roughly equivalent to the gross national product of France.

Brokerage houses, went the joke, now had a new investment strategy for their customers: start putting half their money in bonds, the other half in canned goods. And indeed, echoes of the 1929 Crash were heard everywhere, including in the voice of the president, who insisted that the "economic fundamentals remain sound." After all, Reagan's hero, Calvin Coolidge, had said essentially the same thing as he handed the government over to Herbert Hoover just months before the collapse of the twenties' market lit the path on which the world

Mikhail Gorbachev defied the stereotypical Kremlin mask: he actually smiled. And once it became clear that his charm was not some new Soviet ploy, windows all over the East flew open. Here, communism's heroic reformer arrives to a hearty welcome in Prague, where the last big Soviet appearance had been the tanks that crushed the reform movement of 1968.

dragged itself into the Great Depression. And there was no doubt that the memory of that resulting cataclysmic event hovered over this moment, too. The great bulk of ordinary people now invested in stocks were baby boomers whose aggressive market investment strategies had broken radically from the conservative approach of their parents, and with the market now undergoing a collapse, a look of "I told you so" could be seen in the eyes of America's senior generation, the people who had actually lived through the Depression's darkest hours.

As it turned out, economists were as baffled by this crash as they had been by the one in '29: some fingered an overvalued market, others pointed to pending legislation aimed at cooling the mergers-and-acquisitions fever that had been driving much of the economy. Considerable blame was attached to the Reagan budget deficits, which, growing deeper and deeper, had put interest rates in jeopardy, and to those computer trading models that had functioned brilliantly under stable market conditions but had not been programmed to react to a panic. Still, over the next year, just about everyone looked on in amazement, waiting for a depression that never came. The market, though decidedly more tentative at first, bounced back, and many traders resumed their pre-Crash mentality. Indeed, a little more than a year after Black Monday, corporate raiders grabbed RJR Nabisco for $25 billion, up to then the largest takeover in history, and went about restructuring yet another company, this one the maker of such venerable American brands as Oreo cookies, Ritz crackers, and Winston cigarettes.

At the same time that America was reeling from the tremors of what one trader described as "capitalism gone mad," the Soviet Union was undergoing the most dramatic change since the 1917 revolution. It was an interesting pairing of moods: the American system roaring forth with such speed it had begun to frighten the passengers; the Soviet's, so long stalled, finally prompting someone to look under the hood and replace the engine. And it marked the beginning of an extraordinary episode in human history, the final chapter of the protracted struggle that attended the lives of so many throughout this century. The Cold War was coming to an end.

Ever since the mid-1970s, Americans had grown used to a kind of unfortunate stability in superpower politics, the implacable gray stare of Soviet leadership having become all too familiar, a caricature of the stagnated state, fetid in its own bureaucracy. But with the arrival of the fifty-four-year-old Mikhail Sergeyevich Gorbachev in 1985, fresh air began to blow throughout the Kremlin, and with that, the possibility of a new Soviet Union began to slowly emerge. Few believed it at first. After all, Gorbachev was an unlikely candidate for such a formidable task as the reinvigoration of the ossified communist system. A longtime party functionary, he had been promoted to the top job by the same decrepit leaders who had constructed the present Soviet monstrosity: a Third World country, really, as far as the living standards of its people, with a First World military composed of 3.7 million troops and some 25,000 nuclear weapons.

Even if Gorbachev were sincere in his desire for reform and even if his reforms had the potential of reversing the nation's long economic slide, there was the history of tragic failure attached to those who had attempted such dramatic change. Six men had led the Soviet Union since its inception, and the only one to depart from power before his death was Nikita Khrushchev, whose "thaw" of

Daring the Soviet censors: "I knew that I would be expelled from the Party, but I had to make this film"

In the mid-eighties, I was working at the central television station in Moscow. I had worked for many years as a newsreel camerawoman in different departments of television — making television programs on politics, on literature, art, social life, public affairs. This took half of my year, and the other half of the year I was a filmmaker for Ekram, a special film studio within the television station. It was a very special studio financed by the government, where the filmmakers could do many interesting things. All media in the USSR was heavily censored and television was probably the most censored of them all. Everything we did was controlled by our administration. Every year we had to submit several proposals for the films for the next year. Usually I submitted fifteen or twenty proposals for films, and very often not a single one was passed. All of the proposals and concepts had to go through what was known as the council of editors. Once the proposals made it past the studio level, they went on up the ladder all the way for approval by the chair of the television committee who worked under direct subordination to the Central Committee of the Communist Party. He was the man who worked out the main fields of interest and subjects the media would cover and how they would cover it.

In early 1985, I submitted a proposal for a documentary film version of a book called *At My Mother's*, by Anatoly Streliany. He was a talented writer with independent ideas and a point of view that was not in line with the Communist Party. And he was also a good friend of mine. Because of his views he had a difficult time getting his works published. But this particular book was not overtly political. It described a visit he made to his mother's home in the village he grew up in on the border of Russia and the Ukraine and it gave a very interesting portrait of the village. We got this proposal through all the censors, and it was put into the plan for 1986.

Even before we started working on *At My Mother's*, we got a sense that somehow things were changing. For a long time, it had seemed as if something just had to change because the whole country was stagnating: economically, politically, socially. For so many years, the people who had ruled our country were old and outdated. We were so ashamed when we saw these old faces reading their speeches. They were not able to even read them properly, they were so old. And there were a lot of jokes about it. How they distorted Russian words and made it so funny and meaningless. Then, when [Yuri] Andropov came to power in the early eighties, I was suddenly offered a job to go abroad and be a foreign correspondent for Russian television. Now, this was unheard-of because I am a woman and I am Jewish. And even though I decided not to take the job, it was

—Marina Goldovskaya, born in Moscow in 1941, graduated from the State Moscow Film Institute in 1964 as a cinematographer/director. She won two national film awards for Archamgelskiy Mujik. *She followed that with an equally controversial film about Solovky, one of the first prison camps in Stalinist Russia. In 1990, she came to the United States to teach film. She currently spends half of the year teaching at UCLA and the other half in Moscow, where she continues to make films.*

Goldovskaya filming in Moscow, in the late 1980s.

a sign that things were getting less restrictive that it was even offered.

When Streliany and I started working on this film, I thought that we could take advantage of the changing atmosphere to do something more useful, more interesting. Something that could somehow help to push this process of change. So instead of making a documentary film based on his book — the project we had already gotten approval for — we decided to make a film about farmers and the struggle between the individual and the communal. We knew that our new idea would never be approved by the censors, but we decided to go ahead and make it anyway. We just acted as if we were still making a film based on our original approved proposal.

We traveled around talking to farmers and doing research, and we ended up in this little village called Ust-Vanga. And there I met this farmer named Nikolai Sivkov, who had been a member of the local collective farm but who left in order to start his own little farm, belonging to him and his family. He tried to enlist help from the collective, but they just viewed him as a kulak who was trying to subvert the collective way. From the minute I met Sivkov, I understood that he would be a perfect character for a film. He was eloquent. He was witty. He was biting. In him, you could see all the controversy of our system. This man, who only had about

two years of education, stood before that camera and talked about the advantages of private property and the inefficiencies of the collective, and how the Soviet farming system was preventing him from succeeding. The story of this man and his little farm was the perfect metaphor for the evils of the Soviet system. As I was shooting, I became so afraid. I understood that this could be the end of my career. The things that he was saying would never be shown on television. You just couldn't attack the collective like that. It was impossible. I knew, if I made this film I would be expelled from the party. But it was something beyond me. I had to keep going. It was something that I cannot explain because I am not such a brave woman. I was scared to death, but at the same time, I didn't have the strength to say to myself, no.

By the time I finished the film, which I called *Archamgelskiy Mujik*, which roughly translates to "A Real Peasant from Archamgelskiy," Gorbachev had been in power for about a year, and he was such an inspiration for all of us. He was like fresh air — not only fresh air, he was everything. He was young, brave, and bright — brighter than anybody else. And he was able to get the public to believe in him and to support him. At the time, I lived in a house full of filmmakers and actors. I came home from work one day and I saw Nikolai Bartalov, a very famous Russian actor who lived in the same house with me, sitting in his car and listening to the radio. And I said, "Why are you listening to the radio in the car? You could go inside and listen to it." He said, "Gorbachev is speaking and I am afraid to miss a word."

It was something completely new to us; suddenly there was a lot of hope. We were all absolutely euphoric about Gorbachev. We thought that a new time was coming. Finally, it seemed that people would stop telling lies. We all were fed up with the lies we read in the newspapers. There was a joke that people used to tell that really reflected what was going on. We have two main newspapers in Russia: *Pravda,* which means Truth, and *Izvestia,* which means the News. So the joke was that there is no "News" in the "Truth" and there is no "Truth" in the "News." Everything we read was all fake, all lies. And everybody understood it, but nothing could be done. And suddenly there was somebody, Gorbachev.

When he started talking about *glasnost,* openness, it was exciting. But change came very slowly at first, step by step. And while we were excited by everything, it was a very unsure time. Gorbachev still had a lot of opposition on the Politburo; there were still many of the old leaders around. We didn't know what direction the country would take. When you are floating down the stream, you don't know where the stream goes. And we were living every minute feeling that we were swimming and nobody knows in what direction. So it was in this environment that we presented our film to a consultant from the Central Committee of the party. He was one of the members who was behind Gorbachev and who was ready for change, so he decided to take a chance and approve the broadcast of the film. He said, "I will take the responsibility for what happens. You may have some problems at your work, but for you it will not be as grave as for me — it can ruin all my life."

Archamgelskiy Mujik aired on a Thursday night at 8:00, a prime time on Russian television. The next day, the whole country was talking about it — in the buses, on the subway, in classrooms. I became famous in one minute. The television station wanted to repeat the film two weeks later, but suddenly there came an order to stop the broadcast. And the film was banned. Ultimately, because of the new policy of *glasnost,* they decided to air the film again. The fact that this film survived was a sure sign that Gorbachev was winning against the old guard. This film was kind of a test of the struggle. The feeling that we all had was that now we can start building a new life without lies and with good intentions. We felt that everything would go very quickly in the right direction, that the new life was very close. It took Gorbachev to make the first step, then everyone else just started to push the train.

U.S.-Soviet relations and denunciation of Stalin's "cult of personality" had resulted in his forced ouster in 1964.

But even the crusty and senile Politburo members understood that the situation was desperate and that the country needed young blood. Industrial production was pitiful, hampered by alcoholism, absenteeism, and equipment failures. Housing shortages forced nearly a quarter of the nation's urban population to share bathrooms and kitchens. And food was scarce, though the party always did make sure that there was bread. (After all, it had been a bread riot that had brought down the tsar.) The May Day parades had come to feel even more absurd, with their overly rehearsed "outbursts" of joy. Surely, something had to be done. Still, it is likely that in choosing Gorbachev the old guard expected that it was doing nothing more than livening up an old act, not closing it down.

Gorbachev, too, saw himself as the savior of the communist state, not its undoing. And he presented his tripartite program — *glasnost* (openness), *perestroika* (restructuring), and *demokratizatsiya* (democratization) — not as a break with tradition, but as a way of reconnecting with it. For particularly in these early years, as he juggled the hot coals of Soviet politics, the new leader continued to embrace Lenin as the guiding spirit of the Soviet state. Far from abandoning the revolution, his government, he said, would represent a *return* to Leninism. After all, it was not Lenin who had corrupted the system; it was those who had inherited the government from Lenin, in particular Joseph Stalin, whose policies of random terror had done so much destruction. And Gorbachev knew Stalin's crimes all too well. As he later revealed, both of his own grandfathers had been imprisoned by "the Great Genius Leader" in the 1930s.

There was some substance to Gorbachev's bonding with Lenin, whose New Economic Plan of the 1920s tolerated limited private property and private enterprise as a "transition to communism." But by connecting with the founder of the Soviet state, Gorbachev was really looking to do essentially the same thing that Reagan had done by invoking Roosevelt: make it easier for those who stood by recent traditions to accept radical reforms, in particular those in the party who had dedicated their lives to the state, and who, as members of the elite, continued to benefit from it. In reality, Gorbachev planned a wholesale reconfiguration of the system long before he came to power. "Everything pertaining to the economy, culture, democracy — all spheres — had to be reappraised," he later wrote, including "the erosion . . . of moral values." Yet just how far could he go? And how fast?

By July of 1987, an uncharacteristic mood of excitement filled the streets of Moscow. Newspaper articles revealed corruption and mismanagement; once-taboo abstract paintings now hung in art fairs; and even private conversation took on a new liveliness. American writer David Remnick, who arrived as the *Washington Post*'s Moscow correspondent a few months later, recalls the almost child-like enthusiasm with which Russian friends now spoke critically of the regime. Coming to the American reporter's home for dinner, where they almost certainly would be monitored by KGB microphones, they would act like defiant teenagers, laughingly pronouncing rebellious slogans into the chandelier. And yet such was the level of reform that Gorbachev was proposing and so great the risk he took in proposing it that it was hard to know just what slogan now *was* rebellious — the

" Now comes a man who has stirred up the sleeping
kingdom. He did not come from outside, but arose
from within this very system, possibly as our last
chance of survival . . . He dared, it would seem, the
impossible — a revolution of minds."

Soviet writer Chengiz Aitmatov, on the arrival of Gorbachev

one that condemned Gorbachev or the one that praised him.

Small-scale profit incentives were returned to industries. For the first time since the earliest days of the Soviet state, elections, *real* elections, were held. And while public appearances by the old guard leaders had always been carefully orchestrated affairs in which the politician was propped up behind a bannered podium to wave mechanically at a distant crowd, now Gorbachev took on the behavior of a Western politician, moving himself out into parks and onto streets to press the flesh.

The most exciting reform by far was *glasnost*. And in some ways the most exciting part of *glasnost* was the "return of history." It is hard for Americans to comprehend a state that practiced not only repression but a wholesale lie about its own past, a fiction forced upon the people to ensure their continued subjugation. But for seventy years the population of the Soviet Union had been enduring just that. And now, with *glasnost,* Gorbachev intended to come clean, to replace the overly constructed texts and their grand fabrications, and not just with some other self-serving narrative, as might befit the transfer of power from one despotic leader to another, but with something radical to Soviet, even Russian, experience: the truth. Meeting with Western reporters in early 1987, Gorbachev cautiously pronounced the need to fill in history's "blank spots," declaring that "history must be seen for what it is." But his words took on a new seriousness when he directed them toward the keepers of the tradition, the Soviet power structure itself.

On November 2, 1987, Gorbachev made his way to the podium of the Kremlin's Palace of Congresses for what was, to date, the most significant address of his two-year regime. Marking the seventieth anniversary of the revolution before an audience that included not only the Soviet high command but also the communist chiefs of East Germany, Poland, Romania, Czechoslovakia, Nicaragua, and Cuba, he began to dismantle history's "Great Lie." The language was cautiously chosen, so cautiously that only those who knew the long sad tale of Soviet rhetoric understood it for what it was. Yet there was no denying the monumentality of his mission when he declared "Stalin and his immediate entourage" as responsible for "wholesale repressive measures and acts of lawlessness" and then, as if to tweak the old guard, followed by insisting that this was "a lesson for *all* generations."

Gorbachev restored, partly, the reputation of Khrushchev. And he praised Nikolai Bukharin, a Lenin aide, who had opposed Stalin particularly after Stalin scuttled Lenin's New Economic Plan. Bukharin had been murdered by Stalin's henchmen in 1938. At least for now, Gorbachev neglected to tell the "whole truth." He still refused to condemn Lenin, for instance, and declared continued support of Stalin's decision to join in the infamous 1939 pact with Hitler, but those in the know understood that the new leader was only able to open the door to history slowly, and there was no doubt that he had opened the door.

A few months later, in early 1988, David Remnick walked across the Arbat, a pedestrian mall in Moscow, and saw something shocking: a young woman collecting signatures on a petition. Even now, this remained a risky venture. *Glasnost* had eased the controls on expression but not all expression, and Remnick had seen people get arrested for doing just what this woman was doing. He watched

Intellectuals, fearing the punishment that answered free thought, had led secret lives under Stalin and his successors. Now, with glasnost, *long-suppressed plays and books (even those by Russia's beloved Boris Pasternak) were retrieved from their hiding places and poets, left, took to the street.*

The anger that poured forth from the Soviet people after so many years of forced silence was palpable. There were even calls for a public trial of Stalin. As one writer observed, "Had there not been a trial at Nuremberg, Nazi atrocities at Auschwitz and Buchenwald might have been denied by later generations." Here, a woman holds a picture of her father, a victim of "the Great Terror."

as a few people gathered around her and listened to her explain her campaign, a new "historical, anti-Stalinist" movement called Memorial, which intended to give "names" to the victims of the Stalin era.

Prompted by Gorbachev's speech and by the release from internal exile of the great Soviet physicist and dissident Andrei Sakharov, the organizers of Memorial had been inspired to promote not just the rewriting of textbooks but the publication of secret archives and the erecting of monuments to the victims of Stalinist terror. Memorial began its campaign by attempting to gather signatures from people in their offices, then expanded to the streets, where supporters held aloft a sign quoting Gorbachev's declaration that history should have no "blank spots." People were tentative at first, but by the spring of 1988, thousands had signed the petition (lining up, said one volunteer, as if to "buy sausage"), particularly after Memorial's leaders stoked the fires with the publication of a radically subversive collection of essays entitled *There Is No Other Way.*

The book, which had an initial print run of 100,000 copies, laid out the need for truth, and the fear that anything less than the truth might leave open the possibility of a return to Stalinism. And its publication was followed by an equally courageous demonstration in which people held aloft signs condemning repression. Most of the signs named Stalin. But one participant raised a banner that spoke directly to his victims, and it reconfirmed the need for an accounting of the dead. Quoting a line written by the great dissident poet Anna Akhmatova, it said simply, "I would like to call you all by name."

When the 19th Party Congress convened a few days later, the members of Memorial brought enormous bags to the hall, containing the petitions they had been laboriously collecting over months, and, remarkably, their forthrightness was rewarded. On the last day of the congress, Mikhail Gorbachev finished his address with a request, delivered casually, as if to blunt its full impact on the hard-liners in his audience: a memorial to the victims of Stalin's terror, he said, must be built.

Nineteen eighty-nine was a year like 1914, 1945, or 1968, a time when life didn't simply change, it was *transformed*, as if going from one evolutionary stage to the next — not only in the Soviet Union, which continued to slowly taste the fruits of freedom, and the satellite nations of what was soon to be called "the *former* Soviet bloc," but also in Communist China, of all places, where students marching for reform crowded Tiananmen Square, a plaza that had once been red with banners bearing the face of Chairman Mao. Now, in an incongruity that seemed all by itself to demonstrate the end of the East-West conflict, the students there defiantly constructed a replica of America's Statue of Liberty at the same time that they carried pictures of the new *Soviet* leader, chanting: "In Russia, they have Gorbachev . . . In China, we have whom?"

No one, maybe not even Gorbachev himself, had quite understood the sweeping power of his reforms. Once he announced that the Soviet Union would no longer prop up the communist leaderships of the Eastern European states, the threats of brute force that had long taken the place of political legitimacy in those nations turned hollow. And with that, the once-dominating power structures of Poland, East Germany, Romania, Czechoslovakia, Bulgaria, and Hungary all fell to dust. Even after China ordered in tanks to abruptly put down the students' hunger strike in Tiananmen Square, killing hundreds, there was still the feeling the world over that the students had won at least a moral victory, though China's Deng Xiaoping, who rose to power in 1977 and had already begun to institute market reforms, continued to have little interest in joining those reforms with political freedoms.

The Tiananmen Square riot had also provided the year's most poignant picture, in both video and still. As if scripted, it showed the meeting between a tank and a man. The tank rumbled toward its task: the putting down of the stu-

The Chinese students crowding Tiananmen Square had been inspired by plans for Gorbachev to visit Beijing, which they hoped would cast a negative light on their own nation's leadership. But by the time the Soviet leader arrived in mid-May, his visit had been overshadowed by the plight of thousands of hunger strikers. With the world's attention turning to Beijing, the students called upon China's paramount leader, Deng Xiaoping, and Premier Li Peng to resign.

On June 4, 1989, troops and tanks
arrived in the square, overrunning the
encampments and crushing the students' replica of the Statue of Liberty.
It will never be known exactly how
many were killed. Still, the strikers'
bravery was not to be lost upon the rest
of the world, particularly with images
like this one, in which students lock
arms to form a human barrier against
the mechanized power of the state.

The revolutions of 1989 sometimes had the feeling of being ordained by some higher power. "For guidance, we were always looking to the metaphysical stage director," said Vaclav Havel, looking at this picture of a rally in Prague's Wenceslas Square. "And I think the man [in the foreground] is turning to him."

dent rebellion. The man walked in front of it. The tank stopped and angled to move past him. The man moved to block it again. And on it went for fifty-seven seconds, the classic confrontation of the twentieth century played out in a pixilated performance for the world to see: there, on a Beijing street, man against brute force, and this time man was winning.

For Americans, it was amazing to watch as the postwar order collapsed not under the force of bombs or the iron fist of a tyrant, but at the power of an idea and one very close to their hearts: liberty. In the midst of the rebellion in Czechoslovakia in November, a worker actually stood at a platform and recited, "We hold these truths to be self-evident, that all men are created equal . . ." And yet the questions rippling from the events in Europe and Asia remained puzzling. Was it possible that the Cold War was over and that the Americans had won? Or was it better to simply say that the Soviets had lost? And just what lesson for the American system, if any, *was* there in the collapse of communism? Surely it demonstrated that the West had prevailed, and yet was there not something also chastening in the way that the rebellions grabbed at the most elemental symbols of American pride, the Statue of Liberty, the Declaration of Independence? And did not many Americans receive that, if only by inference, as a call to reexamine their own ways, to look at their own society with fresh eyes?

There were numerous heroes to the new times, not only Gorbachev and Sakharov, but for many, Reagan, too, for while he had left office by now, conservatives in particular gave him credit for forcing the Soviet Union to back down. In this argument, it was the Reagan arms buildup that had finally forced change; Gorbachev simply realized that to continue to compete, he would have had to strangle Soviet society beyond its limits. The Polish dockworker Lech Walesa remained a champion, for despite the imposition of martial law, his Solidarity union had never given up the fight. So did the Polish pope, John Paul II, who continued to inspire his countrymen to stand up to the Soviets. And in Czechoslovakia there was the remarkably principled writer-dissident Vaclav Havel.

Havel had been active in the "Prague Spring" of 1968. Yet unlike others who gave up after the tanks crushed Alexander Dubcek's "Socialism with a Human Face," he had stayed on. Since that time, he had been jailed off and on for terms that together amounted to five years, once being forced to share a twelve-by-seven-foot cell and another time nearly dying when prison doctors — perhaps purposely — neglected to treat his pneumonia. Havel's most recent jailing had come in the autumn of 1989, when the mood in Prague was already changing. He had been arrested for participating in a memorial ceremony honoring Jan Palach, a youth who burned himself to death to protest the 1968 invasion.

Repeatedly, through the years, the authorities had offered Havel the chance to recant, to disown his writings or at least temper them in an exchange for an end to his harassment. He refused. Words to him were sacred. Indeed, he had become world famous in the seventies as the leader of Charter 77, a human rights group that aimed to force Czechoslovakia to do nothing less than live up to its own words, to follow its own constitution. "If an outside observer who knows nothing at all about life in Czechoslovakia were to study only its laws," he argued, "he or she would be utterly incapable of understanding what we are complaining about." The authorities jailed him again after that remark, then pretended they had released him when in fact they put him under an unacknowledged house

Poland	10 Years
Hungary	10 Months
East Germany	10 Weeks
Czechoslovakia	10 Days
Romania	10 Hours

A sign in Prague, describing how long each anticommunist rebellion took to oust the ruling government

Faced with the overthrow of his regime in Romania, President Nico-lae Ceausescu ordered the army to put the rebels down. The result was Europe's bloodiest 1989 confronta-tion. The rebels finally won, where-upon they forced the dictator and his wife to endure a mock trial, then lined them up for execution. But free-dom had come at a price. When some of the dead were carted off by truck to a Bucharest cemetery, the mournful gave an emotional salute.

arrest. In the kind of doublespeak that for Havel, in particular, must have provided a delicious irony, they let him live "free" at his home but erected a sign outside it saying "Entrance Forbidden."

When the time came to force apart the Czechoslovakian state, the people looked to their poet to lead them. In late 1989, it was Havel who put the demands upon the authorities to step down, and when they finally did, it was Havel who emerged from his office to lead a triumphant march through the streets of the capital city. Like many other Prague institutions, the Czech Philharmonic had been on strike through the autumn, but with the news of the government's collapse the musicians hastily arranged a celebratory concert for that night. They planned to perform, appropriately, Beethoven's Ninth, with its stirring last movement, "Ode to Joy," as a way of honoring the rebirth of their nation. The concert audience had already assembled when Havel entered the hall, and as he did, the people, noticing his arrival, rose as one in applause. They then pointed the way to the seat they had reserved for him, the one in the *presidential* box.

Only the story of Germany topped such drama. And how could it not? For if in fact the world had long been rumbling to the shocks and aftershocks of a single uninterrupted tremor, a century-long clash between East and West, then Berlin was surely the quake's epicenter. After all, it was from Berlin that the soldiers had left in 1914 to start the First World War, it was in Berlin that Hitler built his criminal state in the 1930s, perfected his perverted ideology, and masterminded his campaign against the Jews. It was the Soviet soldiers' arrival in Berlin that ended the European war in 1945 and the struggle over Berlin that set the definition of the Cold War. Surely there are few scenes in human history more chilling, more eerily representative of the human struggle against the iron fist, than the barbed-wire and brick barrier that had divided that city since 1961, the one that had prompted John Kennedy, chopping the air with his hand in that distinctive gesture of emphasis, to implore those who doubted the evils of communism to "come to Berlin." And finally, it was at the Brandenburg Gate in Berlin that Ronald Reagan, in 1987, offered his stirring challenge to Gorbachev. Still skeptical of the new Soviet leader's intentions, Reagan demanded that he demonstrate his sincerity through the most dramatic of actions. "If you seek liberalization, come here to this gate," shouted Reagan. "Mr. Gorbachev, open this gate! Mr. Gorbachev, tear down this wall!"

In the twenty-eight years that the Wall had stood, one year for each of its treacherous miles, eighty desperate people had died trying to scramble over it, or under it, or gripping the underside of cars as they passed through it. But by midsummer of 1989, with the increasing liberalization of the Eastern bloc, no one even bothered trying. For there were suddenly so many easier ways to get to West Germany than challenging the border guards. East Germans simply entered Hungary or Czechoslovakia, a relatively smooth passage from one Soviet bloc state to another, then got approval from the Czechs or the Hungarians to exit into the West and freedom.

What started as a trickle developed into a mass exodus, complicating relations between the Germans and their Warsaw Pact allies. By autumn, nearly a quarter of a million people, almost three hundred an hour, had departed through

"Gorby, Gorby!"

East German youth taunting police, 1989

Bringing down communism in Leipzig: **"We are the people . . . please come with us"**

Tension between the United States and the Soviet Union was mounting throughout the 1980s, and, in East Germany, we were worried about being caught in the middle of a nuclear confrontation. In my town of Leipzig, young people began to gather to pray for peace at the St. Nikolai church. As time went by, the group started to discuss other problems they had with their lives in the East. More and more, these meetings resembled a form of protest.

I never attended any peace prayers, but I used to pass by the church in the evening on my way to the Gewandhaus, where I was the music director. I noticed that police would keep watch over the church and would observe people as they came out of the meetings. The atmosphere in Leipzig was growing uneasy. Even some of my musicians started to have difficulty playing, because we could sense that something was going on which might destroy our whole order of life.

In the summer of 1989, I got a letter from a citizen of Leipzig asking me to help musicians who were put in prison for performing in the street without permission. The government would never allow people to sing songs and play music out in the open like that. Such actions were seen as subversive and dangerous. So I invited all the street musicians of Leipzig, the police, the secret police, party members, and the city council together to the Gewandhaus for a meeting. More than six hundred people came to this talk. At the beginning, the meeting was lively and fun, but as the discussion grew more serious, it became clear that we weren't just looking for the freedom to play in the street, the real issue was political freedom. This was really the first time that people began to talk very openly about what was going on in Leipzig. It was really just a dress rehearsal for what was to come.

Political changes were taking place across central and Eastern Europe. In summer 1989 Hungary opened its borders, allowing thousands of East Germans to flee to Austria. In Leipzig, things were different. People were gathering to protest the government, but they didn't want to leave East Germany. I didn't think that leaving for the West would be such a good idea, either. As director of the Gewandhaus, I had received many offers to go to the United States to work. It would have been the easiest way out for me, but I felt I was conducting one of the best orchestras in the world, and I didn't want to leave them. The point for me was not to escape, but rather to help.

On the seventh of October, we celebrated the fortieth anniversary of the founding of the German Democratic Republic [the communist state of East Germany]. The government tried to stage a celebration that would

Masur, at left, leading a public discussion, 1989; below, freedom demonstrators gathered in Leipzig.

—Kurt Masur was born in 1927 in Brieg, Silesia. After a disease paralyzed several of the fingers in his right hand, he left his study of piano for conducting at the famous Hochschule fur Musik in Leipzig. In 1970, he became the music director of the Gewandhaus in Leipzig and led the orchestra on its first tour of the United States in 1974. In 1991, Masur was appointed music director of the New York Philharmonic.

show the world, as well as the people of East Germany, that everything was still okay. I thought this was really the worst mistake our prime minister, Erich Honecker, could have made. Mikhail Gorbachev, the head of the Soviet Union, attended this celebration, and even he warned Honecker to take note of the popular discontent in East Germany. There were harsh confrontations between the police and the protesters in Berlin and other cities that day. We had a sense that something similar might soon happen in Leipzig.

The most crucial day for us was the ninth of October. The number of people attending the meetings had been growing week by week. We knew there would be a mass demonstration after the meeting that night. The Gewandhaus orchestra was scheduled to perform a concert that day, and so I spent the morning at a dress rehearsal. After practice, a member of one of the youth organizations came to tell me that the government had placed security forces all around Leipzig to beat down the demonstration. After the rehearsal I went home to rest a little bit and then I got a telephone call from the head of the government's Cultural Affairs Department. Five people were to come to my house to discuss the action for that afternoon. Three party members and three nonmembers, including me, sat together in my house to try and figure out what to do. For maybe thirty minutes, the six of us tried to come to an agreement. We insisted that the demonstration not be aggressive, and in return, we asked the party members to ensure that the military, police, and secret police remain peaceful. After the meeting we headed back to the Gewandhaus to put our plan into action. It was very difficult to get downtown. Seventy thousand people were gathering in preparation for the demonstration. We relayed this message of peace to all the churches holding prayer meetings, and we made a tape of the agreement and had it broadcast all across Leipzig.

We were gearing up for something big. It was like a military action before going to battle. We knew that things could have gone either way. The peace prayers

ended around six o'clock, and then the people gathered in the street for a peace march. This was a very tense moment because we knew exactly what might happen. The slightest provocation from either side might trigger an explosion. The military and the police were waiting in the streets, and the tanks were all around the outskirts of Leipzig. Some of the younger demonstrators had said farewell to their parents: "I'm going to a demonstration, and I don't know what will happen."

As the prayer meetings ended, the people left the churches and began chanting, "We are the people. Please come with us." They marched around the inner city of Leipzig, carrying candles in a demonstration of peace. Then they started to talk to the soldiers, and the real young ones placed flowers in the barrels of the soldiers' guns. It was a miraculous moment. By seventhirty, the demonstrators had marched around the entire city and come back to the Gewandhaus again.

Our concert was scheduled to start at eight o'clock. I wanted the concert to continue as planned just to show the government that we weren't afraid to go on with our lives. Even though people were fearing for their lives, the house was packed full. All my musicians came to play. We performed our regular program that night, which included Richard Strauss's *Till Eulenspiegel* and Brahms's Second Symphony. My hands were shaking as I conducted, and I know the musicians were nervous. At the end of the concert, the audience just stood up. And this was not a standing ovation to applaud the music, it was just to say, "We made it through this day peacefully." There was never any point in my life when I felt so strongly that music can do much more than entertain.

The next morning everybody went to work as usual. We had no way of knowing that this demonstration would change so much in the GDR. But it got the ball rolling for the rest of the demonstrations, because everybody said, "Wow, this works." The young people had their dream, and it was wonderful. And I must say, that October was one of the happiest times of my life, to see hopeful eyes and to feel freedom.

this end run. Then, frustrated, and hoping to buy some goodwill, the new East German communist leader did something his predecessor had only recently said would not happen for one hundred years: he reluctantly ordered the opening of East Germany's borders.

Almost instantaneously, people poured into East Berlin's streets and approached the Wall's guards with shouts of *"Tor auf!"* (Open the gate), while on the other side, West Berliners gathered, ready to greet them, many of them holding deutsche marks they intended to pass to the newly freed as they came across. After all, East German currency was worthless in the West and these people needed money to celebrate. When the order took effect at midnight, the crowd pushed forward with a roar. They had been waiting for this moment for over a generation, and many had given up hope that it would ever come.

Thirty-four-year-old Angelika Wache became the first East German to cross the border into the new era. "I just can't believe it," she shouted. "I don't feel like I'm in prison anymore." She was followed by thousands and then tens of thousands more "Ossies," as the West Germans called them, each one of them, it seemed, smiling wider than the last. A wild party erupted and all sense of order collapsed. Champagne rained down on each car as it passed, poured from above where youths pranced atop the Wall's once-forbidden parapets. With no sense of danger, people climbed up and, without looking, simply fell into the other side, certain they would be caught in the arms of excited Westerners. Even the guards themselves joined in the fun. "When we got the word," announced one policeman, "we were as surprised as everybody else."

"The Wall is gone, the Wall is gone," chanted the people, delirious with celebration. And soon everywhere one looked there was a hammer or a chisel or a pickaxe, turning the hated symbol into a collection of souvenir rocks. It had risen with such evil fanfare and had stared back at Berlin ominously for decades, and yet within days, it was nothing more than a denuded totem, a simple slab of harmless concrete, filled with Swiss-cheese-like holes. Travelers stopping at Checkpoint Charlie now asked the guards to pose for pictures with their children, and the more than three hundred dogs who had been trained to attack freedom-seekers were quickly sold off to new masters. After all, who needed them now?

The mood was giddy the world over, but for the Germans, in particular, this newfound liberty tasted like sweet nectar. The night that the borders were opened, a man living near the now abandoned crossing at Staaken went outside to make a routine late night check of his greenhouse when he saw a woman in a nightgown dancing along on her tiptoes, past the empty wooden customs booth. The woman, as if in a dreamlike trance, stopped abruptly, searched the ground, and then looked up at him. "Where is the borderline here?" she asked. The two looked carefully for the point that only hours before had been impassable. And when they found the line, the woman whirled atop it in a whimsical pirouette; then, satisfied, she returned home.

Members of West Germany's environmentally
conscious and leftist Green Party recommended
"the breaking off of the work of breaking [the
Wall's] stone" until "orderly waste management" could be administered. But their appeals
were pointless. No one wanted to wait for the
"system," of all things, to tear down this wall.

12

Machine Dreams

1989–1999

Previous spread: Man ended the century much the way that he started it, caught up in a whirlwind over the promise of technology. In the setup shot here, a photographer portrayed family life in the hi-tech nineties: Mom with a laptop computer, Dad on a cellular phone, and both, along with their child, in the grip of the fantasy environment provided by "virtual reality goggles."

Above: The end of the Cold War brought forth a ferocious new era of world capitalism that was American inspired, if not led. When that quintessential American consumer icon McDonald's (or, in Chinese, Mai Dan Lau) opened in Beijing in 1992, a record 28,500 customers queued up. By 1998 there were nearly two hundred McDonald's throughout China, inspiring an Americanization of some local customs, among them clean rest rooms and waiting in line.

Machine Dreams 1989–1999

A few seconds before making his fortieth move in the sixth and final game of one of history's most celebrated chess matches, Garry Kasparov reached across the table at the Pennsylvania Convention Center and retrieved his watch. It was February 17, 1996, and the thirty-two-year-old Kasparov, generally acknowledged to be the greatest chess player ever, was displaying a bit of his characteristic arrogance. When the game is in hand, when he feels he has his opponent in an impossible position, the Armenian grand master traditionally reaches for his timepiece and buckles it to his arm as a way of taunting the other player. After all, he is saying, with the game essentially over, it is time to gather my things together and think about getting a head start on the traffic heading home. And yet the gesture here had to have been prompted more by habit than design, for sitting opposite Kasparov tonight, matching him gambit for gambit, was an opponent impervious to such psychological games: an impassive, calculating computer.

The match between Garry Kasparov and IBM RS/6000 SP, or Deep Blue, had been conceived as sport, but many saw in it issues that raised this contest into a higher realm. Because it calls upon both the intellect and sheer cunning, chess had stood for centuries as the ultimate demonstration of at least a certain kind of human intelligence, and if a computer could now be programmed to seriously compete with the world's foremost chess mind, well, then, what did that tell us? That the human brain could be duplicated by science? That machines could go beyond the performance of functions, beyond "problem-solving," and actually "think"? And if a computer could play chess like Kasparov, how long would it be before it could compose a fugue worthy of Bach? A poem every bit as impressive as those from the pen of Wordsworth? Kasparov won the Philadelphia match, four games to two, yet the champion nervously acknowledged that he had, at times, felt "the stirrings of genuine thought" coming from his opponent, and the mere fact that the computer had beaten him in two of the games was enough for the IBM programmers to declare a victory of their own. Now, as the weeks counted down to a 1997 rematch, many people began to speculate: what if this time Deep Blue wins?

"Deep Blue is just a machine. It doesn't have a mind any more than a flower pot has a mind . . . and its chief meaning is this: that human beings are champion machine builders."

David Gelernter, *Yale computer science professor*

"There's really a tragic sense here; it's the dying of an age. Man may no longer be king of this universe . . ."

Chess expert Bruce Pandolfini, on the man-versus-machine chess match

To poet Charles Siebert, who participated in a *Harper's* magazine panel earnestly assembled on the subject, the anxiety many people attached to the man-versus-machine chess match demonstrated the feeling, pervasive in the nineties, that science had begun an assault on human specialness, one that resonated deeply with advances in fertility research and cloning. "People [are beginning] to think," he declared, ". . . that this is all we are, an assemblage of biological juices — line them up the right way and we can be reproduced." Similarly, computer scientist Jaron Lanier detected a growing public nervousness as to precisely what a person is, and "the better computers get at performing tasks that people find hard to do, the more that definition is threatened." But author James Bailey attributed the fear to a misguided premise, and in that he saw an opportunity. "We, as a species, made a decision at some point to define human uniqueness around our intelligence, our ability to do mind tasks," he argued, ". . . [and] that purported strut . . . is about to get kicked out from under us, by Deep Blue, among other things . . . but if in that process we come to understand that we're not essentially analytical beings, that our essence is something higher, then that's a positive development."

As a rule, Kasparov and all other human players limit their thinking to a handful of positions, pre-edited by their experience (a process known in computer chess circles as forward pruning), and at first chess-playing computers were programmed to "think" that way, too. But gradually, over the years, programmers began to understand that the computer would do much better if it remained true to itself, playing not like a human, but like a computer, and so the IBM team's machines were programmed to follow a process known as brute force, a plan that involved essentially starting over again with each move, considering literally a billion options in a matter of a few seconds, and then choosing the best one. The shift of strategy, which occurred long before Deep Blue, had catapulted the computer into a significantly more competitive position, and in the end it also helped to focus the big question posed by the man-versus-computer match: just how should one determine that the machine had finally equaled the capacity of the human brain — if it could mimic human process or using its own process simply achieve results equal to those achieved by the smartest humans?

When, in May of 1997, Kasparov arrived at a Manhattan office building to play Deep Blue in the much-anticipated rematch, he saw himself as representing nothing less than the entire human race. And in game one, while spectators followed the contest both in person (twenty-five dollars a seat) and through an Internet Web site (*www.chess.ibm.com*), he did humanity proud, forcing Deep Blue to play like "a numskull," as one former U.S. champion declared. Yet, afterward, Kasparov acknowledged that the computer's capacity to consider millions of options at once had forced him to "calculate, calculate, calculate" at a tiring pace and he was not at all sure he could keep it up. He was right. By the end of game five, the computer was still holding its own — one game to one, with three draws — and Kasparov was exhausted. Uncharacteristically addled, he began the sixth and final game with a risky sequence of moves that forced Deep Blue to sacrifice a knight. But that left Kasparov's king exposed, and moments later, realizing his mistake, the champion abruptly stood up and resigned. The game had lasted just nineteen moves.

For so many people, the final decade of the twentieth century began with the kind of fuzzy-headed state of mind that accompanies a dramatic transition, as when one arrives in a new country where the natives speak a different language or settles in to live in a new community where there are no familiar faces or sights. There was now simply no denying that this was a different time, no longer the modern era, but the *post* modern era, no longer the Cold War world, but a *post* Cold War world. And as spent as the modern dogma had become, and as much money and creative thinking as had been exhausted in the hostile competition between the superpowers, at least these had formed a well-known state of affairs.

The new, emerging world, by contrast, felt strange — not necessarily bad; in fact quite good in many ways — but undeniably different. The Cold War had been such a defining element of Western life for so long that it was rather as if some enormous lifelong pain had finally been lifted, a crippling pain, and now, with atrophied muscles, it was time to learn how to walk all over again. In Europe the collapse of communism was followed by puzzling questions. Could West Germany absorb East Germany without undermining its own stability and prosperity? And if it did, could it quell the worries of those in the rest of the world — those who, remembering all too well that the emergence of a strong and ambitious German state had preceded the twentieth century's two most violent episodes, now feared that a happy, unified Deutschland would be the prelude to World War III?

However corrupt or venal, Yugoslavia's Communists had provided the glue that held that fragile nation together. Here, a Croatian boy weeps at the death of his father, a policeman killed by Serbian guerrillas, in the post–Cold War violence that gripped one of many former Soviet bloc states.

The Eastern European peoples found themselves with a different kind of confusion. Since their leaderships had been propped up for so long by little more than the threat of state violence, the very absence of the oppressive, powerful state now allowed for the reemergence of age-old ethnic conflicts and too-long-suppressed political grievances, confirming the maxim that the greatest violence and political chaos come not in revolution, but in the period following a revolution, when a nation attempts to assemble its new identity in an atmosphere dominated by competing interests.

There were many casualties to the emerging new order, most notably the Soviet Union itself, which by 1992 had ceased to exist. Its constituent states now formed a handful of new countries, among them a new Russia, whose people, seeking even greater change than that tentatively offered by their heroic reformer, saw fit to toss Gorbachev *and* the Communist Party onto the dust heap. Czechoslovakia, a peculiar joining of populations with no shared ethnicity and little shared history, split into two states, one Czech and one Slovak. And what became known, for lack of a better phrase, as "the former

"The United Colors of Benetton"

Nineties advertising slogan for Benetton clothing stores, suggesting the joining of the world's consumers

In the eighties he led an empire, but by 1997 Mikhail Gorbachev, out of a job, was shilling for Pizza Hut. "I thought that it is a people's matter — food," explained the man many would rank as among the three or four most important leaders in modern history, "[and] if my name works for the benefit of consumers, to hell with it . . . ."

Yugoslavia" was rent into warring ethnic factions, an eerie development when one considered that it was ethnic strife in the Balkans that had given impetus to the archduke's assassin and the firing of the shot that initiated the bloodbath that was World War I. Was it possible that the great East-West conflict had been a mere interruption of history, a detour from which humanity now returned to link up with the path it had departed from in 1914?

Yet even with the issuing forth of ancient blood feuds, there were many signs of a growing democratic — and capitalistic — consensus, and with that, a growing interconnectedness between national economies. Not only were the Eastern European states holding elections, *real* elections, for the first time in fifty years, even places with a tenuous connection, at best, to the collapse of the Cold War were extending their compliance with democratic principles. In 1994 South Africa's blacks were allowed to vote for the first time, and immediately elected African National Congress leader Nelson Mandela to the presidency (he had only recently emerged from twenty-seven years in captivity). And in many places that had long shunned the profit principle — not only Russia and Eastern Europe but also China and Vietnam — capitalism was now taking hold, a development rapidly producing a single mammoth global marketplace. It was almost as if the "one world" that Marxist ideologists had declared to be an inevitable conclusion of progress was emerging — not, as they had predicted, in the unity of the world's workers, but in the unity of its *consumers* and the assertion of the capitalistic principles that Marx found most abhorrent. By 1997 even Gorbachev had become a willing participant, appearing in American television commercials as a spokesman for Pizza Hut.

One writer, noting this trend, declared the "end of history" — a rather bold pronouncement meant to suggest a worldwide convergence around the ideas of liberal democracy and market economics — and his declaration was greeted by some Americans with smugness. Yet there was no denying that this new form of capitalism, while supranational in character, was decidedly American in style, penetrating beyond markets into the public culture to create what another historian called "McWorld," a community tied together not only by commerce but also by communications, information, and entertainment, much of it originating in the United States. Certainly there was no denying that the new market economics suited America well. By the late nineties the nation had seemed to have arrived at an economic Eden: negligible inflation, negligible unemployment, and 4 percent growth (up from a twenty-year average of 2.4 percent).

The arrival of the twenty-four-hour American cable news channel and the availability of Music Television (MTV) throughout the world contributed enormously to the trend toward an American-driven world economy. So did the development of the ubiquitous Internet, which gave fresh credence to Marshall McLuhan's prediction of a global village, a kind of electronic world society gathered somewhere out *there*, in the ether. Indeed, by the nineties technology had ceased to be something to be turned on or off — it was now the very landscape in which daily lives were lived. And while its scenery was perhaps best enjoyed by traveling the "information superhighway" (to use the most popular metaphor associated with the Internet), one didn't need to be on the Net to feel surrounded, even overwhelmed, by the information age. How else to explain the decade's day-to-day obsession with the minutest details of distant scandal, its

The end of South Africa's apartheid system, which had denied blacks the most basic rights for decades, was one of the century's more glorious triumphs. It was also proof that the new democratic spirit sweeping the world did not confine itself to the former communist nations. Above, newly enfranchised South Africans campaign for Nelson Mandela, who, gathering 60 percent of the vote, would easily become the nation's new president.

"The computers are down . . ."

Nineties lament, stopping all but the most elemental commerce and exchange of information

sensational court trials blown up to carry mythic symbolism, and the oversentimentalizing of the death of public figures than as the arrival of a kind of extraordinary group awareness shared across thousands of miles and the breach of cultures? Now, thanks to the stretch of the techno-environment, it was virtually impossible not to be aware almost instantaneously of every new gory detail about O.J., Diana, even Monica Lewinsky.

And yet these new communications toys, the logical descendants of the century's other communications toys, were just one way in which technology was reasserting its place as the primary engine of social and political change. Like no time since the beginning of the century, science in the nineties promised a new and different life both through the multifaceted advancements of the computer and through the dramatic, and sometimes frightening, developments of medical science. Indeed, from the vantage point of this decade, with its surrogate mothers and selective abortions, its donor eggs and donor wombs, its new definitions of life and death, and its fascination with genetics and the "mad scientist" possibilities inherent in cloning, the test tube as an agent of conception, so radical when it first appeared in 1978, looked as quaint as a midwife.

And in that sometimes dissonant relationship between the society that seemed to be departing and the one that seemed to be emerging lay the nineties dilemma, the *post* modern, *post* Cold War, *post* industrial society dilemma. For how could the new instantaneous world of communications, the one that wired humanity together into a single nervous system, coexist with the kinds of atavistic

With hundreds of Kuwaiti oil wells set ablaze by the Iraqis burning behind them, a group of U.S. soldiers race toward Kuwait City. Desert Storm was mounted for moral purposes — President Bush went so far as to compare Iraqi's Saddam Hussein to Hitler — but economics was a driving force, too. Western oil prices depended upon a free Kuwait.

hatreds that consumed, say, Bosnia, or, for that matter, drove America's own race wars and the paranoia of its growing right-wing militias and their supporters? How could the race-based tribal loyalties of the *jihad,* as historian Ben Barber worried, commingle with the cosmopolitan McWorld? How could man's need to remain true to his humanness endure with the increasingly commanding visions of science? And how could life in the twentieth century meet the long-anticipated arrival of the twenty-first?

When it comes to naming "defense initiatives," there are few choices that can rank with "Desert Storm." Besides its obvious evocations of sand-blown landscapes, the name could also work as the title of a pulp novel or B movie, even as a video game. In early 1991 more than two dozen allied nations began an assault on Iraq in an attempt to extract that nation's forces from positions in neighboring Kuwait. It was a simple rout. In just over forty days of mostly American air attacks (followed by fewer than one hundred hours of ground fighting), thousands of new hi-tech bombs (PGMs, or "precision guided munitions" in official Pentagonese) rained across Iraqi positions, driving the enemy back to Baghdad and international humiliation.

For the United States the war was the first since the debacle in Vietnam, and throughout the fall of 1990, as President George Bush pushed for congressional backing and the American public entered into an anguished debate over whether to strike at the Iraqis, the nation's situation reminded one of a pilot tentatively climbing back into the cockpit years after a traumatic and crippling crash. For who could know if Iraq would not become to the nineties what Vietnam had been to the sixties and seventies, a protracted affair robbing Americans of their young and returning the nation to the kind of internal feuding from which it had never quite recovered?

Still, there was no denying that these were different times. Among the nations standing with the United States against Saddam Hussein's seizure of the oil-rich Kuwaiti sands was the Soviet Union, the first instance since World War II in which Americans and Soviets had fought on the same side. If this was to be America's first war since Vietnam, it was also then to be the first of what the president described as a "new world order," a post–Cold War "order" that positioned the allied nations as a kind of international police force putting down acts of raw aggression.

The idea hearkened back in some ways to the foreign policy of Teddy Roosevelt, who insisted that the advanced civilizations carry the responsibility for maintaining an international morality, the "white man's burden," to use Kipling's imperialist phrase. And yet Roosevelt could never have imagined a police action as pyrotechnically alert as the one that lit the skies over Iraq. For just as significant as the Persian Gulf War's new alliance and purpose was the way that the war was fought. World War I had advanced combat into the sphere of mechanized warfare; World War II had taken technology even further and made civilians targets. Now, in Iraq, computer technology advanced both the tools and the strategy of war to where it resembled science fiction, with bombs programmed to sweep down chimneys, slip through air shafts into bunkers, and take out not just a bridge, but the crucial center span of a bridge, assuring its destruction. Beginning with the launching of a Tomahawk cruise missile from the deck of the USS *Wis-*

consin at 3:00 A.M. on January 17, 1991, Baghdad became the site of one of the most devastating air raids in history.

Later reporting would demonstrate that the Pentagon's much-heralded computer programs were not as precise as then claimed, but there was no doubt that warfare itself had entered a new and impressive epoch, a "military millennium," as defense experts called it. And with satellites mapping the globe with increasing accuracy (within a few years, it would become possible to locate any point on the ground within a five-meter radius), it seemed possible that war would soon become as simple as the deleting of a computer file: a battlefield scanned, the position of principal targets determined and systematically destroyed.

America's new strategy had created the image of a "clean" war, precise and efficient, suspect perhaps in the way that it distanced the fighting man from the reality of his fight — young pilots described their work in the Persian Gulf as reminiscent of computer games — and yet a war well suited to a people whose patience for war remained thin. "The specter of Vietnam has been buried forever in the desert sands of the Arabian peninsula," declared Bush, an unfortunate comment that made the defeat of Iraq seem to be motivated more by Americans' need for psychological relief than the righting of any international wrong. But after the ugly experience of Vietnam, most people did feel it amazing that a war could be fought so fast it hardly demanded more attention than a television miniseries, with so few American losses (148 dead versus around 200,000 Iraqis) and such undeniable results (Iraq out of Kuwait).

New bombs equipped with "video eyes" allowed pilots to closely monitor the progress of their missions. This image confirmed a successful allied strike: destruction of an Iraqi munitions depot.

Both by using advanced technology and by targeting the technology of the enemy, America had seemed to have arrived at a more acceptable way to fight a war, hardware striking hardware, and in that fact military historian Edward Luttwak detected an irony. In 1945, toward the end of World War II, Berlin had been devastated by five years of heavy bombing, yet electrical power, water systems, and sewage disposal were still functioning adequately, and Hitler, from his bunker, continued to direct his troops by telephone and radio. By contrast, only forty-eight hours after the onset of the attack on Baghdad, the Iraqi capital city, while more or less physically intact, had been bombed out of the twentieth century: no telephone service, no electricity, no television, no water, no sewage disposal. Iraqi strongman Saddam Hussein could not communicate with his troops or his people. And his war was already effectively lost.

The American people followed the progress of the Persian Gulf War on television not only through the coverage provided by the three main commercial networks but also through a relative newcomer, the Cable News Network. Because CNN was allowed to install its own dedicated copper phone line before the war even began (separating it from the fate of Baghdad's municipal phone system), the network's correspondents Bernard Shaw, John Holliman, and Peter

Tales of a Gulf War pilot: "This was my generation's war"

When I was a teenager, I really wanted to have a motorcycle, but my father was a doctor and he flatly refused. He said, "I've pronounced too many kids your age dead. You can't have a motorcycle. But if you'd like to do something exciting, I'll help you learn how to fly." So I started flying gliders when I was in seventh grade. I had already known that I wanted to fly airplanes, even then. And when I discovered that there were airplanes that landed on ships, well that sealed it for me. I entered the Naval Academy in 1974, the year after I graduated from high school.

In 1990 I was assigned to a squadron called VFA-81 in Air Wing 17, or the Sunliners, and we were attached to the USS *Saratoga*. We were scheduled to go on a normal deployment to the Middle East in August, so we were as trained and prepared as anybody when the Iraqis invaded Kuwait on August 2. To be quite honest, I wasn't all that concerned with what was going on over there. I was the maintenance officer of the squadron, so I was very focused on just one thing and that was to make sure all my airplanes and all my people were ready by the time our deployment date came. As we were about to leave, the maintenance officer from another squadron nudged me in the ribs and I said, "Hey, this thing in the Middle East is really heating up. You guys may have a chance to shoot down some MIGs." But we really had no idea of what we were about to face. We made it to the Red Sea, on the western side of the Saudi peninsula, by August 20 or 21. By that time Kuwait had been captured and there was this furious churn to get forces into the region to be able to deter any further aggression. We stayed there for five months before the war actually started. Now, I have a Christian faith, which helped me deal with the possibility of my own death. I felt that if the Lord called me home on this, then that's where I'd want to be. On the other hand, the idea of killing people was distasteful to me. Fortunately, with the technology and tactics at the time, we were far more precise about pinpointing the bad guys who were carrying weapons and driving tanks or airplanes. We could strike our targets with a minimal loss of life.

On January 15 we got word that the diplomatic efforts had failed and that we would soon initiate our opening sequence of strikes against Iraq. We had been training for these strikes for months, so there was a certain level of excitement — and a little bravado — at the anticipation of finally seeing action. At the same time, there was a lot of soul-searching and serious thought given to the fact that, no kidding, we're gonna do this. The opening strikes from the *Saratoga* were designed to suppress the defenses around Baghdad. Our first planes were sent out at midnight for time-on-target of about three or four o'clock in the morning. I wasn't on that

— Mark Fox, born in 1956, was commissioned in June 1978 upon graduation from the U.S. Naval Academy and earned his wings in March 1980. During Desert Storm, he led four major air wing strikes and flew eighteen combat sorties. His awards include the Silver Star Medal, the Defense Meritorious Service Medal, two Meritorious Service Medals, seven Air Medals, two Navy Commendation Medals, and the Navy Achievement Medal. He is currently assigned as the Joint Strike & Aviation Programs Liaison officer for the navy's Office of Legislative Affairs in Washington, D.C.

Lieutenant Commander Mark Fox in the cockpit, 1991.

first mission, but as I was being briefed for the second strike, we learned that one of our pilots was shot down and killed in the central part of Iraq. It was like ashes in our mouths. He was a good buddy of mine, a father of two, our children went to the same preschool together. It really helped bring home the realities of what we were doing.

My first combat mission was the first daylight strike on the seventeenth. The target was an airfield in western Iraq. This airfield had six SA-6 sites, which is a pretty lethal surface-to-air missile system. From the Red Sea, over Saudi Arabia and into Iraq is somewhere between 650 and 750 nautical miles, one way. And there are no tactical airplanes that can go that distance without refueling, so on each mission we had to hook up with air force tanker planes. Typically there would be a sum total of maybe four or five air force tankers spaced out in a five-mile area in the sky, and there might be five navy airplanes attached to each tanker getting gas. So in that five-mile patch of sky there might be twenty-five to thirty navy jets all gassing up at the same time. It was an amazing sight, especially at night with all of the lights. It looked like the Empire State Building flying on its side through the sky.

As we were nearing our target, we got word from an early-warning airplane that there were Iraqi fighters in front of us. I was carrying a lot of iron, four 2,000-pound bombs, so I wasn't really configured for classic air-to-air combat with a MIG. But I got a lock on an Iraqi MIG about ten miles on my nose and closing fast. He was supersonic, at about Mach 1.2 or Mach 1.3. I fired a heat-seeking missile. In the old days you had to be behind the guy to shoot a heat-seeking missile. But we were using a more sophisticated Sidewinder that had an all-aspect seeker on it, meaning I could shoot it from

just about anywhere. The bad news was that I didn't realize that it was a smokeless motor missile, which means it had no trail. So it disappeared when it came off my rail and I had no idea if it fired properly. I had a huge wave of self-doubt, and the MIG was closing in on me very fast. So then I selected a radar-guided missile, a Sparrow, and fired it. As it turned out both the Sidewinder and the Sparrow worked just fine.

We were about thirty miles south of the target at this point. And we were just now getting into the heart of the Iraqi surface-to-air missile envelopes. We got a radar lock on another group of airplanes flying very high and very slow just above our target, which is not where fighters defending a target would normally be. And so at this point, I'm thinking, man, you know in the Iran-Iraq war there were some cases where the Iraqis would put up an airplane to do something stupid as a piece of bait. And then when the Iranian F-4s committed on this guy, the Iraqis would have a MIG do a low-to-high intercept. It was a relatively sophisticated bait-and-drag type of tactic. I wound up looking behind me for about the next minute, trying to see if this was a trap. These planes then turned and flew away from us. I had to decide whether to run these guys down or just go ahead and complete my mission. I thought to myself, I came here to drop bombs, not to chase MIGs around. So I let him go and rolled in on the target. I dropped the bombs and did my jinks [erratic evasive maneuvers]. Now, I wasn't gonna come 640 nautical miles and not see my bombs hit their target, so I looked to see my four 2,000-pound bombs falling together like four little fish in a pond. It was a really nice sight. But I could also see the muzzle flashes and the smoke and the dust coming from all over the field. There were literally dozens and dozens of little corkscrew-bottle rocket-looking things shooting up every which way down below me. It was clear that with all of this antiaircraft fire, it was no time for me to speculate any more. So I went back into another series of adrenaline-fed jinks and peeked back at the target just in time to see my four 2,000-bombs hit their target. And that was the first time I smiled all day. I turned back and headed for the carrier. Less then two hours after I landed, I was being briefed for my next mission.

In the Persian Gulf, soldiers turned to CNN for news on the very war they were fighting. Here, enlisted men watch at an American base in Saudi Arabia.

Arnett were in Baghdad as the first bombs arrived, offering Americans one of the most exciting moments of news television ever, a chilling picture of war "as it happened." CNN's dispatches formed the modern counterpart to Edward R. Murrow's live radio reports from London during World War II, only this wasn't radio, this was television, *live* television; and through the miracle of satellite transmission all of America saw what Shaw and his other CNN correspondents saw, an instance when those reporting the news, in a sense, became less important than the technology delivering it: a direct, unfiltered picture of the event itself.

CNN had been around since 1980, and the network had already shown its capacity to deliver viewers instantly to breaking news events like the crash of Pan Am 103 in December 1988, the San Francisco earthquake in October 1989, the American invasion of Panama in December 1989, and the release of Nelson Mandela in February 1990. While the three big broadcast networks were forced to make judgments on whether to interrupt other programming to present such news (and, if so, for how long), the producers at CNN faced no such decision — news was their network's *raison d'être*. Journalism was changing. Back when television became a viable news medium in the 1960s, newspapers struggled to keep up, and since they could no longer beat television to the news, they settled for reporting it in more depth and analysis. Now, in the hi-tech nineties, the older broadcast networks were themselves suffering much the same fate (and turning to the same solutions), for with the exception of the biggest stories, it was virtually assured that CNN, with its twenty-four-hour window to the world, would get the news on the air first.

Those other events had brought the network passing attention, but the Gulf War was CNN's coming-out party. On that first night, the fledgling network achieved ratings near those of CBS, NBC, and ABC, and throughout the war's six weeks, it sustained its largest audience ever. Yet, just as important as the numbers of Americans who now tuned to CNN was the stretch of the network around the world. Expanding first to Japan and then Western Europe, and finally to the former Soviet bloc states and the Arab countries, CNN had become the first truly global network (by 1998 its cable links would reach 73 million American homes, 120 million homes overseas). In fact, it was the Iraqis' familiarity with CNN that prompted them to allow that network access denied to the other big commercial American television news operations. For, with CNN's Peter Arnett in Baghdad throughout the war, they had an opportunity to get their side's story across to Americans *and* the rest of the world.

Arnett's presence in Iraq prompted some to see him as a traitor to the American cause, a tool of Iraqi propaganda. Yet the CNN reporter could now claim (and did) that his responsibility was first and foremost to his CNN audience, an *international* audience. And indeed, with the persistent sense that the world was now transfixed by a single television image, tuned to CNN, it was hard not to feel that national loyalties were becoming increasingly less significant. How else, asked journalist William Henry, were we to "explain Kenyans lined up six deep in front of electronics stores to watch footage of a war they had no soldiers fighting in" than as the arrival of a kind of electronic brotherhood? And how else to explain Russian President Boris Yeltsin resisting the attempted hard-line coup in the Soviet Union a few months later by climbing atop a tank in full view of CNN cameras and delivering a picture of hope not only to the rest of the world but also to at least 100,000 Muscovites for whom CNN remained the only news source not in control of the coup's leaders? (Days later, a diplomat from one of the newly independent Baltic states actually called CNN to thank them for assisting in the defeat of the hard-liners and the eventual freeing of his country from the Soviet vise.)

CNN was just one of many networks in the historic Senate Caucus Room on October 11, 1991, when a forty-three-year-old federal judge sat before the Senate Judiciary Committee some one hundred days after being nominated to serve as the next justice of the Supreme Court. The Senate's consideration of Clarence Thomas had been politically contentious but, as far as the wider public was concerned, uneventful. Now that would all change. In a mood electric with the sensational, Thomas had arrived to face down charges that he had been guilty of sexual harassment.

While there were many who had challenged Thomas's qualifications for the High Court and cynically suggested that he had been chosen by President Bush only because he represented a rare combination — he was both black *and*

"When there was a disaster, it used to be that people went to church and all held hands . . . Now the minute anything happens they all run to CNN and think, 'The whole world is sharing this experience with me.'"

Don Hewitt, producer of
CBS's 60 Minutes

Peter Arnett
Baghdad, Iraq
CNN

"I was in Baghdad for the people who watch CNN," affirmed correspondent Peter Arnett, not for the United States government. But the sense that the press now attached its loyalty to a new borderless world embittered many.

"No job is worth what I have been through," declared Clarence Thomas under the glare of the klieg lights. *The private lives of public officials were a nineties preoccupation, with both liberals and conservatives employing the personal smear as an effective tactic of political warfare. Seven years later, when President Bill Clinton was accused of far worse behavior than Thomas, the tables simply turned, with Republicans trumpeting sexual harassment, Democrats playing it down.*

conservative — it was hard not to be struck by the judge's inspiring life story. Born poor, the grandson of a black sharecropper, at a time when Georgia still operated according to the principles of Jim Crow, he had risen to complete a degree from Holy Cross and Yale Law School, leading to a career at the heart of Washington. The fact that he now rejected the liberal philosophy that may have been the engine of his success rankled some, yet there were just as many who saw in that fact an opportunity to assert a more mature attitude toward race relations: a sort of declaration of independence for black conservatives, eager to break free of the stereotype that had long depicted the black community as unquestioning supporters of liberal politics.

Thomas's accuser had a similarly attractive life story. Anita Hill had been born poor, too, one of thirteen children. Like Thomas, she was devoutly religious, and she, too, had gone to Yale Law School. In 1981 Hill had joined the Reagan administration, where her path crossed with Thomas's, and it was there, while she worked for him at the Department of Education and the Equal Employment Opportunity Commission (EEOC), that, as she now claimed, he had brought her considerable pain by pestering her for dates, attempting to engage her in discussions of pornography, and boasting of his talents as a lover.

Prim in a light blue suit, her voice calm and assured, Hill was the epitome of the believable witness, and as a fellow conservative, what motivation would she have to come forward if it were not to tell the truth? Yet when Thomas took the chair to deny her charges, it was hard not to feel sympathy for him, too. The Senate committee room was not, after all, a court of law, and if, as he claimed, Hill's charges were untrue, then why was the committee giving her a public stage, subjecting him to such torment, such scurrilous accusations before the eyes of the world? Feminists and others were outraged when Republican senators began a vicious attack on Hill, insinuating that she was a psychotic or a liar. Yet it was a frustrated and angry Thomas who finally declared the hearings to have devolved into a circus, a travesty, a national disgrace. "Confirm me if you want. Don't confirm me if you are so led," he stormed, then followed on with a description of the scene as a "high tech lynching for an uppity black."

By then, discussion of the Hill-Thomas affair had become a national obsession. There was something undeniably intriguing, after all, in seeing two people — each of them with eyes forward, voices strong — offer such incompatible memories that it seemed certain that one of them was lying. There was, too, something perverse in seeing the Senate Caucus Room, the setting for the Iran-contra and Watergate hearings, and so many other pieces of grave national business, now echoing with words like "penis" and "pubic hair" and descriptions of the anatomy of porn stars. With no way to determine the truth with any certainty ("he said, she said"), most viewers had quickly turned a public event into a personal one, reflecting back on their own behavior (men) or experience (women), or they had decided instead to look upon the hearings for their symbolic value, asserting that the truth was less important than the fact that Thomas and Hill had focused the nation on the long-suppressed issue of sexual harassment. And yet when it was over, and Thomas had been narrowly confirmed by the Senate (52–48), there was among people on all sides the uncomfortable feeling of having just been party to an ugly public spectacle of extraordinary insensitivity, if not a "high tech lynching" then at the very least a "high tech humiliation" of two people whose murky relationship had been picked apart by a bumbling Senate panel and a television audience of voyeurs.

At the same time that the nation was in the grip of the televised image of the Hill-Thomas hearings, attorneys in Los Angeles were preparing their defense of several police officers accused of brutality. Normally such a story would have received scant national attention, but the presence of a compelling videotape of the beating of Rodney King, a twenty-five-year-old black man, had made the trial of Stacey Koon and three other white officers a powder keg. When, in the early morning hours of March 3, 1991, plumbing parts salesman George William Holliday focused his camcorder lens on the scene outside his Los Angeles apartment window, he had provided all the evidence most people needed to see King as a tragic victim, his tormentors as racist brutes. Surely this film, showing the victim receiving fifty-six blows over eighty-one seconds, was undeniable proof of a serious crime and a clarion call to examine police behavior nationwide. As many blacks asserted, the grotesque attack was no anomaly; blacks were regularly held in greater suspicion than whites and suffered harsher treatment from law enforcement officers.

Many women heard Anita Hill, above, as a voice of courage — the Rosa Parks of the sexual harassment issue — and they accused the all-male Senate panel of an insensitivity born of gender. "They just don't get it" became a familiar cry.

"The judge was wronged, Anita Hill was wronged, the process was wronged . . ."

Senate Judiciary Committee chairman Joe Biden, conceding mistakes in the handling of the Hill-Thomas hearings

"Can we get along?" pleaded Rodney King poignantly, in an attempt to end the Los Angeles riots of 1992, seen below, but much of both white and black America was no longer sure that they could. Twenty-seven years after the "first" L.A. riots in Watts helped set in motion well-intentioned efforts to end the misery in America's blighted urban communities, poverty, crime, and racial animosity appeared to be even worse than before.

The Rodney King beating, right, was one memorable video icon in a video icon age.

In fact, so many people had seen the video (which was telecast over and over again) and been outraged by its contents that it was hard to determine just where Koon and his colleagues could get a fair trial; certainly, it seemed, nowhere in California, or America, for that matter, and not even throughout much of the world. Frustrated, Judge Stanley Weisberg finally settled on overwhelmingly white Simi Valley, sixty miles from downtown Los Angeles. But the strategy of the officers' lawyers would in the end be as key as the racial composition of the jury. Aware that they were up against a compelling piece of evidence, the defense attorneys decided to counter by running the videotape in slow motion and freezing frames — disassembling it, in effect — to assert that King, who had been drunk and fleeing arrest in a high-speed chase, had been more threatening in his resistance of the police than the full tape might suggest. Their argument reversed the perspective of the jurors. Instead of seeing what the camera saw, they began to see what the police saw (or what the lawyers claimed they saw), and when that combined with what many interpreted as a nascent racism, they did the incredible: despite the seemingly incontrovertible evidence pointing toward conviction, the jurors voted to acquit.

When the verdict was read, Los Angeles erupted into what would be the worst scene of civil unrest in America this century, bigger than Watts, bigger than Detroit. Hundreds of fires burst forth throughout the city, inspiring looters to crash through store windows and run off with millions of dollars of merchandise. Motorists were dragged from their cars and brutalized. Stores in South-Central L.A. taped signs to their windows, declaring black ownership, in the hope of appealing to the sympathies of the rioters, but the violence was indiscriminate, and much of it, in the end, was black on black. In three days of unrest, fifty-four people were killed and more than $900 million worth of property damaged.

Smaller riots broke out in other American cities. In New York, as in many places, shop owners closed down early when they heard the verdict, nervously pulling metal shutters over their windows even as they worried what they might find there when they returned the next morning. Many white-collar operations suspended business, too, and sent their workers home in anticipation of violence. It seemed as if the King verdict had put all of white America in fear of black America and all of black America in a mood to make an angry point. "It's good for them to be afraid," said one enraged black woman, watching hordes of white commuters rush to trains in New York's Pennsylvania Station. "Now they know how we feel every day."

With the tragic scene in Los Angeles captured live and delivered throughout the nation and the world, one piece of video grabbed attention above all others. It showed an enormous red eighteen-wheel truck arriving at the intersection

The 1965 Watts riots had pitted black against white, but by 1992 Los Angeles was a more ethnically diverse city. Latinos, Koreans, and other Asian-Americans were well represented in hard-hit South-Central L.A. Here, a Korean armed with a semi-automatic weapon guards against looters.

When your shop becomes a looter's paradise:
"The lottery machine and telephones were gone, so were the dishes and our rice cooker"

I had seen the Rodney King video on television and I did not agree with what the policemen did. I thought they were guilty of overreaction. And I believed that if he was a white guy instead of an African-American, then they would not have done what they did to him. But I was not prepared for the riots. I first heard about the rioting on a Korean radio station. They described how the truck driver, Reginald Denny, got dragged from his truck and I later watched the video where they were hitting him. It was awful. Since the center of the rioting was in South-Central, I got worried because there are a lot of Korean businesses there, including my family's liquor store.

I came to America from Korea in 1978 when I was a senior in high school. My parents felt that my brother and I would receive a better education here. They opened a grocery store in Santa Monica. Then, in 1983, they sold that and bought the liquor store in South-Central Los Angeles. My brother and an employee were in the store when the riots began and my parents told them to shut the store down and come home.

In the first hours of the rioting, my brother and I watched the coverage on TV and my parents listened to the Korean radio. Because so many Korean shop owners were affected, Korean radio spent twenty-four hours a day doing nothing except coverage of the riots. The reports were scary and we were worried about our store. Then, around seven-thirty, my parents were listening when the station interviewed this one guy who started announcing the name of our store and saying that people were breaking the door in and taking some stuff out. And he said, if the owner is listening to this radio station, please call me at this number, and he gave out his cellular phone number.

So we called him. And it turned out that this guy was on the top of the roof across the street from our store and he was watching it get looted! He told us to get down there quick before everything was gone. So my parents went there and I joined them later.

The store was my parents' life. My daddy, he opened up at six-thirty or seven in the morning every single day. We all go to church. But my daddy couldn't go to church because we would have to open the store on Sunday, too. A lot of Koreans are like that. They work really hard. Twelve hours, fourteen hours. Seven days a week.

Ours was a small store, a neighborhood store. And the majority of our clients were African-American. We had black employees, too, and I treated them like, you know, my brother and they treated me like their sister. But who starts looting our store? It's not neighborhood people. It's people coming from other areas. And they

Chang, far left, with her parents outside the family's store.

— Connie Chang was born in Busan, Korea, in 1960. After her parents moved to the United States, she attended Santa Monica High School and Santa Monica College. She received her real estate license in 1989 and works for George Chung Realty in West Los Angeles in addition to managing her family's liquor store. She says the store has only recently recouped the business it lost due to the riots.

think it's all right because they don't know us and they think that all Koreans make money from out of their pockets.

So many people were in front of our store taking stuff away that my parents couldn't get near it. They went around the block several times and they honked their horn at the looters. They'd go around and come back to the store and then they'd honk again. And they did this like three, four times. After a while a lot of people disappeared.

When we got to the store, it looked terrible. An African-American neighbor helped us get through the mess and into the store. Inside, we found that the lottery machine was gone. The telephones were gone. Even dishes and our rice cooker. There was no structural damage to the store, but the looters took a whole lot of merchandise and when they took it, you know, they dropped it so the whole place smelled of alcohol. One lady was still sitting on the floor. She couldn't get up. And you know why? She was drinking inside the store. She didn't take the stuff home. She just sat down and drank. And she got so drunk she couldn't get out.

We were angry, but I put some of the blame on the TV, at what they showed on the news. Early on in the riots, they showed a whole lot of people taking stuff from the FEDCO [appliance] store. And a lot of people watching this thought, why don't we go down there and take it, too? They didn't feel guilty or anything. They just thought, let's go and take it. And I think the television coverage gave them the motivation to take somebody else's merchandise.

My two brothers and my cousin and my father all got up on the rooftop and stayed all night with guns, protecting the store. And they stayed on the rooftop I think three or four days. We were so worried about them we couldn't sleep. And yet even with my parents around, people were still trying to break the door down and get inside. We called the police but they didn't come. They have so many things going on they didn't have the time to, you know, take care of a small store. On the other hand, people say if my store was in Beverly Hills they would have come in a minute.

In the days after the riots, a lot of people came to the store and said they were so sorry about the damages to our store. But of course they didn't know who took the merchandise. Eventually, we just forgot about it and decided to start all over again, even though the damages put my parents back five or ten years. I think the damage to our store was around $50,000 or $60,000 and insurance only paid half of that.

Afterward, my parents considered leaving America and going back to Korea. You know it had hurt our feelings so much after the riot to see what it had done to our store. It's like all our hopes and dreams were gone. But by that time we had already been here fifteen years. And if we went back to Korea we would have to start all over again there, too. A lot of Korean Americans did return to Korea, though. And I know of one man who was so upset when his store burned down he thought about committing suicide.

After the riot, I told everybody to put a smile on their face all the time. Just to show that we are human beings, too. I am sometimes, you know, in a bad mood and I find it hard to smile. But I still try hard to be nice to the customer. And sometimes my parents they make nice Korean barbecue and give it to the people in the neighborhood. And when I see other Korean business owners, I tell them to try to be nice to people. When you are nice to people they won't be mean to you. They will be nice to you, too. Or at least we hope so.

of Normandie and Florence on the night of the verdict, just before seven o'clock. Reginald Denny later said that he had noticed the band of looters there, but knowing that he was only carrying sand, he figured that they would be uninterested in him and he could "tiptoe across the intersection." He was wrong. One of the rioters opened the door of the cab and Denny was pulled onto the street, starting an almost unbelievable barrage. Denny was kicked and beaten with a claw hammer. A five-pound piece of medical equipment, stolen from another truck that had just escaped the intersection, was hurled at him. In what was the scene's most horrific moment, a man threw a slab of concrete at Denny's head and did a victory dance while the innocent truck driver lay unconscious. As the news helicopters hovered overhead, the attacker then looked up at them and pointed to the nearly dead Denny. What, he seemed to be saying, would be the meaning of his crime if the cameras did not record it?

Over the next few days, some declared the Denny attack as a kind of parallel to the attack on King, a piece of "video revenge" that, with the disappointing verdict, satisfied a basic need for justice. It mattered little, as journalist Lou Cannon later wrote searingly, that King and Denny were vastly different stories: one a panicked, violent, and perhaps racist-inspired attempt to subdue someone who had refused to respond to police commands; the other an indiscriminate mob attack on a purely innocent bystander (Denny was listening to country music as he drove along, unaware that the city had erupted in riots) whose injuries were far more serious (Denny's skull had been fractured in ninety-one places, with pieces of it embedded in his brain, and although he survived, his face revealed a permanent crater uncorrectable even with reconstructive surgery). The two videos had come to symbolize the worst kind of racial caricature, one demonizing whites, the other demonizing blacks, and the truth had become an afterthought to a greater argument that reasserted America's long-standing racial divide.

Ironically, on the second night of the riots, much of America had gathered around the television to watch the concluding episode of *The Cosby Show*, an enormously popular situation comedy that portrayed a warm and loving black middle-class family with which both white and black viewers found it easy to identify. Now, as the Huxtables, Bill Cosby's television family, departed from the screen (and into a future of reruns), so, it seemed, did the fiction of racial peace.

Like Cosby, Orenthal James Simpson had a long and attractive history in the public eye. As a running back for USC and the Buffalo Bills, he had thrilled football audiences in the 1960s and 1970s. And after his playing career ended, Simpson's charm and charisma had kept him in view, as a commentator on network football telecasts, as a movie actor, and as an advertising pitchman for Hertz car rental. But all that innocent fame and much of the goodwill that came with it dissolved on June 17, 1994, when "the Juice," as he was known in his playing days, suddenly became the focus of the nineties', perhaps the century's, most drippingly lurid real-life saga: the double homicide of his ex-wife, Nicole, and her friend Ronald Goldman.

The scene that announced the transformation of Simpson from legend to fugitive to accused murderer formed one of the most memorable moments in television history. It was five days after the killings and three days after Simpson had stood with his children at Nicole's funeral, possessed of a mournful dignity

> *"Don't feel sorry for me. I've had a great life, great friends. Please think of the real O.J. and not this lost person.*
>
> *Thanks for making my life special. I hope I helped yours.*
>
> *Peace and love,*
>
> *O.J."*
>
> From the alleged "suicide note" left by O. J. Simpson, written the night of June 17, 1994, as police pursued him for the murder of his former wife, Nicole

The Bronco chase was a surreal experience on television *and in real life. Spectators pulled up lawn chairs to the San Diego Freeway overpasses to wait for O.J. and wave him on.*

Kato Kaelin
Johnnie Cochran
Marcia Clark
Christopher Darden
Barry Scheck
Robert Shapiro
Lance Ito
Mark Fuhrman
Philip Vannatter
F. Lee Bailey
Robert Kardashian
A. C. Cowlings
Faye Resnick

*Familiar names in the cast
of the O. J. Simpson drama,
Trial of the Century*

owed either to his natural instincts as an actor, the magic of powerful sedatives, or, as so many hoped, the simple, though increasingly unlikely, possibility that he had had nothing to do with the brutal attack on his wife and her friend. Now with the great American sports hero fleeing dozens of police cars in a low-speed chase on a Los Angeles freeway, television helicopters buzzing overhead, all of America was drawn into an on-air suicide watch: Simpson, in the backseat of a white Ford Bronco, gripping a steel revolver in one hand, a cellular phone in the other, and announcing that he would pull the trigger on himself if he didn't get the proverbial criminal defendant's wish: a moment with his mother.

For sixty-five minutes America and the world sat transfixed by the scene, bizarre as it was. The police, moving cautiously at sixty miles an hour, appeared more to be accompanying Simpson on a celebrity motorcade or, as *Newsweek* commented, a "demented victory lap" than pursuing him in a manhunt; on the various overpasses, spectators gathered to watch and cheer Simpson on, as if he were still in uniform and looking for the "daylight" that might lead to another miracle touchdown. Hastily constructed signs were held up from roadsides; "Go O.J.," they read. And on call-in radio shows, friends and former teammates telephoned, urging him to give up. "I love you, my mother loves you," pleaded one former USC quarterback.

Simpson finally did surrender, in the driveway of his Brentwood mansion, but this was just the opening episode of what would become the decade's defining soap opera, a messy story of sex and race and celebrity, justice and injustice, media hype and media self-examination — a national fixation in which on-air pundits and overreaching columnists, not to mention prosecutors and defense lawyers, desperately searched for deeper public meaning to what was still, at root, a monstrous private tragedy.

At first, the Simpson case became the symbolic awakening to the subject of domestic abuse or, as one journalist described it, "the ferocious violence that may erupt when love runs awry." (Simpson had been arrested before for striking Nicole, and it was later revealed that his continuingly violent posture toward her made her fear for her life, as a tearful 911 call, played in court, demonstrated.) Then, as it always seems in America, it came down to race. Simpson had never been a favorite in the black community (many blacks saw him as too interested in pleasing whites). But, in the shadow of the Rodney King episode, it was impossible for his defense lawyers, and for that matter many observers, to resist the thought that the LAPD

The decision to ask Simpson to try on the "bloody gloves" was a crucial prosecution mistake. "If it doesn't fit, you must acquit," rhymed defense lawyer Johnnie Cochran in his summation, but latex undergloves (required to prevent spoilage of the evidence), shrinkage, and Simpson's control over the demonstration (he was said to have crooked his fingers) could have been factors in a scene that led many to see the state's lawyers as incompetent.

may have had a role in fabricating the case against him, particularly after it was revealed that Mark Fuhrman, the policeman who gathered some of the evidence, was possessed of such a racist vocabulary he could serve as a poster boy for bigotry. And once that equation was made, O.J., long among the most assimilated of black public figures ("Hertz told me in all their surveys that I was colorless," he bragged to an interviewer in 1992), became, for many, a symbol of black America.

The trial occupied eight months and nine days, every moment of it telecast live to the living rooms and offices of the world, and over that time, as the myriad details of a complex story began to build — the barking dog, the bloody gloves, the 911 calls, the Bruno Magli shoes — it began to resemble a nineteenth-century novel, as essayist Bruce Handy wrote, "one of those ripping, 800-page doorstops from college." The prosecutors had much evidence on their side, but Simpson had his "dream team" of legal experts and one shining master of courtroom performance, the expansive Johnnie Cochran. The race defense had been Cochran's idea, and he flaunted it in the trial's last hours, even appearing at the courthouse surrounded by bodyguards from Louis Farrakhan's Nation of Islam, an organization whose leader was well known for his antiwhite and anti-Semitic sermons.

Cochran's final summation posed the case to the jury as less about the merits of evidence than as an opportunity to send a message about police behavior (he denied, however, suggesting that they consider "jury nullification," the determination by which the breaking of the law is tolerated in exchange for the recog-

Watching a handheld television, a young L.A. black man cheers the news of the Simpson verdict. Ironically for a defendant who had once been a football hero, Simpson's trial had come to resemble a national sporting event — a "judicial Super Bowl" — with people across the country tuning in to see if their "team" won.

nition of some "higher" purpose). But by then, the case had so polarized the nation that one could fairly predict how just about anyone felt about it: to whites, Simpson was a double murderer; to blacks, he was the victim of a frame-up; and there was no space, it seemed, for considering anything in between. "You *can* be a clean-cut cop like Mark Fuhrman and still be a racist liar," insisted Julianne Malveaux, the African-American host of a Washington radio talk show, "or be a nice guy like O.J. who smiles all the time and still beat the hell out of women." But for this moment at least, few were willing to admit such complexities.

On the morning of October 3, 1995, the nation and much of the world paused and looked toward their televisions and their radios, for "the word." It seemed amazing that sixteen months later this double murder, awful as it had been, had grown in meaning to where so many had invested so much in the outcome of a single trial. But there it was, and when the jury pronounced not one word, but two, "not guilty," you could almost hear the final tug of a nation splitting completely into two, most black Americans deliriously cheering their victory and most whites recoiling in disgust.

There were many who saw in the sad adventure of O.J. a travesty of the nation's criminal justice system. By insisting upon a representative jury, one well screened for race, asked an editorial in the *New Republic,* had we abandoned the long-respected principle of judicial deliberation to race-based politics? In insisting upon the retrial of exonerated defendants, had we abandoned the Constitution in favor of satisfying the instincts of the masses? (Both Simpson and the police in the Rodney King case were tried again — Simpson in civil court, Koon and the other policemen in a new civil rights case — with results more satisfying to the majority constituencies.) In televising trials, had we transformed every judicial exercise into a symbolic electronic referendum on a nation's social ills? And in so doing, sacrificed our respect for the truth?

But most of all, people looked upon the trial as the sign of the continuing American race dilemma. It was now thirty years since the landmark civil rights legislation of the 1960s, and the nation had made great strides (there was not only an African-American on the Supreme Court, there was, in General Colin Powell, an African-American chairman of the Joint Chiefs of Staff who was being talked about as a candidate for president), yet the dream of true integration, the kind that would give substance to the American claim of equality and unity, was perhaps even more remote than before. And when, two weeks after the Simpson verdict, Louis Farrakhan led a march on Washington, a "Million Man March," as he called it, excluding both women and whites, it appeared to be another call to separatism, the kind that had characterized some of the angriest moments of the black American experience in the twentieth century.

Farrakhan's was not the only voice leading black America, and his march had been organized with at least some noble aims. The main goal of the event was to address the image of the black American male, and to that end its speakers stressed both comradeship and a renewed dedication to a few unarguably positive values (respect for women, responsibility to families, and a condemnation of violence). And yet because it was an act of exclusion, it was impossible not to hear in the march echoes of the rhetoric of Marcus Garvey and Malcolm X (even, in a less angry way, the call to black self-reliance of Booker T. Washington) and a firm rejection of the ideal that had inspired that other march on Washington, the

*The Million Man March, above, was a bittersweet
expression of black community — a "statement
that black life is to be rescued from within," wrote
African-American social critic Gerald Early,
"without white help or intervention."*

"Another" march on Washington: "All black . . . all male"

There is a perception in America that black males are the lowest, dirtiest, most conniving criminal people on this earth. Even black people think that. I know. I'm black and I am male and I have to overcome that image every day of my life. I am an attorney at a Houston law firm. And I'm a pretty good lawyer. I work on the forty-third floor of this modern sixty-four-story building. It's a class building, the kind of place where everybody wears suits every day. One day I was riding the elevator up to my floor when a white woman got on and as soon as she saw me she started clutching her purse, as though to protect it from me. I thought, this cannot be happening. Surely, I do not look as though I could ever be a threat to this woman or her purse. But, for some reason, to her I did.

So when they announced that there was going to be this Million Man March and that one of the goals of the march was to try to change the negative perception of the black male, I knew that I had to go. I didn't care how I got there or what I had to give up to go. It would be worth it to start changing the perception of black males. Louis Farrakhan and the Nation of Islam were attempting to demonstrate to black males that they could do something on a grand scale in a positive way and do it with a sense of cohesiveness. They were also trying to make a general statement that there are a lot of black males who don't go to prison, who are not beating their wives and girlfriends, and who are not out to rob everybody they see on the street.

I flew up from Houston and met a friend of mine from Michigan, and we made it down to the march site by about 4:45 A.M. My friend was an executive pretty high up in a Fortune 500 company — the only African-American at that level — and he was trying to make some moves to get even higher up. So he didn't want anybody to know he was at the march. He was worried that it might affect his position in his company. But he also felt that the march was too important to miss, so he made the trip from Michigan and we went down to D.C. together. When we got to the grounds things were still pretty empty. And then I started seeing people coming out of the woodwork. I mean they were coming from all directions. Just thousands and thousands of people. About an hour after I got there, there were people as far as I could see. And everyone was so nice. They were all talking about their trip to Washington. Where they came from. What they did back home. Why they came. What they thought they would get out of this event. I was surprised at how many men brought their sons with them. Young kids. I mean they were ten, twelve, thirteen, fourteen. Since I don't have any kids, I hadn't really thought about that. But these men wanted their children to see this event, to be part of it. There were also a lot of older

—T. Deon Warner, born in 1959 in Fayetteville, North Carolina, went to Howard University Law School, clerked for the Southern District of Texas Federal District Court, and served as a board member for the Texas State Securities Board. He currently practices corporate law at Chan Warner P.C. in Houston, Texas.

Warner, above, in his Houston law office, 1998.

people who had been to some of the earlier marches on Washington, and they talked about what it was like being back on the steps of the Washington Capitol and around the reflecting pool. They talked about how long they had had to wait before there was another march that really talked about doing something positive for black people. They also pointed out how the previous marches dealt with bigger issues and were more multiracial, but they said that in this march — with all men — the crowd seemed like it was a lot closer and there seemed to be more energy and more participation. And they were right, the people were really part of the event. There was no pushing, no shoving; I don't recall any fights. Instead, people would help you get through the crowd. And if someone stumbled, they would say, "Oh, are you okay? Can I help you?"

There were many speakers throughout the day. And they came from different parts of the community: various religions, various backgrounds. And they all seemed to have a very common theme which was we all need to pull together to continue to sort of exemplify this cohesiveness and this community-type approach. Even though Farrakhan's speech was a little long, I think he made a very good point, which was that we need to think in terms of getting together to do things in a positive way rather than just reacting to things on the back end. And this point was made by other speakers time and time again all day long.

One of the speakers was a twelve-year-old kid. And

he gave a speech about how proud he was that he had a black father and that he was there at the march. He said that he represented the sons and daughters of each of the black males that were there. And then he made a demand of the audience. He asked that each person who was at that march go home and, if need be, rearrange their life so that they become a more positive role model in the communities. That they become better husbands to their wives. And a better father to their children. And then he asked everybody at the closing of the speech, "Will you do that for me?" Here's a twelve-year-old kid and in a very eloquent way he made a request that just seemed so simple and so basic and yet so compelling.

This march was about the fact that we're not all criminals. We're not out beating our girlfriends. It was about black pride and male redemption. After the march I started paying a lot more attention to the way black males are perceived. Every time you turn on the TV or read the newspaper, you see black males getting arrested. Yet numbers-wise, black males don't commit more crimes than other groups. And you see ads that talk about personal security and safety. Who do they show as the antagonists in those ads? Black males. Black males have been painted as a subculture in our society. So the point about black pride and black male redemption is that we need to change our image. I don't think we need to change, necessarily, what we do. Because I think we do a pretty good job of being citizens in this community. I think we need to change the image of what people think we do. If we don't take charge to create and mold the perception that we want people to have of us, nobody else will. People need to understand that black males come in all different shapes and sizes just like white males or any other people in America. And if you can't generalize as to the other groups, the white males, the Asian males, etc., then you shouldn't generalize as to black males.

When I was in grade school, we had to stand up and sing "God Bless America." We'd sing it every morning, but I never knew what it meant. I never felt any of those words of that song. I just sang it because that's what we were supposed to do. But during the march, during the middle of the day, when all this stuff was going on and all the people were being so nice and just so congenial and so pleasant, and somebody on the ground started singing, "God bless America, land that I love," it really hit home that in an America where people can be treated equally it really can be a land that you can love. A land that's beautiful and shines bright and has all this meaning to it. If we could get to the point where people treated each other on an equal plane, I think everyone, including blacks, could really feel as though this was a place that you could truly love.

one led by Martin Luther King. Indeed, if any voice seemed now to be a part of history, it was the one that had challenged the Birmingham bigots and their power hoses and, dreaming of a tolerant, integrated America, brought the nation to tears back in 1963. "The whole non-violent, turn-the-other-cheek business just isn't getting anywhere," declared African-American filmmaker Spike Lee. "That is one of the reasons why people aren't walking around with a 'K' on their hat."

Of course, in the nineties, so much of Americans' recent experience — indeed the entirety of life in the twentieth century — appeared rapidly on its way to becoming "history," something to be tidied up and stored on the shelf where it could gather dust next to Gibbon's study of the Roman Empire. The century was ending, and that event, which last time around had prompted the *fin de siècle* of the 1890s, was once again serving as something more than just numerological importance. The old laws, increasingly, did not apply; the new ones were still being written. And, in turn, many people were directing their focus beyond the life they knew and toward the life they imagined they would soon know. Cable television and the global marketplace were merely the beginning. The *real* future was still to come, and, to listen to the heralding voices, what a future it would be!

The believers had been gathering in the church for some time now, listening to preachers like the well-known futurist Alvin Toffler (the fact that there was such a profession as "futurist" proved the excitement with which people regarded the time ahead). It was Toffler, writing way back in 1980, who predicted that the world was undergoing a transformation so dramatic it could only be compared to that experienced ten thousand years ago, when the agricultural revolution took hold; or with the equally monumental Industrial Revolution of the nineteenth century. This new revolution (what Toffler called the Third Wave in recognition of the other two) would be a post-smokestack revolution, an *information* revolution, changing lifestyles as much as economies, and — in what many then saw as the writer's most radical statement — it would be achieved primarily through the mysterious device known as the computer.

The *computer*. The very name betrays the modesty with which its inventors saw it, an instrument to *compute*, as in the adding of numbers, a glorified abacus. And yet for decades after the first one was built by the University of Pennsylvania in the forties — the monolithic ENIAC with its eighteen thousand vacuum tubes — sorting, filing, and the manipulating of numbers were principally what it did. The computer was bureaucracy's tool, and anyone alive in the sixties and seventies is likely to recall it through memories of the "punch card" ("do not fold, spindle, or mutilate") or the standardized test forms that forbade the stray pencil mark lest the "computer" misread it. Computers then were colossal structures found in government offices or enormous basement machine rooms at universities where programmers applied for time to hook in and use them. And they were as fascinating to watch as they were impossible to comprehend, with their magnetic tape drives spinning back and forth — shuddering and trembling, remembers author David Gelernter, "like a priestess of Delphi about to disclose an oracle."

Toffler's amazing claim was not simply that the computer would begin to do more than count and sort but that the computer would become a home appli-

"Typically, one big machine served an entire organization. Often it lay behind a plate glass window, people in white gowns attending it, and those who wished to use it did so through intermediaries. Users were like supplicants."

*Author Tracy Kidder,
describing the early computers*

ance, as ubiquitous as the washing machine or the vacuum cleaner and yet ever so much more powerful than any machine humans had ever owned. In part to report from the future he was proclaiming, Toffler even proudly wrote the second half of his book on a "word processor," a device so foreign then to common experience it prompted a typewriter-bound reviewer for *Newsweek* to describe it ("a keyboard which displays words on a screen for editing") as if he were looking at the control panel to the space shuttle.

The development that would make the personal computer possible was miniaturization, specifically the transistor and even more specifically the microchip, a tiny block of integrated transistor circuits. The chip had been around for twenty years or so (providing, among other things, the technology necessary for the pocket calculator and the electronic wristwatch) when the "garage entrepreneurs" Steven Jobs and Stephen Wozniak began, in the late seventies, to explore the possibilities for a computer so small it could be mounted onto a desktop. And yet even then, there were few people who could envision the computer as a practical home device (Xerox, which had funded much of the research that would become the basis for today's desktop interfaces, decided to pass on it, a decision marked by many as among the worst in American business

Equipped with Macintosh laptops, students at Stanford University in 1996 experienced the "flexible classroom," an interactive multimedia method of learning. Teachers, sighed one university president, are no longer the all-knowing fonts of knowledge; now they are mere guides to the student's own discovery through electronics.

history). While one could easily see the computer as essential to, say, polling or mass mailings, just what set of functions could ever justify a space next to the stereo in the den?

In fact, there was no immediate need for the personal computer (in this sense, as David Gelernter has also pointed out, it defied the patterns of invention that almost invariably followed need), and yet it was irresistible all the same. Once Jobs and Wozniak came out with the Apple II and IBM followed on quickly in 1981 with its own PC (a 64KB bargain at $2,880), the personal computer joined the automobile in that exclusive club of American dream machines, a device to be marveled at and upgraded with the introduction of each new model or application. Ironically, while people had not exactly needed one, it soon seemed as if they could not do without one.

Almost overnight, computers changed play (video games) and research (access to databases); they changed writing and editing (the word processor programs were the most common way people used their PCs), and they changed bookkeeping (families, not just accountants, could now keep spreadsheets and document their financial histories). They even began to change work itself, for with a trusty "modem" by which to hook into the office network, people could now afford to work more often at home, live farther away from the office, and, among those at the cutting edge of this rapidly changing technology, even participate in conferences by remote tie-ins — arguing with fellow scientists in Mozambique while still sitting in their pajamas in Minneapolis. Indeed, by the late eighties, the question already was less "what can the computer do?" than "what *can't* the computer do?" With each new day, it seemed, there was some function executed better or faster or more efficiently utilizing the "brain" of an electronic wizard.

To many people, the computer was a positively magical device — not a machine in the usual sense, but something else. It was not, after all, like a mechanical wristwatch or a car or any of the traditional kinds of machines with which one was familiar, the kinds that could be opened up and examined, with their levers and gears moving. Open up a computer and it looked nothing like what it did, for information was stored there and retrieved from there in ways invisible to the human eye. And the computer didn't even do "work" in the traditional sense, either. Most machines are like slaves. The automobile, for instance, starts and is propelled forward by its driver's commands, but a computer is more like a partner, a collaborator — performing functions at the behest of its user, yes, but also taking in information, interpreting it, then delivering back recommendations that inform the user's next set of commands.

Still, it was the word "personal" in the "personal computer" that described the most exciting thing about this machine. Now families — families! — were using systems roughly equal in strength to those gargantuan sixties mainframes, prompting many to feel freshly "empowered," to use a favorite word of the nineties. And while they were using them mostly to write letters, balance the checkbook, plan the week's shopping, and keep track of their stocks (following, with Apple's Macintosh and, eventually, with Microsoft's Windows, graphic icons that simplified everything by mimicking a real desktop), there was already the sense that something amazing now sat atop their desks, the key to a thrilling

"*As you come in, you'll be presented with an electronic pin to clip to your clothes. This pin will connect you to the electronic services of the house . . . [The pin] will tell the house who and where you are and the house will use this information to try to meet and even anticipate your needs . . . when it's dark outside, the pin will cause a moving zone of light to accompany you through the house.*"

Bill Gates, describing the new home he is building for himself, in The Road Ahead, *his 1995 book (how old-fashioned of him) describing the future of technology*

future, and, like waiting for a child prodigy to flower, it was exciting just to think of what it might do next. "Imagine . . . ," said the software ads, and *imagine* people did.

Jobs and Wozniak had arrived first, but they and their Apple computer were eventually replaced in the market and the public imagination by the success of an adolescent-looking Harvard dropout with a faded photograph of Henry Ford over his desk. If indeed this was the dawn of a new age, as transcendently important as the last, then William Gates, the chairman of the Microsoft Corporation, was destined to be its defining figure, every bit as significant to these times as Ford was to his own. In fact, Gates and Ford were much alike: neither man had invented the technology with which his success was so identified, yet each had assembled a rudimentary way to get it to the masses (Ford with the Model T; Gates with his MS-DOS operating system) and in the process built an imposing personal fortune.

A billionaire at thirty-one, Microsoft's chairman had easily become the richest man in America. And by the nineties he was almost as famous for his wealth as he was for his work. If Bill Gates dropped a bill on the ground, mused one writer in 1998, just how large would that bill have to be to justify his leaning over to pick it up? After calculating that Gates was making $150 a second and that the process of retrieving the bill would take four seconds, the writer then deemed that anything less than $500 would be a waste of the computer giant's precious time.

It was a chance agreement with IBM that landed Gates on the track toward his software empire. Eager to get its PC out on the market, the company entered into a contract with then tiny Microsoft, promptly making MS-DOS the industry standard (the fact that IBM decided not to develop its own system internally is counted as another of history's worst business decisions). And by the mid-nineties Microsoft so dominated every aspect of the software industry (simply through its stock the company has created three billionaires, including Gates, and several hundred millionaires) it now stood as an international behemoth itself, resented for its market-controlling practices.

For years after the introduction of the PC, Gates and his colleagues in the industry lived off the "upgrade." Whether in hardware (faster machines capable of carrying more memory) or software (sales of Gates's Windows 95 have topped 120 million units worldwide), it was the thrill of "this year's model" that drove the market — just as it had been for so long in the car industry. In fact, the picture of Ford in Gates's office served, he once said, as an admonition as much as a tribute — his real mentor being Ford's competitor Alfred P. Sloan, the 1920s General Motors chairman, in recognition of Sloan's success at keeping ahead of the market (an instinct that Ford lacked, and which almost proved to be his undoing). Still, by 1995, even Gates was surprised to see the future of computing shifting away from software and hardware in favor of a rollicking new development known as the Internet.

The *Internet.* A Cold War relic, it had been built by the Pentagon as an alternative communications system that was, incidentally, capable of withstanding an atomic attack (it was known then as ARPANET, for "Advanced Research Projects Agency Network") and languished for two decades before it began the rapid

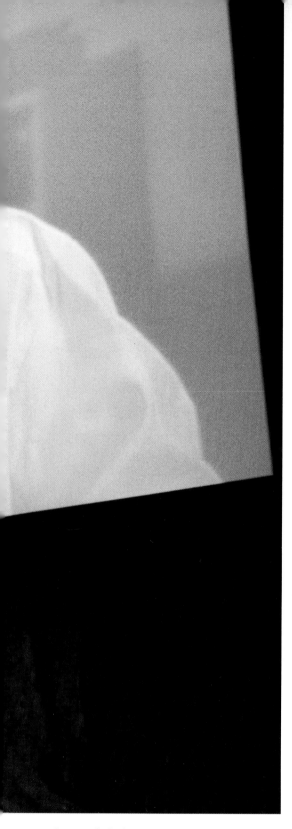

Gates was both admired for his success and resented for his power. Above, he appears on a large screen at the 1997 MacWorld convention with a dwarfed Steve Jobs, left, as the two announce Gates's decision to invest $150 million in Apple, his former rival.

Starting a virtual community: "You throw words out . . . and words come back"

In the mid-1980s the company that I was working for said that I would never move up the corporate ladder unless I had a graduate degree. Now, I wasn't really interested in moving up the corporate ladder — I actually hated it — but I did like the idea of going to graduate school. So I enrolled in the Interactive Telecommunications Program at NYU. I was worried that it was going to be uninteresting. But it turned out to be this wonderful new media program that had a lot to do with community building and bringing people together using new technologies.

When I was in my first semester at NYU, we had to call a place called the Well, and I was an instant addict. The Well is an on-line service based in California. It's a virtual community, where people get on-line to pretty much talk about anything under the sun, and over time, after sharing thoughts and feelings, you get a sense of who's who; it's really a community of personalities. My frustration with the Well was that most of the people were in California. If I started to build a relationship at all with people, I wanted to meet them face-to-face. When I was in my last year of graduate school, I logged into the Well and someone said to me, "Hey, we heard that you were going to start the East Coast version of the Well." I had never said that, but all of a sudden it was like, Duh? Of course, I can do that. So I just typed in, "Yes. I am."

In March 1990 Echo opened to the public. I came up with the name Echo because I had some vague idea like you throw your words out into the world and words come back. I couldn't get any investors interested because in 1989 nobody would believe me that the Internet was going to be hot. This kills me now. I started out of my apartment and I realized that I didn't really need a lot of money to get it going. I started with one computer, maybe a half a dozen modems and phone lines, and software that manages conversations. And that was pretty much it. Getting people interested was very hard at first because in 1990 New Yorkers were not all that wired. I was getting users literally one by one. I'd go to a party and if I met somebody interesting I'd go, "Do you have a modem?" Gradually Echo grew, and today it has over 3,500 subscribers.

When I started Echo, the people on-line were mostly guys and mostly computer people or mathematicians or scientists, and they would talk about computers and science and exchange software. I didn't want that kind of culture at all. I really wanted something more like Gertrude Stein's living room. So I structured Echo so it was made up of different areas, we call them conferences. There's a books conference, a movies conference, an art conference, a New York conference, and within these conferences are conversations that fit under that

general heading. The conversations are in what's called non-real time. So I can go into, say, the books conference and type in whatever I have to say. Then you can log in tomorrow, see what I've written, and add whatever you want to say about the subject. So the conversation keeps going on, and you can talk to these people regardless of who's logged in when. It's actually better than a live conversation. In a conversation that's non-real time, you can take your time and really consider your thoughts and say something more substantial.

On the Internet you get to know someone from the inside out first, whereas in the physical world it's from the outside in. Each way has its pluses and minuses. One of the things that make Echo unique is that, since most of us are in New York, we have a very active face-to-face community as well as the virtual community. But even if the relationship was only virtual, it really isn't a matter of better or worse, it is just different. People are people, and they're no different on-line than they are anywhere else. We don't sit down at our computers and all of a sudden become unreal. If I say, "I love you," to someone on the phone, does that make it not real? So if I say it on a computer, why would that make it not real?

On Echo we don't have anonymity. Everyone goes by their real name. So their name is attached to whatever they say. But even outside Echo on the Internet, where people are role-playing a little bit more, they still can't help but reveal things about themselves. Even in adopting a role you are still revealing yourself. You're showing yourself in the very character that you picked. What happens more often than not is people reveal stuff about themselves that they may not even be aware that they're revealing. Eventually you fall back into your old habits of who you are.

I'm almost like a mayor of a small town. I found whenever disputes break out, if it gets very serious, I'm the one who eventually has to settle things and make a decision. It's similar to how laws are formed within a society. People come in and do very strange stuff and we have to decide what's acceptable and what's not acceptable. We've got this one conference called Feedback. And that's where people talk about what they like and dislike about Echo. And whenever some sort of controversy arises people discuss it there to figure out what to do. We don't have censorship on Echo. You can say whatever you want to say. The only exception is we developed this one rule of no personal attacks. So if you say something that I dislike, I have to attack what you

Horn, left, in 1995. Above, the Echo home page.

—Stacy Horn, born in 1956, has a fine-arts degree from Tufts University and the Museum of Fine Arts in Boston and a master's degree in interactive communications from NYU, where she teaches a course called Virtual Culture. Before founding Echo, she worked for an early computer software company and as a telecommunications analyst for Mobil Oil Corporation. In addition to running Echo, she plays drums with the Manhattan Samba Group and sings with the Grace Church Choral Society.

say and not you.

For the first six years of Echo, I would participate, but only in a very formal way. I felt I had to distance myself a bit so that I could be objective when disputes arose. Where other people might be telling the stories of their lives, I wouldn't. Then someone formed a private conference where they had a very small restricted membership — twelve or eighteen people. They weren't necessarily already friends. They just wanted to see what it would be like if we put a small group of people together — kind of like a biosphere-type arrangement. They asked me to join so I did, and for the first time, I experimented talking about my private life, speaking personally. In this private space, I was not Stacy Horn, the founder and owner of Echo. I was just Stacy, an Echoid like everyone else. And that freed me to talk about my hopes and fears and disappointments. And at first people were like, woah, because they weren't used to seeing this side of me. I would talk about boyfriends and my struggles with learning how to play the drums and the books I was working on. And the people in that private conference became my first friends on Echo. I had had tons of acquaintances over the years, but very few friends. So now I can experience Echo just like anyone else. And even though I'm at the point where I'm ready for a career change, I cannot imagine life without Echo.

growth that brought it to popular attention in the nineties. No technology, not even the computer itself, moved as rapidly into the mainstream of American life as this one, which brought people into the vast space where they could communicate with other computer users around the world, tap into exotic databases at the punch of a key, read postings on personal and corporate "Web pages" (as in the World Wide Web, the most popular way to access the Net), buy cars and subscriptions and clothes and books, and send e-mail (as in *electronic* mail) as quickly and easily to the far reaches of Nepal as to a colleague in an office next door.

The Internet's options for research alone were overwhelming. Way back in the 1930s, the science fiction writer H. G. Wells (*The Time Machine, The War of the Worlds*) had envisioned the establishment of a "World Brain" in which the entire range of human knowledge would be stored for easy access. With the Internet, the brain was here. One could call up on screen the collection of the Louvre art museum in Paris, examine arcane documents in a library in Berlin, and read today's newspaper (both one's own and the daily fare in New Delhi) — all without ever moving from the desk chair. And because the Internet, or more precisely, the Web, was set up with "hyperlinks," allowing a user to jump to a related site at the click of an icon — going, say, from the text of a Shakespeare play to a seminal commentary on it and from there to the play's original manuscript and finally to an essay on life in Elizabethan England — it perpetually stoked the curiosity. Surely man had never possessed a better tool for discovery.

Yet, as significant as it was for accessing information — and there were some who read it to be as significant to this time as the Gutenberg Bible was to the 1400s — the interactive communications capabilities of the Internet had people declaring nothing less than the arrival of a separate plane of existence. The on-line "universe" was often described as "cyberspace," a kind of metaphorical place arrived at through the computer in a way that called to mind Alice's jaunt

" I checked my e-mail . . . made a brisk electronic tour of the Uffizi and the Louvre . . . read some valuable tips on lockpicking written by someone named Ted the Tool . . . browsed the various on-line journals . . . consulted a weather map customized for my neighborhood . . . visited the poetry archive at the University of Toronto and ran a little search on the number of times "thistle" turns up in Byron . . . then found myself sitting by the pool at the Cybercity Hotel, sipping my third or fourth virtual martini. Or, rather, it wasn't me exactly; it was my Net self. Let's call him Chuck. He's 23, 6 foot 4, 220 and has an amazingly sculptured hard body combined with the creativity and passion of an artist."

Writer Charles McGrath, in the New York Times Magazine, *describing his experiences "on-line," December 1996*

The "cyber café" was a nineties invention, combining computer workstations with the decade's drink of choice — coffee. Here, at the Horse Shoe Coffee House in San Francisco, a few generation X'ers (the term referred to the under-thirty crowd that could be said to be the first computer generation) log on.

Living the anti*technology life:* **No computer, no television, no electricity**

Before we were married, my wife and I had many moments when some sort of event like the Clarence Thomas and Anita Hill hearings would make us look at each other and ask, is there another country we could go to? We always felt like outsiders anyway. But as our spiritual lives began to deepen we saw that we needed to actually live out our beliefs more. And the more we tried to do that within the culture we were surrounded by, the more we could see that we had to make a choice between a spiritual life and a modern life.

Our feeling was that while modern life offers all kinds of thrills, they are pretty illusory. And we wanted to get back to living more authentically. We wanted to have a return of texture in our lives, to have a real sense that we're not just cruising from one air-conditioned module to the next, that we are *living* in the old-fashioned sense of that term. At the same time our religious life was becoming more and more important, too. We're Quakers and we were becoming much more concerned about how modern living affects spiritual life.

It seemed to us that our parents had traded a lot of very important values for all those new technological "things" that the century has provided and that the new things not only didn't deliver on their promises, they deprived us of more important things like community. And my wife and I decided that we don't have the energy to repeat that experience, to repeat our parents' disillusionment. To just say, well, we'll just throw ourselves into it and go for an even bigger house and a sport utility vehicle.

We were living in northeast Ohio then. We were both public librarians. We were living the way most people lived. Our income was almost twice what it is now and we had most of the normal appliances of life. But we decided to leave all that behind and kind of create a nineteenth-century existence. And first that meant that we began to use real food to cook with. Food's a good starting place if you want to leave the twentieth century, because food has become very strange in our world. And we decided that we weren't going to live out of a microwave oven anymore and that in fact we would make all our meals from scratch. And we found out that we spent more time at cooking, which meant that we had real sit-down meals, family meals. And we found that working with the food made us think more about the quality of the food. And then we began to get more in touch with who was growing the food that we were eating. And so we began making connections with organic farmers and people who really cared about the land.

We were just beginning the journey to back off from modern life, one that would lead us eventually to the Quaker community where we now reside, but the

—Scott Savage, who was born in 1959, is the editor and publisher of Plain magazine, a journal devoted to simple living that is typeset by hand and printed on a hand-fed solar-powered printing press. He still keeps a car, but spends more time traveling around with his horse (named Techs) and buggy. The Savage home in Barnesville, Ohio, has no electricity, and while there is a phone, he says that it is "subject to review." He declined to appear in a photograph, saying that the world already suffers from an "image glut" and that pictures can sometimes confuse a person's message.

Savage's Plain *magazine, left, stressed the joy of the simple life.*

more we did, the more we saw modernity as the anomaly that it is. When you look back through the last five or six hundred years of history and study how average people lived, you realize that they were peasants and farmers and country people. And that, until the 1900s, the thread from generation to generation had been continuous. And it seems like we have gone through some big firestorm in this century and emerged on the other side of it knowing little more than how to use computers. Certainly nobody knows the great reservoir of wisdom that once carried people along — the wisdom tied to the earth. And so, by reacquainting ourselves with that simplicity, we feel like we're uncovering long-term human truths and spiritual truths that have really been with mankind for thousands of years.

Take tools, for instance. The hand tools that I use function as an extension of the user. But look at modern tools. You don't have to understand anything about them intrinsically to use them. You can use a computer without really understanding computers. Modern tools involve essentially plugging into power; they are what we call "power multipliers" and they do all the work. We wanted to get away from that and back to some essential relationship with our world.

I have to admit that the switch has not always been that easy. After all, the twentieth century is my first language. Modern culture is my first language. And that means that I have had to, in modern terms, "counter-program." Like when we traded car travel for the horse and buggy. It was hard, but we wanted to consciously limit our freedom of movement, because we sensed that limiting our options would help us stay at home more. And it did. And it meant that we had chosen to do

something different, something else besides being *mobile*. We actually plan our trips, now, and because we do, we have an entirely different attitude toward distance and place. And that's important, because we grew up watching the disintegration of place in this century. I started out in a rural setting where my father built our house in an orchard. And in a few years the orchard was gone. And the woods where I used to play became an oil and gas field. And the city, which was forty miles away when I was born, is right up to the doorstep. And I think that experience was probably true for millions and millions of people. You know, that feeling that "I lived in a place that disappeared." Having a community. That's what I mean by being in place.

People rave now about their "virtual communities," the ones they find on-line. But virtual people are not there when your house burns down. Virtual people do not share physical space and eye contact. Virtual people do not have to like each other. In our life if you really want to live in a community with other people, you have to accept them. Where they are. And you can't just pull the plug if you decide you don't want to be there anymore. And that commitment and accountability is necessary, because I think anything that takes us away from being present here in the real world is a real danger. Television. Computers. The way we work. Long commutes. Driving in cars by ourselves. There are so many ways that we have found to not be present in the real world. To opt out. People in virtual communities get to know each other as disembodied brains. The community that I have is so much more messy and earthy than that.

Just think about how people "work" these days.

They sit in a chair and stare at a machine. And usually their mouth is hanging open a little bit. And I don't care what they *think* they're doing. Or where they think they're "going." They are sitting in a chair and staring at a screen. And actual minutes are ticking by. That's what I see. I was in an office building recently and I noticed how people would pick up their phones and call someone in one of the other cubicles and they would get that person's voice mail instead. And they would leave a message on the voice mail asking that person to call them back. Then, while they were waiting, they would listen to their own voice mail. And while they were listening to their voice mail the call would come in from the person they had just called. So it would go into their voice mail. And on and on. And this is modern life — interacting with machines.

It's not that we're against machines, totally. But we ask ourselves, what does the machine want to do? What is it best at? What will it do on its own? And then we construct limitations around it. So that those things that matter so much to us aren't lost because we have been channeled in a different direction. We don't want to do that. We want to stay human. We want to stay children of God. We want to continue the thread of humanity as it works out of destiny and not let that be sidetracked by technology.

In trying to do that we're gaining a whole lot of freedoms that people don't have anymore. It's funny. So much of the twentieth century's technologies have ostensibly been about creating new freedoms — but few people talk about the need to be free from those technologies themselves and the stresses they create. In fact, quite to the contrary, they accept them as inevitable. They know these things are bad and yet they believe they need to accept some percentage of defilement to be alive today. We're not perfect and we all have problems. But I think there's less stress and more contentment in the way we live. And that's one of the underlying questions that we should all be asking ourselves about the twentieth century.

The image I like is a corny one. But it's true and that is that underneath the asphalt and the concrete and the built world that we have made in such a short time in this century there is still dirt. I mean it's still entirely possible that we could change direction and renounce the values of comfort and convenience in favor of community and having a spiritual life. And slow down. The reason we publish our magazine is because we want people to know that if they're not comfortable with modern life, they don't have to live it. That they can stop doing it and they won't die. And they won't end up in a cave, gnawing on a bone.

through the looking glass. And indeed, even though communication with others was still limited primarily to the exchange of text, many people felt like they were entering another world, a *virtual* reality, when they communicated with others on-line — the sense of excitement that came with typing a line of text and watching a line of text appear on the screen in response to it feeling roughly to the imagination like the thrill of communicating with another life-form, not dolphins or Martians or even Lewis Carroll's scurrying hare, but some humanlike species reachable only by one's stepping through the computer glass into "cyberville" and becoming an on-line humanoid oneself.

To the chagrin of many parents, the Internet quickly developed a reputation as a place where sexual fantasies could be acted out (in on-line "chat rooms") and as a haven for pornographers. Yet its many other "user groups" and on-line "bulletin boards" prompted proponents to see something much more wholesome and revolutionary: an emerging political consciousness, the purest of democratic havens, an electronic town hall. In fact, many claimed the Net was serving as a truly healthy alternative to the traditional mass media, reversing an information power structure that had long worked from the top down. For where the content of ABC, NBC, CBS, and even CNN was determined by a handful of programming executives in New York (and Atlanta) and sent out to the masses, the Internet's content rose from the bottom up, originating in the postings and chatter of its users. The Internet was virtually lawless: no one owned it, no one controlled it, and those who used it answered to no set of rules. One could be whoever one wanted to be, say whatever one wanted to say. Information was free and all voices were equal, or as a *New Yorker* cartoon quipped, "On the Internet, nobody knows you're a dog."

Whatever the nature of the Net — and it was changing almost daily in the rough and tumble techno-nineties — it was now part, indeed perhaps the most important part, of the evolving sense of a world grown smaller. There were many who believed that the computer and the fax machine had been primary agents to the collapse of communism. No society that depended upon the control of information could exist in the 1990s, when markets had become more valuable than land and information more potent (and certainly more easily delivered) than any piece of military weaponry. Now, with the Internet, there was even serious discussion of the emergence of a virtually borderless world, where national loyalties eroded in favor of electronic ones. The more people became involved with their on-line "communities" — where they could be joined with those of like interests — and connected to each other through global markets, the less they would care about a local bond issue, a state referendum, even an election for president.

Still, the enthusiasm for the Web and its many wonders was matched in the nineties by an enormous skepticism. Intellectuals worried about its impact on society. Did the arrival of the new medium mean that the book (what one writer, mocking the techies, called an "alternative content delivery system") would be directed backward to some corner of history where it would join the illuminated manuscript and the Stone Age scrawl? Did it spell the ultimate corruption of the blessed English language, the devolving of discourse down to the shorthand, image-driven speech popular on screen? With technology assuming a position of such importance in our lives, did we risk an overhomogenization of the human experience and the construction of a "technopoly" in which people would become slaves to a machine god? Would the construction of so many virtual worlds make people indifferent to the nonvirtual one in which they actually lived, mere "tourists of reality," to use Susan Sontag's phrase about photography? And would the new technologies widen the gap between those with access to its machines and those without, making an even deeper division between the world's haves and have-nots and turning our inner cities into little more than the artifacts of a discredited industrial past?

Perhaps the greatest suspicion rang from those with a historical perspective. For it was hard, looking back at the twentieth century, to take the utopian visions of cyberspace's carnival barkers seriously. After all, some of the best thinkers of 1914, in their pre–World War I innocence, actually believed that international trade would make war obsolete. And both communists and fascists had claimed a faith in science, and the building of the "perfect" society, as justification for their bloody crimes. The 1939 World's Fair had declared the wonders of the future just hours before Hitler marched into Poland. And just how much had the "best" ideas of the twentieth century improved life anyway? "Gazing through grimy windows at the chaotic entropy of our cities," wrote curmudgeonly critic Robert Hughes, "contemplating the foil trays of gourmet 'gunk' that issue from our microwave units, locked in the honking metal glacier of the rush hour, wondering what the kids have been sniffing in the suburban mall, we recognize hopelessly degraded lineaments of earlier utopian fantasies . . . and sigh."

No wonder the emergence of the "Unabomber," the Harvard-educated recluse who systematically targeted people in the technology industry (killing three and injuring twenty-three through sixteen attacks) in an insane attempt to undermine the march of science, so grabbed the public fascination. Yet what an irony it was to learn that the easiest way to read Theodore Kaczynski's "manifesto" was to download it from the Net (where it appeared joined by a sampling of critical opinion of his ideas, a list of items found in Kaczynski's cabin on his arrest, and notes on how to recognize a mail bomb) and that the "Unabomber Political Action Committee," urging people in all seriousness to write Kaczynski's name on the 1996 presidential ballot, preached against the "onslaught of technology" from — guess where? — its very own Web site.

Ted Kaczynski was only the second most famous defendant of the late nineties. A twenty-nine-year-old veteran, decorated with the Bronze Star for service in the Persian Gulf War, attracted more attention for his part in the worst terrorist act ever on American soil. At 9:02 A.M. CST on April 19, 1995, a truck bomb exploded outside the Alfred P. Murrah federal building in Oklahoma City, collapsing its nine floors, and for days afterward, as rescue workers pawed through the wreckage looking for survivors, the scene gripped at the nation's emotions like few in American history. "This is why we live in Oklahoma," said one woman, so detached by her horror she seemed to think she was watching something going on someplace else. "Things like this don't happen here."

Families with loved ones caught in the rubble gathered at a local Methodist church, where Red Cross workers hung enormous sheets of paper on which the names of the missing were scribbled in red crayon, an appropriate writing device

"This revolution may or may not make use of violence: it may be sudden or it may be a relatively gradual process spanning a few decades. We can't predict any of that . . . [and] its object will be to overthrow not governments but the economic and technological basis of the present society . . ."

From the "Unabomber" manifesto

The splintered remains of the Murrah office building, below, continued to tremble for days after the bombing, making the rescue workers' task even more dangerous. "The place is in shock," said one Oklahoma City resident of his once-quiet city. "And it will be forever."

For the families and friends of those who died, resentment accompanied resignation. Awaiting the verdict in the 1997 trial of Timothy McVeigh, people turned the fence that now surrounds the Murrah building site into a makeshift memorial. McVeigh was found guilty and sentenced to death.

when one considered that, with a day-care center situated on the building's second floor, dozens of children had been present when the explosion happened, playing with their Barney dolls and eating their breakfast muffins. So vast was the devastation, so desperate the search for survivors, rescue workers occasionally hid inside the concrete mess to allow the search dogs to discover them, for even the canine crew was getting "depressed" over finding only the dead, and losing the will to continue.

In the end, 168 perished, including 19 children, and as the event's many tragic stories came out, the grief of the families was matched only by the outrage of the nation. Jim Denny's three-year-old son, Brandon, had to be identified from a tiny birthmark on his thigh — his face had been so mutilated by the blast. "Hard to believe," said Denny, "a dad can't identify his own boy." Mike Lenz told reporters of his glee the day before the blast, when he and his pregnant wife had an appointment for a sonogram. They smiled at each other as they listened to the tiny heartbeat and glanced at the computer screen holding a picture of the fragile embryo. Now both Lenz's wife and the incipient life she carried within her were gone. So great was Lenz's grief that there was a point afterward, he later declared, "when I actually stuck a pistol in my mouth."

At first, with no justification, suspicion centered upon "Middle Eastern types" seen fleeing the area soon after the blast, but these were little more than racist fantasies. No one wanted to believe that Americans would kill Americans. Yet, in the first hours after the blast, investigators had also begun focusing on a theory that the date might hold some crucial significance, and as it turned out they were right. To a growing constituency of antigovernment extremists, April 19 was not just another day. It was the anniversary of the Bureau of Alcohol, Tobacco and Firearms (BATF) assault on the Branch Davidian commune in Waco, Texas, in 1993, an event that horrified many on the Right as an attack on religious freedoms.

The final hours of the commune, which had been stockpiling guns and resisting federal inquiries into its treatment of its children, was a dramatic and tragic story, witnessed by millions on live television where its similarities to biblical prophecies made it shimmer with millennial overtones. While the BATF's M-60 tanks and tear gas were penetrating the compound, cult members stayed faithful to their leader, David Koresh (born Vernon Howell), whose assumed name identified him, in an elaborate and controversial reading of the Bible, as the "Second Messiah." In the end, eighty-four people died, including Koresh. But in the days after, Waco became a rallying cry for those on the Far Right, April 19 an anniversary to be marked in mourning or, as it now seemed, with an act of vengeful violence.

Slight, even reedy, Timothy McVeigh was arrested within days of the Oklahoma City tragedy and charged with the attack. But like all big public events of this time, the symbolic meaning soon eclipsed the event itself. When he was taken into custody, McVeigh was wearing a T-shirt with "The Tree of Liberty Must Be Refreshed from Time to Time with the Blood of Patriots" emblazoned on its back, and as more information came out about him, it brought attention to a widespread community of people for whom the federal government was anathema, a venal and tyrannical force which, in a union with the United Nations, was out to impose its "new world order" on the citizens of the United States.

Arming to resist another Waco: "Let's do what our founding fathers did . . . let's form a militia"

In 1992 I filled in as pastor of our church in northern Michigan. Now, I've always done the work of the Lord, whether it was lay preaching, interim preaching, filling the pulpit, or selling Bibles. I had also worked as a teacher for seven years, so I was very comfortable speaking in front of people. So I preached on Sunday mornings, and I guess the congregation liked me because they asked me to continue on as their permanent pastor. I gladly accepted.

In 1993 several parents came to me because they were very concerned about a government school program called Goals 2000 [a national framework for education reform]. We viewed this as a measure to remove the control of our children's education from the state and transfer it to the control of the federal government. We had several meetings about Goals 2000, and while the school itself was pushing for this program, there were a lot of people within our church who were fighting hard against it. These people had children in the public school, and they were Christians, and they realized that parents would no longer have control over their children's education. The federal government was now going to start teaching its own educational format — its own curricula with its own agenda. Now, this was frightening to us. Because we had already gone through Waco, and we had gone through Ruby Ridge [the 1992 FBI siege of white separatist Randy Weaver's Idaho cabin]. We had seen the abuses of government. We had seen the tyranny and the oppression. And now the children were going to be pledging allegiance to the federal government? And to the United Nations? This caused a great deal of uneasiness for the parents in the church.

People were still very much afraid about what happened at David Koresh's church in Waco: the smoldering ruins, the lives that were lost, the carnage that was wrought by the federal government as it burned down a church filled with people. They surrounded a church with tanks and armored vehicles, and they tortured and persecuted those people for fifty days and then they burned the place down over top of them. And all the while they laughed and mocked and jeered. That episode left such an indelible mark in our psyche that we realized that if this government was capable of that kind of barbarity, then it was capable of anything. When I saw David Koresh's place burn down, I cried. What almost hurt me the most about it was that, like so many other Americans, we simply watched this happen and didn't do anything about it.

As the meetings about Goals 2000 continued, we started talking more and more about the abuses of the federal government. These were concerns of people from all different backgrounds — Native Americans, white Anglo-Saxons, Jews, Christians — they were

— Norman Olson, born in Detroit in 1946, joined the U.S. Air Force in 1964 and served as a ground communications officer in Guam and Thailand during the Vietnam War. After twenty years in an air force career that brought him to some twenty-two countries, Olson retired, returning to Michigan to become a schoolteacher and eventually pastor of his church. He and his wife, Mary, have three children and two grandchildren.

Olson, right, in his militia garb.

joined by their fear of the federal government. Some were fearful of the education. Some were fearful of the conspiracies of an intrusive federal government. Some people were fed up with property taxes and having the government take their land away if they could not afford to pay. And after Waco and Ruby Ridge, we knew that the government was not well meaning. Ray Southwell, who was the deacon of our church, asked me, "Pastor, what can we do? Is there any way that we can give these people hope?" And I said, "Let's do what our founding fathers did. Let's do what they did two hundred and fifty years ago. They joined the people together in a defensive group, a militia. Let's arm the people against this government that has gone berserk." By April of 1994 we had begun the Michigan Militia.

From the beginning I demanded that the militia be open and public. Many people wanted it to be secretive — underground — because they were afraid. People thought that black helicopters were going to come hovering over their homes. Or that they were going to be assassinated in their sleep or run off the highway by some truck. But I felt that the best way to dispel the fear and the anxiety and the worry was to face it head-on. I named the first year "Operation Visibility." We put on uniforms, we carried guns, we trained in public. And we invited the press in to see what we were doing. We weren't ashamed. No more running away. I even opened up a gun shop to provide the weapons to the militia. By having a gun, many of these people felt safer. Our main focus was to bring the militia to the forefront of America. I wanted to shock the federal government and the Justice Department. I wanted to show them that I was going to raise up a militia millions and millions strong — with uniforms and guns. And we would shake our guns in the tyrant's face. And if there was another Waco, we would go to war. We would start shooting.

Then in 1996 the FBI had another standoff, this

time with the Freemen in Montana. We watched that whole scenario start to develop, much as it did at Waco. The FBI starting to take up its siege posture. Ray and I got on a plane and went on out there to try and do something. Our objective was to try and make the Freemen who were holed up in the Clark Ranch house seem like human beings in the eyes of the press and in the eyes of the FBI. We didn't want them to be just faceless, nameless, antigovernment, right-wing extremists. There were children in there. Ray, a licensed nurse, and I, a pastor, walked right up to the FBI barricade to try and get in. I was carrying a Bible and a big teddy bear to give to the children who were inside. And Ray was carrying his medical bag over his shoulder.

I spoke some very harsh words to the FBI. I stood at the barricade and told the FBI that if they created another Waco, then the militia would strike back at the FBI. There would be assassinations around the country. Well, they listened, they laughed, they jeered, and they mocked. We tried day after day after day to get through the barricades. And every day we talked to the FBI. And we warned them. And it was interesting, that the FBI who were members of minority groups — women, African-Americans, Native Americans — those people listened very intently. They had a sense of injustice. But those FBI men that I refer to as young white bucks — white men from twenty-eight to thirty-five years old who carried big guns and bowie knives — were the ones that wanted to get in there, and slash and burn, and brutalize those people.

We thought that at any time the tanks were going to start rolling in. We thought that they were going to attack that Clark Ranch house and burn those people out. And if that time came, we had to decide what we were going to do. And we decided that we were ready to start shooting. But the attack never happened. After eighty days the Freemen surrendered.

I've got three children, and I would give my life for those children. I would do it automatically, without thinking. I was a soldier for more than twenty years in the military, and I took a vow that I would give my life to defend all Americans. I vowed to do that, and I meant it. As a pastor, I would do that for my people. As a schoolteacher, I would do that for the children. The day that I helplessly watched those people burn in Waco, I vowed to myself that I would never let that happen again.

Michigan's "Gun Stock '95" was just one of the decade's many conventions displaying antigovernment paraphernalia.

"[The enemy is] not just European, not just African, not just Asian, but a hegemony of all of them combined."

Warning in a Far Right movement video: America at Peril: A Call to Arms

Here, too, the Internet was the communications medium of choice, the kind of freewheeling frontier where crackpot conspiracy theories and unfounded rumors grew like weeds (anonymity is easily preserved on the Web), and yet what an irony that was, too, for wasn't the Web a primary agent to the "one world" future the Far Right so wished to undo? After Oklahoma City, membership in "survivalist" groups actually grew (by 1997, reported *U.S. News,* there were antigovernment organizations in all fifty states, nearly four hundred of them armed), while on talk radio, at hundreds of Web sites, and at a new kind of convention called a "Preparedness" Expo, expressions of paranoia gushed forth, among them the belief that the government would soon be planting microchip identification devices in the hands of everyone, that Washington was preparing to wage biological warfare on its citizenry, and, the perennial American backwoods favorite, that the government would soon confiscate the people's guns. Much of the world might already be basking in the green glow of an electronic future, but to an increasing number of people, it seemed as if a kind of eighteenth-century Royalist threat was present, the time to gather the patriot militia at hand.

Was it a mere coincidence that as the century entered its final days, a nonagenarian getting ready to face the inevitable, so much of the news seemed to be about sensational death? There was Waco, Oklahoma City, and the Unabomber, sure. But there was also that Web site nightmare known as the Heaven's Gate cult (their mass suicide note was actually left on the Net); the doctor-assisted suicide advocate and practitioner Jack Kevorkian, aka "Dr. Death"; and the breathtaking outsize pageant that surrounded the funeral of Diana, Princess of Wales. And was it mere happenstance that this preoccupation with life's end coincided with a similar preoccupation with its beginning, in particular with science's increasing success with the spectacular birth — the sixty-three-year-old mom, the McCaughey septuplets, and Dolly, the irresistible sheep clone? A turning was upon the world, not only the death of this century but the birth of the next, not only the expiration of the second millennium but the delivery of the third, and if there was not exactly a sense of the apocalypse present, there was at the very least a nervous bedside awareness that something very important was happening, jostling the traditional sense of existence.

In fact, science had been stretching the definitions of life at both ends for some time now, but society was still struggling to catch up, to adequately address the ethical and moral dilemmas that this work presented. On one side was concern over the way that medicine, particularly American medicine, seemed so unwilling to let the dying die. In the mid-seventies the parents of the comatose Karen Ann Quinlan had petitioned the courts to allow them to remove their daughter from life support and the Quinlans had eventually won (after nine more years in a coma, Karen died naturally in 1985), leading to the establishment, in all fifty states, of laws permitting "living wills" and the now common procedure of passive euthanasia (the withdrawal of life support equipment). And yet in practice doctors also frequently ignored such directives ("Physicians are taught to save lives, that death is a failure," explained the author of one study) or, if they endeavored to follow them, found themselves in messy situations with families insisting upon miracles and patients' own preferences difficult to decipher. What, for instance, was a doctor to do if the person under his care had forbade measures that could, at best, deliver them to a "poor quality of life," when one's definition of "poor quality" would certainly vary according to personality and circumstances?

Medicine was similarly perplexed by the continuing struggle to determine just what constituted death. For a long time, the agreed-upon definition had been based upon the cessation of brain function, allowing for the removal of life-supporting equipment no matter whether there was a directive calling for that or not. And yet there were many cases where the brain continued to show activity, but the patient had devolved into a persistent vegetative state, sustained purely by technology. Even in those cases where the brain had failed, it was evidently arbitrary to call the person "dead," for the heart still functioned, pumping blood to sustain working organs. In 1993 a seventeen-weeks-pregnant, brain-dead woman in Oakland, California, was kept alive for three and a half months (her "dead" body fed, cleaned, and even put through physical exercises) while the fetus, amazingly, developed into a baby boy delivered by cesarean section.

The staff at Oakland's Highland Hospital cheered their success at achieving such a miraculous birth, and yet just what were the implications of their work? The doctors were following their responsibility to preserve life at all costs, but had the woman's wishes been determined or had she simply lost all rights because she was now "dead"? Would the physicians have followed the same heroic path if it had been shown that the fetus had suffered permanent injury (the woman, attempting a robbery, had been shot)? And if they did not, would they be valuing one kind of life over another? Finally, there had to be concern for the woman's dignity — for if in fact she was dead in the eyes of the law, could the hospital be charged with employing her body as a mere "nutrient supplement, disposable after use," as one critic commented regarding a similar case in Germany?

Death's most public dilemma centered on the topic of doctor-assisted suicide. A best-selling 1991 book by Derek Humphry, the then director of the

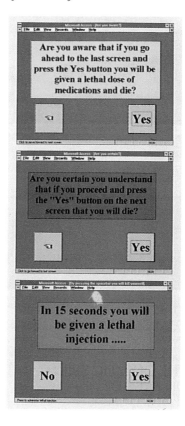

Are you aware that if you go ahead to the last screen and press the Yes button you will be given a lethal dose of medications and die?

Yes

Are you certain you understand that if you proceed and press the "Yes" button on the next screen that you will die?

Yes

In 15 seconds you will be given a lethal injection .....

No   Yes

"I will give no deadly medicine to anyone if asked."

From the Hippocratic oath, under question in the campaign for doctor-assisted suicide

Hemlock Society, included instructions on how to kill oneself with a combination of prescription drugs (in 1992 alone, copies of the book were discovered by the sides of twelve New York City suicide victims), yet while its "how-to" tone was shocking, its publication coincided with the rise of "right to die" advocates everywhere, many of whom insisted that the time had come to consider whether doctors might aid those who felt that their lives had become so hopeless that they would sooner die, and under their own devices, with dignity.

Most people became aware of the subject of assisted suicide through the suicide "machine" created by a Michigan physician named Jack Kevorkian (borrowing from the word "obituary," he preferred the title "obitiatrist"). The contraption, which looked like the kind of deviously complex mechanism the thirties cartoonist Rube Goldberg might have devised, was an elaborate way to get around the law. Kevorkian simply hooked up an IV line to a patient, then allowed him or her to push a switch to inject first a sedative and then the lethal potassium chloride. With the onset of death, the doctor often then called the police to clean up the details, a surgeon signaling for the orderlies.

Kevorkian was a fanatic, full of bluster, self-aggrandizement, and eccentricity (an amateur artist, he favored ghoulish subject matter for his paintings), but the issue he raised was anything but extreme. Many people agreed with him that the termination of one's own life was a right, perhaps even one protected by the Constitution, and they insisted that doctors be allowed the freedom to write deadly prescriptions for terminally ill patients. In 1996 an appeals court even found justification for their claims under the equal protection clause, observing that patients who were joined to life support systems could in a sense "commit suicide" by having themselves disconnected from a ventilator, but that those whose lives were differently compromised — in debilitating pain, say, from irreversible cancer — were being denied that right.

Soon many "right to die" opponents were predicting that doctors would be deciding who lives and who dies and that nature was being subverted for convenience. Others wondered why a right needed to be established at all, when as it was, doctors subtly "assisted" many who wanted to end their lives; legalizing their behavior would only invite abuse. "As a society, do we not want this most fearful act — killing — to be done fearfully?" asked essayist Charles Krauthammer. "If it must be done at all . . . let it be done with trembling, in shadow, in whispered acknowledgment that some fundamental norm is being violated, even if for the most compassionate reasons."

Meanwhile, the justices of the Supreme Court, reconsidering the appellate decision, addressed its practicality. If a constitutional right to die were established, they asked, how would it be limited, and if the grounds were merely patient complaints of intolerable physical or psychological pain, then how could it be denied to anyone who simply wished to die, including a sixteen-year-old suffering from unrequited love?

The issue, in essence, repeated the argument that had been raging for decades over abortion (and the appeals court majority even cited the abortion landmark decision in *Roe v. Wade* as evidence of a right to authority over one's body). For once again, the contest was one that pitted control against fate, the quality of life against the sanctity of life, the man-centered world against the God-centered, and there was simply no consensus building for either side. Even, in

A nineties death watch: Morphine, life support, and "When do we admit it's over?"

Tom Campi, below, and his favorite picture of Christina, and their two children, left, in 1980.

— Christina Walker Campi, born in 1951, studied comparative literature at SUNY Stony Brook. While attending NYU graduate school she took a job with the New York Civil Liberties Union in 1981 and stayed there for six years. She then became the executive director of the New York Food and Hunger Hotline and currently works as a management and fundraising consultant in New York City.

In 1996 my husband, Tom, became sick with what we thought was bronchitis. After antibiotics failed, he went through a battery of tests: chest X rays, MRI, CAT scan, bone scan, liver biopsy, ultrasound. It was like Western medicine at its best and its worst. At the end of it all they diagnosed him with metastasized lung cancer. And what was worse was that it had spread to his trachea and his liver. That night I went home and did a search on the Internet, and I found hundreds of cancer Web sites. What I learned was that only a minuscule amount of people actually survive lung cancer past five years, and that was if it was caught in the early stages. My husband had advanced cancer. The next day, I got our oncologist alone. He said, "What do you want to know?" I said, "I want to know how long he has." He said, "Six to nine months." My knees buckled.

For the next several months, Tom went through round after round of chemotherapy and treatments, but his cancer continued to spread. Ten or fifteen years ago, the oncologist would just keep treating and treating a cancer patient with radiation right up until the last day he or she was alive. Now they give up sooner, which ironically is a good thing. What is incredibly hard, however, is deciding whether or not to keep giving treatment, when you know it's not going to cure him. The day that I decided to stop treatment on Tom, his most recent MRI showed that the cancer had moved to his brain. He had already started to show some neurological symptoms. He still knew who I was, but he was confused in his thinking. Tom was a brilliant guy, who loved to talk, and to see him starting to get confused and losing control of himself was awful. He felt so humiliated. And he was in terrible pain. The cancer had also moved into his bones, which is the most painful cancer of all. I decided to ease his pain with morphine, knowing that this would hasten his death. Both my mother and sister had died of cancer several months earlier, and they both had been put on morphine in the end. With them we didn't know that the morphine would quicken their deaths. The doctors didn't tell us. As a result, my mother died alone. I wasn't about to have that happen to my husband. I knew what I was doing. I was pretty clear-headed at that point. But I'm still tortured by the

possibility that he could have had just a short amount of time more, a couple more days. I feel horrible that I was the one with sole control over this decision.

After Tom and I signed the DNR (Do Not Resuscitate) order, he was moved to a private room and he was put on a morphine drip. After he was on the morphine for a while, a friend of mine, who happened to be a doctor on staff at the hospital, came by and said, "You know, he's not going to last more than a couple of hours right now." And I started to cry, because his children were on their way in from California to say good-bye, and I was afraid he would die before they got there. My friend told me to have them turn the morphine pump off, and then he'd come out of it for a little while. He woke up the next morning, and he saw his kids, and he kissed them, he hugged them. He kind of squeezed my hand a little bit, and he went back to sleep. And that was it, he never woke up again. Luckily, because I had them decrease the dosage, he was able to hold on to see his kids. But I had no guidance, no help, on this at all except that I happened to have this friend who's on staff there. He would've died that night, and not seen his kids, had we not turned the morphine pump off.

We had been helped by the doctors with all sorts of treatment, but their help pretty much stopped when the treatment stopped. These were good doctors, with whom my husband was very attached, but they were trained to prolong life, not to deal with the dying process. I was left with this enormous feeling of having been abandoned. We just needed some more sense of being connected rather than being put in a room with the door closed. At one point, the cardiologist came by and I said to him, "Doc, you know he's dying. This is it." He said, "Yeah it is." And he told me how sorry he was, and how much he liked my husband. And that's the only time any of the doctors addressed the fact that Tom was dying.

The private room my husband was put in had a beautiful view. We could see the East River and the Chrysler Building. I had my son bring the CD player from home and a handful of Tom's CDs. I picked out two of his favorites — a Duke Ellington/Mahalia Jackson CD and a Django Reinhardt CD — really nice early-thirties jazz. I must have played each one of those CDs twenty times as I sat with my husband. I just didn't want it to end. I thought, "You know what? I can stay in this room for a long time. He looks comfortable now. I'm here, I have the couch, there is the shower. Nice view, flowers. Nice music." I didn't want it to end. At that moment, I understood why people want their family members put on life support. Some part of you that thinks, well, as long as the body is there, it's not over.

That night was really hard. He started tossing and turning, so I asked for the morphine to be increased. And then it seemed as if he was strangling to death right in front of me. It was horrifying. I just completely panicked. I called my friend, the doctor, and he told me to ask the nurse to push the morphine all the way up to thirty milligrams. I kept asking him, "Will I be killing him?" And he yelled at me, "No, he's dying from cancer! If he's strangling and choking, push it up!" Almost immediately after the nurse increased the morphine, the strangling stopped, and he started to breathe more comfortably. I sat there and just counted his breaths. At one point, it was eight breaths a minute, and it went down to seven, to six. About two hours later, I was holding his hand when he took his last breath.

This experience made me realize that birth and death are equally important, but we only pay attention to the birth end of it. Whenever you read anything about death or dying, you inevitably read about Dr. Kevorkian and about physician-assisted suicide. That is just a red herring in the whole discussion of death and dying. I think he's helping people commit suicide, which may be a valid discussion, but it has little to do with ordinary illness and dying. Death is like our dirty little secret. We all come to this world, but we pretend we are all not going to go out of it. I think Americans especially are terrified of death. We're a can-do population, so death seems like a terrible failure to us. This is the only culture in the world where if we die we think we did something wrong — the doctor must have screwed up or the person had an unhealthy lifestyle. We assign blame rather than see death for what it is, which is the way it's going to end for all of us.

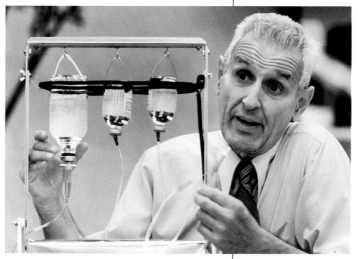

"Oppressed by a fatal disease, a severe handicap, a crippling deformity? . . . Show him proper medical evidence that you should die, and Dr. Jack Kevorkian will help you kill yourself free of charge," read advertisements placed by "Dr. Death" in the 1980s. A few years later, Kevorkian, above, was a bizarre celebrity, casting the cause of assisted suicide in terms of civil rights.

" Technology creates an imperative: 'If we can do it, we will do it.' Ethics asks: 'We can do it, but should we do it?'"

Peter Singer, Rethinking Life and Death

late 1997, as the Supreme Court was unanimously reversing the lower court's decision, firmly denying a constitutional "right to die," Oregon was establishing itself as the first state in the nation to make assisted suicide legal (limited to adults, sound of mind, who — in the considered opinion of two doctors — have less than six months to live), while the House of Representatives in Michigan was adopting a bill making the very same act in that state a felony. And in the meantime, the irrepressible Dr. Death continued his march. By the spring of 1998 Jack Kevorkian had aided in his one hundredth suicide.

The happy Iowa couple staring back from newsmagazine covers in November 1997 looked decidedly Middle American. Innocent, God-fearing (as cover lines declared in proud terms), and now the parents of *sep*tuplets. No one before Bobbi McCaughey had produced seven healthy babies in one pregnancy — one of them weighed in at two pounds, five ounces, and the biggest was just over three — but it seemed likely that she would not be the last. After Canada's Dionne quintuplets were born in 1934, they became a freakish tourist attraction (their father even considered displaying them at the 1939 World's Fair). But by the 1990s medicine had made great strides conquering infertility, pushing the boundaries of the possible, and thanks to the resulting proliferation of fertility drugs, the multiple-birth pregnancy was no longer rare.

In 1995 there were 365 sets of quadruplets and 57 sets of quintuplets and sextuplets in America alone. And there would have been more but for the now common technique of "selective reduction," one of those remarkable medical euphemisms, this one describing the abortion of one or more fetuses in order to relieve pressure on the others. Both Kenny and Bobbi McCaughey — who became pregnant while taking the drug Metrodin, which stimulates egg production — had been unwilling to abort any of their fetuses (they are devout Christians and morally opposed to abortion), even though most experts insist that the dangers are enormous and the chances of taking home healthy children are severely compromised without "reducing to twins." But while the McCaugheys' faith made their decision relatively simple, many couples in the nineties faced agonizing choices over pregnancy, and "selective reduction" was just one of them.

After the delivery of the first test-tube baby in 1978, tens of thousands of American women with blocked or scarred fallopian tubes had achieved success with *in vitro* fertilization, mothering children that in earlier generations would never have been born. But biology had begun to turn its attention to other kinds of disorders, too, developing techniques, referred to as "assisted reproductive technology," that offered new hope to couples everywhere. If a woman had trouble producing eggs, she could, like McCaughey, be dosed with hormones to trick her ovaries into releasing many eggs at once. If she had problems carrying to term, her egg fertilized with her husband's sperm could now be implanted in a "donor womb." If the couple had trouble conceiving, the husband's sperm (or that from a sperm donor) could be injected directly into the egg, then implanted

Pregnancy was truly a family affair when Christa (her last name withheld), above center, opted to have her own forty-five-year-old mother carry her child. Here the "extended" family poses — Christa listening to the heartbeat of her child in her own mother's womb while her father looks on.

"After all those years of sex without procreation, here I lie engaged in procreation without sex. It is a stunning reversal, a cosmic joke . . . a lifetime of trying to be somebody, my whole own woman in the latter half of 20th century America, a lifetime of holding motherhood at bay . . . In my hope and in my angst, I am tempted to roll down the window and shout: 'Hey, hey, Gloria! Germaine! Kate! Tell us: How does it feel to have ended up without babies, children, flesh of your flesh? Did you mean to thumb your noses at motherhood, or is that what we heard?'"

Ann Taylor Fleming, writing in the New York Times Magazine, *on "entering the sisterhood of the infertile" at age thirty-eight*

in her womb or, if necessary, in a donor womb. Or they could visit an "egg donation" clinic and choose the genetic mother of their child, carefully examining hundreds of profiles of women accompanied by glossy photographs and lists of their favorite novels.

The new techniques were exciting, particularly to those whose personal medical histories had long made pregnancy appear difficult or impossible (and to gay couples who wanted children). But they came at a price, and not only the steep financial one that made this more of an option for those of at least the middle class. The parceling-out of the reproductive process placed people in uncharted territory rife with thorny legal, ethical, moral, and social questions. Was it fair to be paying women for eggs, or was that process, in essence, trading money for body parts? And if it was fair, how was that to be regulated so that it did not become a way of life, making poorer women the providers of pregnancies for the rich? Was access to the new methods of reproductive assistance to be granted equally, or should it be limited, preventing situations like that of the sixty-three-year-old Los Angeles woman who, by lying about her age, gave birth to a baby girl, conceived with a donor egg, in the spring of 1997? And what of the many undiscovered issues surrounding extended reproductive "families" now that it was possible for a child to have as many as five parents (his donor father, his donor mother, the woman who carried him, and the two people who would raise him)? Moreover, should the child be told that he actually emerged from his Aunt Judy, or should that information be kept secret? And was Aunt Judy likely to feel some extended claim upon the child, complicating his upbringing? When a friend offered to carry for writer Anne Taylor Fleming, Fleming's first instinct was to regard it as an "offer that transcends love," but when the friend then suggested that she herself would have to breast-feed the infants for the first few days "to get them started," the writer recoiled in a primitive rage. "*My* babies? You will breast-feed *my* babies?"

The new reproductive biology spoke not only to the tremendous advances of medicine but also to an interesting piece of social demography. Having deferred pregnancy to focus on the establishment of their careers, many baby boom women, now into their less fertile years, had become desperate for motherhood. It was, in fact, the needs of these late starters that pushed much of the fertility research, and yet, in the constant tug between fate and free will, one had to ask at some point whether parenthood was a right or a privilege. And whether the pursuit of pregnancy should be allowed to supersede serious social concerns.

In the spring of 1997 a demure Scottish embryologist achieved what even the most optimistic scientists had long considered impossible. Using a single cell from an adult sheep's mammary gland, Dr. Ian Wilmut created a baby lamb he named Dolly and promptly set the imagination of the world on fire. The animal was in essence a clone, a carbon copy of its mother, and while its creation had exciting implications for the propagation of endangered species and the creation of, say, a herd of champion cows, the more frightening possibilities involved human beings. For if man did not step in to regulate the march of progress, it

Making babies in the nineties: "This girl absolutely came from our love. We just had some help"

I didn't always know that I wanted to have a baby. I've always loved children, but I loved my life the way it was. I'm a doctor, and I have a clinical psychotherapy practice in Washington, D.C., which I had built and grown. And I had a very satisfying life with friends, and family, and dogs, and living in the house that we always dreamt of living in. I felt very proud of what I had built. Even so, whether or not to have children was a question that I had been thinking about for a number of years. For Jeff and me, the decision whether or not to have children had to be a very conscious one. It couldn't be "maybe we will, maybe we won't, we'll just see what happens," like many other couples we know. Jeff already had two grown children from a previous marriage, and he had already had a vasectomy when we met. In order to have children, he would have to have the procedure reversed — and there would be no guarantees that it would work.

I am someone who, basically, grew up with the idea that if I worked very hard for something, I could make it happen. Working very hard can get you into the right place and can get you thinking through the right things, but it doesn't necessarily make it happen. It was hard for me to let myself really want something when I didn't really know if I could achieve it. Unlike for my mother, the decision to have a baby was a real struggle for me. For my mother's generation, it was really just an assumption, of course you would have children. Eventually, as I hit my late thirties, it became very clear to me that yes I wanted very much to have children.

We went to talk to Dr. Harry Miller, who was at George Washington University. He had unbelievably high success rates for vasectomy reversal, which is a tricky operation. Despite his successes, Dr. Miller had done very few reversals of men who had had vasectomies for as long as Jeff — twenty years. Dr. Miller checked Jeff out and checked me out to make sure I was fertile, and he thought that we had a good chance of success, so we scheduled the operation. The day before he was to have the reversal, Jeff changed his mind. He really got scared about the surgery. I think he was very afraid that it wasn't going to work, and he didn't know if he could stand disappointing me that way. This was just a devastating time in our marriage. I felt like something was being taken away from me before I even had a chance at it.

Jeff eventually changed his mind and had the surgery and everything went fine. Two or three days later we went back so that they could look into the ejaculate to see if there were swimmers, and there were. Dr. Miller shook Jeff's hand and said, "Congratulations, Dad." Jeff had a high sperm count, mobility, movement, shape, everything looked fabulous. Everything was full steam ahead, and we started trying to get pregnant.

Putchat, left, with her husband and child.

—*Cynthia Putchat, born in 1956, went to Brandeis and Harvard Universities and earned a Ph.D. in clinical psychology from Ohio State University in 1985. She is a psychotherapist with her own practice in Washington, D.C.*

About five months passed, and I had not gotten pregnant. Now, five months is not at all an unreasonable amount of time to be waiting, but I wanted to be careful, so I spoke with a fertility doctor who said that with a lot of men that have vasectomy reversals, there still may be problems with the sperm that are not immediately evident. We had two very new, cutting-edge tests done: the hamster egg test — where they test the sperm with an actual hamster egg — and the acrosome reaction test. It turned out that Jeff's sperm could not penetrate an egg. The only way that we could get pregnant was through IVF [*in vitro* fertilization], with a very new process called ICSI [intracytoplasmic sperm injection]. This process had just been developed a few years earlier and was done successfully at only a few clinics in the world. They take a single sperm and inject it directly into an egg that has been harvested from the mother. Ironically, had we not waited so long, we may never have known about this procedure because the technology was so new. As a matter of fact, just a few years earlier, no one would have even been able to diagnose our problem in the first place.

I did a lot of research about ICSI and found out that Cornell Medical Center in New York had the best program in the world. We met with the head of the program, Dr. Zev Rosenwaks. He went over everything with me and did an exam on the spot. He told us right then and there that he would accept us into the IVF program. I was thrilled. I felt like we were doing absolutely everything on our part to increase our chances of having a baby. Whatever the results were, I could live with it, knowing that we were going all out to make it happen.

As part of the IVF process, I had to take drugs to stimulate my ovaries to produce more than one egg. I had to go into the clinic every day for blood work and sonograms to see how the drug levels were working and how the egg follicles were growing. It is a very delicate balance. You don't want to overstimulate, and you don't want to understimulate, and you want to catch the eggs when they are the right level of maturity. When the time

came, they went in and surgically harvested the eggs. That very day Jeff and I had to produce a sperm sample, and then individual sperm were injected into each egg.

After the fertilized eggs had grown into pre-embryos, they chose the four largest and strongest and put them back into my uterus. After the procedure, the nurses told me, "You know, you can move, you can do whatever you want. They're not going to fall out." It's not logical, but I felt like I wanted to keep my legs crossed. I didn't want to jostle them.

We had to wait a week before taking a pregnancy test to see if the whole thing took. The waiting was the hardest part. I was working the day we were to get the results, and I could not stand the idea of finding out in the middle of the day. I wanted to be with Jeff when I found out. But we also didn't want to wait until I got home at the end of the day. So we decided that Jeff would get the results in the middle of the day, and he would hold on to that information for a few hours until he picked me up from work. Under no circumstances was he supposed to call me and tell me over the phone.

From the time the eggs were put back inside of me, I really believed I was pregnant. I believed, that is, up until that afternoon. When I hadn't heard from Jeff, I was convinced that I was not pregnant. I knew he swore to me he would not call, but I couldn't believe that he would actually be able to resist picking up the phone if I were pregnant. At the end of the day it was pouring rain, and I was in my partner's office when Jeff pulled up in our car. I was so nervous. He got out of the car and just stood there, in the pouring rain, with a dozen long-stemmed red roses. I broke down crying. I said to my partner, "I'm not pregnant, because he got me these roses to make me feel better." I was scared to go downstairs, so I took my time putting on my coat and getting my things together. The whole time, Jeff just stood there in the rain — no umbrella — he just stood there getting drenched. I went outside, and he looked at me, he hugged me, and he said, "You're pregnant." A little over nine months later we gave birth to a healthy baby girl, Sydney Tessa Zev. Zev is her Hebrew name, after Dr. Rosenwaks.

People say to me, "Oh, Cynthia, you went through so much." But I think that all we went through actually enhanced the experience. This baby absolutely came from our love. We just had some help in the process. The doctors, the technology, they all just helped us along in the creation of life. They gave us the opportunity to have a baby. Going through the IVF process for me was as powerful a time as falling in love and the delivery of my baby. This was something that could not have happened a few years before. We were on the cutting edge of technology.

seemed only a matter of time now before people would be photocopied like office memos.

Those awake and about, strolling near the tunnel at the Place de l'Alma at a few minutes after midnight, remembered the noise, a thunderous crash and then an unrelenting sound, like that which might issue from the mouth of an animal caught in a trap, only an animal would wail, and this was constant and unwavering, a single bold note, like an operatic high C with the needle stuck on an old LP. Tourists, approaching the tunnel, peered in and saw a black Mercedes, its cabin crushed. The driver, clearly dead, was leaning full-body into his steering wheel and the mangled car's horn. That was the high C. But it was the fate of the passengers, still unclear, that would make this crash historic.

Over the next hour, emergency workers cut the cabin open and, retrieving a blond woman from the rear, delicately moved her to Pitié Salpêtrière Hospital a little more than three miles away. Early reports said that she had suffered only a broken arm and some cuts, but that was primarily to buy time to get the more tragic truth to two young boys on vacation in northern Scotland. It was their father who jostled William and Harry from their dreaming to tell them that their mother had died. Moments later the world joined the future king of England and his brother in perhaps the greatest piece of collective mourning over a single passing in all human history.

The former Diana Spencer was certainly an odd choice for such a tribute. She had not, after all, been a head of state or in any obvious sense a heroine. She had not even been queen and she never would have been. Her fairy-tale romance with Prince Charles, leading to a spectacular wedding ceremony in 1981, watched live around the world, had devolved into a sordid mess, the kind that kept England's gossip sheets titillated, with affairs and jealousies and the sort of superficiality that only confirmed royalty's hard fall in the twentieth century. These were the empty lives of privilege, long absent the power that had once made their offices fearsome.

The princess's tragic death happened almost exactly one year from the day that a British court declared her divorced from Charles, ending a dream that had been joined vicariously by so many women around the world; but Diana was already such an enormous public figure that it was a foregone conclusion that her fame would outlast her formal connection to the royal family. Charles had chosen well, perhaps too well, for almost from the moment of their wedding it had seemed as if Britain's royal subjects had much more loyalty to the woman they adoringly called "Di" than they had ever had for the present queen or her family, and they had maintained their affection through all her troubles.

The days after the crash were filled with earnest hand-wringing over the circumstances. The car in which the princess and her Egyptian boyfriend, Dodi Fayed, had been driving was pursued into the tunnel by paparazzi, leading many, including Diana's brother, to claim that the press that had, in a sense, made her also killed her. But that ignored the fact that Fayed's limousine driver had been drunk as he tore through the Parisian streets. His judgment might have been hurried, but it was already impaired. More interesting were the swirling rumors that Diana had been pregnant by Fayed at the time of the accident (if so, it would have formed yet another late-century joining of life's two most elemental events) and that their death had been plotted by those who felt threatened by the specter of a

"Goodbye, England's rose . . ."

Pop singer Elton John, at the funeral of Princess Diana

Muslim Arab child as a half sibling to the heir of the British throne. But this was little more than the awkward and bitter chatter that accompanies sudden and unexpected mourning. People were sad and unbelieving; they needed to create distractions.

More than a million lined the streets of London to watch her coffin pass, tossing flowers toward the hearse and weeping at the solemn procession that followed it, one that included, first, Diana's men — her former father-in-law, her former husband, her brother, and her two children — then hundreds of representatives of the charities she had supported, some of them moving along in wheelchairs, each of them a statement that this woman of good means recognized those who lived without: people with AIDS, victims of leprosy and breast cancer, the casualties to land mines. When Mother Teresa, the Roman Catholic nun who spent a life devoted to the "poorest of the poor," died a week later, people noticed the irony — here was a *true* servant of the destitute, devoted, as she once said, "to spoiling the poor, because everyone else is spoiling the rich" — but theater creates its own temporary logic, and if nothing else, Diana's departure was grander theater.

The funeral itself was the most heartrending since England saluted its World War II savior, Winston Churchill, in 1965, but Winnie's parting came at a time before there were satellites beaming live images around the world, and he had been ninety. The rite for Diana, witnessed by billions on television, was the decade's grand cyber event, bigger even than O.J., and its sad evocation of youth and beauty and promise so tragically cut down brought tears to people who

When the whole world descended upon Kensington Palace, bearing tokens of mourning for Diana, England's florists declared a shortage. Similar displays gathered around British embassies throughout the world.

otherwise shouldn't have cared one whit about a thirty-five-year-old divorced British socialite. How else to explain the many alarm clocks waking tens of millions on America's east coast to catch every moment of the procession, and the many other people around the world, all of them well outside the rule of the House of Windsor, who nonetheless had sat up through the night, riveted to the continuous coverage?

To some, the whole week had the feeling of an intense television miniseries, one that might even provide a little embarrassment later when recalling just how much it had gripped at the heartstrings. Cyber*grief*. But when the cameras caught a picture of the white roses atop the coffin and next to them a handwritten card with the inscription "Mummy," it was hard not to well up. Diana may have been primarily famous for being famous, but she was also a mother.

Then again, it was a good moment for a ceremony. After all, the century had begun with one, and with the hour growing late, it was beginning to feel like time for a grand recessional. The same silent streets, the same "noise of the horse's hoofs striking the road," the same "rattle of swords, and . . . chatter of stirrups" had been present in 1901 when the world's churches respectfully tolled at the passing of England's sour, five-foot Queen Victoria and, with her, the 1800s. The glamorous Diana could not have been more different from the monarch for whom an age had been named, and who led an empire so vast and so devoted that even African chieftains reverently referred to her as "the Great White Queen," but then the explosive twentieth century could not have been more different from the steady and reliable nineteenth, and so many of the details around Diana's final moments — the speeding car, the chase of the fame-makers, the electronic global mourning, the inflation of the superficial to the pedestal of gravity, even the immediate crass marketing of T-shirts and key chains and benefit recordings "honoring" her — were icons of the age that was now being passed to the new millennium. They played Chopin and Beethoven at Victoria's funeral; Elton John sang at Di's.

It has become a cliché to remark that life changed more in the hundred years since the reign of Victoria than it did in the thousand years before it, but clichés are clichés because they are so impressively true that one can't help repeating them, and most of the changes the twentieth century brought were for the better. Consider only this: the life expectancy of an American born in 1905 was just forty-nine years; by 1998, it was seventy-six. Or the fact that every second death in the late 1800s was that of an infant. Or that so many in the world at the beginning of the century lived lives not only absent electricity and the telephone and the automobile and the movie house and the radio and the television and the computer and the Internet but, even more important, absent the elemental freedoms that at least the promise of democracy now provided them. Deep within the embrace of the "people's princess" and its corresponding affront to her former royal in-laws was one of the chief lessons of the twentieth century: the stampede of the public will.

That the world did not change even more than this — that is, that it utterly failed to realize the utopian fantasies the century's many dreamers and schemers had concocted for it, that even the sophisticated streets of the 1990s' so-called global community were witness to the bloodshed of the ancient ethnic feud, and

"How, then, shall we live? How must we live to preserve free societies and to be worthy of the blood and the pain? This is the unfinished business of our century . . ."

Theologian Michael Novak, writing for the New York Times *op-ed page, May 24,1998*

that science was now looked upon with skepticism as well as marvel — may have been nothing more than a continued assertion of our subjective humanity. The twentieth century was characterized by the faith so many held that life was knowable, indeed controllable, that the forces of existence could be made subject to the dictates of human will, and that life would only improve, with the golden age almost certainly before us, just over *there,* almost within our reach. Yet with the close of the century and the collapse of the modern era, one could now also detect a new humility, a kind of post-Enlightenment understanding that life might actually be "*un*knowable," and that reason and order may provide answers in laboratories but that in practice, citing the late great essayist Isaiah Berlin, they are too often experienced as "prison houses of the spirit."

Even with its more legitimate governments and mind-boggling machines, it was certainly a humbler world that greeted the twenty-first century, and how could it not be? The number of people connected to an exciting technological future still paled next to the number joined to memories of suffering and death. For there remained no communications medium more powerful than the family story, and the ones handed down from this century popped with the drama of the gulag, the febrile horror of the Holocaust, the primitive injustices of Jim Crow, the pain of AIDS. Within the lineage of every citizen of 1999 was a veteran of 1914, 1929, 1945, 1968, 1989, and while each of those dates ultimately represented a victory — the world *had* survived them — the cost to humanity had been dear. Both politics and technology had made this the killing century; they had also provided people with life and hope. And even now it was hope that carried them forward.

A girl crosses a makeshift bridge connecting the Muslim and Croatian sectors of the Bosnian city of Mostar, 1996. Violence between the rival ethnic factions of the former Yugoslavia had recently destroyed the precious stone bridge that had spanned the spot since 1566. In the fragile peace achieved in 1997, groups on both sides called for the reconstruction of the old bridge as a symbol of reconciliation.

Acknowledgments

A book this ambitious requires enormous effort above and beyond the work of its authors and their staff. We are indebted to Bill Abrams and the late Lionel Chapman of ABC News, who together conceived this book project and offered vital editorial assistance along the way, and to all those who have brought the two mammoth television series of this project, one for ABC and one for The History Channel, to telecast. We are extremely grateful for the work of Terrence Carnes of ABC News, who cleared rights on more than five hundred photographs; Betsy Schorr of ABC, who did the legal review; and Elena Brodie-Kusa of ABC for her expert guidance through the enormous oral history archive assembled for this project. And there would have been no project called *The Century* — television or book — without the steady support of ABC News Chairman Roone Arledge and ABC News President David Westin, and the original vision of Richard Wald and Irwin Weiner, the ABC News executives who offered up the idea for this enterprise more than six years ago. We are equally indebted to Stephen Rubin, Michael Palgon, and our indefatigable editor, Bill Thomas, all of Doubleday, and to Doubleday's Marly Rusoff, Deborah Cowell, Harold Grabau, Kim Cacho, Mario Pulice, Sandee Yuen, and Brian Mulligan, who together shepherded what was a very complex publishing venture from our dreams to your hands, and whose enthusiasm for the concept and execution of this book never flagged. We thank Esther Newberg and David Schmerler of International Creative Management, who brought ABC together with Doubleday. We were also helped immeasurably by our two principal historical consultants, Alan Brinkley of Columbia University and Herrick Chapman of New York University, whose readings were thorough and constructive, and by extensive conversations with historians H. W. Brands, Hampton Carey, William Chafe, Ann Douglas, John Gable, Kenneth Garver, Henry Graff, Nicholas Lemann, David Levering Lewis, Kristin Luker, Richard Pipes, Nat Polish, Fred Siegel, Richard Sylla, and with researchers at the John F. Kennedy and Dwight D. Eisenhower libraries. We thank George Howe Colt for his assistance. Chris Brewster, Tina Brewster, and Daniel Polin offered helpful suggestions on the manuscript. Mindy Lang aided with the initial design concept. And for their incalculable patience and love, we are grateful to our wives, Kayce Freed and Sylvia Steinert, and our children, Christopher and Elizabeth Jennings, and little Jack Brewster, who wasn't yet born when we began working on a then unnamed book on the twentieth century and who will, God willing, live deep into the twenty-first, when much of this work may seem like *ancient* history. May it offer insight still.

Source Notes

To do this history, we relied heavily on contemporary newspaper and magazine accounts and the historical scholarship of others. The New York Times, Washington Post, Time, Newsweek, *and* U.S. News & World Report *were invaluable resources, both in contemporary accounts of events and, in the case of the newsweeklies, in frequent historical overviews published on anniversaries of major events. The list below, while by necessity incomplete, offers a chapter- by-chapter discussion of some of the most essential sources on individual topics. A reading list, composed of one hundred recommended books, follows on pages 584–590.*

Chapter 1

Our essay on the birth of the modern era draws from many sources. The story of Frederick Jackson Turner and the Columbian Exposition comes largely from a reading of Ray Allen Billington's thoughtful biography of Turner, a review of that book by Harry McPherson in *The New Republic,* April 7, 1973, an article by Billington in the April 1958 issue of *American Heritage,* and another by Wilfred McCray in the July 1993 *American Heritage.* Stephen Jay Gould's *Questioning the Millennium* and Hillel Schwartz's *Century's End* were both original, illuminating sources for our discussion of the turning of the century, as was an essay on time and another on the calendar in the *Dictionary of the History of Ideas,* edited by Philip P. Wiener. Thomas P. Hughes's *American Genesis* provided the basis for our understanding of the Industrial Revolution with his explanation of how systems building would shape American society in the twentieth century. Sean Dennis Cashman's *America in the Age of the Titans,* Time-Life's *This Fabulous Century,* and Time-Life's earlier series on the Progressive Era were helpful on immigration and urbanization. For the discussion of Piltdown Man we relied on several essays by Stephen Jay Gould, the most important of which are included in his *Hen's Teeth and Horse's Toes.* We also consulted John Walsh's *Unraveling Piltdown* and a review of Walsh's book by Steve Jones in the February 6, 1997, edition of the *New York Review of Books.*

Our section on the St. Louis fair owes a debt to Robert W. Rydell's *All the World's a Fair.* The story of Joe Knowles comes almost entirely from an essay in *The Call of the Wild 1900–1916,* edited by Roderick Nash. Robert Kanigel's *The One Best Way,* a fascinating biography of Frederick Winslow Taylor, and Spencer Klaw's article in *American Heritage,* September 1979, provided the key details on the story of Taylor and the birth of "Scientific Management." Cashman's *America in the Age of the Titans* was a great help with its discussion of the women's suffrage movement, as was Ann Douglas's *Terrible Honesty.* Our characterization of Teddy Roosevelt benefited from Nathan Miller's and H. W. Brands's biographies of TR, both delightful reads, from Margaret Leech's *In the Days of McKinley,* and especially from Edmund Morris's brilliant essay "Theodore Roosevelt, President," which appeared in the June 1981 issue of *American Heritage.* Morris's biography of the young Teddy Roosevelt, while out of our time period here, is highly recommended reading. Our discussion of Booker T. Washington and W. E. B. Du Bois comes largely from Lerone Bennett's *Before the Mayflower,* John Hope Franklin's *From Slavery to Freedom,* and especially David Levering Lewis's biography *W. E. B. Du Bois.* Dinesh D'Souza's *The End of Racism,* a coherent but very controversial argument on African-American slavery and race relations, was valuable reading as well, particularly for its comparison of the two men. Bennett's article on the Jack Johnson fight in *Ebony,* April 1994, was a frequent reference. Robert Hughes's *The Shock of the New* and his *American Visions* were both valuable sources for our discussion of modern architecture and urbanism, and for the Armory Show and its impact, as were articles from *Time* (April 5, 1963) and the *New Yorker* (April 6, 1963) marking the fiftieth anniversary of the show. David McCullough's informative and entertaining *The Path Between the Seas,* Brands's *T.R.,* and a review of McCullough's book by Gaddis Smith in the *New York Times* (June 19, 1977) were the principal sources for our discussion of the building of the Panama Canal.

Chapter 2

Our description of the Christmas truce was aided by a reading of Lyn MacDonald's *Voices and Images of the Great War* and *Christmas Truce* by Malcolm Brown and Shirley Seaton. The discussion of the Great War's global and historical significance owes a great deal to a reading of Paul Fussell's superb *The Great War and Modern Memory* and, interestingly, Robert Hughes's history of modern art, *The Shock of the New.* Both books trace the century's cynicism to the trauma of this war, and Hughes asks, as we do here, what great minds were lost in the folly of battle. Fussell's book was a particularly good source for the description of life in the trenches, as was Denis Winter's *Death's Men* and an essay by Robert Graves, "Echoes of the Kaiser's War," in the May 17, 1964, edition of the *New York Times Magazine. Life*'s excellent series on World War I, published in 1964 and including a brilliant essay by historian William Leuchtenburg, was also helpful on trench life and all other aspects of the war. John Keegan's *The Face of Battle* and James L. Stokesbury's *A Short History of World War I* were frequent references, as were Martin Gilbert's *The First World War* and J. M. Winter's *The Experience of World War I.* A more recent book on the experience of the soldier in World War I and other wars of this century, *The Soldiers' Tale* by Samuel Hynes, is also recommended reading. All of the above discuss the tragic battles at Verdun and the Somme, but on the subject of the Somme we are equally indebted to Robert Cowley's excellent article in *Horizon,* "The Bloodiest Battle in History." John Williams's *The Other Battle Ground* was essential to our depiction of European life on the home front, and two classic books — Erich Maria Remarque's *All Quiet on the Western Front* and Robert Graves's *Good-bye to All That* — were helpful World War I reading. The story of the Great Migration borrows from Nicholas Lemann's *The Promised Land,* as well as from *Who Built America,* a social history of the United States by the American Social History Project. The story of the Russian Revolution was based upon a reading of the Edmund Wilson classic *To the Finland Station,* as well as Richard Pipes's *A Concise History of the Russian Revolution,* diplomat George Kennan's *Russia and the West,* and *The Russian Century,* which includes text by Brian Moynahan and a stunning collection of pictures, many never before seen. *Over Here* by David M. Kennedy was essential reading for an understanding of the American home front during World War I, as was *Who Built America.* Eric Hobsbawm's *The Age of Extremes* was helpful as an overview for the entire period.

Chapter 3

The discussion of the first night of Prohibition, which opens the chapter, is derived from a reading of Thomas Coffey's *The Long Thirst* and Herbert Asbury's *The Great Illusion,* as well as from contemporary accounts. The description of the complexity of American life during the twenties is based largely on readings of Geoffrey Perrett's excellent study *America in the Twenties,* Sean Cashman's *America in the Twenties and Thirties,* and Ann Douglas's *Terrible Honesty,* which provide not only a general survey of events, but also a look at the cultural trends shaping twenties life. The Time-Life *This Fabulous Century* volume on the twenties, *American Heritage's History of the Twenties and Thirties,* and Michael Parrish's *Anxious Decades* were also useful sources. On the impact of the automobile, *The Car Culture* by David Flink was a great help. The discussion of the early years of radio would have been incomplete without a reading of Erik Barnouw's *A Tower in Babel,* the first in a two-volume series on the history of radio, and Alice Goldfarb Marquis's article on the rise of radio as a medium of communication, appearing in *American Heritage,* August 1983. The section on advertising draws on Roland Marchand's *Advertising the American Dream* and Stephen Fox's *The Mirror Makers.* Sheila Rothman's *Woman's Proper Place* and Ellen Chesler's *Woman of Valor,* on Margaret Sanger and the birth control movement, were essential to the portrayal of the changing lives of women in this decade, as were Paula Fass's *The Damned and the Beautiful* and Harvey Green's *The Uncertainty of Everyday Life,* to which we also referred frequently on other topics of the period. David Chalmers's *Hooded Americanism* was an important source in our understanding of the Ku Klux Klan's widespread popularity, and we turned frequently to W. H. Ragsdale's article in *American Heritage,* June 1975, and *Summer for the Gods: The Scopes Trial and America's Continuing Debate Over Science and Religion* for our discussion of the Scopes trial. David Nasaw's *Going Out* was helpful to our discussion of the burgeoning entertainment industries of the twenties. David Levering Lewis's *When Harlem Was in Vogue* helped in our grasp of urban African-American life in the 1920s. The depiction of Lindbergh and his transatlantic flight borrows much from Leonard Mosley's biography of Charles Lindbergh, as well as from Page Smith's *Redeeming the Time: A People's History of the 1920s and the New Deal,* Perrett's *America in the Twenties,* and other sources.

Chapter 4

Rare as Rain by Nan Elizabeth Woodruff and Robert Cowley's article "The Drought and the Dole" in the February 1972 *American Heritage* helped with the details of the opening story of Homer Coney. *Anxious Decades* by Michael Parrish, *The Great Depression* by T. H. Watkins, *The Great Depression* by Robert S. McElvaine, and John Garraty's piece in the August 1986 *American Heritage* ("The Big Picture of the Great Depression") were central to our explanation of the causes of the Depression and to our understanding of the sense of despair permeating American society in the thirties. The above sources were also helpful in our discussion of the rise of Roosevelt. William Leuchtenburg's beautifully written *Franklin Delano Roosevelt and the New Deal* was a frequent source on the legacy of FDR, as were Otto Friedrich's excellent and thorough essay in *Time,* February 1, 1982, Frank Freidel's *Franklin D. Roosevelt: A Rendezvous with Destiny,* and Arthur Schlesinger's trilogy *The Age of Roosevelt.* The discussion of Huey Long and

Father Coughlin and their mass appeal is based largely on a reading of Alan Brinkley's excellent *Voices of Protest.* Two classics, William L. Shirer's *The Rise and Fall of the Third Reich* and Alan Bullock's *Hitler: A Study in Tyranny,* were critical to our discussion of Hitler's rise and eventual seizure of power in Germany, as were Ron Rosenbaum's "Explaining Hitler," a *New Yorker* article (May 1, 1995) that the author later developed into a book, and *Between Two Fires: Europe's Path in the 1930s* by David Clay Large. Stefan Kanfer's article on Hitler in *Time,* August 28, 1989, part of a special anniversary issue on World War II, was also extremely helpful with its synthesis of the details of Hitler's rise. Otto Friedrich's *Before the Deluge* was a frequent reference on cultural and intellectual life in Weimar Germany, as was Peter Gay's *Weimar Culture: The Outsider as Insider.* To understand what motivated Hitler and Stalin we relied on another of Alan Bullock's studies, *Hitler and Stalin: Parallel Lives,* and for our portrait of Stalin and the description of Soviet life during collectivization, we drew, once again, from Brian Moynahan's *The Russian Century,* and also from Richard Pipes's *Russia Under the Bolsheviks,* Robert Conquest's *Stalin: Breaker of Nations,* Sheila Fitzpatrick's *Stalin's Peasants,* and *Ukraine: A History* by Orest Subtelny. *The Nazi Olympics* by Richard Mandell was helpful for our story on the performance of Jesse Owens at Berlin in 1936.

Chapter 5

The discussion of American life during the latter years of the Great Depression and the onslaught of war in Europe benefited greatly from readings of Richard M. Ketchum's superb *The Borrowed Years* and Doris Kearns Goodwin's *No Ordinary Time,* which focuses closely on FDR during the war. William Manchester's *The Glory and the Dream,* a lively general survey of American history from the early thirties to the early seventies, was also a great help, as was Time-Life's *This Fabulous Century: 1930–1940* and Geoffrey Perrett's *Days of Sadness, Years of Triumph.* Ketchum's book and

Manchester's book were primary sources for our story on the "War of the Worlds," along with *The Panic Broadcast* by Howard Koch and *Orson Welles: The Road to Xanadu* by Simon Callow. Communication's role in the building of the American nation borrows from Warren Susman's excellent *Culture as History* and Erik Barnouw's *The Golden Web,* volume two of his history of broadcasting. The story of the founding of *Life* magazine draws from Loudon Wainwright's *The Great American Magazine,* James L. Baughman's *Henry R. Luce and the Rise of the American News Media,* and Alice G. Marquis's *Hopes and Ashes,* to which we also referred for our discussion of the 1939 World's Fair. *Who Built America* was a frequent source for our discussion of John L. Lewis and the labor movement, for which we also relied heavily upon Manchester. William Shirer's *The Rise and Fall of the Third Reich,* Leonard Mosley's *On Borrowed Time,* Time-Life's *Prelude to War,* and a series of articles in the September 2, 1989, issue of *Time* magazine formed the basis of our interpretation of the road to and eventual outbreak of war in Europe. And we utilized the same sources for the subject of anti-Semitism in the interwar years, along with Michael Berenbaum's *The World Must Know,* Terry Charman's *The German Homefront,* and the more recent and controversial *Hitler's Willing Executioners* by Daniel Goldhagen. For the story of Guernica we relied upon *Franco: A Biography* by Paul Preston. *Voyage of the Damned* by Gordon Thomas and Max Morgan-Witts was essential to the account of the tragic voyage of the S.S. *St. Louis,* as was Ketchum. The story of the invasion of Pearl Harbor is a compilation of details from many of the aforementioned sources and a reading of Otto Friedrich's excellent article marking the fiftieth anniversary of the attack, "Day of Infamy," which appeared in *Time,* December 2, 1991.

Chapter 6

The story of the Lodz ghetto borrows from Lucy Dawidowicz's *The War Against the Jews, 1933–1945,* Paul Johnson's *A History of the*

Jews, Raul Hilberg's *The Destruction of the European Jews, The Holocaust* by Martin Gilbert, *The World Must Know* by Michael Berenbaum, and *Lodz Ghetto: Inside a Community Under Siege,* edited by Alan Adelson and Robert Lapides, which is essentially a collection of excerpts from personal diaries and notebooks that survived the war. Our sense of the overall significance of the war is the result of a reading of several fine volumes on the war itself: John Campbell's *The Experience of World War II,* Stanley Weintraub's *The Last Great Victory,* Martin Gilbert's *World War II,* and Richard Polenberg's *War & Society.* The discussion of the United States home front comes from a reading of Polenberg as well as of John Morton Blum's *V Was for Victory,* Richard Lingeman's *Don't You Know There's a War On,* William Manchester's *The Glory and the Dream,* and Geoffrey Perrett's *Days of Sadness: Years of Triumph,* all of which discuss the government's attempt to bring the American people into the Allied effort and the war's impact on the American economy. We also benefited from Doris Kearns Goodwin's *No Ordinary Time* for our discussion of FDR and the war, and from *Roosevelt and Hopkins* by Robert Sherwood. Our depiction of the soldier's experience during the war is a synthesis of readings of Paul Fussell's *Wartime* and his *Thank God for the Atomic Bomb,* Samuel Hynes's *The Soldiers' Tale,* as well as Eugene Sledge's *With the Old Breed,* which focuses specifically on the experience of the soldier in the Pacific, and Michael C. C. Adams's *The Best War Ever.* Meirion and Susie Harries's *Soldiers of the Sun* was central to our discussion of the Japanese treatment of enemy soldiers and their own morale. Harrison E. Salisbury's classic *The 900 Days* was a frequent reference on the siege of Leningrad, as was *The Russian Century* by Brian Moynahan. Stephen Ambrose's *D-Day* and Otto Friedrich's excellent D-Day anniversary article in *Time,* June 6, 1994, provided the basis of our account of Operation Overlord. Goodwin's *No Ordinary Time* was helpful for the home front reaction to D-Day. Our discussion of the Holocaust borrows extensively from Berenbaum's *The World Must Know,* Dawidowicz's *The War Against the Jews,* and Johnson's *A History of the Jews.* David Wyman's *The Abandonment of the Jews* was helpful on the international community's reluctance to take action, and *Hitler's Willing Executioners* was, once again, an important source on the German people and the Jews. Terry Charman's *The German Homefront* was a valuable source for our discussion of the German people and their waning patience with Hitler. Alan Bullock's *Hitler and Stalin* was valuable for our discussion of Hitler's final days. Our discussion of the Pacific war, from Pearl Harbor to Hiroshima, borrowed much from a series of articles on the war appearing in *Time,* December 2, 1991, and from Howard Chua-Eoan's article in *Time,* August 8, 1995. The story of Tibbets and the *Enola Gay* was largely based on a reading of Richard Rhodes's excellent *The Making of the Atomic Bomb,* Manchester's *The Glory and the Dream,* and Weintraub's *The Last Great Victory.*

Chapter 7

The story of postwar America — including the soldiers' homecoming, the debate over foreign policy, and the rise of the Red Scare — stems from a reading of several survey histories: William Manchester's *The Glory and the Dream,* Geoffrey Perrett's *A Dream of Greatness,* and James T. Patterson's recent award-winning *Grand Expectations.* Joseph C. Goulden's *The Best Years* was an important source on the period as well. These books, along with two biographies of director William Wyler — *A Talent for Trouble* by Jan Herman and *William Wyler* by Axel Madsen — were the basis for our opening scene on the movie *The Best Years of Our Lives.* For more on the dawning of the atomic age we relied on Paul Boyer's *By the Bomb's Early Light.* On William J. Levitt and the construction of Levittown we turned to Perrett, Manchester, David Halberstam's *The Fifties,* and Kenneth Jackson's *Crabgrass Frontier.* John Lewis Gaddis's *Strategies of Containment* and Stephen

Ambrose's *Rise to Globalism* were essential to our understanding of the historic Kennan-Lippmann debate over the shaping of postwar foreign policy. The description of postwar Europe comes largely from Theodore White's *Fire in the Ashes,* a brilliant firsthand account of life in Europe after the war, as well as from the postscript section of Martin Gilbert's *World War II* and Walter LaFeber's *America, Russia, and the Cold War, 1945–1992.* The birth and implementing of the Marshall Plan are taken from White as well as from Forrest C. Pogue's biography of George Marshall and David Ellwood's *Rebuilding Europe.* The discussion of U.S.–Soviet relations and the early years of the Cold War is based on readings of Tad Szulc's *Then & Now,* Alan Bullock's *Hitler and Stalin,* Martin Walker's *The Cold War,* and *Troubled Journey* by Frederick Siegel. The Berlin Airlift story borrows from Manchester, Bullock, and White. The story of the rise of Mao relies upon a reading of another Theodore White book, *Thunder Out of China* (coauthored with Annalee Jacoby), Martin Walker's *The Cold War: A History,* Manchester, and Ambrose. *Nightmare in Red* by Richard M. Fried was a frequent reference on the Red Scare and the origin of American anticommunism, as was Richard Gid Powers's *Not Without Honor.* Both provided the details of the story of Whittaker Chambers and Alger Hiss, as did Alistair Cooke's *A Generation on Trial* and Sam Tanenhaus's biography *Whittaker Chambers.* Of course, Chambers's own *Witness* was invaluable reading, too. On the Korean War and the story of Douglas MacArthur, we turned to two classics, *This Kind of War* by T. R. Fehrenbach and William Manchester's *American Caesar.*

Chapter 8

Once again, the survey histories of America in the postwar period by James T. Patterson, William Manchester, and Geoffrey Perrett provided a general understanding of American life in the fifties and details for our stories of Marilyn Monroe, Elvis Presley, Martin Luther King, Jr., and John Kennedy. David Halberstam's *The*

Fifties was a frequent reference, as was John Patrick Diggins's *The Proud Decades: America in War and Peace 1941– 1960.* On the subject of the Kitchen Debate, both Stephen Ambrose's and Fawn M. Brodie's studies of Richard Nixon's early political career were excellent, and Nixon's account of his trip in his memoirs, *RN,* was essential. Two landmark sociological studies of American society in the 1950s, David M. Potter's *People of Plenty: Economic Abundance and the American Character* and David Riesman's *The Lonely Crowd: A Study of the Changing American Character,* set the tone for our discussion of consumerism and suburban conformity in the postwar period, as did William Whyte's *The Organization Man.* We also turned to Loren Baritz's *The Good Life* and Elaine Tyler May's *Homeward Bound,* an original and intriguing study of family life in the fifties and sixties. On the history and impact of television, we turned to Erik Barnouw's *Tube of Plenty,* Karal Ann Marling's *As Seen on TV,* and museum curator Larry Bird's thoughtful essay in the catalog of the New Museum of Contemporary Art in New York's recent exhibition on television. Our discussion of television advertising owes an enormous debt to Earl Shorris's excellent *A Nation of Salesmen.* Raymond Weinstein's article in the *Journal of Popular Culture,* Summer 1992, helped in our discussion of Disneyland as the first theme park. Manchester's *The Glory and the Dream* was helpful in understanding the growth of marketing aimed at youth and was the source for the study of mothers who reported having been asked to buy something by their television-watching children. Tim Frew's pictorial biography of Elvis Presley and Dave Marsh's *Elvis,* written for *Rolling Stone,* were frequent sources. The story of Marilyn Monroe as a media icon borrows from Manchester, Halberstam, and a reading of *Marilyn* by Norman Mailer, as well as from Pauline Kael's review of that controversial biography, appearing in the *New York Times Book Review,* July 22, 1973. *Time* art critic Robert Hughes's discussions of the cult of celebrity as represented by the life and art of Andy Warhol were also helpful. On the Great Migration, Nicholas Lemann's *The Promised Land,* a lyrical account of the Great Migration told through the story of a black woman who leaves the Mississippi Delta in search of a better life in Chicago, was essential. For the story of the Montgomery bus boycott and the rise of Martin Luther King, Jr., we turned to Manchester, Halberstam, Perrett, and especially Taylor Branch's Pulitzer Prize–winning *Parting the Waters,* the first of a proposed three volumes on King and the civil rights movement. Gerald Early's article in *Civilization,* October/November 1996, was the inspiration for our discussion of King and his use of the media. Daniel Boorstin's *The Americans: The Democratic Experience* provided a unique perspective on scientific progress and how *Sputnik* galvanized the American space program. The discussion of President Kennedy and the climate of idealism surrounding his campaign draws on readings of Richard Reeves's *President Kennedy: Profile of Power,* Arthur Schlesinger's *A Thousand Days,* and Theodore White's *The Making of the President, 1960,* a classic look at the drama of a political campaign.

Chapter 9

The Crosswinds of Freedom by James Mac-Gregor Burns, *Troubled Journey* by Frederick Siegel, *Years of Discord* by John Morton Blum, Geoffrey Perrett's *A Dream of Greatness,* and William Manchester's *The Glory and the Dream* provided detailed accounts of the events of the sixties and insightful analysis. Peter Wyden's *The Wall* and Eleanor Lansing Dulles's *Berlin: The Wall Is Not Forever* helped in telling the story of Peter Fechter's ill-fated attempt to escape to West Berlin. On President Kennedy and the youthful optimism of the early sixties, Theodore White's *In Search of History* and Arthur Schlesinger's *A Thousand Days* were frequent sources (to which we also referred for information on the U.S. and Cuba), as were Michael Beschloss's *The Crisis Years,* Dino A. Brugioni's *Eyeball to Eyeball,* and Richard Reeves's *President Kennedy.* On civil rights, Taylor Branch's *Parting the Waters*

proved, once again, essential, as did Todd Gitlin's *The Sixties,* which was particularly good on how the youth movement and SNCC influenced King, and Steven Kasher's *The Civil Rights Movement,* a recent pictorial history. We were particularly moved by the description of the March on Washington that begins David Levering Lewis's *W. E. B. Du Bois,* with its sad announcement to the crowd that Du Bois had died. Manchester and Siegel also offered good description and analysis of the march. Both Schlesinger and Teddy White, this time in *The Making of the President, 1964,* wrote touching accounts of President Kennedy's assassination and helped us understand the shock and sense of despair across the nation. An essay in *Newsweek,* November 28, 1983, was the source detailing the personal reactions of William Styron and Daniel Moynihan. On the Beatles' invasion of America, Jeff Greenfield's piece in the *New York Times Magazine,* February 16, 1975, was simply marvelous. Luc Sante's essay in the *New York Review of Books,* December 22, 1988, was also extremely helpful. In addition to many of the sources already listed, David Halberstam's *The Best and the Brightest,* Richard Goodwin's *Remembering America,* and Stanley Karnow's *Vietnam: A History* were essential to our grasp of the Vietnam War, from its early years under Eisenhower through the escalation of war under President Lyndon Johnson. In telling the soldiers' story, Samuel Hynes's *The Soldiers' Tale* was indispensable. An article by David Bradley in the December 1983 *Esquire* was helpful for our discussion of Malcolm X. Milton Viorst's *Fire in the Streets: America in the Sixties* aided our discussion of the mid-decade riots. Our discussion of 1968 borrows from Lance Morrow's essay on 1968 in *Time,* January 11, 1988, and the account of Robert F. Kennedy's speech on the eve of Martin Luther King's assassination comes almost entirely from Schlesinger's moving biography *Robert Kennedy and His Times,* Jack Newfield's *Robert Kennedy,* and *Mutual Contempt: Lyndon Johnson, Robert Kennedy, and the Feud That Defined a Decade* by Jeff Shesol. On the rise of Eugene McCarthy, the antiwar

movement, and the tumultuous Democratic National Convention of 1968, David Farber's *Chicago '68* and David Burner's *Making Sense of the Sixties* were frequent sources, as were *Coming Apart* by William O'Neill and *The Unraveling of America* by Allen J. Matusow. Stephen Ambrose's *Nixon 1962–1972,* volume two of his three-volume series, helped in our understanding of Nixon and the conservative backlash, as did James Patterson's *Grand Expectations* and Siegel's *Troubled Journey.* Finally, the story of the moon landing owes a great deal to Michael Collins's *An Astronaut's Journeys* and to *Of a Fire on the Moon,* Norman Mailer's magnificent book on the technological wonder of space travel.

Chapter 10

Our essay on seventies' malaise and the sense of the limits of progress borrows much from readings of Tom Wolfe's sardonic article "The Me Decade" in *New York,* August 23, 1976, and Christopher Lasch's *The True and Only Heaven* and his *The Culture of Narcissism,* a sociological study and criticism of American life in the 1970s. The details of Kathy Boudin's involvement with the Weathermen and subsequent life underground come almost entirely from Peter Collier and David Horowitz's article in *Rolling Stone,* September 30, 1982, and Lucinda Frank's essay in the *New York Times Magazine,* November 11, 1981. On the period's economic woes, we turned to David Calleo's *The Imperious Economy,* which is particularly good on the role of the dollar in international markets. Daniel Yergin's *The Prize* and David Halberstam's *The Reckoning* were both terrific on the politics and impact of the oil crisis. Halberstam's analysis of the troubled automobile industry was also terrific. Otto Friedrich in *Time,* May 2, 1994, Jacob Weisburg in *New York,* May 9, 1994, and Garry Wills in *Esquire,* May 1994, all provided cogent analysis of the Nixon presidency, as did Stephen Ambrose's *Nixon: The Triumph of a Politician 1962–1972,* Tom Wicker's *One of Us,* and Wills's *Nixon Agonistes,* a study of the early years of the Nixon presidency. Our understanding of Nixon was enhanced by our reading of Arthur Schlesinger's *The Imperial Presidency,* a landmark book on the changing nature of the American presidency, and *Troubled Journey* by Frederick Siegel. We referred to George Church's essay in *Time*'s anniversary issue of the end of the Vietnam War, April 24, 1995, on the final days of the war. On the "Balkanization" of American society, Kevin Philips's article in *Harper's,* May 1978, was an important source, as was Theodore White's *America in Search of Itself,* which was particularly good on urban blight. On the women's movement, Carl Degler's *At Odds,* a history of feminism in America, and William Chafe's *The Paradox of Change* were excellent sources, as was J. M. Burns's discussion of feminism in his survey history *The Crosswinds of Freedom.* Kristin Luker's *Abortion and the Politics of Motherhood* provided an original take on the abortion movement. Our discussion of the growing sense of global environmental awareness borrows from Stephen J. Gould's introductory essay on the seventies in *Our Times,* a colossal illustrated chronology of the twentieth century. For the story of the Boston busing fiasco, we drew heavily on J. Anthony Lukas's definitive study of the incident, *Common Ground,* and on an excellent article by Joseph Featherstone in *The New Republic,* January 24, 1976. Our discussion of the first test-tube baby is from contemporary news sources but was also helped by a reading of an essay by Albert Rosenfeld in *Saturday Review,* October 28, 1978. *Newsweek* and *Time* cover stories from April 9, 1979, helped in our discussion of the accident at Three Mile Island. On the rise of the Ayatollah Khomeini in Iran, *Time*'s Man of the Year story, January 7, 1980, was essential, as was Shaul Bakhash's article "What Khomeini Did," appearing in the *New York Review of Books,* January 22, 1988.

Chapter 11

Most historians are reluctant to examine any period until enough time has passed to put that era into perspective. As a result, there are few surveys of the eighties (or, for that matter, the nineties), and most of those that do exist appear now as either dated or limited or both. More specific sources, however, proved to be extremely helpful to us. Our discussion of the story of the design and execution of the Vietnam memorial, for instance, relied upon *To Heal a Nation,* a book by the memorial's organizer, Jan Scruggs, and coauthor Joel Swerdlow, and another book, *Maya Lin* by Bettina Ling, as well as a review of the memorial by art critic Arthur Danto (*The Nation,* August 31, 1985) and a profile of Lin that appeared in *Time,* November 6, 1989. The discussion of the eighties as a decade when history was rewritten was inspired by a reading of *Lenin's Tomb* by David Remnick, where that idea is well developed with respect to the Soviet Union. But the connecting of that theme to what were similar trends in the Reagan presidency and the social fabric of eighties America is fresh here. Remnick's opening reference, in his book, to the Czech novelist Milan Kundera (who is also quoted here in the margin of page 470) prompted us to reread *The Book of Laughter and Forgetting,* a classic eighties fiction that powerfully depicts the chill of life behind the iron curtain. Louis Menand's discussion of the eighties (*The New Republic,* October 9, 1989) was a helpful overview of the entire period, as was Haynes Johnson's *Sleepwalking Through History.* Our discussion of the presidency of Ronald Reagan and its relationship to that of Franklin Delano Roosevelt draws heavily on William Leuchtenburg's excellent study *In the Shadow of FDR,* which addresses Roosevelt's influence on every president from Truman to Reagan. Johnson's *Sleepwalking Through History,* Garry Wills's *Reagan's America,* Richard Reeves's *The Reagan Detour,* Lou Cannon's *President Reagan: The Role of a Lifetime,* and Dinesh D'Souza's *Ronald Reagan* were all helpful studies of the Reagan presidency, too. Wills, in particular, was helpful in the discussion of Reagan as appealing to an idealized image of America. And while his book was written in the mid-1980s, before Reagan had finished his second term, Wills's essay in the *New York Review of Books,* June 13, 1991, provides a continuation of his analysis. Hendrick Hertzberg's piece on Reagan in *The New Republic,* September 9, 1991, was also helpful. Our examination of the eighties economy was aided by a reading of Kevin Phillips's *The Politics of Rich and Poor: Wealth and the American Electorate in the Reagan Aftermath* and an article by him of similar tone in the *New York Times Magazine.* Phillips's ideas seemed a little dated by the late nineties (the image of the Reagan economy had improved in many sectors), which we, of course, took into account. Michael M. Thomas's essay in the *New York Review of Books,* March 29, 1990, was also a helpful study of the eighties economy. Our discussion of the homelessness issue draws from Christopher Jencks's excellent study *The Homeless,* a review of Jencks's book by Deborah Stone in *The New Republic,* June 27, 1994, and a review of Jencks by Brigitte Berger in the *New York Times Book Review,* April 24, 1994. Frederick Siegel's terrific critique of liberal social policy in the inner city, *The Future Once Happened Here,* aided our discussion as well, particularly on the growing tension between haves and have-nots. The story of Bernhard Goetz comes from contemporary news accounts and from an excellent essay by George P. Fletcher in the *New York Review of Books,* April 23, 1987. Our discussion of the *Challenger* disaster was aided by a reading of Tom Wolfe's essay in *Newsweek,* February 10, 1986, and James MacGregor Burns's *Crosswinds of Freedom.* The story of the AIDS epidemic is well told by the late Randy Shilts in a classic, *And the Band Played On.* We also drew much, however, from Susan Sontag's *AIDS and Its Metaphors,* as originally published in the *New York Review of Books,* October 27, 1988. Sontag's essay is a masterful study and her insights are essential to any discussion. The impact of AIDS on the sexual revolution was well discussed in an article in *Time,* February 16, 1987. Our discussion of the rise of Gorbachev draws much from *Time*'s coverage of the late eighties, particularly pieces written by Strobe Talbott, later a Clinton foreign policy aide. Remnick's indispensable

Lenin's Tomb was an essential guide to what the reforms really meant. Gorbachev's memoirs helped, too. The writings of Vaclav Havel were an inspiration to read in reference to the developments of the late eighties. And besides the contemporary news accounts of the collapse of communism, articles by Christopher Hope (*The New Republic,* December 18, 1989), Bennett Owen (*National Review,* December 22, 1989), and Peter Schneider (*Harper's,* April, 1990) were helpful. Schneider's piece is the source of our closing story about the border crossing at Staaken. Jonathan Spence's *The Search for Modern China* helped us understand Tiananmen Square.

Chapter 12

Besides coverage of the "computer versus man" chess match in the *New York Times, Time,* and *Newsweek,* we were helped by the fascinating symposium arranged by *Harper's* ("Our Machines, Ourselves," May 1997) and our own discussions with the IBM team who programmed Deep Blue. Benjamin Barber's superb *Jihad vs. McWorld* helped us come to grips with the new global culture, as did Alvin Toffler's *The Third Wave.* A review of Barber's book by Philip Green (*The Nation,* September 25, 1995) was also helpful. Our discussion of the new high-tech war, as represented by the war in the Persian Gulf, was aided by a reading of "High-Tech: The Future Face of War," a debate in the January 1998 *Commentary.* We were also helped by *The Gulf Conflict 1990–1991, Diplomacy and War in the New World Order* by Lawrence Freedman and Efraim Karsh, and by Edward Luttwak's fascinating piece in the October 11, 1993, *New Republic.* Tom Rosenstiel's superb study of CNN in the August 22, 1994, *New Republic,* William Henry's article on the same subject in *Time* (January 6, 1992), Jay Rosen's piece in *The Nation* (May 13, 1991), and Ed Diamond's piece in *New York* (February 11, 1991) were the basis for that discussion. *Race-ing Justice, En-Gendering Power* is a series of essays on the Clarence Thomas and Anita Hill hearings, edited by Toni Morrison. *Strange*

Justice by Jane Mayer and Jill Abramson was also consulted. Lou Cannon's *Official Negligence: How Rodney King and the Riots Changed Los Angeles and the LAPD* is certainly the most thorough study of that event, and, along with contemporary news accounts, formed the research for that section of our chapter. Our section on O. J. Simpson benefited from a reading of Jeffrey Toobin's *The Run of His Life,* Jack E. White's essay in *Time,* October 9, 1995, Bruce Handy's essay in *Time,* October 16, 1995, and an editorial in *The New Republic,* October 23, 1995. Our discussion of the Million Man March was helped by a reading of Glenn Loury's article in *The New Republic,* November 6, 1995, and the Gerald Early essay in *Civilization,* October/November 1996. Our discussion of the computer and its history owes a great deal to David Gelernter's excellent *Machine Beauty,* one of two recent books by the Yale scholar. His other, *Drawing Life,* is a more personal look at his experience as a target of the Unabomber and was a helpful read to put the story of the Unabomber in perspective. *Computer: A History of the Information Machine* by Martin Campbell-Kelly and William Aspray was also a valuable source, as was *Time*'s "Machine of the Year" story from January 3, 1983. Philip Elmer-DeWitt's essay on the Internet in a special issue of *Time,* Spring 1995, was valuable, and Brent Schlender's article on Bill Gates (*Fortune,* January 16, 1995) was also helpful. There are dozens of new books on the future of communications. Bill Gates's own *The Road Ahead,* Nicholas Negroponte's *Being Digital,* and Michael Dertouzos's *What Will Be* were three we found valuable. Our Oklahoma City bombing section is taken from contemporary accounts and a reading of *Why Waco* by James Tabor and Eugene Gallagher. Peter Singer's *Rethinking Life and Death* addresses the tough ethical issues now facing medicine. George Howe Colt's excellent *The Enigma of Suicide* was also valuable, as was Anne Fadiman's piece on the Hemlock Society in the April, 1994 issue of *Harper's,* as was Anne Fadiman's piece on the Hemlock Society in the April 1994 issue of

Harper's. Besides news reports on the death of Princess Diana, we consulted the very thorough *Death of a Princess* by Thomas Sancton and Scott MacLeod. *Farewell in Splendor: The Passing of Queen Victoria and Her Age* by Jerrold Packard and *Queen Victoria* by Stanley Weintraub helped us understand the last days of the great queen's reign.

One Hundred Books *A Twentieth-Century Suggested Reading List*

1 **The Path Between the Seas** by David McCullough
. . . *the building of the Panama Canal*

2 **W. E. B. Du Bois: Biography of a Race** by David Levering Lewis
. . . *the life of the great civil rights leader, up to 1919*

3 **Booker T. Washington: The Wizard of Tuskegee, 1901–1915** by Louis R. Harlan
. . . *the second of a two-volume biography*

4 **American Genesis: A Century of Invention and Technological Enthusiasm** by Thomas P. Hughes
. . . *wonderful study of America's love affair with technology, beginning with the Age of Invention and going through 1970*

5 **T.R.: The Last Romantic** by H. W. Brands
. . . *along with Edmund Morris's study of his young life, the best of many Theodore Roosevelt biographies*

6 **The One Best Way** by Robert Kanigel
. . . *a biography of Frederick Winslow Taylor, the efficiency expert who inspired Ford's assembly line*

7 **The Strange Career of Jim Crow** by C. Vann Woodward
. . . *how segregation began*

8 **The Shock of the New** by Robert Hughes
. . . *an entertaining and opinionated history of modern art, written in the seventies, when modernism was beginning to fade*

9 **Our Times** by Mark Sullivan
. . . *the multivolume history of our century, as seen from the 1920s*

10 **The Great War and Modern Memory** by Paul Fussell
. . . *the story of World War I, through the letters and poetry of its participants*

11 **The Face of Battle** by John Keegan
. . . *a study of the Somme and two other battles of World War I*

12 **To the Finland Station** by Edmund Wilson
. . . *the story of the Russian Revolution, told by a masterful writer*

13 **The First World War: A Complete History** by Martin Gilbert
. . . *an excellent and thorough study by a prolific historian*

14 **The Guns of August** by Barbara W. Tuchman
. . . *one of the greatest of all popular histories, winner of the Pulitzer, it tells how World War I began*

44 **The Best War Ever: America and World War II** by Michael C. C. Adams
   . . . another excellent study of the war, also from the soldier's point of view

45 **War and Society: The United States, 1941-1945** by Richard Polenberg
   . . . superb look at how war is fought on the home front

46 **The 900 Days** by Harrison E. Salisbury
   . . . the siege of Leningrad

47 **With the Old Breed at Peleliu and Okinawa** by Eugene B. Sledge
   . . . perhaps the best memoir of the Pacific war

48 **The Second World War** by Winston S. Churchill
   . . . the multivolume story of the war as seen by one of its most prominent participants

49 **D-Day** by Stephen E. Ambrose
   . . . the story of Operation Overlord

50 **The Making of the Atomic Bomb** by Richard Rhodes
   . . . the best history of the bomb

51 **The Best Years** by Joseph C. Goulden
   . . . survey of the postwar years, 1945–50

52 **Truman** by David McCullough
   . . . the most popular Truman biography

53 **Witness** by Whittaker Chambers
   . . . beautifully written memoir by the man who turned in Alger Hiss

54 **A Generation on Trial** by Alistair Cooke
   . . . hard to find, but worth it, the best contemporary account of the Hiss trial

55 **Fire in the Ashes: Europe in Mid-Century** by Theodore H. White
   . . .the mood of postwar Europe by an eminent journalist

56 **The Promised Land** by Nicholas Lemann
   . . . the story of the Great Migration, focusing on the years immediately following World War II

57 **Present at the Creation** by Dean Acheson
   . . . the memoirs of Truman's secretary of state, beautifully written

58 **Hiroshima** by John Hersey
   . . . the classic account of the day the bomb was dropped

59 **In the Shadow of FDR** by William E. Leuchtenburg
  . . . how FDR influenced the presidency from Truman to Reagan

60 **Thunder Out of China** by Theodore H. White and Annalee Jacoby
  . . . a gripping look at the rise of Mao, a little dated now, but still a good read

61 **American Caesar** by William Manchester
  . . . biography of General Douglas MacArthur

62 **Crabgrass Frontier** by Kenneth T. Jackson
  . . . the making of the suburbs

63 **The Wise Men** by Evan Thomas and Walter Isaacson
  . . . the postwar brain trust that advised presidents from Truman to Johnson

64 **Making of the President, 1960** by Theodore H. White
  . . . the classic campaign between Nixon and Kennedy

65 **The Fifties** by David Halberstam
  . . . an entertaining cultural history of the period

66 **The Best and the Brightest** by David Halberstam
  . . . the story of the Kennedy team and their failure in Vietnam

67 **A Thousand Days** by Arthur M. Schlesinger, Jr.
  . . . the story of the Kennedy presidency

68 **Eyeball to Eyeball** by Dino A. Brugioni
  . . . the Cuban missile crisis

69 **The Crisis Years** by Michael R. Beschloss
  . . . the Kennedy-Khrushchev years

70 **From Slavery to Freedom** by John Hope Franklin
  . . . a history of the "Negro peoples" as written in the 1960s

71 **Parting the Waters: America in the King Years, 1954–63** by Taylor Branch
  . . . first of a projected trilogy of the civil rights movement, written in the nineties

72 **Pillar of Fire: America in the King Years, 1963–65** by Taylor Branch
  . . . second of the trilogy

73 **Robert Kennedy and His Times** by Arthur M. Schlesinger, Jr.
  . . . biography of RFK with a particularly moving chapter on his reaction to his brother's assassination

Picture Sources

In the course of four years of work on this book, we contacted hundreds of photo archivists, researchers, photographers, curators and other individuals. Generous with both their knowledge and their time, they aided in our search for wonderful pictures. Without their help, and the support and advice of family and friends, this book would not have been possible.

We would especially like to thank:
Linda Bailey/Cincinnati Historical Society; Katherine Bang; Mary Ann Bourbeau; Russell Burrows; Bill Carner/Photographic Archives—University of Louisville; Cathy Cesario/Sygma; Carrie Chalmers/Magnum; Romy Charlesworth; Jocelyn Clapp, Donna Daley and Norman Currie of Corbis-Bettmann; Debra Cohen/Time-Life Syndication; Jane Colihan and Vanessa Weiman/American Heritage; Joseph Cunningham; Virginia Dodier/Museum of Modern Art; Larry Fink Studio; Mary Fitzpatrick; Allan Goodrich and Jim Cedrone/JFK Library; Ellen Graham/Time Inc. Picture Collection; Michael Hashim; Imperial War Museum Photograph Archive; Dennis Ivy; David King; Jonathan Landreth; Penny and Ted Landreth; Gary Mack/The Sixth Floor Museum; Carolyn Marr/Museum of History & Industry, Seattle;Jane Martin; Loring McAlpin; Michele McNally/Fortune; Peter Mitchell; Tex Parks and Mark Renovitch/FDR Library; PhotoAssist; Lisa Quinones; Hilde Randolf, Larisa Khorosh and Blanca Segura/Modernage; Chris Rauschenberg; Allen Reuben and Timothy Feleppa/Culver Pictures; Marcia Lein Schiff/AP-Wide World; Ellen Schlefer; Tara Sherman; Joel Suttles/ CNN; Leslie Swift and the United States Holocaust Memorial Museum; Shigehisa Terao; Anne Tucker/Museum of Fine Arts, Houston; Mike Viola; Margy Vogt/Massillon Museum; Anne Wise.

The following freelancers helped us with expert picture research:
Courty Andrews, Maggie Berkvist, Susan Hormuth, Lindsay Kefauver, Wolfgang Klaue, Pam Sztybel, Hélène Véret, Lynn Weinstein, Karen Wyatt.

CB=Corbis-Bettmann
IWM=Imperial War Museum
LC=Library of Congress
NA=National Archives
UCB=UPI/Corbis-Bettmann

For more than one picture on a page, credits read left to right and top to bottom, unless noted.

Front Cover:
All credits read left to right and top to bottom

First row: Schomburg Center, New York Public Library; Connoly/Gamma-Liaison; Carl T. Gossett Jr./*New York Times* Pictures; Yad Vashem; Orlando Suero/The Lowenherz Collection of Kennedy Photographs at the Peabody Institute of The Johns Hopkins University, Baltimore; Transcendental Graphics.
Second row: Imperial War Museum; Costa Manos/Magnum; Brown Brothers; Brown Brothers; Patrick Durand/Sygma.
Third row: UCB; Personality Photos, Inc.; Dan Weiner/Courtesy of Sandra Weiner; NA; AP/Wide World Photos; Mary Ellen Mark.
Fourth row: UCB; Hulton Getty; Bob Adelman; Brown Brothers; NASA/Courtesy of Dennis Ivy; AKG Photo-London.

Front pages:
i: UCB **ii:** Dan Weiner/Courtesy of Sandra Weiner
vi-vii: NA

Introduction:
ix: LC **x:** Henry Ford Museum & Greenfield Village **xi:** Eudora Welty Collection/Mississippi Department of Archives and History **xii:** Dennis Stock/Magnum **xiii:** Burt Glinn/Magnum **xiv:** Eli Reed/Magnum.

Chapter 1:
pages 2-3: Brown Brothers **4:** Natural History Museum of Los Angeles **6:** Henry E. Huntington Library **7:** NA **8:** Culver Pictures **9:** Courtesy of Mabel Griep; Wright State University **10, 11:** Culver Pictures **12:** © Collection of The New York Historical Society **13:** Courtesy of Alfred Levitt **14-15:** Lewis Hine Collection/New York Public Library **17:** Brown Brothers **18-19:** (both) Courtesy of Eric Breitbart **20:**

From *Alone in the Wilderness,* by Joe Knowles (pub. 1913) **21:** Courtesy of Charles Rohleder **22-23:** Lewis Hine/NA **24:** Brown Brothers **25:** Ford Motor Company, Stevens Institute of Technology **26-27:** Brown Brothers **28:** (both) Courtesy of Lucy Haessler **30-31:** Brown Brothers **32:** (left) Courtesy of Norma Hampson; Courtesy of Carolyn Hicks **33:** U.S. Naval Historical Center **34:** Georgia Department of Archives and History **35:** Smithsonian Institution/Political History Collection/Division of Social History **36-37:** Florida State Archives **38:** LC **39:** LC **40:** Courtesy of Minor Cash **41:** Nevada Historical Society **42:** UCB **44:** Philadelphia Museum of Art: The Louise and Walter Arensberg Collection **45:** CB **46:** Culver Pictures **47:** CB.

Chapter 2:

48-49: IWM **50:** IWM **53:** Culver Pictures; Bildarchiv und Porträtsammlung der Osterreichischen Nationalbibliothek **54:** CB **55:** (both) Courtesy of Joachim Von Elbe **56-57:** Hulton Getty; IWM **58:** Courtesy of Edward Francis **59:** IWM **60-61:** IWM **62-63:** IWM **64-65:** L'Illustration/Sygma **66:** CB **67:** Collection of Eric Sauder **69:** Milton J. Hinton Photographic Collection **70-71:** Brown Brothers **72-73:** IWM **75:** Courtesy of Sophie Koulomzin **76-77:** David King Collection **78-79:** Endeavour Group UK **80:** David King Collection **81:** Courtesy of Alexander Bryansky **82:** UCB; Courtesy of Henry Villard **83:** David King Collection **84:** Stanford University—Hoover Institution Archives; Illinois State Historical Library **85:** (top) New York State Historical Association; (bottom left & right) Courtesy of Leon Despres **86:** (both) Courtesy of Laura Frost Smith **87:** Hulton Getty **88-89:** UCB **90:** Courtesy of Corneal Davis **91:** IWM **92:** San Francisco Chronicle **93:** Courtesy of John Meyerick **94:** NA **96:** Culver Pictures **97:** National Archives of Canada.

Chapter 3:

98-99: Brown Brothers **101:** CB **103:** Henry Ford Museum & Greenfield Village; Cincinnati Historical Society **104-105:** Minnesota His-

torical Society **106:** Courtesy of Betty Broyles **107:** Photographic Archives/University of Louisville **108:** Courtesy of Albert Sindlinger; CB **109:** Minnesota Historical Society **110:** FPG International **112:** *Saturday Evening Post,* June 30, 1928 **113:** UCB; Photographic Archives/University of Louisville **114:** UCB **116:** CB **117:** Minnesota Historical Society **118:** Georgia Department of Archives and History **120:** Swift Collection/Ball State University **121:** Daily News **122:** Culver Pictures **123:** CB **124:** Brown Brothers **125:** UCB **126-127:** Marc Wanamaker/Bison Archives; CB **128:** Culver Pictures **130-131:** CB **132:** UCB **133:** Schomburg Center/New York Public Library **134:** Schomburg Center/New York Public Library **135:** Courtesy of Howard "Stretch" Johnson **137:** UCB **138-139:** Brown Brothers **140:** CB **141:** National Air & Space Museum **142:** Courtesy of I.W. Burnham **143:** UCB.

Chapter 4:

144-145: UCB **146-147:** Schomburg Center/New York Public Library **148-149:** CB **150:** Courtesy of Clara Hancox **151:** UCB **154:** UCB **155:** NA **156:** Courtesy of Bill Bailey **157:** Franklin D. Roosevelt Library **158-159:** UCB **160:** UCB; **161:** LC **162-163:** Courtesy of the Leon Trice Collection, Manuscripts Dept./Howard-Tilton Memorial Library/Tulane University; AP/Wide World Photos **164:** Courtesy of the Leon Trice Collection, Manuscripts Dept./Howard-Tilton Memorial Library/Tulane University; Courtesy of Percy Lemoine **166-167:** AKG Photo—London **168:** (all three) Bayerische Staatsbibliothek **169:** Courtesy of Egon Hanfstaengl **170:** (left) AKG Photo-London; Hulton Getty **171:** Courtesy of Margrit Fischer **172-173:** AKG Photo-London **174:** (both) David King Collection **175:** Roger Viollet/Gamma Liaison **176-177:** Endeavour Group UK **178:** David King Collection **179:** Courtesy of Tom Sgovio **180:** (both) Courtesy of Tom Sgovio **182:** AKG Photo-London **183:** Ullstein Bilderdienst.

Chapter 5:

184-185: Robert Capa/Magnum **187:** Rhode Island Historical Society **189:** FPG International **190:** BBC **191:** Hulton Getty **192:** Dorothea Lange/LC; Photographic Archives/University of Louisville **193:** Marion Post Wolcott/LC **194:** Archives of Labor and Urban Affairs/Wayne State University **195:** AP/Wide World Photos **196-197:** CB; AP/Wide World Photos, **198:** Giraudon/Art Resource, NY, ©1998 Estate of Pablo Picasso/Artists Rights Society, New York **199:** UCB **200:** Courtesy of Karla Stept **201:** Documentation Centre of Austrian Resistance (DÖW) **202:** Wiener Library **203:** Bildarchiv Preussischer Kulturbesitz **204-205:** Documentation Centre of Austrian Resistance (DÖW) **208:** AP/Wide World Photos **209:** CB **210:** David Scherman/*LIFE* Magazine©Time Inc. **211:** (both) Courtesy of Gilda Snow **212:** MGM/UA Entertainment Co. publicity poster for *Gone With the Wind,* Courtesy of Herb Bridges **213:** Ullstein Bilderdienst **214-215:** Ghetto Fighter's House **216:** Courtesy of Peter Pechel; Courtesy of Julian Kulski **217:** Retna Ltd. **218-219:** *LIFE* Magazine©Time Inc., **220:** (left) Courtesy of Paule Rogalin; (right) Hulton Getty **221:** Roger-Viollet **222:** Hulton Getty **223:** UCB **224:** Courtesy of Sheila Black; *New York Times* Pictures **225:** UCB **226:** Courtesy of Henry Metelmann **228-229:** David King Collection **231:** Culver Pictures.

Chapter 6:

232-233: Yad Vashem **234:** NA **237:** U.S. Army/ Courtesy Time Inc. Picture Collection **238:** CB **239:** LC **240:** Tsuguichi Koyanagi **241:** (both) Courtesy of Otto Schwartz **242:** Courtesy of Neal Shine **244-245:** NA **246:** Marjory Collins/LC **248:** NA **249:** NA; Courtesy of Earle Curtis **250-251:** Tsuguichi Koyanagi **252:** Ralph Morse/*LIFE* Magazine ©Time Inc. **253:** Sovfoto/Eastfoto **254:** Sovfoto/Eastfoto **255:** David King Collection **256-257:** Sovfoto/Eastfoto **260:** Yad Vashem **261:** Courtesy of Leon Ginsburg **262-263:** Yad Vashem **264:** Lorenz Schmuel/Courtesy of the United States Holocaust Memorial Museum

265: (both) Courtesy of Ernest Michel 266: UCB 267: Courtesy of Clair Galdonik; Hulton Getty 268-269: Robert Capa/Magnum 270: Henri Cartier-Bresson/ Magnum 271: NA 272-273: Arthur Leipzig/Courtesy of Howard Greenberg Gallery, NYC 275: Courtesy of Tomiko Higa; John Hendrickson/Courtesy of Tomiko Higa 276: Shunkichi Kikuchi 277: Y. Matsushige/ Sygma 279: George Silk/*LIFE* Magazine©Time Inc.

Chapter 7:

280-281: UCB 282-283: AP/Wide World Photos 284: Joe Scherschel/*LIFE* Magazine ©Time Inc. 285: Staatliche Landesbildstelle Hamburg 286: AP/Wide World Photos 288: Courtesy of Sharpe James; Transcendental Graphics 289: Kiwanis International; Irving Haberman/Three Trees Entertainment, Inc./Christie's Images 290: Fred Johs Collection/Levittown Historical Society 291: General Mills Inc. 292: Reproduced with permission from Richard Gerstell's *How to Survive an Atomic Bomb* (pub. 1950) 293: UCB 294: Courtesy of William Hood 295: UCB; Alfred Eisenstaedt/*LIFE* Magazine ©Time Inc. 296: David Seymour/Magnum 298-299: UCB 300: (both) Courtesy of Eva Krutein 301: UCB 302: Ernst Haas/Hulton Getty 303: George C. Marshall Research Library 304: Courtesy of Jack O. Bennett 305: AKG Photo-London 306-307: UCB 308: NA 309: Henri Cartier-Bresson/Magnum; Courtesy of Nien Cheng 310-311: AP/Wide World Photos 312: CB 313: UCB 314: NA 315: Kobal Collection 316: Ap/Wide World Photos; Michael Barson/Archive 317: Courtesy of Len Maffioli 318: UCB, 319: Burt Glinn/Magnum.

Chapter 8:

320-321: Dan Weiner/Courtesy of Sandra Weiner 323: Dan Weiner/ Courtesy of Sandra Weiner 325: Eve Arnold/Magnum 327: Dan Weiner/ Courtesy of Sandra Weiner 328: (both) Courtesy of Harriet Osborn 329: Dan Weiner/Courtesy of Sandra Weiner 330: Courtesy of Northwest Natural Gas Company 331: Personality Photos 332: Minnesota Historical

Society 333: (both) Culver Pictures 334: Campbell Soup Company 335: Cornell Capa/Magnum 336: Courtesy of Maxwell Dane 337: Photofest 338: Wayne Miller/Magnum 339: Costa Manos/Magnum 340: Michael Ochs Archives 341: Courtesy of Bunny Gibson; Dick Clark Productions, Inc. 342: Courtesy of Sam Phillips 343: Elvis Presley Enterprises Inc. 344-345: Jay Leviton-Atlanta 346: Reproduced by Special Permission of *Playboy* Magazine, 347: Bob Henriques/Magnum 348: UCB 349: Dan Weiner/Courtesy of Sandra Weiner 350: AP/Wide World Photos 351: Dan Weiner/ Courtesy of Sandra Weiner 353: Courtesy of Anne Thompson; UCB 354: CB 355: Burt Glinn/Magnum 356: AP/Wide World Photos 357: Courtesy of Semyon Reznik 358: Reprinted from *Popular Mechanics*, August 1959. © Hearst Corporation 359: UCB 361: Orlando Suero/The Lowenherz Collection of Kennedy Photographs at the Peabody Institute of The Johns Hopkins University, Baltimore 363: Cornell Capa/Magnum.

Chapter 9:

364-365: Nacio Jan Brown/Black Star 366-367: Henri Cartier-Bresson/Magnum 369: Burt Glinn/Magnum 371: John F. Kennedy Library 372: (both) Courtesy of Marnie Mueller 373: Lee Lockwood ©Time Inc. 374-375: Bruce Davidson/Magnum 377: *The Tennessean* 378: UCB 379: Joe Alper/Courtesy Jackie Gibson Alper 380-381: Bob Adelman 382: UCB 383: UCB 384: Dan J. McCoy/Rainbow 385: Jim Murray Film 386-387: Jim Deverman Photo; WFAA-TV Collection/The Sixth Floor Museum at Dealey Plaza; *LIFE* Magazine, November 29, 1963© Time Inc.; ©MPI Media Group/Zapruder Film© 1967(renewed 1995) LMH Company; 388: Boston Globe 389: Dan J. McCoy/Rainbow 390-391: Carl T. Gossett Jr. /*New York Times* Pictures 392: Personality Photos 393: Courtesy of Peter Coyote 394: AP/Wide World Photos 395: Frank Wolfe/LBJ Library Collection 396: Courtesy of Larry Gwin 398-399: Larry Burrows Collection 400: Courtesy of

Nguyen Ngoc Hung 402: Danny Lyon/Magnum 403: Dennis Brack/Black Star 404: Bob Adelman 405: UCB 406-407: Larry Fink 408: (both) Reproduced with permission from *An American Requiem* 410: Burt Glinn/Magnum 411: Burk Uzzle/A+C Anthology 412: Gerald S. Upham 414-415: Josef Koudelka/Magnum 416: UCB 418: NASA/Gamma Liaison 419: NASA/Courtesy of Dennis Ivy.

Chapter 10:

420-421: Gilles Peress/Magnum 422: Don Carl Steffen 425: Sepp Seitz/Woodfin Camp 426: Waring Abbott/Michael Ochs Archives 427: Courtesy of Kathy Smith 429: Robert Azzi/Woodfin Camp 430-431: Arthur Grace/Stock, Boston 432: Courtesy of LaNita Gaines 433: John Filo 434: © The Estate of Garry Winogrand, Courtesy of Fraenkel Gallery, San Francisco 435: Courtesy of Tommy Burns 436: Dirck Halstead ©Time Inc. 437: Ken Regan/Camera 5 438: Courtesy of Hugh Sloan 439: Fred Ward/Black Star 440: Mark Godfrey/The Image Works 441: Nik Wheeler/Sipa Press 443: Eugene Richards/Magnum 444: Stanley J. Forman 446: Barbara Confino 448-449: Mary Ellen Mark 450: Courtesy of Midwest Academy 451: Courtesy of Jane Adams; UCB 453: UCB; UCB 455: J.L. Atlan/Sygma 456: Courtesy of Marilyn Noorda 457: UCB 458-459: David Burnett/Contact 460: Arthur Grace/Sygma 461: Fred Ward/Black Star; Sygma 463: Arnold Zann/Black Star.

Chapter 11:

464-465: David Turnley/Black Star 467: Connoly/Gamma-Liaison 469: Louis Psihoyos/ Contact 471: J.L. Atlan/Sygma 472: Arthur Grace 473: Michael Abramson/Gamma Liaison 475: Owen Franken/Sygma 477: UCB 478: J.L. Atlan/Sygma 480: Arlene Gottfried 481: Courtesy of Chris Burke 482-483: Larry Fink 485: (both) Courtesy of Keith Strycula 487: Eugene Richards/Magnum 488-489: Stephen Shames/Matrix 490: (both) Courtesy of the McDaniels family 491: *Los Angeles Times* Photo 492: Bob Sherman/Globe Photos

Inc.; Courtesy of Malcolm McConnell **493:**
Malcolm Denemark/Gamma Liaison **495:**
Scott Thode **496:** Arlene Gottfried; Ellen B.
Neipris **498:** Alon Reininger/Contact **499:**
Mary Ellen Mark **500:** (both) Courtesy of Rob
and Beth Owen **501:** Arthur Grace/Sygma
502-503: Gilles Peress/Magnum **504-505:**
T.Orban/Sygma **506:** Courtesy of Marina
Goldovskaya **508-509:** Chris Niedenthal
©Time Inc. **510:** David Burnett/Contact **511:**
Kenneth Jarecke/Contact **512-513:** Rei
Ohara/Photo Shuttle: Japan **514:** Pavel Stecha
516-517: Peter Turnley/Black Star **519:** (both)
FOTODESIGN: Gert Mothes **521:** Raymond
Depardon/Magnum.

Chapter 12:

522-523: William Mercer McLeod **524-525:**
Huang Zeng/Xinhua/Sygma **527:** Ron
Haviv/Saba **528:** Gamma Liaison **529:**
K.Bernstein/Gamma Liaison **530-531:** Bruno
Barbey/Magnum **532:** J.Witt/Sipa **533:** U.S.
Navy **534:** Dennis Brack/Black Star **535:**
Sygma **536:** David Burnett/Contact **537:** Mar-
tin Simon/Saba **538-539:** Michael Schu-
mann/Saba; Gamma-Liaison **540-541:** Gus
Ruelas/L.A. Daily News/Sygma **542:** Ted Lan-
dreth **543:** Courtesy of KTLA-TV News, Tri-
bune Broadcasting, Los Angeles **544:**
Reuters/Sam Mircovich/Archive Photos **545:**
Michael Owen Baker/*L.A. Daily News*/Sygma
546-547: Eli Reed/Magnum **548:** Grady
Carter **550:** William Mercer McLeod **552-
553:** Jim Bourg/Gamma Liaison **554:** Kevin
Walker/Courtesy of Stacy Horn **555:** Louis
Psihoyos/Matrix **556:** Courtesy of Scott Sav-
age **559:** Jim Argo/*Daily Oklahoman*/Saba
560-561: Ron Haviv/Saba **562:** Nina
Berman/Sipa Press **563:** Jetta Fraser/Impact
Visuals **565:** Courtesy of Dr. Philip Nitschke
566: (both) Courtesy of Christina Walker
Campi **567:** Gamma Liaison **568:** Annie Grif-
fiths Belt/Aurora **569:** Richard A. Bloom **571:**
Peter Turnley/Black Star **573:** Gilles
Peress/Magnum.

Back Cover:

First row: Gus Ruelas/L.A. Daily
News/Sygma; Eli Reed/Magnum; Ron
Haviv/Saba; CB; Natural History Museum of
Los Angeles; Courtesy of Larry Gwin.
Second row: David Scherman/*LIFE* Magazine
©Time Inc.; Sepp Seitz/Woodfin Camp; NA;
Eve Arnold/Magnum; T.Orban/Sygma.
Third row: Cincinnati Historical Society;
Huang Zeng/Xinhua/Sygma; Peter
Turnley/Black Star; Swift Collection/Ball State
University; fred Johs Collection/Levittown
Historical Society; Hogan Jazz Archive/
Howard Tilton Memorial Library, Tulane
University.
Fourth row: Bruno Barbey/Magnum; Retna
Ltd.; Brown Brothers; Lewis Hine Collec-
tion/New York Public Library .

End Papers:

Credits read left to right.
Front: Lewis Hine/NA; Imperial War Muse-
um; Courtesy of Minor Cash; Milton J. Hinton
Photographic Collection; CB; Courtesy of I.W
Burnham.
Back: Courtesy of Karla Stept; Courtesy of
Neal Shine; *Boston Globe*; Courtesy of Peter
Coyote; Peter Turnley/Black Star; Michael
Owen Baker/*L.A. Daily News*/Sygma.

*While every effort has been made to trace the
copyright holders of photographs and illustra-
tions reproduced in this book, the publishers will
be pleased to rectify any omissions or inaccura-
cies in the next printing.*

Index

Index

A

Television Series Staff

Executive Producers
Lionel Chapman (1950-1997)
Av Westin
Tom Yellin

Senior Producers
Todd Brewster (Editorial)
Richard Gerdau
Mark Obenhaus
Robert Roy
Pete Simmons

Operations Producer
Elena Brodie-Kusa

Director of Production
Terrence Carnes

Production Managers
Gerri Bell
Frank Gregal

Producers
Jodi Abramson
Peter Bull
Jeanmarie Condon
Vivian Ducat
John Fielding
Kenneth Levis
Rhoda Lipton
Susan Mitchell
Andrew Pearson
Pamela Ridder
Richard Robbins
Brooke Runnette
Glenn Silber
Martin Smith
Steven Stept
Justin Sturken
Andrea Tucher
Sharon Young

Coordinating Producers
Prudence Arndt
Carrie Cook

Field Producers
Gail Ablow
Caroline Christopher
Jodi Delaney
Shelley M. Diamond
Diana Frank
Annie Leahy
Michael Plante
Pamela Troutman
Mi Ling Tsui

Associate Producers
Nancy Delape
Lisa Doyle
Adi Japhet Fuchs
Linda Hirsch
Michelle Major
ShigehisaTerao

Editors
Ralph Avellino
Lawrence Bruch
Joel Herson
Sharon Kaufman
Marcie Lefkovitz
Thomas Marcyes
John Martin
Peter Mitchell

Photo Editor
Audrey Landreth

Production Associates
Jane Conlin
Brooke Gaffney
Beth Goodman
Izhar Harpaz
Sharon Kay
Sean Kelliher
Paul Kogan
Reginald Lewis
Deborah Runcie
John Schultz
Susan Shipman
Sarah Spill
Susan Stanley
Bryan Taylor
Anna Wild

Production Assistants
Dan Gabriel
Kei Ogushi

*Assistants to the
Executive Producer*
Jennifer Uyei
Natilie Phillips-Colter

Senior Archivist
Hillary Dann

Newswriter
Harry Miles Muheim

Researcher
Barr Seitz

Consultants
Benjamin Barber
Alan Brinkley
Herrick Chapman
Nathaniel C. Comfort
John Steele Gordon
Henry Graff
Thomas P. Hughes
Rita Jacobs
Daniel J. Leab
David Nasaw
Geoffrey Perrett
Rosalind Rosenberg
Bruce J. Schulman
Daryl Scott
Rob Snyder
Jonathan Spence
Peter Winn

Film Researchers
Steve Bergson
Corrinne Collett
Debbie Ford
Lewanne Jones
Wolfgang Klaue
Polly Pettit
Jane Tucker
Robin Wilder
Karen Wyatt
Midori Yanagihara

Executives in Charge
William Abrams
Phyllis McGrady